Kuala Lumpur
The Complete **Residents'** Guide

Passionately Publishing...

Kuala Lumpur Explorer 1st Edition ISBN 978-9948-03-331-8

Front Cover Photograph: Petronas Twin Towers – Victor Romero

Printed and bound by Emirates Printing Press, Dubai, United Arab Emirates.

Explorer Publishing & Distribution
PO Box 34275, Dubai
United Arab Emirates
Phone   +971 (0)4 340 8805
Fax   +971 (0)4 340 8806
Email   info@explorerpublishing.com
Web   www.explorerpublishing.com

Selamat Datang...

Whether you're only just starting to think about a move to Kuala Lumpur, or reading this on the plane, or you're an old-time expat who's lived there for years, well done for picking up the right book. It's not really meant for tourists who are just looking for the best Twin Towers photo op – it's written for you, the intrepid resident who knows the value of year-round sunshine.

The Kuala Lumpur Complete Residents' Guide has been meticulously researched and written by a team of seven city experts – some locals, some expats – who not only know the city inside and out, but love it too. Meet them on the next two pages. This talented bunch have scoured all areas to bring you the lowdown on all the things that are most important to a resident of Kuala Lumpur.

Flick through the **General Information** chapter (p.1) to brush up on some essential facts. It covers the geography, history, environment and culture of the country, and there are also stacks of useful numbers for embassies, banks, airlines and hotels – very handy for when you want to impress people with your encyclopaedic knowledge of the city. The **Residents** chapter (p.43) is the meaty part of the book, and covers all the red tape you'll have to cut through when applying for visas, finding a job, renting or buying a home, getting settled in, changing your driving licence and buying a car, and finding a good hospital or school.

Once you've got all that hard stuff out of the way, get out and about with the **Exploring** chapter (p.155). All the interesting areas are covered, and this chapter will steer you away from the classic tourist traps and show you some great off-the-beaten-track gems. It all starts with the checklist of must-do items on p.157 – whether you're in KL for days or years, these are the things you should not miss.

The **Activities** chapter (p.213) lists hundreds of things to do in your spare time – whether sporty, arty or intellectual – and will definitely make sure you spend less time feeling homesick and more time making new friends. It also covers spas, nail bars, hairdressers and massage for when you want to treat your body right.

Following on from that is the **Shopping** chapter (p.279), and in KL it's a mighty tome of where you can enjoy one of the city's favourite pastimes. Get hundreds of ideas on where to flash your cash, or at least survive on a teeny-tiny budget until payday. It features an A-Z listing of everything you might ever need to buy (from art to wedding stationery), and also has a rundown of the best malls, markets and department stores. Finally, the **Going Out** chapter (p.353) lists over 200 restaurants, bars and nightclubs that have been personally recommended by our team of nightlife writers. You can search by cuisine, or choose from a selection of venues under certain categories, such as cocktails, alfresco or romantic.

Phew! That's a lot of stuff packed into one book. If you can't figure out where to start, turn to the Maps section at the back of the book to get your bearings.

So there you have it – a book that covers just about everything. But if you find something we've missed out, like your Petronas Twin Towers Sketching Society, or your 'Backyard Brothers of Bangsar' Barbecue Club, then go to www.explorerpublishing.com and let us know. Better yet, join the KL community on our Communities section and share the knowledge with your fellow explorers. Enjoy the journey,

The Explorer Team

Explorer's KL

The contrasts of the city make it hard to ever get bored, but while we were there we just couldn't get enough of the following:

The breathtaking view of the Petronas Towers (p.188), especially at night when it's hard to look the other way.

The cocktails in SkyBar (p.404) at the Traders Hotel – beautiful drinks, beautiful people, beautiful view.

Peter Hoe's (p.308) in Chinatown for lovely knick-knacks for the home and a cute little restaurant too.

The range of cheesecakes at Secret Recipe (p.394).

The Canopy Walk at FRIM (p.196); while our legs are still aching from the climb, the suspended walkway above the rainforest was totally worth it.

Alexandra Wong Alex is a fierce patriot who gave up her high-flying day job to freelance full time. Since then she has amassed a huge body of work and has been published in newspapers, magazines and books, with travel, food and human interest stories being her favourite topics. **Favourite daytrip:** Petaling Street (p.327). **Best view:** From the top of inner city carparks. **Best thing about living in KL:** The fantastic food. **Best KL memory:** Taking a lazy Sunday afternoon snooze in the shade of a flyover next to a sleeping pedicab driver.

Brigid Bose Brigid has spent most of the past decade in Asia. She's in danger of becoming what they call a seasoned expat, although has yet to acquire the habit of drinking gin for elevenses. As a freelance writer and editor, she writes about life in KL for a number of expat magazines. She regularly gets lost on the KL roads and discovers something new every time. **Favourite KL cultural experience:** Family Fun Day at the Dewan Filharmonik Petronas (p.249). **Favourite restaurant:** The Magnificent Fish & Chips Bar on Changkat Bukit Bintang (p.383).

David Bowden David is a photojournalist specialising in travel, food, wine and the environment. He is Australian, but has been based in Asia for well over a decade. David has written books about Cambodia and Thailand, and has also worked as an editor for various travel publications. When he isn't globetrotting he relaxes with his wife Maria and equally adventurous daughter, Zoe. **Favourite KL cultural experience:** Going to a hawker stall. **Favourite Restaurant:** Sao Nam (p.384).

David Lavoie David, a retired teacher of English, loves his role as a freelance writer. He has lived and worked in Canada, Cameroon, Ivory Coast, Egypt and Malaysia. Kuala Lumpur, his home for the last four years, is one of his favourite places. Currently a regular columnist for both The New Sunday Times and The Expat magazine, he also enjoys scuba-diving, hashing, and travelling to new places. **Favourite KL cultural experience:** Eating a banana leaf lunch. **Favourite daytrip:** Melaka (p.208). **Worst thing about living in KL:** The drivers, all of them.

*Trying to find your way from the towers to the suburbs, but can't get off Jalan Ampang? Look no further than the **Kuala Lumpur Mini Map**, an indispensable pocket-sized aid to getting to grips with the roads, areas and attractions of the city.*

Lyndsay Avern Lyndsay was born and spent her childhood in KL, so returning to live in the city with her own young family has been quite an experience. She does a bit of writing for the ABWM magazine and helps with the Alice Smith School Alumni Society. **Favourite Daytrip:** Kuala Gandah Elephant Sanctuary (p.204). **Ultimate KL Must-Do:** Spending a morning in and around Little India (p.328) taking in all the beautiful buildings.

Noelle Lim Noelle, who has lived in KL for more than 10 years, writes for a variety of local magazines and loves how this gives her the chance to meet interesting people and attend cool events. A closet bean counter, she still pays her dues to the Institute of Chartered Accountants in England & Wales. **Best view:** The Petronas Twin Towers (p.188) at night. **Reason she would never leave KL:** It's peaceful and earthquake free (so far). **Favourite KL restaurant:** Marmalade cafe (p.389), for its wonderful salad.

*Now that you're settled down in KL, it won't be long before you're playing host to wave upon wave of visiting family and friends – and we've got the perfect guide to help them get the most out of their sightseeing. Packed with info on all the must-do shops, restaurants and tourist spots, you can't go wrong with the **Kuala Lumpur Mini Explorer**.*

Steve Northcott A Canadian by birth but Malaysian by spirit, Steve spends his time as a freelance travel writer, singing and playing the guitar in a local rock band, exploring interesting lands and teaching art. Being in Malaysia has taught him to slow down and that red lights are purely optional. **Favourite KL Cultural Experience:** Thaipusam at Batu Caves (p.189). **Best city memory:** Making the finals of the Malaysian Global Battle of the Bands competition. **Best place to drink with the locals:** Ol Skool Bistro (p.406) or Backyard Pub & Grill (p.405).

Thanks...

Apart from our talented team of local authors who trawled KL for the very best information, there are lots of other people who helped with this book. So a huge big thanks goes out to: the extended Explorer team who mucked in when the deadline got too scary; the two Davids who swooped in to save the day when things were falling apart; Danielle Prenzler for company and for restoring calm when rat-phobia threatened to strike; Mr Tuan Razali Tuan Omar of Tourism Malaysia (UAE, Gulf & Iran) for advice and the picture on p.209; Andy Davison of Expat KL magazine for the introductions; Paddy McHugh for the trio of creme caramel; Justin and Hannah for holding the fort; and finally, the KL team for late nights, hard work and minimal panic – perhaps it was the ginseng tea that did it.

Where are we exploring next?

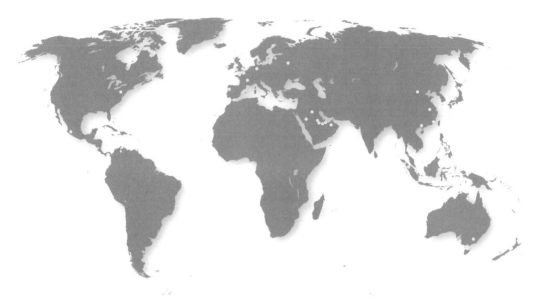

• Abu Dhabi	• Dublin	• Moscow*	• Shanghai
• Amsterdam	• Geneva	• New York	• Singapore
• Bahrain	• Hong Kong	• New Zealand	• Sydney
• Barcelona	• Kuala Lumpur	• Oman	• Taipei*
• Beijing	• Kuwait	• Paris	• Tokyo
• Berlin	• London	• Qatar	• Vancouver
• Brussels	• Los Angeles	• San Francisco*	
• Dubai	• Mexico City*	• Saudi Arabia*	* Available 2008/2009

Where do you live?
Is your home city missing from our list? If you'd love to see a residents' guide for a location not currently on Explorer's horizon please email editorial@explorerpublishing.com.

Advertise with Explorer...
If you're interested in advertising with us, please contact sales@explorerpublishing.com.

Make Explorer your very own...
We offer a number of customisation options for bulk sales. For more information and discount rates please contact corporatesales@explorerpublishing.com.

Contract Publishing
Have an idea for a publication or need to revamp your company's marketing material? Contact designlab@explorerpublishing to see how our expert contract publishing team can help.

www.explorerpublishing.com

Life can move pretty fast, so to make sure you can stay up to date with all the latest goings on in your city, we've revamped our website to further enhance your time in the city, whether long or short.

Keep in the know...

Our Complete Residents' Guides and Mini Visitors' series continue to expand, covering destinations from Amsterdam to New Zealand and beyond. Keep up to date with our latest travels and hot tips by signing up to our monthly newsletter, or browse our products section for info on our current and forthcoming titles.

Make friends and influence people...

...by joining our Communities section. Meet fellow residents in your city, make your own recommendations for your favourite restaurants, bars, childcare agencies or dentists, plus find answers to your questions on daily life from long-term residents.

Discover new experiences...

Ever thought about living in a different city, or wondered where the locals really go to eat, drink and be merry? Check out our regular features section, or submit your own feature for publication!

Want to find a badminton club, the number for your bank, or maybe just a restaurant for a hot first date?

Check out city info on various destinations around the world in our Residents section – from finding a pilates class to contact details for international schools in your area, or the best place to buy everything from a spanner set to a Spandau Ballet album, we've got it all covered.

Let us know what you think!

All our information comes from residents which means you! If we missed out your favourite bar or market stall, or you know of any changes in the law, infrastructure, cost of living or entertainment scene, let us know by using our Feedback form.

Contents

Contents

You're this close to Brits worldwide

Go online at **telegraph.co.uk/expat** for the most comprehensive range of information services available to Brits outside of the UK - and tap into a world network of well-travelled, knowledgeable and friendly expats, many of whom actively contribute to the site and support each other both locally and from afar.

Produced by the publisher's of the Weekly Telegraph, from the home of The Daily Telegraph and Sunday Telegraph, **telegraph.co.uk/expat** is of real value to Brits worldwide. Go online and see for yourself.

Also online, you can subscribe to the **Weekly Telegraph** and have the UK's global newspaper delivered direct to your home or office on a weekly basis. Alternatively, subscribe via our credit card orderline +44 1622 33 50 80 quoting ref. EXP08, lines open 0900 - 1700 BST.

Telegraph.co.uk/expat
the expat community online

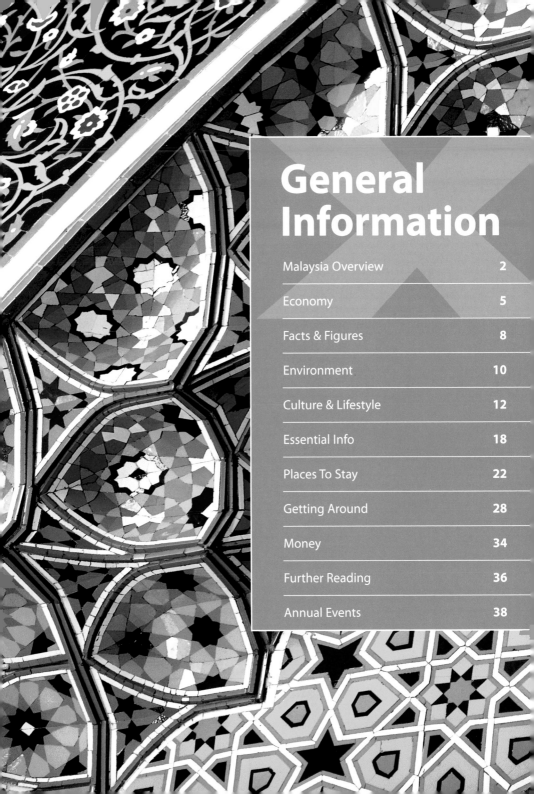

General Information

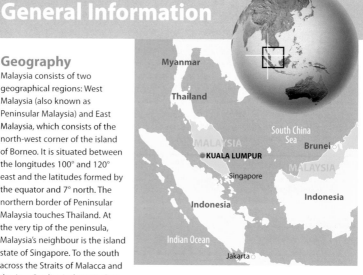

Geography

Malaysia consists of two geographical regions: West Malaysia (also known as Peninsular Malaysia) and East Malaysia, which consists of the north-west corner of the island of Borneo. It is situated between the longitudes 100° and 120° east and the latitudes formed by the equator and 7° north. The northern border of Peninsular Malaysia touches Thailand. At the very tip of the peninsula, Malaysia's neighbour is the island state of Singapore. To the south across the Straits of Malacca and the Java Sea lies Indonesia. Due east of the peninsula, Malaysia shares the island of Borneo with Indonesia. Across the South China Sea are the Philippines, Cambodia and Vietnam. The total land area of Malaysia is about 328,549 square kilometres.

Malaysia is divided into 13 states, two of which, Sabah and Sarawak, are on the island of Borneo; the other 11 are Penang, Perlis, Kedah, Kelantan, Perak, Terrenganu, Pahang, Selangor, Melaka, Negeri Sembilan and Johor. In addition there are three federal territories: the capital city which is Kuala Lumpur, the administrative centre of Putrajaya and the island of Labuan.

About 70% of Malaysia is covered with forest which provides ebony, teak, and sandalwood. There are over 6,000 different species of trees that can be found in Malaysia's fertile forests. A long, narrow range of mountains runs the length of the peninsula, the highest peak being Mount Tahan at 2,200 metres. Sabah and Sarawak in East Malaysia have some swampy coastal areas and are generally quite hilly and mountainous. Malaysia's highest peak, Mount Kinabalu, is located in Sabah. It rises to 4,100 metres. The coast of the peninsula is renowned for its beautiful beaches, the most famous being on the island of Langkawi (see p.196).

Malaysia's largest cities are Kuala Lumpur, Petaling Jaya, Kelang, Ipoh, Johor Baharu, Kuala Terrenganu, and Penang (also known as George Town). The first three lie in close proximity to one another and form what is by far Malaysia's largest urban area.

The skyline of Kuala Lumpur particularly is dominated by skyscrapers ranging from the famous twin spires of the Petronas Towers to the massive sail-like structure of the Malaysia Telecommunications building. Tucked away among the gleaming glass and steel skyscrapers are lovely hints of the past, like the Moorish architecture of the central train station and the buildings around Merdeka Square, handsome colonial structures and old churches, and the quaint shop-houses in Chinatown and Little India. In the suburbs close to the high rise condominiums are the Malay Kampung, small village-like communities. The other cities share this blend, reflecting the cultural mix of Malaysia.

History

Located at the trade crossroads of south-east Asia between the Indian Ocean and the South China Sea, Malaysia has long been a sought-after prize. In the 15th century Indian traders introduced Islam to the rulers of Malacca (modern day Melaka) where it

---

Malaysia: Fast Facts

Longitudes 100 to 120 east and Latitudes 1 to 7 north
Neighbouring countries: Thailand, Singapore, Indonesia, Philippines
Capital city: Kuala Lumpur
Largest city: Kuala Lumpur
Administrative centre: Putrajaya
Total land area: 328,549sq km
Highest point: Mount Kinabalu, Sabah, 4,100m
Total coastline: 4,809km

Inner Tensions

For excellent insights into the history of tensions between the different ethnic groups, try Rehman Rashid's highly readable book , A Malaysian Journey.

Merdeka Square
*Visit Merdeka Square
to experience historic
Kuala Lumpur. A grassy
area called the Padang
where the British once
used to play cricket is
now a revered spot for
Malaysians; it was here
that independence
was declared in 1957.
The gigantic flag
poles dominating the
square are the tallest
in Malaysia and some
of the tallest in the
world. Enjoy both the
traditionally English
Royal Selangor Club
and the blend of
Victorian and Moorish
architecture of the
Sultan Abdul Samad
Building opposite
(see p.185).*

was quickly embraced. It spread rapidly throughout the peninsula resulting in the rise of the various Malay sultanates. The Sultanate of Malacca, the first and most powerful, established strong trade ties with the both the Middle East and the Kingdom of China. After the Sultan of Malacca took one of the Chinese emperor's daughters as a wife, immigration from China along the Straits of Meleka grew quickly. The new immigrants often intermarried with native Malays creating a new class of people called the Baba Nonya, or Straits Chinese.

Malacca's thriving trade in spices drew the attention of the Portuguese who invaded in 1511, bringing Christianity with them. The Sultanate fell quickly. The Dutch drove the Portuguese out in 1641 and held on to power until the end of the 18th century when control was ceded to the British in return for certain concessions in Indonesia.

There was considerable acrimony, and even civil war, among the Malay states during the 18th century. The British intervened, eventually forming West Malaysia into colony states called The Straits Settlements. In East Malaysia, Sabah became a British protectorate, while the Brookes family ruled in Sarawak as the White Rajahs for a full century.

In 1896, Sir Frank Swettenham persuaded four of the Sultans to unite as the Federated Malay States. As Resident General to the FMS, he chose Kuala Lumpur to be its capital. British residents became increasingly influential as consultants to the various sultans on all matters except Malay religion and custom.

Building ports, roads and railroads, the British began to actively exploit Malaya's resources. Rubber plantations, tin mines and trading companies prospered. Chinese immigrants were encouraged to work the tin mines and Indians to work the plantations, while Sikhs manned the police force.

In 1941 the Japanese occupied Malaya for three years until their surrender to Allied forces. Malayan resistance to the Japanese occupation was the birth of modern Malaysian nationalism.

The Federation of Malaya was declared in 1948 with much power going to the Malays. Many Chinese, most of them communists who had actively resisted the Japanese during the occupation, now took to the jungles to engage in a sporadic guerilla war. What was henceforth called Malaysia declared its independence on August 31, 1957 under the leadership of its first prime minister, Tunku Abdul Rahman. By 1963 the new country consisted of Malaya, Singapore, Sabah and Sarawak, although Singapore

Modern skyline

seceded peacefully only two years later. Malaysia became a parliamentary democracy with a constitutional monarchy.

The most traumatic event to face the new country was the eruption of race riots, particularly in Kuala Lumpur, in 1969. The disturbances were the result of simmering tensions particularly between Malays and Chinese-Malaysians. At the root of the conflict was the inequitable division of the country's wealth among ethnic groups. The government instituted a 20 year programme, the New Economic Policy. Henceforth 30% of Malaysia's wealth had to be in the hands of indigenous Malays.

The present government continues to implement the NEP and another ambitious plan, Vision 2020, which aims at Malaysia reaching economic parity with the developed world by that year.

Kuala Lumpur's History

Among the earliest inhabitants of the area now known as Kuala Lumpur were 87 Chinese miners who had been sent upriver from Klang in 1857 to search for deposits of tin at the confluence of the Gombak and Klang rivers. In fact, the name Kuala Lumpur means 'muddy confluence' in Malay. It was with these men that the growth of Kuala Lumpur began. World demand for tin being high, the new settlement grew rapidly. Like many frontier towns it was unruly, but all that changed with the arrival in 1868 of Yap Ah Loy, the 'Kapitan China', a term used for the Chinese man whose job it is to control and discipline all the other Chinese. Brilliant, determined and physically strong, he quickly brought order to the chaos; he is regarded by many as the founder of Kuala Lumpur. Briefly forced out by civil strife between the Malay states, he returned in 1873 to find his community in ruins. He began rebuilding immediately. Peace was brokered by the British between the Malay States in 1874. Bloomfield Douglas, British resident for Selangor, moved his offices from Klang to Kuala Lumpur in 1880 and the city began to take its modern shape. The centre of British administration for the Federated Malay States was Dataran Merdeka, the present day Merdeka Square. Although the Japanese occupation of Kuala Lumpur during the second world war was brief, the city suffered some damage. The British returned only to be ousted in 1957. In 1974 the city was ceded by the Sultan of Selangor and became the Federal Territory of Kuala Lumpur.

Kuala Lumpur Timeline

1400	Malacca is founded. It becomes the first Muslim Sultanate.
1511	The Portuguese conquer Malacca. It becomes a prosperous trading port.
1641	The Dutch arrive and oust the Portuguese from Malacca.
1786	The British open a trading port on the island of Penang.
1824	The British and Dutch agree: Malaya will be a British sphere of influence; Indonesia will be a Dutch one.
1842	James Brooke becomes the first White Rajah of Sarawak.
1874	The British begin actively to influence affairs of the Malay Sultanates. Sporadic wars between the Malay states continue.
1896	The Federated Malay States are formed. British influence and control burgeon.
1941	The Japanese occupy Malaya.
1948	1960 – The Emergency. The government fights Chinese-Malaysian guerilas in the jungles of Malaya.
1957	Independence is declared. Tunku Abdul Rahman becomes the first Prime Minister.
1963	Malaya, Sabah, Sarawak and Singapore unite to become Malaysia.
1965	Singapore secedes from the new union.
1969	Race riots result in new policies favouring Malays.
1997	An economic recession hits south-east Asia. Malaysia does surprisingly well.
1998	The landmark Petronas Twin Towers are completed.
2001	Malaysia's federal government moves its administrative centre to Putrajaya, a new purpose-built city.
2007	First Malaysian astronaut, Dr. Sheikh Muszaphar Shukor, returns to earth from an orbiting Russian space station.

Malaysia Overview

The number one contributor to Malaysia's gross domestic product is the petroleum industry, Petronas being the leading player. The government consistently emphasises technology-intensive industries which are geared to exporting Malaysian products. This has resulted in the establishment of many industrial estates. Malaysia's own car, the Proton, which is heavily protected by the government, dominates the local automotive industry and has become competitive in a number of foreign markets as well. Underpinning the growing industrialisation is the more traditional agricultural sector, producing palm oil, rubber and cocoa beans. Tourism is also a major contributor to the Malaysian economy.

The economy has grown from a commodity-based one in which tin, rubber and timber were the main earners to a solidly entrenched manufacturing economy. Malaysia survived the currency crisis of 1997 which swept through south-east Asia quite well. A pro-business government has lured a number of multinational companies to invest heavily in Malaysia. It has one of the lowest risk ratings among developing countries with an inflation rate of 3.9 %. The World Bank expects the country's GDP of 5.6 % in 2007 to rise to 6% in 2008. Malaysia's current credit rating is A3.

The average annual household income in Malaysia is US$11,531. The lowest 10% of wage earners in the country receive only 1.4% of the country's wealth. The wealthiest 10% enjoy 39% of the wealth.

Employment

With a labour force of 10.68 million, Malaysia experiences an unemployment rate of only 3.5%. The largest portion of the labour force works in the service sector (51%), followed by industry at (36%) and agriculture (13%).

Most foreign nationals who work at high-end jobs in Malaysia are those who have been sent by parent international companies. Spouses of such people are not allowed to work. A few expats do get work permits locally when it is conclusively demonstrated that no local person can do the work, but this is relatively rare. Casual work such as backpackers sometimes rely on is simply not available. There are a large number of illegal immigrants from neighbouring Asian countries, particularly Indonesia, working in Malaysia. Since they provide much of the manual and domestic labour, they are quietly tolerated, but periodically the government does a sweep and several hundred thousand will be sent home. Preference for jobs is always given to Malaysians, and among Malaysians it is given to Bumiputra (this translates loosely as 'sons of the soil'; it means Malay and indigenous people collectively).

Kuala Lumpur Overview

Kuala Lumpur is the beating heart of Malaysia and the focus of most of the country's development. Today, KL contains about 1.5 million people within the city proper, and more than 4.5 million in the surrounding metropolitan area.

Leading Industries

Malaysia's fast paced development in trade and commerce, banking and finance, manufacturing, transportation, information technology and tourism depends on Kuala Lumpur. The city is also the political and cultural centre of the nation, while nearby Putrajaya is the administrative capital. Currently the construction industry is undergoing a tremendous surge.

Speculate To Accumulate

To investigate investment opportunities in Malaysia log on to the website of the Malaysian Industrial Development Authority: www.mida.gov.my.

Major Industries

Malaysia's leading industries are electrical and electronics, engineering support, food processing, life sciences, machinery and equipment, petrochemicals and polymers, rubber products, textiles and apparel, transport equipment, and base metal products. There are no employment opportunities locally for expats – they must be hired abroad. For more information visit the Malaysian Industrial Development Authority at www.mida.gov.my.

Employment

Because Kuala Lumpur is the most prosperous city in the country, it is the focus of the usual rural to urban exodus. Unskilled labourers, many of them Indonesians, flock to Kuala Lumpur looking for manual or domestic work. The government tries to protect the interests of its citizens by requiring that jobs be given to Malaysians first according to a very strict procedure. Some abuses of this system do of course occur. Skilled foreign workers, including the spouses of those legally working in the city, are not normally permitted to work unless it can be clearly demonstrated that there is no Malaysian who can do the job. This means that a foreign national coming to the city hoping to pick up a casual temporary job is likely to be disappointed. Malaysia's unemployment rate is only 3.5%.

New Developments

The most exciting new direction in Malaysia now is the Multimedia Super Corridor (MSC). This hot bed of technology extends from Kuala Lumpur International Airport (KLIA) to the Petronas Towers in the very heart of the city. Supported by a highly developed technology infrastructure, companies from around the world have made the MSC their Asian home. The main node of the MSC is Cyberjaya. Like Putrajaya it is a purpose-built community just outside of Kuala Lumpur proper.

Tourism

Tourism is a major income earner for Malaysia with between 15 and 16 million tourists a year passing through Kuala Lumpur on their way to various destinations in the country. Malaysia has deliberately targeted a combination of tourists from high-end travellers to working holiday travellers, but does not cater particularly to backpackers. The government has undertaken an intensive advertising programme tagged 'Malaysia, Truly Asia', targeted at the global tourist market, which has been paying handsome dividends. In the first six months of 2007, tourists spent RM6.77 billion on shopping sprees. Tourism Malaysia is now seeking to draw in the 'ultra-rich' to its many attractions such as the beaches of Langkawi. There are many reasons why tourists come to Malaysia; its beaches, heritage sites, culture and shopping opportunities are all draws. The top destinations are Kuala Lumpur and the island of Langkawi. Other popular destinations are Penang, the Cameron Highlands, Mulu Caves, Mount Kinabalu, Melaka, Taman Negara and the island of Tioman.

International Relations

Malaysia enjoys cordial relations with its all its neighbours. It is predominantly Muslim, but it follows a generally moderate line in its foreign relations even in such areas as the conflicts in the Middle East. Malaysia belongs to a number of international organisations including Apec, FAO, UN, Unesco, and WHO. It is an important member of Asean. Malaysia's foreign policy has remained generally consistent since the country's birth in 1957.

The hottest point of international disagreement at present is Malaysia's claim to the Spratly Islands which is contested by China, the Philippines, Taiwan and Vietnam. The islands have the potential for large gas and oil deposits.

There has also been contention between Malaysia, the Philippines and Indonesia over the islands off the easy coast of Sabah. There have been occasional kidnappings of tourists by Filipino Abu Sayyaf terrorists in these waters.

Terrorist groups acting in Thailand's predominantly Muslim southern states necessitate a close watch on the Malaysian side and an occasional closing of the border.

Government & Politics

Malaysia's system of government somewhat resembles that of Great Britain. It is a parliamentary democracy with a constitutional monarchy. The government is headed by a prime minister who is the leader of the political party which has the greatest number of seats in parliament. The prime minister governs with the support of his chosen cabinet. Parliament consists of two houses, the senate and the house of representatives. The senate has 68 senators serving six-year terms. Twenty-six of these are appointed by the state legislatures and the remaining 42 are nominated by the prime minister and appointed by the king.

The house of representatives has 180 members chosen in a general election for five-year terms. The system of voting is 'first past the post'. Every citizen over 21 has the vote. Many women hold important positions in both the state and federal governments. Nine of Malaysia's 13 states have royal Malay families generally headed by a sultan. In eight of these states, titles are hereditary; in the ninth, the ruler is elected by a council of peer Malay chiefs. The remaining states are headed by governors who are appointed by the reigning paramount king for a period of four years. Although they need not be Muslim to serve, they must be Malaysian.

Every five years the nine rulers gather to elect one of their number as the 'agong' which in English means 'king'. Each of the sultans must serve as agong before anyone of them can serve a second term. As king, his duties are largely ceremonial.

Loyalty to one party or another is often based on a person's ethnic background rather than policies or actions. The ruling coalition is The National Front (Barisan Nasional) of which the largest political group is UMNO (New United Malays National Organisation). Its most powerful coalition partners are the MCA (Malaysian Chinese Association) and the MIC (Malaysian Indian Congress). The major opposition parties are the DAP (Democratic Action Party) and the PAS (Pan Malaysian Islamic Party). The PAS contests the Malay vote with the Barisan Nasional. It holds power in the two most Islamic states, Kelantan and Terengganu. UMNO won all elections from 1955 until 1974 when it became part of a larger coalition, The Barisan Nasional. The present prime minister, Dato' Seri Abdullah bin Haji Ahmad Badawi, is the fifth prime minister of Malaysia. All have been members of the UMNO. For 50 years, transfer of power has always been peaceful. The military does not intervene in politics in Malaysia.

Berhad building

National Monument

Kuala Lumpur Population – Age Breakdown

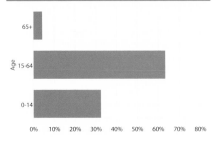

Population

The present population of Malaysia is 27.17 million with an average population growth rate of 1.78% per year. The birth rate, however, has seen a slight decline recently from roughly 19/1000 in 2004 to 18/1000 in 2007. The overall gender ratio is 1.01 male to every female. The average family is 5.4; rural families tend to be somewhat larger than urban ones. The life expectancy for a Malaysian male is 71.8 years; for a female it is 76.3 years. In the graphs opposite, taken from the Malaysian Department of Statistics, 'Bumiputra' translates loosely as 'sons of the soil'. It means Malays and indigenous people collectively. 'Other' is a catch-all phrase for Malaysian citizens who are neither Bumiputra, Chinese or Indian. These include Eurasians, Arabs, Thais and other Asians, even though the family may have lived in Malaysia for generations.

Kuala Lumpur Population – Nationality

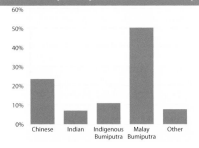

National Flag

The national flag of Malaysia somewhat resembles the stars and stripes flag of the United States, although there is no connection between them. There are 14 horizontal red and white stripes representing the 13 member states and the federal government. The upper left-hand quadrant is a blue field bearing a yellow crescent and a 14 point star. The star, called the Federal Star, represents the unity between the states and the federal government. Yellow is the royal colour of Malay rulers.

The flag is flown prominently throughout Malaysia, not only on government buildings but on structures of all kinds. The most symbolic location is the gigantic flag pole flag in Kuala Lumpur's Merdeka Square where, every year, thousands of people gather to celebrate Malaysian independence on Merdeka Day (31 August). Each of Malaysia's states also has an individual flag.

Education Level

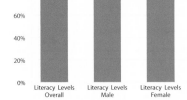

Local Time

Malaysia's time is UTC/GMT + 8 hours. The country does not have any periods when daylight saving time is applied.

Clock This
To set up your Personal World Clock, go to www.timeanddate.com.

Social & Business Hours

The working week in Kuala Lumpur is Monday to Friday. Muslims take some time off on Friday, the holy day, to go to a mosque for prayers. Working hours are consistent throughout the year. Offices, including government offices, generally open between 08:30 and 09:00 and stay open until 17:00. People take about an hour for lunch, often around 13:00. These hours, however, apply to Kuala Lumpur only and vary from state to state.

Shops operate differently. Large supermarkets open about 08:30 and stay open until 22:00 or later. Smaller shops, whether on the streets or in shopping malls, tend to open between 10:00 and 11:00 and stay open until 21:00. In busy malls it can be quite a bit later. Many shops are open seven days a week. Basically, there are no hard and fast rules for opening hours; it depends on when the business's peak hours are likely to be.

Facts & Figures

Time Zones

Dallas	22:00
Denver	21:00
Dubai	08:00
Dublin	04:00
Kuala Lumpur	**12:00**
London	04:00
Los Angeles	20:00
Melbourne	15:00
Mexico City	22:00
Moscow	07:00
Mumbai	09:30
New York	23:00
Paris	05:00
Perth	13:00
Prague	05:00
Rio de Janeiro	02:00
Rome	05:00
Sydney	15:00
Toronto	23:00
Wellington	17:00

Public Holidays

School holidays vary greatly among the international schools depending on the system in the country of origin.

Malaysian schools begin the year in January. In general, school children get around a week of holiday in March, two weeks in May or June, a week in August, and then an extended holiday from the middle of November to the beginning of January.

Government office timings are usually 08:15 to 16:45, Monday to Friday. This is split by a lunch break from 12:45 to 14:00 (from 12:15 to 14:45 on Fridays). Selected post offices are open on the second and fourth Saturdays of each month.

Private sector companies usually operate from 08:30 or 09:00 to 17:30 or 18:00, Monday to Friday. Some open on Saturdays for a half day.

Most major religious celebrations are given as public holidays. However, shopping centres and restaurants will often remain open on these days.

Public Holidays

New Year's Day	1 Jan
Awal Muharram	20 Jan*
Federal Territory Day	1 Feb
Chinese New Year	7–8 Feb*
Prophet Muhammed's Birthday	20 March*
Wesak Day	19 May*
King's Birthday	7 June*
National Day	31 August
Hari Raya Puasa (Hari Raya Aidilfitri)	1–2 October*
Deepavali	
Hari Raya Qurban	27 October*
(Hari Raya Haji)	9 December*
Christmas Day	25 December

Dates change each year.

Past leaders

National flag

Chatting in the park

Climate

Malaysia's climate is both tropical and monsoonal. In the lowlands, where Kuala Lumpur is located, temperatures vary between 21°C (70°F) in the early mornings and 32°C (90°F) in the late afternoon. Humidity is high throughout the year (80%). The highlands are much cooler with temperatures as low as 10°C (50°F). Many people, especially foreigners used to cooler climates, find several air-conditioned rooms in a house to be a necessity.

The average annual rainfall in the lowlands is 254cm (100 inches); the highlands experience as much as twice that amount. Monsoons visit Kuala Lumpur in November and December. There are often violent but short thunderstorms in October and March, so it is wise to carry an umbrella.

Generally Malaysia has two seasons; the dry season from May to September and the rainy season from October until April. In Kuala Lumpur the rainiest months are March, April, October and November. In each of those months rainfall exceeds 200mm (eight inches).

The city copes quite well with heavy rain, but really severe downpours can sometimes bring traffic to a standstill as streets flood and drains are unable to handle all the water. Cars stall in deep, fast-running floods, and taxis are often impossible to find at such times. To deal with the problem of flash floods the city has found an ingenious solution, the Stormwater Management and Road Tunnel (SMART). The tunnel consists of two parts: the stormwater tunnel and the motorway tunnel. Excessive rain is diverted to the stormwater tunnel and held there until it can be safely pumped out. In really heavy rain the tunnel is closed to traffic and both tunnels are used to hold water.

Temperature & Humidity

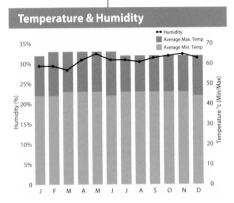

Rainfall

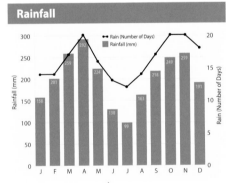

Flora & Fauna

Flowers and flowering trees are everywhere, from bougainvillea to the huge raffia flower which is a symbol of Malaysia. Coconut palms are common. Outside the city and in the forested areas inside it there are many rubber trees which are regularly tapped. Huge plantations of palm oil palms cover the surrounding area.

Kuala Lumpur is a very green city with many parks containing a variety of lowland forest trees like the jelutong tree and bamboo. Macaque monkeys are commonly seen in all but the busiest downtown parts of the city. Monkeys can occasionally pose a problem since they can be quite aggressive, especially in the presence of food. Be particularly vigilant at Batu Caves (p.189). There are also squirrels, colourful butterflies, insects, and birds in their natural habitat. Pigeons are the most common bird.

Environmental Issues

Malaysia is experiencing a number of environmental problems stemming from its drive towards development. Primary among these are deforestation, air pollution from industrial and vehicular emissions, industrial and municipal sewage in its rivers, and oil pollution in the Straits of Melaka. Although faced with these serious challenges, Malaysia has a fairly good record environmentally. A group of international scientists and researchers at Yale and Columbia universities recently ranked Malaysia ninth best on a list of 133 countries for its initiatives in tackling domestic and global environmental problems.

Oil At Sea

The Straits of Melaka is one of the world's busiest waterways – and one of its most polluted. The dumping of oil, sludge and toxic waste by ships into the sea has affected marine life and consequently the livelihoods of local fishermen.

Air Pollution

Air pollution is due to both stationary industry emissions and vehicle exhaust in industrial and urban areas. To some degree the burning of solid waste is also a cause of air pollution. Smog can be a concern under certain atmospheric conditions in the Klang Valley where Kuala Lumpur is located (occasionally schools are closed because of it). The major source of air pollution in Kuala Lumpur is car exhaust fumes from a rapidly growing fleet of private cars, in spite of government efforts to maintain strict emissions standards.

Deforestation

Indiscriminate logging has been a perennial problem. Lowland forests have been cleared for oil palm plantations resulting in erosion, floods and serious adverse effects on wildlife. The latter is particularly true in Sabah, but elsewhere as well, where forests have often been reduced to scattered fragments depriving many animals, notably elephants, of their natural homes. Also affected are orangutans, monkeys and various birds. Deforestation has also caused serious problems of silting and consequent flooding in both rural and urban areas.

Water Pollution

Water pollution still poses a serious threat in certain parts of Malaysia. Studies show that the major contributors to water pollution are agriculture, agro-based industries such as the processing of palm oil and rubber, food and beverage processing plants, textile and leather tanneries, and electronic hardware factories, many of which discharge effluents directly into rivers. Municipal sewage dumped into rivers is also a major contributor to water pollution. In 1995 only 41.7% of Malaysian rivers were classified as 'clean', that is safe for use by humans. There has been a steady improvement since. In 2006, the number of rivers in the 'cleanest' category had doubled from 2005. Only seven of Malaysia's 146 river basins were categorised as 'polluted', down from 15 the year before.

Malaysia's Response

A number of government agencies and NGOs are addressing these issues. Among them are the Department of the Environment, the Department of Fisheries, the

Rainforest at FRIM

Department of Wildlife and National Parks, the Department of Education, and the Forest Research Institute of Malaysia. Non-governmental organisations include the Malaysian Nature Society, the World Wide Fund for Nature, and the Environmental Protection Society of Malaysia. The government seems to be making a serious effort to deal with the various environmental problems both locally and internationally. For instance, Malaysia now produces only CFC-free refrigerators and, in spite of heavy industrialisation, its rate of CFC emissions is only half that of neighbouring Thailand. Kuala Lumpur enjoys a number of parks that are protected areas. The largest and most popular is the Lake Gardens (see p.174). As of yet, recycling and clean-up projects in Malaysia are in their infancy.

Culture

Malaysia is a very forward-looking, progressive country with a strong sense of pride in itself and a clear sense of direction for future development.

The dominating characteristic of Malaysia is that it is multi-ethnic. This is particularly true in Kuala Lumpur. There are three main ethnicities in the country. The Malays, who by definition are all Muslims, form the majority at about 50.8% of the population. Chinese-Malaysians, who are mostly Buddhists, constitute 23.8%, and Indian-Malaysians, who are mainly Hindus, 7.1%. Other groups that make up the population include the Orang Asli, who are the original people of the peninsula, and the more than 50 indigenous groups of Sabah and Sarawak, which are often referred to collectively as Dayak. They make up roughly 10.9% of the population. The smallest group can be crudely classified as 'others'; this group consists of Eurasians and non-Malaysians of dozens of different backgrounds forming 0.6% of the population.

There are also a considerable number of foreign nationals who have happily settled in Malaysia, particularly in Kuala Lumpur and Penang, under a programme called Malaysia My Second Home.

In daily life these ethnicities work well together and there is little apparent friction. Although Islam is the state religion of Malaysia the country is not a theocracy; all religions are tolerated and protected by law. Since the highest government posts are occupied primarily by Malays, however, Islam is a powerful influence in the formation of government policies and approaches, both internally and internationally.

Beneath the surface, however, tensions still simmer stemming from a truly traumatic moment in Malaysia's modern history. In 1969 riots broke out, mostly in Kuala Lumpur, but also in other parts of the country. Particularly involved were Malays and Chinese. The official death count was 196, but unofficial rumours continue to insist that it was many, many more. The government of the day acted swiftly to restore order and then began to address the causes of the violence. At the root was the fact that Malays, although in the majority, enjoyed only 2% of the nation's wealth.

In 1971 the government announced the New Economic Plan, a 20 year project to ensure that 30% of national wealth would be in the hands of the 'Bumiputra'(Malays and the indigenous people of the nation). Non-Malay Malaysians would be entitled to 40% and foreign interests the remaining 30%. The official language of the nation would henceforth be Malay.

Chinese and Indians whose ancestors had arrived in Malaysia a century or more ago, or even the 'Baba' descended from Chinese settlers who had arrived at the time of the Malacca Sultanate some five centuries before, were now non-Malays, or 'Pendatang' (immigrants). Although somewhat successful, the policy does give preferential treatment to Malays at the expense of the other ethnicities, and this is a cause of resentment. There are some recent indications that the government is seeking to move beyond the policy into a more open system that would offer equal advantages to Malaysians of all races.

Boleh Good

One word often heard in Malaysian even when the person is speaking in English is 'boleh' which means something like 'ok'. With a rising inflection it becomes a question, 'can you?' or 'is it possible?'. In small shops and stalls the vendor will often give you the price in dollars, pronounced 'dollah' with no 's' at the end. Don't be alarmed if the price seems high; the vendor is referring to Malaysian ringgit, not dollars. A particular patois of English is often heard in Malaysia and is known locally as 'Manglish'.

Language

Other options **Language Schools** p.243, **Learning Bahasa Malaysia** p.143

The official language of Malaysia is Malay. More commonly it is referred to as 'Bahasa', a word which means simply 'language'. Sometimes it is called 'Bahasa Melayu' to differentiate it from another variant of the same language which is spoken in Indonesia. English, however, is very widely spoken, especially in Kuala Lumpur and Penang. It is not at all uncommon to hear Malaysians speaking English to one another even when no non-Malaysian is present. In some Malaysian families, English is the mother tongue. The quality of English among the educated classes in Kuala Lumpur is very high, with many people being completely fluent. The language of business is English.

In addition, a number of other languages are commonly spoken. These include Tamil, Hokkien, Mandarin, and Cantonese. Many Malaysians, regardless of their ethnicity, speak several languages in addition to Malay and English.

Speak The Language
For easy online translations from English to Malay visit http://search.cari.com. my/dictionary.

In simpler establishments you may run into people who do not speak or understand English, but there is usually someone nearby who does and who will happily help you out. Those who do not speak English are more often Malay rather than Chinese or Indian.

Road signs are often, but not always, bilingual in Kuala Lumpur. If you are planning to drive about, it is wise to learn some of the more common messages on the signs. Shop signs are frequently bilingual, featuring both English and Malay. Restaurants commonly have bilingual, or English only, menus.

Basic Malay

General Words

No	Tidak
Please	Tolong
Thank you	Terima kasih
Yes	Ya

Greetings

Good afternoon	Selemat tengahari
Good evening	Selemat petang
Good morning	Selamat pagi
Good night	Selamat malam
Goodbye	Selamat Jalan
Hello	Hello
How are you?	Apa khabar?
Welcome	Selemat Datang

Introductions

I am from	Saya dari
My name is	Nama saya;
What is your name?	Saya nama awak? (or Siapa nama anda?)
Where are you from?	Anda di mana?

Questions

How much?	Berapa?
How?	Bagaimana?
What?	Apa?
When?	Bila?
Where?	Mana?
Who?	Siapa
Why?	Siapa

Taxi Or Car Related

Airport	Lapangan terbang
Caution	Awas
Detour	Lencongan
East	Timur
Entrance	Masuk
Exit	Keluar
First, Second	Pertama, Kedua
Highway	Leburaya
Hotel	Hotel
Intersection, crossroad	Simpang
Is this the road to?	Ini jalan ka?
Lane	Lorong

Taxi Or Car Related

Near	Dekat
North	Utara
Petrol station	Stesyen minyak
Restaurant	Restoran
Road, street	Jalan
Roundabout	Bulatan
Slow down	Kurangkan laju
South	Selatan
Stop	Berhenti
Straight ahead	Berjalan terus
Traffic light	Lampu isyarat
Turn left	Belok kiri
Turn right	Belok kanan
West	Barat

Accidents & Emergencies

Accident	Kemalangan
Ambulance	Ambulans
Clinic	Klinik
Doctor	Doktor
Hospital	Hospital
Insurance	Insurans
Licence	Lesen
Police	Polis
Sorry	Saya minta maaf

Numbers

One	Satu
Two	Dua
Three	Tiga
Four	Empat
Five	Lima
Six	Enam
Seven	Tujuh
Eight	Lapan
Nine	Sembilan
Ten	Sepuluh
One hundred, two hundred etc.	Satu ratus/seratus, dua ratus etc.
One thousand, two thousand etc.	Seribu, dua ribu etc.

Churches

Churches tend to be much smaller than mosques or temples, which are often tourist attractions as well as places of worship. For a list of Anglican churches, check the website of the Anglican Diocese of West Malaysia (03 2031 2728, www.anglican westmalaysia.org.my).

Religion

The dominant religion of Malaysia is Islam. All Malays are by definition Muslim, most of them belonging to the Sunni branch of Islam. Among both the Chinese and Indians there are also some Muslims. About 60% of all Malaysians are Muslims.

Buddhism is the predominant religion of Malaysian Chinese. Roughly 20% of Malaysians are Buddhist. Most Malaysian Indians are Hindus, although a number, known collectively as 'Jamek', are Muslim. Many Chinese and Indians are also Christians, numbering about 9% of the population. Many of the indigenous people are Animists, or believers in spirits of the forests, mountains, animals and rivers. Some are Muslims. The religions are very tolerant of one another, and the religious festivals of each are joyfully celebrated by all. The most significant religious holidays are outlined below.

Religious Holidays

Muslims in Kuala Lumpur celebrate the Prophet Muhammad's birthday and also the end of Ramadan. Hari Raya Korban marks the end of the annual Hadj to Mecca, while Hari Raya Aidilfitri (also known as Hari Raya Puasa) is the Malay name for Eid. Buddhists celebrate Wesak Day (honouring the life of Gautama Buddha), while Hindus observe Deepavali (the Festival of Light) and Thaipusam (the Festival of Atonement). Dates for all these religious celebrations vary. One which is the same date every year is the Christian celebration of Christmas Day on 25 December.

Places of Worship

Bangsar Lutheran Church	Bangsar	03 2284 5928	http://blc.net.my
Batu Caves	Gombak	See p.189	na
Cathedral of St John (Catholic)	KLCC	03 2078 1876	www.archway.org.my
Chan See Shu Yuen Temple	Chinatown	03 2070 6511	na
Christ Lutheran Church	Ampang	03 4023 0374	www.clc.org.my
Church of the Assumption (Catholic)	Petaling Jaya	03 7782 5854	www.rc.net/kualalumpur/assumption
City Discipleship Presbyterian Church	Selangor	03 5621 2844	www.cdpc.org.my
Masijd Jamek (Jamek Mosque)	Little India	03 2693 6661	na
Masijd Negara (National Mosque)	Chinatown	03 2693 7784	na
Masijd Wilayah Perseketuan	Jalan Duta	03 6201 8791	na
National Evangelical Christian Fellowship	Petaling Jaya	03 7727 8227	www.necf.org.my
Sin Sze Sin-Ya Temple	Chinatown	na	na
Sri Maha Mariamman Temple	Chinatown	See p.190	na
St Andrew's Presbyterian Church	Bukit Bintang	03 2031 1223	www.standrewschurch.org.my
St. Mary's Cathedral	Little India	03 2692 8672	www.stmarycathedral.org.my
Thean Hou Temple	Mid Valley	03 2163 3664	na
Wesley Methodist Church	City Centre	03 20720 338	www.klwmc.org

National Dress

Like so many other things in Malaysia, how you dress depends on who you are and what the occasion is. Business suits, summer dresses, open collar shirts, jeans, shorts and T-shirts are all common. Western dress is prevalent everywhere and among all classes of people, but Malaysians will also wear ethnic clothing fairly regularly as well.

For women this involves a wide variety of styles. Malay women are much more likely to dress traditionally than others. This means a brightly coloured, ankle-length, full-sleeved, batik dress called 'baju kurung' with a coordinated head scarf. Malay men, on the other hand, sometimes wear a black hat called a 'songkok'. During formal occasions, Malay men will wear their traditional costume.

Culture & Lifestyle

Buddha

National Mosque

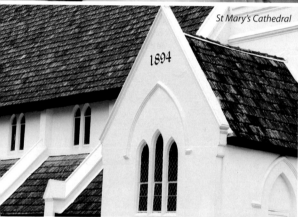
St Mary's Cathedral

1894

Religious sculpture at Thean Hou Temple

Thean Hou Temple

Chinese, Indians and other groups will also put on their traditional dress for special occasions. Chinese women wear the 'cheongsam' and Indian women will 'sarees'. For very formal occasions, such as a wedding, women will dress in their very best traditional clothing. Men will also dress traditionally or wear a colourful silk batik shirt which hangs out over their trousers. This is the equivalent of a tuxedo and much more comfortable.

Should you visit a bar or night club downtown, you might be surprised at the number of beautiful, flirtatious and somewhat scantily-clad young ladies present. However you might wish to approach these nymphs of paradise with some caution. Not all are female.

Masjid Jamek

Batu Caves

Thean Hou Temple

Food & Drink
Other options **Eating Out** p.355

Eat The World
One of the best things about living in KL is that you have virtually all the world's cuisines within reach. Taste authentic Chinese and Indian foods in Chinatown and Little India respectively or enjoy fine dining at many of the five-star hotels, and don't forget to try the local Malay cuisine. See the Going Out section, starting on p.353, for more info on KL's many restaurants, bars and pubs.

Malaysia's cuisine is one of its greatest pleasures. Traditional Malay food, itself delicious, has been strongly influenced by the various styles of Chinese and Indian cooking. It's quite common to find a fusion cuisine of these three in many restaurants. There are also frequent hints of Thai dishes. One of Malaysia's most interesting cuisines is that of the Baba Nonya or Straits Chinese. Chinese men immigrating to Malaysia over the centuries frequently took Malay wives who created a fiery, delicious style of cooking of their own. Restaurants which serve only Chinese or Indian dishes are also common. Vegetarian restaurants are often Indian. Otherwise, if you wish to dine out, there is no style of restaurant which Kuala Lumpur does not offer; western steak houses, Spanish bodegas serving tapas, Japanese restaurants with low tables, Tex-Mex, Italian, Mongolian, Thai, it's all there. Korean restaurants abound.

Malaysians and foreigners alike delight in what are called hawker stalls. These roadside food stalls usually have a few simple tables and plastic chairs available for customers and offer a wide variety of Malaysian dishes, many not available in fancier restaurants. Some care should be exercised when eating from these stalls. Prepared dishes have often been sitting for quite some time and may not be your best bet. Look for a busy place with lots of customers.

Chop Shtick
If you are given chopsticks and a ceramic spoon, hold the spoon in your left hand and use the chopsticks to place small amounts of food in it. Add spices and seasoning liberally from the condiments on the table. Put it into your mouth using the spoon. Enjoy.

There are no staples of western cuisine which are not available in the many supermarkets. New arrivals soon discover which ones are best, however, for fresh greens or fish or beef. Increasingly, any small differences between supermarkets are disappearing. Prices are generally quite reasonable, but imported meat, generally from Australia, can be costly. Buying fruit and vegetables in the small local markets (pasars) is very inexpensive and the quality is generally good.

Almost all supermarkets offer beer, wine and liquor for sale, and so do many restaurants. The exception is, of course, Muslim restaurants which serve no alcohol. Since there are a number of Indians who are Muslim as well, some Indian restaurants also may not serve alcohol. If you want a beer with your meal the safest bet is to look for a place run by Chinese. Fruit juices are very commonly consumed with meals. A special treat is the water of a chilled, freshly-opened coconut.

Muslims do not eat pork and Indians do not eat beef. Otherwise, anything goes. Rice, noodles, chicken and fish are staple food and each can be prepared in an astounding variety of wonderful ways. Pork is particularly taboo for Muslims. Butcher shops, restaurants and stalls selling pork are always placed well away from Halal places. Many restaurants of all types will announce prominently that they are Halal, which means that they serve only meat which has been butchered according to Islamic requirements. In supermarkets there are commonly two butcher shops: one for Halal meat and the other for non-Halal. They are always on opposites sides of the store.

Malays, and many other Malaysians as well, never with their left hand, which is regarded as unclean. Like so many things in Malaysia there is no hard and fast rule about eating with your hands. Some people do; some don't. Except for in high-end restaurants, diners are never given a knife. The usual utensils are chopsticks, a fork and a soup spoon. Many Malaysians watch with quiet glee as westerners politely try to eat rice with chopsticks. They use a fork or a spoon. It's much easier.

In Emergency

Kuala Lumpur has the full range of emergency services and they operate much as they do anywhere else.

Like in every big city there is a range of crime in Kuala Lumpur. Physical assault is infrequent, but snatch and grab robberies, pickpocketing, burglaries and walk-up cons are more common. Snatch and grab robbers often use motorcycles, so walk on the side of the street away from the traffic. Otherwise, exercise all the usual precautions that you would anywhere. Police are helpful and polite, but are not able to do much except fill in a report if you are the victim of a snatch and grab or pickpocketing crime. In areas where tourists are common, the tourist police keep a careful eye out for con artists and thieves, but unless what is lost is very big and obvious, you are unlikely to recover stolen property. Be particularly vigilant with credit cards. It is best not to let them out of your sight anywhere. The emergency number for the police is 999. From a mobile phone dial 112.

Hospitals

Ampang Puteri Hospital	03 4270 2500
Damansara Hospital	03 7722 2692
Gleneagles Intan Hospital	03 4257 1300
Heartscan	03 2287 0988
National Poison Centre	1800 888 099
Pantai Medical Centre	03 2296 0888
Selangor Medical	03 5543 1111
St. John Ambulance of Malaysia	03 9285 1576
Sunway Medical	03 7491 9191

Lost & Stolen Documents

It is wise to keep a photocopy of your passport ID page, your visa page and other travel documents in a secure place in case of theft. It is not necessary to constantly carry your passport with you in Kuala Lumpur.

Hospitals & Ambulances

There are a number of first-rate medical facilities and ambulance services in Kuala Lumpur and the personnel who staff them regularly speak English. The emergency number for an ambulance is 999. From a mobile phone dial 112.

Gay & Lesbian

Other options **Going Out** p.354

Kuala Lumpur has a fairly active gay and lesbian scene in spite of the fact that same-gender sexual activity is illegal. Although homophobia is rare, it is wise to act discreetly and avoid unwanted attention – remember that even between straight couples overt displays of affection are considered inappropriate. There are some gay and lesbian bars and clubs in the Central Market area, on Jalan Sultan Ismail, and on Jalan Changkat Bukit Bintang.

Women

Women can generally feel safe anywhere in Kuala Lumpur, including public transportation, but they should exercise the same caution as anywhere else in the world. Dark and seedy-looking areas late at night should be avoided. Physical assault, although it does happen, is still relatively rare. Much more frequently, women are the victims of purse snatchers using motorcycles.

Examples of harassment are rare in Kuala Lumpur, especially in Chinese and Indian areas. In Muslim areas, harassment is very unlikely if women are modestly dressed. This can be confusing since in other parts of

Embassies & Consulates

Australia	03 2146 5555
Belgium	03 2162 0025
Canada	03 2718 3333
China	03 2142 8585
Denmark	03 2032 2001
France	03 2053 5500
Germany	03 2142 9666
India	03 2093 3507
Ireland	03 2161 2963
Italy	03 4256 5122
Japan	03 2142 7044
Netherlands	03 2168 6200
New Zealand	03 2078 2533
Russia	03 4256 0009
Singapore	03 2161 6277
South Africa	03 2168 8663
Spain	03 2142 8776
Sweden	03 2052 2550
UAE	03 4257 1932
UK	03 2170 2200
USA	03 2168 5000

the city, no such stricture applies. Still, better safe than sorry. When visiting a mosque, women must have all limbs covered and wear a head scarf. Malaysians, no matter what ethnicity, never go topless at a beach.

If you are being harassed, try appealing to Malaysians passing by. They will be mortified by such unsavoury behaviour and immediately come to your rescue.

Children

Although Kuala Lumpur is generally child friendly, special facilities for children and childcare in shopping malls are rare. Mid and high-range restaurants usually have high chairs and special children's menus, but no such thing as toys and colouring books to keep little hands busy. Many hotels offer babysitting services. Mums' and tots' groups are usually located through either schools or expat groups like The Association of British Women in Malaysia (www.abwm.com.my) or the Malaysian Australian and New Zealand Association (MANZA, www.manza.org). Kuala Lumpur has a zoo, a bird park, a butterfly park, and several theme parks such as Cosmo's World (p.241) in the Berjaya Times Square Mall. Sunway Pyramid (p.341) has a small skating rink and various other attractions for children.

People With Disabilities

People with disabilities do not fare particularly well in Kuala Lumpur, although the situation is slowly improving. Pavements are sometimes uneven, often having several different levels in one block, and ramps for wheelchairs are few and inconsistently distributed. Kerbs are very high. Airports, hotels and tourist attractions usually have elevators to accommodate those with disabilities, but not always. Parking spots for people with disabilities are largely non-existent. Public toilets (with the exception of airports) probably do not have a disabled toilet. However, as a general rule, the newer a facility is, the more likely it is to have made some accommodation for those with disabilities. The modern light rail systems such as the Monorail, however, are reasonably accessible. Both Malaysia Airlines and KTM (the national rail service) give 50% discounts to travellers with disabilities.

What To Wear

Since the temperature in Malaysia is fairly consistent (and hot) throughout the year, light clothing is always preferable. Generally very brief shorts and tiny tops are not appropriate anywhere but on the beach or at a holiday resort. That said, many young women wear mini-skirts and tight jeans. Shorts and T-shirts for men are also common. If you are invited to someone's home, however, you will want to dress a little more elegantly. Men should eschew T-shirts in favour of shirts with collars and also wear long trousers. If the person who invites you is Muslim, you must dress conservatively. This means sleeves and modest skirts for women and long trousers for men.

Should you go to the highlands, you should take along a light sweater or jacket since the evenings can be cool.

Dos & Don'ts

There are few dos and don'ts in Kuala Lumpur that would surprise a visitor or new resident. The residents of Kuala Lumpur like their city to be free of litter, so dispose of wrappings appropriately. Don't expect beer in every restaurant; many won't serve it. People usually don't smoke in restaurants unless they are outside on a terrace.

Photography

Photography is widely accepted, especially in tourist areas, and Malaysians usually enjoy having their photo taken. Often they will flash a big grin and a 'v' for victory sign for the photographer. Like everywhere else you should, of course, ask permission before photographing people. Photographs of military installations, military personnel and police and airports are not permitted.

Crime & Safety
Other options **In Emergency** p.18

The government recently released figures showing a rise in the crime rate of 13.4 % in 2007. The greatest number of felonies by far were gang robberies without the use of firearms. Public anxiety has made the rising crime rate a major issue in the upcoming federal elections. Kuala Lumpur, nevertheless, remains a safe city, although it is best to avoid Pudu and Sentul after dark. Stay away at all times from Jalan Choo Cheng Khay which is the scene of much drug-related crime.

There is a demerit system for driving infractions although it is laxly administered. In theory, for instance, you lose two points for speeding or illegal parking, even though both are endemic in Kuala Lumpur. Driving while intoxicated is treated somewhat more seriously. If a breathalyser test reveals that you are over the legal limit, your car is temporarily impounded and a fine of RM300 is levied.

All traffic accidents by law must be reported to the police, but especially any in which there are casualties. Not reporting an accident is a serious offence.

Should you be arrested, you will be read your rights and allowed to contact a lawyer (the state does not provide lawyers). You will be taken to a police station holding cell, and how long you can be held without charge depends on the severity of the crime of which you are suspected. In the case of homicide, for instance, it is seven days. Bail may be set by a magistrate.

At present, the prison system is not particularly rehabilitative in nature except for those convicted of drug-related offences. Because of the problem of persistent overcrowding, however, it is moving in that direction. Prisoners have the right not to be physically mistreated; Malaysian prisoners do not lose their right to vote. Visiting hours vary from institution to institution. As an effort to alleviate crowded conditions in penal institutions, parliament passed a bill instituting a parole system in December

Guard at Royal Palace

Police HQ

2007. However, it will be some time before the infrastructure to implement the parole system is in place. Malaysia has the death penalty and it is administered equally to convicted Malaysians and expats. Death is by hanging for homicide and possession of drugs in quantities suggesting intent to sell. Two hundred grams of cannabis or 15 grams of heroin will get you the rope. If you are tempted by drugs, please take the next sentence very seriously. Don't do it.

Police

The Royal Malaysia Police Force is a centralised force with a number of roles ranging from traffic control to intelligence gathering. Ordinary police wear dark blue uniforms, incorporating berets or baseball caps. Whether or not they carry a sidearm depends on their assignment. Tourist police look similar and can be distinguished only by their shoulder patch. They are stationed in places frequented by visitors because they speak English and know their area of the city well. Highway police on motorcycles wear black riding trousers with black boots, a black Sam Browne belt and white shirts. When not wearing motorcycle helmets, they wear black baseball caps. At road blocks it is common to see them together with regular police. Highway police carry a sidearm. There are also undercover police in civilian clothes at work, particularly in areas where drugs are present.

Malaysia also has a Federal Reserve Unit which is called in during times when crowd control is required, such as a demonstration or other large public event. They are distinguished by red helmets and dark blue uniforms with prominent patches of red on their shirts.

There are also General Operations Forces including Special Action Units modelled on SWAT teams, and the Special Operations Force, a commando battalion for combating insurgents in the jungle (you are most unlikely to see these in the city). Both wear plain green uniforms, not camouflage.

Another branch is the rakan cop which means literally 'friends of cops'. It is an auxiliary police force called in wherever needed to support the regular police. They have only a few police powers. For instance, they can hold suspects for the regular police, but not formally arrest them. They are often used for security, for protecting bank money transfers, and for crowd control. They wear a uniform of dark blue trousers and a light blue shirt. Their shoulder patch says 'Rakan Cop'.

Many large residential building complexes, shopping malls, schools and other public areas employ private security services which come in a bewildering variety of uniforms. Their responsibility is security within and around their respective building complexes. Often the officers of these services do duty as traffic policemen outside their buildings in hours of congestion as well. They are not armed. Within their jurisdictions they can levy parking fines, clamp cars and hold people suspected of an offence for the regular police.

Tourist Information

Tourism Malaysia	Jalan Tun Ismail	03 2615 8188
World Express Tours	Ampang	03 2148 9601
MATTA	Desa Pandan	03 9287 6881

City Information

The best source of information about tourism in Malaysia is Tourism Malaysia, the government agency. It specialises in domestic visits and offers assistance with such things as trip planning and accommodation. The organisation's website also has many links to other agencies (log on to www.tourism.gov.my). World Express Tours offers both domestic and foreign tour services. Its expertise is in special events, meetings, hotels and cruises (see www.worldexpress.travel). MATTA, The Malaysian Association of Tour and Travel Agents is also a useful contact (visit www.matta.org.my).

A comprehensive list of tour operators in Malaysia can be found at www.eguide. com.my. See also p.200.

Places To Stay

Kuala Lumpur offers a wide range of hotel accommodation ranging from five-star to budget. There are a number of international chains, such as Hilton, Marriott, Sheraton and Holiday Inn represented. Mid-range and budget hotels are usually locally owned and operated. Motels and campsites are not found in Kuala Lumpur, where space is at a premium. Resthouses still exist in smaller towns in the countryside, but are somewhat too closely associated with the colonial past to still be in existence in the nation's capital.

Hotels

Five Star	Phone	Website
Equatorial Hotel	03 2161 7777	www.equatorial.com
Hilton Hotel KL	03 2264 2264	www1.hilton.com
JW Marriott KL	03 2715 9000	www.marriott.com
Ritz Carleton KL	03 2142 8000	www.ritzcarleton.com
Four Star		
Concorde Hotel	03 2144 2200	www.concorde.net
Crown Princess Kuala Lumpur	03 2162 5522	www.crownprincess.com.my
Dorsett Regency	03 2715 1000	www.dorsettregency.com.my
Three Star		
Allson Genesis	03 2141 2000	www.allson-genesis.com
Royale Bintang Hotel	03 2143 3134	www.royale-bintang.hotel.com.my
Two Star		
Bintang Warisan Hotel	03 8787 3894	www.bintangwarisan.com
One Star		
Cardogan Hotel	03 2144 4883	www.cardogan.com
Budget		
Backpacker's Travellers Lodge	03 2031 0889	na
Hotel Grand Olympic	03 2078 7888	www.kl-hotels.com
Le Village	03 2026 6737	na

Hotels

Other options **Landmark Hotels** p.23

Hotels are rated by the international star system; however, many of the lower end hotels and hostels carry no star classification at all. The city has a total of 20 five-star and 24 four-star hotels. In 2007, Tourism Malaysia recognised a total of 229 hotels in Kuala Lumpur, offering 30,401 rooms. They are conveniently located all across the downtown area, but many of the best are in the Golden Triangle and Kuala Lumpur City Centre (KLCC) areas. Hotels of all types are relatively inexpensive given the value and services they offer. Rooms are of international standard in the best hotels; in the budget ones, they are clean and comfortable if somewhat spartan. The very cheapest of rooms in Kuala Lumpur goes for around $10; five-star hotels cost up to $250. A night in a suite at the landmark Carcosa Seri Negara (p.23) might cost you between $500 and $1,000.

A five or four-star hotel offers all the amenities one would expect including a pool, a gym, boutiques and restaurants. A budget hotel will offer only rooms, many with fans but not air conditioning. Most of the best budget hotels are found in Chinatown. Some recommendations are Le Village, Backpackers' Travellers Lodge, and the YMCA. Kuala Lumpur's location in the Klang valley places it far from any natural features which would allow for eco-lodges or mountain retreats. Spas and holistic treatment centres tend to be separately run businesses close to the hotels rather than part of the facilities offered directly by the hotels themselves.

Landmark Hotels

Carcosa Seri Negara

Taman Tasik Perdana
KL Sentral
🚇 *KL Sentral*
Map 6 F1

03 2282 1888 | *www.ghmhotels.com*

Located in the lovely Lake Garden Park, the Carcosa Seri Negara, one of Kuala Lumpur's top five-star hotels, was originally a two-mansion retreat for the governor and his guests. Now the hotel provides 13 luxurious suites for those with deep pockets. A 24 hour butler service and a range of first-class dining options will make sure you live the high life for the duration of your stay here.

Crowne Plaza Hotel

Jalan Sultan Ismail
KLCC
🚇 *Raja Chulan*
Map 11 B4

03 2148 2322 | *www.ichotelsgroup.com*

An award-winning four-star hotel situated in landscaped gardens in the heart of KL's business, entertainment and shopping area. With a well-equipped health and fitness centre and a huge spa, this is a good choice when you want to treat your body right. Six eating and drinking outlets cater for those who want some good grub and fine wine in pleasant surroundings.

Federal Hotel

35 Jalan Bukit
Bintang
Bukit Bintang
🚇 *Imbi*
Map 13 B2

03 2148 9166 | *www.fhihotels.com*

Built in 1957 to celebrate Malaysia's independence, the four-star Federal is a historical landmark. It is situated among luxurious tropical gardens and boasts Malaysia's first revolving restaurant, the Revolving Bintang Restaurant, which is the perfect romantic setting. There are seven other food and beverage outlets in the Federal, which is also a very short distance from KL's lively Bintang Walk.

Hotel Istana

73 Jalan Raja Chulan
Bukit Bintang
🚇 *Raja Chulan*
Map 11 B4

03 2141 9988 | *www.hotelistana.com.my*

A central location and a high level of luxury make this five-star hotel a safe bet for accommodation and leisure. The Sompoton Spa features traditional Malay treatments, and the hotel's five restaurants and bars offer a range of cuisines in beautiful settings. Rooms are spacious with conveniences such as broadband internet and a butler service on the Club Floor.

Hotel Maya Kuala Lumpur

138 Jalan Ampang
KLCC
🚇 *KLCC*
Map 11 A1

03 2711 8866 | *www.hotelmaya.com.my*

Timber floors in the 107 suites (there are over 200 rooms in total) and floor-to-ceiling windows make this a luxurious choice of five-star hotel in KL. The all-marble Sky Lounge, reserved for hotel guests, has a huge balcony offering spectacular views of the city's characteristic skyline. The hotel is noted for its excellent Anggun Spa.

Hotel Nikko

165 Jalan Ampang
KLCC
Ampang Park
Map 11 D1

03 2161 1111 | www.hotelnikko.com.my

Hotel Nikko, part of the well-known Japanese chain, is the five-star choice of discerning business travellers, thanks to its proximity to Jalan Ampang and the business district. Of course, the levels of luxury and the superb cuisine available in the hotel's five restaurants keeps hotel guests happy too, while the leisure facilities provide the perfect wind down for any businessman or holidaymaker.

Impiana KLCC Hotel & Spa

13 Jalan Pinang
KLCC
KLCC
Map 11 B3

03 2147 1111 | www.impiana.com

Catering to both business and leisure travellers, this four-star hotel is known for its excellent health and fitness facilities, where both aerobics and yoga classes are available, as well as a designer infinity pool. Discover your inner connoisseur at the hotel's very own cigar bar, or enjoy an end-of-the-day tipple at the Oswega wine bar.

Mandarin Oriental

Jalan Pinang
KLCC
KLCC
Map 11 B2

03 2715 8818 | www.mandarinoriental.com

Kuala Lumpur's most sumptuous hotel, located next to the Petronas Towers and the high-end shopping of the Suria KLCC, the Mandarin Oriental is a five-star haven for both business travellers and tourists. This elegant, art-filled hotel also has six award-winning restaurants offering a range of cuisines, including Cantonese, Japanese and European.

Novotel Hydro Majestic

2 Jalan Kia Peng
Bukit Bintang
Raja Chulan
Map 11 C4

03 2147 0888 | www.novotel.com

Offering comfortable accommodation at reasonable rates this four-star hotel is centrally located between the Bukit Bintang area and the Petronas Towers. It is also close to the nightlife of KL's famous Bintang Walk. There is a restaurant and bar inside the hotel, but the surrounding area is home to countless bars, restaurants and nightclubs, as well as shopping hotspots.

Parkroyal Hotel Kuala Lumpur

Jalan Sultan Ismail
Bukit Bintang
Bukit Bintang
Map 13 C2

03 2147 0088 | www.parkroyalhotels.com

This beautiful five-star hotel, in the heart of the Golden Triangle, incorporates 348 rooms and suites, and a range of fine restaurants enabling you to sample Asian, western, Chinese and Brazilian cuisine without leaving the hotel. With such a central location, there's plenty going on in the area's many nightspots and shopping destinations.

Putrajaya Shangri-La

Taman Putra Perdana
Presint 1, 62000 Wilayah
Persekutuan
Putrajaya
Putrajaya

03 8887 8888 | *www.shangri-la.com*

Surrounded by beautifully landscaped gardens, this stylish hotel sits on a hill overlooking the picturesque city of Putrajaya. Each of the 118 guest rooms has a private terrace so you can enjoy the view. Enjoy international and Malay cuisine in the hotel's two restaurants, or take in a bit of rest and relaxation in the health club and spa, complete with seven semi-alfresco villas and suites.

Renaissance Hotel KL

Cnr Jalan Sultan
Ismail & Jalan Ampang
KLCC
Bukit Nanas
Map 10 F2

03 2163 6888 | *www.marriott.com*

This two-wing hotel features all the usual five-star extravagances including several award-winning restaurants, what is perhaps Kuala Lumpur's most opulent lobby, and an olympic-sized pool. You'll also find an aromatherapy spa and a fitness centre on site, as well as a number of recreation and nightlife attractions nearby.

Shangri-La

11 Jalan Sultan Ismail
KLCC
Raja Chulan
Map 11 A3

03 2032 2388 | *www.shangri-la.com*

In the centre of the Golden Triangle, the five-star Shangri-La is one of Kuala Lumpur's most elegant hotels. Tucked slightly back from the bustle of Jalan Sultan Ismail and surrounded by lush vegetation, it welcomes you to an oasis of green tranquility. A selection of classy eateries and bars are worth a visit, even for non-hotel guests.

Sunway Resort Hotel & Spa

Persiaran Lagoon
Bandar Sunway
Selangor
Setia Jaya

03 7492 8000 | *www.sunwayhotels.com*

This five-star resort is situated right by the Sunway Lagoon theme park, and has nearly 450 beautiful rooms, including 73 luxurious suites. You can eat in one of several restaurants on site, or in over 200 outlets in the adjacent shopping mall. Unwind in the Mandara Spa, stroll round the landscaped gardens, take a dip in the pool, or enjoy a game of rooftop tennis at this destination resort.

Traders Hotel

Kuala Lumpur
City Centre
KLCC
KLCC
Map 11 C3

03 2332 9888 | *www.shangri-la.com*

The ultimate business hotel in Kuala Lumpur, Traders offers a complete 24 hour business service including wireless internet in all public areas, private meeting rooms, secretarial services and video conferencing facilities. This four-star destination is also home to the Sky Bar (p.404), a buzzing nightspot with unbeatable views of the Petronas Towers.

Hotel Apartments

Kuala Lumpur has a number of hotel apartments which are not rated by a system. They are usually available for the period of a month or longer, although lengths of stay and price can be negotiated (shorter stays are often allowed too). All offer kitchenettes, entertainment centres, security, parking and safes. Apartment blocks usually have gyms and pools as well.

Hotel Apartments	
Berjaya KL Plaza Suites	www.berjayaresorts.com
Crown Regency Serviced Suites	www.crownregency.com.my
Duta Vista Executive Suites	www.tancoresart.com
Holiday Villa Apartment Suites	www.holidayvilla.com.my
Lanson Place Serviced Residence	www.lansonplace.com
MiCasa Hotel Apartments	www.micasahotel.com
Pacific Regency Hotel Suites	www.pacific-regency.com
PNB Darby Park Apartments	www.apartmentsmalaysia.com
SuCasa Service apartments	www.sucasahotel.com
The Ascott Kuala Lumpur	www.the-ascott.com
The Maple Suite	www.themaplesuite.com
The Zon All Suite Residences	www.zonhotel.com.my
Wedgewood Serviced Residences	www.wedgewoodresidences.com

Guesthouses

Kuala Lumpur has guesthouses, which are more commonly called 'homestays'. Establishments which advertise as 'bed and breakfasts' are more often small budget hotels which include a simple breakfast in their price rather than what you might expect when you hear 'bed and breakfast'. Most guesthouses and homestays are simple, clean and comfortable. Often the friendliness of the staff is the greatest asset of the establishment. There is no rating system for either and often online travel services will provide you with contact information but will not make reservations for you. It's simply not worth it to them since guesthouses and homestays run in the RM30 to RM40 range. However, homestays can provide a cost-effective, authentic way to experience the 'real' KL.

Guesthouses	
Anjung KL Guesthouse	www.anjungkl.com
Attapsana	03 2142 0710
Eight Guesthouse	www.numbereight.com.my
The Haven Guesthouse	http://thehavenkl.com

Hostels

Hostels in Kuala Lumpur are usually independent, rather than members of YHA. They cater particularly to backpackers. Looking for a hostel anywhere in Malaysia can be confusing because of semantics. Terms like hostel, guesthouse, homestay and bed and breakfast are used very casually. What is advertised as a hostel may, in fact, be a budget hotel with only single and double rooms.

Hostels offer both private and dorm accommodation. Prices vary according to several factors, such as air conditioning, private or communal bathroom, and how many beds per room. A single room costs from RM50 to RM80, a double room from RM70 to RM100. Beds in a six-bed dorm run from RM25 to RM35 per bed.

The best, and more expensive, hostels like the YMCA offer a number of facilities such as cafes, launderettes, internet access and child care. Singles and doubles at the YMCA cost RM80; triples are RM100; quads are RM120.

Whatever the price range, hostels, like budget hotels, are usually clean and centrally located in the Bukit Bintang or Chinatown areas. Breakfast is normally included in the price. There are no age restrictions.

Hostels		
Equator Hostel	03 2145 2120	www.equatorhostel.com
Pudu Hostel	03 2078 9600	www.puduhostel.com
Red Palm KL Backpackers Hostel	03 2143 1279	www.redpalm-kl.com
Trekker Lodge	03 2142 4633	www.thetrekkerlodge.com
YMCA Hostel	03 2274 1439	www.ymcakl.com

Great things can come in small packages…

Perfectly proportioned to fit in your pocket, these marvellous mini guidebooks make sure you don't just get the holiday you paid for, but rather the one that you dreamed of.

Explorer Mini Visitors' Guides
Maximising your holiday, minimising your hand luggage

Getting Around

Other options **Exploring** p.156

The most common modes of transportation in the city are taxis, private cars and the various light rail systems (usually referred to as LRTs). Kuala Lumpur does not have trams or underground/metro systems.

Many people use both a car and an LRT on the same journey. They drive to a convenient train station, park, and use the light railway to enter the inner city thereby avoiding congested one-way streets, aggressive drivers and the often complete unavailability of parking. Driving downtown is generally a challenge best left to those born to it.

Moving across the city by car or taxi means getting onto one of the larger arteries such as Jalan Duta, Jalan Ampang, Jalan Kuching or Jalan Tun Razak. Inevitably these are busy; traffic jams are long and the patience of other drivers is not. Another option is to use the federal highway which cuts through the city, or the North Klang Valley Expressway (NKVE) which sweeps around it. Both are toll roads and consequently not so busy. Since the road system in Kuala Lumpur continues to develop rapidly, but on a rather ad hoc basis, there is little likelihood that there will be vast improvements in the near future. The one hope is the expansion of the various light rail systems which are clean, rapid, efficient and inexpensive.

Air Travel

The Kuala Lumpur International Airport (KLIA) is the country's major air hub. From it regular and frequent flights connect to various cities in Asia, North America, the Pacific, the near east and Europe. Common destinations are Auckland, Melbourne, Los Angeles, Rome, Paris, London, Frankfurt, Bangkok, Singapore, Hong Kong, Shanghai, Seoul and Taiwan.

Many domestic flights also leave from KLIA to all the major urban areas of West and East Malaysia including Penang, Ipoh, Kuala Terengganu, and Kota Kinabalu.

The airport is quite large and consists of two terminals. The second terminal is for passengers only and connected to the first by a rapid monorail train. Although busy, KLIA is blessed with excellent organisation, world-class facilities and an efficient staff. A few electronic check-in terminals are available although most travellers still check in in the traditional way.

Flight information for departures and arrivals is prominently displayed on large electronic bulletin boards and kept up to the minute. Stored luggage, lost luggage, emergency services, limousines and taxi services are all available.

Immigration, customs and security agents are brisk and business-like and waits are seldom long. There are a number of duty-free shops and restaurants available once you

Airlines

American Airlines	03 2078 1168	www.aa.com
British Airways	03 2167 6188	www.british-airways.com
Cathay Pacific	03 2078 3377	www.cathaypacific.com
China Airlines	03 2142 7344	www.china-airlines.com
Emirates	03 2058 5888	www.emirates.com
Eva Air	03 2162 2981	www.evaair.com
Garuda Indonesia	03 2162 2811	www.garuda-indonesia.com
Gulf Air	03 2141 2676	www.gulfairco.com
Japan Airlines	03 2161 1722	www.ar.jal.com
KLM Royal Dutch Airlines	03 2711 9811	www.klm.com.my
Korean Airlines	03 2142 8460	www.koreanair.com
Lufthansa	03 2161 4666	www.lufthansa.com
Malaysia Airlines	03 7843 3300	www.malaysiaairlines.com
Northwest Airlines	03 2161 0203	www.nwa.com
Qatar Airways	03 2141 8281	www.qatarairways.com
Qantas	03 2167 6000	www.qantas.com.au
Royal Brunei Airlines	03 2070 7166	www.bruneiair.com
Saudia Arabian Airlines	03 2166 4488	www.saudiairlines.com
Singapore Airlines	03 8776 6425	www.singaporeair.com
Swiss International Air Lines	03 2163 5885	www.swiss.com
Turkish Airlines	03 2713 6199	www.thy.com
United Airlines	03 2161 1433	www.united.com

have cleared customs. There is also an in-airport hotel for weary travellers in transit. Airport Customer Service can be contacted at 03 8776 4911. Besides the two regular terminals at KLIA, there is a third, the Low Cost Carrier Terminal (LCCT). Located across the vast expanse of landing strips from the main buildings, it is the home of AirAsia (03 8776 4777, www.airasia.com), a no-frills budget airline efficiently serving destinations in Asia.

Kuala Lumpur International Airport

AirAsia is currently looking at expanding its operations to include flights to Europe and Australia. For short flights into destinations like Bangkok or Siem Reap, near Angkor Wat, AirAsia is well worth looking into. The terminal, like the airline, is no-frills but efficient.

About 65 kilometres from the city centre, KLIA is easily accessible by a variety of means, including private car, taxi or the KLIA Ekspres train which can be caught at the KL Sentral train station. Baggage check-in is available at the KLIA Ekspres terminal. It costs RM35 and takes around 28 minutes. One interesting quirk is that although you can take a city taxi to the airport, you cannot hail a city taxi there for the ride back into town – you must use an airport taxi service. Immediately after exiting customs you will come to a counter called Taxi Services. Purchase a ticket there. It is much cheaper than running into the taxi touts as you exit. Unless you have mountains of luggage, ask for a budget taxi and expect to pay between RM60 and RM90.

The national carrier is Malaysian Airlines, which has an excellent reputation. In 2006, *Travel Weekly*, a British magazine, named it the best airline to Asia, and in 2005, *Skytrax*, UK, named it as one of the top five airlines in the world.

Bicycle

Other options **Cycling** p.226

Bicycles are rarely used for transportation by either locals or expats, and you won't find any cycle paths in the city. Heat and traffic are both factors in the lack of popularity of the bicycle as a mode of transport; it's too hot and sweaty, and the traffic varies from the busy to the downright crazy. There are some mountain bike enthusiasts – contact the Kuala Lumpur Mountain Bike Hash Club by logging on to www.bikehash.freeservers.com (or see Activities, p.213).

Boat

There is no body of water big enough in Kuala Lumpur to warrant the use of boats. The closest ferry connections are in Klang, some 40 kilometres away. The ferry crosses the Straits of Melaka to Indonesia.

Bus

There is an extensive city bus system, but it is rarely used by non-Malaysians because of time, crowding, and language difficulties. City buses are run by different companies. The biggest by far is RapidKL, the government-sanctioned company (www.rapidkl.com.my). Its buses are red and white. Other private companies serving some routes around KL include Metrobus and Setara Jaya.

Car

Other options **Transportation** p.144

In Malaysia motorists drive on the left, and the slow lane is the one furthest to the left. Speed limits are usually posted on all major arteries. Malaysians blithely ignore them. It's generally best to keep up with, but not be faster than, the traffic around you. The road signs are understandable, but you may find a few that aren't in English. When you see a familiar red sign with the word 'berhenti' it clearly means 'stop'. Directional signs can be more confusing since they tend to include so much information that it is sometimes hard to read them while keeping up with the swiftly moving traffic. Using a map to get around is not always helpful because signs tend to tell you what lies ahead, but not what road you are on. As forks and clover-leaf interchanges are frequent, this can quickly become a problem.

For the driver, even one born in the city, getting around can be a challenge. Roads and streets are not laid out in a grid system, but seem simply to have grown around the many natural obstacles of the terrain. Roads and streets curve and loop, climb and dip, until your sense of direction is totally challenged. Most people will tell you that they learn to get from point A to point B through trial and error and that the longer they live in KL the more the list of places they can comfortably drive to grows.

Kuala Lumpur has a major problem with parking everywhere. There are simply never enough spots. Double parking is an epidemic in many quarters of the city. Sometimes drivers double park on both sides of a street allowing only one narrow lane down the middle. It's usually best to park in a car park (such as a multi-storey). You may pay more, but you will be able to leave when you want.

Many drivers, particularly motorcyclists, show a similar disregard for traffic lights. Jumping red lights at high speed is common, so when the light changes to green, accelerate cautiously.

Roads are often quite congested. Those who can afford to regularly use the various toll roads. On some the driver pays a few ringett at a toll booth and proceeds to the next one. On others you receive a ticket on entering the system and pay a graduated toll when you exit. Most people who use the toll roads frequently take advantage of the smart card system, which allows you to prepay a set amount and use the card to move through the tolls swiftly.

Car owners pay annual road taxes and the appropriate sticker must be exhibited on the left-hand side of the windscreen. Usually the car owner's insurance company will take care of procuring the road tax sticker for the client.

Cars are available in a number of locations for hire and lease. Please refer to the Residents section for more information (p.43).

Watch Out!
A common modus operandi among pickpockets is to swipe your handbag or mobile phone out of your hand as they speed past on a motorcycle. It's best to walk as far away from the kerb as you can, and always hold anything valuable on the opposite side to the traffic.

Motorcycles

Small motorcycles are everywhere in Kuala Lumpur and pose a serious hazard to car drivers, pedestrians and the other motorcyclists. A significant number of people on motorcycles are not licensed and they drive quite recklessly. Going through red lights and stop signs, changing lanes violently to dart in front of cars, and blocking off whole lanes of traffic under bridges during rain storms are all normal occurrences in the city.

Taxi Companies

Airport Limousine	03 8787 3030
Comfort Cab	03 8024 2727
Hotline Cab	03 2095 3399
Khidmat Saujana Cab	03 2162 8888
KL Taxi	03 9221 4241
New Supercab	03 7875 7333
Outstation Taxi	03 2078 0213
Public Cab	03 6259 2020
Radion Cab	03 9221 7600
Shah Alam Taxi	03 5543 1455
Sunlight Cab	03 9057 5757
Wira Cab	03 4042 2643

It should come as no surprise that 65% of traffic fatalities in Malaysia are motorcycle drivers and their pillion passengers. However, even though it's dangerous, some expats do choose to ride one.

Taxi

All taxis have meters. To avoid any hassles, you should verify that the meter is turned on as soon as your trip begins. If you ask the driver to use the meter, there will invariably be a sad story about how the meter isn't working, but persevere, since a metered journey is almost always cheaper than the 'special price' offered by the driver.

There are a number of independently operated taxi companies. Kuala Lumpur has approximately 200,000 taxis. They are easy to find everywhere except on the most residential of streets. You can phone for a taxi pick-up, although this service is sometimes unreliable during rush hours. It is expected that you add at least RM1 to the metered fare if you are picked up. Tariffs are quite low, which is why you will often see three passengers in one cab; this way it is actually cheaper than taking the light rail. Fares depend on distance driven and time taken. In traffic jams or rain you can expect to pay more. For most destinations downtown a typical fare would be RM5 to RM10. To get from downtown to one of the outlying neighbourhoods might cost RM10 to RM15. Sometimes a driver, all of whom are male, will quote a price before accepting you in the cab. This might be for several reasons. If your destination is on the outskirts of town, he might not easily get a fare while returning to his usual routes so he is losing money. If it is raining heavily, traffic may come to a standstill and for many drivers it is cheaper to save fuel by parking than to spend an hour driving for a few ringett. Lastly, he might quite simply be trying to cheat you. Judge each occasion this happens separately and decide whether it is worth a few more ringgit to you. Quietly refusing an inflated fare and walking away is your other option.

Taxis are always available at the entrances of hotels, but they cost more, because they are higher-quality cars than those used by most taxi companies. A relatively new addition to the KL taxi fleet is 'executive taxis' – these are bright royal blue in colour and although they are slightly more expensive, they are comfortable and reliable. They are operated by Pempena Executive Taxi Services (PETS), and you can find out more info by calling 03 2161 6911.

Generally public taxis are multicoloured and their meters are set at the lowest rate. Most commonly they are a Malaysian-produced car called the Proton. More luxurious taxis are coloured white and their meters are set slightly higher.

Most taxi drivers know the city extremely well. At first it can be disconcerting when a driver takes you down narrow alleys to avoid traffic jams, but it is not a cause for alarm. His time is money; the more fares he has in a day, the more able he is to make ends meet. He is saving you both time. If your destination is far from his usual haunts, the driver may ask you if you know the way. He will know how to get to the general area but may not be sure of the location of a specific building. If you don't know the way, once you get to the general area, the driver will stop to ask a local taxi driver for directions.

Stories abound of taxi scams in Kuala Lumpur, but the truth is that most drivers are honest and polite. A few are even quite chatty. If you find a driver that you particularly like, it's worth asking him for a card and using his services regularly. Should you run into any unpleasantness, simply take the number of the cab and the driver's name. By law both must be prominently displayed on the dashboard of the car. Phone the authorities at 03 8886 6400 to lodge a complaint against a particular taxi driver.

Hailing Without Failing

You can hail a cab from the side of the road but even an empty one might not stop on a busy street. It's best to pick a spot allowing the driver room to pull over without impeding traffic, or looking for one of the many taxi stops where you might have to queue. There is no light system to indicate that a cab is busy. Just hail any one that looks empty by raising your arm, or holding it straight out from your body. Malaysians do not shout to hail cabs. It would be considered very rude behavior.

Taxi companies in Kuala Lumpur do not normally have websites or email addresses. Bookings for pick-ups are made by phone. You will be asked for a home phone number and will receive a call when the cab is on the way. If you do not get a call within a quarter of an hour, phone the company back. If you are using a mobile phone, you will usually have to call back yourself to ensure that a cab is coming.

Train

Malaysian Railways has tracks to all the major towns on the peninsula and connects to Thailand and Singapore. Cars are air conditioned and are divided into first, second and economy class. First and second class offer sleeping berths for overnight passengers. Trains have dining cars. Fares are reasonable.

Light Rail Trains & KTM

The rail systems serving Kuala Lumpur are efficient, clean and safe, but not always easy to use until you know the ins and outs. Because they were built by different companies at different times, the lines are not particularly well integrated. Changing from one line to another may mean walking a block or two, and purchasing a new ticket in many cases. You will often need to combine a taxi ride and a train ride to get to your destination; fortunately, you'll find a line of taxis outside most stations.

RapidKL operates two above-ground light rail systems, the Ampang line and the Kelana Jaya line (formerly the Putra line). The Ampang line joins Ampang to both Sentul Timur and Sri Petaling. Not all signs for the renamed Kelana Jaya line have been changed yet and this can cause some confusion. The Kelana Jaya line joins Kelana Jaya to the Putra Terminal, a distance of around 29km. You can buy tickets from the desk or a ticket machine (ticket machines accept one note only, so if you've got a bunch of RM1 notes, you'll probably have to go to the desk. Machines do give change for larger notes). Log on to www.putralrt.com.my for more information.

KL Monorail operates from KL Sentral railway station to Titiwangsa station, a distance of 8.6km. Check out their website at www.monorail.com.my for more information.

KTM (Keretapi Tanah Melayu), the national railway, operates two commuter services in Kuala Lumpur, joining the suburbs and outlying communities to downtown at very low fares. One line runs from Rawang to Seremban, a distance of 153 kilometres; the other runs from Sentul to Port Klang and covers exactly the same distance. Tickets may be purchased from a machine in most stations. The KTM website is www.ktmb.com.my.

Express Rail Link (ERL) connects the Kuala Lumpur International Airport (KLIA) to KL Sentral station with two services. The KLIA Ekspres is an express train joining KLIA and KL Sentral directly, while KLIA Transit is a commuter train joining the same two destinations but with three additional stops in between.

The largest hub serving these various systems is KL Sentral station. Kelana Jaya line, KTM Komuter, and KL Ekspres all use this station. Across the street one can access the KL Monorail. Immediately outside the station are RapidKL buses to various destinations as well as AirAsia buses to the LCCT terminal at the airport.

Walking

Other options **Hiking** p.236

Nobody walks far in Kuala Lumpur as a means of transportation – it's simply too hot for most of the year, so people walk for short distances only. Crossing streets can be an adventure; use the cross walks wherever possible. There are few pedestrian bridges and no underpasses. Brisk walking as a recreation on weekends is, on the other hand, quite popular, and you'll see armies of walkers striding round any of the city's main parks. The Forest Research Institute (FRIM) is a popular destination for walkers (p.196).

Five Simple Steps
Once you understand the train system, you will be able to get to most places without too much bother, but actually getting to understand it is pretty challenging. Pick up a copy of the book 5 Simple Steps Using Kuala Lumpur Transit System (available in bookshops) – it lists important attractions, shopping malls and hotels, and then tells you how to get there on the train. It's an invaluable guide to getting around.

KL modes of transport

Money

Malaysian currency notes come in colour-coded bills of one, two, five, 10, 50 and 100 ringett. The RM2 and RM100 bills are rarely seen. One ringett is divided into 100 sens. Coins come in one, five, 10, 20 and 50 sen pieces. The ringett is pegged to the US dollar and is generally considered to be a fairly strong Asian currency.

By far the most common method of payment is cash. Credit cards are also common although their use tends to be restricted to larger stores and supermarkets. Debit cards are used only for transactions such as cash withdrawals at ATMs. Only Malaysian ringgits are accepted as payment.

Banks

Banks are easily accessible almost everywhere. The main branches and head offices tend to be in the Golden Triangle but smaller branches are numerous. There are also some foreign and international banks in Kuala Lumpur, the biggest being HSBC. Malaysian banks have international status. They offer all the usual services such as deposit, withdrawal, money transfer and bill payments. They often do not have facilities to exchange money, this being the job of Kuala Lumpur's many currency exchanges. Banks are generally open from 09:00 to 16:00, Monday to Friday.

Some of the major banks are ABN AMRO, Alliance, Bank of America, Bumiputra-Commerce, Citibank, EON, Hong Leong, HSBC and Maybank. Please refer to the Bank Accounts section of the Residents chapter for more information (p.64).

ATMs

ATMs are quite easy to find. Look for them at the entrance to banks, in hotel lobbies, in malls and in large department stores. It is not common to see them on the street

HSBC bank

or in supermarkets. Visa, MasterCard, Maestro, Cirrus and Plus are available on some of the ATMs but not all.

Although it is hard to come up with solid statistics, it seems that cyber crime involving ATMs is on the rise. This includes using counterfeit access devices to retrieve information. Be vigilant about your own security while using ATMs – if the machine looks as though it has been tampered with in any way, or if there are too many people hovering nearby, it's wise to walk away (check that you've got your own card and not somone else's, as card switching is a common trick) and find another ATM.

Money Exchanges

Authorised money changers are dotted throughout the city. They are usually ensconced in glass-fronted booths allowing you to easily see the rates on the bulletin board behind them. Rates change depending on the daily bank rate, but they are generally very similar between changers. One might offer a slightly better rate hoping to attract more business, but unless you are changing a very large amount of money, it's usually not worth the bother of shopping around. Exchange booths are found both on the street and in malls. They tend to be small businesses rather than major companies. Hours vary from changer to changer but most open between 09:00 and 10:00 and close between 20:00 and 22:00. Many are open seven days a week.

Some banks also offer money exchange services but only at larger branches. As their rate is fixed daily by the central bank, the money changers are able to undercut them easily, and so services at banks are not popular. Larger hotels will exchange money as well but their rates are not as good, after service fees, as the smaller money changers.

Credit Cards

The most common credit cards in Malaysia are MasterCard and Visa. Some banks also offer credit cards to their customers. Normally only large retailers and restaurants will accept credit cards. Occasionally a smaller retailer will accept a credit card with a small service charge levied. Such shops proudly have the card's logo exhibited in their front window; however, this is the exception rather than the rule. Debit cards are not used except in ATMs.

Debt: The Latest Fashion Accessory
Credit cards have only fairly recently come into common use; they are seen as a status symbol by young Malaysians much taken with their ability to provide instant gratification. The result has been high levels of personal debt and bankruptcy.

Exchange Rates

Foreign Currency (FC)	1 Unit FC = RM	RM1 = FC
Australia	2.87	0.35
Bahrain	8.69	0.12
Canada	3.19	0.31
China	0.45	2.21
Euro	4.83	0.21
Hong Kong	0.42	2.39
India	0.08	12.01
Japan	0.03	32.5
Kuwait	11.99	0.08
New Zealand	2.51	0.4
Oman	8.49	0.12
Qatar	0.9	1.11
Russia	0.13	7.45
Saudi Arabia	0.87	1.15
Singapore	2.28	0.44
South Africa	0.47	2.12
Sweden	0.51	1.95
Switzerland	2.99	0.33
Thailand	0.11	9.11
UK	6.4	0.16
United Arab Emirates	0.89	1.12
USA	3.27	0.31

Rates calculated as of March 2008

Credit Cards

American Express	03 2050 0000
Diners Club	03 2161 1055
HSBC	03 2072 8608
MasterCard	1800 804 594
Maybank	03 2070 3333
Visa	1800 802 997

Credit card fraud is prevalent in Malaysia and you should not let your card out of your sight if you can help it. Employees at even very high-end establishments have been implicated in such fraud. Generally you are safer using cash as much as possible. Should you lose a card, immediately phone the card provider to put a stop on it and report it at a police station as soon as possible. Not much is likely to come of this in terms of recovering your card, but at least you have protected yourself against unauthorised use.

Tipping

Tipping is still not common in Malaysia except in very high-end, international establishments. In restaurants, a service charge is often added to the bill, but staff don't see much of this. Usually tips go into a common kitty to be shared out at the end of the shift, but this is not always the case.

A tip is often greeted with delight. Use your discretion about when to tip; if service has been prompt, efficient and polite, a small tip ensures that when you next use the service, you will be welcomed with a friendly smile. This applies to all sorts of situations, from waiters to salon staff. Should you find a particularly pleasant taxi driver, tip him and ask for his card. He will become invaluable to you.

Tipping with your credit card is rare and only seen in the most impressive of places.

Newspapers & Magazines

Malaysia's main English language dailies are *The New Straits Times*, *The Star* and the *Malay Mail*. In Malaysian Borneo, you'll find *The Eastern Times* and *The Borneo Post*. The average cost of a daily paper is RM1.20. Most hotels provide free copies to guests. The first three papers are easy to find anywhere; news agents, street vendors, grocery stores and supermarkets all sell copies. *The New Straits Times* is the most conservative of the three, generally supporting the government party line, although not slavishly so. *The Star*, with its slightly more sensational approach, is the most popular. *The Malay Mail* is similar to *The Star* with a slightly different demographic readership. Although open censorship is not practised, more subtle forms of media control are never far out of sight. The *Sarawak Tribune* came under a lot of government criticism for publishing the Prophet Mohammed cartoons in 2006, and shut down as a result.

There are a number of glossy magazines like *Malaysia Tatler* and *Expatriate Lifestyle*, which cost around RM10.

Fresh Foreign Fodder

No matter how good your local paper is, when you're an expat you miss your newspapers from back home. Newspaper Direct has a licence to print over 500 publications from 74 countries, and deliver them to you on the very same day they are published in your home country. Check out their website (www.newspaperdirect.net.my) or call 03 2161 0800.

Books

Other options **Websites** p.37

There are several attractive coffee table books available featuring Kuala Lumpur. All contain highlights of the city and gorgeous photographs. *A Random Walk in Kuala Lumpur*, *Journey Through Kuala Lumpur*, *Portrait of Kuala Lumpur* and *This is Malaysia* are all wonderful books that will remind you of the time you spent in KL, no matter how short or long.

For something more practical, you'll find a number of guidebooks (although not as many as you might find for other Asian cities). Thomas Cook, Globetrotter and Insight Guides all publish guidebooks on the city, and although these are mostly aimed at the tourist market, they can be useful, especially when you first arrive.

Local mag stand

For a deeper insight into Malaysia and Kuala Lumpur, get your hands on *A Malaysian Journey* by Rehman Rashid. All of these books are widely available at major booksellers, Kinokuniya in Suria KLCC being the city's largest (p.341). Other book sellers like Borders, Times and MPH have a number of branches scattered around the city. There is a paucity of entertainment guides, the best being *The Finder*, a free publication found in malls and other public venues.

Further Reading

Websites

There is a wide range of websites available on Kuala Lumpur. Many are aimed at tourists, although the government websites in particular are frequently used by residents. There are also a number of blogs, the most useful being www.travelblog.org and http://dir.blogflux.com/country/malaysia.html.

Websites

Business & Industry

www.btimes.com.my	Online version of the Business Times
www.fmm.org.my	The website of the Federation of Malaysian Manufacturers
www.miti.gov.my	The official portal of the Ministry of International Trade and Industry
www.msc.com.my	Information on Malaysia's Multimedia Super Corridor

City Information

www.kualalumpur-city.com	A guide to Kuala Lumpur with many links
www.expatkl.com	Useful information for people relocating to Kuala Lumpur
www.kualalumpur.gov.my	The Kuala Lumpur Tourism Action Council website

Culture

www.heritage.gov.my	The official portal for the Malaysian Ministry of Culture, Art & Heritage
www.kualalumpur.gov.my	This site gives an overview of the various art and culture centres in Kuala Lumpur

Directories

www.eguide.com.my	A free search engine that allows you to seek out companies, brands, products and services
www.gov.my	The Malaysian government's official website giving information on public services
www.matta.org.my	The website for the national umbrella body for the travel industry
www.pos.com.my	This is the Malaysian post office site; it provides postcodes and other postal information
www.yellowpages.com.my	This site provides listings for all of Malaysia

Kids

www.asia2kids.com	A lifestyle directory for children
www.kakiseni.com	A directory of art classes and performing arts events

Living & Working

www.imi.gov.my	The website for the Immigration Department of Malaysia, Foreign Worker Division
www.mm2h.com	Website about Malaysia My Second Home, a government programme aimed at comfortably heeled expats
www.msc.com.my	The website of the Malaysian Ministry of Human Resources

News & Media

www.bernama.com	The official government news agency website
www.nst.com.my	*New Straits Times* website. This is one of Malaysia's oldest English language newspapers
www.thestar.com.my	*The Star* is Malaysia's most widely read English language newspaper

Nightlife

www.dinemalaysia.com	A dining and bar guide for all of Malaysia which focuses on high-end locations
www.kualalumpur-city.com	A general guide to the city's hottest nightlife areas

Online Shopping

www.mycen.com.my	A directory of websites and listings of online shopping providers, web stores and e-commerce sites

Other

www.itis.com.my	Up-to-the-minute traffic information for Kuala Lumpur
www.klia.com.my	Flight information from Kuala Lumpur International Airport

Travel Within Malaysia

www.islands.com.my	Website containing a great deal of useful information about Malaysia's many island destinations
www.mocat.gov.my	The official Ministry of Tourism website with many links
www.mtc.com.my	The website of the Malaysia Tourism Information Centre.
www.tourismmalaysia.gov.my	This government website for tourists is packed with events and travel ideas
www.virtualmalaysia.com	A website of general travel and tourism information about Malaysia

Annual Events

Two of the largest annual celebrations in Malaysia are the Islamic religious feasts of Hari Raya Puasa (or Hari Raya Aidilfitri) and Hari Raya Korban (or Hari Raya Aidil Adha). These are known more commonly in other Islamic countries as Eid Al Fitr and Eid Al Adha. Both celebrations are dependent on the Islamic calendar (which is lunar), and move forward by around 10 days per year. The whole Malaysian community, Muslim and non-Muslim alike, join in with the spirit of these celebrations.

Hari Raya Puasa marks the end of Ramadan, a month of fasting observed by Muslims around the world. Only the first two days are officially observed as a public holiday in Malaysia, but many Muslims take a few extra days off work. Hari Raya Korban is a celebration of the completion of the period of pilgrimage to Mecca. Well-off Muslims will have animals ritually slaughtered, prepared and then distributed among the poor. The rest of the day is spent visiting friends and relatives, or entertaining guests at home. In 2008, Hari Raya Puasa will occur in October and Hari Raya Korban will occur in December.

Various Locations
Jan/Feb

Chinese New Year

Held in January or February depending on the first day of the Chinese Lunar calendar, this major celebration lasts for 15 days. Elaborate fireworks fill the sky, dragon dances are everywhere, everyone eats oranges and honeyed cakes and small red envelopes of hong bao (gifts of money) exchange hands.

Batu Caves
February

Thaipusam

Every year at the beginning of February a million or more people visit the Hindu shrines at Batu Caves just north of Kuala Lumpur (p.189) to celebrate and to marvel at Thaipusam. The three-day Hindu festival of atonement begins in Chinatown at Sri Marimahaim Temple when pilgrims start the 15km trek to Batu Caves. At the height of the festival, men pierce their cheeks and bodies with multiple skewers and hooks bearing oranges and limes, and climb the 272 steps to the shrines in the caves, in a state of trance and carrying huge structures called kavadis. In spite of the crowds, it's a spectacle not to be missed.

Various Locations
February

Federal Territory Day (City Day)

On 1 February each year, Kuala Lumpur celebrates Federal Territory Day along with Putrajaya and Labuan. The location is not fixed, but parades, fireworks and live entertainment can be found in various places in the city, and it is a state holiday so many offices and schools are closed.

Various Locations
April/May

National Water Festival

The National Water Festival is held in April and early May each year and moves about Malaysia with different sorts of events in each venue. Modern and traditional watersports are featured on the beautiful vacation island of Langkawi. On Labuan the focus changes to game fishing, cross channel swimming, and kayaking. The closing ceremonies held in Melaka draw a crowd from Kuala Lumpur as do the other events.

Sepang International
Circuit
March/April

Petronas Malaysian Formula One World Championship

www.malaysiangp.com.my

This world-class Formula One racing event draws the sport's top drivers who battle it out around the Sepang International Circuit. The event draws huge crowds in March or April each year. The 2007 race saw Fernando Alonso beat Lewis Hamilton to the top post in a close finish. Tickets aren't cheap, with 'hill-standing' tickets at RM100 and Diamond Area tickets going for a whopping RM1,950. Still, it's one of the most exciting events you'll get to see, so it may well be worth getting your hands on one.

Various Locations ◄ Colours of Malaysia
May/June
This month-long festival celebrates the many sides of Malaysia, showcasing definitive local crafts, cuisine and culture. It takes place in various locations around the country – watch the press for a schedule of events, which include parades, dance shows, exhibitions and plenty of delicious food.

Various Locations ◄ Kuala Lumpur Festival
July
www.heritage.gov.my
Every year the Ministry of Culture, Arts and Heritage, the Ministry of Tourism and the KL City Hall team up to organise this arty festival celebrating Kuala Lumpur's cultural achievements. There are various film screenings, art exhibitions, music and dance displays and theatre productions throughout the city during July.

Sarawak ◄ Rainforest World Music Festival
July
www.rainforestmusic-borneo.com
This event, held in Sarawak each year, is not to be missed if you enjoy broadening your music horizons. Catch musicians from the deep heart of Borneo performing on the same stage as people from the Amazon Basin, Africa, Mongolia and northern Europe. Jamming sessions, mini concerts and lectures on ethnic music will keep those toes tapping, while the many food stalls serving exotic cuisines will keep hunger at bay.

Various Locations ◄ Floral Festival
July
See the city go pretty in July when gorgeous floral displays are installed in parks, malls and hotels. The festival's high point is the spectacular international floral parade. Running side by side with the Floral Festival is the Food and Fruit Fiesta, when KL celebrates Malaysia's diverse and delicious food choices. Expect to find your usual favourite Malay, Chinese and Indian dishes pepped up with a variety of tropical and sub-tropical fruits.

Independence Square ◄ Merdeka Day
August
www.tourismmalaysia.gov.my
This national holiday on 31 August celebrates the occasion of Malaysia's independence from Great Britain in 1957. Marked every year with a grand parade, free concerts in Dataran Merdeka (Independence Square) and speeches, this is one of Malaysia's proudest days.

Flowers outside Hindu temple

Deepavali decorations

Lantern Festival

Penang
September

Also known as the Moon Cake, or Mid-Autumn, festival, this celebration began in 14th century China. It is celebrated on the 15th day of the eighth lunar month in the Chinese calendar, usually sometime in September. At night children carry lanterns, and families gather to eat moon cakes. There are many different stories of the origin of this festival. Many people try to make it to Penang for the event.

Deepavali

Various Locations
September

Deepavali (also called Diwali in some countries) is the Hindu festival of light celebrating the triumph of good over evil and light over darkness. It takes place in the seventh month of the Hindu lunar calendar, which usually falls in October or November.

Malaysia A1 Grand Prix

Sepang International
Circuit
November

www.malaysiangp.com.my

Held each year at the Sepang International Circuit, this hugely popular event brings together A1 teams from around the world. Malaysians arrive at the circuit in their droves to cheer on the drivers who often struggle with extreme heat and wet conditions. Tickets aren't cheap, but they still get snapped up quickly.

Malaysia International Gourmet Festival

Various Locations
November

www.migf.com

Malaysia's best chefs team up in November to present a selection of the country's most delicious delicacies. Thirty KL restaurants offer special menus, often featuring a fusion of Malaysian and international cuisines.

Monsoon Cup

Kuala Terengganu
November

www.monsooncup.com.my

The Monsoon Cup, held in the waters off Kuala Terengganu, is part of World Match Racing Tour international sailing circuit, and the tour's first Asian venue. It is one of nine international venues along with such places as Denmark, Brazil and Italy. This world-class event is usually held in late November when conditions are the roughest.

Terengganu International 4WD Rainforest Challenge

Terengganu
December

www.rainforest-challenge.com

Every year participants from over 30 countries take part in this rigorous test of physical and mental endurance, driving 4WD vehicles through rough jungle terrain and facing a number of daunting challenges. In 2007 over 130 participants had to be rescued when swollen rivers trapped them in the jungle.

International Busker's Festival of Kuala Lumpur

Various Locations
December

www.malaysiabuskers.com

For nine days in December, buskers from all parts of the world join in this festival of street theatre. The Grand Buskers' Parade at Dataran Merdeka opens the event. The event is free, although the buskers, of course, appreciate a contribution.

Christmas

Various Locations
December

For the many non-Christians in Kuala Lumpur, Christmas has become a secular rather than a religious occasion. Children of all backgrounds love Santa. Retailers are quick to take advantage of the appeal of the season so shop assistants dressed as elves, artificial pine trees, plum puddings, colourful lights and decorations, reindeer and candy canes can be found in abundance.

Life in the fast lane?

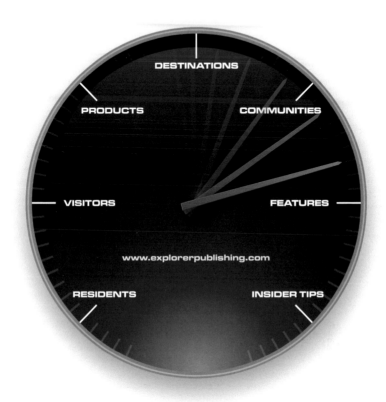

Life can move pretty quickly so make sure you keep in the know with regular updates from **www.explorerpublishing.com**

Or better still, share your knowledge and advice with others, find answers to your questions, or just make new friends in our community area

www.explorerpublishing.com – for life in real time

Residents

Residents

Overview

Twenty years ago KL was a bit of an Asian backwater, overshadowed by modern Hong Kong and Singapore and lacking the excitement of Bangkok. The city was plagued by traffic problems, lacked modern infrastructure and was hemmed in by geographical circumstance. Fast forward to the 21st century and there've been plenty of changes – the city centre is almost unrecognisable. The central horse racing track has given way to the iconic Petronas Twin Towers (p.188), grand colonial bungalows have been replaced by glass and steel skyscrapers and a network of elevated and underground roads and railways alleviate traffic flow. That's not to say everything is perfect, but the city is not resting on its laurels. Numerous active construction sites are evidence of the continuing effort to transform this area into a showcase for modern Malaysia. The transformation has been financed by oil wealth and this sector is the major employer of expats in the city.

To the newly arrived expat, KL can seem alien and overwhelming, but it's surprisingly easy to settle in here. The constant comings and goings of the expat population have resulted in a system that's well adapted to helping newcomers. You'll find professionals such as relocation agents, estate agents, school staff and human resource departments, as well as volunteers at expat associations, who are happy to help you get settled and deal with the inevitable hiccups along the way.

Malaysians are proud of their capital city and you'll find crowds of local tourists at the major landmarks. Family bonds are strong and at holiday times the city empties out and it seems like the entire population has *balik kampung* (gone back to their home town).

Urban Myths

KL is a Muslim city (Malaysia is an Islamic country). Although the majority of Malaysians are Muslims, Malaysia is a secular state. You are just as likely to see a woman dressed in a vest and skinny jeans as you are to see one in a tudung *(headscarf). Men and women mix freely in daily life and alcohol is widely available.*

Considering The City

This city certainly has a certain charm although it isn't known for being one of the most exciting places in the world. For a major capital city it's surprisingly small – outside the rush hour it'll rarely take you more than 20 minutes drive to cross the city. At peak times however, the journey times can rise to well over an hour for the same trip. Its small size doesn't make it easy to navigate either and getting lost is a frequent hazard, even for long-term residents. The city is built on a series of hills and the road system goes around (and occasionally through) them creating a confusing network of loops and turns. Add idiosyncratic signage and notoriously bad driving to the mix and it's easy to see why the recently arrived GPS is catching on fast.

The hills do have the positive effect of keeping the area green. Their steepest slopes have so far outwitted developers, leaving pockets of forest among the skyscrapers. There are several formal parks in the city, best visited in the early morning or evening. Few can resist the charms of a good air conditioner in the heat of the day.

Malaysia's multicultural society has plenty to offer the expat resident. The three major ethnic groups in Malaysia, Malays, Chinese and Indians, are all represented in sizeable numbers in the city. Food, religious festivals, art, music and handicrafts are all influenced by this multicultural mix, producing something uniquely Malaysian.

Rules regarding the issuing of work permits mean that expats tend to be in senior positions, and as a result a high standard of living can be expected. Salaries are high compared to the local cost of living, even in lower paid jobs such as teaching. If however, you buy a car, drink alcohol and consume a lot of imported products you may not find yourself saving much as these are comparatively expensive.

The vast majority of working expats come to the city because they are posted here by their companies. The oil and gas industry is the major employer, while other popular sectors are telecommunications and teaching. The broadcaster Al Jazeera has a large office here, although KL isn't a popular location for other media organisations. There is a sizeable diplomatic community staffing the various embassies. It is possible to arrive on a dependents' pass or social visit pass and find an employer who will apply for a work permit for you, but this is definitely unusual (see the work section on p.55 for more details).

Once you've got over the initial paperwork and house hunting it is easy to feel at home. English is widely spoken and it's easier to make sense of what's happening around you than in many other Asian cities. It won't be long before you're switching lanes without indicating, double parking outside your favourite food stall and washing down your plate of *nasi kandar* (p.372) with a *teh tarik* (p.396).

Before You Arrive

Expat Experts

So you're thinking of moving to a new country – a big step. Consider using the services of expat specialists like Xpat Migrate. They can help with work visas, spouse permits, MM2H paperwork and many other personal and business-related issues that come with moving abroad. Find out more on www.xpatmigrate.com.

A little bit of forward planning before you leave will make your arrival much smoother, so it's worth investing some time thinking about your move, gathering together everything you need and making preparations to ease the transition.

- Make sure all your documents are in order and make a copy of everything. Check that your passport has at least six months left after your arrival date before it expires.
- Decide what to do with your current home. If you're renting it out, or even just leaving it empty, you'll need to let your insurance company know.
- Organise shipment of your possessions if necessary. It will take a while for you to find a place, so don't ship too far in advance of your departure date or you'll end up paying unnecessarily for storage.
- It's a good idea to keep your bank accounts open in your home country. Many expats keep a credit card too. Obtain a letter from your current bank stating how long you've been their customer, as this can help when opening a new account in Malaysia.
- If you're from the UK, you can keep your National Insurance payments up to date by making direct contributions.
- Sort out your tax status. Let the tax office in your home country know you're going and how long you expect to be gone. You may get a refund for the current tax year.
- You will need a return ticket when travelling into Malaysia until you have a work permit or dependent pass, so don't buy a one-way ticket, even if you have a job.
- If you'll be looking for work when you arrive, try to research the local job market as much as you can before leaving. See p.59 for some ideas on where to look.
- Online resources for Malaysia are patchy but you can start researching areas to live and book your temporary accommodation online (for more on accommodation see p.78.)
- If you have children, start sorting out schools as early as possible. KL's international schools (p.136) are oversubscribed and you may have to join a waiting list.

When You Arrive

Extra Expat Benefits

Now that you're a bona fide expat living in KL, you can sign up for the Expat Card. This card gives you great savings at a number of restaurants and bars, hotels, golf courses and many other goods and services. It costs just RM125 per year to join. Find out more at www.expatcard.com.

Try not to feel overwhelmed by the seemingly endless list of things to do. With every move to a new city there's an unavoidable settling in period where it might feel like all you're doing is filling in forms and making yet another copy of your passport. A little patience is required as some of the paperwork will take weeks and though it's hard to feel really settled if you're still waiting for your work permit, there's plenty you can do to make yourself at home in the meantime.

- Make sure your company starts the application process for your work permit as soon as you arrive. You can start work before the permit comes through.
- Register with your embassy or consulate.
- If you have children, get them started at school.
- Look for somewhere to live. Serviced apartments are a good temporary solution while you figure out which area you'd like to live in.

- Contact an expat association (see p.60). Many have welcome groups for newcomers to help you get settled.
- Open a bank account.
- Buy or rent a car.
- Start getting to grips with the roads and transport system and work out your commute.
- Convert your driving licence (you have three months to do this)
- Get into KL life – read the newspapers, eat the food, talk to people and get out and about.

Essential Documents

Kids On Paper

If you have children, you should bring their immunisation records and any school records. If you are divorced and are the custodial parent of your children you should bring documentation to support this.

Apart from your passport, you will need your marriage certificate, your children's birth certificates, your home country driving licence and an international driving permit, not to mention plenty of passport photographs. If you're planning to look for a job while you're here, you should also bring your education certificates and any professional certificates you have. If you already have a job, you should check with your employer exactly what certificates you need to bring (if any) to support your application for a work permit. You will need to supply originals of your passport plus photocopies for work permit applications, converting your driving licence, securing a lease on a property, getting a car loan, opening a bank account and many other processes. Some applications will require notarised copies (your embassy or company will be able to recommend a notary public for you). It's cheap and easy to get passport photos in KL and it's worth getting plenty done at a time.

If your documents are in a language other than English, you will need to get them translated into English by your home country's embassy in Malaysia.

Bring medical and dental records if you can, especially if you have a chronic medical condition, although some countries will not release them.

When You Leave

Your Stuff Helps Others

Sell or give away anything you don't want to take with you. Put up ads at schools, clubs and supermarkets, have a garage sale or donate useful items to charity. Call 03 4297 7022 for Pertubuhan Amal Seri Sinar (pass.my.diip.net), a charity that recycles and reuses unwanted belongings. They'll come to your house to pick up bulky items.

Moving out of accommodation is pretty much hassle free. Check your lease and make sure you give your landlord the appropriate amount of notice. If you're invoking your diplomatic clause (see accommodation, p.70) you may have to give proof that you're fulfilling the requirements. If you don't give enough notice you may end up losing your deposit. Attitudes to wear and tear vary. Some landlords are quite relaxed while others will insist you return the property to the condition it was in when you moved in, and you'll have to do the necessary touching up if you want your deposit back.

Utility bills are usually in the landlord's name, so arrange for the meters to be read on the day you leave and pay the bills so that you can get back your utilities deposit (see p.113 for more details). You will have to disconnect your phone a couple of weeks in advance to get your hefty expat deposit back from Telekom Malaysia. The same goes for mobile phone contracts. It's best to switch to a prepaid SIM card for the last few weeks. Shipping costs can vary, so get at least three quotes. Relocation companies (p.104) can help you return your property to order and sort out your utilities but these services can add extra expense to your move. If you have bought bamboo or wicker furniture you may need to have it fumigated before shipping.

Allow a couple of months to sell your car. Cash transactions are ideal, as it can take time for a buyer to get financing approved. If it's refused, you can be left with no time to find another buyer. Cars tend to get bought and sold between expats, so try asking around to see if anyone you know is looking for a car. Selling to a dealer is the easiest option, but you'll get less for your vehicle than if you sell privately. Given the high cost of vehicles in Malaysia, you'll probably want to get as much of your investment back as possible. Expat-friendly City Motors (see buying a car, p.148) will allow you to continue to use your vehicle for a short time after selling it to them.

Documents

As an expat you will probably find you have far more uses for your personal documents than you ever would have at home. Make photocopies of all your documents before you leave and keep them separately from the originals. This will help if you ever need to get a replacement. Exactly which documents you will need depends on your purpose in coming to Malaysia. At the very minimum you should bring birth certificates for yourself and all family members and your marriage certificate. You may also want to bring your education certificates and membership details for any professional bodies. Come armed with plenty of passport photos; you will find you need to supply multiple photos with most forms for visas and permits. Employers will usually process all the documentation necessary for work permits and dependents' passes, although if you work for a small company they may employ an agent to do this.

Entry Visa

Regulations have recently changed and now residents of most countries are entitled to enter Malaysia on a social visit pass valid for between 14 days and three months. Social visit passes are not issued to travellers holding passports issued by the following countries: Afghanistan, Angola, Bangladesh, Bhutan, Burkina Faso, Burundi, Cameroon, Central African Republic, China, Colombia, Comoros, Congo Democratic Republic, Congo Republic, Cote D'Ivoire, Djibouti, Equatorial Guinea, Eritrea, Ethiopia, Ghana, Guinea-Bissau, India, Israel, Liberia, Mali, Mozambique, Myanmar, Niger, Nigeria, Pakistan, Rwanda, Serbia & Montenegro, Sri Lanka, Taiwan, Western Sahara and Yugoslavia. Citizens of these countries should check on the Ministry of Foreign Affairs website at www.kln.gov.my or contact the Malaysian embassy in their home country as the visa regulations differ for each country.

It is important to check the validity of your passport. On arrival, you must have more than six months left on your passport. This rule applies each time you leave and re-enter Malaysia. Since most residence visas are issued for a year at a time, it's worthwhile renewing your passport anyway if it's due to expire within twelve months as all stamps and passes will have to reissued.

Work Permits
Your employer will usually take are of all the paperwork for your work permit, but if you do find yourself having to make a trip to the immigration department avoid going on Mondays and Fridays as these are the busiest times.

If you are coming to Malaysia to work and you have a job already, you do not need to get a special visa as your employer will apply for your work permit once you are in the country. Any family members who are travelling with you will also be issued with a social visit pass, and when your work permit is approved they will get dependents' passes which will be valid for the same length as your work permit. This process can take a few months, although recently the wait seems to have got much shorter. If your social visit pass is due to expire and your work permit hasn't been issued, you will need to leave and re-enter Malaysia to get another social visit pass.

Malaysia no longer issues business visas for short-term visits. A list of activities covered by the social visit pass can be found on the Immigration Department website at www.imi.gov.my; it includes business meetings, factory inspections, journalism and taking part in sporting competitions.

Health Card

Currently there is no requirement for a health card in Malaysia. Expatriates may access treatment at government hospitals and clinics, but in practice this is difficult if you're not a fluent Bahasa speaker.

Foreign workers classified as 'expatriates', earning over RM3,000 per month and in managerial/professional positions do not require medical checks when they apply for or extend their work permits. If you employ a foreign domestic helper, she will need to have a yearly medical check before her permit can be renewed. This is simple to organise and will usually be arranged by your agent if you're using one (see Domestic Help p.107).

Residence Visa

Strictly speaking there's no such thing as a residence visa in Malaysia. A work permit (sometimes called an employment pass) allows you to remain in Malaysia for a stated period of time (at least one year, usually two) to work for a particular company. If you change jobs, you can't take this work permit with you and your new employer will have to make a fresh application. Your work permit and family members' dependent passes will be issued at the same time. The passes will be valid for the same period as your work permit, which allow them to stay in Malaysia but not to work.

It's up to the company that wishes to employ you to satisfy the government's conditions for employing an expatriate in a given post. Immigration department guidelines state that expatriates should be at least 27 years old (for IT posts this is set at 21 years) in line with Malaysia's policy that expatriates should be qualified and experienced in their field. These guidelines are not hard and fast rules and it is possible for younger expatriates to be issued work permits if the company can demonstrate their suitability for the position. For a new application, the minimum contract is two years and the minimum salary is RM3,000 per month. When your employer applies for your work permit, you will need to provide a full copy (every page) of your passport, your CV and academic/professional certificates alongside a passport photo.

Work permits are usually renewed for a total of 10 years, after which your employer will have to make a special application to have the permit renewed and this will be done on a year by year basis. Fees for issuing and renewing a work permit will usually be paid by your employer, but the cost is RM200 or RM300 depending on how your post is categorised. Once your work permit is issued, you can employ a foreign maid. See domestic help p.107 for more information on how to do this.

Spouses & Children

If you're applying for dependents passes for your family members you will need to provide your marriage certificate and birth certificates for your children as well as their passport photos. A single parent who has a work permit may apply for dependents passes for their children. If you're divorced, you may be asked to prove that you are the custodial parent. Each dependent pass costs RM90, and this fee is normally paid by your employer. If your spouse wants to work in Malaysia, they will have to find a company that is prepared to apply for a work permit under the same terms and conditions described above.

Setting Up A Company

Another way to work legally in Malaysia as a foreigner is to set up your own company. As this is quite an expensive option, it isn't popular with expatriates who are not planning to live long-term in Malaysia. A company that is 100% foreign owned must have a paid-up capital of RM250,000 in order to apply for a work permit for an expatriate, even if the expatriate is the owner. If you go into partnership with a Malaysian, the paid-up capital requirement is reduced to RM200,000. The company must be established before a work permit application can be made and the whole process takes several months.

Student Pass

All foreigners studying at educational institutions in Malaysia are required to hold a student pass. This also applies to expatriate children studying at international schools and the school will give you details on how to apply. If you're over 18 and coming to Malaysia to study independently, you will need to make your application for a student pass through your educational institution before arriving in Malaysia. Your institution will advise you of the specific requirements relating to your course of study, but at a

---

Permanent Residence

It's extremely hard for a foreigner to get permanent residence in Malaysia and even harder to get citizenship. Even foreign spouses of Malaysian citizens have to wait several years for their applications to be considered. It's highly unlikely as an expat that you'll qualify for either.

Kids Born In Malaysia

Children born to foreign parents in Malaysia aren't entitled to Malaysian citizenship. After applying for a passport for your child from your embassy, you should submit an application for a dependents pass, which will be issued with the same expiry date as appears on your work permit.

---

minimum you will need to provide your offer letter from your institution, two copies of your passport, two passport photos and copies of your up-to-date education certificates. Student passes cost RM60 for a full year or part of a year. Holders of student passes studying at postgraduate level are allowed to bring their immediate family members with them to Malaysia and they will be issued with social visit passes valid for the duration of the student pass.

Malaysia My Second Home (MM2H)

Retire In The Sunshine
Find out more about the MM2H programme, and read about what others have to say about their experiences of moving to Malaysia under the scheme, on www.mm2h.com.

Originally set up as a programme for foreign retirees and fetchingly called the 'Silver Hair' programme, Malaysia My Second Home (usually shortened to MM2H), is open to expatriates of any age who meet the following capital and income requirements:

• Those aged below 50 need to provide a fixed deposit of RM300,000 in a Malaysian account. After one year, up to RM240,000 may be withdrawn to pay for approved expenses but the balance of RM60,000 must remain in the account for the duration of your stay in Malaysia.
• Those aged 50 and above have the option to provide a fixed deposit of RM150,000. After one year RM90,000 can be withdrawn for approved expenses leaving a minimum balance of RM60,000 or, they can provide proof of an offshore income (e.g. pension) of at least RM10,000 per month.
• All applicants and their spouses/dependent children must produce a medical report from a private hospital or approved clinic in Malaysia and show proof that they hold valid medical insurance.

Participants in MM2H are issued with a 10 year renewable visa. They are not allowed to work in Malaysia, but may remit offshore income to Malaysia for instance from consultancy work or from an overseas business. More information about MM2H can be found on the website www.mm2h.gov.my.

Expatriate Card

Biometric ID Cards
The Malaysian government is currently rolling out a new biometric ID card for foreigners, called the I-Kad. All foreigners living in Malaysia will be expected to carry this card, which will be issued at the same time as your work permit, dependent's pass or student's pass. The I-Kad will mean expats no longer need to carry their passports around with them as ID.

Work permit holders, but not their spouses and children, will be issued with an expatriate card. This is the size of a credit card and has the holder's employment details and photo. It will usually be mailed to the HR department of your employer (or whoever has taken care of your work permit application) some time after your work permit is issued. The card enables you to use a quick line at immigration and acts as a local ID, proving your residence status. It has the same validity as your work permit; if you end your employment before your work permit expires you must return the card with your passport when your work permit is cancelled.

ID Card

Malaysian citizens and permanent residents are required by law to carry their ID cards with them at all times. Fines of up to RM20,000 or a prison sentence of up to three years can be imposed on those who can't produce their ID when asked. Over the past few years, Malaysia has been replacing old ID cards with a new smart card, called the MyKad. Foreigners are not issued with MyKads and instead are supposed to carry their passport with them at all times. Officially photocopies are not acceptable, but many foreigners prefer not to carry their originals around with them and in practice this seems to be fine. You will find many forms require your ID card number – you may be asked for it at the doctor's surgery, when signing for a letter or parcel, or even for gym membership. Using your passport number is fine, but if you're concerned about the security of your personal information don't write it down, just show the staff your ID if they ask to see it. Often they won't, unless ID is required by law, for example when buying a new SIM card for your mobile phone.

Driving Licence
Other options **Transportation** p.144

The legal age for driving in Malaysia is 17, although you won't find too many Malaysian teenagers on the roads due to the expense of car ownership. Holders of overseas driving licences can drive legally in for up to three months using their regular licence or an International Driving Permit. You should definitely apply for an International Permit if your original licence is not in English. Once you have a work permit you can get a permanent Malaysian licence. Keep your licence with you while driving, as you can be asked to produce it by uniformed policemen during a spot check or at the scene of an accident. You will be fined if you fail to produce your licence when asked. Malaysia operates a system of demerit (penalty) points for driving offences, points last for a year and if you accumulate over 15 points in a year your licence will be suspended for six months. Driving under the influence of drugs or alcohol is an offence and the blood alcohol limit for Malaysia is 0.08%. See Driving p.145 for more information.

Temporary Licence
Before arriving, get an international driving licence from the authorities in your home country. This will allow you to drive legally in Malaysia for three months and comes in handy as you must have a valid work permit before applying for a licence. Spouses of work permit holders may also apply. Some overseas licences may be valid for this three month period but if your licence doesn't have a photograph or isn't in English, you may have problems when hiring a car or if you are stopped by the police for any reason. As with many rules in Malaysia, there seems to be some flexibility and many long-term expats drive on their home country licences for years. Since converting to a Malaysian licence is relatively simple, it doesn't cost much and you get to keep your original licence, so it's worth doing to be on the safe side.

Permanent Licence
How you go about getting your Malaysian licence depends on which country issued your original licence, and this falls under three different categories. People from countries which have a reciprocal agreement with Malaysia fill in a form JPJ L1, which can be downloaded from the Road Transport Department (more commonly known as the JPJ) website (www.jpj.gov.my). This should be taken to the nearest office

Jalan Tuanku Abdul Rahman Crossway

with originals and copies of your passport, work permit and dependents' pass, your original licence and a colour photograph. If your licence is not in English you must also bring a translation certified by your embassy. The fee for the Malaysian licence is RM30 per year. You can check on the JPJ website to see if you fall into this category, which includes Australia, New Zealand, France, Germany, Italy and Singapore. The second category is countries that don't have a reciprocal agreement with Malaysia but which issue licences recognised by Malaysia. Officially you can be asked to retake your test, but in practice this very seldom happens. You must get approval from the Driving Licensing Division at JPJ headquarters in Putrajaya, by filling in form Lampiran B2, downloadable from the website, before following the procedure with JPJ L1 outlined above. Again, the JPJ website has a comprehensive list of countries in this category, including the UK, USA, South Africa, Canada and Ireland.

If you're unlucky enough to have a licence issued by a country that doesn't fall into either of the above two categories, you must take the driving theory and practice tests as if you were a new driver.

If all this sounds like a lot of hard work, you can ask an agent to do the conversion on your behalf. Since the process involves your personal documents only use an agent if they have been personally recommended to you by someone you trust.

Driving Test

Anyone over 17 can learn to drive in Malaysia. Driving lessons may only be given by a licensed instructor and the learner must pass a series of tests before getting a Malaysian licence. Before you can even start lessons, you must pass a theory test. This is taken after attending a five-hour course followed by a paper or computerised test. Your driving school will give you study material if you need it and you must answer at least 40 out of 45 multiple choice questions correctly to pass. The course used to only be available in Malay, but it is now taught in English too.

Once you've passed the theory test you can start lessons and you must have a minimum of 16 hours instruction with a registered school before you can take the driving test. This consists of two parts – car park and open road. Your driving school will also help you with the necessary forms and application procedures along the way. Expect to pay approximately RM20 for an hour of instruction or RM900 for a complete package including theory lectures, driving instruction, help with paperwork and transport to and from test centres.

The procedure is quite complicated and learning to drive on the mean streets of KL can be hair-raising, so many expats (or their children) who don't already drive choose to take their tests in their home countries and then apply to convert their licence.

Motorcycle Licence

If your existing licence is valid for motorcycles, its validity will be converted like a car licence. You may be asked to submit details of the engine capacity of any motorcycle registered in your name if your licence is only valid for specific categories. You must be 16 to ride a motorcycle in Malaysia.

Driving Schools

If you're learning to drive in Malaysia, or you are unable to convert your licence and have to retake the test locally, you must use a local driving school. One of

Driving Schools

Name	Address	Area	Phone	Web
AAM	191/191A Jalan Tun Razak	City Centre	03 2162 5777	www.aam.org.my
Jaya Driving School	22 Lorong Ara Kiri 2, Lucky Garden	Bangsar	03 2094 1457	na
Kepong Driving Institute	39 Jalan Ambong, Kampung Bahru	City Centre	03 6258 5717	na
Metro Driving Academy	28A Jalan Tun Mohd Faud 1	TTDI (Taman Tun Dr Ismail)	03 7725 9737	na
Sekolah Memandu Rakyat	17A Jalan Travers	Bangsar	03 2273 5568	na
Wong Driving School	23 Jalan Ampang Batu 5	Ampang	03 4257 2768	na
Yew Driving School	45 Jln SS22/11, Damansara Jaya	Petaling Jaya	03 7727 5443	na

the requirements for acquiring a Malaysian licence is the completion of 16 hours' instruction with a certified school. Driving schools can also help prepare for the theory test, offer advice on driving on Malaysia's roads and assist with the licence application process. Schools usually use manual Kancils or other very small cars for instruction. The Automobile Association of Malaysia (AAM) runs courses in defensive driving which may help anyone who feels nervous about facing KL's notorious traffic.

What's Your Name?
Sounds like a simple question, but many Chinese Malaysians have English and Chinese names and sometimes the family name will be written before the given name. If you're in doubt about which name to use, you can always ask someone what they like to be called.

Birth Certificate & Registration

You should register the birth of your baby born in Malaysia within 14 days of the birth at your nearest National Registration Department (JPN) Office. For KL residents this is located on the sixth & seventh floors, Maju Junction Mall, 1001 Jalan Sultan Ismail, 50551 Kuala Lumpur (03 2692 5044). The Petaling Jaya office is on the first floor, Bangunan Persekutuan, Persiaran Barat, Jalan Sultan, 46551 Petaling Jaya (03 7956 2634), and the Selangor office is on the seventh floor, Plaza Masalam, 2 Jalan Tengku Ampuan Zabedah, E9/E Section 9, 40100 Shah Alam. Ask at the hospital where your child is born if you are not sure where to go to register the birth.

Complete form JPN.LM01 and bring along proof of birth (from your doctor), your marriage certificate and the passports of both the mother and father. If you are not married and want the father's name to appear on the birth certificate, you must both be present to register the birth and the father and mother must both sign the register. Otherwise a number of people may legally register the birth including the father or mother, a person who witnessed the birth, or a person/guardian taking care of the child.

A child born in Malaysia to non-Malaysian parents is not entitled to Malaysian citizenship. After getting the birth certificate from the JPN, you can apply for a passport for your child from your own embassy and once the passport is issued you can then apply for their dependent's pass from the immigration department. It's a good idea to get your baby a passport as soon as possible. Each country has its own requirements for registering and issuing passports to their nationals – check with your embassy first to find out exactly what you need. If the parents are of different nationalities your child may be entitled to dual nationality but you should confirm this with the authorities of both countries before registering your child. If one parent is Malaysian the child is entitled to Malaysian citizenship and may also be entitled to the citizenship of the non-Malaysian parent.

Adoption

You will usually have to have been resident in Malaysia for at least two years before adopting and as the process can take many months to complete, you should expect to be staying for a significant period of time. Most adoptions are through a doctor, orphanage or other facilitator and contact is made through an informal network – other families who have adopted can help. The facilitator will require some personal information which they will keep on file. They will contact you when a baby is available. Following placement, you will need to instruct a lawyer to deal with the paperwork. The first court date is around three months after the child arrives at your home, followed by a social services visit and a second hearing after six months. At this point, the child is legally part of your family, but it may be another few months before you receive the final adoption paperwork which allows you to register the child and apply for a passport from your home country.

Most adoptions in Malaysia are closed, but it may be possible for you to meet the birth mother, sometimes before the baby is born, or you may be able to get photos or other details from your facilitator to share with your child later.

Here Comes The Bride
*If that's you,
congratulations. If
you're getting married
in KL, there are plenty
of bridal and wedding
experts just waiting to
get their hands on you
– check the Weddings
section of the Shopping
chapter (p.280) for all
the information you'll
need for that perfect
big day.*

Marriage Certificate & Registration

It's not that common for expats to get married in Malaysia, partly due to demographics, but with the Tourism Ministry actively promoting romantic tropical beach weddings, it may become more common as it's a surprisingly easy process.

There are two different systems for registering a marriage in Malaysia: a civil registration for non-Muslim couples and an Islamic procedure for Muslim couples. If one partner is Muslim, the other will be required to convert before marriage. Other religious ceremonies are not recognised as legal marriages without a civil registration also having taken place. Legal marriages conducted in Malaysia are recognised overseas – there's no need to get married again in your home country, although you may be required to register your marriage with your embassy.

For non-Muslim couples, the civil registration ceremony is generally low key and there may not be any celebration. The big affair is the traditional or religious marriage ceremony, generally followed by a reception on an epic scale. Hindus will hold a ceremony in a temple or wedding hall that may go on for hours, while the Chinese community observe traditional rituals such as the tea ceremony. Christians may have a church ceremony, in one of the many churches of various denominations in KL. You may be able to find a religious official who is also an Assistant Registrar; this means you'll be able to combine your civil and religious ceremonies but you may have fewer choices of location. Receptions can vary from the extremely grand – dinner for a couple of hundred at a five star hotel is not uncommon – to simple at home affairs. Malaysia's multi-cultural society means you may have the opportunity to attend many different types of wedding. If you're invited to a friend or colleague's wedding it's a great way to get a taste of real Malaysian life and you're guaranteed great food!

The Paperwork

To register your forthcoming marriage, go to the National Registration Department (JPN) Office. For KL residents this is located on the sixth & seventh floors, Maju Junction Mall, 1001 Jalan Sultan Ismail, 50551 Kuala Lumpur (03 2692 5044). The Petaling Jaya office is on the first floor, Bangunan Persekutuan, Persiaran Barat, Jalan Sultan, 46551 Petaling Jaya (03 7956 2634). The Selangor office is on the 7th Floor, Plaza Masalam, 2 Jalan Tengku Ampuan Zabedah, E9/E Section 9, 40100 Shah Alam. Take your passport with you and photocopies of the data page showing your date of entry into Malaysia, passport photos, affidavit of marital status, and proof of the termination of any previous marriages, and fill out form JPN KC01. Forms are available from the Registrar of Marriages, Malaysia National Registration Department, 46551 Petaling Jaya, Selangor Darul Ehsan (03 7955 1255, Fax 03 7955 1608, Kuala Lumpur Office, 03 2692 5018). You may also need a letter from the embassy of your home country stating there is no objection to the marriage. You must both have been resident in Malaysia for at least seven days prior to the application and you will have to wait another 21 days before the marriage can be solemnised. If the marriage isn't solemnised within six months, you must apply again. You will need two witnesses and the cost of solemnisation is RM30.

You can also get a special licence which is valid for 30 days. For this you can apply as soon as you arrive in Malaysia, but both parties must be present and you must wait for seven days before solemnisation. For this express service you pay RM100 when the application is approved and RM20 on solemnisation.

Once you have registered your civil marriage, you're free to have whatever marriage ceremony or celebration you choose. Many hotels in KL and Malaysia's resorts do wedding packages and the wedding industry is well developed with planners, caterers, photographers and all manner of experts ready to take care of the last detail. See the Shopping chapter on p.280 for some ideas to get you started.

Death Certificate & Registration

In The Event Of A Death

If a member of your family or a friend dies in Malaysia, you should notify the authorities as soon as possible. If the death occurs in hospital, the staff will help you through the procedures required to get a death certificate from a doctor and register the death with the Malaysian National Registration Department (NRD). If the death is sudden, you should contact your embassy immediately for advice on how to proceed. All deaths in Malaysia which happen outside hospital must be reported to the police regardless of whether the death is sudden or expected. In all cases of sudden death there will have to be a post mortem. This is a police requirement and is compulsory regardless of nationality and whether there are any suspicious circumstances surrounding the death.

Life Expectancy
Between 1970 and 2005, average life expectancy in Malaysia rose from 61 to 74 years. With a retirement age of 56, older Malaysians are finding themselves having to finance a much longer retirement and there are plans to increase the number of working years.

Registering A Death

You must register the death in Malaysia and get a Malaysian death certificate even if you intend to repatriate the body. This service is normally provided by local funeral directors who will obtain the death certificate for you. Your embassy will be able to put you in touch with a funeral director. The NRD is required to issue a death certificate within 24 hours of the death being reported. This certificate will be in Bahasa Malaysia and you will need to take it to your embassy along with the passport of the deceased in order to register the death in your home country.

Investigation & Autopsy.

All sudden deaths require a post mortem and this will usually be carried out within 24 hours of the death being reported to the police. If the deceased was terminally ill or had a chronic medical condition and died outside hospital, the police will either ask to see the medical records or they will contact the treating doctor directly. After the post mortem, the pathologist will return the completed report to the police who will then decide if any further action will be taken. Suspicious deaths will be investigated by the police; it is not common practice to hire an independent investigator.

A Shoulder To Cry On
The death of a relative or friend can be a very traumatic experience and being overseas can make the situation even harder to deal with. Sadly, there aren't any formal groups in KL to support the bereaved. If you need to talk to someone about how you're feeling and don't know where to go, call the Befrienders 24 hour helpline on 03 7956 8144/5.

Returning The Deceased To Their Country Of Origin

Once the death certificate has been issued and any police enquiries completed, you can make arrangements to return the body to the deceased's country of origin. The local funeral director will make arrangements with a funeral director in your home country to repatriate the body. Your embassy will be able to help you make contact with funeral directors in Malaysia and in your home country. The funeral casket will be sealed before the flight and an officer from the local health authority is required to be present at this point to witness the sealing of the casket and examine all the relevant documents. You may also need to get a letter from your embassy confirming that the body can be transported to your home country. On arrival in your home country, a funeral director will take over the arrangements.

If you have the funeral in Malaysia, arrangements can be made for either cremation or burial. If the deceased was insured, the insurance company may appoint the funeral director, who will take care of all arrangements and red tape for you.

A Malaysian death certificate may not be accepted by overseas insurance companies as proof of death, although of course you won't have a problem with any local insurers. If you need to deal with an insurance company outside Malaysia you will need to register the death with your embassy and get a death certificate from them, or have a certified translation made of the Malaysian death certificate.

Organ donation isn't common in Malaysia, but there is a national register based in KL. See Organ Donation on p.122 for more information.

Working In Kuala Lumpur

Malaysia doesn't have a huge population of expat workers. The Malaysian Office of Statistics puts the expat population at around 35,000 in a population of almost 25 million people. But because they're concentrated in the oil and gas industry and many of them live in KL, sometimes it can seem like they are everywhere.

Since the 1997 Asian Financial Crisis, Malaysia has been on a steady upward course, but some legacies remain. Many expats were pulled out of the country and some sectors of the economy contracted dramatically; construction shrank by 23.5% and manufacturing by 9%. Malaysia entered a recession and many construction projects were simply abandoned by their developers. Significant government intervention helped to pull the country out of the crisis, but asset values are only now returning to their pre 1997 levels. Malaysia isn't seen as a 'hardship posting' these days and many companies are looking to cut back on expat packages. Even so, expats in KL could hardly be said to be suffering, and for the most part they lead a far more glamorous lifestyle than they would at home.

The weakening dollar hasn't had as dramatic an effect on the standard of living here as it has in some other regions. Salaries seem to have kept pace with rising costs and since many expenses are covered by employers directly (such as school fees), rising costs don't impact on the employee's pocket. Prices on just about everything are beginning to creep up though and there is talk of the government reducing its petrol subsidy, which will push prices of most goods and services up further. Compared to the average Malaysian though, expats are still in a very favourable position.

Work Ethic ◀

It's a commonly acknowledged among both Malaysians and expats that the work ethic differs between Malaysia's main racial groups. Malays are perceived to value quality of life over making money, while Chinese are the opposite – all work and no play. Indians fall somewhere in the middle, and as for expats; they'd probably say they work and play equally hard.

Expat Jobs

Opportunities for expats are quite restricted. Most expats work in Malaysia because they've been posted here by their company for a specific period of time, often two to three years. Those who arrive looking for work have limited opportunities, although it is possible. Every non-Malaysian must have a work permit and many local companies are reluctant to go through the hassle of applying for one. Local salaries are low and although the minimum salary for a work permit holder is set above the average at RM3,000 per month, most expats wouldn't want to work for this amount. So if you're being compared against a local candidate for a position, you'll look expensive and a lot of bother.

One of the conditions of a work permit being issued is that a local candidate can't be found for the job. Another is that the job is a managerial position and that the expat filling it can demonstrate that they have the skills and experience that will be of benefit to Malaysia. There is a guideline minimum age for a work permit of 21 for the IT industry and 27 for all other sectors. As a result, KL isn't a great place to try to start your career if you're a fresh graduate and it's not a conducive environment for changing direction either.

The majority of expats work in the oil and gas industry, which is the source of Malaysia's wealth. Other areas where significant numbers of expats are employed are education, hotels and hospitality, banking and finance, IT and business consultancy. There's also a large diplomatic community. The job market for expats isn't very fluid so it's hard to judge the level of vacancies. Jobs are seldom advertised and tend to be filled by internal transfers or by using headhunters.

Depending on your field, a degree or equivalent professional qualification will be essential, but in some circumstances extensive professional experience relevant to the position being offered may be enough. It's very unusual for a degree holder with no work experience to get a work permit, even in IT where the qualifying age is 21.

As Malaysia moves further towards being a fully developed country, the government hopes the dependence on expats to fill some senior positions in companies will be reduced. Companies are encouraged to hire local staff for positions where possible, and should demonstrate that they have made efforts to do this before being allowed to offer the position to an expat. As more Malaysians step in to fill these posts, there will be an inevitable downward pressure on salaries, and employment in this region will be less attractive for expats. This scenario is still a fair way off, but sectors such as IT and banking are beginning to see more competition for expat posts from well-qualified Indians, who are generally cheaper to hire.

On the plus side, Malaysia is still a generally pleasant and rewarding place to live and work and the contribution of expats to the economy is welcomed.

Expat Packages

Although anecdotal evidence suggests that some employers are cutting back on expat packages, it's still possible to live very well. Expat packages vary enormously but standard features are: relocation allowance, rent allowance, medical insurance, school fees and annual air tickets to your home country. More generous packages will include a car and sometimes a leave allowance for holidays. The best packages are usually available to those who are posted in from overseas. If you're looking for a job while you're here, you may find you're offered an expat salary minus a lot of the perks and allowances.

If you're negotiating a package for KL from abroad, you should expect the company to be paying for your flight and temporary accommodation for a stated period while you house hunt. Any expenses that aren't covered by your package will have to be met out of your salary, so be sure to take into account possible differences in your lifestyle between your home country and Malaysia. Although housing may be cheaper, your children will have to be educated privately and the fees can quickly add up. Cars are more expensive to buy in Malaysia than in many other countries, although this expense is somewhat offset by cheaper running costs. Medical insurance is essential as you won't have access to government healthcare, so if your employer doesn't provide this you will have to buy your own. Do your homework; what looks like a good salary at first glance may not cover all these expenses.

Benefits and salaries are usually better if you're working for an international company. Many local companies struggle to compete with the generous packages offered by multinationals, although you should still get some benefits, particularly if you've been

Job requirements

Kuala Lumpur Convention Centre

hired from overseas. If you're hired by a local company once you're already in KL, you may not get any special benefits over and above your salary.

Make Friends
Check out the Communities section on www.explorerpublishing.com, where you can post comments, join groups, network with other expats and search for updates.

Business Culture

The business culture in Malaysia is based on the concept of 'face'. The ideal outcome of any transaction or interaction is that everyone involved comes out looking good. It's not a good idea to go into a meeting or negotiation without having thought of some way to get what you want, while allowing the other party to also get something they want. Issuing ultimatums is a bad idea, as the other party inevitably loses face if forced to comply. To a westerner this approach can appear soft, or too wishy-washy.

Losing your temper or shouting in a business meeting should be avoided. Try not to reprimand staff in front of colleagues, especially their juniors. Set up a private meeting if you need to speak to someone about their job performance. It's rude to use your left hand to pass something to another person. You'll notice many races, including Malays, support their right arm with their left hand when giving you papers or money – this is a form of politeness. You should not accept something that's offered to you with your left hand unless it's totally unavoidable.

Business cards are essential, and you should make sure you have a good supply with you at all times. At a meeting, you should hand your business card to everyone present, with the text facing them. Use both hands to present your card, or your right hand with your left hand supporting the arm. If someone gives you their card, take it in both hands or in your right hand. Look at it and put it away carefully rather than stuffing it in your bag or pocket and don't write on it.

Meetings can be very long winded and it may take several meetings to reach a decision. In your own company you may have some control over how meetings are conducted, but with outsiders you'll have to go with the flow to a certain extent. Personal contact is still favoured over phone or video conferencing. Meetings may involve lots of people, although often only a few key players actually speak.

KL isn't a major fixture on the international conference and seminar circuit. You'll find more of these events are held in neighbouring Singapore.

Malaysia attracts foreign businessmen from a variety of backgrounds. As well as Europeans and Australians, businessmen from the Middle East, Korea, Japan and India are often around KL, although they often don't stand out as much as their western counterparts.

Networking

Even if it's not essential for work, networking can help you become more established in the city and broaden your social circle. If nothing else, attending networking events will get you out of the house in the early days when you're at a loose end after work.

KL is a small society and locals often use overlapping business, family and social networks extensively. This is a 'who you know' society, with a great deal of information spread by word of mouth. While you may not be able to tap into these local networks to find out where the best Rojak stall is or who's planning a big takeover of whom, there are some useful networking groups for expats.

If you're starting your own business, networking will be a valuable way of spreading the word and getting some insider tips. If you're looking for work, you may have more luck with networking than conventional methods such as using a recruitment consultant or scanning the classifieds.

Many countries have established a chamber of commerce or trade commission and these are the best places to start (Business Councils & Groups on p.58). Some of the larger groups are the American Malaysian Chamber of Commerce, the British Malaysia Chamber of Commerce, the Malaysia Australia Business Council, The Malaysian

International Chamber of Commerce and Industry, and the National Chamber of Commerce and Industry of Malaysia. These groups hold a variety of events from industry-specific workshops and seminars on business topics to purely social drinks evenings.

Work Ethics

Most expats find that the work ethic in Malaysia is rather laid back, which can be frustrating in the workplace. This is not to say that Malaysians don't spend long hours in the office. It's more to do with a general feeling of calm and a lack of urgency that can be exasperating to people who are used to a fast-paced working environment. English is widely spoken and is the language used in most workplaces. Although people will appreciate any efforts you make to learn Bahasa Malaysia, it's not a requirement for working here.

Isn't It A Public
Holiday Today?
Some public holidays apply only to particular states. So it's quite possible for your neighbour who works in Selangor to be legitimately enjoying a day off while you're still toiling away in your KL city office.

Culture Shock

Culture shock can be just as much a factor in the workplace as it is in other areas of your life. Even if you've visited KL before and think you know what it's like, being here permanently can be a challenging experience. If there are other expats in your workplace, try to find out from them what the office culture is like. In some multinationals, it may be very westernised, while other companies will have a distinctly Malaysian flavour. If you're one of a very few, or the only expat in the office, and you are in a senior position, you may find yourself being deferred and feel that you never get a straight answer to anything. This may be your Malaysian colleagues trying to tell you what they think you want to hear, a kind of second guessing that can be extremely frustrating. Malaysian bureaucracy can be incredibly slow moving and especially when you first arrive you may feel like you're in limbo, constantly waiting for your work permit to be issued, waiting to move into your home, and waiting to open a bank account. Try to be patient and work off your frustration away from the office.

Working Hours

Broadly speaking, the standard working week is Monday to Friday, 09:00 to 17:00, but you'll probably find you spend rather more hours than this at work. Certain sectors, such as education, tend to start and finish earlier (partly to avoid the worst of the rush hour traffic) – most teachers will find their day starts around 07:30 and finishes at about 15:00. Other industries, like oil and gas, can have very unpredictable hours as problems can crop up at any time, and some expats work offshore following a two-weeks-on and two-weeks-off pattern. Many expats find their working day is extended because of the need to be in contact with offices in different time zones. On Fridays some companies and many government departments either close early or take a break for prayers. Public holidays (p.9) in Malaysia are very generous, as the major

Business Councils & Groups

American Malaysian Chamber of Commerce	www.amcham.com.my
British Council	www.britishcouncil.org.my
British Malaysian Chamber of Commerce	www.bmcc.org.my
EU-Malaysia Chamber of Commerce & Industry	www.emcci.com
Japanese Chamber of Trade & Industry of Malaysia	www.jactim.org.my
Malay Chamber of Commerce	www.dpmm.org.my
Malaysia Australia Business Council	www.mabc.org.my
Malaysia Belgium Luxembourg Business Council	www.mblbc.com.my
Malaysia Canada Business Council	www.malaysia-canada.com
Malaysia Dutch Business Council	www.mdbc.com.my
Malaysia New Zealand Business Council	www.mnzbc.com.my
Malaysian Danish Business Council	www.ambkualalumpur.um.dk
Malaysian French Chamber of Commerce & Industry	www.mfcci.com
Malaysian German Chamber of Commerce & Industry	www.mgcc.com.my
Swiss Malaysian Business Association	www.myswiss.org

religious holidays of the main ethnic groups are celebrated as national holidays. There are also some state-specific holidays to add to the total, which can be up to 18 in a year. How many leave days you'll get on top of this depends on your company.

Finding Work

The vast majority of expats working in KL haven't actually sought work here, but have been posted here by their company or organisation. It's not common for expats to arrive in the country and start looking for work unless they have another reason for being in Malaysia, for example if they're married to a Malaysian or are the non-working spouse of a work permit holder. If you've made the decision to come to Malaysia to work, you may find you have to take a creative approach to job hunting. A search through the classified section of Malaysian newspapers won't turn up many 'expat wanted' ads!

Employers will be looking for a degree, a professional qualification, a substantial amount of verifiable work experience relevant to their vacancy, or a particular technical skill that's in short supply. This is because they need to satisfy the conditions attached to issuing a work permit, and they're unlikely to initiate this process if they think the application may be turned down.

Application is usually by CV, although some companies may have a standard form that you must fill out to be considered for a vacancy. Some employers, for example international schools, use an agent in their target country to screen potential applicants or attend recruitment fairs. You'll have to do some research to find out what methods are commonly used in your sector.

Finding Work Before You Come

Be proactive and cast your net as widely as possible. You can access the classifieds in *The New Straits Times* and *The Star* online, and you can also look on websites like *Jobs DB* and *Job Street* see table. The more effort you put into independently searching for work, the quicker you're likely to find something. Do many companies in your sector have offices here, or is it regarded as a backwater? For example, if you work in oil or gas, or related service industries, there are plenty of opportunities here. If you work in the media, there's only one employer with a significant number of expatriate staff.

Identify potential employers and approach them to see if they have vacancies in KL. Many employers looking to fill expat posts won't advertise them in the local media but will use headhunters or recruitment agencies to identify suitable candidates. If your profession or sector has a trade journal or website where jobs are advertised, you may have more luck finding vacancies there than in general newspaper classifieds or employment websites. Some international agencies specialise in recruiting expats, try www.international-job-search.com, www.worldwideworker.com or www.expatengineer.net.

Finding Work While You're Here

If you're already here, you'll probably find networking is the most effective route to finding a job. It can be hard to establish a network if you've only just arrived, but joining national associations, chambers of commerce and professional associations will give you a head start. Many Malaysians attend university abroad and there are several active alumni associations here; check with your old university to see if there's one you can join. Print up some business cards with

Recruitment Agencies

CL Search	03 2148 3088	www.clsearchsb.com
Job Street Malaysia	03 2176 0333	www.jobstreet.com.my
Jobs DB Malaysia	03 2161 0000	www.jobsdb.com.my
Kelly Services	03 2078 8833	www.kellyservices.com.my
Knowledge Worker Exchange	03 8315 6038	www.kwx.com.my

your contact details, degree and professional qualifications on and hand them out to people you meet.

The New Straits Times and *The Star* have recruitment advertisements every day. This can give you a good idea of what's available and what salaries are like in your field. You can post your CV on *The Star* website www.star-jobs.com. There's nothing to stop you cold-calling the HR departments of companies you'd like to work for to find out what their hiring policy is and whether they have any vacancies.

Local recruitment agencies may also be able to help, although none are particularly recommended for expat jobs. With some agencies you can register simply by sending in your CV, but you'll get a better response if you call first. An agency will interview you first to get an idea of your experience and expectations before putting you in touch with potential employers, and should help with salary negotiations.

Spouses ◄

Voluntary & Charity Work

KL isn't a great place to look for work if you come over as a non-working spouse, but there are possibilities. Some embassies and business councils employ their nationals for certain local jobs, and many recruitment companies employ established expats to accompany newcomers on 'look see' visits.

Many spouses who come with their partner to KL, but aren't working themselves, get involved in voluntary or charity work. There are a variety of options available, some of which require only a few hours' commitment a week or month, and others which can begin to resemble a full-time job! Some skills are in demand – teachers, medical professionals and counsellors will almost certainly be able to find work in their skill area. Many opportunities don't require any special skills or give you the chance to learn new ones. You can do voluntary or charity work if you're here on a social visit pass or dependent pass, but you won't be able to apply for a work permit in your own right due to the income requirement.

The Befrienders

Volunteers help man Befrienders' 24 hour confidential phone counselling line for people experiencing personal crises of any kind, or with one to one counselling. There is a seven-week training course for volunteers and they are supported by senior volunteers. To find out more about volunteering contact 03 7957 1306 (not the counselling line) or visit www.befrienders.org.my.

Expat Associations

Associations and organisations that support expats in KL, like ibu (p.257), are run by volunteers. You can take up a committee position, help with publications or fundraising, or organise events. Most associations support particular charities and they may organise groups of volunteers to provide a playgroup for an orphange, visit prisoners or teach special needs children. They are a good first point of contact if you're interested in volunteering. See Expat Associations (p.60) for individual contact details.

Hospis Malaysia

With opportunities for skilled and unskilled volunteers, medical professionals are welcome to offer their services while volunteers with no experience will be given on-the-job training and an induction course to learn about the principles of palliative care. As well as visiting and helping to care for patients, volunteers assist with office work and fundraising. Visit www.hospismalaysia.org or call 03 9133 3936.

Malaysian Association For The Blind

MAB is always on the lookout for volunteers to help in a variety of ways. You can help with administrative tasks such as taking calls at reception or organising events, or help produce talking books – if you are fluent in English, Mandarin or Malay, help is required to record books onto CDs for the visually impaired. Call 03 2272 2677 or visit www.mab.org.my.

Malaysian Mental Health Society

Expat volunteers help with rehabilitation activities for recently-discharged psychiatric patients, do office and admin work, and help raise funds. Counsellors with a recognised qualification are also needed, but the society doesn't provide training. For more details see www.mentalhealth.org.my or call 03 7782 5499.

Montfort Boys Town

Volunteers are needed to teach English and to give classes or lead activities in dancing, crafts and music. The centre is located in Shah Alam, about an hour's drive from central KL. Contact 03 5519 1735 for more information.

National Society for the Deaf Malaysia

Volunteers help with pre-school work, speech therapy and counselling parents of deaf children. Experience may be needed for some areas, others are open to anyone. Contact the society on 03 9287 0739 or log onto www.nsd.org.my for details of its current requirements.

PAWS Animal Welfare Society

PAWS rescues unwanted pets and provides veterinary treatment if necessary. It rehomes healthy animals with new families. Volunteers can help with kennel work, inspection duties, give talks to raise awareness about pet care, and raise funds. Call 03 7846 1087 to find out more.

Riding for the Disabled (RDA)

You don't need any previous experience with horses or riding to volunteer with the RDA. Volunteers help by leading the horse or pony, walking alongside the rider, or helping with children or adults who are waiting while others ride. You can volunteer for as little as an hour a week. Contact the RDA at www.rda-malaysia.org or call 03 4256 4531.

Working As A Freelancer Or Contractor

If you're coming to Malaysia to work on a short-term contract that will last for longer than a social visit pass (see Entry Visa on p.47) but less than a year, your employer can apply for a temporary employment permit for you. This permit saves you the hassle of leaving the country every time your social visit pass expires, but doesn't have the same advantages as a work permit – you can't apply for a Malaysian driving licence or employ foreign domestic help, and your family won't get dependent passes. They can stay in Malaysia on social visit passes, but this might be a problem for families with older children who, strictly speaking, need a student pass to attend school.

There's no way to legally freelance in Malaysia as work permits are tied to specific jobs, so most expats are freelancers for employers outside Malaysia. Local freelancing tends to be poorly paid by international standards so it's hard to make a living purely from local work. For this reason expats who freelance are usually spouses of Malaysians or work permit holders, as small amounts of cash-only work will generally slip under the radar of the authorities.

Setting up a company is an option for expats looking to get around the work permit issue (see Setting Up A Company on p.48 for more information), but as this is so expensive, it may not be worthwhile if you think you might only be here for a couple of years.

Employment Contracts

When an employer offers you a job, they'll send you a letter of offer outlining your employment. These can be very comprehensive, and can be over 10 pages long. Read this carefully and make sure that everything you have agreed with your employer during negotiations is included. If it's not on the offer letter, it may not appear on your contract. Your contract should be issued within one month of starting employment.

You should insist on a written contract, and it will usually be in English. If it's not, ask your employer for a translated copy. The contract should cover all aspects of the agreement with your employer including salary, allowances, any benefits in kind, hours of work, leave entitlement and notice requirement. If the contract is for a fixed term the termination date should be stated along with details of the renewal process, if any. Most expat contracts are issued for a fixed term, subject to renewal. If you're given an open-ended contract, it will usually be from a local employer. Even if there's no end date on your contract, you won't get an unlimited work permit – two years is the standard period.

Your employer has certain obligations under Malaysian law, such as allowing the employee a minimum of eight days annual leave on top of public holidays. Expatriate contracts are usually much more generous than the minimum legal requirements, which are designed to protect Malaysian employees at the lower and less secure end of the employment market. There is no minimum wage in Malaysia, but the minimum monthly salary for a work permit holder is RM3,000.

Probation is normally three months, with the option to extend for another three months if necessary. Companies will expect you to sign your contract during this period, and will then provide a letter confirming employment once you've successfully completed your probation. Some allowances, most commonly payments for furniture or relocation may be dependent on you completing your contract, and if this is the case it should be clearly stated under what circumstances you will be required to pay them back.

Your pay slip may show all your allowances listed separately from your basic salary, depending on how your package is structured. Some benefits or allowances may be paid directly by the company to the supplier, and in this case the money won't show up in your pay cheque, but will be included on your payslip for income tax purposes. If you're entitled to any annual bonus, it will normally be based on your basic salary. Some Malaysian employers pay a 'thirteenth month' as a bonus once a year. Standard maternity leave entitlement is 60 days' paid leave, but many companies, especially multinationals, will provide a more generous entitlement and you should check with your HR department. You aren't entitled to any statutory benefits.

Maternity Leave Lottery

Read your contract carefully to be sure of your maternity leave entitlement. Malaysia only allows 60 days, but many multinationals will stick with the policy of their home country or the country where they originally recruited you and allow a more generous leave. You'll be in a stronger position to negotiate better terms if you do it at the start of your employment rather than six months into a pregnancy.

Labour Law

Malaysia's employment and labour laws are complex, with several different acts of parliament covering various groups of employees and circumstances. Some apply to expats, others don't; for example The Employment Act 1955 (Malaysia's main piece of employment legislation) only covers employees earning under RM1,500. If you need advice about labour law, your rights and entitlements, you should consult a lawyer (see Law Firms p.69). If you find yourself in a dispute with your company over your or their contractual obligations, you can take legal advice on what is the best course of action. Your contract will normally state the conditions under which your employment can be terminated. If your employment is terminated and that policy is not followed, you can sue your company for breach of contract. If you're employed by a multinational, your contract may be subject to the laws of the country where it was issued and signed. Again, you should consult a lawyer for advice.

Changing Jobs

Although uncommon, since the job market isn't very fluid in KL, it is possible to change jobs. As your work permit is tied to your employer it will be cancelled when you leave your job. If you leave before your work permit or contract expires, you will need a letter from the company confirming that they are releasing you from their employment before you can get your work permit cancelled. You will then have to leave the country and return on a social visit pass. Your new employer can then apply for a fresh work permit for you. The process for this application is exactly the same as if you were applying for a work permit for the first time.

There is an official 'cooling off' period of six months before a work permit can be issued to a new employer, but this can be waived if you finished your contract with your first company, if they went out of business, or if you produce a letter from your first company saying they do not object to your new employment, so do your best to stay on good terms with your employer, at least until your new work permit is issued! If you have any family with you, their dependent passes will be cancelled and they will get new passes once your new work permit is issued.

Company Closure

If the company you work for closes down, the likelihood of you being compensated is remote. Unpaid employees will join the list of creditors who will be partially reimbursed once any remaining assets of the company have been liquidated. Jobs at start ups or small companies may be better suited to spouses of working partners or single people who can more easily afford to take the risk than to the main earner in a family. If your company closes down, your work permit is no longer valid and you have two choices: you can leave Malaysia and return on a social visit pass and look for another job, or you can go elsewhere to look for work. If you find yourself caught in this situation, take legal advice on the best course of action.

Butterfly Park

KL Railway Station

Bounced Cheques ◀

If you write a cheque that bounces, you'll usually be charged RM50 to RM100 by your bank. The second time, you'll get a warning letter too. If you bounce three cheques, your name is put on a black list circulated to all Malaysian banks and you won't be able to write cheques or open another bank account for a year.

Bank Accounts

You'll see some familiar names in the banking industry in KL – Citibank, HSBC, Deutsche Bank and ABN Amro all have branches here. For convenience however, local banks dominate the scene with Maybank the preferred choice as it has plenty of ATMs and the best online banking service for paying bills.

Most banks offer both savings and current (checking) accounts, credit cards, loans, insurance and accounts for children. Cheques are not used much in Malaysia – most shops will not accept them as payment – so many expats do without a current account. Cash and credit cards are the main methods of payment; a debit card system called 'Bankcard' has been launched recently but is yet to catch on.

You need a work permit to open a bank account, but you may be able to open a savings account with a letter of guarantee from your employer stating that they have applied for your work permit. You'll be expected to produce the permit at the bank once it's issued. Take your original passport, plus a letter of introduction from your company or home bank to open an account. All parties to a joint account must also be present. If you have an account overseas with one of the big international banks, they may open a local account for you before your work permit is issued.

It's unusual to have to keep a minimum balance in your account, but as an expat you're unlikely to be allowed an overdraft.

Banks are open from Monday to Thursday, 08:45 to 17:45 and Friday 08:45 to 16:45. Some branches are also open on Saturday mornings. Many banks have machines for depositing cash and cheques outside banking hours. Most banks won't charge you for regular transactions like ATM withdrawals if your account is in credit. If you withdraw cash from another bank's machine, you may be charged up to RM10 per withdrawal, so it's a good idea to choose a bank with ATMs close to your home or work. Bounced cheques are costly, with fees ranging from RM50 to RM100.

Banking Comparison Table

Name	Phone	Web	Online Banking
CIMB	1300 880 900	www.cimb.com	✓
Hong Leong Bank	03 7626 8899	www.hlb.com.my	✓
HSBC	03 2070 0744	www.hsbc.com.my	✓
Maybank	1300 886 688	www.maybank2u.com.my	✓
Public Bank	1800 883 318	www.publicbank.com.my	✓
RHB Bank	03 9206 8118	www.rhb.com.my	✓

Financial Planning

If you're lucky enough to find yourself working in Malaysia on the equivalent of a London salary with allowances on top for your car, house, children's education and flight home, you'll probably be saving quite a bit of money. Even if you're not so lucky, expat salaries are generally high compared to the local cost of living and you should find yourself able to save. Many expats prefer to keep the bulk of their savings and investments outside Malaysia, particularly if they're only staying for a relatively short time, but it's a good idea to keep a small emergency fund in a local savings account to cover unforeseen expenses.

The Ringgit is currently strong against the US dollar, but with global uncertainty about which way the markets will go and Malaysia's history of protectionism, most expats would rather keep their money in a more liquid currency. It's up to the individual whether they choose to keep their savings in their home country or offshore and what currency they choose to hold. There are usually tax advantages to keeping savings offshore while you're not resident in your home country and your bank or financial adviser can discuss the options with you.

Bank near Jalan Raju

Before the 1997 economic crisis, KL's stock market was the busiest in the world. It's not operating at quite the same pace these days, but foreigners are allowed to invest. Visit www.bursamalaysia.com for more information. Other investment options in Malaysia include fixed-term deposits and property, but this is not considered as a short-term option as you'll pay 30% tax on any capital gains if you sell within five years. If you're interested in property as an investment, see Buying A Property p.74 .

If you find yourself with money left over every month it is a good idea to get some advice about financial planning. If you're not planning to stay in Malaysia long term, choose an adviser who specialises in expat finances. Your bank will usually offer free advice. If you bank offshore you will be assigned an adviser you can contact by phone and international banks like HSBC and Citibank will periodically send advisers to meet with their clients in person.

Financial planners offer independent advice and may have access to a wider range of products than banks. Three Sixty Financial (www.threesixtyfinancial.net) come highly recommended for KL-based expats. Its team of expatriates offers advice on wealth creation, wealth management and tax minimisation, covering structured savings, mortgages, retirement planning, school fees planning, bank accounts and healthcare. Montpelier is based and registered in the UK but makes frequent visits to KL to meet clients and provide personalised wealth management services.

The Fry Group specialises in providing tax and financial advice to British expatriates and UK residents, including retirement planning. Infosolve is a tax and investment specialist advising Americans in KL.

If you want to invest in a property in your home country you'll be better off bypassing local agents and dealing direct with an agent in the area of the country you'd like to buy in. You can get advice on mortgages in your home country from your bank or financial planner. Buying a property in your home country may affect your tax status there, even if you're a non-resident. Check with the relevant tax authority to find out what the regulations are.

Pensions

You won't receive a Malaysian pension, although some employers may offer you the choice to opt into the Employees Provident Fund (EPF). This covers all Malaysian workers and is intended as a fund for retirement savings. You will contribute 11% of your income to EPF each month, while your employer contributes 12%. When you leave Malaysia, you can withdraw the money from your EPF account and do whatever you want with it.

If you've been transferred to Malaysia by your employer, you'll probably keep your existing pension arrangements. Multinationals may pay an allowance or match your payments into an approved savings scheme, or you can make your own pension arrangements with a financial planner.

Offshore Accounts

This type of account is popular with expats as it offers a tax-effective way of managing your finances while you're not resident in your home country. Not all countries treat offshore investments in the same way, so make sure you take advice from someone who is familiar with the regulations in your home country.

Offshore accounts operate in the same way as regular accounts. You can have a savings or current (checking) account, fixed-term deposit and a debit card and credit card with your offshore bank. Some expats use these accounts as their main account and others just use them for savings. HSBC (www.offshore.hsbc.com) is a popular choice with expats because of its worldwide presence. Standard Chartered (www.standardchartered.com) is another recommended choice with branches in multiple countries. Having an offshore account with an international bank can be an advantage when you move to a new country as they may be able to set up a local bank account for you before you arrive. Minimum balance requirements vary so shop around for an account that suits you. You can usually choose which currency you keep your offshore funds in.

Small Change
From April 2008, Malaysia is phasing out the 1 sen coin. Bills ending in 1,2,6,or 7 will be rounded down to 0 or 5, and bills ending in 3,4, 8 or 9 will be rounded up to 5 or 10. Expect lighter purses and less time spent at the checkout as people scrabble around in the bottom of their bags for small change.

Cost Of Living

Apples (per kg)	RM7.50
Bananas (per kg)	RM2.80
Bottle of wine (restaurant)	RM95
Bottle of wine (supermarket)	RM45
Burger (takeaway Big Mac)	RM8.25
Camera film	RM12.50
Can of dogfood	RM3.50
Can of soft drink	RM1.20
Cappuccino	RM5.20
Car rental (basic model, per day)	RM145
Carrots (per kg)	RM2.65
CD album	RM40
Chocolate bar (200g)	RM7
Cigarettes (pack of 20)	RM8.20
Cinema ticket	RM9
Dozen eggs	RM4
DVD (new release)	RM75
Film developing (colour 36 exp)	RM22
Fresh beef (per kg)	RM24
Fresh chicken (per kg)	RM6
Fresh fish (per kg)	RM12
Golf (18 holes)	RM120 – RM200
House wine (glass)	RM22
Loaf of bread	RM2.10
Milk (1l)	RM4
Mobile to mobile call (local per minute)	RM0.36
Newspaper (international)	RM5
Newspaper (local)	RM1.20
Orange juice (1l)	RM5
Pack of 24 aspirin/paracetamol tablets	RM8
Petrol (1l)	RM1.92
Pint of beer	RM18
Postcard	RM0.50
Potatoes (1kg)	RM2.40
Rice (1kg)	RM3
Salmon (per kg)	RM60
Salon haircut (Female)	RM50 – RM150
Salon haircut (Male)	RM30
Six pack of beer (local)	RM38
Strawberries (per punnet)	RM8.99
Sugar (2kg)	RM3
Takeaway pizza (large)	RM34.50
Taxi (10km journey)	RM14
Text message (local)	Free – RM0.10
Tube of toothpaste	RM4
Water (1.5l, restaurant)	RM12
Water (1.5l, supermarket)	RM0.89

Taxation

The Balance

Malaysia is a strange mix of the very cheap and the very expensive, with some locally produced commodities costing a fraction of their price in the west and some imported goods being significantly more expensive. Unless you go exclusively for upmarket imported goods when you shop, these extremes usually balance out into a fairly average shopping bill.

Malaysia's tax year runs from January to December and expats pay tax on income earned in Malaysia. Income from overseas is not subject to Malaysian income tax. Expats are considered resident for tax purposes when they have been in the country for more than 182 days in the first tax year and 90 days in subsequent tax years. Salaries, housing allowances, car allowances, health insurance, school fees and any other benefits in kind are included as taxable income. Tax starts at 0% for the first RM2,500, going up to 28% for annual income exceeding RM250,000. Many expats will find they are in this top tax bracket. You must file your income tax return by April 30, the year following the tax year. The forms are in Bahasa Malaysia and many employers will help with these or you can employ a local accountant. Staff at the tax office may help you with the forms, but bear in mind that the offices will be very busy as the filing deadline approaches. You can post the form, deliver it in person or use the new e-filing service. The Inland Revenue Board office for KL is in Wisma KWSG, Jalan Kampung Attap in Chinatown (you can find additional information on their website www.hasil.org.my).

When you leave Malaysia you may be entitled to a tax rebate. These can be a long time coming but recent improvements to service delivery have shortened the wait to a few weeks in some cases.

If you rent your home, taxes related to the property will be paid by the owner. If you've bought property in Malaysia, you may be liable for two types of taxation, quit rent and assessment. Quit rent is charged on landed (freehold) property at one to two sen per square foot which adds up to an annual charge of less than RM100 for most properties. Assessment, which includes local government services such as street lighting and rubbish disposal, will be between RM500 and RM1,000 per year unless your property is extremely large. The exact charge varies depending on which area you live in and the size of your property, and is billed annually.

Sales tax is included in the sticker price of goods in retail shops, but will be usually be added onto the stated price in restaurants and hotels at 5%.

You may still have tax obligations in your home country, especially if you have property there. Check with the relevant tax office to avoid being subject to late fees or fines.

Financial Advisors

360 Financial	03 2143 4212	www.threesixtyfinancial.net
Financial Planning Association of Malaysia	03 2095 7713	www.fpam.org.my
Financial Planning Malaysia	na	www.financialplanningmalaysia.com
Infosolve	03 2164 9029	na
Malaysian Financial Planning Council	03 2693 1900	www.mfpc.org.my
Montpelier	na	www.montpeliergroup.com
PI LTD	03 6203 2568	www.pioffshore.com
The Fry Group	na	www.thefrygroup.co.uk

Legal Issues

Malaysia is a constitutional monarchy and the King is elected for a five-year term from the sultans of the nine states of Peninsular Malaysia. The King is the nominal Head of State and the leader of the Islamic faith in Malaysia. Executive power rests with the cabinet headed by the prime minister; which is selected from the members of parliament. Parliamentary elections are held every five to six years and there is universal suffrage.

The Malaysian legal system is based on English common law, although, unlike England there are no jury trials. The highest court of appeal is the Federal Court; below this are the Court of Appeal and the High Courts. The Sessions Courts and Magistrates Courts deal with both criminal and civil cases, but are used for less serious offences and have limited sentencing powers. Legal proceedings are usually conducted in English and interpreters are supplied for those who cannot follow in English.

The Syariah Courts operate on a state rather than a federal level and are concerned only with matters of state religious (Islamic) law. They only have jurisdiction over matters involving Muslims and have a restriction on the maximum sentence they can pass. Laws aren't overly strict in terms of what you can and can't do, but capital and corporal punishment apply to a range of offences. Expats rarely find themselves on the wrong side of the law and when they do it's likely to be for a minor offence such as a traffic violation.

Divorce

You can get divorced in Malaysia provided that your marriage is recognised under Malaysian law and you are both resident in Malaysia at the time the petition for divorce is presented. You must have been married for at least two years before you can petition for divorce. The divorce can be either by mutual consent or contested and you will have to prove that your marriage has irretrievably broken down. Proof of an irretrievable breakdown includes adultery by either partner, intolerable behaviour by either spouse such that the other can no longer live with them, desertion, or separation of at least two years.

If your divorce is not by mutual consent you will be required to attend meetings with the Conciliatory Body of the Registrar of Marriages in the district where you live. If after six months of these meetings you cannot resolve your problems, your divorce will be allowed to proceed. Matrimonial property is often evenly split between the two parties and either spouse can be required to pay maintenance to the other, depending on the circumstances. There is no provision for joint custody; one parent will be awarded sole custody of any children and the other parent given visitation rights. Custody of children under 7 will almost always be given to the mother, while older children will have a say in the arrangements made for them. The custodial parent can be prevented from taking the children out of Malaysia if the other parent objects.

Law Firms		
KC Lim and Co.	03 2166 2480	na
Kelvin, Low and Partners	03 6201 8821	www.klplegal.com
Lee, Oliver & Gan	03 9282 3716	www.leeolivergan.com
Sri Murugun & Co.	03 7980 8325	na
Vincent Wong and Partners	03 2166 8030	www.vincentwongpartners.com
Wong and Partners	03 2055 1888	www.bakernet.com

Making A Will

You can make a will in Malaysia yourself, although taking legal advice can help ensure your will is valid and your wishes will be carried out. Unlike many legal documents in Malaysia, a will does not need to be stamped.

Your will should name your executor and the individual beneficiaries, and it should detail what proportion of your estate or specific item of property they are to inherit. You must sign the will and your signature must be witnessed by two independent witnesses who must not be beneficiaries or the spouses of beneficiaries. The executor and/or their spouse may be witnesses provided they are not also beneficiaries. If you want to change your will, you must write a new one and you cannot make corrections or additions to the original.

You should make sure your executor knows about the will and where it is kept. If you decide to keep it with a lawyer, you should give the details to your executor so that they can contact the lawyer in the event of your death.

Adoption

It's possible for non-Malaysians to adopt children in Malaysia. The children are usually Malaysian born and inter-country adoption is rare. See Adoption in the Certificates & Licences section (p.52) for more information.

Crime

KL expats are generally a law abiding lot – in general professionals in their 30s and 40s are statistically unlikely to be involved in crime either as victims or perpetrators. That's not to say expats are never involved in crime in KL, but when they are it is the exception rather than the norm.

The crimes expats are most likely to encounter as victims are burglary and snatch theft. Direct assault or mugging is quite unusual, but snatch theft can be a very dangerous form of street crime. Snatch theft involves a thief riding past on a motorcycle driven by another person, leaning over and grabbing your bag before making off at high speed. Obviously this can result in serious injury for the victim – if you hang on to your bag or the strap is around you and doesn't break straight away, you can be pulled over or even dragged along the road. Snatch thefts can happen in broad daylight as well as at night; often when there are other people around and even if you are walking with someone or in a group. Always walk against the flow of traffic and carry your bag on the side away from the road. Never try to hang onto your bag.

Burglary is less common and is usually the work of opportunists who take what they can carry. Keep your valuables out of sight and lock them up if you can.

If you are the victim of a crime, you should make a police report at the nearest police station. This is especially important if you have lost valuable possessions or documents. Some insurance companies will insist on seeing a police report before settling a claim, and you may also be required to show one when replacing bank cards, credit cards, your driver's licence or passport.

Anecdotal evidence suggests expats seldom end up in jail, although statistics are hard to come by. Malaysia's prisons are not pleasant environments – overcrowding is an issue and general hygiene is poor. The main prison for KL is at Sungai Buloh, although the old Pudu Jail in the city centre is still used for some remand cases. Prisoners are allowed to receive visitors who need not be family members.

If you are arrested, you are entitled to a phone call. You should ask to call your embassy and speak to someone in the consular department who can help you find a lawyer. An embassy representative will usually make visits to any nationals of their country held in prison in Malaysia. If you are convicted of a crime in Malaysia, it may not show up on your criminal record in your home country depending on what agreement exists between Malaysia and your home country and the nature of the offence. Normally there are no international criminal record checks when applying for Malaysian visas, bank accounts and so on.

Court Complex

Incidences of expats being in trouble with the law for anything other than traffic violations are extremely rare. Malaysia has strict laws on drug offences, including the death penalty for the possession of relatively small quantities, and drugs are not part of the entertainment culture. If you are involved in a minor traffic accident or are caught drinking and driving, you may be able to smooth things over with the police. If the accident involves a serious injury or a fatality, you will almost certainly be charged and prosecuted. The penalty for causing death by dangerous driving is a maximum fine of RM10,000, imprisonment of up to five years, or both. For drinking and driving the penalty is a fine of RM2,000, a prison sentence of up to six months, or both for a first offence. The maximum penalties are doubled for a second offence. In both cases your licence will be suspended for 12 months.

Housing

There's a huge variety of accommodation available, from old colonial bungalows with huge gardens to shiny new high-rise apartments. Ampang is a popular family suburb with plenty of greenery and large houses, and for the convenience of city living there are some great apartment buildings just minutes from the iconic twin towers. Most expats prefer to rent (p.73) because they tend to come to Kuala Lumpur on work contracts lasting two or three years. The only restriction concerning non-nationals who wish to buy is that the property must be worth more than RM150,000 (see p.73 for more information).

Location, Location Location

Location is an important factor when finding a home and it pays to get it right. If you're not familiar with the city, it's a good idea to get to know the different areas a bit before making your choice. Consider factors such as the commute time to work and school, local shops and amenities, and the types of housing available.

Renting In Kuala Lumpur

Most expats live in rented property and there's a wide selection on the market. Many employment contracts include rent allowance. Some companies prefer to sign the lease and pay the rent directly while others will include an allowance to cover rental costs in the employee's salary. The advantage of the former is that it's the company that stands to lose the deposit if you are transferred at short notice, but getting an allowance offers more flexibility. Although there are certain areas of the city favoured by expats, there are no areas that are off limits. Some companies and embassies have strict policies on security, which may restrict your choice, but this is rare.

Finding A Home

There are two approaches to searching for rented property. There's the 'look see' visit, which many companies will pay for (especially for senior staff) or there's the option of renting somewhere on a short-term basis, be it a hotel or a serviced apartment, and finding something more permanent once once you arrive.

The advantage with the former is that everything is signed up before you arrive. On the down side, it means choosing a location without really knowing the city.

Serviced apartments are popular with families and those on short-term contracts, and are plentiful in the city. These come fully furnished, and the rent includes all bills, apart from phone calls.

Estate Agents

To help you get your bearings, get an estate agent to show you round the different property options. The landlord pays the agent, so if an agent asks you for money, refuse and find another one. You can also house hunt by driving around looking for 'To Let' signs or using the classified ads in newspapers – *The Star* has the best property listings. You will still end up dealing with an agent in most cases, but you will have more control over the properties that you see.

It's common for landlords to show property for rent in shocking condition. Then once they have a tenant they will arrange for the repairs and make improvements. Rents are highly negotiable and often depend on how much work you want done. That said, major repairs will take time so if you're in a hurry, tell the agent that you only want to see new properties or houses in move-in condition. If an agent can't find you what you're looking for, you're free to try another one. Be very specific about what you want and your budget as sometimes agents have a fixed idea of the kind of property an expat will like.

The Lease

Leases are usually for a year with an option to renew on expiry. Rent is usually paid monthly. A security deposit of two months' rent, plus one month's rent in advance, and half a month's rent as a utilities deposit are normal on signing the lease. Tenants are responsible for all utility bills while the landlord will usually take care of maintenance fees. Rents are fairly stable, but expect to pay a premium for a brand new development.

Accommodation options

Real Estate Agents

The best way to find an estate agent is through word of mouth. Your company may have an agent it always uses, or it may be able to reccommend a few for you to choose from. Agents are paid by the landlord and so you should never be asked to pay an agent for showing you property. If you're unhappy with the service you're getting from an agent you're free to choose another one, although you may end up seeing the same properties again. Try to keep track of which agent was the first to show you a property, if you end up renting it it should be that agent who gets the commission.

Real Estate Agents

Carey Real Estate	03 6203 3399	www.carey.com.my	Rental & Sales
Countrywide	03 2287 3873	www.countrywide.com.my	Rental & Sales
Cy Harta	03 2283 3866	www.cyharta.com	Rental & Sales
Kiara Realty	03 2093 7777	www.kiararealty.com.my	Rentals
Kim Realty	03 2282 9399	www.kimrealty.com.my	Rental & Sales
Mega Harta Real Esate Agency	03 7728 2433	www.megaharta.com	Rental & Sales
Reapfield	03 2713 3399	www.reapfield.com	Rental & Sales
Yap Burgess Rawson International	03 2712 0033	www.yapburgessrawson.com.my	Rental & Sales
Zerin	03 2092 2008	www.zerinproperties.com	Rental & Sales

The Lease

The exact terms of a lease are a matter of negotiation between the tenant and the landlord, but there are some common features. Leases run for one or two years. One-year leases are usually renewable. If there's anything you're unsure of, ask someone to take a look at the lease before signing.

• Rent is negotiable, so make sure the amount agreed is what appears in the contract.
• Standard deposits are two months' rent as security deposit and half a month for utilities. This should be paid on signing the lease, together with one month's rent in advance.
• Rent is payable monthly. Discounts can sometimes be negotiated by paying several months' rent in advance. Be warned though, if maintenance becomes a problem and the landlord has a few months' rent in hand, it might be more difficult to get him to help out.
• The lease should be in English, signed by the tenant and landlord, as well as a witness for each party. Some landlords will only sign a lease once the tenant has been issued a work permit. When signing, bring a notarised copy of your passport. The agent will usually draw up the lease and take care of the stamp duty. Make sure that the termination of lease notice period is clearly stated. This is usually one month. Your company may insist on this as a standard clause in the event that it needs to transfer you.

• Generally, once signed, the lease is binding for the period stated. Otherwise, the tenant stands to lose their deposit. It's in everyone's interest to resolve any disputes amicably and if problems do arise with your property or landlord, ask the agent who helped you find it for help.
• Leases are usually renewed if both parties agree to the terms. The landlord may ask for an increase in rent while the tenant is entitled to ask for extra work such as repainting as a condition of the new lease.

Housing Abbreviations

4r3b	4 bedrooms, 3 bathrooms
5+1	5 bedrooms, 1 maid's room
b/ins	built in cupboards
b/u	built up area
bungalow	detached house set in grounds
cor	corner plot
d/s	two storey
inter	intermediate terrace
l/a	land area
link	terraced
reno	renovated/improved
s/f	square feet
s/s	one storey
semi-D or s/d	semi detached

Main Accommodation Options

Bungalow Lowdown
*Bungalows offer great
space and privacy but
this also means you
may sometimes feel
isolated behind those
big gates.*

Bungalows

The bungalows on offer are often sprawling 1960s and 1970s designs, some of which have been modernised. Those still in their original state are cheaper to rent but you may have to put up with fairly grotty kitchens and bathrooms. You can get a three or four bedroom house with a decent size garden and off-street parking for about RM3,000 per month in Petaling Jaya. Prices start rising steeply in trendy neighbourhoods and a newly modernised six or seven bedroom house with a pool in Bangsar or Bukit Damansara will cost over RM25,000. There's plenty of choice in the RM8,000 to RM12,000 range; this covers a five bed family house with a pool and electric gates in areas such as Ampang, Bangsar or Bukit Damansara.

Spy On The Neighbours
*Be warned, if the build
quality isn't good in
your semi-detached,
you may hear more of
your neighbours than
you'd bargained for.*

Semi-Ds

Semi-Ds or semi-detached houses are joined on one side to another house. They can be as big as bungalows but usually have smaller gardens and it's rare to find a semi-D with a pool. Most housing areas have some, but they aren't as common as bungalows and link houses. Expect to pay about RM6,000 per month for a four bedroom semi-D in Bukit Damansara or Bangsar, and RM4,000 for a four or five bedroom semi-D in Ampang Jaya or Taman Hillview. Semi-Ds are a good option if you need a lot of space and can't afford a bungalow.

Turn On The Lights
*Link houses are a
good budget option
as you get a lot of
space for your money
but they can be quite
dark inside.*

Link Houses

These are terraced houses, joined to another house on either side. They may have little or no garden – although it's rare to find a house fronting right onto the street. The outside space is often used for parking. Some link houses have a yard at the back; others have just a narrow lane separating them from the house behind. Few have gardens although corner houses will have bigger yards than those surrounded on both sides. Three or four bed houses near the trendy Jalan Telawi area of Bangsar rent for between RM2,200 to RM4,000 per month; a four bed in Desa Sri Hartamas will rent for RM3,000 per month and in Taman Seputeh a similar size house will cost around RM2,500.

*The Good,
The Bad & The Condo*
*Condo life is pretty
social, and the facilities
are a big plus. On the
downside, outdoor
space is minimal and
privacy can be an issue
at times.*

Condos & Apartments

There's a huge variation in condo standards and prices. Older units are good value for money but the facilities may be run down, and newer buildings command premium prices. There's always a pool, and some condos have underground parking, a laundry and shop, gym, tennis courts and a children's playground. At a well-established premium condo in the city centre expect to pay RM12,000 monthly for a three bed unit. Mont Kiara condos range from RM2,500 for a one bed unit to RM15,000 for a large four bed unit. A five bed duplex at the brand new Bangsar Loft goes for RM23,000 a month, while just round the corner at the Tivoli a small one bed apartment will set you back RM1,800.

Living The Expat Dream
*These developments
are popular with expat
families and offer good
security and facilities.
On the downside, value
for money is
not optimum.*

Gated Developments

Gated developments are the latest trend in KL housing and they're popping up all over the city. Facilities vary but houses usually share a pool and gym with other larger developments, and may include a clubhouse, park, shop and golf course. The entrance gate is guarded, as it would be in a condo, so vehicles are recorded entering and leaving the compound. Prices are higher than the going rate for a similar size house in a similar neighbourhood. A four bedroom semi-D at iDamansara rents for RM15,000 per month but you could get a five bedroom bungalow with its own pool in Bukit Damansara for a similar fee.

Other Rental Costs

The tenant is responsible for paying utility bills while the landlord will pay assessments (similar to council tax) that cover services such as rubbish collection and street lighting. If you're living in a house with a large garden you may end up paying for a gardener (RM300 to RM500 per month for weekly service) and if you have a pool you might be responsible for cleaning and maintenance. If mosquitoes are a problem, contact a pest control company (see p.109) to arrange a contract for regular spraying.

Most tenants don't bother their landlords for small repairs and maintenance. But some of the more professional landlords will be happy to send their contractor round to deal with anything that arises. Air conditioners need to be serviced regularly to keep them working efficiently. Find out if your landlord has a contract in place; if not you will need to arrange one.

Weaving The Web

For information on buying property, from the rules and regulations to financing and a list of estate agents and property listings, visit www.property inmalaysia.com.

Buying Property

There are few restrictions on foreign ownership of property in Malaysia. Foreigners, whether resident or not, can buy freehold and leasehold property so long as the value of the property exceeds RM150,000. This is really a technicality though as most property sells for a lot more. It's also possible to buy land to build on. Some developers sell individual plots within a gated community where you can build a house to your own specifications. Until recently, property purchases of over RM250,000 by foreigners required approval from the Foreign Invest Committee, but this rule has been dropped in a move to encourage more foreign investment. In all new developments a number of units will be reserved for Bumiputera (Malays) and sold at a reduced price. This is part of a government incentive to improve the economic standing of Malays.

Cashing In On Your Digs

There are no special procedures for renting out property. You can either rent through an agent or privately by advertising on noticeboards of expat associations and international schools. The advantage of using an agent is that they will manage the property for you. Under the terms of the MM2H programme, visa holders can buy two properties in Malaysia, so it's possible to buy one place to live in and one to rent out.

Most houses are freehold, while condominiums are leasehold. After purchase the developer issues the unit owners with the Strata Title, a document proving ownership. Real capital gains tax for non-citizens is 30% if the property is sold within five years of purchase and 5% thereafter, making buying property as a short-term investment less attractive. ING rates Malaysia's property market as medium risk.

Common problems encountered usually involve properties bought off the plan that are not completed on time, or sometimes, not at all. When buying off the plan, go for a reputable developer with a history of delivering on time.

Expats on short contracts don't tend to buy. It's usually the longer term residents including those on Malaysia My Second Home (MM2H) visas that are more likely to invest. Popular areas include Mont Kiara, the city centre, Damansara Perdana and the many new gated developments around town. See p.76 for a rundown of the areas. When searching for a new property, check out advertisements in newspapers like the *New Straits Times* and *The Star*. Alternatively, enlist the services of an estate agent.

The Buying Process

If you're buying off the plan, you pay the developer 10% of the agreed purchase price as soon as you sign the purchase agreement. You then pay the balance in instalments once specified stages of construction have been completed, up to 100% of the total when you take possession of the property. This can be an expensive process if you're taking out a loan to buy as you'll be paying interest on the loan before you're able to live in it or rent it out. Legally the developer has up to 36 months to complete the property, so buying off the plan is really for the longer term investor.

Buy To Let

Once you have bought your property, there are no restrictions on letting it out.

There are no fixed rules when buying a freehold property or a completed apartment where the strata title has been issued, but the practice is to pay 10% of the agreed price on signing the sale and purchase agreement, with the balance due to the seller within three months. A memorandum of transfer must be completed under the National Land Code in order to transfer the title from the seller to the buyer.

Property Developers

Beneton Property	03 2715 1166	www.benetonproperties.com
Capital Land	03 7981 7887	www.capitalland.com.my
Malton Group	03 2776 6188	www.malton.com.my
Sunrise	03 6201 2288	www.sunrise.com.my
Tan and Tan	03 2283 2266	www.tantan.com
YTL Property	03 2142 6633	www.ytl.com.my

Selling Property

You can sell your property either by advertising privately or going through an agent. If you sell within five years of purchase, you will have to pay 30% tax on any capital gains. After five years, this drops to 5%. The property market is fairly buoyant and prices of landed (freehold) property in the areas popular with expats appreciate well. It's harder to call with newer developments and condos, as a lot depends on how the property is maintained after completion. A poorly managed property may lose value over time and be hard to sell.

Mortgages

As a foreigner you may find you're not eligible for the mortgage deals banks offer. In most circumstances a foreigner will get a mortgage for a maximum of 60% of the property value, and banks usually require the property to be worth more than RM250,000. Loans can run for anything up to 20 years. Terms and conditions are not standard so you may be able to negotiate early redemption terms if you think you might be selling the property before the loan period is up.

Foreigners who live in Malaysia under the Malaysia My Second Home programme (see Residence Visa, p.48) are subject to different rules. They may be able to get a loan for up to 85% of the property value but loan periods may be restricted by age requirements. All the major banks offer mortgages so shop around to find the deal that suits you best.

Mortgage Providers

CIMB	1300 880 900	www.cimb.com
HSBC	03 2072 8608	www.hsbc.com.my
Maybank	1300 886 688	www.maybank2u.com.my
UOB	03 2612 8121	www.uob.com.my

Other Purchasing Costs

Legal fees in Malaysia are fixed. For property purchases they are based on the value of the property. This starts with 1% of the first RM100,000, plus 0.5% of the next RM4,900,000 and 0.25% of the remaining purchase price. Stamp duty is 1% of the first RM100,000, and then goes up in increments according to the value of the property. It's 2% between RM100,000 and RM500,000, 3% between RM500,000 and RM2,000,000 and 4% for anything above RM2,000,000. The seller must pay the estate agent's fees.

Real Estate Law

It's advisable to hire a Malaysian lawyer to help with real estate transactions. They will know the details of local laws and practices and can advise on the best course of action. Your estate agent will be able to recommend a law firm (see also p.69). Legal fees are set by law and are based on the purchase price of the property.

If you're buying off the plan, there is a standard sales and purchase agreement that must be used, with clearly set out obligations for both the buyer and seller. The buyer must pay the developer 10% of the agreed purchase price as soon as they sign the purchase agreement. They then pay the balance in instalments once specified stages of construction have been completed up to 100% of the total when they take possession of the property. If there are any significant delays in the construction process, the developer is obliged to inform the buyer. It's possible to take legal action seeking compensation over late delivery but this can take years and be very expensive.

Since there are no fixed rules or agreements for sales of freehold or strata title property (sometimes called a sub-sale), it's vital to use a lawyer.

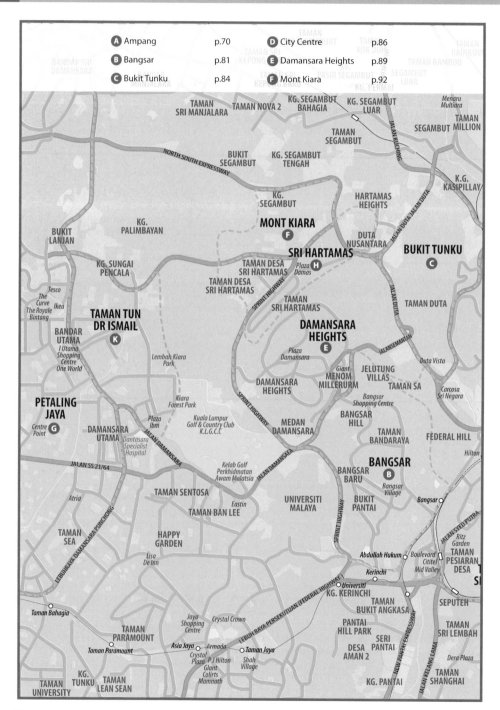

A Ampang   p.70   D City Centre   p.86
B Bangsar   p.81   E Damansara Heights p.89
C Bukit Tunku   p.84   F Mont Kiara   p.92

TAMAN
SRI MANJALARA   TAMAN NOVA 2   KG. SEGAMBUT   KG. SEGAMBUT   Menaru
                                  BAHAGIA   LUAR   Multiara
                                                                   TAMAN
                                  TAMAN   SEGAMBUT MILLION
                                  SEGAMBUT

NORTH SOUTH EXPRESSWAY   BUKIT   KG. SEGAMBUT
                         SEGAMBUT   TENGAH   K.G.
                                                                             KASIPILLAY
                              KG.   HARTAMAS
                              SEGAMBUT   HEIGHTS

            KG.   MONT KIARA   DUTA
            PALIMBAYAN   F   NUSANTARA
BUKIT   BUKIT TUNKU
LANJAN   SRI HARTAMAS   C

      KG. SUNGAI   TAMAN DESA   Plaza   H
      PENCALA   SRI HARTAMAS Damas
                       TAMAN DESA   TAMAN DUTA
Tesco   SRI HARTAMAS
The   Ikea   TAMAN
Curve   SRI HARTAMAS
The Royale   TAMAN TUN   DAMANSARA
Bintang   DR ISMAIL   HEIGHTS
BANDAR   K   Plaza   E
UTAMA   Damansara
I Utama   JALAN SEMANTAN
Shopping   Lembah Kiara   Giant JELUTUNG
Centre   Park   MENOM VILLAS   Duta Vista
One World   MILLERURM TAMAN SA
                           Kiara   DAMANSARA   Carcosa
PETALING   Forest Park   HEIGHTS   Bangsor   Sri Negara
JAYA   Kuala Lumpur   Shopping Centre
          Plaza Ibm   Golf & Country Club   BANGSAR
Centre G   K.L.G.C.C   MEDAN   HILL
Point   DAMANSARA Dantasara   DAMANSARA   TAMAN
         UTAMA   Specialist   BANDARAYA FEDERAL HILL
JALAN SS 21/64   Hospital   Hilton
                           Kelab Golf   BANGSAR
                           Perkhidmatan   BARU
Atria   Awam Malatsia   B
                                                   Bangsar
       TAMAN SENTOSA   UNIVERSITI Village
TAMAN   Eastin   MALAYA   BUKIT   Bangsar
SEA   TAMAN BAN LEE   PANTAI
                                                                JALAN SYED PUTRA
TAMAN   HAPPY   Ritz
SEA   GARDEN   Garden
          Lisa   Abdullah Hukum Boulevard TAMAN
          De Inn   Cititel PESIARAN
                                           Kerinchi   Mid Valley DESA
Taman Bahagia   Universiti
                          Jaya   KG. KERINCHI
       TAMAN   Shopping   TAMAN   SEPUTEH
       PARAMOUNT   Centre   Crystal Crown   BUKIT ANGKASA
       Taman Paramount Asia Jaya Armada Taman Jaya PANTAI   TAMAN
                        Crystal PJ Hilton   HILL PARK   SRI LEMBAH
                        Plaza Glant Shah   SERI
KG.   Colirts Village   DESA PANTAI   Dera Plaza
TAMAN TUNKU TAMAN   Mamnath   AMAN 2   TAMAN
UNIVERSITY   LEAN SEAN   KG. PANTAI   SHANGHAI

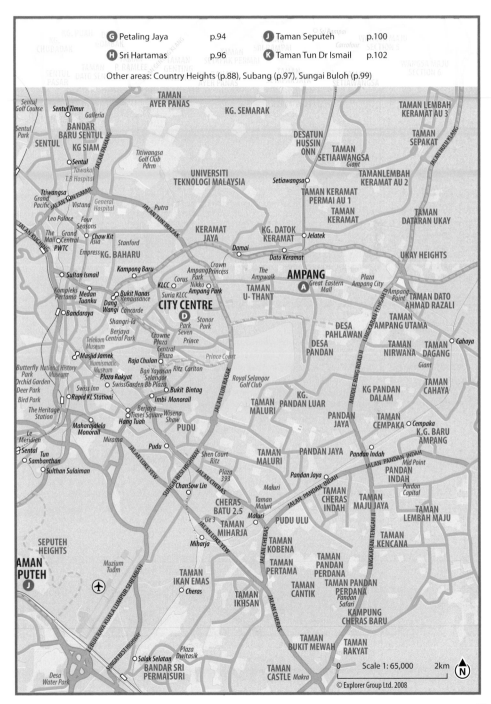

G Petaling Jaya — p.94
J Taman Seputeh — p.100
H Sri Hartamas — p.96
K Taman Tun Dr Ismail — p.102

Other areas: Country Heights (p.88), Subang (p.97), Sungai Buloh (p.99)

Scale 1: 65,000 — 0 — 2km

© Explorer Group Ltd. 2008

Residential Areas

Other options **Exploring** p.156

KL is a small city, even when you include areas which are officially in another state, like Ampang, Petaling Jaya, Subang and Sungai Buloh. Expats and affluent locals tend to use the same shops, hospitals, schools and leisure facilities regardless of where they choose to live. Even though historically there's been a bit of an Ampang-Bangsar divide, the improved road network means that outside of the peak commuting times it will be a relatively quick drive from where you live to most other parts of town. Once you've sussed out the route, you'll be popping across town on a regular basis to make the most of everything KL has to offer.

Area **A** p.76-p.77
See also Map 5

Ampang

Most KL residents refer to the area east of the junction of Jalan Tun Razak and Jalan Ampang as 'Ampang'. In truth this covers a large and diverse area, with the town of Ampang itself being in the neighbouring state of Selangor. Ampang is a popular upmarket residential area, although the parts closest to the city centre (postcode 50000) are becoming increasingly urbanised, with many older houses being torn down to make way for businesses or apartment blocks. Many embassies are located along Jalan Ampang and the area is home to many diplomats and their families. On the Selangor side, (postcode 68000) the neighbourhood borders a forest reserve and is relatively underdeveloped. Ampang is home to a number of international schools and is well served with shops and other amenities, if a bit lacking in nightlife.

Best Point
Great for families – big houses, big gardens, good schools and a quick commute to the city centre too.

Worst Point
Not much happens here in the evenings – you'll be travelling in to town in search of some nightlife.

Accommodation

Along Jalan Ampang, between Jalan Tun Razak and Jalan Ulu Klang, you will find a number of condos and apartment blocks. The apartments in this area tend to be low rise and low density, in older buildings with swimming pools and maybe a gym. Individual apartment sizes tend to be quite large, and the build quality and finishing of a high standard, although bathrooms and kitchens may be a bit dated. Security is usually a feature of these buildings as many diplomats live in these blocks. There is likely to be a guard on duty 24 hours a day. Expect to pay from around RM4,000 per month for a one or two bedroom apartment and RM8,500 per month for a 2,800 square foot three bed in an older but well-maintained block. If you're looking to buy, a similar flat will cost between RM850,000 to RM1 million. A few newer blocks have sprung up recently, especially along Jalan Ampang Hilir and Jalan U-Thant, and these have more modern facilities and styling. Expect to pay RM8,000 for a one or two bed and RM15,000 for a three bed. There are some serviced apartment blocks on Jalan Ampang where you will be able to secure a short term lease and move in with just a suitcase. These are better value than those located in the city centre. There are fewer houses in this area, and those that haven't been knocked down to make way for more modern developments are very pricey, costing over RM20,000 per month for an 18,000 square foot house with a pool. Many are on long term leases with embassies or companies and you may have to wait for a while if you have your heart set on a house close to the city centre. There are also a small number of townhouse developments clustered around Jalan Damai; these usually have a shared pool and will rent for between RM9,000 and RM15,000.

Further out past Jalan Ulu Klang, also known as the middle ring road, there are fewer apartments and more houses. There's plenty of greenery out here and it can be hard to believe you're only a 15 minute drive from the city. Houses in this area were mostly built in the 1960s and 1970s and you'll either love or hate the distinctive period touches. Large open plan living spaces are the norm, and many houses will have a bathroom for each bedroom. Large bungalows rent for anything from RM5,000 to RM15,000, depending on the internal condition and whether or not there is a pool. Similar houses sell for RM3,000,000 and upwards. Some modern rebuilds are available, but expect to pay a hefty premium for these. There are a few older style apartment blocks with rents from RM2,000 upwards – good value but you may not get a pool or lift for this. Prices are highest in the Taman TAR and Ukay Heights neighbourhoods, as these are closest to the city centre and enjoy easy access to the Ampang-KL elevated highway. Moving further out along Jalan Ulu Klang; Taman Hillview, Bukit Antarabangsa and Taman Melawati offer lower prices but a longer journey to the city centre.

Shopping & Amenities

The Ampang Hilir area is well served with neighbourhood shops, and you may be able to walk to your local shop. Hock Choon, a well-stocked supermarket popular with expats, is on Jalan Ampang, and opposite is a small mall, The Ampwalk, which has an excellent deli, a 7-Eleven, beauty salons and a great Thai massage place. The main neighbourhood mall is Great Eastern, with a large Cold Storage supermarket, bookshop, boutiques, a soft play centre and a spa.

In other neighbourhoods you may find yourself faced with a short drive for even the most basic necessities, so life without a car can be quite restricted. Ampang Point, at the junction of Jalan Ampang and Ulu Klang, is a busy local shopping centre with a Giant supermarket, post office, banks and numerous small shops.

Parking can be a problem as it's incredibly popular but you can find just about anything here. Hypermarkets Carrefour and Tesco have branches in Ampang; Tesco is on Jalan Ulu Klang and Carrefour is at Wangsa Maju and on Jalan Ampang past Ampang Point. Most neighbourhoods have a few small shops, and ATMs can be found at many petrol stations. The Ukay Heights Bakery is a very popular meeting place, with a small cafe attached. Ampang residents are lucky to have Phang Trading (03 4257 3468), popularly known as 'the van lady', a mobile supermarket with an astonishingly wide selection that makes home deliveries throughout the Ampang area.

Entertainment & Leisure

Ampang is short on public open spaces, and most residents are content with their gardens or condo facilities. The nearest parks are at KLCC, in the city centre, and Titiwangsa, north on Jalan Tun Razak. KLCC has an excellent playground and running tracks. It's tidy and well maintained. Titiwangsa is larger, with an older style playground, lake, running tracks and picnic spaces. It's popular with kids on bikes and their parents. The National Zoo (Zoo Negara) is located in Taman Melawati.

Clubs are a popular way of accessing recreational facilities and Ampang has two, the Raintree in Ampang Hilir and the KDE in Taman TAR. The Raintree is smaller but has more modern facilities including tennis and squash courts, a pool and gym. The KDE is older but has the advantage of having a nine-hole golf course. The circuit around the KDE is a popular walking route.

Ampang doesn't have much in the way of nightlife, but its proximity to the city centre means this isn't too much of a disadvantage.

Healthcare

Two large private hospitals, Gleneagles (03 4257 1300) and Ampang Puteri (03 2296 0888), offer round the clock care, including accident and emergency. Many expats rely on hospitals for all their medical care, although they can be an expensive option if you don't have medical insurance. Pharmacies at Ampang Point and Great Eastern Mall are open until 22:00 each night.

There are a few neighbourhood private clinics used by expats and their families as GP services. Klinik Segara in City Square (03 2163 2140) is popular, as is Dr Prakash (03 4253 0768) at Naan Corner near ISKL. Both Gleneagles and Ampang Puteri also offer dental services.

Education
There are a few international schools in Ampang providing primary and secondary education. The International School of Kuala Lumpur (American) has its Elementary campus in Taman Melawati and Middle and High schools in Ampang Jaya. Next door to the ISKL senior campus is Mutiara International Grammar School offering the British system from preschool through to secondary. In Ampang Hilir, Fairview and Sayfol international schools offer the British system. There are several popular nursery schools in the area including the Children's House on Jalan Ampang Hilir and Sunshine Rabbits and Kindicare in Ukay Heights. See the Education section on p.136 for more information.

Transport
Ampang is a series of sprawling neighbourhoods and in some you will find life difficult without access to a car. Public transport is sketchy; there is an LRT station at Ampang Park on the edge of Ampang Hilir and at Jalan Jelatek near the Great Eastern Mall. Plenty of buses run along Jalan Ampang to and from the city centre, but away from this main artery buses are less frequent and do not serve some residential areas. Some residents have reported problems calling taxis; offering to pay a supplement over the meter charges may help if you're having problems calling a cab. Driving around the neighbourhood is pretty stress free and traffic isn't bad by KL standards, although parking can be a problem in some commercial centres. Ampang is linked to KL by the Ampang-KL Elevated Highway (sometimes signposted as AKLEH) and this cuts journey time to the city centre dramatically, especially at peak times, for the price of the RM1.50 toll. The AKLEH has an exit straight into the carpark at KLCC, making commuting a breeze if you work in the Twin Towers.

Safety & Annoyances
Monkeys can be a problem in Ukay Heights, Taman Tar, Hillview and Melawati. They swing through the neighbourhoods in large groups, much to the amusement of children, but they can be destructive and there have been reports of some being

Ampang housing

aggressive. Keep small children inside when monkeys invade your garden. Walking around can be a problem due to the lack of pavements and motorists' general lack of respect for pedestrians. Most areas are not well lit at night. There have been reports of motorcycle snatch thefts in some areas. Be aware of your surroundings when walking, walk against the flow of traffic and carry your bag on the side away from the traffic. Overall though, Ampang is a safe and pleasant area to live in.

Area **B** p.76-p.77
See also Map 6

Bangsar

Home to KL's cafe society, there's always something new happening in this upmarket suburb. Located between KL city and Petaling Jaya, Bangsar has good transport links and is popular with expats and trendsetting locals. Bangsar isn't dominated by any one of Malaysia's main ethnic groups; there's a good mix of all races and a large dash of expats too. There's a wide variety of housing, excellent shopping facilities and plenty of nightlife. It's more urban than Ampang although hardly a concrete jungle. Being a well-established suburb, there are plenty of mature trees and some green spaces. Its popularity as an entertainment centre means that traffic and parking around major commercial centres can be a problem, but Bangsar residents have the advantage of having their every need catered for within their own neighbourhood.

Best Point

Fantastic shopping and entertainment hub, everything you could possibly need or want can be found in Bangsar.

Worst Point

Its popularity means it can be busy and clogged up with traffic. Parking can be a problem, especially in the afternoon and evening.

Accommodation

There's a great variety of housing available in Bangsar and although you will pay a premium for living in this trendy suburb, there's still plenty that's affordable. A three bed terraced house in the streets around the Jalan Telawi shopping and entertainment hub will cost from RM2,500 per month to rent and just under RM1,000,000 to buy. Large bungalows in the Bukit Pantai neighbourhood cost around RM6,500 to RM20,000, or more if there's a pool, and sell for RM4,000,000 upwards. Jalan Maarof is the main road through Bangsar. Although it's still lined with houses, many have been converted into business premises to take advantage of the substantial passing trade. Similar bungalows can be found in the streets behind. Apartment blocks tend to be older style. Most come with swimming pools and other facilities, with rents from RM2,500 for a two bed two bath older condo, up to RM10,000 for a large apartment opposite Bangsar Shopping Centre. A few new apartments have been built and for RM12,000 per month (rent) or RM2.7 million (buy) you'll get a generous 3,400 square foot living space in a brand new block. A couple of major developments are under construction, including One Menerung behind the popular Bangsar Shopping Centre.

Shopping & Amenities

Being the shopping paradise that it is, Bangsar residents will seldom need something that can't be found in their neighbourhood. The main road, Jalan Maarof, has a large shopping centre at each end; Bangsar Shopping Centre (BSC) at the Damansara side (north east) and Bangsar Village I and II in the Bangsar Baru district near to Jalan Bangsar (south west). BSC is currently undergoing a major renovation that will see it double in size. It's a popular and well-established shopping centre with an excellent Cold Storage supermarket, deli, bookshop, boutiques selling clothing, accessories, home furnishings and toys and a soft play centre. It's also home to several restaurants and bars and is busy well into the night. Bangsar Village has two separate buildings joined by an overhead walkway. The older, known as Bangsar Village I, has an upmarket supermarket, an electrical store, bookshop and a number of specialist shops. There's a good alterations shop in the basement. The new building, or BVII, has a more chic feel, with branches of several European fashion chains, Turkish baths, some trendy hangout places and a large gym. There are banks and a post office nearby in Jalan Telawi, and an excellent stationery supplies shop, Czip Lee. The Jalan Telawi area is home to a number of small boutiques and specialist shops and is well worth exploring. The Sunday evening pasar malam (night market) at Bangsar Baru is well worth a visit.

Across Jalan Ara from Bangsar Village is the equally useful but less trendy Lucky Garden. This commercial centre has the supermarket TMC, a less expensive alternative to those glossy shopping centres. There's also a wet (fresh food) market here in the mornings. There's a host of useful businesses here, from motor mechanics to appliance repair shops, printing, DIY and hardware. Bukit Bandaraya also has a small commercial area with some specialist shops, bars and restaurants.

The Bangsar Beat
Find out more about Bangsar in the Exploring chapter (p.81).

Entertainment & Leisure

If there's one thing Bangsar lacks, it's a cinema. The nearest is at Mid Valley, a stone's throw if the traffic is in your favour, a frustrating crawl if it's not. It does have the Actors Studio (03 2094 0400 www.theactorsstudio.com.my), a small theatre located at BSC which stages both local and international productions.
The municipal Bangsar Sports Complex (03 2282 2360), on Jalan Terasek 3 has a playground, swimming pool and squash, tennis, basketball and badminton courts. Rates are very reasonable and there's plenty of car parking. There's no big park, but there are other playgrounds at Jalan Kurau, Jalan Tempinis 5 and Jalan Tersaek 7. Bangsar's nightlife is much talked about, although some say its trendy reputation was simply the result of demographics and is now fading. The bars, pubs and restaurants clustered around Jalan Telawi tell a different story, while those at BSC attract a more mature, wealthier crowd.

Healthcare

Pantai Medical Centre is a large private hospital located on Jalan Bukit Pantai and it is used by expats as well as affluent local residents. The accident and emergency department is open 24 hours. Although not in Bangsar, the Universti Malaya Medical Centre (03 7957 4422) is a large public hospital about five minutes' drive away with a 24 hour accident and emergency unit and ambulance service.
A government clinic, Pusat Kesihatan Umum Bangsar, is on Jalan Bangsar, and there are also numerous small private clinics around Bangsar. Try Poliklinik Bangsar (03 2282 3753) on Jalan Telawi or the Japan Medicare Clinic (03 2287 0988) on Jalan Maarof. An excellent family dentist is Yee Dental Surgery (03 2095 1102) at Bangsar Shopping Centre. Mamalink (www.mamalink.com.my), a centre promoting natural birth and breastfeeding, is located in Lucky Garden.

Education

There are no international primary or secondary schools in Bangsar itself but its central location means most schools are easily accessible. The Alice Smith School primary campus (03 2148 3674) at Jalan Bellamy is the closest and the schools in Mont Kiara are a short drive away. There are many nursery schools, including a branch of the Children's House (03 2283 4825) on Jalan Tempinis Kiri, Child's Playworks (03 2093 9592), Chiltern House (03 2095 5500), a bilingual English/Mandarin school, and Tadika Sunbeam (03 2287 7899), a Reggio Emilia school.
Universiti Malaya, Malaysia's top government university, is located close to Bangsar on the borders of KL and Petaling Jaya.

Transport

Driving around Bangsar can be a pain. Local traffic is often heavy throughout the day, and parking around the major commercial and shopping centres hard to find. Some streets have speed bumps or strips to slow the traffic on Bangsar's steep hills or to discourage motorists from taking shortcuts. Some speed bumps are unexpectedly high – slow right down to avoid bumping the undercarriage of your car. Bangsar is encircled by major roads so it's easy to access other parts of the city. Several toll roads link Bangsar with other suburbs, and the New Pantai Expressway connects Bangsar with Subang Jaya via Pantai Dalam, Old Klang Road and Bandar Sunway. To the north, at the opposite end of Jalan Maarof, the Sprint Highway links to the New Klang Valley Expressway, the Damansara Puchong Expressway and the Kerenchi Link.

It can take as little as 10 minutes to drive to KL city centre, or as much as an hour, depending on the traffic.

Residents of Bangsar can easily get by without a car. It's possible to live close enough to shops and entertainment to walk, cabs are easier to come by than in some other parts of the city and there are several bus routes running through the area – see www.rapidkl.com.my for maps and details. Bangsar LRT station, on Rapid KL's Kelana Jaya line, is on Jalan Bangsar and offers quick connections to KLCC, KL Sentral and Petaling Jaya. KL's main rail station, KL Sentral, is a five-minute drive away.

Safety & Annoyances

Parking is possibly the biggest bugbear of Bangsar residents, so leave your car behind if you can or arrive early in the day to beat the crowds. Bangsar is generally a safe neighbourhood and many roads have pavements so it's more pedestrian friendly than some other parts of the city. There have been some media reports of *Mat Rempit* in the area. These are gangs of young motorcyclists who get their kicks racing along Jalan Maarof, usually late at night on weekends. Police action, including roadblocks and confiscating unlicensed motorbikes, seems to have put a stop to this, but be on the alert when driving in this area at night.

Bangsar housing options

Area **C** p.76-p.77
See also Map 4

Bukit Tunku

One of the older suburbs, Bukit Tunku (sometimes known as Kenny Hills) is an oasis of green located just outside the city centre. Hidden in its forest-covered slopes are some of the city's most expensive homes. This area was traditionally the home of Malaysia's top politicians as it is close to the parliament building. Today's residents are a mix of wealthy Malaysians and expats living in old-style splendour.

Best Point

Lovely homes, if you can afford them, in a very central location with good access to and from the city. Easy access to the Lake Gardens; KL's biggest park.

Accommodation

Palatial bungalows built on a grand scale are the order of the day here. Most houses have pools and many were built with separate staff quarters and guest houses. Prices are high with bungalows selling for RM10 million upwards and renting for RM15,000. There are a few older style condo blocks and a couple of new gated developments. Tijani is popular with families and a four bed semiD will rent for around RM15,000, while Impian Bukit Tunku is very exclusive with rents from RM16,000 to RM30,000. A three bed apartment in one of the few older blocks rents for RM8,500. There's really nothing at the lower end of the scale here, although if you're very lucky you may uncover an unmodernised gem. If you're on a tight budget it's probably better to look elsewhere.

Worst Point

There's not much here apart from those lovely houses, so you may find yourself driving outside the area for many essentials. You'll be dependent on a car too, since public transport here is poor.

Shopping & Amenities

There is a small shopping area with a bank, restaurant, general store and drycleaners. For anything else you'll find yourself driving to Bangsar or the city centre, which are each about 10 minutes away.

Entertainment & Leisure

The green hilly surroundings and quiet roads make this a pleasant area for walking, and this is a good area to live if you have a dog. There aren't any pavements though, so pedestrians must be aware of traffic. Bukit Tunku is located very close to the Lake Gardens, a large park with playgrounds, paths and jogging tracks. The very upmarket Carcosa Seri Negara hotel (03 2295 0888) is just next to the Lake Gardens – the Sunday curry tiffin and afternoon tea are very popular. This area is also home to KL's Bird Park (03 2272 1010) and Butterfly Garden (03 2693 4907). The Islamic Arts Museum (www.iamm.org.my) and Planetarium (03 2273 5484) are also close by. For bars, restaurants and nightlife, head for Bangsar or the city centre.

Healthcare

Pantai Medical Centre (03 2296 0888) in Bangsar is the closest hospital with 24 hour accident and emergency. For clinics and dentists, you'll have to travel into the city centre or Bangsar.

Education

There aren't any schools or nurseries in Bukit Tunku. The Alice Smith primary campus (03 2148 3674) is nearby and has a bus service. Parents of younger children tend to choose nursery schools in Bangsar or Damansara Heights, and outside of peak hours it's a drive of 10 to 15 minutes to these areas.

Transport

You'll definitely need a car if you're living here. The lack of amenities in the immediate area means you'll be driving to almost everything. It's not usually a problem to get a taxi because of the central location, but you will have to call one since there's not a lot of traffic passing through. Bukit Tunku is centrally located with easy access to most areas of the city. Traffic on the main connecting road, Jalan Duta, can be very heavy at peak times and this can affect journey times but outside peak hours you'll be within a 15 minute drive of most parts of KL.

Safety & Annoyances

Bukit Tunku is regarded as a very safe area. Monkeys living in the surrounding forest may be a problem in your garden, and you should keep pets and children inside if the monkeys are around. If you're walking around the area watch out for passing cars – drivers may not be looking out for pedestrians.

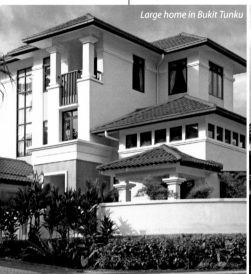

Large home in Bukit Tunku

Affluent neighbourhood

Bird Park

Orchid Gardens inside the Lake Gardens

Area **D** *p.76-p.77*
See also Map 5

City Centre

This is the place to be if you like to have everything on your doorstep. The city centre is quite compact and there's still plenty of residential accommodation in among the office blocks, hotels and shopping malls. It's possible to live and work in adjacent buildings and that certainly cuts down on commuting! Although KL is not exactly the city that never sleeps, there's plenty going on and you'll be spoilt for choice when it comes to bars and clubs.

Best Point

Everything the city has to offer, right on your doorstep. It's still a surprisingly liveable area with large pockets of residential buildings in among the malls and office blocks.

Accommodation

The main areas where expats live in the city centre are Bukit Ceylon, around Jalan Kia Peng and Persiaran Hampshire. New residential developments are springing up all around KLCC; they're pitched at the luxury end of the market but it's possible to find city centre accommodation to suit a wide range of budgets. A 3,200 square foot apartment in the brand new Marc Residence sells for RM4.3 million or rents for RM22,000 per month. Studios in the same building rent for RM4,500. Similar sized apartments in an older building like 1A Stonor rent for RM2,500. At the bottom end of the market you can get a studio for around RM1,000 off Jalan Bukit Bintang. There are still some houses in the city centre but it's rare to see them on the market for rent or sale as they're usually snapped up by developers.

Worst Point

All that traffic makes for a fairly polluted environment – if you're after a bit of clean air you'll be better off in one of the greener suburbs.

Shopping & Amenities

If retail therapy is your thing, you'll be right at home in the city centre. From the glossy malls at the top end of Bukit Bintang to the night market on Changkat Bukit Bintang there's shopping everywhere you turn. Unlike many city centres, KL is well served with the basics too. There are supermarkets at Isetan Department Store in Lot 10 and KLCC malls and branches of Cold Storage at KLCC and Times Square. There's a large Maybank branch on the corner of Bukit Bintang and Jalan Sultan Ismail and HSBC is on Jalan Sultan Ismail. Most malls have least one bank branch and there's a post office at KLCC. Convenience store chains 7-Eleven and Kiosk have many city centre branches and some are open 24 hours.

Entertainment & Leisure

Changkat Bukit Bintang is a small street lined with bars and restaurants that comes alive at night. There's a gourmet burger bar, Relish (03 2145 3321), the Magnificent Fish and Chips Bar (03 2142 7021) and The Green Man pub (www.greenman.com.my). Jalan Doraisamy, popularly known as Asian Heritage Row (www.asianheritagerow.com) is an upmarket development of restored shop houses with restaurants, bars and clubs. Jalan Alor, off Changkat Bukit Bintang has some delicious Chinese food stalls open to the street.

There are several large gyms, including a branch of Fitness First (www.fitnessfirst.com. my) at Menara Maxis on Jalan Ampang and a brand new True Fitness (www.truefitness. com.my) at the Pavilion. If you prefer the great outdoors, KLCC park is landscaped and manicured to perfection. There's a great playground here and a popular jogging track. Bukit Nanas forest recreational park is at the bottom of KL Tower in the heart of the city. It's a bit wilder and has marked trails through the forest. There's a fantastic flying fox here too.

Cinemas can be found at KLCC and the Pavilion, and for something a bit more highbrow, the Dewan Filharmonik Petronas (www.malaysianphilharmonic.com) is at KLCC.

Healthcare

The Twin Towers Medical Centre at KLCC (03 2382 3503) provides GP and dental services. Klinik Segara at City Square (03 2163 2140) is easily accessible from the city centre. Gleneagles (03 4257 1300) on Jalan Ampang used to be the nearest major hospital but the new Prince Court Medical Centre (03 2160 0000), just off Jalan Tun Razak on Jalan Kia Peng, is a much closer option.

Education

Although there aren't any schools in the city centre, there's easy access to the Alice Smith primary school (03 2148 3674). There are a few nursery schools in Ampang that are easy to get to from the city. Children's House (03 4257 7273) on Jalan Ampang Hilir, and Building Blocks (03 2142 0611) on Jalan Murni are probably the closest.

Transport

You certainly won't need a car if you're living in the city centre. It's compact, so most shops and amenities, and perhaps even work, will be within walking distance. There are plenty of taxis to be found, but around popular tourist spots and hotels you may have trouble finding a driver who will use the meter. The LRT and Monorail each have several stops in the city centre and there are frequent bus services run by RapidKL. The LRT provides a fast connection to KL Sentral for domestic train services and the express train to the airport.

Safety & Annoyances

The city centre is a remarkably safe place to walk around, but if you look like a tourist you may be pestered by touts in areas like Bukit Bintang. If you walk in the city be extra careful to watch out for motorcyclists when crossing the road, as they often ignore pedestrian lights. Some areas around KLCC and Persiaran Hampshire are still seeing a lot of new construction and this can be noisy and dusty.

View over city centre

Best Point ◄

Large, modern houses perfect for families and a good location if you have children at Alice Smith Secondary School or the Australian International School.

Worst Point ◄

It's a long commute into KL from here. Despite this being a gated community, there have been reports of problems with safety and security.

Country Heights

This new upmarket residential community was established in 1992 and is located in Kajang, between KL and Putrajaya. It's about a 30 to 45 minute drive into KL, depending on traffic. Guarded by a 24 hour security system, this self-contained community is set in a beautifully landscaped environment on what was once a rubber plantation. The development was conceived before the economic crash of the 1980s when it was anticipated that many embassies and business would move out of KL to Putrajaya, the new administrative capital. This hasn't happened yet, but Country Heights is still a good location for families who want to be near the Australian International School or the Alice Smith secondary campus. It's also popular with people who work in the Multimedia Super Corridor or in Cyberjaya.

Accommodation

Unlike many modern housing developers in KL, the company behind Country Heights didn't build all the houses. They sold plots of land to individual owners and developers and the result is that there is a variety of architectural styles, including some stunning showpiece homes. Houses are large, often with private pools and are good value for money for the size and quality. A four bed detached house with private pool is RM11,000 per month and you can buy a similar one for RM2.6 million. Three bed terraced villas at the Country Heights Resort, which is located within the estate, can be rented on a long-term basis from RM2,200 per month.

Shopping & Amenities

Community facilities include a grocery shop, volunteer run charity shop, restaurant, tennis courts and swimming pool. Outside the development you'll find local shops, banks and a post office in Kajang and the nearest big mall is at the Mines. You'll have to drive here or to KL or Putrajaya for most of your shopping.

Entertainment & Leisure

The quiet country location is the big draw here, with golf, swimming, walking and biking all popular outdoor pursuits. At the nearby Mines complex (www.mines.com. my) you'll find lake with an artificial beach where you can waterski and wakeboard. The Selangor Turf Club (www.selangorturfclub.com) horse racing track is also nearby at Sungei Besi if you fancy a flutter. For nightlife and a selection of bars and restaurants you'll be looking at a fairly long drive into town.

Healthcare

For emergency treatment Putrajaya Hospital (03 888 0080) is the nearest with a 24 hour accident and emergency department. For non-emergency cases most expats living here will visit one of the popular private hospitals or clinics in KL itself.

Education

One of the biggest plus points of Country Heights is its proximity to the Australian International School (03 8943 0622), which is about 10 minutes away in Bangi, and the Alice Smith secondary campus at Equine Park, about a 20 minute drive. There aren't any popular nursery schools in this neighbourhood, although the Australian school does take children from age 3 in its early years department.

A new international school, run by the Taylors Educational Group who also run the Australian and Garden International Schools, will be opening in Putrajaya in late 2008.

Transport

You'll need a car to get around, although the KTM Komuter station at Kajang may be a possibility for commuting into KL. A frequent train service runs from here to KL Sentral where you can continue your journey by taxi, LRT or monorail. Country Heights is located off the major North-South Highway linking Malaysia to Singapore. The international airport KLIA is a 30 minute drive away and outside the rush hour it'll take about 30 minutes to drive to KL. Putrajaya and Cyberjaya are both 15 minutes' drive away.

Safety & Annoyances

Despite being a guarded community, there have been reports of house break-ins in Country Heights. Generally though, this is a safe neighbourhood where you will see children riding their bikes on the street. More housing developments are planned for the area, and this could have an adverse effect on local traffic in the future.

Area **E** p.76-p.77
See also Map 4

Damansara Heights

Also known as Bukit Damansara, this is one of KL's ritziest neighbourhoods, and a lot of wealthy families live here. Like neighbouring Bangsar, Damansara Heights is built on a hill and some houses have excellent views of the city. Jalan Beringen is the main road circling through. Initially this suburb can be confusing to navigate as many roads have similar sounding names like Jalan Setiabakti and Jalan Steiabistari. Once you get the hang of it though, the layout is fairly logical. The general feel is of a quieter and less commercial suburb than neighbouring Bangsar, although there is a reasonable range of local shops and some popular restaurants. Damansara Heights has good connections to other suburbs via a network of highways although it's not well served by public transport.

Best Point

Well planned residential area with very little traffic off the main roads. Ideal for families – quiet and peaceful with some excellent neighbourhood dining options.

Worst Point

There's not much shopping locally and the small commercial areas can get very congested. A proposed new major mixed use development may spoil the peace and quiet.

Accommodation

You'll find many large bungalows here, often with swimming pools. Sprawling 1960s and 1970s designs predominate. Some have been extensively remodelled and modernised and these are the most expensive, with a large detached six bedroom house with pool renting for RM25,000 a month. Like most KL areas, you can pick up a bargain if you're prepared to rent an older, unmodernised property. Although you won't get as much for your money here as in Ampang, RM6,000 will get you a four bedroom bungalow without a pool. There are also areas with semiD and link houses which are a cheaper option. These are usually closer to shops and other amenities, which can be an advantage if you don't have a car. There are only a few apartment buildings in this area with rents ranging from RM5,000 for a three bed unit. Damansara Heights is now home to several pricey gated housing developments, although you may find that prices are creeping down a bit in the older developments as each new arrival opens for business. Well-established gated developments include Jelutong Villas and Semantan Villas, while newer names to look out for are iDamansara and Seri Beringin. Expect to pay RM14,000 for a large four bed semi-D at Semantan Villas.

Shopping & Amenities

Although it's not known as one of the city's great shopping areas, Damansara Heights has a good selection of local shops located at several small commercial centres. There's no really big supermarket so you'll probably have to go to Bangsar for your weekly grocery shop, but Hock Lee on Jalan Batai is a good mini market. There is a small mall at Plaza Damansara and banks and a post office at the Pusat Bandar Damansara complex. You'll find a few upmarket boutiques catering to the area's affluent population located in converted bungalows. A number of interior designers and upmarket dressmakers have showrooms here.

Entertainment & Leisure

You'll find some excellent restaurants here ranging from family favourites like pizzeria La Risata and the deli-style Jarrod and Rawlins to more grown up affairs like Klimts and The Courtyard. Medan Damansara and Pusat Bandar Damansara are the best areas for eating out. If you're after a livelier scene, it's only a ten minute drive in one direction to Bangsar's Jalan Telawi or in the other direction to Desa Sri Hartamas. The nearest cinemas are in Mid Valley, about 20 minutes drive away.

Lonely?
Don't be – it's usually pretty easy to make friends when you're living away from home. The trick is to get out and about - see p.257 for a list of social groups that are friendly and always welcome newbies.

The national science centre, Pusat Sains Negara (03 2092 1150) is at Persiaran Bukit Kiara on the edge of Damansara Heights. Nearby Bukit Kiara Club (www.berjayaclubs.com/kiara) is popular with expats and has good sports facilities including swimming, horse riding, a driving range and tennis courts. There's a Fitness First gym (www.fitnessfirst.com.my) at Pusat Bandar Damansara.

Healthcare

The nearest hospital is Pantai Medical Centre in Bangsar which has a 24 hour accident and emergency department. There are number of small private clinics in Damansara Heights including Klinik Segara (03 2095 2227) at Pusat Bandar Damansara, and Global Doctors on Jalan Dungun (03 2092 1999). In the same building as Global Doctors there's the highly recommended KL Sports Medicine Centre (03 2096 1033) and a dentist, Dr Loke (03 2094 6088).

Education

You're well located for the Alice Smith primary campus (03 2148 3674) and the international schools at Mont Kiara, both of which are about a 10 or 15 minute drive. There are several nursery schools popular with expats including Magic Years (03 2095 2496) and Children's House (03 2094 2090). Help University College is at Pusat Bandar Damansara as is the Berlitz Language Centre (03 2093 1619).

Damansara housing

Transport

As you'll have to travel outside the area for most amenities and services, you'll need a car if you live here. The area isn't well served by public transport with no major stations nearby. The Sprint Highway runs between Bangsar and Damansara Heights with links to the New Klang Valley Expressway, the Damansara Puchong Expressway and the Kerenchi Link. On the opposite side of the hill, you can access the Kerenchi Link and the Penchala Link. It's quite easy to get a taxi here.

Safety & Annoyances

This is a pretty safe area, with no major safety concerns. Some residents have reported bogus contractors in the area trying to gain access to homes, so be sure to check the ID of anyone who comes to your house. The area around Pusat Bandar Damansara can get extremely congested as this busy business centre has limited access. Parking can also be a problem here.

Are you always taking the wrong turn?

Whether you're a map person or not, these pocket-sized marvels will help you get to know the city – and its limits.

Explorer Mini Maps
Fit the city in your pocket

Area **F** p.76-p.77
See also Map 4

Mont Kiara

Probably the newest neighbourhood in KL, Mont Kiara is a planned community consisting of a mixture of high-rise condominiums and modern gated housing complexes. It's been purpose designed as a complete neighbourhood with schools, nurseries, a shopping mall and office buildings. It's on the west side of the city, next to Sri Hartamas. Some people find the environment here rather sterile, and it's the closest you'll get to a concrete jungle in KL. Others find the modernity, convenience and order reassuring and it's not surprising that it's home to a large expat population. The well-maintained pavements make walking to the shops with a pushchair a possibility – a rare prospect in KL – and there are fewer reports of problems with getting taxis here. On the downside there is little local flavour to the neighbourhood and there's a limited choice of mainly upmarket shops and businesses.

Best Point
Modern, purpose-built neighbourhood with excellent amenities and two international schools. Plenty of new condos with resort-style facilities to choose from.

Worst Point
It's a bit of a concrete jungle. Some people find it's rather soulless and lacks a local flavour.

Accommodation

You won't find as much variety as in other KL neighbourhoods, and this is deliberate. Mont Kiara was planned as an upmarket suburb with accommodation to match. There are several high-rise condominiums with excellent leisure facilities and on site shops, restaurants and even a spa at Damai Sari. Prices start at RM2,500 for a one bed condo to RM16,000 for a six bed unit. If you'd like a house, your choice here is limited to one of a handful of gated developments. These houses are large and modern in design with high quality fittings. You'll find, detached, semiD and link houses but typically you don't get much outside space around your house so if privacy is important this type of accommodation may not be for you. Houses in gated communities usually have shared facilities such as a playground, clubhouse and pool, but some have private pools and a five bed house rents for RM15,000. Mont Kiara is a popular area for expats to purchase property, condos range from RM500,000 to over RM2 million and houses from RM2 million to RM4 million.

Transport

You should be able to walk to most of your local shops and other amenities and you could easily live in Mont Kiara without a car. Commuting options are limited though – without a car you'll be dependent on taxis. Some condos have a shuttle bus that runs on a set route to major destinations in the city and this could be used for commuting. There's poor access to public transport other than taxis. In theory Mont Kiara should be well connected to other parts of KL by road, in practice the ramps connecting it to the highway system don't seem to have been completed yet. Rush hour bottlenecks are common at the entry and exit points, but in the last year an access road has been opened up to Jalan Duta on the west side and this has alleviated some congestion. Bottlenecks aside, Mont Kiara is linked to TTDI and Petaling Jaya by the Penchala Link to the Federal Highway, Damansara Heights and Bangsar by the Kerenchi Link; and to the city centre via Jalan Duta. Commutes can be long – well over an hour to the city centre at peak times – but outside these hours getting around will be fairly hassle free.

Shopping & Amenities

There are two main commercial centres; Plaza Mont Kiara is the larger with a Cold Storage supermarket, banks and a post office. There's also a nail bar, hairdressers and beauty salons. There's a smaller mall further up Jalan Mont Kiara towards Mont Kiara International School. This is currently being redeveloped but there is a bakery, cafe and small supermarket here. Energy Day Spa has a branch here located at Damai Sari next door to Bijou restaurant. There's a wider range of shops in neighbouring Desa Sri Hartamas, which is in walking distance. Regular night and flea markets help to liven up the shopping scene, but there's no big mall or department store. It's just a 10 minute drive through the Penchala Link to the excellent shopping at Mutiara Damansara and 1 Utama, where you'll find IKEA, Tesco, Borders, Mothercare, Marks and Spencer, Jusco and a branch of just about every retail outlet in Malaysia.

Entertainment & Leisure

Most condos here have excellent facilities. With gyms, pools, playgrounds and even tennis and squash courts on site, Mont Kiara residents have little need for communal recreational facilities. A regular night market held on Thursdays, and a flea market on Sundays liven things up somewhat. There are a couple of bars and restaurants in Mont Kiara itself, including the laid back and classy Bijou and family favourite Marmalade, but there's a lot more nightlife in neighbouring Desa Sri Hartamas, which is buzzing most nights of the week. The National Science Centre (p.188) is a short drive away and The Bukit Kiara Club (www.berjayaclubs.com/kiara) has excellent outdoor sports facilities. The nearest cinema is The Cathay Cineplex, a ten minute drive away through the Penchala link at the Curve shopping centre.

Online Communities

There are numerous expat-focused websites offering advice and advertising services especially for expatriates. See p.37 for a list. And check out www.explorerpublishing.com, where you can join an online community for your city, share tips, get updates, ask questions and make friends.

Education

Probably the most convenient neighbourhood for families, Mont Kiara has two large international schools. Garden International School (see p.140) offers the British curriculum from nursery to A-levels while Mont Kiara International School (see p.140) follows the American system from kindergarten to High School. Both have modern, purpose-built campuses with playing fields and swimming pools. There are also several nursery schools in the area; Kidscool (03 6201 7350) and Children's Discovery House (03 6203 7001) are popular choices. A special needs nursery school, The Learning Connection (www.thelearningconnection.com.my) caters to children with a variety of learning difficulties.

Housing in Mont Kiara

Healthcare

Global Doctors (03 6203 3999) has a clinic here and there's a branch of Klinik Segara at Plaza Mont Kiara. There's no hospital in Mont Kiara and the nearest with 24 hour accident and emergency is Damansara Specialist Hospital (03 7722 2692) in Damansara Utama.

Safety & Annoyances

One of the safest areas to live in KL, Mont Kiara has regular security patrols provided by the area's developer, Sunrise. As almost all the housing is in gated and guarded condos or housing enclaves, general security is very good too. Ongoing development means new construction sites will continue to spring up for some time, bringing plenty of dust and noise.

Area **G** p.76-p.77
See also Map 6

Petaling Jaya

Actually a city in its own right rather than a suburb of KL having been granted city status in 2006. Petaling Jaya, commonly known as PJ, was established by the British administration in the 1950s as a way of keeping Chinese communists in check. PJ consists of a number of neighbourhoods or sections and is located to the south-west of KL on the Federal Highway. It has several neighbourhoods popular with expats including the areas around Jalan University and Jalan Gasing, Bandar Utama, and the new developments at Mutiara Damansara and Damansara Perdana. PJ has excellent shopping and recreational facilities and on the whole you get more for your money here compared to KL.

Best Point
Great value for money compared to KL city; a diverse mix of Malaysians and expats live here.

Accommodation

All types are available, but this depends on location. Older style bungalows near Jalan University are good value, starting at RM3,000 for a three bed. Unrenovated three beds here sell for RM800,000 onwards. A studio near the LRT rents from RM1,000 upwards, while a three bedroom condo is from RM3,000. You'll pay slightly less in areas that aren't served by the LRT. In Bandar Utama a four bedroom house rents for RM1,750 and sells for RM500,000 upwards. Mutiara Damansara and neighbouring Damansara Perdana have mostly new condo developments. A four bed condo in the popular Armanee Terrace rents for RM4,500 and sells for RM600,000. Smaller one bed condo units start at RM1,000.

Worst Point
Residential areas are isolated pockets among industrial and commercial developments. Many residential roads are used as shortcuts between neighbourhoods so traffic past your front gate can be heavy.

Shopping & Amenities

PJ has excellent shopping facilities. The huge 1 Utama mall has a branch of just about every major retailer in Malaysia, plus a Jusco supermarket, Marks & Spencer and a soft play centre with drop and shop services. Close by a major new shopping development at Mutiara Damansara houses IKEA (www.ikea.com.my), Tesco (www.tesco.com.my), Cold Storage, furniture retailer Courts, Borders and Mothercare among others. The two major complexes here are Ikano and The Curve (www.thecurve.com.my). The Curve is newer and has a good selection of bars and restaurants. IKEA has a drop and shop service for children over three. Back in the more established sections of PJ, the Amcorp Mall on Jalan Timur has a great weekend flea market and Sunway Pyramid (www.sunway.com.my/pyramid) has more than 350 outlets including a Pet Lovers centre. There's a large organic grocery store, Country Farm (03 7880 9936) on Jalan PJU 3/49.

Entertainment & Leisure

PJ is well known for its wide variety of neighbourhood restaurants and everyone has a favourite. Out of Africa (03 7955 3432) is popular with families and Fatty Crab (03 7804 5758) in Taman Megah is a great Chinese seafood place. Raju Restaurant (03 7956 1361) is recommended for Indian food, and they do catering too. Rennie's (03 7955 2541) on Jalan Gasing is a popular bar with older expats while Laundry (03 7728 1715) at The Curve attracts a younger crowd. Next door to the Curve is the Cathay Cineplex (www.cathaycineplexes.com.my) which hosts live events as well as showing films. Sunway Lagoon (www.sunway.com.my/lagoon) in Bandar Sunway is an enormous theme park with a large water park section and some great rides. There's also a petting zoo and ice rink here at Sunway Pyramid. After all that eating and excitement, calm down at the Asian Arts Museum (03 7967 3805) on Jalan Universiti.

Healthcare

Universiti Malaya Medical Centre (03 7957 4422) is the largest government hospital in the area with 24 hour A&E. Popular private hospitals include Assunta Hospital (03 7680 7000) on Jalan Templer, Damansara Specialist Hospital (03 7722 2692) in Damansara Utama and Sunway Medical Centre (03 7491 9191) in Bandar Sunway, all of which have

Residential Areas

24 hour A&E. Outpatient treatment is available at Megah Medical Specialist Group (03 7803 1212) on Jalan SS23/15 and from Dr Junaidi (03 7724 1832) who also makes house calls in the Damansara Perdana area.

Education
The German International School (03 7956 6557) is in PJ, and there's good access to the Alice Smith primary campus (03 2148 3674). A popular nursery school is The Playhouse (03 7875 5491). Several local universities have their campuses in PJ including the International Islamic University Malaysia, Tunku Abdul Rahman University and Tun Abdul Razak University. Assunta Hospital has a nursing college.

Transport
Central PJ is well served by public transport with the Rapid KL LRT Kelana Jaya line passing through. If you live near a station such as Universiti or Asia Jaya you can be at KLCC in half an hour. This compares well with driving times as the Federal Highway, the main road linking PJ to KL, is notoriously congested. A planned extension of the LRT system will link Kota Damansara in the north of PJ with KL, further improving the local transport network. It's relatively easy to get a taxi in PJ, so it's possible to manage fine without a car. Rapid KL buses serve PJ with routes to all the major neighbourhoods.

Safety & Annoyances
Like all mixed urban neighbourhoods, petty crime can be a problem, so keep an eye on bags and purses. Although not common, motorcycle snatch thefts do occur and you should always walk against the flow of traffic with your bag held on the side away from traffic. That said, PJ isn't unsafe and crime rates against expats are low.

Petaling Jaya Housing

Area **H** p.76-p.77
See also Map 4

Sri Hartamas

Located to the east of Mont'Kiara are Sri Hartamas and Desa Sri Hartamas, on either side of the Sprint Highway. An established upmarket suburb, Hartamas has a wider variety of housing types than Mont'Kiara, with condos and gated communities alongside link houses, semi-detacheds and bungalows. Extremely well served with local shops, entertainment and leisure facilities, there's plenty of life here. Well-maintained playgrounds are dotted around the area and there's generally a family friendly atmosphere. The area has always been popular with local young families and it's becoming increasingly popular with expat families too.

Best Point
Popular with families; there's a wide selection of housing options from budget right through to luxury. Vibrant local shopping and entertainment scene.

Accommodation

Rents tend to be better value here than in the adjoining areas of Bukit Damansara and Mont'Kiara. Hartamas lacks the new sparkle of Mont'Kiara or the big old money of Bukit Damansara, and succeeds at being a pleasant family neighbourhood with good local amenities. Basic four bed link houses rent from RM3,000 per month and sell for RM800,000. Small studio apartments start at RM1,100 and three beds from RM3,000. There are two new gated communities in the area, Duta Nusantara and Duta Tropica. Rents for five bed houses here start at RM12,000 and sell for RM3 million.

Worst Point
Limited access points into and out of the area create traffic bottlenecks at peak times and parking can be extremely hard to find in the commercial areas.

Shopping & Amenities

Hartamas Shopping Centre is an air-conditioned mall, not large by KL standards but with a general supermarket, a Japanese-Korean supermarket, several boutiques selling ladies' and children's clothes, and a soft play area. Adjoining the mall is Plaza Damas, an integrated open-air retail and business development. There's a selection of spas, beauticians and hairdressers. Across the road, Desa Sri Hartamas has an eclectic mix of shops, bars, cafes and restaurants, plus branches of major banks and a post office. Parking here can be a nightmare, with cars double parked all down the narrow streets, but its popularity is well deserved. It is one of the best areas in KL to eat out if you're looking for non-halal food, as plenty of establishments here serve pork.

Entertainment & Leisure

Kids will be kept amused by the Kidzone soft play centre in Hartamas Shopping Centre, which has a drop and shop service. There are a number of small playgrounds in the area which are often crowded in the morning and early evening. They don't have much shade, so aren't a good option for daytime play. For adults there is a branch of Yoga Zone (www.yogazone.com.my) at Plaza Damas and a huge True Fitness (www.truefitness.com.my) gym at Desa Sri Hartamas. Sri Hartamas can be a little quiet at night, but Desa Sri Hartamas has a good selection of pubs and bars including Souled Out (03 2300 1955) and Finnegans (03 2300 0528). There's no cinema, and driving to the nearest ones at either Mid Valley or The Curve could prove frustrating during heavy evening traffic. Just next door to Desa Sri Hartamas, the Bukit Kiara Club (www.berjayaclubs.com/kiara) has excellent outdoor sports facilities.

Healthcare

There's no hospital in Sri Hartamas and the nearest are probably Damansara Specialist Hospital in Damansara Utama or Pantai Medical Centre in Bangsar. Klinik Segara (03 2300 0400) has a branch at Desa Sri Hartamas.

Education

Garden International School (British) and Mont'Kiara International School (American) are a five-minute drive away in Mont'Kiara. Both take children from 3 to 18 years. There are a number of popular nursery schools in Mont Kiara too.

Transport

If you're happy to do most of your shopping and socialising locally you could probably live in Hartamas without a car. Commuting is an issue, as with no nearby station a car or taxi is the only option. The Sprint Highway, dividing Sri Hartamas and Desa Sri Hartamas, links both neighbourhoods to the Kerenchi Link (Federal Highway, Bukit Damansara, Bangsar, Petaling Jaya) in one direction, and to the Penchala Link and Jalan Duta (Mont Kiara, TTDI, city centre) in the other. This main traffic artery can become extremely congested at peak times, although the biggest jam will be at the access points in and out of neighbourhoods rather than on the main road. There are usually plenty of taxis around, although you may have to call one if you live away from the commercial centres.

Safety & Annoyances

Parking, especially in Desa Sri Hartamas, can be a problem. There have been reports of petty crime around the bars and pubs. On the whole, the residential parts of this neighbourhood are quiet and safe.

Best Point ◄

Value for money housing and good local facilities. Close to Subang airport for domestic and regional flights.

Subang

Subang is a planned township, developed in the 1970s, which has now grown into a municipality. It's about 30 minutes' drive south-west of KL. Subang was the location of KL's international airport before KLIA opened, and the airport is still used for some domestic flights. Because of its proximity to the airport, Subang was perhaps more popular with expats once than it is now, but the area still has its fans, and as Air Asia is currently in talks to operate flights from Subang Airport, it may experience a resurgence. Subang is divided into two sections: Subang Jaya is the original township, while USJ is the second phase of the development.

Worst Point ◄

Major construction projects are expected to continue for the next few years and have a major impact on traffic flow in and around Subang.

Accommodation

Housing here dates from the 1970s onwards, with construction still ongoing. There are some major integrated developments being built in Subang in anticipation of the planned extension to the Kelana Jaya LRT line, which will improve commuting times to KL. Four bed link houses rent for RM1,000 upwards and sell for RM295,000. Houses at the Saujana Lakeview gated development start at RM6,000 per month for a semi-detached and go up to RM14,000 per month for a five bedroom bungalow with a private pool. Condos in Subang start at under RM1,000 per month, rising to RM5,000 for a large apartment with a lake view.

Shopping & Amenities

Subang has plenty of local shopping with a Giant Hypermarket at USJ1 and a Carrefour supermarket at Jalan SS16/1. Subang Parade mall has recently undergone extensive refurbishment and has the nicest mothers' room in KL. There's a Parkson Grand department store here, as well as over 160 retail outlets. The Summit USJ mall is the largest in the area with over 400 outlets. There are branches of all the local banks and a post office in Subang. JoJo Bali Spa at the Saujana Hotel is the best place in town for pampering beauty treatments.

Entertainment & Leisure

The Saujana Golf and Country club has two 18 hole golf courses, swimming pools and restaurants. You're also not far from all the excitement at Sunway Pyramid, including the Lagoon water and theme park and ice skating rink. There is a cinema at USJ Summit.

Healthcare

Subang Jaya Medical Centre (03 7491 9191) has a 24 hour accident and emergency department and a comprehensive team of specialists providing both inpatient and outpatient care. Sunway Medical Centre (03 7491 9191) is also within easy reach.

Education

Subang isn't well located for the international schools and children living here face a long commute each day. For this reason the area doesn't attract many expat families. A number of local colleges are in Subang Jaya, including Segi College and Taylors College. Australia's Monash University has its Malaysian campus nearby in Bandar Sunway.

Transport

Subang Jaya has a KTM Komuter station which makes commuting into KL from here a possibility. An extension to the LRT Kelana Jaya line is in progress, which will improve links to PJ and on to KL. Road connections are good, with the Federal Highway linking Subang to KL, PJ, Shah Alam and Klang. The New Pantai Expressway provides a quick route into town. The old international airport is experiencing a revival and it's now possible to fly to a number of domestic destinations from Subang. See www.fireflyz. com.my for more details.

Safety & Annoyances

As Subang is still undergoing extensive development you can expect a lot of construction noise and disruption to traffic, especially along those roads where the LRT extension is being built. Construction is likely to continue for a number of years, so bear this in mind.

Housing in Hartamas

Condominium

Best Point ◀

Fabulous resort-style facilities may mean you never want to leave your gated community.

Worst Point ◀

If you do venture out, there's not much in the immediate area and you'll have to drive to access any amenities not available on site.

Sungai Buloh

This area is well known as a former leper colony and some of the lepers (now cured) still live in the area. Because of this, many Malaysians have a negative feeling about this area, which has now been transformed by the development of two large gated communities, Valencia and Sierramas, into an upmarket residential area. It's popular with expats as you can get a high standard of resort-style living for the price of a regular house in KL. Sungai Buloh isn't far from popular areas of PJ such as Damansara Perdana and Bandar Utama and is about a 25 minute drive from KL.

Accommodation

Expats live in one of the two gated communities here, Valencia and Sierramas. Valencia is set in 280 acres and has around 900 homes. It has a clubhouse with tennis courts, a 50 metre pool, a gym and a restaurant, a nine-hole golf course open to residents only and a 'village square' with shops and services. Rents start at RM53,500 per month for a link house, rising to RM19,000 for a five bed bungalow. Sale prices are from RM750,000 – RM4 million. Sierramas has similar amenities, and although it doesn't have a golf course rental and sale prices are about the same as at Valencia.

Shopping & Amenities

Sungai Buloh is well known in KL as a great place to buy plants, pots and other garden supplies. You'll see the shops set up along the roadsides. It's just a short drive to the malls of Mutiara Damansara though, so all the shops and facilities of Ikano and The Curve are just 10 minutes away by car. There you'll find Tesco and Cold Storage supermarkets, IKEA, Mothercare and Borders. There's a post office in Sungai Buloh itself, and branches of some local banks.

Entertainment & Leisure

With so much on site, residents of Valencia and Sierramas hardly need to go out. But if you fancy a night at the cinema, the Cathay Cineplex (www.cathaycineplexes.com.my) is a 10 minute drive away at the Curve, where you'll also find plenty of bars and restaurants.

Healthcare

Damansara Specialist Hospital (03 7722 2692) is your closest hospital with a 24 hour accident and emergency department. There are some popular clinics in Mont Kiara, which is about a 20 minute drive away for non-emergency medical care.

Education

ELC International School (03 6156 5001) is located on Jalan Sierramas Barat. It follows the British national curriculum and takes children aged 3 to 16 years. If you're looking for a nursery school, Mont Kiara has some popular ones and it will take about 20 minutes to drive there.

Transport

You'll probably want a car if you live out here, since the main shops are some distance away. There is a KTM Komuter station in Sungai Buloh with regular trains to KL Sentral, and this could be a possibility for commuting.

Safety & Annoyances

Security at both Sierramas and Valencia is very strict and there haven't been any reports of lapses. Sierramas has a well-lit network of paths for residents who like to walk or jog at night. Although many people love living in a gated community, it's not for everyone and you may find it feels claustrophobic after a while.

Area ❶ p.76-p.77
See also Map 7

Taman Seputeh

This is the closest residential neighbourhood to the Alice Smith Primary school campus and is fast developing a more expat-friendly character. Historically, it's considered a haunted area by Malaysians and there are many graveyards in the hills behind. This hasn't put off developers and a major new housing project, Mutiara Seputeh, is under construction. It's centrally located with easy access to the city centre, PJ, Bangsar and Sri Hartamas or Mont'Kiara. It's popular with international school teachers for the good value rents and central location.

Best Point

Its central location means you can get to most parts of the city and Petaling Jaya quickly. It's the closest residential area to Alice Smith primary school.

Accommodation

There's a wide variety of housing here, encompassing good value link houses, several condos, older style bungalows and new developments of houses. Four bed link houses rent for around RM2,600 per month while larger five bed link houses in Bukit Robson are RM3,500. There are some good value condos, with a three bed in Robson Condo renting at RM2,000 and selling at RM360,000. Further up the scale Sri Langit condo has large apartments and is popular with expat families. A three bedroom condo here rents for RM10,000 per month. There's a shuttle bus to Alice Smith primary and other key locations in KL for residents. Sri Tiara is a serviced apartment block that also has a bus to Alice Smith, and this can be a useful short-term option for families.

Worst Point

Most local facilities are in the mall, otherwise local shopping is poor. Not a great range of housing options, although a soon to be completed major new housing development may make it more attractive to expat families.

Sierra Seputeh is a new development of semi-detached houses on Bukit Robson, with rents at around RM10,000.

There's a gated development of very upmarket houses at Seputeh Heights, where the rents start at RM20,000 and sales at RM5 million. You can also buy land here to build your own house.

Shopping & Amenities

There are some small shops in Taman Seputeh near the station and near the entrance to Robson Condo on Bukit Robson, including a laundry, dry cleaners and small grocery store. The major shopping attraction in Taman Seputeh is Mid Valley MegaMall, located just over the Federal Highway. This enormous shopping mall has recently added a new upmarket wing, called the Gardens, with a branch of Singaporean department store Robinsons. Mid Valley has Metrojaya and Jusco as anchor tenants, with a Carrefour supermarket in the basement. The Gardens has a Cold Storage supermarket and several upmarket food shops including a butcher and an organic food shop. There's plenty of fashion stores; Gap, Zara, and Mango all have branches here. Downstairs there is a post office and several banks have branches here. It's just as well that the large soft play area, Megakidz, has drop and shop facilities.

Entertainment & Leisure

MegaMall has a cinema complex and a branch of California Fitness, which has a swimming pool. There are plenty of places to eat here and a Finnegans Irish Pub (03 2284 8157) if you fancy a drink. Over in the Gardens, Alexis is a popular bistro. Outside the mall, there's not really anything in Taman Seputeh itself, but the bars of Bangsar are a 10 minute drive away or you can get into the city centre in about 15 minutes. Brickfields, KL's 'other' little India, is the next door neighbourhood and there's plenty of great food to be had there, as well as a bustling night market.

Healthcare

Pantai Medical Centre (03 2296 0888) in Bangsar has the nearest 24 hour accident and emergency department although in an emergency it may be quicker to get to Universiti Malaya Medical Centre (03 7957 4422) in Petaling Jaya. Most residents go to clinics in Bangsar or the city centre for non-urgent minor medical matters.

Education

Much of Taman Seputeh's appeal for families lies in its proximity to the Alice Smith primary campus, which is a 10 minute drive away. The international schools in Mont Kiara are about a 20 minute drive. There aren't any nursery schools in the area, but there are several in nearby Bangsar.

Transport

Taman Seputeh has a KTM Komuter station and there's another one at Mid Valley. These go to nearby KL Sentral, where you can change onto the LRT or monorail to get to the city centre. Many buses pass by Mid Valley, although the bus stops have a rather hair-raising location at the side of the Federal Highway. You could manage to live here without a car as Mid Valley is within walking distance. The area is well connected by road to Petaling Jaya and the centre of KL via the Federal Highway. Sri Hartamas and Mont Kiara are reached in 15 minutes using the Kerenchi link, and Bangsar is a 10 to 15 minute drive depending on traffic. It's reasonably easy to get a taxi here, although you may have problems during rush hour.

Safety & Annoyances

This is quite a safe area, although there have been reports of bag snatching outside MegaMall after dark. It's not terribly well lit at night, so walking alone may not be a good idea for women. Once the new housing development at Mutiara Seputeh is complete the extra traffic may make the access road to the area congested, although at the moment it's generally fine.

Mid Valley Megamall

Views over Taman Seputeh

Area **K** *p.76-p.77*
See also Map 4

Taman Tun Dr Ismail

TTDI is a well-planned suburb on the border of KL city and Selangor State. It used to be hard to access from the city, but with the opening of the Penchala Link tunnel and the Kerenchi Link it's become a lot more popular. The area takes its name from Tun Dr Ismail, a former deputy Prime Minister of Malaysia. It was developed during the 1970s and is now well established. It was planned to promote neighbourly interaction and there is a generous amount of public space here and a good community spirit.

Best Point

Strong community spirit means residents work together to maintain and improve the area. There's a diverse range of local shops and a lovely park. The wet market is famous throughout KL.

Accommodation
Housing options here are mostly link, semi-detached and bungalow houses but there are a few condos. Rents are good value with a six bed bungalow at RM6,500 per month and a four bed link house at RM2,300. Link houses sell for RM580,000 onwards, and you can buy a 7,200 square foot bungalow for RM3.8 million. A three bed apartment sells for RM400,000 and you can rent a similar unit for RM2,200 per month.

Shopping & Amenities
TTDI is known for its market, where you can buy meat, fish, spices, vegetables and all sorts of dry goods. There's also a pharmacy here. TTDI has a post office and branches of all major banks. It's also home to a number of small independent shops and businesses including a great cycle shop (03 7727 5173) and an independent book shop (03 7725 7085). 1Utama mall is a short drive away.

Worst Point

A little isolated from the rest of KL. It's a long commute into town and the traffic can be terrible.

Entertainment & Leisure
TTDI Park is very popular, with a small children's playground and large mature trees for shade. It has a small stream running through and a lake where you can feed fish and tortoises. You can hike up TTDI hill, which has a paved path and is popular with cyclists too. The nearest cinema is the Cathay Cineplex (www.cathaycineplexes.com.my) at The Curve, about a 10 minute drive. There aren't many pubs and bars in TTDI, but Desa Sri Hartamas is a five minute drive along the Penchala link – you'll find plenty of nightlife there.

Healthcare
The nearest large hospital with 24 hour accident and emergency cover is Damansara Specialist Hospital (03 7722 2692), a short drive away in Damansara Utama. In TTDI itself, Apollo TTDI Medical Centre (03 7726 6911) provides 24 hour cover although it has fewer facilities. There's also an outpatient clinic here. There are several small clinics in TTDI; try Klinik Khoo (03 7728 2379).

Education
The international schools at Mont'Kiara are just a short drive away, with a choice of the British curriculum at Garden International School (www.garden.edu.my) or the American at Mont'Kiara International School (www.mkis.edu.my). Mont Kiara also has several nursery schools popular with expat families.

Transport
Recent improvements to the road links have made getting to and from TTDI much easier. The Penchala Link enables quick access to Mont Kiara and Sri Hartamas and on to the city centre. The Kerenchi Link connects TTDI to Petaling Jaya, Mid Valley and Bangsar. You'll need a car if you live here, as without one you will have to rely on taxis.

Safety & Annoyances
TTDI has a 24 hour security patrol scheme operating in many areas. The neighbourhood is generally considered to be quiet and safe.

Not big, but very clever…

Perfectly proportioned to fit in your pocket,
this marvellous mini guidebook makes sure
you don't just get the holiday you paid for
but rather the one that you dreamed of.

Beijing Mini Visitors' Guide
Maximising your holiday, minimising your hand luggage

Setting Up Home

Finding a place to live is only the first part of the challenge. Next comes moving in your furniture and possessions and getting your household running smoothly – it may sound straightforward enough but things don't always go to plan. Luckily you won't have to do much of the hard work yourself as moving services are good value and pretty reliable. If you're lucky, the agent who found you your house will also do a lot to smooth the transition – so don't throw their business card away as soon as you've signed the lease!

Smooth Moves
To make your move go as smoothly as possible, enlist the support of your estate agent and relocation agent. Between them they should be able to take care of the essentials like making sure all the utilities are connected and the house is cleaned, leaving you free to decide where to put your furniture.

Moving Services

Expats in KL are lucky to have a wide choice of both furnished and unfurnished accommodation, so it's up to you if you want to bring all your worldly goods with you. Contact your local Malaysian consulate or embassy to check if there are any restrictions on what you can bring, or ask your moving company for advice. If you're moving to KL from overseas and have shipped your household goods, one of two things will happen. If the shipping or relocation company has an office in Malaysia, they will be handling your incoming shipment and you will contact the local office with the details of your new home. If the company doesn't have a local office, it will allocate your shipment to a local handling company that will take care of all the importation paperwork. You can contact the local company when you're ready to move.

Relocation Companies

Allied Pickfords	03 6253 6553	www.alliedpickfords.com
Crown Relocations	03 5636 9166	www.crownrelo.com
Crownline Move Management	03 6275 1830	www.crownline.com.my
Felix	03 5636 5511	www.felixrelo.com
Santa Fe Relocation Services	03 7805 4322	www.santaferelo.com

The advantage of using a relocation company is that they will provide a host of services designed to help you settle in smoothly. These can include home search, helping to find schools, showing you around the city and help with paperwork. Your company may pay for these services, but if it doesn't remember that costs can vary so it's worth shopping around.

If you've been in KL for a while and just fancy a change of scene, local moving companies will give you a better deal for a move across town than the full-service international relocation agents. You can hire a truck and labour fairly easily and cheaply: just look out for 'lori sewa' signs around your neighbourhood or in the Classifieds in the *New Straits Times* or *The Star* – it should cost about RM80 for a single cross-city trip. This is a good option for moving a couple of large pieces or something you've bought second hand, but unless you are on hand to supervise all the time this may not be the most secure option if you've got a lot of small things.

Removal Companies

AGS Four Winds	03 6251 7175	www.ags-worldwide-movers.com
Allied Pickfords	03 6253 6553	www.alliedpickfords.com
Ambassador Worldwide Movers Malaysia	03 4253 2000	www.ambassador.com.my
Baltrans	03 7785 7794	na
Continental Movers and Transport	03 7843 0575	www.ContinentalMovers.com.my
Crownline Move Management	03 6275 1830	www.crownline.com.my
Inter Grace Movers	03 7954 4908	www.intergrace.com.my
Intermovers	03 6187 7777	www.intermovers.com
Santa Fe Relocation Services	03 7805 4322	www.santaferelo.com
Transpo Movers Malaysia	03 5511 3788	www.asiantigers-malaysia.com

Furnishing Your Home

Rented accommodation can be kitted out to an extremely high standard – serviced apartments will come with crockery, cutlery, sheets and towels – or be completely bare. Most places are somewhere in between, with kitchen appliances and fitted cupboards in the bedrooms fairly standard. Houses tend to be very large, so even if you've brought all your furniture with you, you may find yourself looking for some extra pieces to fill the space.

If you do find yourself shopping for household appliances, local chain HSL (www.hslg.com.my) is a good place to try. Appliances may not be the same models as you're used to at home. Large American-style fridges and washing machines are sometimes available but very expensive and front-loading washing machines aren't common. Free-standing cookers are a very rare breed since the trend is for built-in hobs. Choice is limited and the models tend to be low spec; see Household Appliances (p.298) for more options.

Renting furniture is an option if you're only staying for a short time, or while you wait for your own to arrive. If you're likely to need the furniture for more than a year it may work out cheaper to buy. MK Homes (03 6189 3331, www.mkhomes.com.my) will rent out anything from a single item to a complete house full of furniture. There's even an option to buy if you become too attached to something to part with it!

If you are looking to buy, IKEA (www.ikea.com.my) has the usual selection of flat-pack furniture with the added benefit of an affordable delivery and assembly service to remove the hassle of DIY. Cavenzi (www.cavenzi.com) is a Malaysian company offering modern looks at bargain prices. Fella Design (www.fella.com.my) has a wide range of sofas which it will cover in your choice of fabric – its Urban Culture brand is trendier than its main line. At Barang Barang (www.barang.com.sg) and Homelife (www.homelife.com.my) you'll find a comprehensive selection of contemporary furniture and accessories with an Asian twist.

Malaysia is a great place to buy teak and other hardwood furniture, but check before buying that the wood used has come from a sustainable source. Try Gotic (www.gotic.com) for a good quality range sourced from managed forests. Allison Tasker (012 905 4089) has many original and antique teak pieces imported from Indonesia. There are plenty of antiques and 'antiques' around – if you're serious about collecting do your homework first and check the provenance of any pieces carefully. The Tomlinson Collection (03 2283 2196) is the place to go for the real thing – staff are very knowledgeable and will talk you through the features of a piece.

If you've always longed for furniture made exactly to your requirements try Allison Tasker for pieces made to order from recycled Indonesian teak. Although it's located a three-hour drive away in Melaka, Malacca Woodwork (06 315 4468) is popular with KL residents; they produce good quality pieces and deliver to KL.

Add the finishing touches with accessories from Courtyard (03 2163 2868) or Peter Hoe (03 2026 9788) or see the Home Furnishings & Accessories section of the Shopping chapter on p.280 for plenty more ideas.

Second-Hand Furniture

There is a constant stream of expats arriving in and leaving KL, so it's worth looking out for second-hand furniture if you don't want to buy new. This is an especially good route to go down if you're looking for furniture that you might only use in your KL home, for example large garden pieces, sun loungers or extra furniture to fill the cavernous living spaces of some older bungalows. Look for ads on notice boards at schools, expat associations (see page 60) and supermarkets such as Hock Choon (03 2141 6062) on Jalan Ampang.

The IKEA Factor

They say that the true measure of whether or not you've settled into KL is whether or not you can find your way to IKEA. This furniture giant is, as you might expect, huge, reliable and cheap. For this and other great furniture shops, see p.306 of the Shopping chapter.

Tailors

Other options **Tailoring** p.323

IKEA (www.ikea.com.my) offers a sewing service and will make up curtains, cushions and blinds to your requirements using their own fabrics. Prices are very reasonable, but the choice of fabrics is limited. Kamdar (www.kamdar.com.my) is another good budget choice with a much wider choice of fabrics and several stores around town. With both IKEA and Kamdar you will have to do your own measurements, but they will give advice on how much fabric you need to buy depending on the style of curtains you're after. Doshi's (03 2161 2678) has an impressive array of fabrics and will make curtains and upholster furniture. For an upmarket selection try Janine (03 2148 2840) or Thamsea (03 2144 7985) where you will find a wide selection of imported designer fabrics that can be made into cushions, curtains or upholstery. Macy (www.macyhomefurnishings.com) is a popular local choice for curtain making with a wide selection of fabrics and reasonable prices. Several tailors specialise in home service – they bring samples to your home so that you can see the fabrics in situ and they can get a better idea of what's required. Try Miss Wong (03 7727 1733), Stewart Chee (03 8945 9098) or Putih Ekar (03 2092 5269). You'll find more ideas in Tailoring (p.323) and Textiles (p.324).

Strong sunlight can fade and damage fabrics very quickly, so bear this in mind when making your choice. If you've set your heart on expensive designer fabric, make sure you get your curtains lined to protect them from sunlight, and position any large upholstered pieces of furniture out of direct sunlight.

It's always worth asking when you're negotiating your lease if curtains can be included – many landlords are prepared to provide them. This can save you a significant amount of money depending on the size and number of windows you have; the downside is that you may have to put up with your landlord's taste in fabric.

Tailors

Doshi's	Lot 3.18, Ampang Park Shopping Complex	City Centre	03 2161 2678
IKEA	No. 2 Jalan PJU 7/2, Mutiara Damansara, 47800	Petaling Jaya	03 7726 7777
Janine	Level 1, Great Eastern Mall	Ampang	03 4260 2743
Janine	2F, Bangsar Shopping Centre, Jalan Maarof	Bangsar	03 2094 9530
Kamdar	1st Floor, Mid Valley Mega Mall	Mid Valley	03 2938 3052
Kamdar	429-435 Jalan Tuanku Abdul Rahman	City Centre	03 2693 9513
Macy	1st Floor, Ikano Power Centre	Petaling Jaya	03 7726 8100
Thamsea	237-241 Jalan Ampang	Ampang	03 2144 7985

Household Insurance

If you are renting, you landlord will be responsible for insuring the property itself, but you can insure your household contents separately. These policies are sometimes known as householder policies. The independent website www.insuranceinfo.com.my has a list of insurance providers in Malaysia and gives general information about what you can expect from a policy. Your bank may also be able to help with insurance queries. Malaysians rarely have household contents insurance and many expat residents also go without it.

Household Insurance

Allianz Insurance	03 2162 3388	www.allianz.com.my
American International Assurance	03 2056 6111	www.aia.com.my
AXA Insurance	03 2279 8282	www.axa-insurance.com.my
Berjaya General Insurance	03 2141 3323	www.bgi.com.my
ING Universal Insurance Bhd.	03 2161 7255	www.ing.com.my

Two types of policy are available if you've bought your home and want to insure it. The basic fire policy will cover loss or damage to the property by fire, lightning or explosion. More expensive house owners' policies will cover extras such as loss or damage to the property due to flood, burst pipes and so on. If you've bought an apartment in a condo block (sometimes referred to as strata title or leasehold properties), the management company is responsible for insuring the building as a whole and you can ask to see the certificate to check that they have bought the necessary cover.

Malaysians take security very seriously and almost all houses have lockable iron grilles covering doors and windows. Many will have a burglar alarm or security system where a guard regularly checks the property. Some embassies and companies pay for this checking service. Despite this there are reports of burglaries; they tend to be opportunists who take what they can carry, so keep valuables locked away.

Laundry Services

You'll find a laundry (kedai dobi) in every neighbourhood and shopping mall. These are not self-service laundrettes; the only option is to leave your clothes with the staff. Charges are usually by the piece. You may get a discount if you have a lot of clothes or are a regular customer. Dry cleaning is also easily available and generally good value, although services run by the five-star hotels are considerably pricier than neighbourhood shops.

Laundry Services		
City Laundry	Bangsar	03 2282 3785
Cleanair Laundry	Ampang	03 4257 8425
Jetson Laundry & Dry Cleaning	Petaling Jaya	03 7956 7035
Modern Fabricare	Ampang	03 4252 1498
My Laundry Station	Various Locations	03 7980 6900
YS Dry Cleaning	Various Locations	03 2142 2096

Consumer rights aren't strong in Malaysia so there's not likely to be any redress for lost or damaged items. If you have something very special or expensive, the Oriental Hotel's Valet Service at KLCC or Micasa Shoppes Dry Cleaning on Jalan Tun Razak are recommended.

Domestic Help
Other options **Entry Visa** p.47

This is both affordable and easily available. Whether you opt for full or part-time help, live in or live out, will largely depend on your personal circumstances and preferences. Most locals and expats employ domestic help; the workers tend to come from less well-off Asian countries such as Indonesia, the Philippines and more recently Cambodia and Vietnam, although some locals also work in this sector. Most houses and apartments in KL will have a room intended for use by your domestic helper – even if you don't intend to have live-in help, don't be too quick to earmark this room for a storeroom or study, as a part-time or live-out helper will also need space to work and take breaks. There are a few cultural considerations to bear in mind when hiring domestic help. Muslims will not cook pork, and will normally not use utensils that have been used to cook pork. They should not be expected to touch or look after dogs. Hindus do not eat beef although some may not mind cooking it; being sensitive and asking first is a good strategy. Your helper will usually want to take her annual holiday around her main religious or cultural festival; Hari Raya for Muslims, Deepavali for Hindus, Christmas for Christians and Chinese New Year if you have a Chinese helper. It's usual to pay a bonus of a month's pay at holiday time (pro rata if she's been with you for less than a year). Check the legal status of your helper if she isn't local. If she doesn't have the right to live and work in Malaysia, you are committing an offence by employing her. You must have a work permit yourself before you can legally employ a foreign helper. You can employ an agency to help you with the paperwork to bring in a foreigner or to transfer someone who is already working legally in Malaysia. You can also do this paperwork yourself. Forms and a checklist are available to download from the Immigration Department of Malaysia website (www.imi.gov.my/eng/Forms/im_forms.asp) but you must make the application in person.

Part-Time Help

If you are looking for part-time help and you live in a condo or apartment block, the easiest thing to do is to ask around your neighbours or the building's management staff and find out if there are any maids currently working in the building who are looking for extra work. You may then be able to talk to her other employers to get a reference, as well as an idea of an appropriate rate of pay. Part time rates can be between RM15 and RM20 an hour, which is usually paid as a monthly flat rate for an agreed number of hours worked or tasks completed. Be reasonable when deciding how many hours help you need – don't expect your helper to be superwoman and pack a day's worth of cleaning and ironing into a couple of hours. Agencies do not commonly place part-time or local helpers.

Using An Agency

Agencies usually specialise in recruiting live-in helpers from overseas who come to Malaysia to work on a fixed-term contract. You will not normally be able to interview candidates or even meet them before they start work, although you will be shown a selection of biodata (usually with photos) and asked to choose. Most agencies recruit from a particular country, although some larger agencies may offer candidates from different countries. Many expats prefer Filipino helpers as they generally have a good standard of spoken and written English, which makes communication easier. Their salaries tend to be higher and are set by the agency. Generally you can expect to pay a fairly hefty fee of up to RM4,000 to the agency which will include finder's fees, airfare, medical insurance, Malaysian government levy, processing fees and possibly a set number of months' salary in advance. You may have to wait for up to three months, and she will then be on a fixed two-year contract. Not surprisingly, the placements do not always work out, and most agencies will offer a replacement should the first one not be suitable, although you may have to wait for replacements to arrive. You should expect to pay around RM1,000 to RM1,400 a month for full-time help.

Community noticeboard

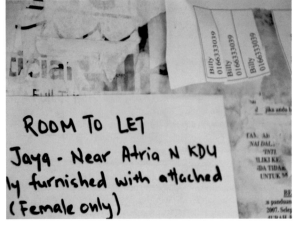

The Informal Option

This involves using word of mouth and essentially enlisting everyone you've met so far in KL in your search. Check noticeboards at schools, supermarkets and expat associations (see p.60), where you may find expats who are leaving and are recommending their helper for a new position. Ask around to find out if anyone's helper has a friend who is looking for work. Where possible, talk directly to the former employer or get a reference by email. The informal route allows

Domestic Help Agencies

Agensi Pekerjaan ASK	03 9058 1440
CCS	03 7727 5478
Citylink	03 5636 5952
Ma'Clean Services	03 7785 3688
Malindo	03 2282 9262
Philip Cleaning Services	03 7983 1852
PT Maids	012 238 8338
Susan's Domestc Services	03 9221 8482

you to meet and interview possible candidates, and this can be especially helpful if you're looking for a helper who will live with you, as it's very important that you get along. Prepare a job description before the interview so that you are both clear about the tasks involved in the job, and set some sample tasks if you like. If childcare is part of the job, watch how the candidates interact with your children. If you can, arrange for a couple of trial days so that you can get a feel for whether things are likely to work out.

If you decide to employ someone, write out a contract that you both sign, setting out expected working hours, time off, expected tasks and stating whether and when overtime will be paid, for example for evening babysitting or weekend work. Remember that a domestic helper is an employee like any other and deserves to be treated with respect and consideration. Experienced helpers who have worked for expat families are much in demand so expect to pay a higher salary.

Babysitting & Childcare

Most people rely on their domestic help for babysitting and childcare, although there are limited other possibilities. Some shopping centres have soft play areas where they operate a 'drop and shop' programme, usually for children over 3, where children can be left on an ad hoc basis. Hotels and serviced apartments will provide babysitting services for guests, and if you've used one already, you may be able to get the same babysitter on a freelance basis once you've moved out. Some gyms do have creches, but this is not a common facility.

Full-time group daycare isn't very common, and in Malaysian families where both parents work, childcare is provided by other family members, a domestic helper or a babysitter who looks after children in her own home, sometimes overnight. Most expats who need full-time childcare opt for a domestic helper. Schools aren't really geared up to the needs of two working parents, so before and after school care or extended hours aren't common.

If you're just looking for occasional babysitting rather than a full-time helper, you could try asking friends if their domestic helper has any free time and would like to earn some extra money. You might be able to find an older teenager keen to earn some extra pocket money – this is a good possibility if you live in a gated community or a condo. One of the staff from your child's school might be interested in earning some extra cash, and you have the added advantage of the babysitter being a familiar face for your child. If you're looking for a nursery school, check the education section on p.136.

You may also see ads on the noticeboard at Hock Choon Supermarket (241 Jalan Ampang, 03 21416062) from individuals offering babysitting services – it goes without saying you should check anyone out carefully before leaving them with your children. Malaysia doesn't have a formal system of qualifications for childcare workers, so you're

Babysitting & Childcare

Kizsports & Gym	03 7726 6313	www.kizsports.com
MegaKidz	03 2282 9300	www.megakidz.com.my

unlikely to find someone with paper qualifications and there's no system of police checks for people who work with children. The best way to find someone reliable is through word of mouth.

Domestic Services

KL's frequent heavy rains and electrical storms make leaky roofs, burnt out wiring and flooded drains a fact of life. Usually your landlord will be the person responsible for repairs, and they will make the arrangements. If you live in a condo or apartment block, there may be a manager or other employee on site who will deal with these matters and minor repairs. Luckily the cost of calling out a plumber or electrician is still quite reasonable. Check your lease to see if you're responsible for maintaining the air-conditioning units, as they need regular servicing to ensure that they are running efficiently. Even if you're responsible for doing this, you may find the landlord already has an arrangement in place and all you have to do is pay the bill.

If you've bought your property, you're on your own, although if your home is part of a gated development or a condo, you may find the management company can help you find repairmen and contractors.

Walls are usually concrete and very hard to drill into. Most people use a professional to hang pictures rather than risk damaging the walls. If you've used a relocation company, they may include services like picture hanging – even if it's not included in your contract they will be able to recommend a handyman to you. You could also ask your landlord or real estate agent if they can suggest someone.

The hot and humid climate is a breeding ground for all sorts of pests. While some are merely irritating, others such as mosquitoes spread dangerous diseases and need to be kept under control. Do everything you can to eliminate breeding grounds by making sure there is no standing water in your home or garden. You can hire a pest control service to spray chemical insecticide if the problem is very bad. Most pest control companies will also deal with ants, termites, rats, bats and any other pest you might encounter around the home. They will do one-off treatments, or you can set up a contract where they will visit at fixed intervals (usually monthly). A contract will work out cheaper than calling out a company several times on an ad hoc basis; the cost depends on the size of the area needing treatment. Look on the Pest Control Association Malaysia website (www.pcam.com.my) for a list of its members. Malaysian Pest Control and Ridpest are popular.

Domestic Services

Ace Pest Control	013 353 4900	Pest control
Allied Locksmith & Trading	03 2148 4270	Locksmith
Francis Ng	016 225 3849	Handyman
Hoan Sheng Renovation	03 4251 0285	Plumber/Builders
Kok Wah TV & Radio Service	03 9131 1422	TV and video repair
Malaysian Pest Control	03 4257 7401	Pest Control
Mani Garden & Pool Maintenance	03 4253 5509	Gardening and pool maintenance
Multiaire Services	03 7981 2780	Air-conditioning service and repair
Pied Piper	03 5633 3744	Pest control
Ridpest	03 4143 0888	Pest Control
Viscell Sdn Bhd	03 2095 2528	Handyman/picture hanging
Wee Locksmith	03 2145 6500	Locksmith
Wind Flower Air-Conditioning	03 9284 3782	Air-conditioning services

DVD & Video Rental

The prevalence of pirated DVDs, despite the best efforts of law enforcement to stem the flow, means there's not much of a market for DVD rental in KL. One online option is www.eflix.com.my where you can rent unlimited DVDs for a RM63 monthly subscription. Videos are considered prehistoric, and you will be met with astonished looks if you go shopping for a VHS tape or a VCR machine. It's up to you whether or not you choose to buy pirated DVDs. Many KL residents just can't resist the temptation to get the latest films or TV series as soon as they're released overseas, particularly as the pirates stock a wider and more varied selection than any legitimate shop. Legitimate DVDs are relatively cheap and if you aren't concerned about quality you can pick up legal VCDs for under RM20. If you are strongly against buying pirated DVDs, check carefully before you buy, since pirated discs are often sold at quite legitimate-looking shops in malls and neighbourhood shopping centres. It's often hard to tell the difference between a real and a fake.

Pets

Pets haven't traditionally been part of Malaysian life, but as society becomes increasingly affluent, owning a pet is often seen as one more way to demonstrate that you have money to spend on luxuries. That's not to say Malaysians aren't responsible pet owners, but there certainly are cases of animals being kept in less than ideal conditions and some, dogs in particular, being abandoned once they're no longer cute and cuddly. Dogs are considered unclean by Muslims and so you will find most dog owners are Chinese or Indian.

Bringing Your Pet To Malaysia

If you have a pet (cat or dog) that you would like to bring with you to Malaysia, contact the Malaysian embassy or high commission in your home country or the Malaysian Department of Veterinary Services (03 8870 2000 or www.agrolink.moa.my/jph) well in advance to find out if there are any requirements you must fulfil. Some requirements are specific to the country you're relocating from or the breed of your dog, but generally speaking cats and dogs must have the following:

• An import permit from the Department of Veterinary Services. This permit is issued for a period of one month, but can be extended for up to 60 days.
• A health certificate from a vet in your home country. This should be dated within seven days of the animal's date of travel.
• A certificate of vaccination against rabies. The vaccine should have been administered more than 30 days but less than 180 days previously.
• Dogs and cats should be up to date on all routine vaccinations.

Your pet may be kept in quarantine for up to 30 days, although costs for this are low – dogs are charged at RM4 per day. If your cat or dog was not born in your current country of residence, you will not be able to bring it to Malaysia. Your removal or relocation company may be able to help with relocating your cat or dog, or your vet can help you locate a specialist animal relocator in your home country.

KL is a large, urbanised city with relatively few open spaces. It's not the best environment for a large dog, although some residential areas are more suitable than others. There are also rules governing dog ownership which affect where you can live with a dog, and a Muslim landlord may not allow you to keep a dog. If you live in an apartment, you

Snake at KL Aquaria

cannot keep a dog. Residents of terraced or semi-detached houses can keep one dog and those in detached houses can keep two. If you have more than two dogs, you will need a special breeder's licence.

All dogs must be licensed. This costs RM12 per year and licences are available from DBKL Headquarters in Jalan Raja Laut (03 4021 1682) if you live in KL city, and from your local municipal centre if you live outside the city, for example in Ampang or PJ. Licensed dogs are issued with a tag which must be permanently attached to the collar. If caught, unlicensed dogs will be taken to the pound and not released until a fine is paid and a licence bought. As the

Pet Boarding & Sitting

Dr Sharon	03 4257 2896	Vet, also provides pet boarding
Pet Care	03 4106 7515	Pet boarding
Pet Epicure	03 4107 2973	Cat boarding only
Scallywags	03 7787 1507	Cat boarding only

owner, you are fully responsible for your dog's behaviour both outside in public and on your property. If neighbours complain about your dog's behaviour, pest control officers have the right to enter your property to investigate. Dogs must be kept on the lead at all times in a public place, including parks, and are not allowed at all in many parks. You should always pick up after your dog, but instances of this rule being enforced are rare. Taman Desa Community Park is dog friendly, and many dog owners walk their dogs in the forest at Bukit Gasing in Petaling Jaya. The Malaysian Kennel Association (www.mka.org. my) has useful information for dog owners. You can find out about dog shows and other activities for dogs and their owners in KL and around Malaysia at www.puppy.com.my.

Pet Grooming & Training

Animal Medical Centre	03 4042 5873	www.petscorner.com.my	Home grooming
Pet Epicure	03 4107 2973	na	Cat Boarding
Purina Puppycom Agility & Obedience Training	03 4297 8281	www.puppy.com.my	Training and agility classes
The Pet Family	03 7727 8771	www.thepetfamily.com	Grooming

Cats don't need to be licensed and are not subject to the same ownership restrictions as dogs, although some condos may not allow them. The website www.kitten.com.my has information for cat owners, including events for cat owners and cat shows.

Pet ownership is a relatively recent trend for Malaysians but the retail industry has been quick to catch on. Pets Wonderland (www.petswonderland.com.my) and the Pet Family (www.thepetfamily.com) are local chains selling animals and all things related. Fish are very popular and shops selling tropical fish and aquarium supplies abound. If you're interested in fish, visit the Sentul Park Koi Centre on Jalan Strachan off Jalan Ipoh, where you can find out about the esoteric Japanese art of koi breeding and maybe even get some of your own. If you're interested in adopting an animal from a shelter, PAWS (www.pawsmalaysia. com) and the Society for the Prevention of Cruelty to Animals (www.spca.org.my) both have homeless pets in need of rehousing.

Services for pets such as grooming, training and kennel services can be hard to come by. The prevalence of domestic help means that many pet owners rely on their helpers rather than outside providers to care for their animals while they are away. Pet Epicure (03 4107 2973) is a service that provides boarding and grooming for cats; for dog boarding you may need to ask around. The SPCA will sometimes recommend its volunteers, or your vet may be able to suggest someone suitable.

Veterinary Clinics

If you're unable to take your pet to a clinic a home visit service is available from Dr George (019 276 0885) covering the Ulu Klang, Ampang, Kenny Hills, Bangsar and Damansara areas. In an emergency try the Animal Medical Centre at 8 Jalan Tun Razak, near the Jalan Ipoh junction (03 4042 7642) which is open 24 hours.

Veterinary Clinics

Animal Medical Centre	Wisma Medivet, 8 Jalan Tun Razak, 50400	03 4042 5873
Bangsar Vetinary Clinic	94 Lorong Maarof, Bangsar 59000	03 2284 4051
Damansara Heights Vetinary Clinic	Plaza Damansara, 79 Medan Setia 1, 50490	03 2095 6877
Dr Dhillon Animal Clinic	19 Jalan 11/2, Section 11, Petaling Jaya	03 7955 1370
Dr Singham	437 Jalan Ampang 50450 Ampang	03 4256 3175
Ukay Animal Centre	6 Medan Damai Ukay, Jalan Pinggiran 1, Ulu Klang 68000 Ampang	03 4042 6742

Utilities & Services

Basic utilities such as water, sewage and electricity are provided by monopoly companies, so unlike in some countries there's no chance to switch provider to get a better deal. Generally the main companies are quite efficient though, and while breakdowns in service do occur these are often dealt with remarkably quickly.

Both the electricity and water services have 24 hour numbers you can call to report problems. Staff usually speak English and if you're not the first person to report the problem they will tell you what they're doing about it and how long they expect it will take to fix.

It is common practice for landlords to keep electricity and water bills in their name and request a security deposit from you against unpaid bills. This means that services remain connected so you do not have to worry about contacting the companies when you move in and out of rented accommodation (see Housing, p.70).

Fixed line telephone services are also provided by a monopoly, while broadband, dial-up and mobile internet services are available from several different suppliers.

Gas is the preferred fuel for cooking. It's not usually piped in to houses (although some apartments do have this) but comes in cylinders which you can have delivered to your home. It's always a good idea to have two in case one runs out mid-meal.

Electricity

Blackout?
Don't Freak Out
If there is an electricity blackout in your area, you can call 15454 to report it and get information on how long it is likely to last.

Tenaga Nasional Berhad (TNB) supplies electricity to both business and residential customers in Malaysia. If you have any queries you can contact the call centre on 15454 from anywhere in the country. In most rental situations the tenant is responsible for paying electricity bills, although the account remains in the landlord's name. The exception is serviced apartment rentals, where utilities are often included in the rent. There will be a clause in your lease explaining your obligations and the landlord will take a specific deposit, which is usually half a month's rent, to offset against any bills left unpaid when you leave. The billing system is computerised and very efficient – a meter reader will visit once a month and will usually issue you a bill on the spot based on your reading. If you're not in when the meter reader calls, you will get an estimated bill, but after three months you will be asked to arrange a time for your meter to be read. When you're moving in and out you can request a reading on the day so there's no dispute about who is responsible for paying what.

If you've bought your property or find the service has been disconnected, you will have to register as a new customer and pay a deposit of two months' estimated bills. The main TNB building is in Bangsar, at 129 Jalan Bangsar (03 2296 5566), and district offices are located all over town. Check the Kedai Tenaga section at www.tnb.com.my for your nearest one. Opening hours are 08:00 to 13:00 and 14:00 to 17:00 Monday to Thursday and 08:00 to 12:15 and 14:45 to 17:15 on Fridays.

The electricity supply is 220/240 volts AC, 50 cycles, three phase. Sockets are most often square three pin (UK style), although some older houses and apartments may have other types. Appliances sometimes come with two-pin plugs, either round or square, but adapters are easily available.

Electricity bills can be very high, especially if you use your air conditioning a lot. You can minimise your bills by keeping air-conditioning units well maintained and switching them off when you're not in the room. Close doors and windows when the air conditioning is on and use fans whenever possible. Ceiling fans are very popular and effective – if none are installed in your home ask your landlord about getting some; they cost between RM100 to RM200 and are easily installed by an electrician. If you have a pool, the pump will add on a significant chunk to your electricity bill. Expect to pay anywhere from RM150 to RM1,000 a month for electricity, depending on the size of your property and how much you use air con.

The Pressure's
On (Or Off)
Some areas of KL
experience fluctuating
water pressure. It's
sometimes announced
in advance if it's due to
cleaning or maintenance
and sometimes not if it's
just due to unexpectedly
heavy demand on the
supply or a leak. Don't be
too concerned if you're
shower slows to a trickle,
normal service will
usually resume shortly.

Water

Water bills are pretty reasonable, usually under RM50 per month and often much less. A single person in a small apartment could pay less than RM10. If you have a pool, or a large garden that requires watering, your bill can start creeping up. Water services in KL, Selangor and Putrajaya are provided by Syabas (www.syabas.com.my). Like TNB, it has an efficient billing system, with meter readings followed by a computer printout of your bill once a month. As with electricity, the account will usually remain in the landlord's name although the tenant pays the bills. If you do need to reconnect your water supply, contact Syabas to find out the location of your district office. For most expats it will be in Bangsar on Jalan Pantai Baharu (03 2282 6244) or in PJ on Jalan Templer (03 7781 4455). You will have to pay a fee of between RM50 and RM300 depending on the meter size, and the supply will be reconnected by the next working day.

If you have any problems with your water supply, Syabas has a call centre on 1800 88 5252 with English-speaking operators who will investigate the fault and send an officer if necessary. Interruptions in supply are not that frequent, but they do happen every so often for a few hours. If there is a planned disruption to your supply, you will usually be notified by letter. It's a good idea to keep a supply of bottled water at home for emergencies. The majority of houses have a water storage tank, which should be enough to see you through most situations.

Most people do not drink tap water, although you can install a filter for your household water supply. There are a number of different filter systems available. At the bottom end you can get one for less than RM100, but you will need to change the filter regularly. More sophisticated systems that don't need much maintenance can cost over RM1,000 so it may not be worth installing one if you don't plan to stay for long.

Water Suppliers	
Atlas	03 9223 4014
Cactus Water	03 6274 8888
Ocean Water	03 5634 1788
Pure Water	03 8961 5200
Sterling Pure Water	03 6274 7088
Total Water	03 7859 1122

Many people opt for bottled water at home. There are a choice of companies that will deliver large bottles to your door; some will also supply the cooler unit if you take out a long-term contract with them. Units are also available to buy (see Shopping, p.280) if you don't feel like committing to a single supplier.

Gas

Gas is the preferred fuel for cooking in Malaysian homes. It's likely you'll find a fitted gas hob in your kitchen, fuelled by a gas canister containing LPG (liquid petroleum gas) either under your kitchen counter or outside the kitchen. These are easy to obtain, and your supplier will deliver them to your house. Each canister costs around RM25, and you will usually have to pay a deposit of RM50. How long a canister lasts depends on how much you cook, but a rough estimate is about six months. Always keep a spare canister – even though the delivery service is quick a replacement isn't likely to arrive in time to save a half-cooked meal. Major gas suppliers include Shell Gas, Petronas and BHP. If there isn't a canister already in the kitchen when you move in, ask at your nearest petrol station to find out who delivers in your area. Check the regulator and hose that connect the canister to your cooker regularly. Regulators should be replaced every five years and hoses every two years, so if the ones you have look old it's worth getting a new set. Your gas supplier can help with this or you can buy new ones at most hardware stores.

Gas Suppliers	
Ace	03 7876 5517
BHP Gas	1300 883 533
Gas Malaysia	03 9206 7800
Mesralink (Petronas)	1300 888 181
See Enterprise	03 4256 2953
Shell Gas	1300 885 808

Piped gas is a rarity in KL, but it is possible to get a residential connection. Make sure you inform your landlord of your intention to connect to a new utility before you go ahead. Contact Gas Malaysia for more information. If there is piped gas in your building, you will have to pay an RM35 connection fee and RM60 deposit. Bills are sent quarterly and are pretty cheap – about RM10 to RM20 per quarter.

Sewerage

Most houses have a septic tank in the garden for sewage. These are emptied on a schedule once every two years free of charge, but you can ask to have it emptied at any time as long as your regular sewage payments are up to date. If your home has been empty for a long time, it may be worth having the septic tank emptied before you move in. Although it may not sound particularly pleasant, the staff make every effort to ensure the process is quick and clean. Domestic sewage charges are RM6 or RM8 per month and are billed every six months. The sewage service is provided by Indah Water (1 800 88 3495).

If you live in a condo, the building may have a septic tank or it may be connected to a sewage treatment plant. Indah Water provides both kinds of sewage service, but if there's a problem with the sewage in your block contact the building management first. If you feel there's an unresolved problem you could then contact Indah Water directly. Internal piping in both houses and condos is the property owner's responsibility. See Domestic Services on p.109 for plumbers, or ask your landlord if he or she has a regular plumbing service they'd prefer you to call.

Rubbish Disposal & Recycling

If you live in a condo or apartment block, there will be a chute, either in your flat or in a communal area, where you will deposit your refuse – and that's the last you'll see of it, unless you are unlucky enough to have to pass the giant bins from where it's all collected. Rubbish from large blocks is usually collected daily – Malaysia's heat means day-old rubbish is not pleasant.

If you live in a house, you will have to be a bit more organised. Rubbish collections vary in frequency – it could be every other day, or it may be twice weekly. Ask your landlord or neighbours what day it's collected, or keep an eye (or a nose) out for the truck coming down the street. Many houses have a special section of the boundary wall or gatepost where rubbish is kept. There is a lockable door on the inside where you put in your full bin bags, which are then collected from another door on the outside. This is a good system that keeps pests and scavengers away from the rubbish. If your house doesn't have one, invest in a bin with a secure lid or you may find your rubbish scattered all over the neighbourhood by dogs or monkeys. If you are using a bin, you must put it outside your gate for collection. Rubbish is collected by Alam Flora (1 800 880 880, www.alamflora.com.my). Payment

Recycling

for rubbish collection is included in local government assessment charges, which are paid by the property owner. If you're renting your landlord will pay these for you, and if you've bought a property you'll receive an assessment bill annually. Assessment charges are quite reasonable and are based on property values; they will be between RM500 and RM1,000, depending on the location and size of your property.

Recycling

Recycling is still a bit haphazard in KL, but efforts are being made to encourage more people to recycle household waste. Bins for paper, glass and plastic have appeared in several neighbourhoods, and there are manned points where you can bring recyclables. There is a complete listing of times and locations on the Alam Flora website.

Telephone

Landline services are provided by a monopoly, Telekom Malaysia, or TM (www.tm.com.my). Once connected at home you'll find your phone bill for local calls is quite low. TM provides a 'Home Country Direct' service to allow you to use an overseas calling card account

Telephone Companies

Celcom	1300 111 000	www.celcom.com.my
Digi	016 221 1800	www.digi.com.my
Maxis	1800 821 123	www.maxis.com.my
Telekom Malaysia	100	www.tm.com.my

without incurring local charges. Phone boxes are plentiful and use either cash or cards, or you can get a pay-as-you-go SIM card with a local provider and use this until you have your own line. If you're staying in a hotel when you arrive, you may find yourself charged several times the TM rate for calls made from your room. TM charges 80 sen for the first two minutes of a local call and 40 sen for each additional minute. There's no peak time rate for local and international calls, but long-distance calls within Malaysia are about 50% cheaper from 19:00 to 07:00. International call rates available for TM's IDD service have recently been drastically reduced to 90 sen a minute to Australia, Canada, the UK and US, and RM1.80 per minute to New Zealand and most countries in Europe; but cheaper rates are available using prepaid cards sold at convenience stores or from mobile phone companies.

Although the practice with other utilities is to keep the account in the landlord's name, tenants will be expected to open their own account with TM. Service is generally fine once you're connected, but some expats report problems with the set-up process. This is partly down to all the forms being in Bahasa Malaysia; TM staff will sometimes help to fill them in, but to be on the safe side you may want to take a BM speaker with you when you apply. You will have to pay a deposit (RM1,000 for expats) plus stamp fee (RM10) and installation charge (RM50) to TM. It will then send an independent contractor to physically connect the line, and this is where the process tends to come unstuck. It may take a couple of attempts before the contractor visits. You pay between RM30 and RM50 directly to the contractor plus RM5 for every extra metre of cable used over five metres. Expats pay much higher deposits for both fixed line and mobile services than Malaysians, because of the fear you will skip town leaving a large IDD bill behind you. Terminate your services and switch to a prepaid mobile before you leave to be sure of getting these deposits back. Extra services available from TM include ISDN lines, call waiting, voicemail, call transfer and caller identification.

Mobile Phones

Often called handphones, mobiles are everywhere in Malaysia, and many people seem to have more than one. There are three main service providers: Maxis (www.maxis.com.my), Celcom (www.celcom.com.my) and Digi (www.digi.com.my). Celcom is run by TM while Maxis and Digi are independent firms. All three operate both pre and post-paid services, and provide good coverage across Malaysia, plus international roaming. Maxis and Digi both offer very low IDD rates and are popular with expats for this reason.

Malaysia Telecom

Recent legislation requires all mobile phone numbers to be registered, so you will be asked to show your passport before you can buy and activate a local prepaid number. So long as you remember to take your passport along you'll be connected in minutes. Frequent promotions and stiff competition make prepaid SIM cards very cheap (SIM cards for Maxis' prepaid Hotlink network are currently just RM8.80), and they're widely available with at least one retailer at every mall. If you lose your mobile, registration means you can keep the same number when you get a new phone.

Area Codes & Useful Numbers

The city code 03 for Kuala Lumpur also includes Selangor and Putrajaya.

Cheap Overseas Calls

Look beyond Telekom Malaysia and its affiliate Celcom if you want the best rates for overseas calls. Mobile phone operators Digi and Maxis offer IDD rates of around 20 sen per minute to fixed lines in a number of countries, including Australia, Canada, the UK and US. Digi offers good rates for calls to mobiles too. Maxis users dial 132 before the international number to access the cheaper rates from both post-paid and its Hotlink branded prepaid service, making this an excellent choice for calling home when you've first arrived.

Prepaid calling cards are available from convenience stores and can be a better value option if you're calling the Indian subcontinent or the Middle East. Check headline rates carefully, as the price listed is often for a 10 or 20 second block so price comparison is difficult. Popular brands include TMs i-Talk (which uses VoIP), OneComm and TimeKontact.

Area Codes & Useful Numbers	
Directory Enquiries	103
Emergency	999
International Operator	108
Johor	7
Kelantan, Terrenganu	9
KL	3
Melaka, Negri Sembilan	6
Penang, Kedah and Perlis	4
Penang, Kedah and Perlis	4
Sabah	88
Sarawak	82
Service Problems	100

Cheap Overseas Calls		
i-Talk	na	www.tmonline.com.my
OneComm	03 8991 7090	www.onecomm.com.my
TimeKontact	03 2730 5287	www.time.com.my

Internet

Other options **Internet Cafes** p.397, **Websites** p.37

Broadband Deals
Internet connections aren't KL's strong point, but the recent entry of mobile phone providers into this market has consumers looking hopeful. Mobile USB modems and wireless broadband hotspots are popping up everywhere, but time will tell if they're any more reliable than the much maligned Streamyx.

Internet connections in KL are generally less than stellar, with frustratingly slow connection speeds and service interruptions. The major provider of domestic dial-up and broadband services is TMNet, a division of Telekom Malaysia. Its broadband service, Streamyx, is now available in most residential areas, and it has a full range of dial-up services including prepaid cards. Other providers include Jaring Communications and mobile phone companies Maxis and Celcom.

Streamyx broadband services offer bandwidths of 512K up to 2Mbps. Monthly packages start at RM66 for unlimited 512K access, not including a modem. Unlimited 2Mbps access will set you back RM188 monthly, including a modem. The minimum subscription period is 12 months, and there are charges of RM75 for activation and RM88 for installation on whichever package you choose.

Jaring's broadband service starts at RM69 per month for 1Mbps, including a modem. There's no extra charge for activation but installation is RM80. Coverage isn't as wide as for Streamyx, so the service may not be available in your area.

Wireless broadband, available from Maxis and Celcom, is new to the market. Early feedback reports some problems with speed and connection strength. A modem plus unlimited monthly usage costs RM138 from Maxis and RM120 from Celcom.

Dial-up internet access is also available; it's cheap but slow. Jaring has a 10 hour package for RM5 per month, with additional minutes charged at 1 sen. Normal fixed-line call charges apply. TMNet has a 10 hour package for RM10, with extra minutes at one sen. TM fixed-line subscribers can access the internet on an ad hoc basis by dialling 1315. The charge is four sen per minute and appears on your monthly phone bill.

Internet Service Providers		
Celcom	www.celcom.com.my	na
Jaring Communications	www.jaring.com.my	03 8991 7080
Maxis	www.maxis.com.my	na
TMNet	www.tmnet.com.my	1300 888 123

Prepaid cards are available from TMNet in denominations of RM10, RM20, RM50 and RM100. The RM30 start-up card gives you an email account, dial-up time and access to TM's network of wireless hotspots.

Wireless access is available through TM wireless hotspots and at many hotels and cafes. Internet cafes tend to be located in areas popular with students and budget travellers and are a cheap way to check your email.

Local internet sites are suffixed with '.my'. There is some censorshiop but it's mainly related to political and religious sensibilities and won't have much impact on the casual expat surfer.

Bill Payment

Most utilities are billed monthly, with the exception of piped gas, which is quarterly. You can pay most bills in person over the counter at your bank, at any post office branch or at the office of the relevant company. If you have an account with Maybank you can pay bills online. Some bills can be paid by posting a cheque to the company, but with personal payment you have a receipt in case of any dispute. Some shops may also accept bill payments, but they will charge for the service.

If you miss a bill, you will generally just get a reminder with your next bill. It's unlikely you'll be cut off unless you miss several bills. Most mobile phone companies will put a limited on a post-paid (billed) account. If you exceed this you won't be able to make any more calls until you pay the bill.

If you have any problems with your bills, call the relevant service provider listed in this section.

Postal Services

Most people have their post delivered to their door by POS Malaysia, which has branches all over KL and in many shopping malls too. You can post letters and parcels, pay many of your bills, and buy money orders at post office counters; queues can be slow moving as a result. Most post offices operate a queuing system where you take a numbered ticket and wait your turn. Opening hours are excellent with some post offices opening on Saturday mornings and until 22:00 on weeknights.

Courier Companies		
City-Link	03 5033 3800	www.citylinkexpress.com
DHL Worldwide Express	1300 881 188	www.dhl.com.my
FedEx	1800 886 363	www.fedex.com.my
Nationwide Express	03 5512 7000	www.nationwide2u.com
POS Malaysia	1300 300 300	www.pos.com.my
Poslaju EMS – National Courier Service	03 2263 2626	www.pos.com.my
TNT Express Worldwide	03 5569 1951	www.tnt.com
UPS	03 7784 1233	www.ups.com

Stamps are only available through POS Malaysia outlets, although there are stamp machines in popular locations, like shopping malls, that don't have a post office. There are mixed reports on the reliability of the postal service, but it's generally pretty quick. Letters arriving to or from the UK and Australia take about a week and it will take 10 days to two weeks to or from the USA. Small parcels may be delivered with your letters, but you will probably have to go and pick up larger parcels from the main sorting office for your area. You will get a card delivered telling you where to collect your parcel. If packages don't arrive, you can report the loss to the post office, but unless a signed-for or similar tracking system has been used, you're unlikely to have any luck tracing them.

You can post your letters at the post office or at the red post boxes located in all neighbourhoods. The boxes usually have two slots: KL and lain-lain for everywhere else. A standard airmail letter to the UK is RM1.50 and a 500g airmail parcel will cost

RM48.10 with an insurance limit of RM3,000. If you're sending something valuable, it's a good idea to use a courier service, either Pos Lajau from the post office or a commercial company like DHL.

Courier Companies

POS Malaysia has its own courier company, Pos Lajau, that delivers throughout Malaysia and internationally. Nationwide Express is a popular local courier that delivers to East and West Malaysia, Singapore and Brunei. International courier companies FedEx, UPS, DHL and TNT all operate in Malaysia.

Radio

Radio is as multicultural as television and you can tune in to broadcasts in Bahasa Malaysia, Chinese, Tamil and English. Some stations switch between languages at different times of the day. The majority of stations are owned by the government broadcaster RTM (www.rtm.net.my) or satellite TV operator Astro (www.astro.com.my).

RTM has an English station on 90.3 and 100.1 FM called Traxx. There's also a classical music station, Klasik Nasional on 98.3 FM.

Astro owns three English language stations: HITZ.FM on 92.9 FM, Mix on 94.5 FM and LiteFM on 105.7 FM. There are two independent radio stations, Red on 104.9 FM and Fly (www.flyfm.com.my) on 95.8 FM, both broadcasting in a mix of English and Bahasa Malaysia.

There's not much variety, with all channels airing a mix of conversation and music with regular news bulletins. LiteFM specialises in classic pop music, while the others play current chart music from the UK and USA. Playlists on all radio channels are limited, so if you're a frequent listener you may find yourself switching between channels to get some variety. Competitions are popular and prizes range from a CD or meal voucher to a new house or car. Competitions for big prizes tend to be long running. If you're keen to enter radio competitions, check the rules as some may only be open to Malaysian citizens. Stations broadcast nationally but the frequencies vary throughout Malaysia so you'll have to retune your radio several times on a long road trip.

Television

Digital television hasn't yet arrived in Malaysia and conventional free to view channels are provided by a mix of government and privately owned broadcasters. There are six free to view channels that are available throughout Malaysia. Programmes are broadcast in Bahasa Malaysia, Mandarin, Tamil and English, although not all at the same time. Some of these programmes will be subtitled in English. Scenes of an overtly sexual nature are censored and there is some censorship for political reasons, which probably goes unnoticed by most expats.

Radio Televisyen Malaysia is the government broadcaster and information about its channels RTM1 and RTM2 can be found online (www.rtm.net.my). RTM1 broadcasts mainly in Bahasa Malaysia and includes locally made soap operas that provide an interesting insight into local life and its preoccupations. RTM2 broadcasts in several languages and has many imported programmes from around Asia. RTM isn't known for up to the minute programming choices; current English language films being shown in the prime Saturday night slot on RTM2 include You've Got Mail and Space Jam. There's also limited children's programming, including some imported cartoons dubbed into Bahasa Malaysia.

Of the privately owned channels, expats will find NTV7 (www.ntv7.com.my) and 8TV (www.8tv.com.my) the most interesting. NTV7 has some American series and syndicated chat shows including *24*, *CSI* and *The Martha Stewart Show*. NTV7 also makes a number of Malaysian reality TV shows which are very popular locally. 8TV broadcasts popular American reality series such as *Project Runway*, *The Apprentice* and *American Idol*. The remaining two privately owned channels, TV3 (www.tv3.com.my) and TV9 (www.tv9.com.my) don't broadcast in English.

None of the free to view channels broadcast exclusively in English, but you'll find nightly news bulletins in English on RTM2 and NTV7 and at least one English language programme to watch at most times of the day. For a choice of English language programmes, the satellite service provided by Astro (see below) is the only option.

Satellite Television

Satellite television is provided by a single company, Astro (www.astro.com.my, 03 7491 9888) and you'll see their dishes sprouting from almost every house and condominium in upmarket areas. Satellite radio hasn't taken of in the same way and many expats listen to radio stations from their own home via the internet.

Astro has many English language channels covering the news (BBC, CNN, Al Jazeera, CNBC), movies (HBO, Cinemax, Star Movies), lifestyle (Discovery Home and Health, Travel and Living), Sports (ESPN and Star Sports) and many more. There are several children's channels broadcasting in English including Playhouse Disney, Nickelodeon and Cartoon Network. Subscriptions start from RM37.95 per month for the basic package and various add-ons are available. To receive all available English language channels you'd pay about RM120 per month.

To view Astro at home you'll need a dish and a decoder box. Landlords don't usually have a problem with you installing Astro and you may find the cabling is already there. Individual condo units and apartments need their own dish. Installation costs around RM100 and is done by a contractor recommended by Astro. Astro also sells the Astro Max decoder and recorder for RM549, which allows you to record a programme while watching another.

Many hotels and serviced apartments subscribe to Astro, although they may not offer the full range of channels. Sports coverage is pretty good, with a strong focus on football (soccer). Some sports fixtures are shown on a pay per view basis. Popular venues for watching sport include Legends (03 2166 6603) and Barfly (03 2145 9198), both on Jalan Sultan Ismail, and Finnegan's in Bangsar (03 2284 9024), Mid Valley (03 2284 8167) and Desa Sri Hartamas (03 2300 0538).

Sultan Abdul Samad Bldg

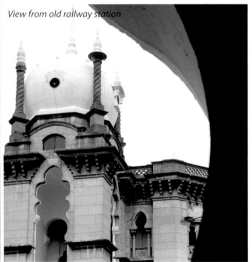

View from old railway station

General Medical Care

Malaysia has both public and private healthcare, but as an expat you're unlikely to use the former. It's targeted towards Malaysians and, other than doctors, staff rarely speak English. Government hospitals are publicly funded, providing medical care at little or no cost. Wealthy patients can pay for better facilities, such as a private room. You need a Malaysian ID card (MyKAD, p.49) to access public healthcare, except in emergencies, when the nearest hospital (whether public or private) is obliged to provide treatment. Many expats rely solely on private hospitals, but this is expensive, especially if your insurance doesn't cover outpatient care. Expats tend to use private clinics as they would a family doctor or GP back home, and these offer better value than hospitals for minor illnesses and immunisations.

Malaysian doctors have often been trained overseas (the UK and Australia are popular) and speak excellent English. Culturally, however, the doctor-patient relationship may be more formal than you're used to.

Attitudes to treatment tend to be conservative, with maternity care particularly old fashioned. Good dental care is available, and cosmetic surgery is on the rise. Some private hospitals have begun actively courting the international market for medical tourism, much of which is for cosmetic work.

Government Healthcare

This is free (or comes with a minimum charge) and geared towards Malaysians. Other than doctors, most staff in government facilities will speak little English. Signs and other information are in Bahasa Malaysia, and only holders of a MyKAD (Malaysian ID card) are eligible for anything beyond emergency care. This effectively rules out expats. Government hospitals are heavily used and resources are tight. Malaysians with money usually opt for private care. Many doctors who have had their training paid for by the government serve a minimum term in state hospitals before going into private practice. This can mean that there's a lack of experienced doctors at government hospitals, although some do stay in the public sector.

Private Healthcare

Most Malaysians who can afford private healthcare choose to pay for the convenience it offers. Private clinics are dotted all over town. Standards of care vary, so ask around for a recommendation in your area. There are several large private hospitals in the city, including Ampang Puteri (p.124) and Gleneagles (p.125) in Ampang; Pantai Medical Centre (p.125) in Bangsar; Damansara Specialist Hospital (p.125), Sunway Medical Centre (p.124) and Assunta (p.124) in Petaling Jaya; Tawakal Medical Centre (p.126) in the city centre and Subang Jaya Medical Centre (p.125) in Subang Jaya. All of these offer 24 hour accident and emergency facilities as well as inpatient and outpatient specialist care.

Health Insurance

Most employers will include this as part of your terms of employment, although outpatient care and dental treatment may not be covered. Insurance usually covers the employed person and their dependents. It's possible to buy individual medical insurance (p.122, although choice is limited) or you can arrange cover through an international provider like BUPA or PPP before you arrive.

Health Insurance Companies	
Allianz	03 2168 6868
American Home Assurance	03 2058 5000
Great Eastern	03 4259 8888
ING Insurance	03 2058 4838
Manulife	03 2719 9112
Van Breda International	03 2032 5333
William Russell	03 2171 2071

Pharmacies

Doctors often dispense their own medicine, which saves you a separate trip to the pharmacy. For minor ailments, you can visit a pharmacy for advice and may be able to get the necessary drugs without seeing a doctor. Malaysia's drug control laws mean that pharmacists can't dispense painkillers containing codeine, but you should be able to get antibiotics, asthma medication and antihistamines without a prescription. Pharmacists will also fill repeat prescriptions from your doctor. The two major chains are Watson's and Guardian – you'll find branches of both in all major shopping centres. Pharmacies are usually open from 10:00 to 22:00, and 24 hour pharmacy services are available from the major private hospitals (p.124).

Calling An Ambulance

Most private and some government hospitals have ambulance services, but these are solely a means of transporting a patient to hospital. There is no paramedic service. At best, ambulance personnel will give basic first aid, at worst, nothing. Unless you suspect the patient has a severe injury to their spine or neck, the best and quickest option is often to take them to hospital by car or taxi. If you need to call an ambulance, try the St John's Ambulance Service (03 9285 5294) or Lifeline (03 7956 9999), or one of the major private hospitals on their emergency line: Gleneagles (03 4255 2880), Pantai (03 2296 0999) or Ampang Puteri (03 4260 7060).

Health Insurance

This isn't mandatory for expats, apart for those who fall under the MM2H programme (see p.49) who must have health insurance for themselves and any dependents as a condition of their visa. Although private healthcare is relatively cheap in Malaysia, costs can quickly mount up if you're seriously ill or in an accident, so having private health insurance is certainly recommended for all expats.

Many expats will have health insurance included for themselves and their dependents as part of their salary package, although outpatient care and dental treatment may not be covered. It's possible to buy individual medical insurance locally and there are now some policies specifically geared towards expats. ING offers a policy called I.ExpatCare, which offers very comprehensive coverage including inpatient and outpatient care, maternity, complementary therapy and medical aids. Annual premiums depend on age and start at RM4,044 for adults under 30, rising to RM14,816 for ages 61 to 70 for annual coverage of RM950,000. William Russell has the Global Health Malaysia essential plan, offering cover from around RM2,800 per month, which has been approved for MM2H visa requirements. Health insurance is also offered by local providers, although few cover outpatient care. Payment policies vary, with some insurers requiring the annual premium upfront and others happy to accept monthly payments. Alternatively you can arrange cover with an international insurer such as BUPA or PPP before you arrive, but this will be more expensive than buying insurance locally.

Prince Court Medical Centre

Donor Cards

Organ donation is managed by the National Transplant Resource Centre based at Hospital Kuala Lumpur. It's not a common practice in Malaysia, with only 25 organ donors in 2007, although the centre is hoping that growing awareness of the facts about organ donation and transplants will result in more donors. Information about organ donation is available from the centre on 03 2615 5555, ext 6576.

Giving Blood

Blood donation in Malaysia is coordinated by the National Blood Centre (www.pdn. my). Blood donation is widely promoted and blood drives at companies, government departments and colleges are common. The minimum age for blood donation in Malaysia is 17. You can donate blood at Gleneagles Intan Medical Centre on Jalan Ampang, where they have a satellite unit of the National Blood Centre. Call 03 4257 1300, ext 7129, for details of opening times and donor criteria.

Giving Up Smoking

There's a lack of formal support for giving up smoking. You may be able to drum up an informal support group through one of the expatriate associations, or you can ask your doctor for advice and help. Alternatives such as hypnotherapy and acupuncture are available – see the Alternative Therapies section on p.136 for details.

Hospitals

While you probably won't be visiting a government hospital for regular treatment, it's important to know where they are and what facilities they offer in case of an accident or other emergency. Limited resources and plenty of patients means facilities are often overstretched and all but the most severe cases are likely to have a long wait in accident and emergency. Most nursing and ancilliary staff will speak Bahasa Malaysia, while doctors will usually speak English. Signs, forms and other information are often printed only in Bahasa Malaysia. It's common for a full service hospital, either government or private, to be called a medical centre.

Cnr of Jalan Pahang
& Jalan Tun Razak
City Centre
 Chow Kit
Map 8 E1

Kuala Lumpur General Hospital

03 2165 5555 | *www.hkl.gov.my*

This is KL's busiest hospital, and it has a 24 hour accident and emergency department as well as a comprehensive range of medical services. It's very crowded and you will have to wait a long time for treatment, so in all but the most immediately life-threatening situations, where this is the closest hospital, you should seek treatment elsewhere.

145 Jalan Tun Razak
City Centre
 Chow Kit
Map 9 B2

National Heart Institute

03 2617 8200 | *www.ijn.com.my*

The National Heart Institute (Institut Jantung Negara) is a centre of excellence providing cardiovascular and thoracic care for adults and children. Formerly part of Kuala Lumpur General Hospital, IJN was set up as an independent facility in 1992. This hospital has 24 hour accident and emergency facilities for cardiac patients only. For all other emergencies you should seek treatment at another hospital, such as Kuala Lumpur General which is next door.

Jalan University
Off Federal Highway
Petaling Jaya
 Universiti
Map 6 D3

Universiti Malaya Medical Centre

03 7956 4422 | *www.ummc.edu.my*

Malaysia's largest teaching hospital is part of Universiti Malaya and located on the huge UM campus between Bangsar and Petaling Jaya. It offers a full range of medical services including a 24 hour accident and emergency department. It's very busy and you're not advised to seek treatment here except in life-threatening emergencies. Most signage is in Bahasa Malaysia.

Hospitals			
Kuala Lumpur General Hospital	City Centre	03 2165 5555	www.hkl.gov.my
National Heart Institute	City Centre	03 2617 8200	www.ijn.com.my
Universiti Malaya Medical Centre	Petaling Jaya	03 7956 4422	www.ummc.edu.my

Main Private Hospitals

You'll most likely find yourself visiting a private hospital if you need any kind of specialist medical care. Facilities are generally good, and in some cases excellent. If you come from a country with a government health system, you may take a while to get used to the private system – don't forget to pay the bill before you leave! Some expats feel private hospital doctors over medicate, so feel free to ask what each medicine prescribed is for and refuse any you don't want or need.

1 Jalan Mamanda 9
Ampang Point
Ampang
🚇 *Ampang*
Map5 F4

Ampang Puteri Hospital

03 4270 2500 | *www.apsh.kpjhealth.com.my*

Ampang Puteri is the older of the two private hospitals in Ampang. It's a popular choice with expats living in the UK Heights and Taman TAR areas, since it's very close by. It provides a full range of medical services, including a 24 hour accident and emergency department and a wide range of outpatient clinics. It has 250 inpatient beds, an ICU and day surgery facilities. There is a home nursing service for recently released patients living within 10km of the hospital.

68 Jalan Templer
Petaling Jaya
🚇 *Jalan Templer*

Assunta Hospital

03 7782 3433 | *www.assunta.com.my*

Upgraded in 2006, the PJ location of Assunta means it's better value than hospitals in the smarter suburbs. There is a nursing college attached to the hospital, and the

Private Health Centres & Clinics

Global Doctors	B3-05 Bayu Walk, Mont Kiara Bayu	Mont Kiara	03 6203 3999
Japan Medicare	107/109 Jalan Maarof	Bangsar	03 2287 0988
Klinik Goh Dan Rakan Rakan	A1205 12A Floor, Wisma Lim Foo Yong, 86 Jalan Raja Chulan	City Centre	03 2141 0362
Klinik Kaulsay	9A Jalan Setiapuspa Medan Damansara	Bukit Damansara	03 2094 8280
Klinik Segara	4th Floor, City Square Complex Jalan Tun Razak	Ampang	03 2163 2140
	B-08-06 Block B, Plaza Mont Kiara	Mont Kiara	03 6411 8007
	No 1 Jalan 26/70A, Desa Sri Hartamas	Sri Hartamas	03 2300 0400
	2 Pusat Bandar Damansara	Bukit Damansara	03 2095 2227
Klinik Tan Mano	10 Jalan Wangsa 2, Wangsa Ukay Bukit Antarabangsa	Ampang	03 4108 0177
	13th Floor Plaza OSK, Jalan Ampang	City Centre	03 2166 2050
Klinik Toh & Lim	52 Jalan SS22/25, Damansara Jaya	Petaling Jaya	03 7729 1991
The Medical Practice	18A Lorong Kolam Air Lama 1 (Naan Corner)	Ampang	03 4253 2768
Twin Towers Medical Centre	Suria KLCC	KLCC	03 2382 3500

Other Private Hospitals

Chinese Maternity Hospital	106 Jalan Pudu, City Centre	03 2078 2055	na
Damai Service Hospital	Jalan Ipoh, City Centre	03 4043 4900	www.dsh.com.my
Kelana Jaya Medical Centre	Jalan Perbandaran, Petaling Jaya	03 7805 2111	www.kjmc.com.my
Pantai Cheras Medical Centre	Jalan 1/96A, Taman Cheras Makmur	03 9132 2022	www.pantai.com.my
Sambhi Clinic & Nursing Home	Medan Tuanku Abdul Rahman	03 2692 4594	na
Sunway Medical Centre	Bandar Sunway, Petaling Jaya	03 7491 9191	www.sunmed.com.my
Tun Hussein Onn National Eye Hospital – THONEH	Lorong Utara B, Petaling Jaya	03 7956 1911	www.thoneh.com.my
Tung Shin Hospital	102 Jalan Pudu, Chinatown	03 2072 1655	www.tungshinhospital.com.my

standard of nursing care has been praised by patients. It offers inpatient and outpatient specialist services, including a dedicated angiography room. There is a special care baby unit as well as adult intensive care. The hospital allows a family member to stay overnight in hospital with the patient. You can also donate blood here.

119 Jalan SS20/10
Damansara Utama
Petaling Jaya
🚇 *Taman Bahagia*
Map 6 B1

Damansara Specialist Hospital

03 7722 2692 | *www.dsh.kpjhealth.com.my*

DSH is a full-service hospital offering inpatient and outpatient care with a 24 hour accident and emergency department. There are a number of specialist clinics here, including a sleep disorders clinic, oncology unit, haemodialysis centre, and a well woman clinic offering health screening packages. The hospital offers a discount card to regular patients, giving discounts of between 5% and 20% for cash payments.

282 Jalan Ampang
Ampang
🚇 *Jelatek*
Map 5 E3

Gleneagles Intan Medical Centre

03 4257 1300 | *www.gimc.com.my*

Opened in 1996, Gleneagles is extremely popular with the expat community in KL. The main hospital has 330 beds and the outpatient clinics are housed in an adjacent building with 110 consulting suites. Gleneagles provides a high standard of care and comprehensive services including a neonatal ICU, adult ICU, fertility services, rehabilitation and behavioural counselling. The executive screening programme and well woman clinics are recommended. There's a 24 hour accident and emergency department with a private ambulance service (call 03 7956 9999).

8 Jalan Bukit Pantai
Bangsar
🚇 *Abdullah Hukum*
Map 6 E3

Pantai Medical Centre

03 2296 0888 | *www.pantai.com.my*

Pantai probably ties with Gleneagles as the most popular hospital with expats and has recently introduced an international ward to tap into the medical tourism market. It offers a full range of inpatient and outpatient services and has a 24 hour accident and emergency department. Specialist departments include hand and micro surgery, plastic and reconstructive surgery, foetal medicine, endocrinology and clinical and medical oncology. There's also a dental clinic here.

39 Jalan Kia Peng
City Centre
🚇 *Bukit Bintang*
Map 11 F4

Prince Court Medical Centre

03 2160 0000 | *www.princecourt.com*

Only just opening at the time of writing, this new hospital promises to be one of the largest and best equipped in KL. Funded by Petronas in a joint venture with the University Hospital of Vienna, it has 35 intensive care beds and 300 regular care beds. Centres of excellence include dermatology, men's health, oncology and cosmetic surgery.

1 Jalan SS 12/1A
47500 Subang Jaya
Subang
🚇 *Subang Jaya*

Subang Jaya Medical Centre

03 5630 6466 | *www.sjmc.com.my*

SJMC is a joint Malaysian-American venture governed by US hospital standards. The 24 hour emergency service is specialist supported. Specialist departments include a cancer and radiosurgery centre, fertility clinic, kidney stone centre and liver transplant surgery. It offers a range of support services to patients, including counselling and support groups for cancer patients, a healthcare library, nutrition advice and antenatal and parentcraft classes. Because of the location it's not as popular with expats as hospitals closer to the city centre, but those who do use it are very happy with the quality of care offered here.

202A Jalan Pahang
City Centre
Ⓜ *Titiwangsa*

Tawakal Medical Centre

03 4023 3599 | *www.tawakal.kpjhealth.com.my*

The smallest of the major private hospitals, with 147 beds, 40 resident consultants and 20 visiting consultants, Tawakal is part of the same group as Ampang Puteri and Damansara Specialist Hospitals. This is a less expensive option than some of the larger hospitals. It has an intensive care and coronary care unit, physiotherapy department, maternity services and a haemodialysis centre. It offers a comprehensive range of health screening services for men and women and a discount scheme for regular patients. The hospital has a 24 hour accident and emergency department.

Dermatologists

Dr Chow	Pantai Medical Centre, 8 Jalan Bukit Pantai	Bangsar	03 2282 6558
Dr Chu Siew Mun	Subang Jaya Medical Centre, 1 Jalan SS12/1A	Petaling Jaya	03 5630 6118
Dr Gan Ain Tan	Suite 611, Gleneagles Intan Medical Centre 286 Jalan Ampang	Ampang	03 4257 2690
Dr Ruban Nathan	7th Floor Wisma I-Perintis, 47 Jalan Dungun	Petaling Jaya	03 2092 4007
Dr Tan Lay Peng	11 Jalan 2/71	TTDI (Taman Tun Dr Ismail)	03 7728 1733
Nathan Skin Clinic	1st Floor, Wisma PKNS, Jalan Raja Laut	City Centre	03 2691 5858
Ting Skin Specialist Clinic	136 Jalan Imbi	City Centre	03 2144 4848

Maternity

Other options **Maternity Items** p.312

It's common for expats to give birth in Malaysia, although some do choose to go back to their home country if there are issues surrounding citizenship or they feel they'd like a lot of extended family support.

Maternity care is hospital based, and you will have regular appointments with an obstetrician throughout your pregnancy who will then be present to deliver your baby. There's no formal midwife service at hospitals, although some independent midwives practise here providing antenatal and postnatal support. Jenlia Maternal Services in TTDI (03 7726 7002) holds antenatal classes and will visit you at home after the birth. Mamalink in Bangsar (www.mamalink.com.my), run by a UK-trained midwife, holds antenatal classes that have a strong focus on natural birth and has a breastfeeding support service. Home births and water births aren't currently available in Malaysia.

Maternity care may be covered by health insurance, but there is often a waiting period of a year after cover starts. Some insurers will not cover you for maternity unless your spouse is insured by the same company.

Pain relief is commonly used, with natural birth being the exception rather than the rule. Gas and air and epidurals are the most widely used and you will usually have access to pain relief on demand.

Some hospitals restrict access to the delivery room and you may only be allowed one support person (usually the father) with you. Although Malaysia is a conservative society and single parenthood or unmarried parents are unusual, there are no special laws or regulations for these circumstances.

After the birth, you have 14 days to register your child with the Malaysian authorities. Once you have the birth certificate you can register the child at your embassy and get a passport. There's not usually a time limit for this, but you can't travel outside Malaysia until your baby has a passport, so most expats get one soon after birth. See Birth Certificates & Registration on p.52. for more details.

There may be issues regarding citizenship for children born overseas. Check with your embassy well before your due date if you have any questions or concerns regarding this.

Confinement ◀
Malaysians of all races traditionally observe a period of confinement for the new mother and baby after birth, which lasts for up to a hundred days. During confinement the new mother must wrap up warmly in long sleeves, trousers and socks despite the tropical heat, and fans and air con are not allowed. Special foods are prepared to help her recover from the birth and the new mother is not supposed to wash her hair or body.

Choosing A Hospital

Non-Malaysians must use private hospitals for maternity care. Most people choose a hospital based on ease of access, cost, comfort and the equipment and services available. Which hospital you choose may also depend on your obstetrician, who may only work at one or two hospitals. Popular choices for maternity care are Gleneagles Intan Medical Centre, Pantai Medical Centre, Subang Jaya Medical Centre, Damansara Specialist Hospital and Assunta Hospital.

Costs vary between hospitals, but some offer all in one birth packages, usually one for a natural delivery and one for a c-section. You will usually pay for antenatal visits as you go, and one way to keep costs down is to see your obstetrician at a clinic rather than at the hospital. The packages usually include all the costs relating to the birth including pain relief. Many doctors are happy for you to write your own birth plan, but there are mixed reports as to whether these carry any weight with nursing staff when the doctor isn't there. There aren't any doulas currently practising in KL, and you can usually just have person in the delivery room with you. The rooms are fairly basic and not well set up for active birth, but some doctors may allow you to bring in aids such as a fitball. Private rooms aren't too expensive; Gleneagles has single rooms from RM230 a night.

Going Home To Have The Baby

Most airlines start restricting travel by pregnant women after 28 weeks, and may insist on a doctor's letter stating you're fit to fly. Most airlines won't allow you to travel at all after 36 weeks. Newborns over one week old are usually allowed to fly by airlines, but many parents prefer to wait until after the first set of immunisations before taking their new baby on a plane. You must apply for a passport for your baby before you can return to Malaysia. Your baby will then be issued with a social visit pass which you can convert to a dependent pass. Arranging postnatal care and healthcare for your baby won't be a problem – just call the hospital to make the necessary appointments. If you can, bring all your medical records regarding your pregnancy with you to your home country and bring back any information about the birth and your baby's health to Malaysia.

Antenatal Care

Antenatal care is provided by obstetricians, either at private clinics or at a hospital outpatient department. Antenatal classes are provided at some hospitals and by independent midwives. Care is of a very high standard and you will normally be offered an ultrasound scan at every visit. At each check up you will be weighed, have your blood pressure taken and your urine checked for protein and sugar levels. Screening tests are carried out to detect possible birth defects.

Some obstetricians will only see patients at the hospital where they plan to deliver. Others may have an independent clinic and offer a choice of hospitals for delivery. Most people choose their obstetrician based on personal recommendation or on the hospital where they want to deliver if they have a strong preference. You will normally see the same doctor throughout your pregnancy and they will manage your labour and deliver your baby.

There's a high level of intervention in the birth process, including induction of labour, forceps and vacuum deliveries and c-sections. If you're strongly in favour of an active or natural birth, choose your doctor carefully as many are not supportive of this. Dr Choong Kuo Hsiang at Pantai Medical Centre is highly recommended for women who want a natural birth. The c-section rate is high, and doctors will usually agree to an elective c-section, although this may not be covered by insurance. Most mothers stay in hospital for two or three days after birth, or up to a week after a c-section.

If you're over 35, the risks for some birth defects increase and you may be offered extra screening. Your doctor will be able to advise you on the risks and benefits of each test. Ibu (www.ibufamily.org) has a pregnancy support group where you can meet other women and get advice on maternity care. Mamalink (www.mamalink.com.my) offers antenatal classes, as does Jenlia (03 7726 7002). Fit For 2 (www.fitfor2.com.my) offers a range of fitness classes for pregnant women from a UK certified instructor.

Postnatal Care

PND

Postnatal depression can strike any new mother, and it's important to seek help as quickly as possible. Health professionals may not seem as concerned about your emotional wellbeing as at home but help is available and you should talk to your doctor or a midwife from Jenlia if you're at all worried about PND.

Once you leave hospital with your new baby, you can arrange for a private midwife to visit you at home. Jenlia (03 7726 7002) offers this service. After the birth, your baby will be seen by a paediatrician while in hospital, and you will usually be given an appointment for a follow-up visit after six weeks before you leave the hospital. At this first check up the doctor will examine your baby, check for proper growth and any signs of problems. You should also have a check up after six weeks. You'll be asked questions about your general health and perhaps about your emotional well-being, as well as being examined to make sure your body is returning to normal after the birth. Many doctors offer a pap smear test at this visit.

Breastfeeding support is available from Mamalink (www.mamalink.com). Attitudes towards breastfeeding are generally positive. It's ok to feed discreetly in public, but probably not a good idea to let it all hang out! Ibu (www.ibufamily.org) offers a well baby clinic staffed by volunteer expat doctors and midwives, and a new baby group which is a great way to meet other new mums. Fit For 2 (www.fitfir2.com.my) has antenatal exercise classes that you can do with your baby.

Having a new baby can be hard work emotionally and physically and it can be extra hard if you're away from family and friends. Many women encourage family visits around the time of the birth so that they have some extra support. Luckily, with household help being easily available you can concentrate on your new baby without having to worry about cooking dinner or getting the ironing done.

Maternity Leave

Under Malaysian law women are entitled to 60 days' paid maternity leave for each birth. If you work for a multinational company, you may find your entitlement differs and you should check your contract. It's possible to negotiate additional unpaid leave, but employers are not obliged to agree to this.

If, during your maternity leave, you decide not to return to work, you may be asked to repay some or all of the maternity pay to your employer. Individual companies differ in their approach to this; you should consult your HR department to find out the policy at your company.

At the moment, there's no formal entitlement to paternity leave in Malaysia, but employers will normally allow a few days of compassionate leave.

Maternity Hospitals & Clinics (Private)

Assunta Hospital	68 Jalan Templer	Petaling Jaya	03 7782 3433
Chinese Maternity Hospital	106 Jalan Pudu	City Centre	03 2078 2055
Damansara Specialist Hospital	119 Jalan SS20/10, Damansara Utama	Petaling Jaya	03 7722 2692
Gleneagles Intan Medical Centre	282 Jalan Ampang	Ampang	03 4257 1300
Jenlia Maternal Services	46A Jalan Datuk Sulaiman	TTDI (Taman Tun Dr Ismail)	03 7726 7002
Mamalink	2 Jalan Taban4, Lucky Garden	Bangsar	03 2095 1206
Pantai Medical Centre	8 Jalan Bukit Pantai	Bangsar	03 2296 0888
Subang Jaya Medical Centre	1 Jalan SS 12/1A, 47500 Subang Jaya	Subang	03 5630 6466

Contraception & Sexual Health

While you may be used to visiting a family planning clinic or GP's office for contraception and sexual health matters, the healthcare system in KL is organised differently. Although the pill may be more easily available here than in your home country and you may be able to buy supplies over the counter, it's common to visit the gynaecologist for any issues relating to this and other contraceptive methods and for sexual health check ups. See Gynaecology and Obstetrics.

Gynaecology & Obstetrics

As with so many things in KL, word of mouth is the best way to find a gynaecologist you feel comfortable with. There are both male and female doctors to choose from and many have trained overseas, usually in the UK or Australia. It's usual to visit a gynaecologist for anything to do with sexual and reproductive health, so for example rather than having a cervical smear test at a GP practice, or visiting a family planning clinic for contraception, you would see your gynaecologist.

Contraception is widely available; you'll find condoms in pharmacies, supermarkets and convenience stores and both oral contraceptive pills and emergency contraceptive (morning after) pills are available at pharmacies without prescriptions to women over 18. For other methods such as the cap, diaphragm or coil you'll need to visit the doctor. The majority of HIV and Aids cases in Malaysia involve injecting drug users, with 75% infected in this way. 90% of those infected are men. The government runs an awareness campaign which promotes the use of condoms as a means of preventing transmission in the general population. For more information about sexual and reproductive health see the Malaysian Aids Council website (www.mac.org.my) or contact the Federation of Family Planning Associations Malaysia on 03 5633 7514.

Gynaecology & Obstetrics

Bangsar Women's Specialist Centre	22K Jalan Telawi, Bangsar	03 2282 1828
Dr Choong Kuo Hsiang	Suite 37 Pantai Medical Centre, 8 Jalan Bukit Pantai, Bangsar	03 2283 1411
Dr Gunasegaran PT Rajan	Suite G21 Damansara Specialist Hospital, 119 Jalan SS20/10 Damansara Utama, PJ	03 7722 2692
Dr Jean Woo	Suite 217 Gleneagles Intan Medical Centre, 282 Jalan Ampang	03 4257 7288
Dr Ravi Chandran	Suite 202 Gleneagles Intan Medical Centre, 282 Jalan Ampang	03 2457 7500
Dr Theresa Chow	Suite 606 Gleneagles Intan Medical Centre, 282 Jalan Ampang	03 4253 4460
Dr Thomas Ng	Ground Floor, Pantai Medical Centre, 8 Jalan Bukit Pantai, Bangsar	03 2282 7395
Klinik Pakar Wanita Hartamas	4-1 Jalan 31/70A, Desa Sri Hartamas	03 2300 1990

Paediatrics

Most expats see a paediatrician at one of the private hospitals. Some paediatricians also consult at their own clinics and this can be convenient if you don't live close to a big private hospital. If you have medical insurance that covers outpatient care, paediatrician visits should be covered, but many policies do not cover vaccinations and these can be quite pricey.

It's important that you're happy with your child's doctor so if you're not, feel free to try someone else. It's not unusual for parents to try two or three doctors before finally settling on one they really get on with. Word of mouth can be very useful in finding someone who suits your culture and personal preferences; you can also try contacting the ibu family resource group (www.ibufamily.org) for a list of paediatricians other expats have used.

The Malaysian vaccination schedule may be different from that in your home country due to local incidence of disease. A child born in Malaysia needs to be protected against the diseases he or she may encounter here. Paediatricians are usually happy to discuss any differences with you and will take your wishes into account. The most common differences are that the tuberculosis vaccine (BCG) is commonly given at or around birth and that Hepatitis B is a routine vaccination.

MMR is usually given as a single injection. If you would like to have your child immunised separately for each disease, you should discuss this with your paediatrician. In the private healthcare system there is more flexibility than is often the case in government-funded systems such as the NHS in the UK, so you can ask for extra vaccinations such as chicken pox or meningitis and your paediatrician will usually be happy to do them.

You may not find familiar brand names of medication for infants and young children in Malaysian pharmacies and many expats bring supplies with them from home. If in doubt, always check with a doctor before medicating your child. Some medications commonly available over the counter elsewhere (such as Infacol for colic symptoms) are not available in Malaysia.

Once your child starts mixing with other children at nursery, toddler group or playgroup, he or she is bound to pick up a few common illnesses. Apart from the usual coughs and colds, watch out for occasional outbreaks of chicken pox and hand, foot and mouth disease, a virus which causes fever and blisters on the tongue and mouth, palms of the hands and soles of the feet. Diarrhoea can be spread through poor hygiene at nurseries, so make sure your child learns to wash their hands properly after going to the toilet and before eating. Because of the heat, any illness involving diarrhoea or vomiting is potentially serious because of the risk of dehydration. Give your child plenty of water or electrolyte solution to drink and take them to the doctor or hospital if the illness is severe.

Be warned that many doctors, including paediatricians, run their surgeries on a first come first served basis. This can result in very long waits. Call first to check and try to arrive towards the beginning or end of consulting hours to minimise the waiting time.

Paediatricians

Name	Address	Area	Phone
Dato' Dr Iean Hamzah Sendut	Room 318 Gleneagles Intan Medical Centre 282 Jalan Ampang	Ampang	03 4253 4373
Dato' Dr Vernon Lee	Suite 608, Gleneagles Intan Medical Centre 282 Jalan Ampang	Ampang	03 4251 2648
Dr Ananda Dharmalingham	Suite 515, Gleneagles Intan Medical Centre 282 Jalan Ampang	Ampang	03 4251 1022
Dr Azizi, Dr Matthew, Dr Nordin	Ground Floor Damansara Specialist Hospital 119 Jalan SS20/10, Damansara Utama	Petaling Jaya	03 7722 2692
Dr Chin Yoon Hiap	Suite 24, Pantai Medical Centre, 8 Bukit Pantai	Bangsar	03 2296 0402
Dr Eric Lee	Suite A303, Pantai Medical Centre 8 Jalan Bukit Pantai	Bangsar	03 2296 0734
Dr Lam Shih Kwong	Room 5, Megah Medical Specialist Group 79 Jalan SS23/15	Petaling Jaya	03 7803 1212
Dr Lim Miin Kand	Suite 109-110, Gleneagles Intan Medical Centre 282 Jalan Ampang	Ampang	03 4251 9333
Dr Patrick Chan	Suite 712, Gleneagles Intan Medical Centre 282 Jalan Ampang	Ampang	03 4252 8712
Dr Tan Teong Wong	Room 206 Sunway Medical Centre 5 Jalan Lagoon Selatan, Bandar Sunway	Petaling Jaya	03 7491 2606
Klinik Kanak Kanak	42 Jalan Datuk Sulaiman	TTDI (Taman Tun Dr Ismail)	03 7732 3812
Klinik Kanak-Kanak Tay	1st Floor, #16/1 Jalan 31/70A Desa Sri Hartamas	Sri Hartamas	03 2300 0380

Children With Disabilities

If your child has a disability, you may find that you have to do a lot of the leg work yourself to access medical care, education and therapy that meet your child's needs. There's no formal liaison between different service providers and you will almost certainly be entirely dependent on the private sector for your needs. Your child's doctor should be your first point of contact for information on what is available locally for your child.

Children With Disabilities

If your child has a disability, or you are concerned in any way about their development, you should ask their paediatrician for advice. A range of therapies, services and support is offered, mostly by the private sector and NGOs. The website www.disabilitymalaysia.com is an excellent resource with links to many specialist organisations. See Disabilities p.19.

Dentists & Orthodontists

Dental care is widely available and generally good value with a high standard of care. Prices vary widely with dentists based at hospitals being more expensive. A full range of dental services are offered, including orthodontics for adults and children, cosmetic dentistry and whitening treatments. As with doctors, many dentists have trained overseas and speak excellent English. Unless there is an apparent problem, most children should have a first dental check up at around 3 years old when all the first teeth are present. Good dentists for children include the Yee Dental Surgery at Bangsar Shopping Centre, Wong Dental Clinic in the city centre and Dr Kartina Stephens at Gleneagles.

Dental Matters (www.dentalmatters.com) is open seven days a week, and right up until 22:00 on weekday evenings, so should be able to see you should you have any dental emergency. If they are closed and you need help urgently, try calling their mobile number, 019 238 5148.

Not all insurance policies cover dental treatment, but some employers will reimburse the costs of essential dental work.

Dentists & Orthodontists

Chai Dental and Implant Centre	59 Jalan Bangkung	Bangsar	03 2094 6882
Damansara Orthodontic Clinic	Level 3, FIMA Building, Plaza Damansara	Bukit Damansara	03 2093 6160
Dental Matters	7A Tingkat 1, Lorong Ara Kiri Satu Lucky Garden	Bangsar	03 2092 1002
Dr Kartina Stephens	Suite 713 Gleneagles Intan Medical Centre, 282 Jalan Ampang	Ampang	03 4251 4988
Dr Perlin Loke	6th Floor, Wisma Perintis, Jalan Dungun	Bukit Damansara	03 2094 6088
Mont Kiara Specialist Dental Clinic	5-03 Block B, Plaza Mont Kiara	Mont Kiara	03 6203 1061
Twin Towers Medical Centre Dental Clinic	4th Floor, Suria KLCC	KLCC	03 2382 3503
Wong Dental Clinic	31 Jalan Medan Tuanku	City Centre	03 2698 9530
Yee Dental Surgery	S2 Bangsar Shopping Centre, Jalan Maarof	Bangsar	03 2095 1102

Opticians & Ophthalmologists

Most shopping malls will have at least one optician who can perform eye testing and sell glasses, prescription sunglasses and contact lenses. Popular opticians include England Optical (branches at KLCC, Bangsar Shopping Centre, Great Eastern Mall), Better Vision in City Square, and Supreme Optical in Sungei Wang Plaza. You'll also find opticians at hospitals as well as ophthalmologists offering more specialist care. Contact

Opticians & Ophthalmologists

Arthur's Eye Care Centre	29 Jalan SS2/75	Petaling Jaya	03 7876 3848
Better Vision	1st Floor, City Square Centre, Jalan Tun Razak	Ampang	03 2161 4137
Dr Ho Hong Bing	Pantai Medical Centre, 8 Jalan Bukit Pantai	Bangsar	03 2296 0741
Dr Tan	Twin Towers Medical Centre, 4th Floor Suria KLCC	KLCC	03 2382 3500
Supreme Optical	LG Floor, Sungei Wang Plaza, Jalan Sultan Ismail	City Centre	03 2148 7893
Tun Hussein Onn National Eye Hospital (THONEH)	Lorong Utara B	Petaling Jaya	03 7956 1911
Vista Laser Eye Centre	101 Block B Phileo Damansara 2	Petaling Jaya	03 7956 1415

lenses are widely available and you can buy solution from pharmacies. See Eyewear in the Shopping section (p.280) for more options.

Lasik surgery to correct short sightedness is becoming increasingly popular, with clinics springing up in shopping malls offering great deals. As with any kind of elective surgery, you should consider the procedure carefully beforehand and consult a doctor you trust before going ahead. Lasik surgery is also available at the major private hospitals and at the Tun Hussein Onn National Eye Hospital in Petaling Jaya. This is also the best place to go to if you need specialist eye treatment.

If you're worried about your child's sight, consult your paediatrician and ask them to recommend an optician or ophthalmologist who is experienced in treating children.

Cosmetic Treatment & Surgery

Cosmetic surgery is becoming increasingly popular in Malaysia, both among expats and the local population. Some hospitals even court the medical tourism market for cosmetic procedures. Sadly cosmetic treatment is poorly regulated and there have been some high-profile cases where operations have gone tragically wrong. Always use a reputable hospital or clinic, get a word of mouth referral whenever possible and research treatments thoroughly before agreeing to anything. Popular treatments include laser surgery to remove pigmentation or scars, botox for wrinkles, face lifts and liposuction. If you're not keen to go down the surgical route, many spas offer a variety of peeling, microdermabrasion, body wraps and cellulite treatments.

Cosmetic Treatment & Surgery			
Dr Benjamin George	Suite 706 Gleneagles Intan Medical Centre, 282 Jalan Ampang	Ampang	03 4252 5755
Dr Kim Tan	Suite 3802 Pantai Medical Centre 8 Jalan Bukit Pantai	Bangsar	03 2283 1459
Kayshaa Plastic Laser and Cosmetic Surgery	31-11 The Boulevard	Mid Valley	03 2282 9811
Promenade Plastic Surgery Centre	Megan Phileo Promenade, Jalan Tun Razak	City Centre	03 2166 5661

Alternative Therapies

A wide variety of alternative therapies is available in KL. Historically this is a result of the different ethnicities and cultural groups that make up Malaysian society bringing their traditional healing practices with them. More recently, there has been a trend towards popular therapies being adopted by people of many different cultural backgrounds, and this has made them more accessible to expats. Reflexology has proved exceptionally popular and is available in many neighbourhoods , particularly those with a large Chinese population. The reflexology practitioner applies pressure to your foot to relieve symptoms manifesting themselves in a particular part of the body. There is a 'map' of the foot showing which areas correspond to which body part. Reflexology isn't for the fainthearted – traditional therapists operate on the principle that you have to pass your pain threshold to experience any real benefit! An experienced practioner will inform you about the worst excesses of your dissolute lifestyle just by looking at and touching your feet and recommend ways you could treat your body more kindly.

Acupressure & Acupuncture

Acupressure treatments such as shiatsu are available at some spas. Energy Day Spa (p.272) has experienced shiatsu therapists, with treatments available at their Ampang and Mont'Kiara branches. Both acupuncture and acupressure treatments are available from Oran Kivity at her clinic in Bangsar. Bill Deng is an experienced Shiatsu therapist practising in KL. Klic offers acupuncture by a qualified Chinese practitioner at its city centre clinic.

Tummy Tuck Tourism ◄

Although Malaysians aren't as body conscious as their Thai and Singaporean neighbours, some KL hospitals have jumped on to the medical tourism bandwagon. Much of this work is cosmetic and tourists are being offered new breasts and slimmer thighs as well as a tan. Rumour has it that the newest private hospital in town is strongly promoting its cosmetic surgery department locally and overseas.

Aromatherapy

Aromatherapy is widely available at many spas in KL. Individual spas blend their own unique oils, often based on local plants and herbs with traditional healing properties. Oils are also widely available for home use. For a spa with a strong emphasis on Malaysian traditions, try Vila Manja, located just off Jalan Ampang. Aromatherapy isn't commonly seen as a treatment therapy in Malaysia, more as a pampering or de-stressing treat. For a spa listing, see p.272.

Homeopathy

Homeopathic treatments are readily available in KL. They are often linked to a particular healing philosophy such as Chinese herbal medicine or ayurveda. Try the Homeopathic Medical Centre in Kampung Baru, or the Homeopathy Holistic Centre in Petaling Jaya. Klic has a Chinese Herbal Medicine practitioner.

Reflexology

This very popular treatment is available at many locations around KL, from neighbourhood shopfronts with just a few chairs to reflexology spas with massage chairs, herbal foot baths and pampering lotions. Try Asianel at Starhill Gallery for a top of the line experience, or Siam Bodyworks' Thai-trained therapists at their branches at Mid Valley and Jalan Ampang. Alternatively take a stroll around the Jalan Telawi area of Bangsar, down Bukit Bintang or around Chinatown to see a host of small places all offering reflexology.

Alternative Therapies

Reflexology	
Asianel Reflexology Spa	03 2142 1397
Bill Deng	016 209 8040
Energy Day Spa	03 4256 8833
Homeopathic Medical Centre	03 2692 6549
Homeopathy Holistic Centre	016 683 8019
KL Integrated Heathcare Centre	03 2166 1599
Oran Kivity	012 934 8040
Siam Bodyworks	03 2166 9351
Vila Manja	03 2161 5418

Acupressure & Acupuncture	
Bill Deng	016 209 8040
KL Integrated Heathcare Centre	03 2166 1599
Oran Kivity	012 934 8040
Samkyya	03 2287 2111

Aromatherapy	
Cah'Ya Aromatherapy	03 6203 4500
Energy Day Spa	03 4256 8833
Evlyn	012 614 7508

Healing Meditation	
Lightworks	03 2143 2766
Manjushri Kadampa Centre	03 6272 1098
Yogashakti	03 4252 4714

Homeopathy	
Dr Saw	03 7710 2678
Dr Wong	03 2094 1335

Reflexology & Massage Therapy	
Asianel Reflexology Spa	03 2142 1397
Blind Massage	03 2274 0813
Energy Day Spa	03 6201 7833
Samkyya	03 2287 2111
Siam Bodyworks	03 2282 0233

Physiotherapy

Most private hospitals have a physiotherapy department for post-operative rehabilitation and injuries. You may need a referral from a doctor at the hospital before you can get an appointment with the physiotherapy department. Services offered at hospitals range from general physiotherapy to specialist neurological rehabilitation following a stroke. There are also some specialist clinics providing physiotherapy and one highly recommended clinic specialising in sports medicine.

Physiotherapy

Dr Marc Daniel	18G Blok C, Jalan 9/11 6B, Sri Desa Entrepreneur's Park, Off Jalan Kuchai Lama	Mid Valley	03 7981 2142
Jireh Physiotherapy Centre	6 Jalan 8/1 Jalan Sungai Jernih	Petaling Jaya	03 7958 4276
Kinesis Care	P-1-16 Plaza Damas	Sri Hartamas	03 6201 5259
KL Sports Medicine Centre	Wisma Perentis, Jalan Dungun	Bukit Damansara	03 2096 1033
Oasis (Ampang Puteri Hospital)	1 Jalan Mamanda 9	Ampang	03 4272 7199

Back Treatment

If you suffer from back problems, a chiropractor or osteopath may be able to help. Chiropractors use spinal adjustment and other soft tissue and joint manipulation to treat back, neck and joint pain. Osteopaths employ several different manual manipulation treatments together with advice on diet, posture and occupational matters to treat musculoskeletal disorders including spinal symptoms such as lower back pain. There are several popular chiropractors and osteopaths in KL, and some treat babies and children as well as adults.

Back Treatment

Bangsar Chiropractic	4-1 Jalan Telawi 2	Bangsar	03 2282 9975
Contour Health	B-06-08 Plaza Mont Kiara	Mont Kiara	03 6201 5168
Damansara Chiropractor	205 1st Floor, Block A Phileo Damansara	Petaling Jaya	03 7660 5733
Green Chiropractic Centre	257 Jalan Tun Sambanthan	Little India	03 2272 5318
KL Integrated Heathcare Centre	A-5-2 Wisma HB, Megan Avenue II Jalan Yap Kwan Seng	City Centre	03 2166 1599
Natural Harmony (osteopathy)	8-5 Jalan Batai	Damansara Heights	03 2094 1335

Nutritionists & Slimming

Slimming is big business in KL, with specialist clinics offering the holy grail of weight loss without exercising or feeling hungry. Amazing before and after pictures and celebrity endorsements fill their windows together with details of their latest promotional packages. If that sounds too good to be true and you're after a more traditional approach, registered dietician Mrs Rekha Naidu offers workshops and one-to-one counselling, and some expat asociations have weight loss support groups. If you have digestive disorders you could try consulting a gastroenterologist at one of the larger hospitals, and Mrs Naidu can help with suitable diets.

Nutritionists & Slimming

Body Perfect	Ground Floor, The Boulevard, Mid Valley	03 2938 8883
Chu (personal trainer)	Damansara area only	012 373 3088
Esthetika Slimming Beauty Centre	33 Jalan Mamanda 7, Ampang Point	03 2166 3551
Jenny (personal trainer)	na	012 381 7313
Marie France Bodyline	Level 4, Suria KLCC	03 2161 1895
Mrs Rekha Naidu (registered dietician)	na	03 7729 5216

Psychiatrists

A list of psychiatrists in KL can be found on www. psychiatry-malaysia. org. Psychiatrists recommended by expats are listed below.

Counselling & Therapy

For cultural reasons, issues surrounding mental health aren't discussed as openly in Malaysia as they often are in western societies, although help is available for people suffering from mental health problems. Clinics don't formally specialise in specific problems such as eating disorders or depression, but you will find that some are more experienced than others in these areas. It's difficult to find effective help for serious psychiatric disorders and you might have to consider returning to your home country for treatment.

Many expats experience mild depression as a result of culture shock after moving to a new city. If you find yourself feeling depressed, calling the Befrienders helpline on 03 7956 8144 can be a good place to start getting help. Doctors at general clinics may prescribe anti-depressants or suggest other ways to help alleviate your depression. Exercise, yoga and meditation can all help you to achieve a more positive frame of mind, and socialising can help. Contact one of the expat associations to find out if there are any activities you can join in, or try socialising with work colleagues if you don't know many people in the city. Some people find maintaining close contact

Counsellors & Psychologists

Name	Area	Phone	Speciality
Access Counseling Services	Ampang	03 4106 7307	General
Agape Counseling Centre	Petaling Jaya	03 7785 5955	Emotional and family problems
Coralie Leong	Ampang	03 4257 6607	Psycho-educational assessment
Dr Brian Scott	KLCC	03 2382 2000	Clinical psychologist
Dr Kana Kanagasingham	Sri Hartamas	03 2300 6077	Children and teenagers
Dr Sandra Chin Beek Yuen	City Centre	03 2161 6261	Teenagers and adults
Gleneagles Intan Charter Behavioural Health Services	Jalan Ampang	03 4255 2960	Emotional and behavioural problems for children, adolescents and adults
Shantini R Vanniasingham	Bangsar	03 2092 4969	Clinical psychologist, child and family

with friends and relatives at home via phone or email helpful, while others find it's counterproductive as it prevents them from getting fully involved in life in KL. There aren't any formal organisations for marriage or family therapy, but some counsellors may help with this. If you're worried about your child's behaviour, their school or paediatrician should be the first point of contact. If they feel that more help is needed, they can refer you to a recommended counsellor.

Psychiatrists

Dr Fadzilman	Ampang	03 2161 6729
Dr Lim Chee Min	City Centre	03 2166 2241
Dr Rabin Gonzaga	Jalan Ampang	03 4255 2971

Addiction

Alcoholics Anonymous meets at two locations in KL, call 03 2078 0564 for details. Al Anon meetings for relatives and friends of alcoholics are also available; call 03 2031 1223. Narcotics Anonymous meets at St Andrew's Church, call 03 2031 1223.

Support Groups

Although life in KL certainly has its frustrations, it's not considered a very challenging place to live for expats. There's the inevitable homesickness and culture shock, but once this has passed most expats enjoy their life here. There are no

Addiction Counselling & Rehabilitation

Al-Anon	03 2031 1223	www.standrewschurch.org.my
Alcoholics Anonymous	03 2078 0564	www.aakualalumpur.com
Narcotics Anonymous	012 420 3110	na

Support Groups

Joining a national association, expat organisation or cultural group can be a help in settling in and making new friends. Many of the national associations are open to people of all nationalities; if you live in Ampang you may find you get more out of joining the American Association that's located in your area, rather than your national association that's located in Bangsar. See Social Groups (p.257) in Activities for more details.

specific support groups for expats, but several groups exist to support people who are coping with illness or addiction and these are open to expats. You may find that the conversation isn't always in English, as people will use the language they feel most comfortable in when talking about feelings and issues they might find hard to express. Support groups exist for pregnant women, breastfeeding and new mothers. Ibu (www.ibufamily.org) can give information on these and other support groups for specific parenting issues including adoption, multiple births and bilingualism. The Befrienders operate a 24 hour helpline open to anyone who is going through a personal crisis.

Support Groups

Al-Anon	03 2031 1223
Alcoholics Anonymous	03 2078 0564
Amanita Breast Cancer Support	03 2162 8215
CancerLink Foundation	03 7956 9199
ibu Family Resource Group	03 2094 2234
MMA Aids Counselling Line	03 4045 4033
Narcotics Anonymous	03 2031 1223
National Cancer Society of Malaysia	03 2698 7351
Pink Triangle (counselling on sexuality)	03 4044 5455
The Befrienders	03 7956 8144

School buildings

Education

For the vast majority of expat children in KL, education takes place at one of the many international schools, although a few foreigners choose to home school their children. Generally speaking, non-Malaysian children may not enrol in government schools. Fees at international schools are quite high, so research your needs in advance, and factor the cost into any salary negotiations. International schools can have long waiting lists too; if you arrive in KL in the middle of an academic year you may find it impossible to get a place in the school of your choice, so register as far in advance as you can. As people come and go all the time, you may not have to wait long for a place but the experience can be stressful. Some families prefer to wait until the start of the new school year before joining the working parent in KL.

The Malaysian school year follows the calendar year, and runs from January to November. Children start primary school at the age of 6 or 7, and before this most will go to a private nursery school or kindergarten. Education isn't compulsory, so there's no minimum leaving age; secondary education finishes at 18. The school week runs from Monday to Friday, and some schools hold extra classes or activities on Saturdays. International schools usually follow the school year of the national curriculum they teach, but take Malaysian public holidays. Many international schools have an 'early years' department, taking children from age 3, and some stop at 16 but most go up to 18. Fees range from RM8,000 to more than RM50,000, depending on the school and age of the child, and there are usually extra charges such as enrolment fees. Class sizes are generally kept quite small; around 18 to 22 children is the norm. Many schools offer clubs and activities after school, but don't provide wrap-around care so working parents will have to make their own childcare arrangements.

When you're ready to enrol your child, bring their school reports, transcripts, records and certificates if they're older and have already started school, as the admissions department will want to see them. Some schools may also ask to see vaccination records or ask for a medical. You may need to show proof of your (or your child's) nationality at some schools.

Many Malaysians choose to go overseas to pursue post-secondary studies, with Australia, New Zealand, the UK and the US being popular choices. This trend has resulted in several international universities setting up campuses in KL to capture a bigger share of this lucrative market. In addition there are many colleges offering external degrees from overseas universities, as well as Malaysia's own universities and colleges. Most expats tend to pursue post-secondary education outside Malaysia, usually in their country of origin.

KL has become a popular centre for English language learning, attracting students from across Asia and the Middle East. International students can also be found in Malaysia's universities and colleges.

Evening classes and further learning opportunities for adults are fairly thin on the ground. Studying a language is a popular option, as is learning to teach English as a foreign language. Internationally recognised Montessori nursery teaching courses are available at a few colleges. You may also be able to pursue a distance learning qualification from an overseas institution.

Nurseries & Pre-Schools

Malaysian children start primary school at 6, but for children under this age there are a wide variety of privately run nursery schools, kindergartens and preschools offering early years education. These are often referred to as taskas or tadikas, or both. A taska is for children up to 4 years old, and will generally offer a play-based learning experience. Tadikas are for children aged 3 to 7, and essentially act as formal preparation for starting primary school, teaching basic literacy and maths in a structured way. Many are popular with expats and people tend to choose a school in their residential area. Programmes based on the Montessori philosophy are very popular, although they are often structured more formally than they would be in Europe or the US. Bilingual (English/Bahasa Malaysia or English/Mandarin) programmes are also popular, and Reggio Emilia is available too. Preschool or early-years programmes at international schools follow the national curriculum or educational philosophy of the institution's home country.

Schools at this level do not have to be licensed or inspected, and staff at local schools may not have formal qualifications in childcare or education. Staff at international schools will usually have the same qualifications as they would in schools in their home country, and will usually be expats.

Visit any school you are interested in and observe for yourself how the staff interact with the children, what approach they use and what kind of activities are offered to the children. Ask around for recommendations, or get a list of schools in your area from ibu (www.ibufamily.org), an organisation that offers help and support to families in KL. As well as providing information it has playgroups every weekday, which you can attend with your child. These are a good alternative if you find the local nurseries too structured, as it allows your child to interact with others and develop social skills in an informal environment.

Many schools are located in converted residential buildings and children will have access to a garden for outside play. School fees for local preschools are very reasonable, from about RM750 per term, and the staff to child ratio is good.

1 Lorong Steiarasa
Bukit Damansara
 Kerinchi
Map 6 D1

Big Blue Marble
03 2095 6527
Big Blue Marble exposes children to Bahasa Malaysia, Mandarin and English through play and fun activities. As you would expect, the children come from a wide range of nationalities. This nursery is consistently praised for having a warm and caring environment. Classes run from 09:00 to 12:30.

21-3 Jalan 15/48A
Sentulraya Blvd
Sentul
 Ampang Park
Map 9 E4

Building Blocks
03 4044 1397 | *http://buildingblocksmalaysia.org*
This small school, for children aged 2 to 4 years, is based at the American Association of Malaysia. Building Blocks offers an American-style preschool education based on learning through play, and follows the US school calendar. Open from 09:30 to 12:30.

40 Jalan Bangkung
Bukit Bandaraya
Bangsar
Bangsar
Map 6 E1

Child's Playworks
03 2093 9592
The emphasis here is on play, and with a teacher to child ratio of 1:5, there's plenty of individual attention to help children develop. Child's Playworks accepts pupils from the age of 1 to 6 years. It is popular with expats who prefer a less structured approach to early-years education. Open from 08:30 to 12:30.

137

Children's Discovery House

Ground Floor
i-Zen @ Kiara II
1 Jalan Kiara
Mont Kiara
Map 4 D3

03 6203 7001

Children's Discovery takes youngsters from 18 months to 6 years, and the focus here is two-fold: for younger children the emphasis is on play-based learning, with more structured activities for the older ones. The school is spacious and has an indoor play area to beat the KL heat.

The Children's House

7 Jalan Ampang Hilir
Jalan Ampang
🚇 *Ampang Park*
Map 7 D4

03 4257 7273

The Children's House is a small group of nursery schools that uses the Montessori method of teaching, and has other branches in Damansara and Bangsar. The Ampang branch has a toddler department and takes children from 18 months, while the other branches start at 2 years old. Children can attend all branches until the age of 6. The Children's House is very popular with expats and as such is one of the more expensive schools, with fees around RM1,500 per term.

Chiltern House

123 Jalan
Bukit Pantai
Bangsar
🚇 *Kerinchi*
Map 6 E2

03 2095 5500

Chiltern House is a new school offering a bilingual education in Mandarin and English for children aged 3 to 6 years. The school is well equipped with a nice outdoor play area and is popular with both locals and expats. It opens from 08:30 to 12:30.

Magic Years

1 Jalan Beluntas
Medan Damansara
Bukit Damansara
🚇 *Kerinchi*
Map 6 D1

03 2095 2496

A popular school, Magic Years offers optional after-hours care until 17:00, which makes it an attractive option for working parents. It takes children from the age of 18 months to 5 years and follows the Montessori method. Normal school hours are from 09:00 to 13:00.

Sunshine Rabbits

14A Jalan Chong
Khoon Lin
Ukay Heights
Ampang
Map 5 F3

03 4251 1335

Sunshine Rabbits is a small Montessori school that's very popular with expats living in the area. It takes a maximum of 24 children, aged 2 to 6 years, who learn and play together. There's an emphasis on good manners and learning to get along with each other.

Tadika Sunbeam

53 Jalan Terasek
Bangsar
🚇 *Bangsar*
Map 6 E2

03 2287 7899

This is currently the only school in Kuala Lumpur offering the Reggio Emilia integrated learning method. It offers extra activities,

Nurseries & Pre-Schools		
Blue Daisy	Mont Kiara	03 6203 1669
Buzzy Bee	Ampang	03 4251 6278
Kidscool	Mont Kiara	03 6201 7350
Kindicare	Ampang	03 4256 7591
My Little Home	Bukit Damansara	03 2093 5078

including cooking and Mandarin, outside normal school hours. The school accepts children from 2 to 5 years, with a 5:1 child to staff ratio. Normal school hours are 09:00 to 13:00.

Primary & Secondary Schools

Since many international schools are full and operate waiting lists, you may find your choice of schools in KL very limited. If you're already living in KL and your child is reaching school age, you'll have the luxury of visiting the various schools before deciding which to choose, although even at this stage long waiting lists are common. Some schools operate preferential admissions policies based on nationality, language spoken by the child or parents, or the type of school previously attended. It can also help if either parent is a former pupil of the school or if there are siblings already attending. Check the admissions policy with each school, as it can dramatically affect your child's chances of getting a place.

In all circumstances, it's best to register with a school or schools as early as possible, before arriving in KL. If you do arrive after the start of the school year and find that there are no places, you may have to home school until a place becomes available. Schools may be willing to offer help and guidance in these circumstances, or even recommend a tutor, but this situation is far from ideal.

The following school systems are available in KL: American, Australian, British, French, German, Indian, Indonesian, International Baccalaureate, International Islamic and Japanese, and each follows the school year of their home country. School fees are not cheap and can add up if you have a large family. Some schools cost up to RM50,000 per child per year, but others can be cheaper. Generally the more expensive schools have expat teachers and better facilities, although not always. Schools don't offer scholarships or rebates on the fees, so either you or your company will pay.

Schools take advantage of the cultural opportunities offered by their Malaysian setting, celebrating the festivals of the country's different communities and involving students in the world outside the classroom. Most schools admit pupils from a wide variety of national and cultural backgrounds so even if you stick to the educational system of your home country, your children's education will have a distinctly international flavour. Traffic in KL being what it is, most families try to live reasonably close to the school their children attend. Schools have bus services to popular neighbourhoods so if this is an important factor check bus routes first before deciding where to live. Schools tend to start and finish early to avoid the worst of the congestion.

All students over the age of 6 are required to have a valid student's pass. Your child's school will help you to apply for this.

The Alice Smith School (Primary)

2 Jalan Bellamy
Nr Royal Palace
🚇 *Tun Sambanthan*
Map 7 B2

03 2148 3674 | *www.alice-smith.edu.my*

Alice Smith offers preschool and primary education based on the British national curriculum. Located in KL city, a short drive from many popular suburbs, the school has a good reputation and strong academic results. It is staffed by UK-trained teachers and locally trained teaching assistants. Excellent resources and facilities at the primary campus include libraries, a swimming pool, gym, playing fields, music and performing arts rooms, plus a variety of after-school clubs and activities. Fees start at around RM30,000 per year.

The Alice Smith School (Secondary)

3 Jalan Equine
Taman Equine
43300 Seri Kembangan
🚇 *Sungai Besi*
Map 1 B4

03 9543 3688 | *www.alice-smith.edu.my*

Offers secondary education based on the British national curriculum on a new greenfield campus about 40 minutes' drive from central KL. The secondary school places a strong emphasis on academic excellence, but also provides good facilities for creative and expressive arts, sport and social development. Teachers are predominantly UK trained, and top facilities on the spacious campus include specialised science labs, ICT suites, a library, a design centre, playing fields, a 50m swimming pool and a gym. Fees start at around RM40,000 per year.

Australian International School Malaysia

22 Jalan Anggerik
The MINES Resort City
🚇 *Serdang*
Map 1 C4

03 8943 0622 | *www.aism.edu.my*

The Australian International School provides a 'school away from home' for Aussie expats. Starting from early-years education (for children aged 3 and up) through to year 12, the school has age-appropriate activities and curriculums for all students. It follows the Australian Board of Studies NSW curriculum. The school's facilities are diverse, with science and IT labs, design and art rooms, a music room, large swimming pool, gym, playing field, and a well-stocked library. Fees range from RM18,000 to RM42,000 per year.

ELC International School

Lot 3664
Jalan Sierramas Barat
Sungai Buloh
🚇 *Sungai Buloh*
Map 1 A2

03 6156 5001 | www.elc.edu.my
The school is about 30 minutes' drive from KL and is located in an up-and-coming suburb. Following the British national curriculum for ages 3 to 16, ELC caps enrolment at 600, and has a good student-to-staff ratio. Classes normally have 18 children or less. The campus has plenty of green space and good facilities for sport including a large sports field, courts for volleyball, basketball and badminton, and a swimming pool. Fees are lower than at some of the city centre schools, ranging from RM8,145 to RM19,830 per year.

Garden International School

16 Jalan Kiara 3
Mont Kiara
Map 4 C3

03 6209 6888 | www.gardenschool.edu.my
A large British curriculum school located in the popular Month Kiara suburb, Garden International offers education for expat children aged 3 to 18 on a single site. Extensive facilities support all areas of the curriculum and a wide range of after-school clubs and activities are offered. Fees range from RM22,000 per year in the nursery to RM40,000 per year in years 12 and 13.

International School of Kuala Lumpur (Middle & High School Campus)

Jalan Kolam Air
Ampang
Map 5 F4

03 4259 5600 | www.iskl.edu.my
ISKL's middle and high school campus is situated in the heart of the popular Ampang residential district. Catering for children aged 11-18, the school provides American courses, as well as the International Baccalaureate for the 16 to 18 age group. ESL tuition is provided to students who have difficulty accessing the curriculum in English. Facilities at the Ampang campus include a swimming pool, library, computer labs, and dance and drama studios. Annual tuition fees for the high school are RM53,160.

International School of Kuala Lumpur (Elementary Campus)

Jalan Melawati 3
Taman Melawati
Ampang
Map 1 C2

03 4104 3000 | www.iskl.edu.my
Established more than 40 years ago, ISKL elementary school offers an American education for ages 3 to 10 (up to grade 5) at its well-resourced campus in the Melawati area of Ampang. Students come from more than 50 countries, and there is a strong English as a second language programme. Facilities include a gym, swimming pool, library and playground, and there are specialist teachers for art, music, physical education and modern languages. Fees start at around RM26,000 per year.

Mont'Kiara International School

22 Jalan Mont Kiara
Mont Kiara
Map 4 D3

03 2093 8604 | www.mkis.edu.my
This relatively new international school opened in 1994 in the modern residential suburb of Mont Kiara. It offers education from ages 3 to 18 on a single purpose-built campus, including US high school diplomas and the International Baccalaureate, as well as extensive ESL support. Its 870 students represent 49 different nationalities. Parental involvement is encouraged, and mums and dads play a large part in organising clubs and activities. Sporting facilities include a swimming pool, dance studio, gym, weights room, climbing wall and sports field, all on site. Annual fees start at around RM22,000.

Jalan Kerja Ayer Lama ◄
Ampang Jaya
Ampang
🚇 **Jelatek**
Map 5 F4

Mutiara International Grammar School

03 4252 1452 | *www.migs.edu.my*

Mutiara follows the British national curriculum from foundation stage (age 3) to IGCSE (age 16). There's a strong emphasis on academics, with internal examinations held three times a year on top of external examinations for key stage assessment and IGCSE. A variety of clubs and after-school activities are offered to suit different age groups, and the school has a gym, library, computer room, science labs and an art room. A bus service is provided to main residential areas in KL.

University & Higher Education

Most expat students travel abroad, usually to their home country, for higher education, but it is possible for a foreign resident to attend university in Malaysia. To do so you'll need a 'student pass visa', which your educational institution applies for on your behalf. Students who study at postgraduate level are allowed to bring their immediate family to live with them in Malaysia. Family members will be issued with 'social visit' passes, valid for the same length of time as the student pass (see Visas, p.48).

KL is home to Malaysia's largest and most prestigious public university, Universiti Malaya. International students who do not speak Bahasa Malaysia must take a language course. Private universities such as Limkokwing, KDU and HELP offer a variety of degrees and diplomas, often in partnership with universities overseas. A few international universities have set up campuses in KL, including Monash from Australia and Nottingham from the UK.

Most final school qualifications offered by international schools, including A Levels, International Baccalaureate, US high school diplomas and Australian HSC will be accepted for entry into local universities.

Adult Education

Adults can apply to study at any of the universities mentioned above. Many degree and masters courses are offered on a part-time basis, although classes for these are often held during the day, so you'll have to negotiate with your employer if you're working. Two open universities, the Open University Malaysia and Wawasan Open University are geared specifically towards working adults, and hold classes in the evenings and at weekends. If your field is specialised and you can't find a suitable course offered in Malaysia, a university from your home country that offers distance learning may be your best option. See Activities (p.214) for details of non-degree courses and classes.

SS22/41 ◄
Damansara Jaya
Petaling Jaya
🚇 **Kelana Jaya**
Map 6 A2

KDU College

03 7728 8123 | *www.kdu.edu.my*

KDU offers pre-university, degree and diploma courses for both full and part-time students. Degree courses are offered in association with partner universities overseas, and sometimes part of the course is completed at the partner institution. Partners include the University of Northumbria and Oxford Brookes University (both UK), and Murdoch University (Australia). Courses are offered in business, engineering, IT, law, tourism & hospitality and mass communications.

University & Higher Education

Help University College	Bukit Damansara	03 2094 2000	www.help.edu.my
Monash University Malaysia Campus	Petaling Jaya	03 5514 6000	www.monash.edu.my
Nottingham University Malaysia Campus	Selangor	03 8924 8000	www.nottingham.edu.my
Open University Malaysia	City Centre	03 2273 2002	www.oum.edu.my
Wawasan Open University	Ampang	03 9281 7323	www.wou.edu.my

23 Jalan Sultan Ismail
City Centre
🚇 *Sultan Ismail*
Map 11 B4

Limkokwing University of Creative Technology

03 2143 0005 | *www.limkokwing.edu.my*

Limkokwing is a private university with a contact centre in KL and a large modern campus out of town in Cyberjaya. It offers arts and social science courses at foundation, diploma, undergraduate and postgraduate levels. Courses concentrate on design, media, business and IT.

Jalan Universti
Petaling Jaya
🚇 *Universiti*
Map 6 D2

University of Malaya

03 7967 7022 | *www.um.edu.my*

Established in 1905, the University of Malaya is the country's top-ranking academic institution, offering undergaduate and postgraduate courses in the arts, sciences, social sciences, law, medicine and education, as well as an MBA programme. International students enrolling at the university will have to demonstrate their proficiency in Bahasa Malaysia, or take a compulsory language course. Science courses are taught primarily in English, but social science courses may be taught in Bahasa. The university occupies a huge campus on the borders of KL and Petaling Jaya, and has its own LRT station.

Special Needs Education

Educational facilities for children with special needs are thin on the ground in KL. Mild learning difficulties such as dyslexia may be accommodated within mainstream international schools, and some are able to provide more support than others. Contact schools directly to find out what help you can expect. Two learning centres cater for children with mild autistic spectrum disorders and ADHD, although most help seems to be targeted at younger children. Try The Learning Connection, which is run by an American teacher trained in special needs, or Sri Rafelsia, which supports children up to the age of 16. Some international schools are trying to rectify the lack of facilities by recruiting more teachers with special needs qualifications. Assistance in areas such as speech or occupational therapy may be available, so consult your child's school or paediatrician for a referral.

Local organisations set up to support people with specific disabilities, such as deaf and blind people, can be helpful, but some resources and materials may not be in English.

H-3-4 Plaza Damas
Jalan Hartamas 1
Sri Hartamas
Map 4 D3

Hilslearning

03 6201 5595 | *www.hilslearning.com*

Hilslearning provides consultation, assessment, training and therapy for children who are challenged by the mainstream school environment.

University

It works closely with schools to ensure children are supported in their regular classes. Run by an experienced expat teacher, this centre is highly recommended for children with mild learning difficulties including dyslexia, ADHD and Asperger's.

The Learning Connection

15C 12-5, Aspen Tower
Mont Kiara Pines
Jalan Mont Kiara
Mont Kiara
 Kerinchi
Map 4 D3

03 2094 5971 | *www.learningconnection.com.my*

Set up by Sara Brenneman, an experienced American special needs teacher, The Learning Connection is a small centre providing a special needs kindergarten for children aged 4 to 6 who require early intervention. For older children, one-to-one sessions are planned to take into account the child's specific areas of difficulty and to support mainstream schooling where necessary. The Learning Connection also runs a programme for children with attention deficit disorders.

Malaysian Association for the Blind

Kompleks MAB
Jalan Tebing
KL Sentral
Tun Sambanthan
Map 7 A2

03 2272 2677 | *www.mab.org.my*

Set up with the aim of giving blind people in Malaysia equal opportunities and the chance of living the same quality of life as sighted people, the Malaysian Association for the Blind can help put parents of blind and visually impaired children in touch with facilities and resources available in KL.

Pusat Majudiri Y for the Deaf

YMCA KL
95 Jalan Padang Belia
KL Sentral
Tun Sambanthan
Map 7 A2

03 2274 1439 | *www.ymcakl.com*

The YMCA-affiliated Pusat Majudiri Y for the Deaf provides a range of services for deaf people and their familes, including clubs for children and teenagers. It also has a support group for parents. Not specifically set up to cater for expats, so some resources may not be in English.

Sri Rafelsia

38-2 Jalan 24/70A
Desa Sri Hartamas
Sri Hartamas
Kerinchi
Map 4 A4

03 7710 0372 | *www.srirafelsia.com*

Sri Rafelsia provides learning support in group sessions for younger children (aged 2 to 8) with mild learning difficulties, and one-to-one sessions for older children and those with more severe problems. The organisation caters to children with mild to moderate learning difficulties such as developmental delay, hearing impairment, dyspraxia, dyslexia, downs syndrome and autism. Children can either attend the centre full time, or have after-school sessions to support them in mainstream schooling.

Learning Bahasa Malaysia
Other options **Language Schools** p.243

Although you can get by without learning any Bahasa Malaysia, it helps smooth your path in many situations if you can at least say a phrase of greeting or a few words. Most international schools include Bahasa Malaysia classes from primary school upwards as a second language, and many local nurseries will use both Bahasa Malaysia and English. Several language schools offer lessons, and many will come to your workplace if you can get a group together who are interested. If you're free during the day, some expat associations such as the ABWM and AAM run popular courses.

Learning Bahasa Malaysia

ALS	03 7804 4915	na
American Association of Malaysia	03 2142 0611	www.klamerican.com
Association of British Women in Malaysia (ABWM)	03 2095 4407	www.abwm.com.my
ICLS (Inter-Cultural Language School)	03 2144 2060	www.icls.com.my

Transportation

Other options **Getting Around** p.28, **Car** p.30

Getting around KL can be one of the biggest challenges to living here. The lack of a coherent strategy in the past has resulted in a poorly integrated transport network that can be very frustrating to use. You will probably find yourself using a car – either your own or a taxi – for most journeys around the city. The climate doesn't lend itself to walking, and pedestrians seem to be bottom of the heap when it comes to town planning.

Public transport is available but options are usually limited by where you live and work. Buses and the LRT network now come under a single operator, RapidKL, and there have been reports of improvements in services, especially bus feeder lines that connect neighbourhoods to LRT stations. A monorail line also runs through the city centre. The road system in KL takes some getting used to. The regular road network is supplemented by a series of toll roads, run by private companies under contract to the government. Parking can be a problem in all areas of KL and parking illegally on the street or double parking in car parks is common.

KTM Komuter

The national rail company KTM (www.ktmb.com.my) runs air-conditioned commuter (KTM Komuter) trains connecting outlying suburbs to KL. If you've chosen to live further out from the city centre where some of the international schools are located, you may find the train makes your commute quicker. Fares start at RM1, with most journeys costing under RM10. Neighbourhoods served by trains include Sungai Buloh, Taman Seputeh, Petaling Jaya, Subang Jaya and Kajang. Putrajaya is connected to KL by the KLIA Transit line. All Komuter lines pass through KL Sentral where you can connect to the LRT. Peak hour trains can be very crowded.

Taxi

Taxis are relatively cheap and are a popular option for commuters. The fare is RM2 for the first two kilometres and 10 sen for each further 200 metres. Fares haven't gone up for several years despite the rising price of fuel, so prices may change soon. Rather than flag down a taxi each morning many people prefer to make an arrangement with a regular taxi driver to pick them up. This can cost more but has the advantage of reliability. Ask around at work to find out if anyone else has a regular taxi – their driver will often be able to put you in touch with someone. You can also chat to the driver of any taxi you use to see if they are interested in taking you to work regularly. During rush hour many taxis will refuse to use the meter and demand inflated fixed prices for journeys. This is illegal but widely practised, and it's a matter of individual choice whether you get in and pay up or try another cab.

LRT art

Monorail

Running through the city centre from Titiwangsa to KL Sentral, the monorail (www.monorail.com.my) gives an excellent view of the city. It's useful for commuting if you work in the Bukit Bintang or Jalan Sultan Ismail area and for quick trips around the city centre, although connectivity to major residential areas isn't good. Fares range from RM1.20 to RM2.50, and you can use Touch 'n' Go to pay at the barriers. The monorail is quick – the journey from one end to the other takes about 20 minutes. The KL Sentral stop is a long walk from KL Sentral itself, so take this into account when planning a commute.

RapidKL LRT

Previously operated by two companies, Putra and Star, the Light Rail Transport (LRT) network was unified under RapidKL in 2004. It operates three lines: Kelana Jaya, Sri Petaling and Ampang. You can find maps and other information at www.rapidkl.com. my. The lines pass through the city centre and intersect at a single station, Masjid Jameck. You can connect to the monorail at Dang Wangi, Hang Tuah, KL Sentral and Titiwangsa stations, although some of these 'connections' involve a long walk. Some expats use the LRT to commute into the city centre, but many find themselves having to drive or take a taxi to the nearest station. Residential areas popular with expats that are served by LRT include those in the city centre, Bangsar, Petaling Jaya and parts of Ampang. Fares range from 70 sen to RM2.50 for a single journey; commuters can buy stored-value tickets to cut down on queuing, or a monthly travel pass which costs RM100 and covers travel on the entire LRT network. You can also use a Touch 'n' Go card to pay LRT fares by tapping it at the barrier. The advantage of commuting by LRT is speed – trains run every four minutes during peak times and you can get to Petaling Jaya from KLCC in about 25 minutes. The same journey could take well over an hour by road. The major disadvantage is overcrowding, although thankfully this hasn't reached the intolerable levels of cities like Tokyo.

Bus

Bus services within the city are run by RapidKL (www.rapidkl.com.my) and Metrobus. You can ride the extensive RapidKL bus network for RM2 for the whole day. Metrobus has a smaller network and you pay for each trip you make with fares ranging from 90 sen to RM2.50. Buses are not so popular with expat commuters since there are few bus lanes and they often get stuck in traffic. They are very crowded at peak times and traffic congestion can affect their reliability. Outside peak hours buses are handy for quick point-to-point trips, such as from Ampang to the city centre.

Traffic Updates ◄

A network of electronic signboards is going up around KL to give drivers real time information about traffic and road conditions. The only problem for expats is they're in Bahasa Malaysia. It's worth learning a few words of traffic vocabulary to help you decipher the warnings and avoid the worst of the jams.

Driving In Kuala Lumpur

Driving in KL is certainly not for the fainthearted! Many residents will suggest you make your first driving excursions on a Sunday morning when traffic is likely to be light. It's not really the volume of the traffic that's the problem for most expat drivers though, it's the unpredictability. If it's not motorbikes zooming every which way around you, it's other motorists making multi-lane changes without indicating, or overtaking on the inside – so the fewer other drivers around the better while you concentrate on navigating your way around the idiosyncratic road system.

Most maps are often out of date or simply inaccurate, but *The Street Directory* published by Rimman is the best option. Roads have many twists and turns and it's extremely hard to double back if you realise you've made a wrong turn. Getting lost is part of KL life though, and eventually you'll find the road network starting to make sense. GPS has recently arrived in KL, and although there are mixed reports about the accuracy of the maps, it can be a big help.

When it comes to getting hold of a vehicle, cars are expensive. A new Honda Civic will cost around RM110,000, while a five year old second hand one will cost around RM65,000. Local brands Proton and Perodua, as well as locally assembled models by

145

Toyota, Nissan, Hyundai and Kia, offer more car for your money; a new Proton Waja comes in at around RM60,500. Despite this, cars are popular and 'new' sales are strong. Petrol is cheap (it's subsidised by the government), with a litre costing about RM1.90, so once you've invested in your car, or if you're lucky enough to get a company car, running costs are relatively low.

Jaywalking pedestrians can be a hazard to drivers, especially in the city centre and around shopping centres, so it pays to be cautious. Cyclists are a rare sight in the city centre but are sometimes found in the suburbs.

Traffic at peak times is heavy. The morning rush will start to build up at around 07:00 and clear by 09:30, while 17:30 to 19:30 is the worst time for evening traffic. Most radio stations have regular traffic updates during peak hours and will report on any problems through the day as they happen. Major roads have electronic signboards providing real-time information on traffic and road closures. Note that the messages are written in Bahasa Malaysia, and, although it's easy enough to understand a warning about a jam, some of the more complicated messages are a mystery to most expats. If you can commute outside peak hours or against the flow of traffic you'll spend much less time in the car. Car pooling doesn't have any tangible advantages like being able to use special lanes, but you may be able to share a ride with someone who works with you and lives nearby.

You can avoid some of the traffic by using the network of privately operated toll roads but these can get jammed too, especially around toll plazas and exit ramps.

Traffic Rules & Regulations

Malaysians drive on the left and, in theory, follow similar road rules to those in the UK. It's not illegal to use a right-hand drive vehicle, but you may find it awkward at toll and parking booths. Front-seat passengers are required to wear seatbelts but there are currently no laws regarding rear seatbelts or child safety seats. Lane discipline is generally poor, but you should overtake on the right, and give way to your right at roundabouts. You should never stop in a junction box marked in yellow, and you must stop at a berhenti (stop) sign, even if there doesn't seem to be any traffic about. Speed limits range from 50kph on residential roads to 120kph on major highways, and speed traps on highways are common. During peak hours traffic lights at busy junctions may be overridden by police instructions. Always obey the signals of the police officer in this instance, although the lights will continue to change as normal. The limit for drink driving is 80mg of alcohol per 100ml of blood, and you'll lose your licence for six months on the first conviction.

Alcohol

Drink driving is against the law, although there isn't a zero tolerance policy and few expats end up on the wrong side of this law. KL driving is hard enough to deal with sober; only a fool would have a go after a few drinks.

Driving Habits

Before driving it's a good idea to travel as a passenger a few times to observe local etiquette. Safety seems to be a minor concern – it's not unusual to see people chatting on their mobiles, driving with one hand on the wheel and a small child in their lap. Vehicles will frequently turn or change lanes without indicating, and it's common to be overtaken on the inside. Lane switching in traffic jams is a frequent occurrence, although you may find that other drivers won't let you in to a merging lane; winding down the window and waving at the car behind often helps to open up a gap. At major holidays and festivals roads are very busy, and the police run regular holiday safety campaigns with the focus usually on speeding.

Motorcyclists seem to be everywhere all the time – always check both sides of your vehicle before turning or changing lanes. They often ride against traffic or the wrong way on a one-way street, so look both ways at all junctions. Despite the traffic snarls and long jams, KL drivers are generally quite mild mannered and incidents of road rage are rare.

Driving Licence

You can drive in Malaysia using an international licence for up to three months, after which time you should convert it to a Malaysian one if you intend to continue driving in the country. See p.145 for information on how to do this.

Parking

Parking at your home won't be a problem. Houses are built back from the road and will have space to park at least one car, often two or three. Most apartments or condos will come with on-site parking too. Away from home it's a different story. You may get a season ticket from your employer to park at work, if not you can usually pay to leave your vehicle in the building's public carpark. Expect to pay RM4 to RM8 per hour to park in the city centre. Cheaper options are the open-air carparks that appear on every empty piece of land in the city centre, although be aware that security at these may not be as good as at building carparks. On-street parking is cheaper still but very hard to find. You pay for this at parking meters, usually at a rate of RM1 per hour (you can use 10, 20 and 50 sen coins). Shopping centres have their own carparks, and these are usually cheaper in the suburbs than the city centre, although all parking is cheap by European standards. Expect to pay about RM20 to park for the day at a city centre office building. Illegal parking is a common problem, but parking enforcement is sporadic and you'll seldom see a car being clamped or removed.

Petrol Stations

Major petrol retailers in Malaysia include the national oil company Petronas as well as international names such as Shell, CalTex and Mobil. Petrol is subsidised and costs around RM1.90 per litre, but with rising global oil prices the cost is susceptible to increases. At many stations you can pay at the pump with your credit card and fill your car yourself, but service is usually available if you want it. If you're paying cash you should pay the cashier before filling up. Some stations have car washes and larger ones have pretty well-stocked shops, ATMs, mobile phone top ups, bill payment and other facilities.

Vehicle Leasing Agents

Advantage Car Rental	03 2142 5855	www.advmsia.com.my
Avis	03 9222 2558	www.avis.com.my
Hertz	03 2148 6433	www.hertz-malaysia.com
Mayflower Car Rental	03 6252 1888	www.mayflowercarrental.com.my
Orix Car Rental	03 9284 7799	www.orixcarrentals.com.my
Pacific Rent a Car	03 2287 4118	www.iprac.com

Vehicle Leasing

Private vehicle leasing hasn't taken off yet in Malaysia, but if you don't want to buy a vehicle, long-term hire is an option. A number of car rental companies will rent vehicles on monthly or yearly contracts as well as the usual daily or weekly rates, and the longer the contract, the better the rate. Although there's not much flexibility in the market, you may get a better deal from a local company rather than a multinational.

Usually all costs are included in the rental rate, including insurance, maintenance and recovery services, but coverage from a small company may not be as comprehensive. The selection of vehicles available may be limited and choice may be restricted to just one or two vehicles in each category. Be aware that many hire companies will not allow you to drive their cars over the border to Thailand or Singapore, so check before heading off on a road trip.

Company Cars

Senior staff may get a company car as part of their contract, but the car will usually be owned by the company rather than leased. In some cases you will be paid a vehicle allowance and it will be up to you whether to spend that money on hiring or buying a car.

Buying A Vehicle

Although they are expensive, many expats opt to buy a vehicle simply because of the lack of a reasonable alternative form of transport. You don't need to wait until your work permit comes through before buying a car, unless you need a loan to buy one. Take a good look around at what's available before you buy as you may not find many familiar brands or models, especially if you've come from the US.

Locally made cars dominate on the roads as tax breaks make them cheaper to buy, and they are easier to get fixed if things go wrong. Perodua is currently the biggest-selling brand, and you'll see its miniature Kancil, Kelisa and Kenari models everywhere. It also has a very popular small SUV, the Kembara, and two more modern small cars, the Myvi and Viva. Perodua has a better reputation than Malaysia's other car maker, Proton, although recent launches have revived this company's fortunes somewhat. Popular Proton models include the Saga, Wira, Waja, Persona, Gen-2, Savvy and Perdana. A new Saga starts at about RM31,500.

New Car Dealers

Brands	Name	Area	Phone	Web
Alfa Romeo	Milan Auto	Petaling Jaya	03 7956 8525	www.alfaromeo.com
Audi	Auto Dunia	Petaling Jaya	03 7781 5511	www.audi.com
BMW	Auto Bavaria	Selangor	03 5569 3900	www.bmw.com
Chevrolet	Hicomobil	Ampang	03 2052 5000	www.hicomobil.com.my
Citroen	Directional	Ampang	03 4251 2151	www.citroen.com.my
Ford	Ford	Petaling Jaya	03 7783 2000	www.ford.com.my
Honda	DRB Oriental Hicom	Selangor	03 2052 8777	www.honda.com
Honda	New Era Sales	City Centre	03 2032 4423	www.honda.com
Land Rover	Land Rover Malaysia	Petaling Jaya	03 7960 2800	www.landrovermalaysia.com.my
Mazda, Mercedes, Kia	Cycle & Carriage	Petaling Jaya	03 7957 2422	na
Nissan	Edaran Tan Chong Motor	City Centre	03 4041 1044	www.nissan-global.com
Perodua	Zamahan	Bangsar	03 2283 5687	www.perodua.com.my
Proton	EON	Selangor	03 7803 1111	www.proton.com
Toyota	Toyota	Ampang	03 4270 6866	www.toyota.com.my
Volkswagen	Volkswagen Malaysia	Bangsar	03 2295 9995	www.volkswagen.com.my
Volvo	Volvo Car Malaysia	Mid Valley	03 2287 7781	www.volvocars.com.my

You'll see a lot of locally assembled models of Korean cars too – Hyundai (Innokom) and Kia (Naza) both have regional partnerships. Over the past couple of years the choice of new models on the market has improved, while waiting times for new cars have reduced. At the beginning of 2006 you would have had to wait seven months for a new Toyota Innova or nine months for a Perodua Myvi, but now you'll probably have your car within a few weeks.

Despite the extra duty there are plenty of imported brands out on the streets, including Honda, Toyota, Mercedes Benz, BMW and Volvo. As a guide a new Honda Civic will cost you RM110,000 (in Britain the base price of a Civic is around £13,000, and $16,400 in the US). Second-hand cars are correspondingly expensive, and even a six or seven year old Proton Saga will set you back RM12,000.

If you're buying second hand, there are few reliable dealers, so beware. City Motors caters specifically to expats and offers a good service. It will help with all aspects of car ownership, including insurance, transfer of ownership and paying road tax.

Private Sales

You can sometimes get a good deal on a second-hand car from an expat who is leaving – look out on the notice boards at expat associations and international schools for

Transportation

Used Car Dealers

| Car World Group | Ampang | 03 4260 1888 | www.carworldmotor.com |
| City Motors | Bangsar | 03 2282 3795 | www.citymotors.com.my |

ads. Recent regulations stipulate that all private vehicles must be inspected before ownership can be transferred. This is done at Puspakom for a fee of RM30. Puspakom inspection centres can be found in Cheras, Wangsa Maju, Bangi, Petaling Jaya and Gombak – see www.puspakom.com.my for branch locations. If the vehicle passes the inspection, which is mainly to detect illegal modifications, the certificate is transferred online and you should visit the road transport department (JPJ) office within 14 days to complete the transfer. Ideally the seller should come with you; if they can't you will need a copy of their ID card or passport, a notice of release of their ownership claim, proof of you having insured the vehicle and two copies of completed form Borang JPJ K3 (see p.150 for details).

Importing & Exporting Cars

Under the Malaysia My Second Home programme, visa holders are entitled to import their previously owned car tax free. If you are using a relocation agent, they can advise you on the procedure for importing cars. In other cases, import duties can be up to 300% of the vehicle value, making this option prohibitively expensive. You can export a car from Malaysia, but it will be up to you to make sure the vehicle is considered roadworthy in your destination country. As cars are so expensive in Malaysia compared to many other countries, most expats sell their cars when they leave as the resale value elsewhere would be significantly less.

Vehicle Finance

Most car dealers, both new and second-hand, will offer finance, but if you need a loan to finance a private car purchase you will have to approach a bank. For each of these options you will usually be unable to get a loan until your work permit is approved, and some finance companies may ask to see three months' payslips as proof of income, or a letter from your company confirming your position and salary. Strict regulations govern hire-purchase loans. The maximum loan amount is 90% of the value of the vehicle, with a maximum interest rate of 10%, fixed for the duration of the loan (a maximum of nine years).

Vehicle Finance

EON Bank Group	03 2612 8888	www.eonbank.com.my
Hong Leong Bank	03 7626 8899	www.hlb.com.my
Maybank	1300 886 688	www.maybank2u.com.my

Interest rates vary, and are better for new cars. Maybank's interest rates hover between 2.5% and 4.75% on new car loans, and from 3.5% to 10% on used cars, depending on age and model. Promotional rates can be even lower, with Honda offering a rate of 1.38% in early 2008. A limited number of banks offer independent car loans, but the best deals are usually through dealers.

Vehicle Insurance

Only third-party insurance is compulsory in Malaysia, although comprehensive policies are widely available. Despite high car prices, insurance is quite affordable and is calculated based on a number of factors: the value insured, the number of passengers

Vehicle Insurance

AIA	1300 881 899	www.aia.com.my
Allianz	03 2168 6868	www.allianz.com.my
AXA Insurance	03 2279 8282	www.axa-insurance.com.my
Berjaya Sompo Insurance	1800 889 933	www.bgi.com.my
MSIG	1800 881 789	www.ms-ins.com.my

the vehicle is licensed to carry, the engine capacity, and any no-claims discount you're entitled to. Insuring a new Honda Civic will cost about RM3,100 per year, assuming zero no-claims discount. Policies run for a calendar year.

If you buy a new or used car from a dealer, they will usually sell you insurance at the same time. You're tied to using repair shops approved by your insurer, and these may not always be in a convenient location. If your car is over four years old and you need replacement parts for an insurance claim, you will have to pay a percentage of the value of any new parts used or accept a repair with second-hand parts. It's not really worth shopping around in the hope of a better rate as the insurance industry is highly regulated, so policies are almost identical and prices are fixed.

Insurance ◀

Before you leave your home country, bring with you records of your no-claims status from your vehicle insurance back home. It may secure you a discount with insurance companies here in KL.

Registering A Vehicle

All vehicles driven on the roads in Malaysia must be registered, and the motor vehicle licence must be renewed annually. If you buy a new car the dealership will take care of the initial registration, and many used-car dealers, including City Motors, will register a second-hand car for you. To renew your motor vehicle licence you must bring your original registration certificate and provide proof of insurance. The cost of renewal is RM50. You will have to go to your local JPJ office to do this. Road tax is also payable annually and ranges from RM20 to RM2130 depending on the engine capacity (CC) of your vehicle. Driving without valid road tax or registration is an offence, and the maximum fine is RM2,000. There's no official grace period, but you may get away with it if you miss the renewal date by a couple of weeks.

The Automobile Association of Malaysia (AAM) provides renewal services for members, and City Motors also provides renewal services – even if you didn't buy your car from there, it may still offer the service.

Registration Service	
AAM	03 2162 5777
City Motors	03 2282 3795

There have been rumours that Malaysia will introduce mandatory scrapping for vehicles over a certain age, but this seems unlikely to happen any time soon. Even if a car dies on you and you want to scrap it, the chances are you will be able to get someone to take it off your hands, although you may not get much for it. Outside KL, you'll see the most amazing cars on Malaysia's roads, seemingly held together with bits of string and tape.

Traffic Fines & Offences

If stopped for offences such as speeding, running a red light, or driving without wearing a seatbelt, while holding a mobile phone, or in a bus lane, the police will issue you with a ticket which you will have to sign, and a compound (fine), usually RM300. You can pay the fine at any main police station that has a Traffic Police Division before the expiry date shown on the ticket. In KL this is at Jalan Tun H S Lee (03 2072 9044). It is illegal to offer the policeman money (a bribe) to settle the matter on the spot, although anecdotal evidence suggests this is possible. If you do decide to make an offer and the policeman warns you not to, stop there as you must be warned before being charged with offering a bribe – if convicted the penalty is a heavy fine or even a prison sentence.

Tinted windows are permitted, but very dark windows are illegal. Use a reputable installer if you're getting tinted film on your car to ensure it complies with Malaysian law.

More serious offences carry heavier fines, penalties on your licence or even prison sentences. Driving while drunk (more than 80mg of alcohol per 100ml of blood) carries a fine of RM2,000 and/or a prison sentence of up to six months for the first offence. You will also lose your licence.

Breakdowns

It's well worth joining the Automobile Association of Malaysia for its 24 hour breakdown assistance service. Membership covers the whole country, although AAM will not provide assistance if you are off road (it may be able to put you in touch with a local garage who can assist you, however). It's a good idea whenever you're driving in Malaysia to keep bottled water in the car and have your mobile phone with you to call for assistance if necessary. If at all practical you should move your prone car to the side of the road in the event of a breakdown. If you have to leave your car where it is, put on your hazard lights to warn other motorists.

Emergency telephones are provided on highways managed by PLUS (toll roads), which will connect you directly to its assistance centre; alternatively you can dial 1 800 880 000 from your mobile phone. PLUS has dedicated highway patrol personnel (PLUS Ronda) who will come to assist you if you break down. They will do minor repairs and if necessary tow your car to the nearest toll plaza or rest stop.

Recovery Services/Towing (24 hour)		
Automobile Association of Malaysia (breakdown)	03 2161 0808	www.aam.org.my
PLUS	1800 88 000	www.plus.com.my

Traffic Accidents

Other options **Car** p.30

Expect The Unexpected
Changing lanes without indicating, overtaking on the left, tailgating, queue jumping, slowing to a crawl in the outside lane, backing out of a wrong turn off the highway, illegal U-turns, jumping the lights, not stopping at a stop sign – it's an average day on the roads of KL. Be aware of all the traffic around you when driving and don't be surprised by any manoeuvre another motorist makes.

Accidents are an all-too-frequent occurrence on Malaysia's roads, and KL is no exception. While most of these accidents are minor shunts involving little damage to people or property, there are also many fatalities. In 2006 there were 341,252 road accidents reported in Malaysia, resulting in 6,287 fatalities. Although there are no particular accident hotspots in the city, rain always increases the chance of a collision. When driving you should always have your licence with you, as failing to produce it when asked is an offence.

If you're involved in a minor accident where no one is injured, it's common practice to settle the matter immediately at the scene, with the party at fault paying for the damage. If you don't reach an agreement you must report the accident to the police within 24 hours and notify your insurance company if you intend to claim. You will need a copy of the police report in order to make a claim.

If the accident is more serious and someone is injured, call the police on 999. Make the accident scene as safe as possible by using hazard lights to warn other drivers, and keep your car headlights on if it's dark. Make sure no one smokes around an accident scene to reduce the risk of fire or explosion. You must make a police report within 24 hours if a person has been injured or killed, or if livestock are involved in an accident and the owner is not present.

You should take down the name, address, vehicle registration number and insurance details of the other vehicle, and give your details when asked. Get details of any witnesses if possible and take pictures of the scene if you have a camera with you. You should not admit liability – once the police arrive they will assess the situation and ask you to make a report at the station.

If you're involved in an accident in a rural area the advice commonly given is not to stop or get out of your vehicle. You should drive straight to the nearest police station and report the incident. See Crime (p.69) for more information.

In KL you should report traffic accidents to the Traffic Police – this office is at Jalan Tun HS Lee in Chinatown, and is open 24 hours.

Although KL traffic can be frustrating, the incidence of road rage is remarkably low. It's better to just let things go rather than stress about bad driving.

There is a points system in operation for traffic offences. Points stay on your licence for one year and if you accumulate more than 15 in a year you'll lose your licence for six months. See Driving (p.145) for more details.

Vehicle Repairs

You'll need to have a police report if you want to claim for repairs to your car on your insurance, but no paperwork is required if you're paying for the repairs yourself. There is an approved list of workshops for repairs claimed on insurance, drawn up by the General Insurance Association of Malaysia, and insurance firms can choose who to use from this list. Work carried out by these workshops is guaranteed for six months. If you insist on using someone else, your insurance company may not settle the bill in full. How much excess you will have to pay depends on the terms of your policy.

Driving conditions in Malaysia are tough on brakes, shock absorbers and tyres, so you may have to replace them more often than you're used to. You can choose whether to have your car repaired by the manufacturer's service centre or go for an independent mechanic. There are a number of good general mechanics. Some, such as Ann Heng Auto and Keu Fong Auto Service, will come to pick up your car and deliver it after servicing or repairs.

Vehicle Repairs		
Ann Heng Auto	Ampang	03 9287 9818
CKL Group	TTDI (Taman Tun Dr Ismail)	03 7727 7377
Damansara Auto Repair Centre	Petaling Jaya	03 7725 9620
Keu Fong Auto Service	Ampang	03 4143 5797
Leng Seng Workshop	Ampang	03 4291 6472
Lim Tayar	Petaling Jaya	03 7876 8175
Vision Auto Care	Bangsar	03 2282 4899
Volcare Service Centre	Ampang	03 4256 5827

Popular transport options

Is getting lost your usual excuse?

Whether you're a map person or not, this pocket-sized marvel will help you get to know the city like the back of your hand – so you won't feel the back of someone else's.

Kaula Lumpur Mini Map
Fit the city in your pocket

Exploring

Exploring

Kuala Lumpur is a city that, on first impression, seems to incorporate characteristics from so many cultures, countries and eras that it can't possibly have its very own character. You have the huge, modern, steel and glass beauty of the Petronas Twin Towers (p.188), and then you have the dark and dingy wet markets in Chinatown, with their bubbling pots of tofu and rather alarming rat populations. You have beautiful Chinese temples and imposing, architecturally striking mosques. And you have the bustling markets of Little India and Chinatown competing with the serene surroundings of designer shopping malls. Add the humidity, the traffic (more motorcycles than you've ever seen), and a seemingly endless mix of nationalities, and it can be a hard city to define.

However, the longer you stay there, the more you are able to put your finger on KL's intricate character. Its unique blend of Malay, Chinese and Indian cultures, as well as a large expat population, make it a place where everybody feels at home. It's a city that retains its character, no matter how modern it becomes.

Compared to other Asian cities (like Bangkok or Manila), KL is small and relatively easy to get around. The train system may seem complicated at first, but once you get the hang of it you'll be able to navigate the city easily. The trick is to be prepared to combine your train journey with a short cab ride once you reach the nearest station. And once you master the trains, you should make the effort to head to those out-of-town locations – while there is plenty to see and do in KL, if you stay within the city limits you'll miss out on some amazing attractions just a short trip from the city. The Batu Caves, where hundreds of thousands of Hindus come to worship each year, and the Forest Research Institute of Malaysia, or FRIM, where you can walk high above the rainforest on a canopy walkway, are just two examples of amazing activities that are only a short trip from the city.

Further afield, Malaysia has much to offer the city dweller. From the beautiful beaches of Langkawi to the cooler climes of the Cameron Highlands, there are many wonderful destinations that can be covered within a weekend break (see p.205).

Dancing Fountains outside Suria KLCC

Checklist

Splash Into Aquaria KLCC
This is the largest oceanarium of its kind in south-east Asia, and it is a wonderful opportunity to get up close and personal with the many fishy characters found under the sea. The main aquarium has a fascinating walk-through tunnel where you can see the various species (including lots of sharks) on both sides and swimming above your head. See p.182.

KL Kraft Kompleks
Catch skilled craftsmen making beautiful batik, weaving traditional cloth called songket, or painting colourful artworks in this lovely outdoor craft centre. You can try your hand at making your own piece of batik art, and of course there are many items for sale, both from the craftsmen directly and from the shops inside. See p.188.

Spend A Day In The Lake Gardens
Just west of the old colonial quarter of downtown KL lie the expansive Lake Gardens, also known as Taman Tasik Perdana. This green lung of the city has broad lawns, rolling hills and clusters of ancient trees, all surrounding a lovely man-made lake, which you can either stroll around on the two-kilometre path or sail across on a colourful rowboat. See p.174.

Understand Islam At Masjid Jamek
Masjid Jamek is the oldest mosque in KL, and arguably the most charming. The multi-domed red brick and marble building sits at the confluence of the Gombak and Klang Rivers, between the old colonial quarter and Chinatown. Visitors are welcome outside of prayer times. Dress modestly. See p.190.

Shop Till You Drop
You don't have to go very far in KL to find somewhere to offload your hard-earned cash: shopping is a very popular pastime here. The huge Suria KLCC shopping mall (p.341) gets a nod for its sheer size and range of brands – it would take you at least a day to get round all the shops and stop for sustenance in one of the many restaurants and cafes. See p.280.

Central Market
Head for Chinatown to find the Central Market, where you can browse through corridor after corridor of arts and crafts, jewellery, clothing, toys and souvenirs. The market is air conditioned and covered, so it's a great pitstop when you find yourself in the area during a rainstorm, or when the humidity gets too much to bear. See p.333.

Find A Feathered Friend At The Bird Park
Spend a tranquil afternoon in the bird park when you need to unwind – with birdsong in the air and secluded pathways winding through lush vegetation, you'll feel a world away from the bustle of the city. Catch the entertaining bird show if you can – who would have thought a parrot could do sums? See p.194.

Enjoy Afternoon Tea In The Drawing Room

Carcosa Seri Negara (p.184), the former home of the last colonial ruler of Malaysia, is a luxurious hotel set among the beautiful lawns of the Lake Gardens, and staying there is reserved for those with serious cash. You can, however, experience the splendour by having a traditional high tea, complete with scones and cucumber sandwiches, in The Drawing Room. See p.397.

Thean Thou Buddhist Temple

This amazing Buddhist temple is just a few minutes away from downtown KL. Visitors will love its wild and gaudy wall paintings and swathes of bright red. As it is on top of a hill, you'll have a wonderful view across the city to the north on a clear day. A lack of signs can make it difficult to find, but any cab driver should know it. See p.191.

Canopy Walk At FRIM

Take a short trip out of town to enjoy the Forest Research Institute of Malaysia (FRIM) – there are several walks that you can take, but the best is surely the canopy walk. After a rather challenging hike up a forest path, you can walk along a suspended walkway 200 feet above the trees, enjoying the view of four levels of rainforest. Highly recommended. See p.196.

Malaysian Philharmonic Orchestra

The MPO stands out in KL's cultural scene. With world-class musicians from 25 other countries making up this popular orchestra, and over a hundred concerts per year on their schedule, this is a top-quality operation. Housed in the magnificent philharmonic hall on the ground floor of the Petronas Towers, an evening out to enjoy the musical talents of the MPO should not be missed. See p.249X.

Chinatown

Leave the gleaming skyscrapers of the city centre and head to the gritty streets of Chinatown, which may not be as modern but which reverberate with character. From the dingy but fascinating wet markets (watch out for rats) to the old architecture and the many interesting shops, there's plenty to see in this area. Peter Hoe's (p.308) is well worth a visit for beautiful home decor. See p.280.

Genting Highlands

Take a break from the humidity and head for the cool, misty climes of Genting, just a 90 minute drive away. Situated on top of a 1,500m high mountain, Genting offers great views of Kuala Lumpur. It is also home to Malaysia's only casino, the biggest hotel in south-east Asia, and a huge amusement park. It is a popular destination for daytrippers and overnighters. See p.170.

Petronas Twin Towers

The big daddy of attractions in KL, this gleaming pair of towers is visible from almost anywhere in the city, and forms a striking addition to the skyline. At night the towers are mesmerising, thanks to their beautiful silver glow, and a few cocktails in a bar with a view is an essential KL experience. Get your free ticket to go up to the sky bridge for panoramic views of the city. See p.188.

Checklist

Strut Along Bintang Walk
For extravagant shopping by day and great nightlife once the sun goes down, head for Bintang Walk in Bukit Bintang. With malls like Lot 10 (p.338) and Starhill Gallery (p.341), hotels like the JW Marriott and the Westin, and streets lined with cafes, bars and nightclubs, this is where the city's heart beats. See p.354.

Sample Street Food
Even the squeamish should find some tasty morsels to try from street food vendors. Sample hokkien mee (noodles with pork or seafood in a sticky sauce), kway teow (flat noodles, usually with beef) or nasi lemak, the traditional Malay dish with coconut rice and accompaniments like prawn paste, peanuts and fried anchovies. See p.357.

Enjoy The Views
Head for a bar or restaurant with an amazing skyline view, so that you can enjoy your martini while you gaze at the Petronas Towers. One of the best views in town, and one of the trendiest settings, belongs to the Sky Bar in the Traders Hotel. Set around a rooftop swimming pool, it has a good food menu, and extensive cocktail list, and that all-important view. See p.404.

Batu Caves
This important Hindu shrine is a must-do experience. It's just a short trip out of town, and is instantly recognisable thanks to the giant golden statue of Murugan, which stands nearly 50 metres tall. Walking up the 272 steps to the Temple Cave is the most obvious place to start, but you could spend at least half a day exploring this and the other caves and statues. See p.189.

Independence Square
When you see the cricket pitch laid out on the vast lawns of Merdeka Square, you can almost imagine a team of colonial British gentlemen playing there. While it's rarely used for cricket these days, Merdeka Square is home to the Independence Day celebrations, the Royal Selangor Club, Malaysia's giant flagpole, and St Mary's Cathedral. See p.184.

Sri Maha Mariamman Temple
Strangely, KL's oldest Hindu temple lies right in the middle of Chinatown. It is an active place of worship and a favourite place for Hindus to get married. Visitors are welcome but must remove their shoes at the door. Be sure to buy a fragrant string of flowers from the vendors outside, and enjoy the intricacies of the impressive gateway tower that looms over the entrance. See p.190.

KL Tower
It may only look higher than Petronas because it stands on a hill, but the Menara Kuala Lumpur – or KL Tower – is the place to go for unfettered, panoramic views of the city. Take the super-quick lifts up to the viewing deck (nearly 280 metres high) and learn about KL from a lofty perspective. Audio guides and headphones are available. See p.187.

The Complete **Residents'** Guide

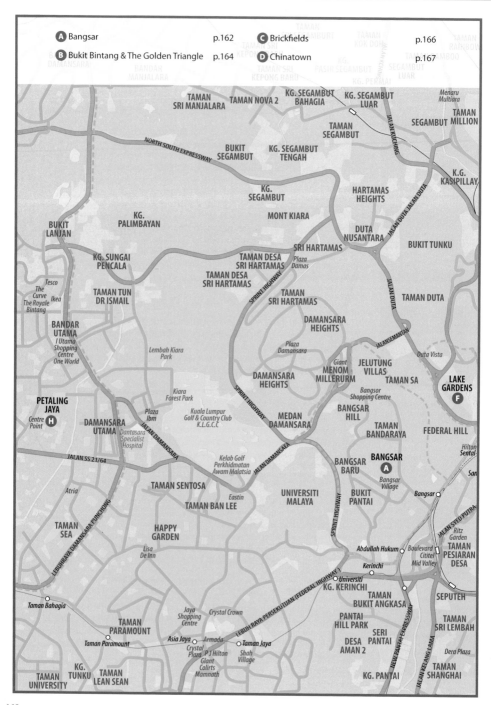

A Bangsar   p.162   **C** Brickfields   p.166

B Bukit Bintang & The Golden Triangle   p.164   **D** Chinatown   p.167

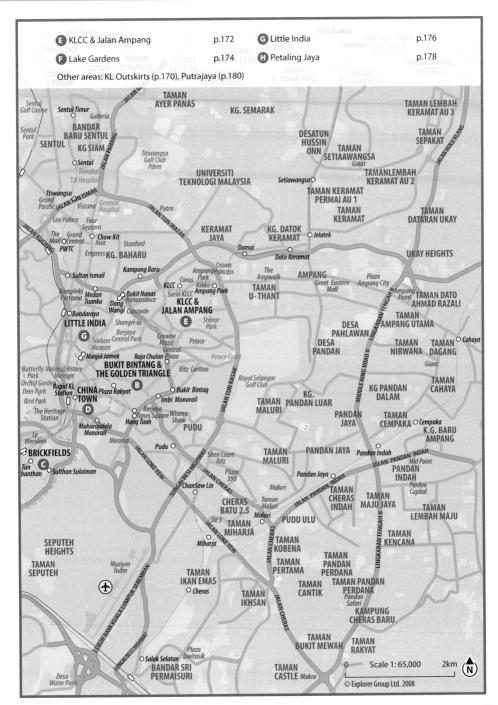

Area ● p.160-p.161
See also Map 6

Bangsar

A little over 30 years ago Bangsar was mostly a rubber plantation, but now the area known as Bangsar Baru has developed into one of mixed residential and low-rise commercial space. Most people call this central area of Bangsar Baru simply Bangsar, but the greater area also includes the neighbouring suburbs of Bukit Bandaraya, Taman Lucky, Taman Bukit Pantai, Taman Bandaraya, Taman Bangsar and Taman SA. Greater Bangsar is roughly bordered by Jalans Maarof and Bangsar, and the University Malaya.

Bukit Bandaraya has many excellent views of KL and it seems that every square inch of land has been given over to towering blocks of condominiums or large and exclusive homes. The older and flatter parts of Bangsar are dominated by terraced housing or free-standing bungalows.

Around 15 years ago the central part of Bangsar Baru was little more than an open area that was used as a parking lot for the newly emerging commercial activity and entertainment outlets. Now it is has been developed and is considered one of the trendiest parts of town, with a community mall called Bangsar Village (p.336) being the focal point for designer

Bangsar Village

The Lowdown
Bangsar is a mostly residential area not far from the city centre. For many it is also a trendy place to hang out, with bars, clubs, restaurants and cafes and some great community shopping malls.

The Good
An upmarket area with some smart dining and shopping options and a favoured residential area for upwardly mobile Malaysians and expats.

The Bad
For a residential suburb, there are surprisingly few large open areas for recreation.

The Must-Dos
Shop in Bangsar Shopping Centre, Bangsar Shopping Village, visit the bars and restaurants of Bangsar Baru and attend a performance by Actors' Studio.

shops, fashionable boutiques, contemporary restaurants and some slick bars.
Over the past few years, Bangsar has had its ups and downs, going from being the epicentre for partying, to experiencing a lull of subdued activity and now, to being an upmarket urban village again. In the early 1990s, KL city centre was where most people went to party and to be entertained. A short time later, Bangsar evolved as an entertainment area and this all happened very quickly with the granting of what seemed to be a disproportionate number of outlet licences for such a small area. Soon certain areas of Bangsar, in particular Jalan Telawi 2 and 3, were pumping with bars, restaurants and cafes that opened onto the streets, and the crowds flocked here to flit from bar to bar, to see and to be seen. Establishments came and went quickly and a popular activity at the time was to try and recall what outlet used to be where. Ronnie Q's (p.407) is one of the early pubs that has survived, and very little has changed since its inception, although an open-fronted bar bench has been added in recent years. Many of the patrons haven't changed either, and they probably still sit on the same stools that they have for years – it's just that kind of place.
Bangsar was very much the public face of Malaysia's booming economy in the early 1990s. Back then, the streets were lined with partygoers driving luxury cars which mostly double parked in total disregard for anyone else. The 1997 Asian economic crisis quickly curtailed a lot of these excesses. While Bangsar has clawed back, it has never regained the euphoria of these glory days. Today, there is still a buzz in Bangsar, but now other areas in the city have opened up. So although once it was the place – and the only place – to be, there are now so many other options for nightlifers.
Bangsar is now more a place for the local residents to wine, dine and shop and where a few 'outsiders' still come to have a good time. Much of the late night boozing has declined as Bangsar assumes the role of catering to residents on the way home from work seeking a glass of wine or a frothy cappuccino rather than a big night out in the bars.
The recently opened Bangsar Village II is what the developer calls a 'community mall'. It's there more for the convenience of local residents rather than as a destination mall

that people would travel to see. It is connected via a covered overhead walkway to Bangsar Village I, where there is a supermarket selling most essential items (this and Cold Storage in Bangsar Shopping Centre cater to the many expats living in the area by selling imported items not found in many other parts of KL). Village II is home to a range of prestigious boutiques and some famous designer names relatively new to KL, and therefore it attracts a crowd of discerning shoppers who like the small scale and personal attention that it offers.

Bangsar Shopping Centre is located in Bukit Bandaraya at the top of the hill, overlooking much of the rest of Bangsar. Cold Storage supermarket is the main tenant, and perennially popular thanks to its range of premium and hard-to-get items. It is also the location for a KL institution: the Actors' Studio (03 2094 0400, www.actorsstudio.com.my), which is on the third floor of the west wing. Since 1989 the Actors' Studio has raised the bar for live theatre by providing a venue for local writers and actors to have their work performed in a city that has yet to fully embrace the arts. It has regular performances of local plays, as well as popular overseas plays and acting classes for children. In the past it has also demonstrated a willingness to perform controversial theatre and political satire.

Settle Down

If you fancy setting up home in Bangsar, one of the most popular residential areas for expats, turn to p.81 in the Residents chapter for the lowdown on living here.

At the bottom of Bukit Bandaraya, off Jalan Maarof and facing Jalan Bangkung, you can find a small collection of restaurants, cafes and shops. This very quiet part of Bangsar is surrounded by residential properties. One of the great advantages of dining in this part of Bangsar is that there is plenty of free parking immediately in front of the restaurants. Komplex Sukan Bangsar, or Bangsar Sports Complex (2284 6065), is on Jalan Terasek 3 in Bangsar Baru. This council-administered complex provides a facility for those who don't live in condominiums (apartments) which are fully equipped with sporting facilities. There's a swimming pool and tennis, squash and badminton facilities, and a canteen and children's playground. The rates for court hire are very modest and the facility is open daily from 09:30 to 24:00.

A popular *pasar malam* (night market) is held on Sunday night from late afternoon to late in the evening. Like many held in other parts of the city, the markets create havoc with traffic but there is sufficient off-street parking in several covered carparks. Many locals love to shop here for fresh vegetables, fruit, seafood and a multitude of takeaway snacks.

Bangsar Station on the Putra LRT, located along Jalan Bangsar and KL Sentral, is within minutes of most places in Bangsar. This adds to the area's appeal as a place to live as KLIA is just 28 minutes away by fast train and many inner city destinations can be accessed via train.

Bangsar is definitely one of KL's best-known suburbs, with a reputation for entertainment and a good night out. While this has changed over recent years, as it embraces more of a village atmosphere, it remains an area that appeals to many.

Chutney Mary Restaurant

Area **B** *p.160-p.161*
See also Map 5

The Lowdown
This is KL's golden heart, where all the cut and thrust of commercial life is played out. It is KL's premier address for many businesses, five-star hotels, boutiques, shopping malls, night clubs and restaurants.

The Good
Everything that glistens with gold in the city is found here.

The Bad
Recent road changes and general congestion in the city have resulted in the main arterial roads becoming jammed, especially in the evening peak hour. Getting around on the monorail is a good idea, particularly around Bukit Bintang.

The Must-Dos
Menara KL for views of the city; a short walk through the only protected rainforest in the middle of a city at Bukit Nanas; enjoy the designer shopping at Pavilion KL; ride the monorail between destinations.

Bukit Bintang & The Golden Triangle

The Golden Triangle is recognised as KL's central business district (CBD) and is bordered by Jalans Imbi, Sultan Ismail and Tun Razak. However, it is a term that has been lost in translation and most city residents probably couldn't mark it on a map. To most, it refers to the expensive part of the city centre, where there are many five-star hotels, office headquarters, smart shops and upmarket restaurants.

Menara KL (KL Tower, p.187) soars 421 metres into the sky and is the natural place for first-time visitors to KL to go to get their bearings. Views are best on a clear day. The Seri Angkasa revolving restaurant is situated near the top of the tower (see page 380).

Bukit Nanas Forest Reserve surrounds the base of Menara KL between Jalan Ampang and Jalan Raja Chulan. While the origins of the name Pineapple Hill (Bukit Nanas) are

Bintang Walk

unknown, the 10.5 hectare reserve is a natural haven in the heart of Kuala Lumpur. Few cities claim their own natural rainforest in the city precincts. The land was declared a forest reserve in 1906 and survives to provide a recreational area and a place for visitors to see some rainforest features within the safe confines of several well-developed and signed trails. It was later changed to a wildlife reserve and bird sanctuary and in 1950 parts of it became a virgin jungle reserve, a status which supposedly means it cannot be developed. One of the entrances to the trails starts at the far end of the Menara KL carpark.

The Golden Triangle is home to several shopping malls with large department stores as anchor tenants. Lot 10 (p.338), Starhill Gallery (p.341), Sungei Wang Plaza (p.341), KL Plaza (p.338), Berjaya Times Square (p.336) and the Pavilion Kuala Lumpur (p.340) are the biggest shopping complexes in the area. These include international designer brand boutiques in addition to large department stores such as Isetan, Tangs and Metrojaya. While most are modern, well designed and spacious, Wang Plaza is a rabbit warren of rows and rows of small shops packed with bargains and is very popular with the locals. Prices are reasonable and bargaining is acceptable in some outlets. Low Yat Plaza (p.339) is the place for cheap computers and accessories but be warned that some may not always be authentic items.

One of the hottest precincts is Bintang Walk (p.327), along Jalan Bukit Bintang from Jalan Sultan Ismail to The Westin KL. It is an excellent example of re-engineering KL social habits, as many locals, once confined to the air-conditioned hotels and bars, have now taken to the streets. People want to be seen enjoying the good life and are now happy to sit outdoors. While there has always been a tradition of open-air dining in hawker stalls, KL has come of age with the arrival of Dôme, Starbucks, Gloria Jean's, San Francisco Coffee and The Coffee Bean brands.

The young and impressionable parade down Bintang Walk or lounge about in places like Planet Hollywood (p.359) and sidewalk cafes along Jalan Bukit Bintang. If you want to be seen, this is definitely the place to be.

The Pavilion KL is the most recent addition to the shopping scene, with Tangs (p.340) and Parkson (p.330) as anchor tenants but supported by an impressive cast of around 450 retail outlets such as 128 Faubourg, Clinique, L'Occitane, A/X Armani Exchange, DKNY, Guess, Jaspal, Paul Frank, Raoul, Ted Baker, Jean Paul Gaultier and Versace. There are also cinemas, restaurants, foodcourts, bookshops and a fitness centre. Emporio Armani is located immediately opposite, in front of the JW Marriott.

Kompleks Budaya Kraf (p.287) on Jalan Conlay sells Malaysian handicrafts such as batik, songket, carved wood, baskets and beadwork from Borneo. There are also some displays where visitors can see articles being made, and to even have a go at making these crafts themselves..

Nearby at 2 Jalan Stonor, the headquarters for Malaysia's Heritage Trust, or *Badan Warisan* (p.185), is located in a delightful 1920s British colonial bungalow. Badan is a non-profit, non-government organisation established to promote the preservation and conservation of Malaysia's built heritage. There is also a traditional wooden Malay house in the grounds that is well worth inspecting. Badan Warisan has an excellent resource library, a small but well-stocked gift shop, and is one of KL's lesser known assets. It holds talks and leads guided trips across the city and the country, and anyone interested in Malaysia's built heritage should consider joining the organisation. Visitors are welcome between 10:00 and 17:00 (Monday to Friday) and 11:00 to 16:00 (Saturday).

Away from the glass and aluminium of the modern Golden Triangle there remain pockets of 'old' KL. Just off all the retail action of Jalan Bukit Bintang, Jalan Alor is a good place to visit. In the evening, hawkers set up their plastic chairs and offer a delicious array of dishes to enthusiastic diners.

This is an authentic Malaysian dining experience with reasonable prices, great variety, lots of noise and a fantastic atmosphere. First-timers should visit all the stalls, making a note of what looks good. Then it's best to choose a location that offers lots of variety and order whatever takes your fancy.

The dishes on offer along Jalan Alor are principally Chinese and mostly from the island of Penang. Indian and Malay hawker stalls can be found here, but they are in the minority. The stalls often remain open until the early hours of the morning, giving the city life around the clock. There are no set hours for meals and Malaysians will snack and drink at all times, so join in the fun. At such stalls, if you are unsure what something is, take a chance and order it anyway – it's always really cheap so if you don't like it you can just bin it and try something else instead. The Jalan Bukit Bintang area of the city offers the best of several dining experiences, from local hawkers stalls to fine dining in modern international restaurants and smart coffee shops under the stars.

Bintang street scene

There are various public rail stations that service the Golden Triangle. Use the monorail stops of Imbi (for Times Square), Bukit Bintang (Jalan Bukit Bintang), Raja Chulan (Istana and Crowne Plaza Hotels) and Bukit Nanas (Bukit Nanas Forest Reserve). Imbi Station is also near the Pudu Star LRT line and Bukit Nanas is the access station for Dang Wangi Station on the Putra LRT line.

*Area **C** p.160-p.161*
See also Map 7

The Lowdown

Brickfields was once infamous for its unsavoury nightlife. It is now cleaned up and a favourite haunt of many locals, especially for its restaurants.

The Good

It's the place to come for authentic, delicious and cheap Indian food.

The Bad

Like so many areas of Kuala Lumpur, Brickfields seems in danger of losing its unique character to uncontrolled development.

The Must-Dos

Eat some satay skewers and a roti pisang at a hawker stall.

Brickfields street scene

Brickfields

Although the area around Masjid Jamek just to the north of Chinatown is called 'Little India', Brickfields might also have a legitimate claim to the name. The largest number of the inhabitants of this fascinating part of Kuala Lumpur are Indian-Malaysians, and how this came to be is a fascinating story. In the 1870s, Kuala Lumpur was expanding fast and the demand for building materials was high. An enterprising businessman, Yap Kwan Seng, saw the potential of the rural area now known as Brickfields. One of its main features was a huge clay quarry which would provide excellent material for the fabrication of high quality bricks. Yet the area also retained its agricultural character for a long time after it became a centre for the production of bricks; hence the blending of the two words, 'brick' and 'fields'.

Meanwhile, the British were developing the KTM – Malaysia's railway system. Having already put an excellent rail system in place in India, they knew that it was the place to go for trains and an efficient, cost-effective work force. Many of the new workers settled in Brickfields, where their descendants remain until this day. The colourful Jalan Rosario still has scores of the original railway quarters built at this time.

Modern Brickfields is roughly between Bangsar and Chinatown and retains much of its historic character. Old shophouses operate next to modern skyscrapers. It's a hustling, bustling, vibrant community famed for its many restaurants and hawker stalls where delicious local food is sought out by local connoisseurs. This is the place to go for a banana leaf lunch, or to sample thosai or roti pisang, both a sort of banana pancake. Another local favourite is curry laksa, a spicy soup.

In spite of its Indian flavour, Brickfields offers a variety of culinary experiences. Jalan Tun Sambanthan bustles with Malay, Chinese, Vegetarian and Indian Muslim restaurants as well as more standard Indian eateries offering some of the best and most affordable Indian fare in town.

After lunch go shopping for gold and silver jewellery, saris and rich silks. Be sure to drop by Sri Kota Shopping Center. Wherever you are, bargain hard.

Brickfields is also known as the 'Divine Location' because of the many famous temples and shrines in its streets, not all of them Hindu. Don't miss the Buddhist Maha Vihara Temple, the Aminmegu Sree Veera Haouman Temple, the Lutheran Church, or the Three Teachings Chinese Temple on Jalan Thambipillay.

Brickfields also has a lively nightlife, which may explain why one of Kuala Lumpur's four police district headquarters is located there. Once known for its relatively high crime rates, Brickfields' reputation is now much better.

It is bordered roughly by Jalan Travers in Bangsar, Jalan Tun Sambanthan 4 and Jalan Sayed Putra. Kuala Lumpur Sentral Station is in Brickfields and provides the easiest access point to it. Located on the corner of Tun Sambanthan and Tun Sambanthan 4 is the large YMCA, which offers a number of community activities – even lessons in Scottish dancing.

Area **D** *p.160-p.161*
See also Map 7

Chinatown

Chinatowns the world over have their own magical qualities, and the one in Kuala Lumpur does not disappoint. It's difficult not to be excited by the variety of exotic aromas, the bustle of traders, the sense of excitement and the theatre of it all. While it can get hot, busy and sometimes claustrophobic, at least you know you are alive when you are in this part of KL.

Chinatown doesn't actually exist on most KL street directories. It is often referred to as Jalan Petaling (Petaling Street, p.327), which is the best known street and taxi drivers may better understand this as a direction rather than Chinatown. The area is concentrated around Petaling Street and bounded by Jalans Tun HS Lee, Cheng Lock, Hang Lekir and Balai Polis.

Once in the district, walking is the best way to get around and to connect with other places like Central Market. Much of what occurs in this part of town has not changed for decades. You may still see old men pedalling their bicycles, collecting and delivering their wares as they always have for decades. Chinese medicine shops display their various traditional herbs and medicines. There are goldsmiths, basket weavers, dry goods stores, stores selling pots and pans, food outlets and clothes stores. The old residents hold fast as new developments slowly make inroads and it is obvious that the architectural qualities of the shop facades are changing.

There is always something open, no matter what the time, although the wet market running between Petaling Street and Lorong Bandar is most active early in the morning and at sunset. Every conceivable Chinese product is sold here, from fresh fish and meat to dry herbs and spices. Chinese is the most common language spoken, and this is a place to do business and to sell things – not for asking too many questions and having people pose for photos. For many Chinese, being photographed is a very sensitive issue so indicate or ask before blinding a trader with your flash. Various hawker stalls are located in and around the produce with some hawkers having sold the same thing here for eons.

In the morning, dim sum restaurants are popular for breakfast, but then things quieten down. The streets pick up at lunchtime as office workers descend for lunch. The activity quietens down a little in the afternoon, but once work finishes the streets return to their frenzied state of excitement. Food is served around the clock, in makeshift open-air stalls, in fan-cooled coffee shops, or air-conditioned restaurants. Some favourite dishes in Chinatown include dim sum, Hainanese chicken rice, curry laksa, won ton mee, Assam laksa and yong tau foo. The Old China Café on Jalan Bali Polis (see p.363) is one of the more atmospheric restaurants in KL. It is located in what was once the Selangor and Federal Territory Laundry Association and old historic photos line the walls.

In the evening, restaurants spread out onto Jalan Hang Lekir and there is relaxed, open-air ambience. Several restaurants all sell similar Chinese dishes, but at a premium for foreigners. If you don't want to pay the higher price, eat in the adjoining restaurant, off the street with the locals where the prices are cheaper.

For many, Chinatown is a big 'rip-off' as a variety of inexpensive but fake clothes, watches and DVDs are sold everywhere despite it being illegal. Shopping should be treated as fun and ruthless – bargaining is essential to secure a good deal. The five-foot walkways still remain to offer shelter from the tropical heat, but mostly they are filled with traders and their stalls selling all sorts of treasures.

Many of these merchants sell a variety of near 'genuine' brands and seemingly operate with immunity. It's all a bit of fun, so don't be surprised if that 'designer' watch you buy self destructs just months after being purchased (in fact, many of them are excellent watches but you can guarantee the 'diamonds' in the face won't be real).

While prices may be displayed, bargaining is an essential component of shopping in

The Lowdown
This is a high energy part of KL, with parts that haven't changed for eons and night markets that are crowded, active, brash and energetic. The food and shopping are very good and the slowly eroding architecture is fascinating.

The Good
Food, food and food; there's a lip-smacking variety of delicious food available here.

The Bad
The streets are a rabbit warren full of stalls, shops and hawkers. For those who don't like crowds or having to bargain for every item they buy, the air-conditioned designer malls maybe a better place to shop.

The Must-Dos
Check out the Hindu Sri Maha Mariamman Temple, Tze Ya Temple, Petaling Street wet market, and dine in the Old China Café (p.363) or in one of many dim sum restaurants.

Tze Ya Temple

Chinatown. Firstly, choose a price that you are happy with and then start the game of haggling. You can be assured that the trader will always get the better of you, but does it really matter? Pay what you think it is worth, and enjoy the banter.

While the area is known as Chinatown, it is an ethnically mixed area with an Indian temple and Malay curry houses among the predominantly Chinese shops. There are several places of worship in the district that make a peaceful retreat from the streetside mayhem. The colourful and ornate facade of Sri Maha Mariamman Hindu Temple built in 1873 is an arresting sight. It was constructed over a century ago and remains important for Hindus (see p.190).

Malaysia is home to many fascinating festivals, with none more colourful than the Hindu festival of Thaipusam. It is celebrated with the full moon in the tenth month of the Hindu calendar at the end of January or the start of February. The festival proper is celebrated at Batu Caves on the north-western outskirts of the capital; they start in Chinatown. The actual day of the celebrations at Batu Caves is a public holiday for KL residents. However, for Hindus who celebrate, it is three days of festivities that start at the Sri Maha Mariamman Temple in Chinatown and finishes at Batu Caves. The procession to Batu Caves commences as the chariot is pulled by two bulls for the eight-hour journey to the caves. Despite the crowds, congestion and apparent mayhem, this festival is something all residents should experience at least once.

The temple, situated along Chinatown's Jalan Tun S Lee, is well worth visiting. It is KL's principle Hindu temple and like most similar temples, it offers a rainbow of colours and a cast of gods and deities that looks totally confusing to outsiders (see p.190).

Just down the road is the Persatuan Kwong Siew Chinese Temple, built in 1888 by the Kwong Siew Association. Nearby in Jalan Hang Kasturi, Tze Ya Temple is the oldest in Kuala Lumpur. It stands hidden a little back from the street, but look for the colourful facade above the driveway entrance. This small temple is a hive of activity as devotees burn incense, make offerings on the altars and hit big brass gongs to seek help and guidance. Just behind the temple is the large and colourfully decorated Central Market. One of the least active times in Chinatown is during Chinese New Year. Although there are only two days of official public holidays, most Chinese businesses close for up to five. Before and during the celebration, Chinatown becomes decorated with all things red (the colour the Chinese associate with happiness). Red lanterns light the streets and boxes of imported mandarins are sold. Chinatown is best visited before the celebration – it tends to be quiet during the festivities as Chinese merchants close shop to celebrate with their families. Preparations begin weeks before the actual date, when people start buying presents, food and clothing, and decorating their homes and shops.

There are various transport nodes, with Pudu Bus Station (for long distance buses and taxis) and Pasar Seni Station on the Putra LRT. The KL Hop-On Hop-Off (p.199) bus also stops in Chinatown and Central Market.

We're all over Asia

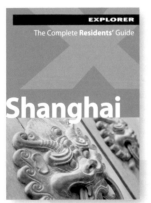

When it's time to make the next stop on your expat Asian adventure, be sure to pack an Explorer Residents' Guide. These essential books will help you make the most of your new life in a new city.

Explorer Residents' Guides – We Know Where You Live

The Lowdown
a number of tour
agencies will offer
guided tours to places
on the outskirts of KL
at hefty prices. The
truth is that you can
arrange all of these
expeditions much
more cheaply yourself.

The Good
Walks in the rainforest
at FRIM and Templer
Park offer wonderful
opportunities to
experience the jungle.
Listen for the chatter of
monkeys overhead.

The Bad
Most of the places worth
visiting on the outskirts
of Kuala Lumpur are
hard to reach without
a car of your own. In
addition, the Genting
Highlands are relatively
expensive to visit.

The Must-Dos
Climb the stairs at
Batu Caves late in the
afternoon when the sun
is not too hot. Buy some
water to drink at the top
and sit quietly watching
the people making their
way up after you.

KL Outskirts

While there's plenty to see and do within the city limits of KL, there is a lot more going on just a little way out of the city. You can literally get to some of these places in 30 minutes or less.

Batu Caves

About 15 kilometres north of Kuala Lumpur is the most popular destination for visitors on the city's outskirts, Batu Caves. But these are much more than a series of limestone caves in a hill overlooking Kuala Lumpur; it's a sacred Hindu shrine and the focal point of the world's largest Thaipusam celebrations. Access to the caves is by way of 272 steep steps climbing, past a golden statue of Lord Murugan, said (at over 40 metres high) to be the world's tallest. Take some care about what you carry, especially food. The dozens of macaque monkeys on the way up are talented, aggressive and relentless thieves. Batu Caves can be reached on the old Ipoh Road or by travelling north west on the Middle Ring Road from the direction of Ampang. See also p.189.

FRIM

Although the Forest Research Institute of Malaysia is first and foremost a legitimate government facility examining techniques of forest regeneration, it also welcomes visitors to its museum and arboretum. You are encouraged to walk the somewhat challenging jungle trails through 1,482 acres of primary rainforest. The most popular attraction is the Canopy Walk, but there is lots more to see. FRIM can be reached from the Middle Ring Road, or the old Ipoh Road. To get more information visit www.frim. gov.my. To book a Canopy Walk call 03 6279 7575. See also p.196.

Genting Highlands

Initially criticised by some because of the destruction of virgin tropical jungle and the negative environmental impact caused by its construction, Genting Highlands has become, nevertheless, enormously popular with Malaysians and expats alike. Among its attractions are a casino, a theme park, convention centres, excellent restaurants, nightclubs featuring world-class entertainers, and a cable car ride, the Genting Skyway. It's best accessed from the Karak Highway (driving in the direction of Kuantan), or from Jalan Hulu Kelang. There is also a bus service from various parts of the city. For more information visit www.genting.com.my.

Kampung Kuantan & The Fireflies

Some nine kilometres east of Kuala Selangor, the tiny village of Kampung Kuantan is a popular destination for visitors wishing to see spectacular displays of synchronised flashing by thousands of fireflies in the Mangrove swamps along the Selangor River. The fireflies are at their best between dusk and midnight and can be visited on a locally hired boat. For those not wishing to return to Kuala Lumpur so late, nearby Kuala Selangor offers accommodation and dining, the best bet probably being the Firefly Park Resort (www.fireflypark.com).

Templer Park

This 2,966 acre primary rainforest park is around 20 kilometres from Kuala Lumpur, just off the highway E1 (the North-South Expressway) in the direction of Ipoh. Take the exit at Rawang. It's an excellent venue for hikes through the jungle on any of a number of marked trails. Don't miss the Kanching Waterfalls, and bring swimwear so you can enjoy a dip in one of the artificial lake's many lagoons. A climb up the 350 metre-high Bukit Takun, stopping on the way to explore some of its caves, is a popular pastime.

The many sights at Batu Caves

Area **F** *p.160-p.161*
See also Map 5

KLCC & Jalan Ampang

Petronas is the acronym for Petroliam Nasional Berhad, which is the Malaysian state-owned petroleum company (it sponsors an F1 racing car, so the branding is internationally recognised). The Petronas Twin Towers dominate the skyline and once were the world's two tallest buildings. Now the national spin doctors refer to it as the world's tallest twin towers, to maintain national pride and not to be outdone by 101 Tower in Taipei which is higher, and the Burj Dubai in the United Arab Emirates, which, although incomplete, is now officially the tallest building in the world.

The Lowdown

The glistening 452 metre-high Petronas Twin Towers are the focal point for the city and a symbol of the growing Malaysian economy. If you do nothing else in KL, stand at the base of the Twin Towers and marvel at their architectural grandeur.

The parkland, office and entertainment area was once home to the Royal Selangor Turf Club (now relocated to Sungai Besi, see page 238). The club moved just before 1992 when the KLCC development commenced. In April 1996, the pinnacles were installed to top out the towers at 451.9 metres.

Designed by Boston-based Cesar Pelli & Associates, the towers are now the most photographed building in Malaysia. They are also a magnet for tourists and shoppers, as well as a beacon for Malaysian nationalism and its desire to be part of the developed world.

Access to the towers is strictly controlled and only accredited visitors are allowed inside for security reasons. The highest point any other visitor can go is the 58.4 metre-long, two-storey Skybridge: this is 170 metres above the ground (at levels 41 and 42).

The Good

Kuala Lumpur City Centre (KLCC) is indeed the centre of the city, with offices located in the towers, but it also includes the associated Convention Centre (also called some what confusingly, KLCC), parkland and lake, six floors of high-end retail space in Suria KLCC, a philharmonic auditorium, art gallery, hands-on science centre, hotels, transport nodes and, cinemas to make it a place you don't want to leave.

While access to the Skybridge (see p.188) is possible from 08:30 to 17:00 from Tuesday to Sunday, visitors need to be at the ticket office (open at 08:30) early to queue to be allocated one of a very limited number of free tickets (reportedly just 1,300 a day) for a guided tour. Weekends are almost impossibly busy, with weekdays being a better option, but be prepared to queue even then.

The views from the Skybridge are impressive but should you miss out, all is not lost. Head off to the adjoining Traders Hotel (p.25) and ride the elevators to the 33rd floor where the SkyBar (p.404) serves cool cocktails and has intoxicating views of the Twin Towers. The bar opens at 17:00 so plan to arrive before sunset when the lights to the towers are turned on at about 18:30. Order one of the designer martinis (try the lychee) and enjoy the uninterrupted views of the towers and the parklands (do this even if you manage to obtain a ticket to the Skybridge).

Of course, everyone can visit the six retail floors of Suria KLCC (at the base of the Twin Towers). This is the place where Malaysians meet and socialise at all times of the week, but especially at weekends. They come here to be with friends, take in a movie, eat, and of course shop – one of the leading national pastimes. Tour groups are also dropped here for several hours. Such a well-known address attracts leading international brands such as Marks & Spencer, Chopard, Raoul, Adidas, FCUK, Zara, Naf Naf, Christian Lacroix, Gap, Diesel, Polo, Guess, Max & Co and Converse. Several local brands are here, along with the Parkson and Isetan department stores.

The Bad

There are not too many bad things associated with this area but it can get crowded at weekends. Access to the top of the towers is not possible and is restricted, in limited numbers, to just the Skybridge, 170 metres above the ground.

For a change from all the retail action of Suria KLCC, art is on display at Galeri Petronas (p.183) on level three. The art gallery is open daily (except Mondays) from 10:00 to 20:00. Entry is free and it stages regular exhibitions of international and local artists. At the street-level entry is the box office for the Malaysian Philharmonic Orchestra (p.249). The concert hall for the philharmonic orchestra is a world-class space for live music. Ticket prices are very reasonable and often special matinees are conducted for families. Respectable clothing is required – no jeans, T-shirts or sandals at any time and long-sleeved shirts for men in the evening. Annual programmes are arranged well in advance.

Petrosains (p.186) is on level four of Suria KLCC and is a hands-on science discovery centre with a focus on the oil and gas industry. A fun approach to learning is taken and the exhibits are well maintained – kids love it. It's open from Tuesday to Sunday from 09:00 to 17:00. On Fridays you can visit between 09:00 and 13:00, and 14.30 and 17:00.

Kuala Lumpur – Main Areas

The Must-Dos
Visit the Skybridge,
hear the Malaysian
Philharmonic
Orchestra, walk
through the park,
view the evening
lights from the SkyBar
in the Traders Hotel
and take the kids to
discover Petrosains.

A short underground walk from KLCC through to the Convention Centre, leads to Aquaria KLCC (p.182) with over 5,000 aquatic and land-based animals on display. The highlight is the walk-through glass tunnel where it's possible to safely eyeball sharks, rays and many colourful fish. Charges for adults are RM38, and with a MyKad the price is RM28. For kids (aged 3 to 12) it costs RM26, or with a MyKad, RM22. Those younger than 3 get in free. It is open from 11:00 to 20:00 daily; last admissions are at 19:00. MyKad is a Malaysian identification card, so it is a good way of disguising the fact that foreigners pay a premium.

The parklands immediately in front of the Convention Centre and the Twin Towers are a multipurpose area with lots of paths beneath carefully positioned mature rainforest trees. The trails have a special surface for joggers and there are several recreational areas like a big pool and playground which are frequented by families at the weekends. Several other office towers are on the periphery of the park, and modern premium condominium blocks reach ever skyward around the whole area. Inner city living is on the increase.

Tourists can stay in several hotels in and around the area – Mandarin Oriental, Traders Hotel, Impiana, Crowne Plaza, Ascot, Hotel Equatorial, Corus, or Hotel Nikko, with the luxurious Four Seasons currently under construction.

The area is well served by public transport with the KLCC station on the Putra LRT line being the closest railway station, connected via an underground tunnel to KLCC. There are several recognised taxi stands where queuing is expected.

Sky Bar at Traders Hotel

Suria KLCC

Petronas Twin Towers

Area **G** *p.160-p.161*
See also Map 6

Lake Gardens

Most Malaysians know this area as KL's 'green lungs' because of two artificial lakes surrounded by landscaped gardens and a few public recreational areas. While there are other parks in the city (KLCC and Lake Titiwangsa), this is the biggest. It was incorporated into the city as an open space back in 1889. The area was also designated as the official residence of the British Government's representative (Carcosa from 1904) and the king's House (Istana Tematu from 1913). They no longer serve as residences but Carcosa Seri Negara (p.23) is considered one of the city's most exclusive boutique hotels, with a grand restaurant serving excellent French cuisine in stylish surroundings.

The Lowdown
Also known as Taman Tasik Perdana, Lake Gardens were first laid out in 1889 to provide KL with a large open space for the growing population and a botanical garden. Despite the city's rapid growth over the decades, the gardens remain a green lung for residents and visitors.

Tiffin lunch is served in Gulai House from 12:00 to 15:00 every Sunday. The name tiffin is associated with the container that people used to take their lunch to work in, but in this instance refers to the excellent Malay and Indian cuisine served buffet style. Reservations are essential and seats on the open verandah are best.

Every day in the adjoining Drawing Room (p.397) of Seri Negara, traditional English afternoon teas with all the trimmings are served to KL's social set. This never becomes too crowded, so you could find yourself in luxurious surroundings with a battalion of waiters attending to your every need. This is the place to impress overseas friends and relatives when they drop by.

The Good
The gardens are a large, multi-functional public space with lots of things to do; all is close to the city centre.

In the Carcosa section of the hotel (a 200 metre walk through the landscaped gardens from Seri Negara), The Dining Room (p.368) is possibly the city's most elegant dining space. Walking in past the grand staircase is like stepping into a museum, but the excellent French food and wines are fresh and full of life. It's posh, and reserved by many for special occasions. Most guests arrive in their chauffeur-driven limousines or their own luxury cars. Very few arrive by taxi so drivers may not even know where the Carcosa is located – so if this is your mode of transport, have a good map available as you may have to direct the driver.

The Bad
Nothing really although the gardens get crowded at weekends and are sometimes booked up by large groups for functions. However, they are big enough for everyone to find their own solitude.

While few residents get to experience Carcosa Seri Negara, most have enjoyed the open spaces and recreational facilities in the rest of the gardens, which are divided by the main arterial road, Jalan Parlimen, leading to Parliament House.

Tugu Negara (National Monument) is located on the smaller, northern side of the park. There is a similarity between this and the famous Iwo Jima Memorial in Washington DC, as both were designed by sculptor Felix de Weldon. The 15.5 metre-high bronze statue has seven figures – five local servicemen from the various branches of the security forces and two fallen communist terrorists. The statue commemorates those who died fighting for the newly-independent Malaysia during the Communist Emergency from 1948 to 1960. It sits majestically on a white-tiled terrace backed by a pond and a curved pavilion with three golden domes.

The Must-Dos
There are many family activities here and kids will appreciate the Bird Park, Orchid Garden and Deer Park. Grown ups will love the tiffin curry lunch served every Sunday at Gulai House in the Carcosa.

Below the monument are various sculptures in the ASEAN Sculpture Garden. These are prize-winning efforts from leading ASEAN sculptors and provide a distraction for those relaxing in this part of the park.

Cross Jalan Parlimen into Jalan Cenderawasih which leads into the main section of the park. There are directional signs and maps to all the attractions in the park, but sadly some of these are in Bahasa Malaysia only. A few signs indicate that flowers are not to be plucked, there should be no littering, no pets and no close proximity between couples. While there are roads throughout the park, some of them are closed, but there are lots of carparks.

The eastern side of the area has the leafy appearance of being in the park but some of the attractions, like the Taman Burung (Bird Park, p.194), Muzium Polis (Police Museum) and the Planetarium Negara (p.188), are just outside. Muzium Negara (National Museum, p.186), National Mosque (p.188) and the Islamic Arts Museum of Malaysia (p.185) are on the park's periphery so there are many things to do in the area, and while seeing them all involves some walking, it is not impossible to see everything on foot.

Fantasy Planet is a fantastic playground for kids, with swings, slides and magical castles to explore. In other parts of the gardens, there are wooden tables and chairs for picnics, shelters, expanses of grass and lots of shady trees. Small paddle boats can also be hired for a little exercise on the lake.

There are also several attractions with an entrance fee. The Butterfly Park (p.193X) is located on Jalan Cenderasari on the park's eastern fringe. The covered area is full of plants and colourful flowers and, of course, butterflies (around 6,000 of them) and insects. There is an extensive souvenir shop at the exit and a place to buy cold drinks. The park is open daily from 09:00 to 18:00 and entry fees are RM17 for adults and RM8 for kids, but a family pass (2 adults and 3 kids) costs RM24. Additional charges are RM1 (camera) and RM5 (video), but tripods are not permitted. Within walking distance is the Bird Park (p.194) which is well worth visiting.

The Orchid Garden offers visitors a very colourful display of 800 species of local and foreign orchids, as well as some good elevated views of the KL skyline. The garden is open daily from 09:00 to 18:00 and while entry is free during the week, there is a minimal entry fee at weekends and on public holidays. They also sell specimens of plants and flowers and offer useful advice on growing orchids.

Deer Park (p.193) is located just below the Tunku Abdul Rahman Museum. Entry is free for those who want to see Malaysia's mouse deer and rusa deer from a wooden boardwalk in a grassland setting.

Tunku Abdul Rahman Museum (03 2694 7277) on Jalan Dato' Onn is a memorial to Malaysia's first Prime Minister, who helped the country attain nationhood. Entry is free to what was once the residence and office of the PM. The museum is open from 10:00 to 17:30, except Fridays (10:00 to 12:00 and 15:00 to 17:30), and Mondays, when it is closed.

A short walk up the hill from the museum is the National Planetarium (p.188) operated by the National Space Agency. This was established to educate the public about space exploration and the solar system. The displays are quite informative and good for children.

Lake Gardens

Area **H** p.160-p.161
See also Map 5

The Lowdown
Bollywood meets
Malaysia with a busy,
crowded and colourful
streetscape that is best
discovered on foot.

The Good
Just like a Bollywood
movie there's lots of
action, drama and in-
your-face culture.

The Bad
Parking and traffic
here, like in many
parts of KL can be
oppressive, but the
area is well served by
public transport or by
the KL Hop-On Hop-Off
City Tour.

Little India

Little India is the area around Masjid India on the north-western side of the Klang River near Jalan Tuanku Abdul Rahman (still known to many by its original name, Jalan Batu). Masjid Jamek is on the southern side and Jalan Dang Wangi is to the north. Jalan Masjid India dissects the area and it is named after the mosque situated just around the corner from Jalan Melayu. This area is the focus for northern Indian Muslims and is one of the oldest parts of the city. It is located just a few hundred metres from the confluence of the Gombak and Klang rivers where the city first started. The area is always busy and colourful; when people gather for Friday prayers it's particularly active and crowded.

Walking the busy streets is the best way to experience the many facets of Indian culture. Many restaurants and shops in the area were originally opened by the Chettiar – an Indian caste who were traditionally moneylenders, merchants and professionals. Shops spill out onto the road, and there is an extensive range of goods, from colourful saris to jewellery, brassware, stacks of incense, rolls of fabrics, Muslim prayer items, flowers and food. There's sure to be at least one medicine man offering some magical cure for everything from impotence to ingrowing toe nails. While you may not understand the sales pitch, you will definitely enjoy the theatre of it all. There are plenty of budget hotels around here too.

Start exploring the area by alighting from either the Star LRT or Putra LRT, which meet at Masjid Jamek. This is possibly KL's most beautiful mosque; certainly one of its most serene and compact. It is also the city's oldest mosque, built in 1909 using red brick and white marble. Like most of these buildings, the architectural inspiration is Mughal and aesthetically the building is without equal. There are various places to photograph the mosque, both from within the grounds and also on the southern banks of the Klang River. The mosque is particularly busy at prayer times (especially Friday prayers) and visitors should plan to visit at other times of the day. Only Muslims are allowed in the main prayer hall and shoes must be removed before entering. Modest dress is expected of all visitors.

To reach Little India proper, cross the road and head north along Jalan Melayu, which leads into Jalan Masjid India. Masjid India is situated on the western side of the road

Covered market

Ceremonial flowers

just after Wisma Kosas. The original and modest mosque was constructed from timber in 1863 and the present building was erected in 1966. It can accommodate about 3,500 worshippers and is the main Indian Muslim mosque in the city. The three-storey building is representative of a southern Indian mosque, with various onion-shaped domes and arched windows. Non-Muslims are not allowed in but there is enough to admire from the street.

Food is plentiful: from fresh milk to a range of Indian breads, snacks and very sweet cakes. Not all outlets are halal (being Indian Muslim) but some serve food from many regions of India. This is a good dining area for vegetarians as many Indians do not eat meat, and several restaurants in the area cater to their needs. Some restaurants serve dishes based upon traditional recipes that have never changed. One of the most popular dishes is nasi campur (mixed rice), where diners add their own selection of vegetables and curried meats to a mound of white rice. Curry sauce and poppadoms complete the dish.

For general shopping, visit the popular Semua House. From here, just past the Guobna Building, is the Sri Pathra Kali Amman Temple, open from early morning to late in the evening.

The Must-Dos ◄

Masjid India, Masjid Jamek, the many hawker stalls, night markets along Jalan Tuanku Abdul Rahman, dining in the Coliseum Cafe and, if you are up to it, a Hindi blockbuster movie in the Coliseum Cinema.

Around the corner from Jalan Bunus, on the main thoroughfare of Jalan Tuanku Abdul Rahman, are two colonial buildings which have significant heritage value and, as such, are protected under the Antiquities Act. The Coliseum Theatre and Coliseum Cafe & Hotel were built in early in the 20th century. The Coliseum resists change and caters to its loyal group of followers who love the old-fashioned ambience and the mostly Hindi and southern Tamil movies screened these days.

The Coliseum Hotel is locked in a time warp but was once the place to stay in KL. Planters used to travel from various parts of the country to 'live it up' a little in the big city and their hotel of choice was the Coliseum. No doubt they sat in the small bar adjoining the cafe and sipped their gin and tonics. Contemporary visitors drop by today and do exactly the same. While neither the hotel nor cafe would be considered the height of luxury, they don't come much better in terms of their atmosphere.

There is a night market (*pasar malam*) along the one-way street off Jalan Tuanku Abdul Rahman every Saturday evening.

Retail outlets along Jalan Tengu Abdul Rahman include G.S. Gill (for sportswear and equipment) and the modern Sogo Department Store, which is very popular with Malaysians. Globe Silk Store, on the same street, is one of the country's oldest department stores, having been around for 70 years. It sells an extensive array of cloth and clothing. Other shops include Mun Loong Textiles, P Lal Store and Chotimall.

Little India is within easy walking distance of Petaling Street and visitors to the city can explore both at the same time. The best way to get there is to travel by LRT train, whether Putra or Star LRT, as both lines intersect right outside Masjid Jamek. Little India is just a short walk from the station. Buses and taxis are easily available. The KL Hop-On Hop-Off City Tour bus makes three stops along Jalan Raja Laut which is just a short walk from Little India.

Area ❶ p.160-p.161
See also Map 6

Petaling Jaya

The Lowdown
*Petaling Jaya, or 'PJ',
is one of KL's premier
residential suburbs. It
was the first 'new' town
built after the second
world war, and became
a model for other
towns in Malaysia.*

The Good
*PJ has many pleasant
residential areas that
are well served by
freeways and public
transport, such as the
KTM line to Klang and
the LRT system.*

The Bad
*The original new
town was planned to
accommodate 70,000
residents, but with 10
times the population
today, services are
stretched to the limit in
some places.*

The Must-Dos
*Make a trip to Siva
Temple at the summit
of Bukit Gasing and
walk through the
forested trails there.*

The establishment of Petaling Jaya, and later other suburbs, was initially intended to resolve the problem of overcrowding in KL. There was a need to resettle urban squatters located on inner city land that was earmarked for development. The Selangor State Government acquired almost 500 hectares of poor quality rubber estate in 1951 in what is now PJ.

Older residents refer to the Old and New Town sections of central Petaling Jaya. The Old Town is located near the intersection of Jalans Selangor, Othman and Pasar (east of Assunta Hospital). There is a large wet and dry market here and some good hawker stall food.

The New Town is the civic centre located in what the locals call PJ State because of the cinema here near the large council office block named Menara MPPJ.

There are green spaces in Petaling Jaya, with Bukit Gasing Forest Reserve (Gasing Hill) holding out against developers who would love to carve it up and develop more towering condominium blocks similar to those that already line the periphery. There are various walking trails through the secondary forest here and organisations like the Hash House Harriers are known to run along these. Access points are located around the edges and there are some reasonable views of KL and PJ from the highest point. The best access is from Jalan Lembah 5/4, which runs off Jalan Gasing near the ornate Poh Lum Fatt Yuen Chinese Temple. The reserve is home to wildlife including birds, snakes, monitor lizards, monkeys and squirrels. There is an entrance to the park at Jalan Telok, one kilometre up the hill from the temple.

Siva Temple is on the summit of Bukit Gasing and there are some decent elevated views across Petaling Jaya. The hill lies in both PJ and KL territory and town planning policies appear to be different, with KL being more proactive in seeing the hill 'developed'. The temple is reached by turning off Jalan Gasing into Jalan 5/64 which leads to Jalan 5/66A – just head for the Telecom Tower and look for the monkeys playing in the trees. There is another temple (Sri Maha Kaliamman) nearby but this has little tourism interest.

The other main recreation area in Petaling Jaya is Taman Jaya, bordered by the Federal Highway and Jalans Gasing and Timur. There is a large lake that is popular with local anglers, as well as walking paths, large grassy areas and car parks. The park is reasonably well maintained and is popular at sunrise and dusk.

There is a Hindu temple in one corner and nearby, on Jalan Pantai 9/7, there is a church, a Chinese temple and a Thai Buddhist temple. The glittering Thai Chetawan Buddhist Temple is a magnificent example of classical Thai architecture; a sight not commonly seen in Malaysia. Covered in gold, it is a dominant feature of the PJ landscape. It was officially opened in 1962 by the current king of Thailand, King Bhumibol. Being a Buddhist temple, visitors need to remove their shoes before entering. Vesak or Wesak Day, held in May, is a good time to visit so you can join in the celebrations associated with Buddha's birth, death and enlightenment.

Petaling Jaya and the state of Selangor begins along the Federal Highway with a ceremonial archway (Kota Darul Ehsan) located just after the turn off to Bangsar. Universiti of Malaya (p.142) is on the northern side of the road. The archway sprawls across the highway and marks the boundary between the Federal Capital (KL) and Selangor state. It is not advisable to stop here (it's actually illegal unless

What's Your Number?

PJ is divided mostly into sections named as numbers (for example Section 5), and the roads in the suburbs are further numbered (Section 5/56) so it can become a little confusing. The sections were also numbered according to when they were established, so sections 17 and 18 do not adjoin one another.

your vehicle has broken down) so simply drive underneath and admire it; keep your passport in your pocket as it is not required.

The distinction between KL and PJ is not obvious, especially in the location of Universiti Malaya and the adjoining Universiti Hospital (p.123), both of which are actually in KL but could easily be mistaken for PJ. There are several entrances to the university, Malaysia's first institute of higher learning. The main entrances are along Jalans Pantai Baharu (eastern side) and Jalan Universiti (western side). While access is normally restricted to vehicles displaying official stickers, security guards will allow visitors to enter two places of interest – Rimba Ilmu ('Forest of Learning' botanical gardens) and the Muzium Seni Asia (Museum of Asian Arts).

Living In PJ

Petaling Jaya is a huge residential area and quite popular with expats. Find out more about its pros and cons as a place to live on p.94 of the Residents chapter.

There is basically a one way circular road system around the expansive and landscaped university grounds. Look for the signs to Rimba Ilmu, which occupies 80 hectares of the campus near the squash complex and sports field. The entry gate and visitor registration area are located in the Institute of Biological Sciences, a distance past the dormitories called Rumah Universiti. Rimba Ilmu is open Monday to Friday from 09:00 to 16:00, and the first Saturday of the month from 09:00 to 12:00. An exhibition has been established in the registration area, as has a superbly labelled garden trail leading into the gardens themselves. The gardens are divided into wetlands, palms, mixed forest species, fruit trees and medicinal plants. There are many tropical plants growing in a near natural setting, and the gardens remain one of KL's best kept secrets.

The Museum of Asian Arts (7967 3805, www.um.edu.my) is located near the Faculty of Economics and Administration off Jalan Ilmu Baru; this is best accessed via the western entrance (the unmarked entrance to the car park is the first turn to the left after the Faculty of Economics, just 100 metres from the Jalan Universiti or western entrance). The building has a large sign but this is not clear until after you have driven past it. Wahid's Food Court is at the front entrance.

The small but representative collection, spread over three floors, includes local cultural items and Chinese and south Asian ceramics. It supposedly has the world's largest collection of kendi (ceramic water vessels), and the keris (Malaysian dagger) collection is also impressive. The collection of Ban Chiang pottery from Thailand is good and there are some detailed songket textile weavings. The museum is open during office hours from Monday to Friday and on Saturday mornings. There is also a good collection of films, slides and pictures for research purposes and the staff are very helpful.

PJ's busy streets

Putrajaya

While Kuala Lumpur is Malaysia's capital city, Putrajaya, founded only in 1995, is its administrative centre. Lying 25 kilometres south of KL and roughly halfway on the route to Kuala Lumpur International Airport, this purpose-built municipality is an architectural masterpiece. Situated on 12,000 acres of land, it is well worth a daytrip if only to marvel at its many striking buildings conceived and built entirely by Malaysian enterprises and reflecting a very Malaysian aesthetic.

Putrajaya is divided into a number of precincts, the most important being at the city's centre. They are called Government, Commercial, Civic and Cultural, Sports and Recreation and Mixed Development. The land area of the city is huge and attractions are spread out, so being familiar

Putrajaya bridge

with which precincts are home to the various sights you wish to visit is essential. In addition to the core precincts, there are another 15, most of which are residential.

Any visitor to Putrajaya should see the Prime Minister's Office complex and the nearby Putra Mosque. The mosque is massive and can accommodate up to 15,000 people for prayers. It contains a museum, a library, an exhibition hall and an auditorium, as well as the main prayer area itself. Built on five levels, the mosque is a visual message to the faithful. The levels represent both the five pillars of Islam and the five daily calls to prayer.

The blue-domed prime minister's residence next to it is also impressive and reflects a number of architectural influences, although both the arches and onion-shaped domes are unmistakably modern Islamic.

Some criticism has been levelled at the architecture of Putrajaya, claiming it is too exclusively Islamic. Since Malaysia is multi-ethnic, say the critics, where are the buildings reflecting Chinese, Indian, western and even modern Malay influences? You will need to judge for yourself whether or not this criticism is justified, but even the untrained eye is likely to uncover a wide number of cultural styles in the city's fabulous buildings.

Putrajaya is one of Malaysia's three federal territories, the other two being Kuala Lumpur itself and the island of Labuan. The eventual population goal for the city is 300,000 people: at present it is only about a sixth of the way there. Given the vast area of Putrajaya it is little wonder that the city's streets often feel quite empty.

The city is built around a huge waterway, Putrajaya Lake, which afforded the designers the opportunity to construct a total of nine bridges, some of which are visually quite stunning. Most notable among these are the 370 metre-long Seri Perdana Bridge and the two-tiered Putra Bridge.

Putrajaya was designed to be beautiful not only in terms of its architecture, but also its setting. The gently rolling landscape of the city has been carefully groomed to preserve its natural character. Botanical gardens, parks and wetlands adorn the city. Most visitors stop off at the Wetland Park to explore its 800 acres of marsh which are home to dozens of indigenous plants and fish. In addition to opportunities for birdwatching, the park also offers picnic areas and marked trails for biking, walking and jogging. After spotting such inhabitants as the little egret, the little green heron and the cinnamon bittern, visit the Nature Interpretation Centre to see its wetland diorama and handicraft displays.

No trip to Putrajaya is complete without a love boat ride at the Putrajaya Lake. A number of different tours are also available, and some offer dinner and cocktails.

No Car? Take the LRT!

KL's train system appears confusing to the novice, but once you jump in and start taking a few trains, it will all click into place. Check the LRT map at the back of this book, and check each entry for the nearest station. You'll probably have to combine your train ride with a taxi trip to get to most places, but it's still a quick, easy and cheap way to get around.

Tours Of Putrajaya

For more information about tours and facilities, contact the Putrajaya Information Centre on 03 8888 7272, or visit www.ppj.gov.my. Office hours for the centre are from 08:30 to 18:30 (Monday to Saturday). On Sundays and public holidays the office is open until 19:00. Organised tours of the city, including a bus service, are available. For boat cruises in Putrajaya contact Cruise Tasik Putrajaya on 03 8888 5539, or email sales@cruisetasikputrajaya.com.

Putrajaya skyline

Getting There

Any one of a number of expressways will lead the motorist to Putrajaya, depending on what part of Kuala Lumpur you are starting from. The North-South Highway is the most familiar. For the non-motorist, the best choice is the KLIA Transit train which stops at Putrajaya. Trains run every half hour and the trip takes about 20 minutes. Return fares are available and the train leaves from KL Sentral Station. Be warned, however, that the KLIA Ekspres does not stop at Putrajaya, but goes directly to the airport. Be sure that you take the KLIA Transit train.

Taxis also leave from KL Sentral for a fixed price. Buy a coupon at the taxi booth on the ground level.

Both these options do, however, pose a problem for getting around once you arrive in Putrajaya. Public transport within Putrajaya is almost non-existent so bring good walking shoes. Even taxis are rare, so be warned. An organised tour may be a good choice.

Amusement Centres

Other options **Theme Parks** p.192

Berjaya Times
Square
1 Jalan Imbi
Bukit Bintang
📍 *Imbi*
Map 13 B2

IMAX – Times Square

03 2117 3046 | www.timessquarekl.com

Berjaya Times Square is one of KL's biggest shopping malls and stands on Jalan Imbi, right in the heart of the city (one street over from Bintang Walk). It is also home to Malaysia's only IMAX theatre. Here, you can watch amazing 2D and 3D movies especially made for IMAX's signature giant screens. These screens are in fact the largest in south-east Asia. There are normally two or three movies shown in rotation, so check schedules first. Opening hours are daily from 10:00 to 22:00, and the tickets are cheaper than any IMAX experience in the world, at just RM15 for adults and RM10 for kids.

Sunway Pyramid
Petaling Jaya
📍 *Setia Jaya*

Pyramid Ice

03 7492 6800 | www.sunway.com.my/pyramidice

Next to the Sunway Lagoon Theme Park is the Sunway Pyramid Shopping Complex where a 30 metre tall lion forms the entrance. But the biggest attraction is the ice rink on the lower level. This is Malaysia's only public ice rink, and is home to south-east Asia's biggest skating school. Opening hours are daily from 10:00 to 22:00 and the entrance fee is RM20 for as long as you like. Skate rental is available. Check the website for lesson schedules and prices.

Aquariums & Marine Centres

Concourse Level
Kuala Lumpur
Convention Centre
📍 *KLCC*
Map 11 C3

Aquaria KLCC

03 2333 1888 | www.klaquaria.com

This oceanarium is located in the Kuala Lumpur Convention Centre (KLCC), which is, rather confusingly, right next to the better known KLCC, home to the Petronas Twin Towers. It boasts an impressive variety of tropical marine life. There is an amazing plexiglass walkthrough that allows visitors to pass through the giant aquarium and look out – and up – at toothy nurse sharks, hornbill turtles and stingrays. For the little kiddies, there is also an interactive petting zoo. Unfortunately, signs are often poorly lit or offer insufficient information, but on the whole it is a fascinating place to visit – just avoid the school holidays if you can, when the queues get ridiculous. A common

Aquaria KLCC

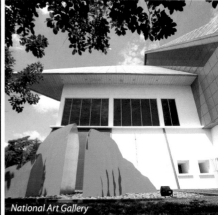

National Art Gallery

grievance is that non-Malaysians are charged nearly 50% more for tickets than locals, for which there seems to be no good reason. Entrance for foreigners costs RM38 for adults and RM26 for children.

Art Galleries
Other options **Art** p.284, **Art & Craft Supplies** p.286

Starhill Gallery
181 Jalan Bukit Bintang
Bukit Bintang
🚇 *Bukit Bintang*
Map 13 C1

Artseni Gallery
03 2144 0782 | *www.artseni.com*
Tucked away on the fourth floor of the very upmarket Starhill Gallery shopping centre on Bintang Walk is a curious and bold art gallery called Artseni. Although it is tiny, there is nothing small about the gallery's commitment to bringing local art to the public. Most exhibitions feature work by Malaysian artists, both traditional and modern. This is a beautiful gallery that is well worth a visit. Open daily from 10:00 to 21:30.

Level 3, Suria KLCC
KLCC
🚇 *KLCC*
Map 11 C2

Galeri Petronas
03 2051 7770 | *www.galeripetronas.com.my*
Head up to the third floor of Suria KLCC to take a break from shopping and enjoy a range of thought-provoking works by Malaysian and foreign artists. With free entrance and a great 'mainstream' location, the gallery does well in achieving its aim of bringing visual arts to the Malaysian public. You can expect to see many forms, from sculpture and photography to abstract and absurd, in the constantly changing exhibitions. The gallery is open from 10:00 to 20:00 every day except Monday, and the adjoining gift shop is tiny but well worth a browse for glossy catalogues of past exhibitions and some interesting local prints. Please note that you are not allowed to take cameras or bags into the gallery – lockers are provided at the entrance.

2 Jalan Temerloh
Off Jalan Tun Razak
City Centre
🚇 *Titiwangsa*
Map 8 F1

National Art Gallery
03 4025 4990 | *www.artgallery.gov.my*
Malaysia's first Prime Minister, Tunku Abdul Rahman, established the National Art Gallery in 1958, just a year after Malaya achieved independence. His intention was to highlight Malayan culture as part of his effort to shape a national identity. The original gallery was in a borrowed corner of the old parliament building and started with a modest collection of four works of art. Today, the new National Art Gallery boasts a permanent collection of 2,500 pieces, along with ongoing visiting exhibitions from around the world. This new National Art Gallery, opened in 2000, takes pride of place in a massive cultural complex which also includes the National Theatre and the National Library. Located just off the main thoroughfare of Jalan Tun Razak, just outside KL's Golden Triangle, the National Art Gallery actually houses six separate galleries, each with its own exhibition. Although the exhibitions are not restricted to Malaysian artists, they are given priority. Parking is easy and any visit is worth at least a couple of hours. The gallery is a short taxi ride from the Titiwangsa monorail station. Entrance is free.

17 Jalan Telawi 3
Bangsar Baru
🚇 *Bangsar*

Valentine Willie Fine Art
03 2284 2348 | *www.vwfa.net*
Valentine Willie, an active local patron of the arts, decided to concentrate on the evolving south-east Asian art scene, recognising the somewhat similar, yet essentially individual, cultures and roots of these nations. The gallery has featured a range of hugely talented artists from throughout the region, and an exhibition at Valentine is often regarded as an up-and-coming artist's official 'debut'. VWFA hosts up to 14

exhibitions per year, and admission is free. The gallery's resource room is open to the public and houses an extensive library of art books, magazines and catalogues.

Wei-Ling Gallery

8 Jalan Scott
Brickfields
Bangsar
🚇 **KL Sentral**

03 2260 1106 | *www.weiling-gallery.com*

The Wei-Ling Gallery, set up by Lim Wei-Ling and Yohan Rajan in 2002, can be found in the 'other' Little India of Kuala Lumpur – Brickfields. The gallery has up to a dozen exhibitions each year, concentrating on works by Malaysian and south-east Asian artists. Its efforts to increase both local and international support for these artists should be applauded, and it ensures that collectors are kept up to date with developments in the local art community, including the rise of young artists. Even if you don't have the funds to treat yourself to a work of art, the gallery is still worth a browse.

Heritage Sites

Carcosa Seri Negara

Taman Tasik Perdana
(Lake Gardens)
🚇 **KL Sentral**
Map 6 F1

03 2295 0888 | *www.ghmhotels.com*

Historical, elegant, tranquil…these are just some of the words to describe the Carcosa Seri Negara, KL's most exclusive hotel. It will cost you a pretty penny to stay here overnight, but it's worth a visit for the afternoon tea in The Drawing Room – a wonderful way to imagine yourself being transported back to colonial times. The hotel is a restored mansion that was the residence of the British colonial governor of Malaya, and whether you simply wander through the hotel lobby or check in for an extravagant overnight stay, it's a fascinating glimpse into the past.

Independence Square

Jalan Tun Perak
City Centre
🚇 **Masjid Jamek**
Map 10 C4

Independence Square (known locally as Padang Merdeka or Dataran Merdeka) is a good starting point to explore KL. Here the national flag flies atop a 100 metre-high flagpole, once the tallest in the world. Within the square is a field fronting the Royal Selangor Club where Malaysians converge every year to celebrate independence (*merdeka* means independence) on 31 August. The club itself is easily recognisable from its black and white tudor facade, and is still an important venue for wealthy residents of KL. The square is also home to some lovely fountains and a vast lawn, so it makes a tranquil spot to rest for a bit – if you can avoid the tourists. Just next to the square is St Mary's Cathedral, one of the oldest Anglican churches in Asia, having been built in its current location in 1895 (www. stmaryscathedral.org.my). Opposite the square is the ornate Sultan Abdul Samad building (p.185), which was built in 1897 by the colonial British, and which has a distinctly Moorish feel about it, complete with a clock tower and copper domes. It is especially lovely at night, when it is lit up by 10,000 lights. It used to be the headquarters of the British colonial administration, but today it houses the Supreme and High Courts.

Malay Tea House

FRIM
🚇 **Kepong**

03 6280 3503 | *www.frim.gov.my*

The Forest Research Institute of Malaysia (FRIM) (p.230) is just a short drive north of KL (and a 10 minute taxi ride from Kepong station). It is a must-visit place for many forest hikes and particularly the canopy walk (p.196). But while you are there, it's well worth popping into the Malay Tea House for a rest and a few refreshments. The tea house is a good 10 minute walk from the Visitors' Centre, but don't miss out on the chance to try a huge range of Malaysian herbal teas – the menu lists the healing benefits of each variety. You can also sample various traditional Malay dishes and desserts. There is a little shop where you can buy the various teas to take home, and also browse through some local crafts. The Malay Tea House is located in a beautifully restored 1929 colonial house.

No. 2 Jalan Stonor
City Centre
🚇 *Raja Chulan*
Map 11 E4

Rumah Penghulu Abu Seman

03 2144 9273 | *www.badanwarisan.org.my*

Just up the road from the KL Craft Complex (p.188) you'll find a magnificently restored traditional Malay wooden house, Rumah Penghulu Abu Seman. It was built in 1924, but was then dismantled and reconstructed in its current location in the grounds of the Heritage of Malaysia Trust (Badan Warisan Malaysia). Step inside to get a clear idea of what a traditional house would have looked like many years ago. It is open daily, with tours starting at 11:00 and 15:00, Mondays to Saturdays. You will be asked to make an RM5 donation. The Heritage of Malaysia Trust also houses a gift shop and a resource centre, and it is well worth combining a visit with the Craft Complex.

Opp Merdeka Square
City Centre
🚇 *Masjid Jamek*
Map 10 C4

Sultan Abdul Samad Building

Featuring Moorish architecture, the copper-domed Sultan Abdul Samad Building was constructed in 1897 by the British, and formed the centre of the KL skyline for decades. Even today its distinctive architecture and impressive location on Merdeka Square command attention, even though it is towered over by many surrounding high-rises. Evenings are a particularly good time to admire the building, as it is lit up with 10,000 lightbulbs. It now houses a branch of the High Court of Malaya.

Museums

Beh National Mosque
Jalan Lembah Perdana
City Centre
🚇 *Kuala Lumpur*
Map 12 B3

Islamic Arts Museum Malaysia

03 2274 2020 | *www.iamm.org.my*

This fascinating venue is part art gallery, part museum, part educational institute. Islamic art from across the world is exhibited in a series of permanent and temporary displays, but you'll also find fascinating exhibits showcasing textiles, coins, jewellery and armour. This is the largest museum of its kind in the region, and the 30,000 square metre space is packed with interesting articles from the Islamic world. Aside from the exhibition space, there is also a well-stocked library of books on Islamic art, as well as a restaurant serving Middle Eastern cuisine. The museum runs various educational programmes for adults and students, as well as a series of Saturday workshops for children, featuring storytelling and crafts. The museum is open from Tuesday to Sunday from 10:00 to 18:00. Entrance costs RM12 for adults and RM6 for students with a valid ID.

Islamic Arts Museum

Malay Tea House

National History Museum

29 Jalan Raja
City Centre
🚉 **Masjid Jamek**
Map 12 C1

03 2694 4590 | *www.nationalhistorymuseum.gov.my*

This museum holds items of historical importance – from prehistoric times to modern history. The three-storey building's architecture is a blend of Victorian and Moorish, dating back to 1910. It is next to the Sultan Abdul Samad building and the old railway station. In truth, the contents are not as interesting as the building itself, although if you are a history buff it's probably worth a visit. If you have the time and the interest, spend an hour or so learning more about the history of the country. Otherwise, simply appreciate the colonial exterior of the building on your way to Merdeka Square. Admission is free. The museum is open from 09:00 to 18:00 daily.

The National Museum (Muzium Negara)

Jalan Mahameru
KL Sentral
🚉 **KL Sentral**
Map 12 A4

03 2282 6255 | *www.museum.gov.my*

Although impressive from the outside, the museum gets mixed reviews. It is made up of four different galleries, each showcasing a particular theme. In the first gallery, the theme is culture, and you can see national costumes, traditional games and historical Malaysian rituals. In the second gallery, there is a range of historical and cultural artefacts, all looking a bit dusty. In the third gallery, there are exhibits on the natural history of the country, and in the last gallery, subcategories of weapons, music and ceramics are covered. There are a further three galleries in the museum that host temporary exhibits, which tend to be better than the permanent displays. Keep an eye on the website for news of upcoming events. The museum is open daily from 09:00 to 18:00, and entrance costs RM2.

Orang Asli Museum

Jalan Gombak
Sungai Buloh

03 2161 0577

Because it is a little way out of town, few expats make the effort to visit this unusual and fascinating museum, but it does make a great stop-off on the way to the Genting Highlands (p.202). Orang Asli means 'original people' in Malay, and the museum displays the many facets of Malaysia's indigenous people, who could once be found in all areas of the peninsula. Exhibits accurately depict the lives of these rainforest people, including their arts, accommodation, medicines, hunting techniques and their animist religion. Particularly interesting are the old photos and the impressive, hand-carved wooden masks on display. The museum is open from 09:00 to 17:00 daily, except for Fridays. Admission is free.

Petrosains

Level 4, Suria KLCC
🚉 **KLCC**
Map 11 C2

03 2331 8787 | *www.petrosains.com.my*

The name is a Malaysian mish-mash of 'petroleum' and 'science' and therein lies the biggest clue to what this museum is about. Start your journey in an oil-drop shaped vessel, and travel back in time. Ride in a helicopter simulator, watch live science demonstrations, explore the world of atoms, and learn all about petroleum and gas production. It is set up primarily for kids, who will enjoy the many interactive exhibits. The museum is open from 09:30 to 17:30 from Tuesday to Friday, and from 09:30 to 18:30 on Saturdays and Sundays. Admission is RM12 for adults, RM7 for kids aged 13 to 17, RM4 for kids under 12, and kids under 4 get in free.

Telecom Museum – Muzium Telekom

Jalan Raja Chulan
Chinatown
🚉 **Masjid Jamek**
Map 10 E4

03 2031 9966

Learn about the history of telecommunications, from manually operated switchboards through to modern technology, at this interactive museum that features old photographs, printed materials, soundbites and a huge collection of related artefacts.

It is housed in the dusty, pillared Victorian building at the very end of Jalan Ampang, across the street from the Maybank building (p.64). It's not for everyone, but if you're in the area it is certainly worth a quick visit. Open from 09:00 to 17:00, Tuesdays to Saturdays. Admission is free.

Other Attractions

Off Jalan Sultan Ismail ◄
Nr Jalan Berangan
Bukit Bintang
🚇 *Bukit Bintang*
Map 13 B1

Ain Arabia

Arabs make up a large percentage of tourists visiting Asia, which is fast becoming the top Muslim-friendly travel destination. Kuala Lumpur has recognised the need to welcome Arab tourists and Ain Arabia ('Eye of Arabia') is a little slice of Arabic life right in the heart of Bukit Bintang. While it is little more than a side road branching off Jalan Sultan Ismail, you'll find some excellent restaurants serving authentic Middle Eastern cuisine, Arabic tea houses complete with shisha pipes (hubbly bubbly), and specialised barbers. Of course, if you're not a tourist from the Middle East, you can still enjoy the atmosphere of this bustling area, which stays open until late at night.

Lake Titiwangsa ◄
🚇 *Titiwangsa*
Map 5 B2

Eye On Malaysia

www.eyeonmalaysia.com.my

This popular ferris wheel towers 60 metres above the water in the Titiwangsa Lake Gardens. Originally meant to operate for the duration of 2007 as part of the 'Visit Malaysia' celebrations, its run has now been extended until the end of 2008. It receives thousands of visitors a day, and queues at the weekend can be unbearably long. The ride (in an enclosed cabin that can seat up to eight people) takes 12 minutes, during which you'll make four revolutions. The Eye operates from 10:00 until 23:00 on weekdays, and up until midnight on Fridays and Saturdays. Tickets cost RM15 for adults and RM8 for children.

2 Jalan Punchak ◄
Off Jalan P. Ramlee
City Centre
🚇 *Raja Chulan*
Map 5 B4

KL Tower (Menara Kuala Lumpur)

03 2020 5444 | *www.menarakl.com.my*

This is the fourth tallest communications tower in the world, after the CN Tower in Toronto, the Ostankino Tower in Moscow and the Oriental Pearl Tower in Shanghai. You'll see it jutting into the skyline from just about anywhere in the city, but it actually stands atop Bukit Nanas, a rainforest reserve right in the middle of the Golden Triangle. It reaches just over 420 metres high and may seem to tower over the Petronas Towers from many viewpoints, but this is because its base is nearly 100 metres above sea level. This makes for an energetic walk from the gate to the base, but it's a pleasant one, landscaped with beautiful greenery and fountains. Get your ticket from the booth on the ground floor (RM20 for adults, RM10 for children); from there you'll be escorted to any of the four express lifts that will rocket you upwards to the viewing deck, 276 metres above ground level.

Eye on Malaysia

Here you can pick up your personal audio set that lets you listen to a guided tour in any one of 11 languages. The views are spectacular. The tower also houses a revolving restaurant, banquet facilities (they do weddings), a cluster of little gift shops on the ground floor, and of course access to the Bukit Nanas rainforest (p.196). The tower is open from 09:00 to 22:00 every day of the year.

Section 63
Jalan Conlay
City Centre
🚇 *Raja Chulan*
Map 5 C4

Kuala Lumpur Craft Complex

03 2162 7459
The Craft Complex was built to increase awareness and promote the commercial viability of Malaysian crafts. This centre features a cluster of wooden buildings in which you can watch local crafters at work, and buy authentic hand-made articles directly from the artist. The art of batik features heavily here, with plenty of different stalls selling finished items and offering you the opportunity to create your very own batik art. Getting the kids to make a batik painting for granny and granddad back home is a popular Christmas activity among expats. Inside the main building of the complex, you'll find a handful of lovely shops packed with traditional craft items for sale.

Lake Gardens
🚇 *KL Sentral*
Map 7 A1

National Planetarium (Planetarium Negara)

03 2273 5484
Learn about stars, moons and galaxies at this interesting planetarium, which includes a dome and a theatre showing space-themed educational movies. It is located in the large, blue-domed building in the Lake Gardens. Admission is free for kids and just RM1 for adults, although if you want to see the show it will cost RM6 for adults and RM4 for children. To get there take a five-minute cab ride from KL Sentral train station.

Persiaran Bukit Kiara
Bukit Damansara
🚇 *Bangsar*
Map 4 C4

National Science Centre (Pusat Sains Negara)

03 2092 1150 | *www.psn.gov.my*
Located in the upscale, leafy suburb of Damansara Heights on the outskirts of KL, this avant-garde building, with its geodesic dome, is an eye-catching architectural attraction in itself. Founded in 1996, this science and technology centre uses themed exhibits to promote learning in a hands-on, practical way. It's a great way to understand the principles of science and its use for daily applications. It's a huge hit with kids, particularly slightly older ones. And it is located right in the middle of three popular expat neighbourhoods – Bangsar, Mont Kiara and Damansara. If you're coming from the city centre, it's best to drive or get a cab; otherwise you can take the RapidKL U83 bus from KL Sentral. The entrance fee is RM6 for adults and RM3 for kids aged 6 to 12. The centre is open from 09:00 to 17:00, Saturday to Thursday.

Suria KLCC
Jalan Ampang
KLCC
🚇 *KLCC*
Map 11 B2

Petronas Twin Towers

www.petronastwintowers.com.my
You've heard the statistics countless times: 88 storeys, 452 metres, $1.2 billion. But nothing can prepare you for the beauty of the Petronas Twin Towers – once the world's tallest buildings, and now simply the world's tallest twin towers (a fact that many a cab driver will point out with a wry smile). By day they are striking, towering over the city and dwarfing the Suria KLCC shopping mall to which they are attached. But by night they are positively breathtaking – lighting up the sky around them with a beautiful silver glow. You can go up to the Skybridge, which is suspended between the two towers on the 41st floor. While you will get better views at the KL Tower (p.187), simply because you are higher, it's still worth going up to the Skybridge for the experience alone. It is free of charge, but you do need to go and get your tickets from the lower ground level of the towers. Tickets become available from 08:30 each morning, and

only 1,300 tickets are issued per day, so they run out rather quickly. Groups of 20 people are taken up at a time, and you'll only have about 10 minutes on the Skybridge itself. In the lift a tour guide will tell you some interesting trivia about the towers, like how they sway in the wind and how the Skybridge is not actually attached directly to the towers, but rather suspended between them.

Petronas reflections

4 Jalan Usahawan 6
Off Jalan Pahang
🚇 *Wangsa Maju*

Royal Selangor Visitor Centre

03 4145 6122 | www.royalselangor.com

The Selangor state is famous for the Royal Selangor brand of pewter, and you can explore the visitor centre to experience how pewter items are made, and even have a go at making something yourself. The tour is free, and takes you through the factory to learn about the various procedures involved in creating a beautiful finished product, from casting and filing right through to hammering and engraving. You can also have a wander through the on-site gallery, where you can see the world's biggest pewter tankard as well as an incredible replica of the Petronas Twin Towers (see p.188) measuring two storeys high. After your tour, try enrolling at the 'School of Hard Knocks', where for RM50 you can make your own bowl by hammering away at a flat piece of pewter. There is also a gift shop, so you can round off your visit with some lovely pewter purchases. The Visitor Centre is open from 10:00 to 17:00 daily, and it is just a five-minute taxi ride from the Wangsa Maju station.

Religious Sites

Gombak District
13km north of KL
🚇 *Taman Melati*

Batu Caves

Undoubtedly the most important Hindu site in the city, the Batu Caves are also one of the top tourist attractions. There are three main limestone caves, as well as a handful of smaller ones, and you could easily spend half a day exploring the many fascinating statues and temples here. Getting there is easy – take the train to Taman Melati station and then get a cab to take you the remaining 10 minutes to the cave. As you drive up you'll see the gigantic gilded statue of Murugan, an important Hindu deity, measuring over 40 metres in height. The statue stands at the bottom of 272 steps leading up to the main temple cave – each one is numbered, so you know exactly how far you've got to go. Just a word of warning: monkeys perch on the sides of the steps, looking cute, but they are cheeky enough to snatch things out of bags or pockets, so take extra care. The cool cave at the top of the steps is a welcome break after the tiring climb, and you can also stop for a while to browse at the stalls selling Hindu ornaments and pictures. During the annual Thaipusam festival, a celebration to honour Murugan and absolve the sins of the previous year, up to a million Hindus descend on Batu within a 24 hour period. Some worshippers pierce their bodies with metal hooks and skewers and carry heavy loads to the top of the stairs as a gesture of penance. Thaipusam normally occurs at the end of January or the beginning of February, depending on the lunar calendar.

Chan See Shu Yuen Chinese Temple

This colourful temple was built in 1906, and is one of the oldest Buddhist temples in Malaysia. The architecture is heavily Chinese, and has a pottery roof in the Qing Dynasty style. A favourite feature of this temple is the display of terracotta friezes displaying scenes from Chinese history and mythology. The temple is open daily from 08:00 to 18:00, but you should come and visit in the mornings when it is at its busiest – Malaysian Chinese of all generations come here to ask the Goddess of Fortune to answer their prayers.

Masjid Jamek

03 2274 6063

the Jamek Mosque is one of the oldest and most significant mosques in the city. It was built in 1907 right at the important confluence of the Klang and Gombak Rivers, which is seen as the historic centre of Kuala Lumpur and the point from which all other areas developed outwards. You'll recognise it immediately, because of the striking red and white stripes, and its moorish architecture. It has three domes: one large central one and two smaller ones, and two striped minarets. Visitors are welcome outside of prayer times, although you will need to dress modestly. You can borrow robes and headscarves from the entrance. Getting to the mosque is easy, as it is right outside the Masjid Jamek train station. It is situated at the edge of the Little India district, which is a fascinating area to explore.

National Mosque

Jalan Sultan
Hishamuddin
nr Bird Park
City Centre
🚇 *Pasar Seni*
Map 12 B2

Recognisable by its concertina-style design, this distinctive mosque is one of the largest in Asia, with room for 15,000 worshippers. Built in 1965, the 75 metre-tall minaret's unusual design was inspired by a royal umbrella, and marks the city's first departure from the more traditional dome style. The prayer hall is built in the shape of an 18 pointed star, representing the 13 states of Malaysia and the five pillars of Islam. Visitors are welcome outside of prayer times, and entrance is free.

Sri Maha Mariamman Temple

Strangely located in the middle of Chinatown, this fascinating Hindu temple is one of KL's oldest. The massive gateway tower (*gopuram*) is a fascinating and intricate carving of numerous Indian gods, and well worth a few photos. Many local Hindus get married here and you'll find a wedding in progress most weekends. In fact, this can be a good time to visit – these are not private affairs, and if you happen to visit during a wedding, you will most likely be invited to join in the festivities. Weddings aside, this is an active place of worship, and although visitors are welcome you should show the necessary respect and decorum. You will be asked to remove your shoes at the door, and to make a small donation on your way out. If you want to take any photos of worshippers in the temple, it is always better to ask their permission first. It is open daily from 09:00 to 18:00.

Sultan Salahuddin Abdul Aziz Shah Mosque

It's quite a way out of town (50 kilometres), but this mosque, known more commonly as the Blue Mosque, is a spectacular sight. It is the main mosque of the Selangor state, and can accommodate upwards of 16,000 worshippers. It also has distinctively tall minarets and a very large dome (which is intricately designed in silver and blue, hence the nickname). The mosque is fully carpeted and air conditioned, and has separate sections for male and female worshippers. Visitors are welcome and it is open from 09:00 to 17:00, although you won't be able to enter during prayer times. As with any mosque, you are required to dress modestly – that means long skirts or trousers, long sleeves and head scarves for women.

Robson Hill
Just off Jalan
Syed Putra
Taman Seputeh
Maharajalela
Map 7 A3

Thean Hou Buddhist Temple

It's only 20 years old and you can tell by its appearance: the riotous colours and wild wall paintings are a far cry from older, more traditional temples. It is hugely popular with wedding couples as a photo backdrop, and on any weekend you can see several couples posing for photos in the front courtyard. Its beautiful gardens, four levels (all featuring distinctive architecture), and wonderful view over KL city make this a definite must-do. The temple is open from 08:00 to 21:00 daily. There are no signposts to guide you; from the Maharajalela station take a 15 minute taxi ride to the temple – your driver should know how to get there.

Masjid Jamek

Blue Mosque

Batu Caves

Thean Hou Buddhist Temple

Theme Parks
Other options **Water Parks** p.192, **Amusement Centres** p.182

Mines Resort City
B1 MIECC
Jalan Dulang
🚉 *Serdang*

Mines Wonderland
03 8942 5010 | *www.mineswonderland.com.my*
This amazing theme park is only a 35 minute drive from KL, and is home to a collection of attractions that are both impressive and bizarre. Stroll through the Coin Garden, where you can walk past gigantic replicas of some of the world's coins, or chill out in the Ice Factory, where the temperature is as cold as -15°C and you can gawp at various ice sculptures while you try to keep warm. Nature lovers will enjoy the Animal Kingdom, home to a variety of species – you can even walk over a bridge where white tigers roam freely underneath. There is also a musical fountain show, a three-dimensional aqua laser show, and various dance performances are on offer. Well worth a visit.

3 Jalan PJS 11/11
Bandar Sunway
Petaling Jaya
🚉 *Setia Jaya*

Sunway Lagoon Theme Park
03 5639 0000 | *www.sunwaylagoon.com*
Just 30 minutes outside KL, in the sister city of Petaling Jaya, lies the huge Sunway Lagoon – Malaysia's premier theme park. The park is easy to find and spans over 80 acres, so it's worth making a whole day of it. The main park is divided into three sections: the Wild Wild West, World of Adventure, and Waters of Africa. Each section has a different theme and caters to a different age group. Recently, a new sub-section called Extreme Park has been added to cater to the growing interest in more extreme adventures. Here you'll find a place to ride all-terrain vehicles (ATVs), practise your shooting skills at paintball, or even learn how to scuba dive. A combined ticket for the Theme Park and Extreme Park is RM55 for adults and RM40 for kids.

Water Parks
Other options **Theme Parks** p.192

Taman Desa

Desa Water Park
03 7118 8338 | *www.desawaterpark.com.my*
If you love coming down water slides but hate that long walk back to the top dressed only in your swimming costume and clutching a big inflatable ring, then Desa may be the place for you. The Thunderbolt is Asia's longest uphill watercoaster, where riders are propelled to the top by jets of water. The park is also home to a massive wavepool, that pulses out a series of metre-high waves for 10 minutes at a time. There are many other fun rides and activities within the park, as well as lockers, snack bars and a souvenir shop. It should take you less than 20 minutes to get there from KL city following the Pantai Expressway. There is plenty of parking. Entrance costs RM18 for adults and RM12 for children.

Shah Alam
🚉 *Padang Jawa*

Shah Alam Wet World Theme Park
03 5510 2588
Shah Alam lies 30 kilometres west of Kuala Lumpur and is easily reached in under 40 minutes using either the Federal Highway or the NKVE Highway. Wet World is a low-key family water park that may not match up to Desa, but that certainly gets the seal of approval from the droves of kids that visit it. And that's who it was designed for – water is never deeper than one metre in any part of the park, so it is ideal for little people. That said, some of the rides are pretty exciting, particularly the Monsoon Buster: a 225 metre-long uphill watercoaster that's a big hit with kids and adults. Facilities include a fast food centre, gift shops and changing areas. Entry fees are just RM7 for adults (RM5 on weekdays) and RM4 for kids (RM3 on weekdays).

Zoos, Wildlife Parks & Open Farms

Lake Gardens
📷 KL Sentral
Map 12 A1

Butterfly Park

03 2693 4799

Only a five-minute stroll from the Bird Park, the 'Taman Rama Rama' is also a delight. Featured are over 120 different species in an environment which has been carefully tailored to imitate the rainforest in which many have been captured. If you are lucky, you will witness the delicate release of these new inhabitants from the gently folded squares of waxed paper in which they have made their trip, usually from the Cameron Highlands. Most of the gorgeous insects, however, are bred in the park's nurseries. The names of the butterflies are almost as much pleasure as the vibrant colours; consider seeing the Green Dragonfly, the Malay Lacewing, the Painted Jezebel, the Red Spot Sawtooth, the Blue Glassy Tiger and the Tufted Jungle King. Open daily from 09:00 to 18:30. The entrance fee is RM15 for adults.

Jalan Perdana
Lake Gardens
📷 KL Sentral
Map 12 A2

Deer Park

The Deer Park is in the north part of Lake Gardens, just beyond the memorial to Tun Abdul Razak. It is home to scores of tame deer – so tame in fact that they will even accept appropriate food from some visitors (before you feed the deer, check with the park staff what is appropriate). In the beautifully lush and landscaped terrain a lucky visitor may even glimpse the tiny, very shy kancil (mouse deer), the smallest hoofed animal in the world. The kancil features prominently in Malaysian folklore, where it is much vaunted for its courage in spite of its size. The park is open from 09:00 to 18:00 daily; entrance is free.

Butterfly Park

KL Bird Park

920 Jalan Cenderawasih
Lake Gardens
KL Sentral
Map 12 A2

03 2272 1010 | *www.klbirdpark.com*

It bills itself as the largest covered bird park in the world, a claim somewhat contested by rival Judong Park in Singapore. This friendly rivalry matters little since the Bird Park, one of the jewels of the city, is high on the list of every resident and visitor. In an area of eight enclosed acres, one can see thousands of different varieties of birds including hornbills, pigeons, flamingoes, storks, egrets, mynahs and peacocks. Many of the birds are native to Malaysia, but some come from other south-east Asian countries and a few from the Americas and Africa. Raptors such as owls, eagles and kites which might prey on other birds are caged; so are some others, such as ostriches, cassowaries and hornbills, which are potentially dangerous to visitors (but most of the park's inhabitants fly gloriously free). Be sure to get your photo taken with some of the gorgeously plumed parrots at the photo booth. Take in some of the feeding times. If you are lucky, you will stumble upon the large open-air amphitheatre during show time – join a large audience of gleeful children howling at the antics of parrots riding tiny bicycles and orangutans (all of whom are shameless hams) playing tricks on their keepers. Open daily from 09:00 to 18:30. Entrance costs RM35 for adults and RM25 for children.

On Your Doorstep

If you've got kids who love getting up close and personal with feathered or furry friends, you could always head to Singapore for a weekend break – it is home to a fantastic zoo and a beautiful bird park. There's also a great nightlife and excellent shopping, which will keep the mums and dads happy too. See p.205.

Kuala Gandah Elephant Orphanage Sanctuary

Kuala Gandah

03 9075 2872 | *www.myelephants.org*

Head east along the Karak Highway for about an hour and you'll reach the Kuala Gandah Elephant Orphanage Sanctuary. It rescues, rehabilitates and relocates Malaysian elephants, and in an effort to raise the funds to continue caring for them the sanctuary opens its gates to visitors. You do not need to pay an entrance fee; however, you will be asked to make a donation to the sanctuary and you should give generously, since the work done here is wonderful. On a visit you can hand-feed the elephants, participate in activities like washing and grooming, and ride on an elephant (although only the first 100 visitors will be able to do this each day).

Zoo Negara (National Zoo)

Hulu Kelang
Ampang
Wangsa Maju

03 4108 3422 | *www.zoonegara.org.my*

Zoo Negara opened in 1963 to become Malaysia's first zoo to meet international standards of care, presentation and diversity. Located in the quiet, leafy suburbs of eastern KL, the 110 acre zoo is home to over 5,000 animals from about 450 species. It is laid out in a well-marked network of trails shaded by massive trees, creating a real jungle atmosphere. The most popular residents of the zoo are the Sumatran tiger, the red-haired orangutan and the elephants. Twice daily, at 10:30 and 14:30, you can watch the highly trained elephants put on a show as their skilled trainers explain to the audience what makes elephants so unique, how they are threatened, and how similar their social structure is to human beings. To get there, take a 10 minute cab ride from the Wangsa Maju station. The zoo is open daily from 10:00 to 17:00, and the night zoo is open until 22:30 at the weekends and on public holidays. Entrance costs RM15 for adults and RM6 for children.

KL's colourful animals

Parks, Beaches & Gardens

As one of the few Asian capitals that is landlocked, KL has no natural beaches within an hour's drive from the city. For a natural beach experience, you'll have to make a daytrip to Port Dickson (p.254). This convenient seaside resort, known to locals simply as PD, may lack charm but the waters are calm and the weather is good. Sadly, several abandoned developments litter the coastline, but if you're after a beach, this is the place to be. There are some wonderful beaches on Malaysia' east coast, but these are three hours away by car, and so perhaps are more suitable for a weekend trip. KL does have one beach though – the man-made one at MINES Resort City (p.196).

With a tropical climate and lots of rain, it's no wonder KL is so green. The city has plenty of green spaces and public gardens where you can while away an hour or two. The humidity and sunshine make shady patches the most popular.

Beaches

Other options **Swimming** p.259

There are no beaches in landlocked KL, unless of course you count the man-made beach at the Mines Resort. There are, however, some glorious beaches out of town. See the section on Daytrips (p.201) and Weekend Breaks (p.205) for more information.

Sungei Besi
🚇 *Serdang*

Palace Beach, Mines Resort City

03 8943 6688 | *www.mines.com.my*

Back in the 1950s, the Hong Fatt tin mine was the largest open mine in the world. When it was abandoned, it slowly filled up with rainwater until it was a vast, 150 acre lake. 15 years ago, the Mines Resort was built along the southern edge of the lake, and a sandy beach was created, complete with beach chairs, barbecue pit, watersports, a volleyball pitch and an open air bar. Nowadays, this beach, recently renamed the Palace Beach, is a favourite hangout for expats, and is a great way to get your seaside fix until you can take your next beach holiday.

Nature Reserves

Nr KL Tower
2 Jalan Punchak Off
Jalan P. Ramlee
City Centre
🚇 *Bukit Nanas*
Map 10 F3

Bukit Nanas Forest Recreational Park

03 2020 5444 | *www.menarakl.com.my*

This 26 hectare place was designated as a nature reserve in 1906, and great efforts have been made to preserve it ever since. Even during the construction of the KL Tower, little damage was done to the area. The result is a beautiful little slice of rainforest right where you would least expect it: smack in the middle of the city. You can follow any one of three well-marked trails through the forest (remember to use insect repellant before going in), and afterwards you can chill out in the picnic area or children's playground. Entrance is free, and the park is open from 07:00 to 18:00 daily.

Kepong
Sungai Buloh

Forest Research Institute of Malaysia (FRIM)

03 6279 7000 | *www.frim.gov.my*

Although it is actually a forestry research centre, FRIM is better known to most KLites as a wonderful place to go for some excellent hikes and picnic spots. This popular rainforest location is just a short drive from the city. The canopy walk is undoubtedly the highlight of any visit to FRIM. Get your ticket from the gift shop before setting off (they charge a nominal fee), and then you have to hike up a forest trail – which can be pretty challenging, especially in the heat, so leave as early in the day as possible – before you get to a wooden hut marking the location of the canopy walk. You will be given quick instructions by the person on duty at the hut, and then you're off, walking along a suspended walkway 200 feet above ground level. You can see four levels of rainforest and a wonderful view of the city (but only on a clear day). Undoubtedly one of the best days out in KL.

Jalan Klinik ◀
Kuala Selangor

Kuala Selangor Nature Park
03 3289 2294 | *www.mns.org.my*
It's nearly 70km north of KL, so you'll need to make a daytrip out of it, but this lovely park reserve is chock full of fascinating insects, birds and mammals. They all live harmoniously in the well-balanced river ecosystem, which has its very own mangrove plantation. The park is protected and managed by the Malaysia Nature Society. You can pick up a self-guided walk booklet from the gift shop, or take a guided tour. Particularly recommended is the night walk – a guided walk leaving at 21:00 during which you'll see the park's wildlife in a completely different light, and plenty of fireflies. If you choose to go on this walk, you may want to stay in the park overnight in a chalet. Accommodation is basic: you'll need to bring your own towels, and don't forget the mosquito repellant (and lots of it!).

Parks & Gardens

Nxt to Suria KLCC ◀
City Centre
🚇 **KLCC**
Map 11 C2

KLCC Park
This vast green space is found next to Suria KLCC and the Petronas Towers. With 40 acres of landscaped gardens, including plenty of shaded benches, a host of trees, shrubs and plants specially planted to attract local birds, and a 1.3km rubberised jogging track, it's little surprise that this park is so popular with people wanting a break from the city for a while. There is an enormous kids' play area stretching over two acres, with a vast collection of climbing frames and a rubberised floor to cushion the blow if there are any nasty falls. Right next to this is the kids' splash pool, which is for kids aged under 12 only. One of the busiest parts of the park is the viewing bridge, which is one of the best places to gawp at the Petronas Towers and pose for a photo. From here you'll also have a good view of the dancing fountains that dominate the park's central lake. Entrance to the park is free of charge, and it is open every day. The kids' splash pool is closed on Mondays.

Jalan Kuantan ◀
City Centre
🚇 **Titiwangsa**
Map 5 B2

Lake Titiwangsa
03 2693 6661
Taman Tasik Titiwangsa, situated around a clear lake, is one of the most popular recreational parks in Kuala Lumpur. With a walking and jogging trail around the lake, workout stations, tennis courts, canoeing and hiking, there's a lot to do and plenty of reasons to keep visiting this large park. At sunset, take time to enjoy the lovely view of the KL skyline, and if you want to stay for dinner, try the floating restaurant. On weekends the park is bustling, with local vendors setting up food and shopping stalls. One of the park's most popular attractions is the Eye on Malaysia (see p.187), a giant ferris wheel that is scheduled to operate until the end of 2008. Entrance to the park is free.

Lake Gardens ◀
🚇 **KL Sentral**
Map 12 A2

Orchid & Hibiscus Gardens
Literally across the road and just up a gentle slope from the Bird Park are the beautiful Orchid and Hibiscus Gardens. During weekdays the gardens are an oasis of tranquility and pleasure. One can enjoy over 3,000 different types of orchids. Some prefer shade and others bright sunlight so be sure to bring water, a hat and sunscreen for your visit. Eight hundred different species of orchid alone are found in Malaysia. Bordering the Orchid garden is the equally lovely Hibiscus Garden with approximately 2,000 species of Malaysia's national flower on display. A small flower market staffed by knowledgeable personnel offers both Orchids and Hibiscus for sale. Entrance to both gardens is free on weekdays; on Saturdays, Sundays and Public holidays there is a nominal fee of RM1.

Tours & Sightseeing

Considering there is so much to see in KL, there are surprisingly few tour companies offering tours. Of course you can get to most places easily by yourself, but often a guided tour will often add value to the experience. A good tour guide is usually a long-term resident who has a seemingly endless supply of facts and trivia about a certain location – and a tour is a great way to find out some little facts that even the locals don't know. You will find several tour operators located in the Malaysian Tourism Office on Jalan Ampang (03 2164 3929), which also has some friendly and knowledgeable staff who can answer just about any question you have on Kuala Lumpur.

Activity Tours

Sungai Slim &
Sungai Selangor

AIDM White Water Rafting

03 016346 0735 | *www.raftingmalaysia.travelbytes.biz*
Experience the thrill of racing down a raging river – all in complete safety with AI Destination Marketing. You can choose from Sungai Slim in Perak, which has over 20 rapids from grades one to three, or Sungai Selangor, with a rafting distance of over seven kilometres, and rapids ranging up to grade four. For both locations, AIDM will collect you from Amcorp Mall in Petaling Jaya, and transport you to the river where you will be briefed and issued with all the equipment you will need for the adventure. The duration of the entire trip is around eight hours, although only two or three hours of that is actual rafting – the rest of the time is spent on travelling and briefing. The rafting tour costs RM285 per person for Sungai Selangor and RM270 for Sungai Slim. The price includes transport, equipment, trained river guides, on-river snacks and lunch.

Various Locations

AIDM Geocoaching Adventure Tours

03 016346 0735 | *www.geocoaching.travelbytes.biz*
Geocoaching is a great way of getting out and about and exploring Malaysia's beautiful outdoors while you search for secret hidden treasures. Armed with a hand-held GPS, you will explore various areas to find the treasure – you can take something from the find, but you will be asked to leave something in return. You log all your 'finds' in a notebook, and later you can check them on the website. After the Geocoaching, you will be taken to a relaxing outdoor location to start the barbecue lunch – the price of RM290 per person includes lunch and refreshments, equipment and transportation.

Lot 11, Jalan Lengal
Off Jalan Tembak
Kuala Kubu Bahru

Tracks Adventures

03 6065 1767 | *www.tracksadventures.com.my*
This company specialises in white water rafting and kayaking, although they can also organise canyoneering, cave exploration trips, camping trips, rock climbing, abseiling and orienteering. No matter what level of experience you have, Tracks can take you on a skill-appropriate ride down the Selangor River. You will be accompanied by an experienced guide, and all safety equipment, such as life jackets and helmets, is provided. You will need to bring some dry clothes and a towel. The excursion lasts around two hours, covers a distance of six kilometres, and costs RM230 per adult (excluding transport from KL).

Boat Tours

Jeti Putra
Jambatan Putra, Presint 1
Putrajaya
🚇 *Putrajaya*

Cruise Tasik Putrajaya

03 8888 5539 | *www.cruisetasikputrajaya.com*
There are not many places in KL where you can take a boat tour. Cruise Tasik offers traditional boat tours in Putrajaya, where there is a huge man-made lake and various

arterial waterways throughout the city. Hop into one of their small boats (each boat takes four to six people) for a 25 minute cruise past some of Putrajaya's most famous sights, including the Putra mosque, the prime minister's office and the Putra Bridge. The traditional cruise costs RM20 for adults and RM12 for children. Other cruises, such as lunch and dinner cruises, loveboat cruises and cocktail cruises are also available.

Bus Tours

Various Stops ◄
Around KL

The KL Hop-on Hop-off City Tour

03 2691 1382 | www.myhoponhopoff.com

The hop-on hop-off bus tour phenomenon has quickly become an important tourism feature in many large cities around the world. It's a wonderful way to get your bearings and decide what things you might like to come back to for further exploration. The KL Hop-On Hop-Off tour has been operating since 2006, and while it may not match the similar services offered in cities like London, New York or Dublin, it is still a good way to see the city in comfort. The bus is completely enclosed, unlike the open-top versions available in other cities, although in KL's humidity it's nice to have the air conditioning. You can hop off at any stop that interests you, and then hop on again once you've finished and carry on to the next destination. A bus comes past every half hour. Stops include the Petronas Towers, Malaysia Tourism Centre, Aquaria KLCC, Bintang Walk, Central Market, Chinatown, KL Tower, National Palace, Lake Gardens, Masjid Jamek, Merdeka Square and Lake Titiwangsa, among others. Tickets are RM38 for adults and RM17 for children, and can be bought on the bus when you board, or at many tourist offices around the city. Tickets are valid for 24 hours from when you first board the bus.

City Tours

Taking a city tour of KL is a good way to get your bearings – you may have already discovered by now if you've just moved here that it's pretty challenging to figure out what's in what area, and what is nearby and what is far away. The hop-on-hop-off bus tour is a good option (p.199), but there are also various tour companies offering this service and you may find that they offer more insight into the items on the tour, thanks to a more personal service and more experienced tour guides. Any basic city tour of KL will take in the National Museum (p.186), the Lake Gardens (p.174), the Jamek Mosque (p.190), Chinatown (p.327), Merdeka Square (p.3) and of course the big daddy of attractions, the Petronas Twin Towers (p.188). Some city tours may also take you to the Royal Selangor Visitor Centre (p.189), where you can learn all about pewter craftmanship. These tours usually last around four hours, and cost anything from RM70 to RM100 – this may exclude entrance fees to any attractions. To find out more about city tours, contact Tour East Malaysia (04 899 8833, www.toureast.com.my) or Shajasa Travel & Tours (03 2026 8668, www.shajasa.com.my).

The KL Hop-on Hop-off City Tour

Helicopter Tours

No 8, Lorong Ceylon
Off Jalan Raja Chulan

Shajasa Tours
03 2026 8668 | *www.shajasa.com.my*
Take off in a four or five-passenger VIP helicopter for a one-hour joyride high above KL. The pilots are very knowledgeable and will tell you about the buildings you fly over. Shajasa will arrange to collect you and transport you to the airfield one hour before take off. The cost is RM3,300 for the four-passenger helicopter, and RM3,500 for the five-passenger one. You can add an extra 20 minutes to the flying time, but this will cost an additional RM1,000. Bookings must be made a week in advance.

Nature Tours
A select group of tour operators, offers tours exploring Malaysia's natural wonders and fauna. You can head up to Kuala Selangor (about an hour's drive from KL) to watch hundreds of thousands of fireflies flicker in the dense mangrove plantations. It's an experience that you're unlikely to have outside of Malaysia, so definitely counts as a must-do, no matter how long you're staying in KL for. Both Shajasa Travel & Tours (03 2026 8668, www.shajasa.com.my) and Tour East Malaysia (04 899 8833, www.toureast. com.my) offer this tour. Tour East also offers other nature tours, including trips up to the Elephant Sanctuary (p.194) and the Forest Research Institute of Malaysia, where you can explore beautiful rainforest (p.196). They also offer a Nature Tour, during which you will visit the Bird Park (p.194) and the Orchid and Hibiscus Gardens (p.197), before enjoying an optional traditional afternoon tea at Carcosa Seri Negara (p.184).

Tour Operators

Sungai Slim &
Sungai Selangor

AI Destination Marketing Tours
016 346 0735 | *www.raftingmalaysia.travelbytes.biz*
AIDM focuses on the thrilling side of life – and therefore is the best company to take you to some of the most undiscovered spots that other tour operators just don't reach. Try their white water rafting tours (p.198), which take you to beautiful rivers in Selangor and Perak, or for something completely new, go on one of their Geocoaching trips (p.198), during which you'll have to find a hidden treasure armed just with a GPS.

No 8, Lorong Ceylon
Off Jalan Raja Chulan

Shajasa Tours
03 2026 8668 | *www.shajasa.com.my*
Shajasa Travel and Tours offers a variety of tour experiences from KL – many of their tours are city based, but they also offer tours further afield. Some of their more popular tours include the Kuala Selangor Fireflies tour, helicopter tours, tours of Putrajaya by night, deep sea fishing tours, tours of the KL countryside and the Batu Caves, and a Malaysian cultural show and dinner.

Various Locations

Tour East – Malaysia
03 4899 8833 | *www.toureast.com.my*
Tour East can whisk you away for a day of leisure and fun at either Genting Highlands or Sunway Lagoon, or they can give you a whirlwind trip back in time with their Kuala Lumpur Heritage Trail tour. Foodies will love the Heavenly Dining Experience tour, which starts with a trip to Central Market and ends with dinner in the Seri Angkasa Revolving Restaurant in the Menara KL (p.380). They can take you up close to elephants, fireflies and rainforests, or show you the wonders of many of KL's most sacred religious monuments.

Tour Operators

Asian Overland Tours	03 4251 0462	www.asianoverland.com.my
Heritage Travel & Tours	03 4147 4788	www.heritagetravel.com.my

Daytrips

Batu Caves

Approximately 13 kilometres north of Kuala Lumpur via Jalan Kuching is the inspiring, famous Hindu place of worship, the Batu Caves. You will instantly know when you are getting close as the newly erected 140 foot gold statue of Hindu deity Lord Murugan will appear, welcoming you to the site. Batu Caves is at its most spectacular during the festival of Thaipusam (January), but it is a memorable place to visit at any time of the year.

Try to arrive at the caves early to enjoy the cool KL air, colourful sunrise, and a chance to see the returning nocturnal fruit bats. Fill your tummy with some delicious Indian hawker delights before you walk up the 272 concrete steps to the shrine within the grotto at the top. Be sure to leave all evidence of food at the bottom of the site as you will pass many mischievous and anxious monkeys throughout your climb that have come to expect treats from visitors. Marvel at the geological wonder but remember that this is a place of worship and respect those around you devoted to prayer. Spend some time exploring the cavernous art gallery to the left. The numerous colourful and elaborate wall paintings depicting Hindu folklore and mythology are truly inspiring.

For the adventurous rock climbers, Batu Caves also offers challenging routes for all levels. You have to bring your own gear, as there is none available for rent. All of the existing routes are bolted but some anchors are a little less than bomber. Try to get there either early in the morning or late afternoon so you don't receive direct sunlight. The climbs are mostly single pitch but there are a few multi pitch climbs.

272 Steps

Ipoh

Malaysians will tell you that 'all roads lead to Ipoh', and it certainly seems that way as you navigate KL's intertwining highways. To see where travellers once came to visit the tin centre of the world, head north on the North-South Highway to Ipoh. Ipoh may be a bit ambitious for the typical daytripper, as travel time is just over two hours, but Ipoh's limted yet unique offerings better suit a one day visit.

Ipoh is a photographer's delight as there are many architectural wonders and interesting street life that will keep you inspired and shooting all day. Visit the Majestic Hotel, known locally as the 'Taj Mahal', the Stesen Hotel, the state mosque, Masjid Negeri, Kellie's Castle and Sam Poh Tong Temple for some great photo opportunities and unique history. Ipoh's older town boasts traditional shop houses offering tailor-made goods and numerous coffee houses. When in Ipoh, try the culinary delights that have made it famous over the years. It is said that it is Ipoh's water supply that is the secret to their delicious mix of Chinese and Malay cuisine. There are numerous offerings but be sure to try the kway teow chicken soup noodle (prawn-based soup with a flat of noodle and chicken slices), bean sprout chicken, dim sum, cuttlefish vegetables, pomelos and the seedless guava.

For the young and young at heart, visit Sunway's, 'Lost World of Tambun' waterpark (www.sunway.com.my/lostworldoftambun). Emerging from the nearby jungle and surrounding rock cliffs, Lost World offers a variety of refreshing and exciting water rides, a chance to see the exotic Malaysian tigers at Tiger Valley, and a hot spring with ancient therapeutic properties. The park is closed on Tuesdays and if you purchase your ticket online, the adult's admission fee is RM30 and RM17 for children.

Genting Highlands

On a clear day, the misty, mountaintop playground of Genting Highlands is visible from Kuala Lumpur. Travelling by car, it takes approximately 40 minutes on the Karak Highway to reach this unique hillstation. Here, trekking shoes are not mandatory as Genting's main pleasures are its numerous entertainment offerings.

For the risk takers, Malaysia's only casino offers both western games of chance in addition to traditional Chinese games such as tai sai. Neck ties and a high tolerance of cigarette smoke are mandatory for entrance. Casino de Genting also offers international quality live shows and entertainment.

Genting's theme park offers indoor and outdoor attractions as well as a water park. Enjoy the numerous amusement rides such as rollercoasters and go-karts with your day pass. Prices vary depending on the package so check www.genting.com.my/en/themepark for the price and package that best suits you. A signature attraction, the Sky Venture, allows you to experience the sensations of sky diving as you travel though 190 kilometre winds. Other attractions include SnowWorld, Ripley's Museum and the X-Pedition Wall. Check the website for additional prices and hours of operation.

Genting Highlands also boasts Malaysia's highest shopping arcade with six themed areas dedicated to shopping, playing and eating.

If you plan on making Genting Highlands a weekend trip, there are over 10,000 rooms with numerous accommodation offerings to suit every budget. Check out the Genting Hotel, Highlands Hotel, Theme Park Hotel and the First World Hotel to see what fits your accommodation needs. For more information see www.genting.com.my.

Fraser's Hill

A hundred kilometres and two hours away by car from Kuala Lumpur is the colonial-era hill station known as Fraser's Hill. To enjoy the cooler temperatures of this 1500m high hill station, take the Karak Highway to the Bentong junction and turn left. Proceed to Teranum. At Teranum, take the left turn towards Gap before the short eight-kilometre ascent up to Fraser's Hill.

Ultimately Fraser's Hill is perfect for those looking for a relaxing getaway from the hot, concrete jungle of Kuala Lumpur. Try a nature hike along one of the eight posted jungle trails. Hemmant Trail is a relatively easy 20 minute trail along a golf course. Bishop's Trail picks up where the Hemmant Trail leaves off with a slightly more challenging path that becomes mildly dangerous when wet. The six-kilometre long Pine Tree Trail is the most physically demanding trail and takes approximately four hours to complete. There are rest stations throughout the path for short breaks. Remember to bring water and protect yourself with sun block and insect repellent.

Fraser's Hill has also become somewhat of a bird watcher's paradise with over 200 species of local and migratory birds being recorded including the wreathed and rhinoceros hornbill. Fraser's reputation of a bird watching haven was recognised by the Malaysian Nature Society with the annual Fraser's Hill International Bird Race. Other activities available at Fraser's Hill include whitewater rafting, horseback riding, fishing, archery and mountain biking. If you wish to make your day at Fraser's Hill a weekend escape try the Shahzan Inn Fraser's Hill, Fraser's Pine Resort or the Fraser's Silverpark Resort (www.fraserssilverpark.com).

Taman Pertanian ◀
Malaysia (Malaysia
Agriculture Park)
This agriculture park is
about 40 minutes out of
KL and makes for a nice
day out of the city. The
emphasis is on nature
and conservation, and
visitors can hire bicycles
to cycle around as they
visit themed gardens and
other attractions (03 5510
6922, Shah Alam station).

FRIM

A few kilometres west of Batu Caves is the nature lover's perfect day out, the Forest Research Institute and Museum, commonly known throughout Malaysia as FRIM. With over 1,500 acres of natural Malaysian forest, nature lovers will enjoy the opportunity to explore the local flora, experimental plantations, botanical gardens, waterfalls, a canopy walk, mountain bike trails and an arboreta.

There are numerous paths and trails for the adventure trekker that range in distance and challenge. Explore the relatively unchallenging 1.5 kilometre Salleh Trail to check out the Malaysian 'Bubble Gum Tree'. The 1.5 kilometre Keruing Trail starts near the fishpond and exhibits the numerous timber species of Malaysia and the famous 'Elephant Tree'. The Engkabang Trail will take you through former wetlands and grasslands. Before embarking on any nature trek, dress appropriately, wear protective sunblock and insect repellent, watch for curious leeches and most importantly, respect the nature around you. If mountain biking is more your thing, be sure to equip yourself with a proper mountain bike, helmet, protective glasses, water, snacks and if available, bring a tool kit. Check FRIM's website at www.frim.gov.my for a visual tour and up-to-date information.

Canopy Walk at FRIM

Kuala Gandah Elephant Conservation Centre

For an unbeatable Asian experience, travel down the Karak Highway, eventually turning left into Lanchang. Further down the road you will discover the Kuala Gandah Elephant Conservation Centre. As there isn't much else to do in the area, it becomes an ambitious three-hour drive for a daytrip, but it is here you will find an elephant sanctuary that acts as a research centre and an ecotourism site that delights all its guests.

The Kuala Gandah Elephant Conservation Centre's main objective is the conservation of elephants and their habitats. The sanctuary does this by ensuring the protection of the elephants within its boundaries, educating the public on the importance of elephant conservation and continuing animal research.

While at the centre, visitors can participate in a wide variety of activities. There is a documentary informing visitors about the centre and visitors are also invited to hand feed the elephants during dinnertime. During these times of close contact with the elephants it is important to follow the instructions of the staff closely. Once feeding time is over, the elephants offer bumpy but charming rides to the river where visitors will then have an opportunity to give them a bath.

Since the doors to the sanctuary have opened in 1989, there has never been an entrance fee. However, those that work with the elephants encourage all visitors to donate generously as it is the support of the public that continues to fuel this project. The sanctuary closes daily at 16:00 allowing plenty of time for the drive home to KL. It is closed on Fridays. Please note that you should dress modestly.

Befriend The Locals

When travelling to locations outside KL, you're likely to encounter fewer English speakers and learning a few key phrases will stand you in good stead.

Please	*Tolong*
Thank you	*Terima kasih*
Good morning	*Selamat pagi*
Good afternoon	*Selamat tengahari*
Goodbye	*Selamat jalan*
My name is	*Nama saya*

Port Dickson

Malaysia is known for its number of world-class, exquisite beaches and crystal clear waters. Port Dickson, regrettably, is not one of these sites. However, with a driving distance of only one hour away, Port Dickson offers the truly desperate a dash of sun and cool, if not clear ocean waters. Travel south on the North-South Highway and follow the signs to Port Dickson. The road approaching Port Dickson, along the Malaysian coastline, is very pleasant and there are numerous places where you can just park your car and set up camp on the beach.

Many resorts and hotels in the area will allow for day passes and there are numerous activities and water sports offered at each. You can spend the day waterskiing, canoeing, snorkelling, sailing, go-karting, windsurfing or just catching some rays on the beach.

As Port Dickson is mainly a resort and oil town, there isn't much to see for the adventurous site seeker. However, North of Port Dickson you can explore the 180 year old Fort Lukut. While the site looks more like a local park than a military fort, climbing the steps to the fort allows for great views of the surrounding area.

Nature lovers come to Port Dickson to enjoy bird watching, as the area is a popular stopover for migratory birds. From early autumn to spring, flocks of sparrows, buzzards and swifts can be witnessed. The Port Dickson area also hosts the annual Raptor Watch in March. The 80 hectare Tanjung Tuan Forest Reserve, located about 15 kilometres from Port Dickson, is an ideal spot for bird watching and to locate Malaysia's diverse flora and fauna. Port Dickson's nicest beach is a worthwhile but tiring walk through this forest.

Port Dickson can easily be made into a weekend stopover, as there are many local resorts to choose from.

Weekend Breaks

Kuala Lumpur is a hectic city: the heat, the traffic, the crowds and the shoppers can all get a bit much at times. Fortunately there are several destinations that are just a few hours away, where you can escape for a weekend to unwind and enjoy a change of scenery.

Nasi Lemak ◄

No matter where in Malaysia your travels take you, you will came across some fascinating food choices. For the true Malaysian experience, try Nasi Lemak – the unofficial national dish consisting of coconut rice, prawn paste, peanuts, egg, and usually a fish curry.

Cameron Highlands

If an escape from the Kuala Lumpur humidity becomes a necessity then head to the cool hills of Cameron Highlands. Located 1,800 metres above sea level, this charming hilltop getaway has numerous leisure and getaway options to suit your tastes. The drive is scenic and depending on the mode of transport you choose (bus or car) it could take between four and six hours. Head north on the North-South Highway, exit at Tapah and follow the signs to Cameron Highlands.

Numerous tea plantations decorate the landscape in this area, and it is worth visiting one of them. Boh Tea Plantations (www.boh.com.my) is one of the largest, with over 8,000 acres dedicated to the farming of delicious tea.

Another unique tourist attraction is the local strawberry farms. The cool highland climate is ideal for the farming of the fruit and it allows visitors the chance to enjoy fresh strawberries and strawberry produce. You will pass the Mountain Strawberry Farm on the way to the Boh Tea plantations. Stop in to pick some fresh strawberries, buy some delicious strawberry jam or enjoy their unique 'petting zoo'.

For the outdoor adventurer there are numerous trails that offer mountain and jungle trekking for all types of fitness levels. For the adventurous trekker, challenge yourself to the peak of Gunung Brinchang, Cameron Highland's tallest peak (over 2,000 metres high). If you are lucky enough to be there on a clear day, the breathtaking view reaches the surrounding forests of faraway Ipoh.

Flora lovers should stop in at Cactus Valley and the Rose Centre Kea Farm. While Cactus Valley (RM4 adults, RM2 children) boasts an impressive collection of cactus plants (some even older than 60 years), their existing range of various other flora is equally as impressive. The Rose Centre's (www.cameron.com.my/rose-centre.html) aromatic atmosphere, unique layout, picturesque views, cheap admission, and variety of flowers is well worth your time. There is not a lot in Cameron Highlands for the dedicated shopper, but there is a nice night market in Brinchang where you can stock up on fresh, local produce and flowers.

Singapore

Singapore is a wonderfully weekend getaway from KL. It is just four hours away by car, five hours by bus, or a quick 40 minute flight. Most bus companies offer frequent departure times and are surprisingly comfortable and affordable. Try Aeroline Bus (www.aeroline.com.my).

For shoppers, hit Orchard Road for mall after mall of everything you could ever need (and many things you don't). Each mall hits a specific demographic – upscale, trendy, sports, technology, bargain. If you can stand the noise pollution and the congested pavements, you will be rewarded with an unbelievable variety and air-conditioned malls. The newly opened Vivo City (www.vivocity.com.sg), 10 minutes from Orchard Road towards the south, has become Singapore's largest retail and lifestyle destination and is a convenient gateway to Singapore's Sentosa resort Island. If bargain hunting and flea markets are more your thing, head to Bugis Street for your traditional Asian market experience. Stock up on souvenirs like T-shirts, accessories, handbags and CDs, and recharge with a stop at one of the many food stalls before heading on to Little India on Serangoon Road or the streets surrounding Chinatown (Pagoda Street). Both neighbourhoods offer a little of everything for discerning shoppers.

Make time to hit Singapore's world class zoo (www.zoo.com.sg), which also boasts the world's first night safari where you can get up close and personal with 120 different

Mini Sin

It's clean, well organised, full of heritage, shopping and great food, and, as it's only an hour's flight from KL, Singapore is a popular weekend break. Pick up a copy of the Singapore Mini Visitors' Guide – it's got all the info you'll need, and it's so tiny that you can fit it in your pocket.

species of animal. Admission is costly but if you have a full day, you can get an adult's pass to the zoo, night safari and the bird park for S$45 (S$22.50 for kids). Alternatively, head to Sungei Buloh Wetlands Reserve (www.sbwr.org.sg) where you can take one of three walking trails that will expose you to over 150 rare and exotic birds, monitor lizards and numerous tropical flora. Admission is only S$1 for adults.

There is never a shortage of activities for night owls in Singapore. The newly opened nightclub district in Clarke Quay offers an intense range of drinking options and beautiful people watching. The Esplanade theatre on the bay is an incredible audio and visual experience offering a range of performing arts.

The Asian Civilisations Museum on Armenian Street (www.acm.org.sg) is 14,000 square metres of 11 galleries that showcase various perspectives of pan-Asian cultures and civilizations. Nearby is the grand Fullerton Hotel (www.fullertonhotel.com) which offers luxurious accommodation and an exquisite Sunday brunch.

Race fans will be pleased to know that F1 is introducing its first ever night-time grand prix race in Singapore (www.singaporegp.sg) in September 2008.

Pantai Cherating

The beach at Cherating is one of those little-known secrets that once you find it, you are almost reluctant to share it with anyone. Located three hours west of Kuala Lumpur along the west coast of Penisular Malaysia, Cherating beach offers a massive, soft-sanded getaway for families, couples and friends. The often-vacant beach is gorgeous and the perfect place to enjoy some warm ocean water. The beach is wide and long, and therefore ideal for beach games. There is even a short surf season from November to January along the shores of Cherating, where surfers can enjoy long breaks and strong swells.

There are numerous resorts in the area including the family-friendly, entertaining Club Med (www.clubmed.com.my), but if you fancy a more tropical beach escape, try Ruby's Resort (www.rubys-resort.com) located just yards away from the beach. Here you will find true peace and quiet in a welcoming setting.

A 10 minute walk along the beach will bring you to the Cherating Turtle Sanctuary. From May to September, you may be able to witness the endangered green turtle approach the shores to nest. Contact Malaysia's Department of Fisheries for volunteering opportunities (www.dof.gov.my/v2).

Cherating also offers some unique natural wonders to its visitors. A short drive towards Kampang Kuantan will bring you to one of the largest firefly colonies in the world. You can go on an organised night tour or hire a boat in order to witness this inspiring natural phenomenon. A night-time dip in the ocean is a must-do experience, as your movements are lit up by the marine bioluminescence.

For a truly local experience, check out the Cherating Cultural Complex. Here you can learn about and participate in traditional Malaysian activities such as basket or mat weaving, batik painting and playing congkak, a traditional Malay board game.

Penang

In Malaysia you can be on a beautiful beach one weekend, and exploring a historical site the next. In Penang, you can do both, and so much more. Known as the 'Pearl of the Orient', Penang is one of Malaysia's most popular islands and, according to AsiaWeek, one of the most livable cities in Asia. Daily flights to Penang on Air Asia (www.airasia.com) are swift and inexpensive. Alternatively you can go on the bus – Aeroline does daily trips (www.aeroline.com.my) – or you could make the six-hour drive yourself.

Many come to historic Georgetown for the delicious and plentiful food options. It can seem like nobody sleeps in Georgetown, as street-front hawker stalls are bustling all night with waiters yelling orders of asam laksa, mamak mee and fried kway teow to the back kitchens. Make a trip here in June for the annual Food and Fruit Festival to make

Need Some Direction?

The Explorer Mini Maps pack a whole city into your pocket and once unfolded are excellent navigational tools for exploring. Not only are they handy in size, with detailed information on the sights and sounds of the city, but also their fabulously affordable price means they won't make a dent in your holiday fund. Wherever your travels take you, from Europe to the Middle East and beyond, grab a mini map and you'll never have to ask for directions again.

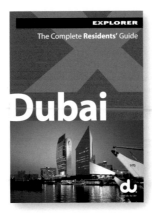

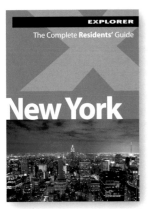

Turn to the team page and ask yourself…

…would you like to see your face?

Explorer has grown from a one-man operation a decade ago to a 60+ team today and our expansion isn't slowing down. We are always looking for creative bods, from PR pro's and master marketers to daring designers and excellent editors, as well as super sales and support staff.

So what are you waiting for? Apply online at www.explorerpublishing.com

the most of the delicious local food. Before leaving, head to Market Street in the heart of Little India to stock up on spices and curries to take back to KL.

About 20km outside Georgetown is Batu Ferringhi, Penang's most popular beach. While there are more attractive beaches in Malaysia, this is perfectly acceptable for some sun, sand, watersports and an entertaining nightlife scene. Be careful in the uncharacteristically murky water though: it often hides jellyfish, which can give a nasty sting. However, the sandy beach is lovely and invites lazy afternoons lounging in the sunshine.

Visit Penang in late November or early December to catch the world-class Jazz Festival (www.penangjazz.com), featuring top-notch international artists, workshops, competitions and exhibitions. In May, Penang hosts the World Music Festival in the Botanical Gardens (www.penangworldmusicfestival.com), where music lovers can enjoy the rhythms of local and international artists in truly inspiring surroundings.

Sightseers can spend days exploring the many architectural, spiritual and historical offerings of Penang. A definite item on anyone's checklist should be the world's third largest reclining Buddha at Wat Chayamangkalaram on Jalan Lorong Burma. The historical Cheong Fatt Tze Mansion (www.cheongfatttzemansion.com), otherwise known as the Blue Mansion, recently won Unesco's Asia-Pacific's Most Excellent Heritage Project award. For just RM10 you can explore all 38 rooms of this unique architectural landmark.

For an inspiring and uninterrupted view of Georgetown and the Penang Bridge, climb Bukit Bendera (Penang Hill), located 830m above sea level on Pulau Pinang. Aim to get to the top in time to witness the panoramic sunset over the Straits of Malacca.

Melaka

Melaka is an excellent choice for a weekend getaway, because it truly feels as though you have escaped from urban Kuala Lumpur. The old city of Melaka charms its guests with its interesting history of Dutch, Portuguese and Chinese heritage, diverse and delicious local food, wonderful shopping and truly artistic vibe. A weekend is all you need to see all of Melaka's historic quarters, shop and catch a break from the hustle of KL's busy life. There are many accommodation options in Melaka from basic two-star lodgings to luxurious five-star hotels. Check the websites below for an option that is best for you.

A good place to start is with a walking tour of the city. Begin your tour in the Dutch Square near Christ Church, where you can visit the Studthuys, Tan Beng Swee Clock Tower, and the beautiful Queen Victoria fountain. Just off the square you'll find a market where you can pick up local handicrafts – you can also have your picture taken with an iguana or a massive python. Head to the St Paul's Hill complex where you can see the ruins of St Paul's Church. This is where St Francis Xavier, a famous Catholic missionary, was buried briefly in the 1500s. Walk across the Malacca River and spend an afternoon exploring the numerous antique shops along Heeren and Jonker Streets. These shops are full of old western and Asian treasures.

If you'd rather not walk, you can hire one of the colourful local tri shaw bikes in the Dutch Square. These guides will transport you around the cobblestone streets, accompanied by whatever music they can pick up on their tiny radios.

Satisfy your spiritual side with a visit to Cheng Hoon Chinese Temple (Malaysia's oldest), the Kampong Kling Mosque and the Sri Vinayagar Temple.

Melaka is home to numerous cafes, hawker stalls and restaurants so during your weekend you'll be able to sample many different foods. Local specialities include the spicy Nyonya-Baba cuisine and the popular Chicken Rice Balls.

Langkawi

For that ideal beach getaway, many choose the short flight (www.airasia.com) from Kuala Lumpur to Langkawi. Made up of 99 islands, Langkawi boasts beautiful beaches, inexpensive and diverse lodging options and the opportunity to buy duty free!

Longing For Lankawi
Nature lovers will also enjoy Langkawi as it boasts ancient mountains and rainforests that over the years have evolved int a very ecosystem of diverse flora and fauna. When exploring the jungles try the canopy walk known as 'Sky Trekking', which allows you to walk among the tree tops. Many tour companies run full-day and half-day trips for jungle trekking, kayaking, mangrove exploration and bird watching. Travel company Langkawi Insider (www.langkawi-insider.com) offers a great variety of tour options for all adventure seekers.

Langkawi provides a laid-back atmosphere, even on it's busiest of beaches. Pantai Cenang is where most of the accommodation and food choices can be found. It is here you can also enjoy a great selection of watersports available right on the beach. Go parasailing for a bird's-eye view of the island, or try jetskiing for thrills and the inevitable spills, or hire a boat to explore the nearby islands. Nearby Pantai Kok is another beach option that offers more traditional chalets and provides a quieter holiday.

Other activities to pursue while in Langkawi include a visit to the Cave of Stories (Gua Cerita Cave) in Tanjung Rhu and Malaysia's best man-made tourist attraction, Underwater World, located among the markets and hotels in Pantai Cenang (04 955 6100). There are also top quality golf courses, weekend cruise options, and for those in need of some rejuvenation, incredible spa packages.

Taman Negara

No matter how long you plan on living in Malaysia, it is simply unacceptable to leave without visiting the world's oldest rainforest of Taman Negara. Considered to be Malaysia's National Park, it has been lucky enough to celebrate over 130 million birthdays and covers an area of over 4,000 metres squared. Take the Temerloh exit from the East Coast Expressway and proceed to the town of Jerantut. Visitors bound for Taman Negara will then have the option of continuing by boat via the nearby jetty or driving an additional 75km to the resort at Taman Negara. In total, expect the anticipated journey to take about three and a half hours from Kuala Lumpur.

There are numerous accommodation options from basic huts with fans to air-conditioned resorts that lie within the park itself and in the surrounding areas. The park can offer advice on the best accommodation options to suit you. Contact them through their website (www.taman-negara.com).

Once you arrive at the park, staff services are set up to take care of your every need. In order to travel throughout the park, you must do so by boat. Taman Negara does an excellent job of making sure the park is tourist friendly. Please show your respect by following all common sense environmental practices. Activities to enjoy once in the park include a thrilling canopy walk, jungle trekking, water rapid shooting, night trekking, and fishing. The park has limited equipment available for purchase so it is wise to arrive at the park prepared with any equipment you may need.

While in the park, a thrilling activity is to spend a night in a jungle hide. These are traditionally small huts on stilts, often near a stream, that place you front row for the

Langkawi (courtesy Malaysia Tourism)

jungle's nocturnal action. Arrive at your hide early and remember to bring a packed dinner, flashlight and patience, and lots of insect repellant. As your eyes adjust to the darkness (use your flashlight when walking, not when observing) you can witness more and more of the fascinating jungle activity. The deer is the most common night creature that may pop into view, with the tapir being a rare welcome sight also. While very, very rare, it is not unheard of to catch a glimpse of an elephant or the majestic Malaysian tiger. You're far more likely to see a variety of spiders and snakes, however, making it an authentic jungle experience!

Taman Negara is also home to Gunung Tahan, which is peninsular Malaysia's tallest mountain. There are numerous paths and trails in which to climb the mountain, but you will need more than a weekend in which to pursue this physically demanding goal.

Holidays from Kuala Lumpur

One of the best things about living in Kuala Lumpur is that it is so central – with just a few hours on a plane you can be in one of many different countries.

Flight time: *6 hrs*
Time difference:
2 hrs 30 mins behind
Best time to visit:
Oct – Feb

India

India is a land of contrasts, from Goa's beautiful beaches to the vibrant city of Mumbai and the imposing mountains of Kashmir. Goa is a top holiday spot with palm-fringed beaches and luxurious hotels. Alternatively, travel to Agra for architecture, handicrafts and jewellery, as well as to visit the legendary Taj Mahal or the rose pink city of Jaipur.

Flight time: *2 hrs*
Time difference:
1 hr behind
Best time to visit:
Aug – Sep

Indonesia

The main destination for most visitors to Indonesia is Bali, the Island of the Gods. Bali's tranquility has been horribly disrupted in recent times, but it is still one of Asia's best destinations. For its remarkable culture, fascinating temples, chillout beaches and the number of reasonably priced hotels, Bali remains unmatched in the region for a relaxing and absorbing holiday. There are numerous options for daily flights to Jakarta.

Flight time: *4 hrs*
Time difference:
3 hrs behind
Best time to visit:
Year round

Maldives

While south-east Asia tops it for culture, few destinations in the world have coastal resorts as stunningly beautiful as the Maldives. Unrivalled for its pearl white sand and spectacular diving, Maldives is not as inexpensive as south-east Asia, but it is soothingly spectacular. Direct flights are available on Malaysia Airlines.

Flight time: *4 hrs*
Time difference:
1 hr 30 mins behind
Best time to visit:
Year round

Sri Lanka

The beauty of Sri Lanka is that whether your budget ranges from basic to luxurious you'll find ways of having the holiday of a lifetime. Capital city Colombo has its attractions, but most holidaymakers head for the beautiful beach resorts. Direct flights on Malaysia Airlines are available.

Flight time: *2 hrs*
Time difference:
1 hr behind
Best time to visit:
Aug – Feb

Thailand

Bangkok is a favourite weekend stop for many KL residents, but if you're from outside the region Thailand is well worth a longer stay. The islands offer great watersports and everything from marine to nightlife. Unmatched for its great food and shopping, interesting Buddhist culture, and a swathe of upmarket bars, clubs and cafes, Bangkok is one of Asia's most fun and engaging cities.

Flight time: *8 hrs*
Time difference:
3 hrs ahead
Best time to visit:
Year round

Australia

Australia's got a bit of everything: beaches, amazing underwater life, hip and trendy culture to soak up in Melbourne and wine districts such as the Barossa and Coonawarra. Most of the cities offer a wealth of cafes, bars, clubs and year-round events. Malaysia Airlines flies to Adelaide, Brisbane, Melbourne, Perth and Sydney.

Flight time: *6 hrs*
Time difference:
0 hrs
Best time to visit:
Apr – Oct

China

In the grip of its pre-Olympics frenzy, Beijing is worth visiting now before it loses too many of its more visible signs of the past. A bustling and frantic holiday destination, the Forbidden City, terracotta warriors and the Great Wall are nevertheless all wonders to behold. There are three direct flights per week on Malaysia Airlines.

Flight time: *4 hrs*
Time difference: *na*
Best time to visit:
Oct – Nov

Hong Kong

Gateway to China and a city of great towers and unrivalled shopping, Hong Kong is a scenic and vibrant destination, with perhaps a little more soul than its rival Shanghai. But when it comes to better prices and greater awareness of how important leisure

Travel Agencies

Heritage Travel & Tours	03 4147 4788	na
ProHighway Travel	03 2282 7979	www.prohighwaytravel.com
Shajasa Travel & Tours	03 2026 8668	www.shajasa.com.my
Tour East – Malaysia	03 4899 8833	www.toureast.com.my

travellers are, it definitely has the edge. People come here for Hong Kong's food, nightlife and new attractions like Disneyland. Malaysia Airlines flies direct to Hong Kong daily.

Flight time: 6 hrs
Time difference:
1 hr ahead
Best time to visit:
Spring and autumn

Japan

In contrast with the 'Asia-lite' of Malaysia, a visit to Japan is like being thrown in the deep end. From the buzzing vast metropolis of Tokyo to the tranquility of Kyoto's atmospheric old quarters or the beauty of its countryside, Japan is a hit with everyone who visits. Not a cheap destination – accommodation can be wallet-draining, but well worth a trip. Direct flights are available with Malaysia Air to Tokyo or Osaka.

Flight time: 10 hrs
Time difference:
7 hrs behind.
Best Time to Visit:
Dec – Mar for summer,
Jul – Sep for skiing

New Zealand

The North Island's bubbling mud pools, hot water beaches and the Bay of Islands' many scenic inlets and coves are well-worth summertime exploration. Wellington is the country's arts capital and a year-round destination, and a short trip by ferry takes you to the winelands of Marlborough. The South Island offers plenty for nature lovers in the way of whale watching, hiking through Milford Sound or the glaciers of the West Coast. In winter New Zealand's ski slopes in Queenstown are a real drawcard. Direct flights are available on Malaysia Airlines.

Flight time: 7 hrs
Time difference:
4 hrs behind
Best time to visit:
Nov – Apr

United Arab Emirates

A gleaming city in the desert, Dubai is the Singapore of the Arab world, a gateway to the Middle East that offers travellers spectacular hotels, vibrant nightlife and great leisure options. Further afield there are many opportunities to explore the deserts and rich cultural heritage of the United Arab Emirates and its neighbours. There are daily flights from Kuala Lumpur to Dubai on Emirates Airlines.

Flight time: 4 hrs
Time difference: na
Best time to visit:
Sep – Apr

Philippines

Seven thousand tropical islands make a wealth of choices for a beach holiday, but many KL travellers head for a handful of palm-fringed isles; like Boracay, Cebu and Palawan. Diving and watersports are popular pastimes, and English is widely spoken. Flights go direct to some resort destinations; for others, you'll need to pass through the chaotic capital of Manila.

Dubai, United Arab Emirates

Auckland, New Zealand

MALAYSIA *Magazine*

The Most Established Golf Publication in South East Asia

*Golfers are also eligible to participate in the Golf Malaysia Irons Challenge on 23 August 2008 at Palm Resort Golf & Country Club, Johor. Tel: 03-7880 5060/13 for more information.

Activities

Wish You Were Here?
If you run a popular expat sports or activity group and you're always on the lookout for new members, you need to get listed in the next edition of this book. Visit www. explorerpublishing. com to find out how to get your name in print.

Sports & Activities

Rest assured that for anyone living in Kuala Lumpur, there is no shortage of things to do, whether you are a sports fan or someone that has a particular hobby or interest. There is always a group somewhere in the city that shares an interest with you and it's often a case of looking at notice boards (at schools or even outside supermarkets) or asking around friends to find some contact details. Social groups such as the Association of British Women in Malaysia (ABWM), Malaysian Australian New Zealand Association (MANZA) or American Association of Malaysia (AAM) are usually very good sources of information. Unfortunately, many groups and venues do not have their own websites (or often they have one which is out of date) so searching the internet is not always very informative or indicative of what's happening out there.

Despite the humidity, Malaysia's climate is conducive to an active lifestyle, so some sports are extremely popular and have a high profile here, particularly football, badminton, squash, golf and motorsports. Meanwhile there are other mainstream sports that don't get a high profile here, including sailing and horse riding, and remain in the realm of the wealthy local or expat for the time being. The presence of so many expats adds another dimension, particularly on the social front, and there are an increasing number of smaller, friendly groups that get together in the evenings and at weekends to play their particular games.

Activity Finder

Aerobics & Fitness Classes

Most health and country clubs are now providing a wide range of fitness classes including conventional aerobics as well as body pump, step, spinning and conditioning classes. Typically each gym has a number of classes which aim to cater for each discipline at differing levels of fitness and ability. The fitness centres listed below conduct Les Mills classes (www.lesmills.com) at all their branches, and therefore you can be assured that all these instructors are being retrained and updated on current techniques on a regular basis.

Aerobics & Fitness Classes

California Fitness	03 2295 0088	www.californiafitness.com	Mid Valley	Body Combat, Body Pump, Step, Aerobics, Boxercise, Spinning, Dance, Body Conditioning
Celebrity Fitness	03 2092 8000 03 7718 8000 03 5163 3000	www.celebrityfitness.com	Bangsar Petaling Jaya Subang	Body Combat, Body Pump, Step, Aerobics, Dance, Body Conditioning
Fitness First	03 2093 8050 03 2711 3299 03 2026 1828 03 7728 0077	www.fitnessfirst.com.my	Bukit Damansara City Centre Suria KLCC Petaling Jaya	Body Combat, Body Jam, Body Pump, Step, Body Attack, Spinning, Dance, Body Conditioning
True Fitness	03 6209 3200	www.truefitness.com.my	Sri Hartamas	Body Combat, Body Pump, Step, Body Attack, Body Jam, Dance, Spinning

Aqua Aerobics

Aqua aerobics is still popular, largely because it is ideal for people who have just started exercising and are not yet fit, and also for anyone recovering from an injury. Classes in Kuala Lumpur however are restricted to shared pools within condominium blocks or gated communities. Once you have a pool and a group of people who want to try it, you will then have to find an aqua aerobics instructor and, believe it or not, it is difficult to source anyone suitably qualified in KL.

If you are keen to try aqua aerobics, keep an eye on expat noticeboards (at the international schools, or outside supermarkets) and ask around, particularly anyone that lives in an apartment or gated community. These frequently have one large but shared pool, so why not see if you can join their group?

Archery

Archery is popular throughout Malaysia, and the national team will be flying the flag at the Olympic Games in 2008. It is perhaps surprising then that there are not more outdoor facilities around KL. For serious archers, or those wanting to take it up properly, there really is only one fully equipped location to go and that is out to the National Archery Association's facilities on the east side of the city, near the zoo. Other, more commercial outlets, are useful for technique practice.

Maju Junction Mall
1001 Jalan Sultan
Ismail
City Centre
 Sultan Ismail

Big Shot Archery

03 2697 1606 | www.bigshotarchery.org

This small but well equipped archery facility in the centre of town has 16 lanes with motorised retractable targets. There is a walk-in fee of RM15 for 30 minutes' play if you need to hire equipment, or RM10 if you have your own. If you are new to the sport, they also offer an archery clinic which provides six hour-long lessons for RM240, inclusive of equipment usage. Regular visitors should consider Privilege Card Membership which costs RM100 per annum, but entitles you to free entry and unlimited arrows for RM30.

Star Archery

Sunway Pyramid
Petaling Jaya
🚇 Setia Jaya

03 5621 1302

Star Archery is an indoor facility for target practice, with 16 lanes for adults (each six metres long), and seven lanes for children (each four metres long). To use the facility there is a charge of RM9 which entitles you to 12 arrows (around 5 to 10 minutes of play). Although there are no classes, there are instructors on hand at all times to provide help.

Art Classes

Other options **Art Galleries** p.183,
Art & Craft Supplies p.286

Apollo Hui

Bangsar Shopping Centre (BSC)
Bangsar
🚇 Bangsar

012 637 8003

Apollo has his own studio located in Bangsar Shopping Centre, and provides lessons in oil painting on canvas to all standards of artists. It's a comfortable, well-lit and peaceful environment with plenty of Apollo's own art surrounding you for inspiration. One month's fee of RM300 entitles you to a weekly two-hour lesson.

Sam Karuna's Fine Art Batik Painting

85B Jalan Tempinis
Lucky Garden
Bangsar

03 2282 9818 | www.samkaruna.net

Sam Karuna, a well renowned batik artist in Kuala Lumpur, offers both professional artists and novices the opportunity to create fine art batik through a carefully designed training programme. A three-month intensive course involves a weekly three-hour session, and costs RM1,200 inclusive of materials. One-off lessons can be organised separately and tailored to groups. Groups consist of no more than 15 students to ensure that Sam can provide individual instruction to everyone.

Try your hand at batik

Astronomy

With Malaysia's first astronaut launched into space in 2007, astronomy is rapidly gaining popularity. The International Year of Astronomy 2009, a global event aimed at promoting the impact of scientific knowledge on our daily lives, will undoubtedly underpin national enthusiasm, and Malaysia is one of many countries that is considering high-profile projects to contribute to the global effort.

National Planetarium

53 Jalan Perdana
Lake Gardens
🚇 KL Sentral

03 2273 5484 | www.angkasa.gov.my/planetarium

Located in the Lake Gardens, the Planetarium is part of Malaysia's space programme and has strong support from the Prime Minister. As such, it has plenty of exhibits that will keep everyone entertained, such as an anti-gravity room and black hole simulator. Entry costs RM1 for adults but is free for children up to 12 years old. For an extra cost of RM6 (adults) or RM4 (children), see a movie shown in the large domed auditorium – these are usually space-related but often about other science subjects such as 'The Human Body.' Parts of the Planetarium can be hired for functions, from RM1,000 upwards. It's a five-minute taxi ride from KL Sentral.

Picture Perfect

Once you've added the final brushwork to your paintings, you may decide to have them framed. Some shops in KL that offer this service include WL Framing and Art in Petaling Jaya (03 7958 1848), Art Case Galleries in City Square (03 2163 5160), and Talens Frames in Taman Tun Dr Ismail (03 7727 9820).

Aussie Rules Football

Club Aman
4 Lorong Damai 5
Ampang
 Damai

Malaysian Warriors
017 696 7204 | *www.malaysianwarriors.com*

The Warriors have twice weekly practices for players of all ages and abilities, and play both friendly games and in local and regional competitions. Training is midweek after work and also on Saturday afternoons at 16:00 at the Club Aman Sports Field. They also organise a Junior Auskick programme (for kids aged 5 years old and over) using smaller synthetic balls, run by coach Matthew Black (0123624970) at 15:00 every Saturday at the same ground. If you are interested in attending, call their President Andrew Mannering on the telephone number above. Note that to play with the Warriors you need to join MANZA (p.221) as well as the Warriors Club (RM150 per annum).

Badminton

Badminton is very popular here in Malaysia and the country's success in the global arena is a strong source of pride among locals. There are plenty of badminton courts around KL, but most within private membership clubs. Irrespective of where you wish to play, booking in advance is essential.

The sport is monitored and promoted by the Badminton Association of Malaysia (www.bam.org.my) which is trying to increase the number of players at international level. The Malaysian section of www.badmintoncentral.com is also worth keeping an eye on for online discussions about new facilities.

Jalan Terasek Tiga
Bangsar
 Bangsar

Bangsar Sports Complex
03 2284 6065

This small sports centre has three good badminton courts which cost RM4 per hour. It is conveniently located and as a result, it is very popular. The courts can be used seven days a week. Coaching is available upon request at the office (open 08:00 to 16:00). Bangsar Sport Complex also has squash and tennis courts and an outdoor swimming pool.

> ### Bad Crowd
> Other places you can play badminton are at the BBBS Sports Complex in Petaling Jaya (03 7957 0880), Raintree Country Club (members only) situated on Jalan Wickham off Jalan Ampang (03 4257 9066), and the Recreation Club on Jalan Jelatek (03 4256 4853).

Jalan Memanda 9
Ampang Point
Ampang
Ampang

Sports Planet
03 4252 0816 | *www.sportsplanet.com.my*

Although primarily an indoor football facility, Sports Planet in Ampang has eight badminton courts that can be hired on an hourly basis, from RM17 upwards for non-members. Equipment appears to be in good order. Unfortunately coaching is not available. Sports Planet also has another venue at Sungai Buloh (036157 2137) with six badminton courts, which opens daily from 10:30 to 02:00 during the week, and from 10:00 to 02:00 at weekends.

Ballet Classes
Other options **Dance Classes** p.227

Block A-3-6
60 Jalan Sri Hartamas 1
Sri Hartamas
Bangsar

ACTS Dance Studio
03 6203 2921

ACTS is a popular and well established dance studio providing ballet (as well as latin, salsa, ballroom, belly dancing, tap, modern and jazz) lessons for beginners through to professionals. Lessons are available for children aged 3 years upwards, and are usually held in the afternoons and evenings. Closed on Sundays. Term fees depend on style of dance, and start from RM225 upwards. Music lessons in violin and guitar are also available. ACTS is 10 minutes from Bangsar LRT in a taxi.

ACTS School Of Performing Arts

73 Jalan Setiabakti
Bukit Damansara
 Bangsar

03 2095 5691

Angeline Yew overseas this small but popular dance school which offers ballet and jazz (as well as music, art, crafts and drama classes) for children from 3 years old upwards. Classes are held throughout the week and Saturday mornings. Call to arrange a trial class at RM25. Situated a five-minute taxi ride from KL Sentral station.

Annabelle School Of Dancing

14-2 Jalan Utara
Off Jalan Imbi
Bukit Bintang
Imbi

017 878 8559 | www.annakronenburg.com

Centrally located off Jalan Imbi, fully qualified ballet teacher Anna Kronenburg oversees weekend ballet dancing classes for children aged between 5 and 17, and follows the RAD syllabus with annual examinations held between March and May. Anna holds the Teaching Diploma from RAD and is also qualified as a Pilates instructor.

Dance Society Of Malaysia

487 Jalan 17/17
Petaling Jaya
Taman Jaya

03 7957 7433

The Dance Society is an organisation aimed at supporting the needs of serious dancers that would like to pursue a career in dancing. Among other events it organises an annual competition, the winners of which are sent abroad (Singapore, Australia and New Zealand to name but a few places) to experience dance with other internationally run dance schools.

Federal Academy Of Ballet

Wisma FAB
1-3 Jalan 14/22
Petaling Jaya
Taman Jaya

03 7957 3413 | www.dancemalaysia.com

The Federal Academy has its own Dance Theatre located in the busy suburb of Section 14. This school provides lessons in ballet (as well as tap, modern, jazz, and rhythm tap) to children and adults of all levels. FAB also has a sub-branch in Bangsar on Jalan Telawi where it also conducts classes.

Karen Barnes School Of Dance

14 Lorong Timor
Section 9
Petaling Jaya
Taman Jaya

03 7954 7558

Karen Barnes spent 12 years as a professional dancer before becoming an international choreographer and subsequently settling in KL. She now runs a successful dance school that specialises in preparing students for a career in dance. However she does teach a variety of classes in ballet, modern stage, tap, as well as speech and drama for children from pre-school to professionals. Weekly classes cost from RM90 per month upwards.

Basketball

Although there is a national team with its own home stadium (see www.malaysia-basketball.com), there are very few organised social teams in KL, particularly for expats. To shoot some hoops, you can always head down to the YMCA near KL Sentral with a few friends, or practise at the court in Bangsar Baru.

Bangsar Sports Complex

Jalan Terasek Tiga
Bangsar
Bangsar

03 2284 6065

BSC has a small hard court with basketball hoops. Anyone can come along and use it at any time but note that there is no court booking system so it will be particularly in demand during the evenings and at weekends. Bangsar Sports Complex is a small but popular centre that is very convenient for expats living in this residential suburb. Facilities also include tennis, badminton and an outdoor swimming pool.

Little Leagues

If your kids are mad about basketball then Mont Kiara International School (MKIS) and the International School of Kuala Lumpur (ISKL) both offer their students plenty of opportunities to participate in the sport.

218

YMCA

95 Jalan Padang Belia
 KL Sentral

03 2274 1439 | www.ymcakl.com

The YMCA is a facility for everyone, not just men. Membership (RM80 for an individual adult annual fee) entitles you to take advantage of the varied activities that take place at this facility, including use of the basketball court. The court can be booked (either by phone or online) anytime between 07:00 and 19:00, at a rate of RM35 (RM55 after 19:00) for two hours or RM210 for one day. Volleyball and tennis court also available.

Belly Dancing

Other options **Dance Classes** p.227

ACTS Dance Studio

Block A-3-6
60 Jalan Sri Hartamas 1
Sri Hartamas
Bangsar

03 6203 2921

ACTS is a popular and well established dance studio providing belly dancing lessons (as well as classes in latin, salsa, ballroom, tap, modern and jazz dancing) for beginners through to professionals. It has brand new facilities which will open in Sri Hartamas in April or May 2008. Lessons are usually held in the afternoons and evenings. Term fees start from RM225 upwards. Music lessons are also available. Once at Bangsar LRT, it's a 10 minute taxi ride to the studio.

The Dance Space

1 Jalan 1 (just off Jalan Ulu Klang),
Taman Sri Ukay
Ampang
Setiawangsa

016 258 1499 | www.thedancespace.com.my

The Dance Space, run by dancesport championship-winners Peter and Lavinie, claim that shimmies, abdominal muscle control, and Arabic gestures are only the tip of the iceberg for attendees. The drop-in fee is RM35 per session, but monthly fees (four sessions) are RM120. Classes are held in the evenings and weekends – look at the class schedules online. It also has a studio in Plaza Damas, Jalan Sri Hartamas (03 6201 8032).

Sherlyn Dance

17 Jalan Sri Hartamas 7
c/o Caterpillar
Sri Hartamas
Bangsar

012 233 3016 | www.sherlyndance.com

Sherlyn is the first Chinese Malaysian belly dancing instructor in KL and when she is not teaching, she performs with her own troupe of belly dancing girls named Sirocco Secrets. She organises both private and group classes, the latter held routinely at Caterpillar's Studios in Sri Hartamas. Classes are held at various times of the day (mornings, evenings and weekends) throughout the week to suit different levels of expertise. One-off classes cost from RM40 although a package of eight lessons will only be RM200. So if you are feeling 'hippy', come along and shake your stuff!

Birdwatching

Other options **Environmental Groups** p.230, **Birdwatching** p.219

There is a vast wealth of bird species found in Malaysia – many endangered and protected – so it is not surprising that birdwatching is very popular here. In the cities, you will find an array of birds such as kingfishers, minivets, and woodpeckers in even the smallest urban garden. You don't need to travel too far out of KL to find freshwater birds hanging out at the ex-mining pools. Alternatively, head off to the forest and feast your eyes on bulbuls, cuckoos, bee-eaters, flycatchers and hornbills among many others. Visit www.birdinginmalaysia.com to get a full list of bird species. Port Dickson is also on the migration path for many raptors and from late February to early March every year, you will be lucky enough to see hundreds of birds flying overhead on their way from Papua New Guinea all the way up to Japan and Siberia.

Kingfisher Tours

11F Bangunan
Yayasan Selangor
Bukit Bintang

03 2142 1454 | *birds@tm.net.my*

This small company organises birdwatching tours in Peninsular Malaysia and Borneo, for private groups (between one and 12 individuals) on a request basis only. So whether you want an introduction to birding in Malaysia or have a particular species that you want to see, then this company can take you. Accordingly, Kingfisher can take you on a day trip up to Fraser's Hill (where you can go for some beautiful walks through the jungle) or arrange short trips of two or three days for a more extensive study. It provides a tailor-made solution, and will organise transport as well as accommodation, depending upon your requirements.

KL Bird Park

920 Jalan
Cenderawasih
Lake Gardens
🚇 *KL Sentral*

03 2272 1010 | *www.klbirdpark.com*

KL's Bird Park features approximately 200 species of local and foreign birds, housed in a huge walk-in free-flight aviary. While some

Ostrich at the KL Bird Park

birds are placed in mini aviaries and cages, a large number are able to roam free as you walk around. Admission is RM35 for adults and RM25 for children. There is also a photography point where you can get a close-up view by holding a selection of bigger birds.

Malaysian Nature Society (MNS)

641 Jalan Kelantan
Bukit Persekutuan
KL Sentral
🚇 *KL Sentral*

03 2287 9422 | *www.mns.org.my*

The birdwatching group within the MNS is an active collection of volunteers that organises everything from birdwatching day trips to evening talks and an annual Raptor Watch extravaganza. However, there is a serious side to it all and that is the monitoring and conservation of these beautiful birds and the environments they live in. For the novice, the group hosts an annual beginners' course. Membership of MNS is RM70 per annum for an individual, although family and corporate memberships are also available; membership also entitles you to a regular copy of the *Malaysian Naturalist* magazine.

Bowling

You will never be far away from a 10 pin bowling alley in KL, although the facilities will differ enormously between those that have been operating for considerably longer than the new alleys just opening. While the older alleys are still perfectly good, the newer facilities are trying to distinguish themselves with new and unusual ways of bowling such as glow bowls for playing in the dark. Shoe rental is usually around RM2, with lane rental starting at around RM5 per game. Most bowling alleys are open daily from 10:00 to 01:00 during weekdays and 02:00 at weekends.

Bowling

Ampang Superbowl	Ampang Point Shopping Centre	Ampang	03 4252 7575
Bangsar Bowl	Bangsar Shopping Centre	Bangsar	03 2094 3498
Cosmic Bowl	Midvalley Megamall	Mid Valley	03 2287 8280
The Mines Bowling Alley	Mines Shopping Fair	Seri Kembangan	03 8945 4125
Pyramid Mega Lanes	Bandar Sunway	Petaling Jaya	03 7492 6307
U-Bowl	1-Utama Shopping Centre	No Area Listed	03 7725 6399

Boxing

41 Bangsar Puteri
Jalan Medang Serai
Bangsar
 Bangsar

Kissaki Defensive Tactics Academy (KDT)

012 202 6111 | www.kdta.com
The Crazy Monkey Defense Programme at the KDT Academy is not just about boxing, it's about personal training and life coaching too. Sessions are highly personalised in small groups, although individual training is also possible. Annual membership is RM100 and after this one month's subscription is RM125 (one session per week). Boxing gloves and a mouthguard are necessary.

Bridge

Whether you are a beginner or have been playing for years, you will find a good selection of groups to play with across the city. Mostly attended by expatriates (the local equivalent is mahjong which is also played in easily accessible groups) which is reflected in the venues. Many of KL's Sports and Country Clubs, notably the Royal Lake Club and the Royal Selangor Golf Club, organise their own bridge meetings, although you have to be a member of the club to join.

12 Jalan Menerung 3
Bangsar
 Bangsar

Association of British Women In Malaysia (ABWM)

03 2095 4407 | www.abwm.com.my
The ABWM House hosts a bridge session every Friday between 09:00 and 13:00, to which everyone is welcome and which costs approximately RM10 per morning. In addition, there are a number of bridge groups run by ABWM members in their own homes (in all areas of town) including a complete beginners' group every Thursday at 10:00, an improvers' group on Mondays at 12:45, and a duplicate bridge club every Wednesday at 19:45. Everyone is welcome.

Royal Selangor Club
Kiara Sports Annexe
Jalan Bukit Kiara
Off Jalan Damansara
Bukit Damansara
Bangsar

Ladies' Bridge Club

03 2284 0250
The Ladies' Bridge Club holds a bridge session on Tuesday mornings at 09:30. If you already have a partner, you can simply turn up. If not, the Ladies' Bridge Club will pair you up with one of their many members, but call beforehand to register your attendance. There is a joining fee of RM20 and a charge of RM10 per session. All welcome. To reach the Royal Selangor Club by LRT, you will need to stop at Bangsar LRT and take a taxi to the club, a journey of about 15 minutes which will cost approximately RM10.

38 Jalan Tempinis
Lucky Garden
Bangsar
Bangsar

Malaysian Australian New Zealand Association (MANZA)

03 2284 7145 | www.manza.org
MANZA hosts a weekly bridge group at its house in Bangsar. The classes are for beginners and are every Thursday at 10:00, although you need to call beforehand to register your attendance so that everyone can be partnered up. Everyone is welcome and you don't need to be a member of MANZA, despite the venue.

Kiara Sports Annexe
Jalan Bukit Kiara
Off Jalan Damansara
Bukit Damansara
Bangsar

Royal Selangor Club

03 2096 2157 | www.rscweb.org.my
This is a smaller group of ladies playing bridge, and all standards are welcome. If you can find yourself a partner, you are encouraged to come along to the club's Kiara Sports Annexe on a Thursday morning at 09:30. It's RM6 per morning which includes refreshments; everyone is welcome and you don't need to be a member of the Royal Selangor Club to join this group.

Bungee Jumping

While bungee jumping itself has no permanent venue in Kuala Lumpur yet, the world-renowned AJ Hackett (who made this sport famous) has a strong presence here in two different locations. Adrenaline junkies need not worry: AJ Hackett is promising to make Kuala Lumpur his largest and most diverse location, so no doubt it will only be a matter of time before we see plenty more activities for the brave hearted.

Menara KL
Jalan Punchak
Off Jalan P Ramlee
Bukit Nanas

Flying Fox By AJ Hackett

03 2020 5145 | www.ajhackett.com/malaysia

Located in the heart of the city at the appropriately imposing 345 metre-high Menara KL (KL Tower), Flying Fox offers the opportunity to strap yourself into a harness, attach yourself to a steel cable with a pulley, and launch yourself from a takeoff ramp over the treetops. Flying Foxes range in length from 120 metres to 150 metres. Flying Fox costs RM30 for adults and RM15 for children for each run.

Sunway Lagoon
Theme Park
Petaling Jaya
Setia Jaya

G-Force X By A J Hackett

03 2020 5145 | www.ajhackett.com/malaysia

G-Force X is the highest slingshot ride in Asia. After strapping yourself into a twin-seat flight capsule, you get catapulted up to 65 metres in the air, reaching speeds of 120 kilometres per hour in less than two seconds. Hold on tight! Costs RM50 per ride. The theme park is open daily from 10:00 to 18:00.

Camping

Other options **Outdoor Goods** p.314

Due to the tropical climate, you can camp in Peninsular Malaysia all year round, although Taman Negara is best avoided during the monsoon season (October to mid February). Aside from torrential rain, certain places are susceptible to landslides and flash flooding so make sure that you are not in a danger zone and don't take unnecessary risks.

Camping in the jungle is very different and special equipment should be considered. Some jungles have rough terrain and you should carry a sturdy yet lightweight machete. Clothing depends on the terrain – sturdy but lightweight clothes (that will dry quickly) are best, but never denim jeans. Lightweight but strong shoes are better than boots. There are a great many off-road places to camp within two hours' drive of KL, depending upon the length of your trip and how experienced you are. While you can, of course, decide to camp independently, it is advisable to go with one of many adventure-type companies based in KL. Some provide you with the tools to camp independently, but bear in mind that a lack of experience and knowledge about trekking or camping in the jungle can lead to potential dangers from nature and wildlife.

Ampang Point
Jalan Memanda 9
Ampang

Asian Overland Services

03 4252 9100 | www.asianoverland.com.my

Asian Overland has a number of programmes depending upon the size of your group and the type of camping you want – whether it is centralised camping around its own private Jungle Lodge in Alang Sedayu (around one hour's drive from KL) or survival camping near waterfalls. The company will also organise island camping, which involves one night at the lodge before setting off to your chosen destination, whether it is Langkawi or Tioman. They have a regular scheduled programme of camping dates, or you can organise your own independent group (ideally 10 to 15 people). All equipment (including four and six-man dome tents) and catering is provided (with the exception of survival camping).

Jungle Geckos

14 Jalan 6/3
Petaling Jaya
🚇 *Jalan Templer*

03 7781 2027 | www.junglegeckos.com

This small company organises a wide range of outdoor activities in and around KL, including camping trips. Every trip is tailor-made to the customer's needs so it can also include riverboarding, mountain biking and trekking. Customers are taken by 4WD to one of many suitable venues just outside of KL. All equipment is provided (dome tents are possible but camp beds under an awning are infinitely more enjoyable, particularly in the rain) including sleeping bags. Cost is approximately RM150 to RM180 per person per day.

Jungle School

Suite 284-14-03
The Heritage
Jalan Pahang
Ampang
🚇 *Titiwangsa*

03 4022 5124 | www.jungleschool.com.my

Jungle School regularly take clients to one of many suitable camping grounds within 30 to 90 minutes of KL, such as the jungles in Ulu Yam, Ulu Kemansah, Pertak and Ulu Gombak. Longer trips may take you into Taman Negara. All are off the beaten track so be prepared for some walking. A common sharing tent can be provided as well as meals, and they will provide advice on additional equipment for personal use.

Malaysian Nature Society (MNS)

641 Jalan Kelantan
Bukit Persekutuan
🚇 *KL Sentral*

03 2287 9422 | www.mns.org.my

MNS has a Pathfinders special interest group which encourages people who enjoy nature conservation to go out hiking and camping on organised trips. Trips are arranged monthly and can be overnight outings or they can be extended expeditions according to the destination. Pathfinders need to have their own camping equipment. Individual membership to MNS costs from RM70 upwards.

Mudtrekker Adventure Travel

132 Jalan KIP8
Taman Perindustrian
KIP, Sri Damansara
🚇 *Kepong*

03 6274 1268 | www.mudtrekker.com

Mudtrekker organises a wide range of adventure packages out of KL. One such offering is the opportunity to camp in a designated site in Negeri Sembilan Wilderness Park (not open to the public), either in a small independent group, or as a larger group accompanied by a Mudtrekker guide. Tent rental is possible. The site is under two hours from KL by road (one hour on the main road, 40 minutes by 4WD) and has shower and WC facilities, plus sheltered areas for cooking. Accompanied groups between 10 and 100 people can be accommodated. Full catering and transportation is available. A two-day (one night) camping trip with all equipment provided will cost approximately RM380.

Canoeing

Other options **Kayaking** p.240, **Outdoor Goods** p.314

Kelab Tasik Putrajaya (Lake Club Putrajaya)

2 Jalan P8 Precinct 8
Putrajaya
🚇 *Putrajaya*

03 8889 5008 | www.kelabtasikputrajaya.org

The Lake Club is a membership club but permits the public to come and make use of its non-motorised watersports facilities. It has a good choice of canoes (see the website for full descriptions), including 15 two-seater ocean-going canoes, 15 single-seaters and 10 Canadian canoes, all of which can be hired on an hourly basis at the cost of RM10 per hour per seat. Instruction is available to groups of five or more.

Messing About In Boats

If you're a fan of canoeing then visit Taman Tasik Perdana (in Jalan Parlimen) and Taman Tasik Titiwangsa (in Jalan Setapak). Both are parks with lakes where you can enjoy your sport.

Caving

Despite being in the middle of a large city, KL residents can easily reach the Dark Cave near the Batu Caves (p.189) which remain the only feasible caving site unless you visit other states. The Dark Cave (www.darkcave.com.my) consists of two kilometres of surveyed passages in a limestone outcrop, and comprises of seven chambers featuring stalagmites, stalactites, flowstones, cave pearls, curtains, columns and cave straws. Visitors can turn up at the Dark Cave and take an educational trip (RM35 adult) which lasts 30 to 45 minutes and enables you to walk around the main chambers, learning about the different features, some of which have taken thousands of years to form. Alternatively, you can contact the Malaysian Nature Society and join its next Adventure trip. The Adventure trip (RM80 adult) take two to three hours and involves crawling and creeping around on your hands and knees. Equipment (helmet, boots, head lamps) are provided, but visitors need to wear proper clothing (long-sleeved top and long trousers, and sturdy shoes) and bring along a change of clothes for afterwards.

641 Jalan Kelantan
Bukit Persekutuan
KL Sentral
🚇 KL Sentral

Malaysian Nature Society (MNS)

03 2287 9422 | www.mns.org.my

The caving group's activities include a basic caving course, explorations, and courses for school children. Among other trips, MNS runs a great tour through the Dark Cave, which is two kilometres of cave systems at the back of the Batu Caves (p.189). Membership of MNS is RM70 per annum for an individual, although family and corporate memberships are also available; membership also entitles you to a regular copy of the *Malaysian Naturalist* magazine.

Climbing

Near Kuala Lumpur, Batu Caves and Bukit Takun (Templer Park) are the best places to climb outdoors, and both organisations listed below will coordinate group trips. These venues have a number of climbing routes suited to all levels, from the beginner (although the best place to start is on the indoor walls) through to the advanced climber. The climbing guide book *Climb Malaysia* (www.climb-asia.com) is an essential piece of reading and provides maps and route information.

In the last two years, climbing has developed a major following in Kuala Lumpur, with the number of climbers growing 100 fold in that time. This is largely down to the courses provided by the indoor climbing venues in controlled environments, but also to the subsequent support shown by local government that has helped to put climbing walls in schools and universities.

One Utama
Selangor
🚇 Kelana Jaya

Camp 5

03 7726 0410 | www.camp5.com

Asia's biggest indoor rock climbing facilities, designed to feature beginner walls, steep overhangs, slabs, aretes, dihedrals, crack lines, roofs as well as a couple of boulders and a 22 metre-high towering arch. One-hour taster sessions are available at a cost of RM45 (includes entry and equipment rental). Suitable for children as well as adults; group packages are also available.

Summit USJ
Persiaran
Kewajipan USJ 1
Subang
🚇 Subang Jaya

Summit Climbing Gym

03 8024 5152 | www.nomadadventure.com

Owned by Nomad Adventure, the Summit Climbing Gym has over 300 square metres of climbing walls, while 30 top ropes provide the potential for more than 120 climbing routes. Has an easygoing atmosphere. Trained instructors are on hand at all times, even on a walk-in basis. The Basic Rock Climbing Safety Course for beginners costs RM15 excluding entry fee and equipment rental. The company also organises outdoor climbing sessions.

Cookery Classes

Association of British Women in Malaysia (ABWM)

12 Jalan Menerung 3
Bangsar
Bangsar

03 2095 4407 | www.abwm.com.my
Priscilla Edwards at the ABWM runs regular Asian and Thai cookery courses, available upon request in your own home for groups of 10. Although very much hands-on, food preparation is done beforehand so that attendees focus on the techniques and ways of cooking. Recipes are provided to take away.

Cooking School for Kids

Mandarin Oriental
KLCC
KLCC

03 2380 8888 | www.mandarinoriental.com
Junior Cooking Class is held on every last Saturday of the month, and teaches children to prepare a three-course meal in small groups, overseen by one of the Mandarin's top chefs. This is a great way to introduce your child to preparing food in the commercial kitchen, by making it lots of fun (with chefs' hats and personalised chefs' jackets) while learning some favourite dishes with the experts. Cost is RM200 each.

Get Cooking At The Hilt

Hilton Hotel KL
KL Sentral
KL Sentral

03 2264 2592 | www.hilton.com
Every month, the Hilton team organises a very popular cookery class during which its head chefs demonstrate simple but delicious recipes from their own collections. Groups are small (up to 20 attendees) so the sessions are very interactive and informative. After the masterclass, lunch is served in the chic surroundings of a Hilton restaurant. Recipes are provided so that you can try them at home for yourself. Costing RM150, these sessions are well attended by the expat set, for good reason.

Malaysia International Gourmet Festival

Various Locations

03 2282 8866 | www.migf.com/classes.html
Towards the end of every year, the residents of Kuala Lumpur are fortunate enough to enjoy the Malaysian International Gourmet Festival during which many top chefs from all the hotels, as well as visiting international chefs, treat their restaurant guests to special menus and dining experiences. Many of these chefs also provide cookery classes during this month-long extravaganza, with sessions ranging in price depending upon the menu being served, usually anywhere between RM50 and RM150.

Local delicacies

38 Jalan Tempinis
Lucky Garden
Bangsar
🚇 *Bangsar*

Malaysian Australian New Zealand Association (MANZA)

03 2284 7145 | www.manza.org

MANZA offers cookery classes at its home in Bangsar Baru, specialising in the wonderfully varied food typically found in Malaysia, from Chinese to Indian to Malay and more besides. These are hands-on classes in which participants work together to produce four dishes that can be enjoyed together afterwards. Four classes are held every Wednesday, from 10:30 to 13:00, followed by lunch.

Bukit Damansara
🚇 *Bangsar*

Natalie Gourmet Studio

017 280 6717 | www.nataliegourmetstudio.com

Natalie hosts two classes each week in her own home, teaching French and Thai cookery to groups of between six and eight people. Each class teaches how to create a three-course meal, and the fee of RM170 includes the ingredients and lunch afterwards. Call her to be added to the mailing list.

Cricket

Alice Smith School
Equine Park Campus
Seri Kembangan
🚇 *Sungai Besi*

KeLawar Cricket Club

019 330 8268 | www.kelawarcc.com

The KeLawar Cricket Club has its home ground at the Alice Smith School campus at Equine Park, where it plays on AstroTurf. No training sessions are held as such, but the team plays 25 to 30 times during the year, participating in the National Interclub League, in the Navaratnum Shield (KeLawar are holders of the 2007 Shield) as well as other competitive games. They play host to touring sides from overseas, and also manage to go on three or four tours each year, typically to Singapore, Jakarta, Phuket or Manila. It is a very social group of men, with a number of non-cricket events organised during the year. Membership for expatriates costs RM200 per annum.

Royal Selangor Club
Kiara Sports Annex
Jalan Bukit Kiara
Off Jalan Damansara
Bukit Damansara
🚇 *Bangsar*

Kuala Lumpur Junior Cricket

012 296 1953 | www.kelawarcc.com

Organised by MANZA and Kelawar Cricket Club, this Junior Cricket Club is open to all boys and girls aged from 7 to 15. Practices are held every Saturday from 09:00 to 11:00 at the RSC nets, Kiara Sports Annexe, with coaching from a qualified coach and his assistants. Games are played as often as possible throughout the year. No previous experience is necessary to join. Registration fee is RM100 per annum. You need to be a member of MANZA or of the Royal Selangor Club to join the Junior Cricket Club.

Jalan Raja
Little India
🚇 *Masjid Jamek*

Royal Selangor Club

03 2692 7166 | www.rscweb.org.my

The Royal Selangor Club is perhaps the oldest sports club in Kuala Lumpur and renowned for cricket matches out on the Merdeka Square lawns. These days, cricket is played at the Bukit Kiara Annexe (off Jalan Damansara, 03 2093 2277), and it is social play on Saturdays but competitive on Sundays. However, you must be an RSC member to play (lifetime membership costs RM14,500, plus a monthly cricket subscription of RM500). The RSC also organises its own Junior Cricket coaching and regular games.

Cycling

Other options **Sports Goods** p.322, **Bicycle** p.29, **Mountain Biking** p.248

Malaysian shops are all run by enthusiastic friendly owners who can give you lots of advice on where to ride and cycle clubs. They can also repair and maintain your bike at very reasonable prices.

Once kitted out with a good bike and all the right equipment (such as helmet, lights, sunglasses and shoes), you can enjoy a totally different perspective of Malaysia. If you cycle in the right places you don't necessarily have to worry about the traffic. There are plenty of places to ride within 20 minutes of KL, including up to Genting in Putrajaya on the big, open, quiet roads (particularly at the weekends). Or you could try riding on trails around the local hills.

Le Tour De Langkawi

Keen cyclists should enter this challenging cycle race, which attracts some of the finest cyclists in the world. Originally staged in 1996, it encompasses several arduous stages as riders overcome the challenging Malaysian landscape. It begins and ends in the city of Kuala Lumpur itself (www.ltdl.com.my).

Various Locations

Pedalphiles Cycling Club (PCC)
www.pcc-cycling.freeservers.com

PCC is an enthusiastic group of cyclists who simply love to get out on two wheels, usually early on a Sunday morning (both on and off-road) but other options include Thursday evening night rides, Saturday kiddies specials (for 7 to 12 year olds) and it also does some long distance outstation rides. Everyone is welcome. To receive the newsletters which will tell you all about forthcoming rides, subscribe by sending an email to pcc_newsletter-subscribe@yahoogroups.com.

Dance Classes
Other options **Salsa Dancing** p.255, **Belly Dancing** p.219, **Music Lessons** p.248

Block A-3-6 60
60 Jalan Sri Hartamas 1
Sri Hartamas
🚇 **Bangsar**

ACTS Dance Studio
03 6203 2921

ACTS is a popular and well established dance studio providing ballet, latin, salsa, ballroom, belly dancing, tap, modern and jazz dance lessons for beginners through to professionals. Lessons are available for children aged 3 years upwards, and are usually held in the afternoons and evenings. Term fees depend on style of dance, and start from RM225. Music lessons in violin and guitar are also available.

73 Jalan Setiabakti
Bukit Damansara
🚇 **Bangsar**

ACTS School Of Performing Arts
03 2095 5691

Angeline Yew oversees this small but popular dance school which offers ballet and jazz (as well as music, art, crafts and drama classes) for children 3 years old and over. Classes are held throughout the week and Saturday mornings. Call to arrange a trial class at RM25.

1 Jalan 1
Off Jalan Ulu Klang
Taman Sri Ukay
Ampang
🚇 **Setiawangsa**

The Dance Space
016 258 1499 | www.thedancespace.com.my

The Dance Space, run by dancesport championship winners Peter and Lavinie, offers belly dancing and latin-style dancing and are also the first to offer pole dancing The drop-in fee is RM35 per session, but monthly fees (four sessions) are RM120. Classes are held in the evenings and weekends – look at the class schedules online. The Dance Space has another branch in Sri Hartamas at Plaza Damas, Jalan Sri Hartamas 1 (0362018032).

14 Lorong Timor
Section 9
Petaling Jaya
🚇 **Taman Jaya**

Karen Barnes School Of Dance
03 7954 7558

Karen Barnes spent 12 years as a professional dancer before becoming an international choreographer and subsequently settling in KL. She now runs a successful dance school that specialises in preparing students for a career in dance. However she does teach a variety of classes in ballet, modern stage, tap, speech and drama for children from pre-school to professionals. Weekly classes cost from RM90 per month upwards.

Sutra Dance Theatre

12 Persiaran
Titiwangsa 3
Titiwangsa
🚇 *Titiwangsa*

03 4021 1092 | www.sutradancetheatre.com
Well known dancer Ramli Ibrahim runs the Sutra House at which dance and culture are intermingled and expressed through music, art and dance (everything from Indian classical dance to Celtic musical performances have been held here within the 200 seater Amphi-Sutra). Ibrahim also provides traditional Indian and Malay dance classes for adults and children alike, in Bharata Natyam and Odissi. Dance is taught in a structured manner and with a methodical approach, with pupils being taught to appreciate the art form. Each year is divided into four three-month semesters. Sutra Academy has produced a number of successful professional dancers.

Temple Of Fine Arts

116 Jalan Berhala
Brickfields
🚇 *KL Sentral*

03 2274 3709 | www.templeoffinearts.org
Provides lessons in traditional Indian dance forms (specifically Odissi and Bharata Natyam) to children aged 6 years upwards, and adults. Everyone is welcome and no previous experience is required. It is entirely suitable for any expats that might wish themselves or their children to learn a local form of dance. Children's classes are held on Tuesdays at 19:30, while adult classes are held on Thursdays at 19:30. Cost is RM50 per month.

YMCA

95 Jalan
Padang Belia
🚇 *KL Sentral*

03 2274 1439 | www.ymcakl.com
The YMCA provides a wide range of dance courses to members including Scottish Country Dancing (Tuesdays at 19:00), Ballroom Dancing (Mondays and Wednesdays at 21:30), Line Dancing (Mondays and Thursdays at 19:00) and Latin American Dancing (Wednesdays at 20:00). On top of membership (RM80 for the first year), there are additional fees for each course, ranging from RM40 to RM200 for three months of classes. All classes are held in an air-conditioned multi-purpose hall.

Diving

Malaysia is a fantastic place to go diving. Unfortunately, much of the west coast of Peninsular Malaysia has been spoilt with shipping up and down the Malacca Straits but you can still head for Langkawi and Pangkor. Off the east coast of Peninsular Malaysia there are several islands where diving is a main attraction, notably the Perhentian Islands, Redang Island, Tioman Island and Tenggol Island. Over in East Malaysia, Sipadan is legendary. Check out the website for the Malaysian Sport Diving Association at www.msda.com.my.

The diving season is February through to November. With such opportunities on the doorstep there are of course many diving schools around the country offering a variety of courses for the beginner and the seasoned diver. As with all instruction check out the qualifications and, perhaps more importantly, experience of the instructors.

Planet Scuba

2 Jalan Telawi 5
Bangsar
🚇 *Bangsar*

03 2287 2822 | www.planetscuba.com.my
Planet Scuba organises diving courses and trips around Malaysia and south-east Asia. From its classrooms in Bangsar, it teaches the theory side for all the PADI courses (Open Water, Rescue, Dive Master, Assistant Instructor and Instructor), and follow this up with pool training in nearby Petaling Jaya. Subsequently, pupils can select which destination they visit (east coast of Peninsular Malaysia or East Malaysia) for their island trip to secure the qualification. Courses are tailored according to the individual, so classes can be for individuals or in groups of up to five. Open Water PADI costs RM850 plus island trip costs.

Sports & Activities

Dog Training
Other options **Pets** p.217

Although dogs are a common sight, Malaysia is perhaps not the ideal place for man's best friend. For starters, the climate makes it rather hot for some to exercise outside. In addition, there are not very many places to simply let your dog off the lead and run around so you'd better have a big garden at home. As if that weren't enough, Muslims are forbidden to touch dogs, so it makes them rather unpopular with a large percentage of the population. Saying that, showing dogs is very fashionable and there is a very definite move to promote animal welfare in Malaysia, so events such as Pet World Malaysia and K9 Day are becoming higher profile.

For general information of a domestic pet nature, visit the Malaysia Veterinary Forum at www.vet.com.my where you can discuss health, breeding and nutritional issues with fellow animal lovers and also vets. For information about government-approved vets and importing pets into Malaysia, you can go online to the government's Veterinary Department website at http://agrolink.moa.my/jph or call them on 03 8870 2000.

Kakiseni
Kakiseni is an online portal through which to keep abreast of arts, theatre, dance, music, film and cultural events in KL. It also provides regularly updated details on courses and auditions being held around the city (www.kakiseni.com).

8A Jalan Tun Mohammad Fuad 2
TTDI (Taman Tun Dr Ismail)
🚇 *Kelana Jaya*

Malaysian Kennel Association
03 7729 2027 | www.mka.org.my
The MKA provides members with information about different breeds, breeders and events in your area. It also helps to promote the welfare of dogs in the Malaysian environment. National MKA membership now surpasses 3,000 members, with local MKA divisions throughout the country. MKA conducts a range of obedience classes for dogs including those for puppies (aged three months and older), beginners (participants will qualify for the Canine Good Behaviour Certificate) and training to more advanced levels. The ten-week programme of classes to complete the CGBC costs RM100.

Taman Desa Community Park
Jalan Desa Jaya
Mid Valley
🚇 *Mid Valley*

Purina Puppycom Agility & Obedience Training
03 4297 8281 | www.puppy.com.my
Dog obedience and agility classes are held every Saturday and Sunday. Organisers will work with you and your dog towards completing the Canine Good Citizen Certificate sponsored by dog food supplier Purina. The Basic Obedience Course is held over 10 lessons, costing RM200. More advanced classes are held (for competition-level dogs) in Obedience and Agility, including Flyball Training. Puppy classes are held for dogs between 3 and 6 months old. One-to-one training at home is also available at a significantly higher cost of RM1,500.

Drama Groups

Sentul Park
Jalan Strachan Ampang
🚇 *Sentul*

The Actors' Studio
03 4047 9060 | www.theactorsstudio.com.my
Classes and workshops for enthusiasts and professionals in the field of performing arts. Courses range from gamelan music, an introduction to musical theatre, creative writing, theatre for the young, and traditional Indian and Chinese dance. Holiday programmes and workshops for children are available, from RM90 upwards. Classes are held at KLPac (www.klpac.com) and also in Bangsar.

Fun Theatre
Gardner & Wife presents fun theatre, ranging from classic farce comedies to quirky, off-Broadway musicals, fringe acts and West End plays. Managed by Producer Chae Lian and Director Richard Harding Gardner. Performances are held at the Actors Studio at Bangsar Shopping Centre (03 2273 1398, www.gardnerandwife.com).

229

Environmental Groups

Other options **Voluntary & Charity Work** p.60

 Kepong
Kepong

Forest Research Institute Malaysia (FRIM)

03 6091 6131 | www.frim.gov.my

FRIM is a government-run body for tropical forestry research. Occupying a 600 hectare site north-west of KL and surrounded by the Bukit Lagong Reserve, FRIM is well worth a visit for everyone in the family. Forest tours provide education as well as an opportunity to go for walks in these beautiful areas. Also good for camping, birdwatching, jungle trekking and nature photography. One of the main attractions here is the Canopy Walkway which is 200 feet high.

Lush local flora

 641 Jalan Kelantan
Bukit Persekutuan
KL Sentral
KL Sentral

Malaysian Nature Society (MNS)

03 2287 9422 | www.mns.org.my

Established in 1940, MNS is a prominent conservation and environmental group that promotes the study, appreciation and protection of Malaysia's natural heritage. For active members, there are special interest groups that are always looking for more volunteer participants. Themes covered include marine life, birding, photography, pathfinding, caving and urban green living (in other words, something for everyone). Membership costs from RM70 per year and includes newsletters and emails, trips, courses, activities and discounts.

Fencing

 Fitness Network
1F Centrepoint
Bandar Utama
Petaling Jaya
Kelana Jaya

Swashbucklers Fencing Club

016 682 0870 | www.fencing4all.com

Swashbucklers offers classes at all levels to children and adults alike, and provides both recreational and competitive programmes. Group sessions are conducted on weekdays (including evening classes), costing from RM150 per month for adults, and sparring sessions are held on alternate Saturdays. Individual training is available starting at RM90 for a 40 minute session.

First Aid

Tingkat 2, Block B
Anjung FELDA
Jalan Maktub
Off Jalan Semarak
Ampang
Damai

Heart Foundation of Malaysia (Yayasan Jantung Malaysia)

03 2693 4709 | www.yjm.org.my

The Heart Foundation is proactive in promoting health issues, and they conduct one-day training courses in Cardiopulmonary Resuscitation (CPR), either at the foundation's facilities or at your own chosen venue (provided you have a group of between 10 and 20 people doing the course). As an individual, you can phone the foundation and register your interest in the next course, and they will get in touch with dates and availability. The course itself covers CPR for infants, children and adults, and includes life-threatening situations such as dealing with choking. Certification is

230

provided by the Heart Foundation upon satisfactory completion and final assessment. The cost is RM150 which includes use of training equipment, face shield, and supporting manual.

St. John Ambulance of Malaysia

41 Jalan Shelley
Off Jalan Peel
City Centre
🚇 *Pudu*

03 9285 1576 | www.sjam.org.my

If you can organise a group of between 15 and 20 people to do a course, an instructor from St. John Ambulance will come to your chosen venue to provide training. Courses include first aid for adults, babies and children, as well as advanced programmes such as First Responder and Home Nursing. Modules can be created to suit your own particular requirements. First aid courses start from RM150 upwards, which includes use of training equipment, face shield, and supporting manual. A St. John Ambulance certificate is awarded upon completion to a satisfactory standard of competency.

Flower Arranging

Other options **Gardens** p.302, **Flowers** p.300

Summer Pots

Podium Block
Menara Keck Seng
Bukit Bintang

03 2145 8252 | www.summerpots.com.my

Summer Pots runs three different classes: a hobby class (RM1,000) consisting of 12 lessons that will cover the basics of shaped designs, hand bouquets, basket arrangements, and bridal bouquets. It also holds two classes for professionals: one consists of 30 detailed lessons (which cover baskets, hand-tied bouquets, wedding and bridal arrangements, as well as some advanced creative floral designs) and the other covers all of the above including some extra lessons to learn different designs and techniques, as well as looking at festive seasonal designs. Summer Pots can, upon request, organise one-off flower arranging classes for groups of between 10 and 15 participants.

Flying

There is no shortage of small but well qualified flying clubs around Malaysia, ranging from the clubs in and about Kuala Lumpur to those in Kedah, Johor Bahru, Penang and Perak. Once you have your Private Pilot's Licence you can charter an aircraft and fly to any of the 40 airports, airstrips and airfields in West Malaysia (flying to East Malaysia is simply too far for a small aircraft). Note that the Malaysian Department of Civil Aviation prohibits night flying in a single-engine craft.

Most clubs require you to take up membership before you can start regular lessons, so taking that into account, together with Ground School, medical, personal materials and examination fees, you are looking at a total cost of around RM30,000 to get your Private Pilot's Licence.

It's fortunate that in KL small craft are still allowed to fly over the city centre itself, which means that many of the clubs offer short flights that will take in the Petronas Twin Towers (p.188) at close range and show you a bird's eye view of the city centre. These are well priced (from around RM300 for half an hour) and make ideal treats for special occasions.

Hot air ballooning and gliding are not popular in Kuala Lumpur, largely because of the weather and the tropical thunderstorms. There is an annual air carnival held down at Nilai (south of Kuala Lumpur) every November and they offer balloon rides to guests, so watch out for advertisements in the local media. Paragliding, however, is starting to gain momentum here and there are now a couple of sites that are certified and sanctioned by the Department of Civil Aviation as being suitable for this. The closest to KL is in Jugra, Selangor, where paragliders jump from the top of a hill. For more information, refer to the website of the Malaysian Sport Aviation Federation (www.msaf.com.my).

Air Adventure Flying Club

Terminal 3 ◀
SAAS Airport
Subang
🚇 *Subang Jaya*

03 7845 4308 | *www.airadventureflying.com*

Chief Flying Instructor (and expat) Andreas Walther provides instruction at all levels, from the enthusiast who has never flown before and wants to try for a Private Pilot's Licence, through to the experienced individual who would like to fly more hours. Flying out of Subang, the club has seven aircraft for lessons (including the Cessna 172, Piper 28, Beechcraft as well as turbo prop aircrafts). The club will provide all assistance in obtaining a flying licence (issued by the Department of Civil Aviation) which normally includes 45 hours' flying (35 hours with an instructor and 10 hours solo) after Ground School theory training. For beginners, the first lesson lasts half an hour during which you will be taken up into the skies above KLCC – a unique experience. Hourly lessons with an instructor costs RM550.

Elite Flying Club

Terminal 3 ◀
SAAS Airport
Subang
🚇 *Subang Jaya*

03 7859 1933 | *www.oxyskygroup.com*

The Elite Flying Club has a membership system (basic cost RM2,500) which accommodates aircraft owners (gold), through to licensed pilots (silver) and student pilots training for their Private Pilot's Licence (blue). If you have your own aircraft, you can store it with the Elite FC and it will provide maintenance. It holds special events such as the Youth Aero Adventure which is a one-day camp for groups of children (between the ages of 7 and 17) to learn all about aviation. The club also offers a Discovery flight which is for up to three passengers who simply want to see what it is like to fly or would just like to see KL from above (RM390 per person).

Royal Selangor Flying Club

Jalan Lapangan ◀
Terbang Lama (old
Sungei Besi Airstrip)
Taman Seputeh
🚇 *Chan Sow Lin*

03 2141 1934 | *www.rsfc.com.my*

RSFC is located at KL's very first airport (built by the RAF) which is now used for military purposes as well as by the flying club. It provides a tailor-made training service for anyone wanting to obtain a Private Pilot's Licence (and who has passed the pre-training medical). Minimum age is 17 years old and there is no maximum age limit, providing students meet the medical criteria. Using a single-engine aircraft (typically a Cessna 172), students have to study theory through Ground School (60 hours) as well as fly approximately 50 to 55 hours. Obligatory membership of the RSFC is RM2,240. Flying lessons normally cost RM400 per hour.

Subang Flying Club

Terminal 3 ◀
SAAS Airport
Subang
🚇 *Subang Jaya*

03 7846 9134 | *www.subanghighflyers.com*

Subang Flying Club provides hangar storage and maintenance for privately-owned planes, as well as full support and training for members wanting to obtain a Private Pilot's Licence. The club has five aircraft (three Cessnas, a TB20 and a Seneca III) which it uses for introductory flying tours over KL, for pilot training, as well as for rental to members. Membership costs RM2,300 and the rental of a Cessna 150 with an instructor for one hour costs RM400.

Football

Gooner? ◀
KL has its own Arsenal
supporters' club, which
meets to watch all
Arsenal's games on TV
(www.arsenalmy.com).

Malaysians are football mad, so there is always a club nearby to play at, and if you are a keen spectator, it is always on the television. Perhaps surprisingly (as we all know about the England team's recent performances), they are fascinated by the English Football League, and you will see well-known players regularly endorsing local products on overly sized advertising billboards around town. There are many venues to play football, both indoor and outdoor, so visit www.gofutsal.com for a full listing. There is an expat team called the Expatriate Lions (www.expatriatelions.com), made up mainly of Scots it would seem, and who appear to be a lively and social crowd to play with, as your might expect. A longer established side is the members-only Royal Selangor Club soccer team (www.rsc.com.my) that play a lot of 7s games, both socially and at friendly international level.

The Summit Subang
Persiaran Kewajipan
Subang
Subang Jaya

Astrodome

03 8024 2288 | www.gofutsal.com/astrodome

Astrodome has three five-a-side indoor pitches, all with 'fieldturf' surfaces, which can also be configured into one five-a-side pitch and one seven-a-side pitch. Fully air-conditioned. Rental of the pitches starts at RM50 for non-members for a five-a-side pitch during weekdays. Membership is only RM20 so if you intend to play here on a regular basis, it is well worthwhile. Facilities include a viewing gallery and cafe.

Sekolah Kebangsaan
Sri Petaling
Section 12
Petaling Jaya
Taman Jaya

The Goal Academy

03 2719 5612 | www.thegoalacademy.com

The Goal Academy trains children aged 3 to 18, with a number of different classes to suit different abilities. It distinguishes itself with its online support which includes access to skills and drills, as well as a regular newsletter for members. Membership costs from RM350 per term. The Academy's structured, age-specific coaching programmes cover the entire range of football skills to ensure all-round development. All programmes are coached by qualified instructors who are all, incidentally, trained and experienced in providing first aid.

Bukit Kiara
Equestrian &
Country Resort
Jalan Bukit Kiara
Off Jalan Damansara
Bukit Damansara
Bangsar

Little League Soccer

03 7710 6101 | www.littleleague.com.my

Little League Soccer provides football coaching to children aged 6 to 18. Qualified coaches organise training through many of the international schools and hold their sessions at Bukit Kiara. Beginners' sessions are run on Wednesdays at 16:45, as well as Saturdays and Sundays at 09:00. More advanced sessions are run on Tuesdays and Thursdays at 16:45. Players can try to join the Centre of Excellence which is an elite group, but this is by invitation only. Membership costs from RM350 per term.

106 Jalan SS2/75
Petaling Jaya
Taman Bahagia

Manchester United Supporters' Club (MUSC)

03 7877 3070

As one of the most famous clubs in the world, Manchester United deserve special mention. The club have a huge following here in Malaysia so their games are televised here on a regular basis. MUSC has its own club venue in PJ where members convene to watch games together and play socially. Annual membership is RM50. Everyone is welcome to drop in at the clubhouse and see what other entitlements come with membership.

Jalan Memanda 9
Ampang Point
Ampang
Ampang

Sports Planet

03 4252 0816 | www.sportsplanet.com.my

Sports Planet has fantastic indoor pitches in six different locations in and around KL, namely Ampang, Subang Jaya, Subang Grand, Shah Alam, Puchong, and Sungai Buloh. The Ampang venue has eight artificial turf pitches and one FIFA international size parquet pitch (as well as a sports shop), although the number and size of pitches at other venues differ, so please check. Very popular among expats and locals alike. Pitches cost from RM40 upwards, depending upon day and time, and whether you are a member. Ampang and Sungai Buloh also have badminton courts.

Golf

Golf has enjoyed unparallelled success in Malaysia in the past 10 years, with the number of championship-level courses growing apace. Most of these have been designed by acknowledged international designers from around the world, so golfers are spoilt for choice. Courses, naturally, vary in their level of difficulty, so ask around for recommendations based on your ability. All are grass, all have caddies, but not all are buggy courses. Play will generally start from around 07:30 every morning. Note that the majority of clubs require you to be a member before you can play, however both Saujana and KLGCC allow non-members on at restricted times (with reasonable green fees). You will also find driving ranges at all of these clubs.

All the clubs have professionals who will give instruction, both on the driving range and on the course. You do not always have to be a member to get lessons, so choose the club you are interested in playing at and give them a call to find out. Saujana has its own Golf Academy which is managed by Director of Coaching Roger Denton (0163516408), and offers private and group packages on the driving range as well as an on-course nine-hole training module and a junior development programme for 6 to 20 year olds. Note that most clubs are very strict about their dress code, so go prepared – wear collared shirts, shirts tucked in, and look the part. Many of the courses are also surrounded by trees and water, so take your mosquito repellant as well as sun cream.

Association Of British Women in Malaysia (ABWM)

12 Jalan Menerung 3
Bangsar
🚉 *Bangsar*

03 2095 4407 | www.abwm.com.my

The ABWM, headquartered in Bangsar, has a members' monthly outing on the third Tuesday of every month, teeing off at 08:00. This social group tries to play on different courses in and around KL every month, including Saujana, Kuala Lumpur Golf & Country Club (KLGCC), Royal Selangor Golf Club (RSGC) and Tropicana Golf & Country Club, on a regular basis. All standards are welcome.

Glenmarie Golf & Country Club

1 Jalan Usahawan
Section U1
Subang
🚉 *Shah Alam*

03 7803 9090 | www.glenmarie.com.my

Glenmarie Golf & Country Club combines business with golf, and has two 18 hole courses (one of which is illuminated for night play, so you can tee-off at 18:30). The typically tropical and rolling Garden Course contrasts with the very steep slopes of the Valley Course where buggies are mandatory. The Club also has a 33 bay driving range and a golf pro is on hand to provide instruction. Glenmarie also boasts tennis courts, squash courts, a swimming pool and other facilities for a family outing. Only for members and in-house hotel guests.

Kelab Golf Negara Subang

Jalan SS7/2
Petaling Jaya
🚉 *Subang Jaya*

03 7876 0381 | www.subanggolf.com

A members-only club, KGNS has two 18 hole courses, the Putra Championship Course (rated one of the best in Malaysia) and the Kelana Course. There is also a 42 bay driving range where golfers can tee off from actual turf bays. Members can take advantage of the swimming pools, tennis and squash courts, gymnasium and aerobics studio. Golf lessons are available for adults. Junior Golf Clinic is on Sunday mornings. Individual membership rates are from RM25,000.

Kuala Lumpur Golf & Country Club

10 Jalan 1/70D
Bukit Damansara
🚉 *Bangsar*

03 2093 1111 | www.klgcc.com

KLGCC is well located for residents near to Bangsar and Damansara. With two golf courses and an excellent driving range (with automatic ball feeder), KLGCC is a very picturesque course to play and afterwards to retire to the 19th hole. Other facilities include a swimming pool, gymnasium and aerobics studio. Non-members can play during weekdays when green fees are RM165 for 18 holes.

Jalan Kelab Golf
Off Jalan Tun Razak
Ampang
🚇 *Ampang Park*

Royal Selangor Golf Club
03 9206 3333 | www.rsgc.com.my
Founded in 1893, the RSGC was one of Malaysia's first clubs and still one of the most prestigious. Currently with 6,000 members, the RSGC is located in the heart of Ampang, and features two 18 hole courses (the Old and the New) as well as the nine-hole Sulaiman Course. All courses are relatively flat, which is a relief when walking. The historic Old Course has hosted many international golf championships. Members only.

Saujana Resort
Section U2
Kelana Jaya
Petaling Jaya
🚇 *Subang Jaya*

Saujana Golf & Country Club
03 7846 1466 | www.saujana.com.my
Saujana is one of the most attractive places to play in Kuala Lumpur, but has a reputation as being one of the hardest too. The two 18 hole courses, named the Palm and the Bunga Raya, feature dog legs, rolling fairways and many lakes, all of which contribute to its popularity. As a result, it has a lot of expatriate members who can also take advantage of the Golf Academy, driving range, squash and tennis courts, swimming pool and (last but not least) its friendly but casual 19th hole. Saujana hosted the 2007 Malaysian Open Championship. Non-members are allowed to play; green fees are RM223 for 18 holes, buggies are RM80, and caddies RM40.

Jalan Kelab
Tropicana
Petaling Jaya
🚇 *Kelana Jaya*

Tropicana Golf & Country Resort
03 7804 8888 | www.tropicanagolf.com
The Tropicana gated community boasts a nine-hole East Course and an 18 hole West Course where residents and members can play in an exclusive environment. The West Course is illuminated for night play and you can also use the driving range until 23:00 at night. There are picturesque holes with plenty of sand and water hazards to look out for. This is a popular course with expatriates. Individual membership costs RM60,000.

Golf

Name	Area	Phone	Web	Length	Par
Glenmarie Golf & Country Club	Subang	03 7803 9090	www.glenmarie.com.my	6404m	72
Kelab Golf Negara Subang	Petaling Jaya	03 7876 0381	www.subanggolf.com	5865m	72
Kuala Lumpur Golf & Country Club	Bukit Damansara	03 2093 1111	www.klgcc.com	6186m	71
Royal Selangor Golf Club	Ampang	03 9206 3333	www.rsgc.com.my	6224m	72
Saujana Golf & Country Club	Petaling Jaya	03 7846 1466	www.saujana.com.my	6692m	72
Tropicana Golf & Country Resort	Petaling Jaya	03 7804 8888	www.tropicanagolf.com	5902m	72

Hashing
Other options **Running** p.254

If you have never tried hashing, KL is undoubtedly the best place to start. This can be a very social sport, and there is even one group which is aimed at getting the kids started. The Hash Heritage Foundation (www.thehashhouse.org) will provide you with your nearest group. The Royal Selangor Club has its own Hash Club (www.rschhh.com) as does the Royal Lake Club (www.rlc.com.my), but membership of the country clubs is required.

Various Locations

Kuala Lumpur Hash House Harriers (Mother Hash)
016 366 8018 | http://motherhash.com

The Mother Hash is the oldest club in Malaysia, having been established in 1938. It remains a men-only group, and socialising is the mainstay. The weekly Monday runs start at 18:00 and normally take over an hour and a half. Enjoying the beer wagon afterwards is recommended, as is the ensuing sit-down dinner. Guest fee is RM35 and the termly subscription thereafter is RM150. Visit their website to find out directions on where to find the next run.

Various Locations

Kuala Lumpur Hash House Harriettes
012 660 0351 | www.klharriettes.org

This friendly group is a mixed hash (men are allowed) that runs weekly on Wednesdays at 18:00, with food after the run at a nearby restaurant. Its runs are usually around one and a half hours long. Look at their website to find directions on where to find the next hash run. The guest fee is RM20 and if you want to run on a regular basis, take out annual membership at RM120.

Various Locations

Kuala Lumpur Junior Hash House Harriers
017 219 1634 | www.kljhhh.org

This family-oriented group is operated along the lines of a traditional hash run but is focused on getting the children involved. Irrespective of the venue (usually within one hour of KL and always through forests, rubber and palm plantations), the hare usually lays two different lengths of run, the longest of which normally takes over an hour, the shortest 30 to 40 minutes. However, with false trails thrown in, frequent rain and sometimes even leeches to contend with, this is no walkover for kids! First-timers can come along and see if they like it (RM10 per child) and thereafter annual subscription costs RM60. Visit their website to find out directions on where to find the next run.

Various Locations

The Petaling Hash House Harriers
012 309 8301 | www.ph3.org

Another of the popular mixed hash groups in the Klang Valley, PHHH was established in 1977, and runs every Saturday at 16:30. Quarterly subscription required. Socialising, as with all hash clubs, is high on the agenda, but if you need an excuse then running for an hour or so through rubber and palm plantations is an excellent way to work up a thirst for the mobile beer wagon which awaits you afterwards. Mosquito repellent is an essential piece of kit.

Hiking
Other options **Outdoor Goods** p.314

39C & 40C Jalan
Memanda 9
Ampang Point
Selangor
🚇 *Ampang*

Asian Overland Services
03 4252 9100 | www.asianoverland.com.my

Asian Overland Services has a number of adventure programmes which include hiking, depending upon your preferred terrain and what other activities you wish to include. You may like to try a short day trip which includes limited hiking as well as a visit to a Malaysian village and a stop at a local aboriginal museum. At the other end of spectrum, it can also organise island trips which include more serious trekking and survival camping. All requirements can be accommodated. The company also has its own private jungle lodge in Alang Sedayu (around one hour's drive from KL) which it uses for shorter programmes. Private groups welcome.

Jungle Geckos

14 Jalan 6/3
Petaling Jaya
🚇 **Jalan Templer**

03 7781 2027 | www.junglegeckos.com

This small company organises a wide range of outdoor activities in and around KL, including hiking trips. Every trip is tailor-made to the customer's needs, so it can also include camping, mountain biking, bamboo rafting and even riverboarding. Customers are taken by 4WD to one of many suitable venues just outside of KL. All camping equipment can be provided.

Malaysian Nature Society (MNS)

641 Jalan Kelantan
Bukit Persekutuan
KL Sentral
🚇 **KL Sentral**

03 2287 9422 | www.mns.org.my

MNS has a Pathfinders special interest group which encourages people who enjoy nature conservation to go out hiking and camping on organised trips. Trips are arranged monthly and can be day outings, overnight or extended expeditions according to the destination. Pathfinders need to have their own camping equipment. Individual membership to MNS costs from RM70 upwards.

Mudtrekker Adventure Travel

132 Jalan KIP8
Taman Perindustrian
KIP, Sri Damansara
Selangor
🚇 **Kepong**

03 6274 1268 | www.mudtrekker.com

Mudtrekker organises a wide range of adventure packages out of KL including trekking and camping trips in Negeri Sembilan Wilderness Park. Clients can trek to a canyon and abseil down to the river running through, enjoying such sights as a 150 metre single drop waterfall. The hikes can also include visits to authentic native villages in the area. If combined with camping, tent rental is possible. Transportation to the hiking area is provided, as is catering. A two-day overnight camping trip (with all equipment provided) will cost approximately RM380.

Pathfinders

Jalan Kelantan
Bukit Persekutuan
KL Sentral

03 2287 9422 | www.mns.org.my

The Pathfinders are a group of enthusiastic MNS members who get together at least monthly to hike into the surrounding rainforests using little-explored trails in an effort to discover new wild places. The going is never easy and involves a lot of sweat, dirt and fun. Their activities include trekking, mountain climbing and camping.

Hockey

Other options **Ice Hockey** p.239

Montpelier Liquorice All Sorts

Kelab Aman
Off Jalan Damai
Ampang
🚇 **Damai**

012 302 0593 | kbrown@talisman-energy.com

So named because the group consists of a very mixed crowd of field hockey players – men, women, children, expats and locals – all with varying levels of experience. Several of the players are qualified coaches that provide instruction. The group plays at Kelab Aman off Jalan Damai every week (dinner and drinks afterwards) and occasional matches are organised with other local teams as well as touring games to Hong Kong and Singapore. Everyone is welcome and hockey sticks can be provided if required. The cost is RM10 each time you play and there's no joining fee.

Royal Selangor Club

Jalan Raja
Little India
🚇 **Masjid Jamek**

03 2692 7166 | www.rscweb.org.my

If you are a member of the RSC (one-off fee of RM14,500 for lifetime membership) you can participate in their Hockey 9s games held twice per week at the outdoor Tunku Abdul Rahman Stadium. Thursday evenings are for RSC members of the Hockey Section (RM10 per month) and include a mix of male and female players. Tuesday evenings are specifically for competitive games organised with other local teams. To reach the stadium take the train to Putra and catch a 10 minute taxi.

Horse Riding
Other options **Polo** p.252

Think hot arenas and sweaty jodhpurs! Since the 1990s, riding has become increasingly popular thanks in part to former Prime Minister Dr Mahathir, and also in part to the current King, both keen equestrians. However, standards vary enormously and you need to visit each riding school, observe and ask lots of questions.
Because of the lack of suitable land for hacking out around KL, most riding takes place within a riding school arena and the focus is on developing skills in show jumping and dressage. A calendar of events can be found on www.equestrian.com.my.

1 Jalan Ekuin
Equine Park
🚇 *Sungai Besi*

Akademi Ekuestrian DiRaja Selangor
03 9543 7878
New Zealander Chris Ladbrooke oversees a stable of over 40 horses, half of which are available for lessons, the rest being private livery. They are looked after by a team of Nepalese grooms and are healthy and well fed. Chris and his team provides lessons for all ages, from novices to those riding to international standard. Group and private lessons are available, and they also host a regular Saturday morning Pony Club which provides an introduction to horse care as well as fun activities. To reach the stables by LRT, disembark at Sungai Besi and take a 10 minute taxi to Equine Park.

Jalan Bukit Kiara
Off Jalan Damansara
Bukit Damansara
🚇 *Bangsar*

Bukit Kiara Equestrian & Country Resort
03 2093 1222 | *www.berjayaclubs.com/kiara*
Bukit Kiara is the largest equestrian school in Malaysia and conveniently located for many expats close to Damansara and Bangsar. Lessons in all disciplines are available, including polo for adults. Bukit Kiara also boasts a great tack shop with a range of quality clothing and tack from around the world. Experienced riders can also hack out on trails on Bukit Kiara itself and there is a 90 by 45 metre indoor arena which is particularly useful during monsoon season. Private livery stables are available. To reach the centre by LRT, disembark at Bangsar and take a 10 minute taxi which will cost approximately RM10.

Lot 1314 Jalan
Ampang Hilir
Ampang
🚇 *Ampang Park*

Royal Selangor Polo Club
03 4257 0508 | *www.rspc.org.my*
The Royal Selangor Polo Club, first and foremost a polo club, also offers dressage and jumping instruction at all levels and ages. The club has over 25 horses available for lessons and can accommodate all levels of ability, irrespective of whether you are preparing for the show circuit, need introductory stable management, regular ongoing clinics, or the Pony Club. Facilities include a 90 by 45 metre indoor arena. To help promote riding in KL, the club provides a riding package priced at RM850 where the participant will receive 28 basic riding lessons, all taught within a three-month timeframe. This is also the home of Riding for the Disabled. Full livery service available.

Jalan Kuda Emas
Selangor
🚇 *Sungai Besi*

Selangor Turf Club
03 9058 3888 | *www.selangorturfclub.com*
At Selangor Turf Club, close to the Mines Resort, lessons are given in all the main disciplines. If you have ridden before, you will firstly be assessed to make sure you are put into a suitable group for your level of expertise. A one-hour group lesson for an adult starts at RM310 for a package of eight lessons. Alternatively, you may wish to opt

for a private lesson (only available during weekdays) which will cost RM350 for eight 45 minute lessons. The club works closely with the Malaysian Equine Council to conduct education and training in horse management, and also offers instructor training.
It has over 45 horses and ponies available for lessons and its facilities include two international arenas and a cross country course. Hacking is also available within the surrounding 225 acre grounds. Pony Club activities are also provided.

Ice Hockey
Other options **Ice Skating** p.239

Sunway Pyramid Rink
Jalan PJS 11/15
Bandar Sunway
Petaling Jaya
🚇 *Kelana Jaya*

Kuala Lumpur Cobras
019 388 3646 | www.klcobras.com
The KL IndoChine Cobras are KL's expatriate ice hockey team, made up of a variety of different nationalities, but all with one thing in common – an interest in ice hockey, no matter how great or small. The club welcomes all new members to get out on the ice with them, either socially or at competition level. Hockey School offers weekly lessons for two levels: beginners and beginner-intermediates.

Ice Skating
Other options **Ice Hockey** p.239

Sunway Pyramid Rink
Jalan PJS 11/15
Bandar Sunway
Petaling Jaya
🚇 *Kelana Jaya*

Pyramid Ice
03 7492 6800 | www.sunway.com.my/pyramidice
Pyramid Ice is a great facility, reputedly the largest skating school in south-east Asia, and can hold 400 skaters at any one time. Admission costs between RM13 and RM19 which includes skate rental. Coaching is well promoted with junior and senior as well as foreign coaches available. Lessons include freestyle, skating for couples and figure skating. Prices range from RM60 upwards for half an hour's instruction. Individual, semi-private and group sessions are possible. Birthday functions are available.

Karting

Quadrant C
Shah Alam Stadium
Section 13, Shah Alam
🚇 *Batu Tiga*

City Karting
03 5512 5868 | www.citykarting.com
If you are relatively serious about karting, visit City Karting which runs several different classes of Sprint Karts for club races and national competitions. These include Formula 100, Formula J, Formula Cadet, Formula 125 and (at club level) Formula V for veterans. At a fun level, City Karting can coordinate karting events however small or large, and their track is open seven days a week until 22:00 at night. It also provides an on-site ambulance service. There's no minimum age but karters must be a minimum four feet in height.

Jalan Lagoon
Selatan
Bandar Sunway
Petaling Jaya
🚇 *Kelana Jaya*

Extreme Park
03 8027 0426 | www.extremepark.com.my
One block from Sunway Lagoon is Extreme Park where you can go fun karting on a 1.3 kilometre track, one of the longest in Malaysia and built recently to international standards. It has been designed to encourage the novice while also challenging the experienced karter. Have a go at RM35 for 10 minutes or RM65 for 20 minutes. Extreme Park is a great fun day out for the family or as a corporate outing. Angling, camping, X Games Park (for skating and BMXing), ATV riding, dirt karting and golf are all available.

Sepang Circuit

Jalan Pekeliling
Selangor
 KLIA

03 8778 2204 | *www.malaysiangp.com.my*

Sepang, famous for its F1 Grand Prix, also has a 1.2 kilometre kart circuit (tarmac, with 11 challenging turns) where racers can enjoy the experience of a full-throttle environment. SIC fun karts, 100cc fun karts and 125cc karts are available for use. Also accessible at Sepang is the F1 circuit (the Malaysian F1 Grand Prix is usually held in March each year) and there are track days where you can take your own car out and push it (and yourself) to the limit.

Kayaking

Other options **Canoeing** p.223

Kelab Tasik Putrajaya (Lake Club Putrajaya)

2 Jalan P8 Precinct 8
Putrajaya
Putrajaya

03 8889 5008 | *www.kelabtasikputrajaya.org*

The Lake Club is a membership club but permits the public to come and make use of its non-motorised watersports facilities. It has a good choice of kayaks (full description on the website) with leisure kayaks, ski kayaks, slalom kayaks and polo kayaks, all of which can be hired on an hourly basis from RM10 upwards per hour per seat. Instruction is available to groups of five or more.

Tracks Adventures

Lot 11, Jalan Lengal
Off Jalan Tembak
Kuala Kubu Bahru
Selangor

03 6065 1767 | *www.tracksadventures.com.my*

Tracks specialises in rafting and kayaking in whitewater, and visits the Selangor River (on the road to Fraser's Hill) for its training programmes. For the beginner, there is an introduction to kayaking which starts students off by teaching them the basics in still flatwaters. After this, students move onto testing their skills in whitewater rapids. For the experienced there is an Intermediate Moving Water Course and an Advanced Whitewater Course. An ACA-credited course on Swift Water Rescue is also available, although students should already have a good understanding of whitewater boating. Equipment (helmet, kayaks, life jackets) is provided if required. This one is for the serious adrenaline junkies.

Kids Activities

Caterpillar

Jalan Sri Hartamas 7
Sri Hartamas
 Bangsar

03 6201 0378 | *www.caterpillar.com.my*

Caterpillar has a popular venue with something for almost everyone, from dance and fitness classes, baking and cookery programmes for kids, arts and crafts, as well as a cafe serving healthy home-cooked meals. Has a very friendly and welcoming environment. To reach Caterpillar by LRT, get out at Bangsar Station and catch a 10 minute taxi ride costing approximately RM10.

Clay Expression

Ikano Power Centre
2 Jalan PJU 7/2
Mutiara Damansara
Petaling Jaya
Kelana Jaya

03 7725 4598 | *www.clayexpression.com*

Cindy Koh, founder of Clay Expression, has created a unique pottery opportunity for both adults and children in KL. Whether it is custom-made orders, pottery classes, corporate functions, or children's clay parties, Clay Expression can offer almost anything required to create a pottery masterpiece, from the techniques to the glazing and firing. This is a fun and friendly place to take the kids, with whom it is extremely popular. Trial classes cost RM48. There is a shuttle bus from Kelana Jaya to the Ikano Power Centre. It also has a small but inviting cafe. Clay Expression has another branch at Block C5, Jalan Subang 3, in PJ (03 5628 1613).

Sports & Activities

Berjaya Times Square
Bukit Bintang
Imbi

Cosmo's World Indoor Theme Park

03 2117 3118 | www.timessquarekl.com

Cosmo's World is the largest indoor theme park in Malaysia, with two main areas: one more suitable for adults and teenagers (Galaxy Station) than the other (Fantasy Garden). As you would expect, the former includes being thrown around in a high-adrenaline rush, whereas the more faint-hearted can enjoy bumper cars, mini train rides and fantasy trails. As Times Square is one of KL's largest malls, Cosmo's World can get very busy. Admission is based on height – for kids under 140 centimetres entry is RM20, while for those over it's RM30 (add an extra RM5 on weekends and holidays). After initial payment all rides are free.

4-1 Jalan 24/70A
Desa Sri Hartamas
Sri Hartamas
Bangsar

Flying Colours

03 2300 8820 | www.flying-colours.org

Flying Colours is an arts and crafts studio where you can paint your own pottery (simply choose an object and get painting). The kids can also make artistic cards, photo frames and jewellery among much more. Offering glass painting, ceramic work and mosaic making, the different programmes offered by this studio show this a great place for unleashing your artistic side. To reach Sri Hartamas by rail, go to Bangsar and take a 10 minute taxi ride.

Berjaya Times Square
1 Jalan Imbi
Bukit Bintang
Imbi

IMAX – Times Square

03 2117 3046 | www.timessquarekl.com

As befits the size of Berjaya Times Square, IMAX is a huge movie screen (the equivalent of five storeys high) and blasts out 12,000 watts of digital sound to cinema-goers. It regularly shows educational feature movies (such as Shark 3D or T-Rex 3D) as well as current movie screenings. It costs RM15 for adults and RM10 for children.

Plaza Ground Floor
Hartamas Shopping
Centre
Sri Hartamas
Bangsar

Kidz Zone

03 6201 8799

Kidz Zone is a popular and well-equipped playland that will appeal to children up to around 12 years old. There's lots of climbing, crawling, hanging, swinging and jumping around, as well as a foam ball shooting gallery which is always popular. Parents can drop and shop or stay and have a coffee from the limited cafe. Socks are essential for the kids. It's a popular place for birthday parties. To reach the Hartamas Shopping Centre by LRT, go to Bangsar Station and catch a taxi which will take 10 minutes and cost approximately RM10.

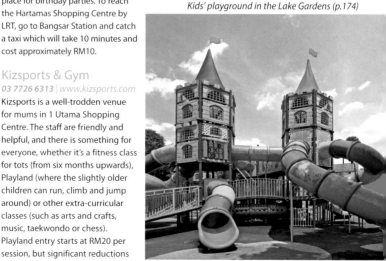

Kids' playground in the Lake Gardens (p.174)

2nd Floor, 1 Utama
Shopping Centre
Petaling Jaya
Kelana Jaya

Kizsports & Gym

03 7726 6313 | www.kizsports.com

Kizsports is a well-trodden venue for mums in 1 Utama Shopping Centre. The staff are friendly and helpful, and there is something for everyone, whether it's a fitness class for tots (from six months upwards), Playland (where the slightly older children can run, climb and jump around) or other extra-curricular classes (such as arts and crafts, music, taekwondo or chess). Playland entry starts at RM20 per session, but significant reductions are possible by taking membership. Socks are essential. Kizsports has another outlet in the Great Eastern Mall on Jalan Ampang (03 4257 2277).

Kompleks Kraf (Craft Complex)

63 Jalan Conlay
Bukit Bintang
🚇 Bukit Bintang

03 2162 7459 | www.kraftangan.gov.my

The Craft Complex is a relaxed, child-friendly venue where you can get close-up to many of Malaysia's most famous exports, including silverware, pewter, art and woven rattan. It's a particularly popular stop for children, who are invited to sit down and create their own batik pictures, both on pieces of silk fabric or even on T-shirts. Items cost from around RM20 depending on the article and design chosen. Great for children over 5 years old.

Mad Science Malaysia

Various Locations

03 7712 0120 | www.madscience.com.my

Mad Science successfully shows children how science can be fun. The team demonstrates experiments and gets children 3 years old and over actively involved in seeing how things work. A huge variety of subjects are covered including gravity, aerodynamics, how a camera works and chemical reactions. The team can come to your venue for a party, or you will frequently see them at places around town (shopping centres, Zoo Negara, the National Science Centre). They also visit schools as part of the kids' extra-curricular activities. During the holidays there are one and two-day camps (limited to 25 places). Keep an eye on the website for upcoming programmes and venues. Standard party packages for up to 20 children in the comfort of your own home will cost RM500.

MegaKidz

Mid Valley Megamall
Mid Valley
🚇 Mid Valley

03 2282 9300 | www.megakidz.com.my

MegaKidz is a large, well-equipped playland where kids can be dropped safely while mums are out shopping (RM30 per hour, the minimum age for the kids is 3). There is a set-aside area for younger children to play (an adult must be with them at all times here) as well as an exciting playland area for independent children. Slides and helter skelters feature here as well as the normal climbing and crawling stations. Great facilities for birthday parties. Membership is also available. Socks are essential.

My Lil Artist

Persiaran Ara Kiri
Lucky Garden
Bangsar
🚇 Bangsar

012 321 0356

Wonderfully located just behind Bangsar Village, My Lil Artist has recently opened for young kids to drop in. Its painting club is open to children from 3 years upwards and the company is a provider of the well established Da Vinci creative programme (www.davinci.com.my) for children from 5 through to 18 years of age. This includes creative kids art, educating them about the different elements of art, as well as creative crafts. My Lil Artist has two classrooms as well as a dance studio, although it also organises children's parties at home. Open Thursday and Friday evenings and throughout Saturdays.

National Science Centre (Pusat Sains Negara)

Persiaran Bukit Kiara
Bukit Damansara
🚇 Bangsar

03 2092 1150 | www.psn.gov.my

Once inside this impressive domed building you'll find an arched aquarium full of tropical fish and enjoy a huge range of different galleries (for all age groups) and interactive exhibits that the kids will love. Optical illusions, dinosaurs, bridge building and, for toddlers, giant Lego and a ball pit, are just some of the things to visit. Outside there is an adventure playground and a mini zoo. This is a great place for the family to come, but note that the cafe is very basic. The entry fee is RM6 for adults and RM3 for children. To reach the centre take the LRT to Bangsar and catch a taxi which will take 10 minutes and cost approximately RM10.

Level 4, Suria KLCC
KLCC
KLCC

Petrosains
03 2331 8787 | www.petrosains.com.my

Petrosains is an enormous interactive science museum that begins with a short journey through space (the 'Dark Ride') which gives you a pleasant introduction to the science behind hydrocarbon recovery. You can enjoy a huge selection of scientific demonstrations which form part of the regular exhibition. Although interesting for everyone, it is particularly good for kids who can run around and try out experiments for themselves. It takes a good two hours to go around properly so make sure you have lots of time and energy. Entry fee is RM12 for adults and RM4 for children aged 5 to 12.

Pernas Sogo Complex
190 Jalan Tuanku
Abdul Rahman

Starz Studio
03 2698 2003 | www.starzstudio.com

Starz Studio is a comparatively new studio for kids aged 5 years old and over, and very unusual in the sense that the teachers provide courses in grooming, manners and public speaking, all focused on giving children more confidence. It hosts holiday courses which include art, music, crafts, cooking and basic maths, so check the website for dates. For shopping mums, there is a very secure playground area where you can 'drop and shop'.

Language Schools
Other options **Learning Bahasa Malaysia** p.143

15 Lorong Gurney
Ampang
Damai

Alliance Française
03 2694 7880 | www.alliancefrancaise.org.my

French lessons can be provided on an individual or group basis, either at your own home or at one of three Alliance Française centres in KL (Lorong Gurney, Damansara and Petaling Jaya). Group courses are held in the mornings, evenings and on Saturdays. Lessons cost from RM85 per hour upwards for one-to-one instruction. Conversational French and a Crash Course can be provided, as can classes in French literature. There are also weekend classes for children aged 7 and older.

Sunway Rahman Putra
Sungai Buloh
Sungai Buloh

ALS Learning
012 339 1675 | mazypuyi@yahoo.com

Lessons in Bahasa Malaysia are provided in your own home (individually or in groups up to four) or you can choose to join weekly group sessions (two hours long) held at the Association of British Women (ABWM) in Bangsar, or the American Association (AAM) in Ampang. The emphasis is on spoken Bahasa for beginners. A group package of 30 hours with either ABWM or AAM costs approximately RM650.

Ground Floor
Wisma UOA Damansara
50 Jalan Dungun
Bukit Damansara
Bangsar

Berlitz
03 2093 1619 | www.berlitz.com.my

Berlitz specialises in the spoken language and has a number of different learning programmes, from the Total Immersion course which will have you proficient by the end of one week, to weekly classes over a much longer period. Languages taught include English, Bahasa Malaysia, Mandarin (all to a high level of fluency) as well as Spanish, French, Russian and Arabic to a basic Level One standard of proficiency. It also has group classes especially for children, in English and Mandarin. Groups are small (up to six students), and private one-to-one lessons are also available. A Level One package of 40 hours will cost from RM1,440. The nearest LRT is Bangsar, where you should take a taxi.

Activities

West Blok, Wisma
Selangor Dredging
142C Jalan Ampang
Ampang
 KLCC

British Council

03 2723 7900 | www.britishcouncil.org

If you wish to improve your English language, the British Council provides both full and part-time courses for adults that are designed to help you become more proficient at communication. It also has a Business Programme which is specially designed to improve your English language usage in the workplace. Programmes are modular according to your requirements and proficiency. The British Council also conducts a very popular Teacher Training course for individuals who would like to teach English to foreign students. The course costs RM7,500 (for both full and part-time courses) and leads to a Certificate in English Language Teaching to Adults (CELTA).

> ### Intellectual Curiosity
>
> The University Book Store has all the academic books you're likely to need during your time in KL. Expand your mind with great literary masterpieces or a range of school age academic books, including educational books for young children (03 9100 1868, www.ubsm.com.my).

A-2-1 Wisma HB
Megan Avenue 2
12 Jalan Yap
Kwan Seng
 KLCC

ELS Language Centre

03 2166 5530 | www.els.edu.my

This teaches students to be proficient in English, focusing on reading and writing as well as spoken English. Programmes are full-time classes held during the week. Instructors are both local and expatriate. Personal instruction is supplemented by the use of computer-supported learning to practise pronunciation and vocabulary development. ELS Language Centres are also in PJ (off Jalan Utara, 03 7958 8530) and Subang Jaya (Subang Square, Jalan SS15/4, 03 5636 5530).

1 Jalan Langgak Golf
Off Jalan Tun Razak
Ampang
 KLCC

Goethe-Institut

03 2142 2011 | info@kualalumpur.goethe.org

The Goethe-Institut offers a number of courses according to how quickly you wish to learn or improve your German language skills. Intensive courses (three hours per day, Monday to Friday for seven weeks) as well as more extensive courses (10 or 20 weeks long) are possible. Group sizes are between 12 and 20 students. Alternatively you can tailor programmes to smaller groups or even individuals. Sessions begin in January and July.

Lot D3, Block D
KL Plaza
Jalan Bukit Bintang
Bukit Bintang
Bukit Bintang

ICLS (Inter-Cultural Language School)

03 2144 2060 | www.icls.com.my

ICLS specialises in Japanese language classes, although it also teaches English, Mandarin and Korean as well as Bahasa Malaysia, French, Spanish, German and Italian. All the courses are flexible to suit your needs and requirements. Group and private lessons available. ICLS will also help you prepare for your Japanese Language Proficiency Test which is held in December each year. It also has schools in Subang (72 Jalan SS15/4D, Subang Jaya, 5635 0393) and in Damansara (67 Jalan SS21/1A, Damansara Utama, PJ, 7722 5250).

Jalan Ampang
Utama 2/2, One
Ampang Avenue
Selangor
Jelatek

The Language Studio

03 4253 5052 | www.thelanguagestudio.net

Director Teresa Chen oversees a very popular language school that teaches English to a high standard, through various different programmes suited to the student's age. Weekday and weekend scheduled classes are possible for pre-school students up to adults and include a strong element of speech and drama to make classes more fun and encourage confidence. School holiday workshops are also available upon request. The US Embassy uses The Language Studio to improve English among its local staff. The Language Studio also has an outlet in Desa Sri Hartamas (28 Crystal Ville 2, Jalan 22A/70A, 0362039721).

Units 8 & 10
Jalan Wan Kadir 1
TTDI (Taman Tun Dr Ismail)
🚇 *Taman Bahagia*

Lorna Whiston Study Centre
03 7727 1909 | *www.lornawhiston.com.my*

Lorna Whiston has extensive experience teaching English and now oversees her own school and team of fully qualified teaching staff who are all native English speakers. The school is designed to teach English to Asian students and has over 700 students aged between 1 and 16, all attending weekly classes suited to their age group and ability. It offers an introduction to English for the very young, and can supplement an international school education for older students. The centre has an extensive library of over 9,000 titles imported from the UK, USA and Australia. To reach it by rail, disembark at Taman Behagia and take a 15 minute taxi ride.

American Association

The American Association of Malaysia has a lending library available. Membership of the association is open to non-members, with 40% being drawn from other nationalities (03 2142 0611, www.klamerican.com).

Libraries
Other options **Books** p.289, **Second-Hand Items** p.318

232 Jalan Tun Razak
Ampang
🚇 *Titiwangsa*

National Library of Malaysia (Perpustakaan Negara Malaysia)
03 2687 1700 | *www.pnm.my*

The National Library is the largest in the country, containing a huge collection of printed publications, maps, newspapers, Malay manuscripts, photos, audio materials, and children's books, plus much more. These resources can be borrowed at the cost of RM1.20 per item for a maximum period of three weeks. The library is also a repository for a huge collection of heritage and cultural material if you are interested in finding out more about the history of Malaysia. Weekends are the busiest times for visits. Certain areas of the library can be hired out (for half and full days) for private or corporate events, according to the number of delegates and the equipment required.

Libraries

Alliance Française	03 2694 7880	www.alliancefrancaise.org.my
Badan Warisan	03 2144 9273	www.badanwarisan.org.my
British Council	03 2723 7900	www.britishcouncil.org
Goethe Institute	03 2144 3717	www.goethe.de/kualalumpur
Islamic Arts Museum Scholar's Library	03 2274 2020	www.iamm.org.my
Japan Embassy Information Library	03 2142 7044	www.my.emb-japan.go.jp
Japan Foundation	03 2161 2104	www.jfkl.org.my
KL City Library	03 2692 6204	http://klcitylib.dbkl.gov.my
Lincoln Resource Centre	03 2168 5000	www.usembassymalaysia.org.my
MATRADE Business	03 6207 7077	www.matrade.gov.my

Martial Arts

6-2 Jalan Dangang
SB 4/2, Taman
Sungai Besi Indah
Seri Kembangan
Selangor
 Sungai Besi

Aikido Shudokan Martial Arts Centre
03 8948 6462 | www.shudokanmalaysia.com
Aikido is a self-defence art that teaches students how to use powerful arm locks as well as sword, staff and knife techniques. This centre has a number of very experienced instructors, all overseen by its Australian-based director, seventh Dan Joe Thambu Sensei. The majority of classes are held at its studio near The Mines, although additional classes are held on Tuesday afternoons at the Australian International School for students based there. An initial registration fee of RM100 provides you with the uniform and after this monthly fees are RM80 (adult) for an unlimited number of classes.

> ### Kickboxing
> Those interested in both learning kickboxing and developing their skills should get in touch with TNT Kickboxing in Sri Hartamas (03 6201 2342, www.tntkickboxing. com), or try Xtreme Martial Arts and Kickboxing in Sri Hartamas (03 6203 4749, www.kickboxing.com.my).

T18 Jalan 32/154
Taman Bukit
Anggerik, Cheras
 Cheras

BTFC Taekwondo Club
03 9101 7955 | www.btfc.com.my
To join BTFC classes, annual membership costs RM50. After this you pay another RM50 which entitles you to join any number of their public classes. Adult classes are held on Tuesday and Thursday evenings at the local school in Kelana Jaya, and also in the sports complex at Taman Tasik Titiwangsa on Sunday mornings at 09:00. Competition training is also possible at dedicated times.

41 Bangsar Puteri
Jalan Medang Serai
Bangsar
 Bangsar

KDT Academy
012 202 6111 | www.kdta.com
KDT (Kissaki Defensive Tactics) conducts classes in Brazilian Jiu-Jitsu, which is a martial art and combat sport that can be used for self defence, sport grappling tournaments and mixed martial arts competitions. Training classes are held twice weekly in the evenings. You must have a uniform (which can be rented at KDT) as well as a mouthguard for protection. You can drop in for a trial class at RM50, or take out a 12 month membership at RM100 and pay RM35 for each class. Various packages are available if you intend to attend regularly.

27 Jalan Gasing
Petaling Jaya
 Taman Jaya

Yoshinkan Aikido Malaysia
03 7783 7700 | www.yoshinkan-aikido.com.my
Sixth-dan black belt Sonny Loke Sensei leads a qualified team promoting Japanese culture through the Yoshinkan form of aikido. Scheduled classes are held throughout the week, including Sundays. There are regular beginners' classes, evening and weekend sessions specifically for children, and a Gold Class during the week for the over 50s. For with a belt grade who wish to progress further there are daily sessions held in the evenings and at weekends. Even if you are already a black belt, there are Instructor Courses held on Sunday mornings between January and June every year. The starter programme for adults costs RM420, which entitles you to three months' unlimited classes. Classes are also held at studios in Taman Maluri (11-A Jalan Jejaka 2, 92864120) and in Subang Jaya (USJ1, Persiaran Subang Mewah, 037783 7700).

Mother & Toddler Activities
A lot of expat mothers do not work in KL, so there is plenty of time to have fun with the kids. Below are some options for mother and toddler activities that are popular with expats. If you'd like to gently push your little one into a musical environment, there are some wonderful musical activities available at the Kidz Talent Lodge (03 7728 0834, www. kidztalent.com) and through Musikgarten Malaysia (03 8024 2131, www.musikgarten.biz).

Sports & Activities

12 Jalan Menerung 3
Bangsar
🚇 Bangsar

Association of British Women in Malaysia (ABWM)

03 2095 4407 | www.abwm.com.my

The ABWM holds a weekly group for toddlers on Tuesday mornings from 10:00 to 12:00 in different child-friendly locations around KL, and at the ABWM House on the last Tuesday of every month. Venues are mostly in Bangsar and include Kizsports (at Bangsar Shopping Centre), Marmalade Cafe (in Bangsar Village II), Kidz Zone in Hartamas Shopping Centre and the ABWM House (for play sessions). Very friendly group, all welcome.

Bangsar Village
Bangsar
🚇 Bangsar

Gymboree

03 2284 5602 | gymboree_malaysia@yahoo.com

Gymboree is a friendly and fun place to take your youngster for a developmental class or even just to play around in a fun and interesting environment with music and bright colours that stimulate. Programmes include play and music as well as gym and yoga, and are designed to develop a child by encouraging them to solve problems, as well as help cognitive development and coordination. Classes are held throughout the week, but after a trial class at RM45 you will have to purchase a package of lessons. A package of 10 playgym drop-in sessions will cost you RM120.

33 Jalan Jelutong
Damansara Heights
🚇 Bangsar

ibu Family Resource Group

03 2094 2234 | www.ibufamily.org

This is an excellent organisation dedicated to supporting mums and young children. By taking out membership (RM120), you are entitled to receive its monthly magazine, pre and post-natal support, attend a Well Baby Clinic, as well as join in any of its playgroups such as the Crawlers' Group for tots over four months old. It also has a Multiple Births Support Group. To reach ibu by LRT, disembark at Bangsar and take a 10 minute taxi.

The Curve
6 Jalan PJU 7/3
Mutiara Damansara
Petaling Jaya
🚇 Kelana Jaya

Tumble Tots

03 7725 7075 | www.tumbletots.com.my

Tumbletots provides weekly programmes for children from six months old to toddlers of four years. All are designed to stimulate and provide children with plenty of opportunity for purposeful play, using creative expression, awareness and motor skills development. The Physical Play programmes are meant to help kids play and learn at the same time, and they are a good way of teaching your young child to interact and socialise with people outside of the family, often for the first time. Don't forget that it's a good way for the mums to develop a social circle too.

Motorsports

Jalan Pekeliling
Selangor
🚇 KLIA

Sepang International Circuit

03 8778 2200 | www.malaysiangp.com.my

Motorsport fans will love Sepang, purpose built for the Formula 1 Grand Prix which attracts lots of interest and support here. Aside from F1, Sepang also hosts MotoGP and the A1 Grand Prix. If you have your own car or bike and want to try it out at top speed then members of the public can visit on regular track days (organised most Sundays). Bikes are invited between 09:00 and 12:00, while cars are allowed onto the track between 14:00 and 17:00. For avid followers there is membership of the Sepang Circuit Motorsports Club which entitles you to discounts off tickets, track days, karting, as well as exclusive invitations to driving events.

Quadrophenia

Forthose who love the thrill of ATV (All Terrain Vehicle) riding, Extreme Park is the place to go, offering an RM60 Scenic Ride (03 5631 0426, www.extremepark.com.my).

Mountain Biking
Other options **Cycling** p.226

Various Locations

Kuala Lumpur Mountain Bike Hash
www.bikehash.freeservers.com
The KLMBH rides once a month on the last Sunday of every month (whenever possible) and incorporates a short run for beginners and families with children, and a long run for more experienced mountain bikers. This long run is always through jungle, palm oil or rubber plantations and can be very physically demanding, not least because of the hot tropical weather. The group of 30 to 40 cyclists always adjourns to a restaurant for a long lunch where the trials and tribulations of the morning's 'torture session' are discussed over a couple of cold drinks and yummy local cuisine.

Music Lessons
Other options **Dance Classes** p.227

Ikano Power Centre
2 PJU 7/2, Mutiara
Damansara
🚉 *Kelana Jaya*

Kindermusik at Kidz Talent Lodge
03 7728 0834 | www.kidztalent.com
Kidz Talent Lodge offers the Kindermusik curriculum, which is aimed at teaching music to children aged from newborns up to 7 years old, using simple percussion instruments and a stimulating and interactive approach. A trial class costs from RM28. Kidz Talent Lodge will also organise musical birthday parties for you. To reach the Ikano Power Centre by rail, go to Kelana Jaya and take the shuttle bus provided.

Various Locations

Musikgarten Malaysia
03 8024 2131 | www.musikgarten.biz
Musikgarten is a programme aimed at teaching music to children from newborns up to 9 years old. Different classes available include an introductory Music Circle for pre-school children, Family Music for babies and toddlers, and more advanced programmes for slightly older children that are capable of learning how to play instruments. Musikgarten is taught by a number of qualified teachers at various venues in KL, including Bangsar (Fit for Two Fitness Services, 75 Jalan Bangkung, 2093 9088) and Mont Kiara (Children's Discovery House, Jalan Kiara, 6203 7001).

Various Locations

Selangor Institute of Music (SIM)
03 7956 6202 | www.simmusic.com
SIM is a private and well established music school, teaching music classes in over 16 different instruments to advanced examination levels. It has a specific course (both in groups and privately) for adults that have no background in music but would like to learn, starting with the piano. SIM also teaches Kindermusik to help children appreciate music, with programmes for newborns upwards. SIM has branches in TTDI (2B Persiaran Zaaba, 77221017) and in The AmpWalk on Jalan Ampang (2163 2218).

Various Locations

Yamaha Music
03 7803 0900 | www.yamahamusic.com.my
Yamaha Music has over 20 retail branches around KL, selling musical instruments of every kind. Its Music School, which operates out of these shops, encourages children from as young as 3 years old to practise and work towards examination levels one to 13. And to make sure that children stay enthusiastic about music, its Pop Music School enables students to learn the flute, saxophone, electric guitar, electric bass, keyboard and drums with a modern approach. For those who want to pursue a career in music, the Yamaha Academy of Music and Arts helps students

Music Lessons

Allegro Music	03 4251 5780
Bentley Music	03 2144 3333
Euphony Musical	03 7725 1377
Harmony Music Centre	03 7727 3034
Kindermusik at Kidz Talent Lodge	03 7728 0834
Mahogany (The House of Guitars)	03 7873 6388
Selangor Institute of Music (SIM)	03 7956 6202
Yamaha Music	03 7803 0900

to study for a diploma or degree recognised by the Ministry of Education. There are branches in Sri Hartamas (Ground Floor, Plaza Damas, Jalan Sri Hartamas 1, 0362013213) Mid Valley (2nd Floor, Mid Valley Megamall, 2287 2682), PJ (2nd Floor, The Curve, 7725 3426) and Subang Jaya (1st Floor, Subang Parade, 56341971). Yamaha also franchises its music programmes through a large number of independent music shops around KL and you can find a full listing on the Yamaha website.

Netball

12 Jalan Menerung 3
Bangsar
 Bangsar

Association of British Women in Malaysia (ABWM)
03 2095 4407 | www.abwm.com.my
The ABWM organises a netball get together every Wednesday at 19:30 at the Garden International School, Mont Kiara. These are social games only and beginners are welcome. Coaching can be provided, followed by drinks. You do not need to be an ABWM member to join the fun. To reach Mont Kiara by rail, disembark at Bangsar LRT and take a 10 minute taxi ride.

38 Jalan Tempinis
Lucky Garden
Bangsar
 Bangsar

Malaysian Australian New Zealand Association (MANZA)
03 2284 7145 | www.manza.org
MANZA organises a Friday morning game on outdoor courts near KLGCC near Bukit Damansara, between 09:00 and 11:00. Everyone is welcome, irrespective of age and fitness level. The cost is RM5 per week. This is a friendly, social group that welcomes beginners and simply wants to have some fun. To reach Sudan Komplek Bukit Kiara by rail, disembark at Bangsar LRT and take a 10 minute taxi ride.

Orchestras & Bands
Other options **Music Lessons** p.248

Dewan Filharmonik
Petronas
Petronas Twin Towers
KLCC
 KLCC

Malaysian Philharmonic Orchestra (MPO)
03 2051 7007 | www.malaysianphilharmonic.com
Established in 1998, Dewan Filharmonik Petronas (DFP) has become Malaysia's premier venue for world-class music performances. It is home to the Malaysian Philharmonic Orchestra (MPO) and hosts an extensive programme of events throughout the year, including visits from many leading international musicians. It operates under the direction of Music Director and Principal Conductor Matthias Bamert and is comprised of over 100 professional musicians of all nationalities, who together make up an orchestra of international calibre.

Paintballing
Other options **Shooting** p.256

Jalan Lagoon
Selatan
Bandar Sunway
Petaling Jaya
 Kelana Jaya

Extreme Park
03 8027 0426 | www.extremepark.com.my
One block from Sunway Lagoon is Extreme Park where you will find Xtion Paintball, the first paintball arena in the Klang Valley. There are a number of different playing courts and a Jungle War Zone. It costs RM60 per person (a minimum of six people are required to play). Target practice is possible for RM10

(10 pellets) and you have the option of renting a chest protection vest at RM6.

132 Jalan KIP8
Taman Perindustrian KIP, Sri Damansara Selangor
🚇 *Kepong*

Mudtrekker Adventure Travel
03 6274 1268 | www.mudtrekker.com
Mudtrekker has a dedicated paintball arena at Kuang, near Sungai Buloh, where you can choose from three programmes: the Urban Field (made up of old houses and good for close quarter combat), the Speedball Field (using oil drums and wooden bunkers), and the Jungle Field (wooded area suited to stealth attacks). The Mudtrekker team is also very good at providing a number of different combat strategy scenarios for your session. Weekend or weekday sessions are available (at RM65 and RM48 respectively) and include two hours' field use, pellets, a gun and a face mask, but exclude camouflage clothing, elbow and knee guards, and chest protectors. The facility is used by the Malaysian Paintball Association (MPA).

> **X Marks The Spot**
> For more paintball thrills, and the opportunity of hiring mobile paintballing for your location, you can also visit Xtion Paintball at the National Sports Complex (03 8027 0658, www.xtionpaintball.com).

Photography
The Photographic Society of Malaysia (www.mir.com.my/psm) provides a forum for photographers to share ideas and get together at informal workshops. Its website will also keep budding photographers abreast of competitions to enter.

641 Jalan Kelantan
Bukit Persekutuan
🚇 *KL Sentral*

Malaysian Nature Society (MNS)
03 2287 9422 | www.mns.org.my
The Photo Group is 'focused' on capturing the beauty of Malaysia's natural heritage. Photos are used to describe better conservation methods to the general public as well as political decision makers. Its activities include an annual beginners' course for Nature Photography. The group undertakes regular exciting Nature Photography Expeditions. These are basically weekend trips to beautiful spots around the country that are off the beaten track, and afford these camera enthusiasts with good subject matter. You need to be an MNS member to join (subscriptions cost from RM70 per annum) and you need to have your own SLR camera.

Photogenic KL

Written by residents, the Dubai Explorer is packed with insider info, from arriving in the city to making it your home and everything in between.

Dubai Explorer Residents' Guide
We Know Where You Live

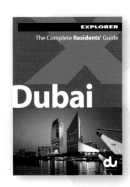

Polo
Other options **Horse Riding** p.238

Jalan Bukit Kiara
Off Jalan Damansara
Bukit Damansara
🚇 *Bangsar*

Bukit Kiara Equestrian & Country Resort
03 2093 1222 | www.berjayaclubs.com/kiara
Bukit Kiara is the largest equestrian school in Malaysia and provides lessons in learning polo as well as other riding disciplines. It has great facilities: Bukit Kiara also boasts a great tack shop with a range of quality clothing and tack from around the world. It has a dedicated polo field with spectators' grandstand. The first month's lessons (with two every week) cost RM360.

Lot 1314 Jalan
Ampang Hilir
Ampang
🚇 *Ampang Park*

Royal Selangor Polo Club
03 4257 0508 | www.rspc.org.my
Although also a riding club, polo is the main activity at the Royal Selangor Polo Club in Ampang. It's played up to four times a week all year round, weather permitting. To help develop the sport in Malaysia, the club has a training programme that offers beginners (even non-riders) the chance to learn the game in three months for RM2,000 (comprising 24 regular lessons and three intensive clinics, culminating in a two-chukka game). The fee includes the use of a polo pony throughout. It's a fantastic opportunity – for anyone interested in taking up the sport this is the place to come. The club is the home of the Royal Malaysian Polo Association (www.rmpa.org.my).

Pottery

23 Jalan Industri
Batu Caves 1/1
Taman
Perindustrian
Batu Caves
Selangor
🚇 *Sentul*

Tenmoku Pottery
03 6187 8601 | www.tenmokupottery.com.my
Tenmoku Pottery is well known in Kuala Lumpur for its distinctive and intricate designs sold through retail outlets in Central Market, Suria KLCC and Mid Valley MegaMall. However, the company's HQ also welcomes visitors and this is where members of the public can attend workshops on various aspects of the pottery process, including clay modelling, glazing, plasticine modelling and hand throwing. A half-day package costs RM100. The minimum group number is 10. Tenmoku is open Mondays to Fridays from 08:30 to 17:00, and on Saturdays from 08:30 to 12:00.

Rafting
Just a short drive from KL you'll find various rivers that are ideal for white water rafting and associated sports. Riverboarding is rapidly gaining popularity as a new extreme sport in which you ride the rapids lying on your stomach grasping a hardboard in front of you – the equivalent of luging in the water. Riverboarding and other types of rafting are available through Jungle Geckos (03 7781 2027, www.junglegeckos.com). AI Destination Marketing (016 346 0735, www.raftingmalaysia.travelbytes. biz) also offers white water rafting on Sungai Slim or Sungai Selangor. All equipment is provided (see p.198).

Fighting rapids with AIDM

Rollerblading & Rollerskating

Other options **Beaches** p.196

Roller sports are rapidly gaining recognition in Malaysia and have recently been included within the schedule of sports for the 2010 Asian Games in China. To help support the growth, the Malaysian Association of Roller Sports (MARS) (http://rollersports-malaysia.blogspot.com) has been established to organise events and put fellow skaters in touch with each other. As well as Skateline Malaysia, two such groups that communicate via their own online forums are the Underdogs (http://underdogsmalaysia.blogspot.com) and the KJ Rollers (http://kjrollers.com/).

18 Lorong Datuk
Sulaiman 1
TTDI (Taman Tun Dr
Ismail)
🚇 **Taman Bahagia**

Skateline Malaysia

03 7727 7758 | www.skateline.com.my

Apart from two shops selling everything you could possibly want for skating (recreational, free-style, aggressive, hockey and speed skating that is), Skateline runs its own skate school which provides scheduled lessons at the weekend in the park behind the TTDI shop. Private groups can also be organised, as can specialist training in aggressive, speed and slalom skating. For doing your own thing, the website offers some suggestions on where to skate in and around KL, such as around lakes and on quieter roads. Another Skateline shop can be found in the Sungei Wang Plaza on Jalan Sultan Ismail (03 2143 2337). Skateline is open Tuesdays to Fridays from 12:00 to 20:00, and on weekends from 08:00 to 20:00. It is closed on Mondays.

Rugby

7 Lorong Utara B
Jalan Utara
Petaling Jaya
🚇 **Taman Jaya**

Cobra Rugby

03 7955 6527 | www.cobrarugby.com

The Cobras were established in the 1960s largely for expatriates wanting to play rugby in their free time. Nowadays, with over 200 members, the club has its own clubhouse and hosts the annual rugby 10s tournament every October. There is a one-off joining fee of RM1,500, and thereafter membership costs RM350 per year which entitles members to discounts in the Clubhouse. Training is held every Tuesday and Friday from 18:00 onwards, and competitive games are organised on a regular basis.

Komplex Sukan
Astaka
Petaling Jaya
🚇 **Taman Jaya**

Cobrats Junior Rugby

013 398 9779 | www.klminirugby.com

Cobrats is run voluntarily by parents, many of whom have gained IRB qualifications to help with coaching. All children aged 6 years and above are welcome, and girls are encouraged to join the touch rugby section. Children are split up into groups according to their age and size. Games with other junior clubs are organised for the older boys. This is also an enjoyable and social way for parents to get involved, and everyone is very welcome.

Royal Selangor Club
Kiara Sports Annexe
Jalan Bukit Kiara, off
Jalan Damansara
Bukit Damansara
🚇 **Bangsar**

Jonah Jones Rugby 7s Tournament

03 2093 2277 | www.rscrugby.com

The British expatriate community established a rugby group at the RSC back in 1892 and it remains to this day an institution. The club stages the enormously successful Jonah Jones 7s tournament, which attracts over 60 visiting teams each year. For RSC and rugby section members (RM5 per month), training is held on Tuesday and Thursday evenings (17:00 to 19:00) at the Kiara Sports Annexe. This is also a great social side with excellent after-game refreshments available on the balcony overlooking the pitch.

Kiara Sports Annexe
Jalan Bukit Kiara, off
Jalan Damansara
Bukit Damansara
 Bangsar

Royal Selangor Club Junior Rugby

019 219 1629 | www.rscrugby.com

Junior Rugby is for children who are aged 6 to 14 (both boys and girls) and who want to play an active team sport. There is always a very healthy turnout of kids and parents every week, as the children learn to tackle, pass the ball, and score tries. Groups are organised according to skill and size or age. There is a Puppies group for the under 6s. Membership of the RSC is not necessary but there is a charge of approximately RM200 per term, which includes a rugby kit (uniform) and half-time refreshments.

Running

Other options **Hashing** p.235

KL has its very own international marathon (www.klmarathon.gov.my) which is normally held in March each year and organised by the City Hall of KL (DBKL) and the Federal Territory Amateur Athletic Association (FTAAA). There are two options for runners – a full marathon (42 kilometres) or a half-marathon (21kilometres). The organisers even plan circuit running events in the run up to the actual marathon to help runners realise their ability levels. Both routes start and finish at Dataran Merdeka.

Bukit Aman Carpark
Tasik Perdana
Lake Gardens
 Masjid Jamek

Pacesetters Athletic Club

www.pacesetters.com.my

Originally established for long-distance runners, the Pacesetters has evolved into KL's largest group of runners, including half and full marathon runners, track runners, and those who simply want to run with a group of fellow enthusiasts. Although there are several splinter groups that organise runs in their own areas (see website for more details), the most regular is the Carcosa Run around the Lake Gardens every Sunday morning (call Jimmy Tong, 012 234 8978). Runners can choose from several different routes ranging between four to 20 kilometres. Everyone is welcome, membership is RM36 per annum, and fees can be paid at the starting point (Bukit Aman Car Park).

Sailing

2 Jalan P8, Precinct 8
Putrajaya
Putrajaya

Putrajaya Lake Club

03 8889 5008 | www.kelabtasikputrajaya.org

Putrajaya Lake Club has a good sailing school (the PM keeps his dinghies here!) with over 10 dinghies (mostly single-handed) available for lessons and rental on the lake. The school is focused on encouraging children to learn to sail, although there are also two 420s and a Streamline 7.1 metre keelboat more suited to adults. All the boats are available for rental if you are already competent, with costs ranging from RM10 to RM35 per hour. Lessons (Basic Level is a two-day course, Intermediate Level is a four-day course) are designed so that each student becomes a competent sailor accredited to Sail Malaysia standards. More advanced tuition in Port Dickson is also possible through the club.

4th Mile
Jalan Pantai
Port Dickson

Royal Port Dickson Yacht Club

03 6647 1635

Just over one hour's drive from KL is Port Dickson where you will find a relaxed, friendly club with an active sailing division. Dinghy instruction is available using single-handed dinghies for adults or optimists for the children, all off the beach. A package of six group lessons (groups usually consist of four to five students) costs RM350 for members or RM450 for non-members. Members or their guests are also welcome to hire a dinghy (single and double Lasers and 420s) after an initial assessment. The club also organises dinghy racing every Sunday at 13:30.

Jalan Shahbandar
Port Klang
Selangor
🚉 Klang

Royal Selangor Yacht Club
03 3168 6964 | www.rsyc.com.my
The RSYC is probably the longest established sailing club in peninsular Malaysia and it still has great facilities on the banks of the Klang River. The sailing school itself offers a range of different courses for beginners (including children from 8 years old upwards) on dinghies and cruisers. Although the courses are not officially RYA registered, they do follow the RYA course content and will give you the same end result. Experienced crew are welcome to come and join in the fun on a Sunday (from noon onwards) for the weekly races.

Salsa Dancing
Other options **Belly Dancing** p.219, **Dance Classes** p.227

F3-2 Plaza Damas
Jalan Sri Hartamas
Sri Hartamas
🚉 Bangsar

The Dance Space
03 6201 8032 | www.thedancespace.com.my
Salsa and rueda classes are held for beginners and more experienced dancers on Monday evenings and on Sunday afternoons at this Sri Hartamas studio. If you are not sure, drop in for a beginners' class (RM30) or alternatively, go for the monthly option of RM100 for four sessions. Other classes provided include Latin dance classes that incorporate cha-cha-cha, samba, rumba, paso doble and jive. To reach Sri Hartamas by rail, disembark at Bangsar and take a 10 minute taxi.

Jalan Datuk
Sulaiman
TTDI (Taman Tun Dr Ismail)
🚉 Taman Bahagia

Havana Estudio
012 280 6969 | www.havanaestudio.com.my
Havana offers a varied schedule of latin dancing, including salsa classes, starting with its popular beginners' group at RM200 for eight weekly classes. However, there is a fixed date for new intakes so it's advisable to register a place. Aside from salsa, there are classes in merengue, bachata and rueda. Havana is open Tuesdays to Thursdays from 19:00 to 22:00, and on weekends from 14:00 to 17:00.

2 & 4 Lorong Sahabat
Off Changkat
Bukit Bintang
🚉 Bukit Bintang

Little Havana
012 280 6969 | www.mylittlehavanakl.com
This latin-styled restaurant and pub is the place to come and practise your salsa at its regular party every Friday night, from 21:30 until the early hours. A basic level of salsa is advisable but not essential. The focus of the evening is to enjoy dancing in a relaxed and friendly environment. The cost is RM10 at the door upon entry.

199 Jalan Bukit Bintang
Bukit Bintang
🚉 Bukit Bintang

Qba
03 2731 8333 | www.starwoodhotels.com
If you really want to get into the latino mood, try the Qba bar, the Westin hotel's own piece of Latin America where, on a Thursday evening, you can join the salsa and bachata dance class on the dancefloor. No booking is required and classes cost RM50 per session. If you are not sure, take a 15 minute trial session at the start of the class which is free of charge.

1st Floor, Wisma
Cosway
Jalan Raja Chulan
🚉 Raja Chulan

Ritmo Latino Dance Studio
016 366 3993
Venezuelan salsa specialist Patricia runs a busy studio with salsa and merengue classes for all levels, run on a monthly basis at RM120 per month (four classes). Classes are held in the evenings between 18:30 and 22:00, with Saturday practice sessions for beginners between 14:00 and 16:00. Private lessons are available.

Scouts & Guides

The Malaysian Scouting Association (www.pengakap.net) provides an online forum to discuss issues relevant to scouting, as well as acting as a useful reference for badges and awards and upcoming events. Scouting has strong support here in Malaysia, with many dignitaries from the Government being part of the movement. In Selangor alone there are many scouting groups, including troops in Titiwangsa, Subang Jaya, Sungai Buloh, Gombak Damansara Utama, Bukit Bintang, Klang, and Petaling Jaya. However, please note that local languages are usually spoken within the troop. For children with a foreign mother language, the international schools offer their own scouting and guiding groups which are usually held as extra-curricular activities.

Scouts & Guides		
Alice Smith School	03 2148 3674	www.alice-smith.edu.my
ELC International School	03 6156 5001	www.elc.edu.my
Garden International School	03 6209 6888	www.gardenschool.edu.my
International School of Kuala Lumpur	03 4104 3000	www.iskl.edu.my
Kolej Tuanku Ja'afar	03 6758 2561	www.ktj.edu.my
Mont'Kiara International School	03 2093 8604	www.mkis.edu.my

Scrapbooking

8 Jalan Murni
off Jalan Damai
Ampang
🚇 *Damai*

American Association of Malaysia

03 2142 0611 | www.klamerican.com

The AAM hosts a weekly scrapbooking group which is very friendly and well attended as a result. It is not a class but rather a group of enthusiasts getting together and sharing ideas. You are, however, advised to phone and reserve a place beforehand. Everyone is welcome but there is an RM10 charge for non-members. The group meets on Tuesdays at 09:30.

The Curve
Mutiara Damansara
Petaling Jaya
🚇 *Kelana Jaya*

Papier Love

03 7725 4815 | http://papierlove.com

Papier Love in The Curve hosts regular weekly classes for children and adults to get them started with scrapbooking, and then teaching more advanced techniques. It is also a stockist of many brands of papers, albums, stickers and tools as well as magazines and books on the subject. To reach The Curve by rail, disembark at Kelana Jaya and take the shuttle bus.

Bangsar Shopping
Centre
285 Jalan Maarof
Bangsar
🚇 *Bangsar*

Scrappingville

03 2284 4302

Scrappingville is a small but welcoming workshop in the middle of Bangsar Shopping Centre, that stocks all the latest designs of papers, accessories and embellishments from Europe and North America. The team organises starter classes for adults and children, as well as workshops to learn new techniques. They will also accommodate privately arranged groups (the maximum group number is six) for special events. Outside of pre-arranged class times, regular scrappers are invited in at a cost of RM10 per hour.

Shooting

Other options **Paintballing** p.250

City Square Centre
182 Jalan Tun Razak
Ampang
🚇 *Ampang Park*

City Square Shooting Gallery

03 2164 9818 | www.shootinggallery.com.my

Right in the middle of KLCC is the City Square Shooting Gallery where you can practise pistol shooting in a safe and controlled environment. If you wish to shoot regularly, take out one of its membership packages (from RM2,000 upwards). Alternatively, if this is something you'd prefer to try on the odd occasion, you can try the walk-in package which is RM202 for one hour and includes a pistol, 50 rounds of ammunition, booth rental and two target papers. Instruction is available, although if you are serious about learning to shoot, you should consider joining one of the group classes.

Skydiving

23 Jalan Indah 13
Taman Cheras Indah
Selangor
🚇 *Pandan Jaya*

Skydive Kuala Lumpur

03 9284 0063 | *http://skydivemalaysia.tripod.com*

Otherwise known as the Wilayah Sport Parachuting Club or Wilayah Skydivers, this group is qualified to provide a basic two-day skydiving course approved by the Department of Civil Aviation (DCA), and which includes two jumps, at the cost of RM750. Subsequent jumps cost from RM150. After an assessment, the club can also provide a progressive freefall course. Equipment is available for rental. Aerial photography possible.

Social Groups

Other options **Support Groups** p.135

With its cosmopolitan population it's hardly surprising that KL has a large number of social and cultural groups for people from all walks of life. Some are linked to an embassy or business group, and can be an excellent way of meeting like-minded people.

33 Jalan Jelutong
Damansara Heights
🚇 *Bangsar*

ibu Family Resource Group

03 2094 2234 | *www.ibufamily.org*

ibu is an excellent organisation that provides all kinds of support to mums and mums-to-be. Membership costs RM120 per year. The ibu house is a welcoming environment if you simply need to share stories with other women in the same situation, and it also arranges specialist support groups focusing on bilingual families, adoption, multiple births and even for breastfeeding. It hosts a well-baby clinic, regular playgroups, first aid courses, and even provides a baby equipment loan service. A monthly magazine is included in the membership. The ibu house is open from 09:00 to 17:00, Monday to Friday.

Social Groups

Alliance Française	03 2694 7880	www.alliancefrancaise.org.my
American Association of Malaysia	03 2142 0611	www.klamerican.com
Association Francaise de la Malaisie	03 019346 9906	www.afmkuala.com
Association of British Women in Malaysia (ABWM)	03 2095 4407	www.abwm.com.my
British Council in Malaysia	03 2723 7900	www.britishcouncil.org.my
Canadian Association of Malaysia	03 017294 3036	www.canadians-in-kl.com
German Speaking Society of Kuala Lumpur (GSSKL)	na	www.kl-post.com.my
Goethe Institute	03 2142 2011	www.goethe.de
Grupo de Damas Latinas en Malasia	03 2094 0350	na
ibu Family Resource Group	03 2094 2234	www.ibufamily.org
International Women's Association Kuala Lumpur	na	www.iwakl.org
Japan Foundation	03 2161 2104	www.jfkl.org.my
Japanese Club	03 2274 2274	www.jckl.org.my
Malaysian Australian New Zealand Association (MANZA)	03 2284 7145	www.manza.org
Malaysian Culture Group	na	www.malaysianculturegroup.com
Royal Society of St George	na	www.stgeorgesmalaysia.com
Scandinavian Society Malaysia	03 9286 4625	www.scandinaviansocietymalaysia.com
Selangor St Andrews Society	na	www.ssas-online.com
St Patricks Society of Selangor	03 012689 4401	www.stpatsoc.org
Swiss Club Malaysia	03 012366 9121	www.swissclub.com.my

Various Locations

Malaysian Culture Group
www.malaysianculturegroup.com

The Malaysian Culture Group (MCG) is a volunteer-run organisation of members from Malaysia and overseas living in Malaysia and who want to know more about this country, past and present, through regular lectures, workshops, and visits. Once you join as a member (RM60 per year), you can join the Explorers Group which arranges a series of events looking at history, art, culture, and literature. There is also a Book Club which focuses on Malaysian literature and sharing ideas. The group has no office but membership forms can be downloaded from its website. Alternatively, you can write to PO Box 7550, 50704 Kuala Lumpur.

Squash
Other options **Sports & Leisure Facilities** p.264

Jalan Terasek Tiga
Bangsar
🚇 *Bangsar*

Bangsar Sports Complex
03 2284 6065

Bangsar Sports Complex has two squash courts that can be rented at RM4 per court per hour. Courts must be booked beforehand at the office which is open from 08:00 to 16:30. Facilities also include tennis and badminton courts and an outdoor swimming pool.

Bukit Bintang
Secondary School
Jalan Utara
Petaling Jaya
🚇 *Taman Jaya*

BBSS Squash
012 658 0622 | *www.malaysiasquashacademy.com*

Located in Petaling Jaya, BBSS has 10 courts available to the public, costing RM8 per hour. Coaching is also available from Kenny Foo, in group classes (beginners through to intermediate) as well as one-to-one sessions. He charges from RM120 per month for an adult.

Level 1, National
Stadium Bukit Jalil
Selangor
🚇 *Sri Petaling*

National Squash Centre
03 8992 9600 | *www.ksn.com.my*

The National Stadium is an enormous sports facility that incorporates the National Squash Centre. Ten squash courts have movable walls which means that they can be converted into eight doubles courts. The Centre Court is even fully glass-sided with seating for a thousand spectators. Courts cost RM8 per hour to book and are open until 20:00. The National Stadium also houses international-standard facilities for swimming, gymnastics and hockey.

Kompleks Sukan
Taman Tasik
Titiwangsa
Ampang
🚇 *Titiwangsa*

Titiwangsa Sports Complex
03 4023 9558

The Sports Centre at Titiwangsa has two squash courts, one glass-backed, that can be booked from RM4 per hour (or RM6 per hour for the glass-backed court) anytime during the day up until 23:00 at night. Coaching is not available here. Booking in advance is advisable. The centre also has tennis and badminton courts.

Stadium Hockey Tun
Razak
Jalan Duta
Bukit Tunku

Tun Razak Sports Complex
03 6201 2699

Tun Razak Stadium has seven courts in reasonable condition, one with a glass back, and all available for use throughout the day until 22:00. Rental cost is RM10 per hour. Note that up until 17:00, the courts are fairly free but if you wish to play after 17:00 you will need to have booked beforehand. Coaching is provided by qualified freelancers so if you want lessons, pop down and speak to them for more information.

Squash	
Titiwangsa Sports Complex	03 4023 9558
Tun Razak Sports Complex	03 6201 5482

Swimming

Other options **Beaches** p.196,
Sports & Leisure Facilities p.264

Residents of Kuala Lumpur are incredibly spoilt when it comes to swimming or, at least, access to a swimming pool, which is just as well with the climate here. If you're not so lucky, then don't despair because there are several pools open to the public around KL, such as the one at Bangsar Sports Complex (03 2284 6065) and MPPJ Swimming Pool in Petaling Jaya (03 7956 3544). Finding a swimming teacher will probably take a little longer, simply because standards of teaching vary so much, and so

Cooling off

you should ask around for recommendations. Many teachers will come to your house or condo, while others are tied to teaching at certain venues such as at the country clubs.

National Sports Complex

National Stadium
Bukit Jalil
Selangor
🚇 Sri Petaling

03 8994 4660 | *www.ksn.com.my*
The Aquatic Centre at the National Sports Complex is no different to the other sports facilities in situ. It's modern, beautifully designed to meet international competition standards, and it is enjoyable to train here. There is a 10 lane Olympic-sized swimming pool, a diving pool and an additional eight-lane training pool (both have temperature controlled water) with grandstand seating on all sides. All the facilities are open for public use, or to conduct classes.

Team Building

Great Adventure Consultants

2-1 Fortune Court
1 Jalan Berangan
Bukit Bintang

012 325 3198 | *www.gacadventure.com*
GAC specialises in corporate team building and it can cover just about any activity you care to include in your exercise. From treasure hunts to educational trips, and jungle walks to specific sports (including zorbing), there are endless opportunities. The focus is on fun and creating adventure, and your trips can be just out of KL or anywhere else in Malaysia. It has a ground team that will make all arrangements for travel and accommodation. If you already like adventures, why not join one of GAC's oversees programmes as an Expedition Guide? There are many expeditions that require people who like working as a team and love the outdoors. Similarly, GAC often have positions available for volunteers as facilitators or guides.

Jungle Geckos

14 Jalan 6/3
Petaling Jaya
🚇 Jalan Templer

03 7781 2027 | *www.junglegeckos.com*
This small company organises a wide range of outdoor activities in and around KL, including jungle treks and camping trips, riverboarding and mountain biking. It is very experienced at corporate teambuilding and can create challenging yet enjoyable programmes that will bring out the best in everyone as individuals and as

team players. Using a fleet of 4WDs, groups of up to 30 can be accommodated. All equipment is provided.

Jungle School

Suite 284-14-03
The Heritage
Jalan Pahang
Ampang
Titiwangsa

03 4022 5124 | *www.jungleschool.com.my*

Jungle School takes groups for team building trips, which can last anything from one to five days. Popular places are camping grounds within 30 to 90 minutes of KL, such as the jungles in Ulu Yam, Ulu Kemansah, Pertak and Ulu Gombak. Longer trips may take you into Taman Negara. All are off the beaten track so be prepared for some walking. A common sharing tent can be provided as well as meals, and Jungle School will give advice on additional equipment for personal use. Survival training for private groups is also available, based on scenarios regularly faced in the jungles here.

Tennis

Other options **Sports & Leisure Facilities** p.264

American Association of Malaysia

8 Jalan Murni
Off Jalan Damai
Ampang
Damai

03 2142 0611 | *www.klamerican.com*

The AAM organises social tennis on Monday mornings between 09:00 and 11:00 at the Jalan Duta courts. Beginners are also welcome – a six-week group beginner course of lessons is RM180 for two hours each week – after which you can join the main AAM group. A ladies' singles tennis ladder is open for anyone to join.

Association of British Women in Malaysia (ABWM)

12 Jalan Menerung 3
Bangsar
Bangsar

03 2095 4407 | *www.abwm.com.my*

British resident Caroline Barber organises the ABWM social tennis group every Thursday morning at the Duta Tennis Centre, off Jalan Duta, near Bukit Tunku. There are eight outdoor courts which can usually be used, as well as three indoor courts for the rare occasions when in rains in the mornings. This is a friendly group of ladies that can accommodate a range of tennis abilities, but things are kept informal. The cost is RM10 which covers court fees and tennis balls.

Bangsar Sports Complex

Jalan Terasek Tiga
Bangsar
Bangsar

03 2284 6065

There are four tennis courts in the middle of leafy Bangsar, all in very good condition, which means that they are exceptionally popular and booked well in advance. You can book a court for RM4 per hour at the BSC office, but don't leave it until the last moment if you want to play first thing in the morning or after work, because these time slots get taken a week or more ahead of time. If you want lessons, pop down to the courts and watch some of the freelance coaches in action (they vary in their teaching methods). Coaching is usually around RM60 to RM70 per hour.

Duta Junior Tennis Academy

Gelanggang Tenis
MSN, Jalan Duta
Bukit Tunku
PWTC

03 6201 5496 | *www.tennismalaysia.com*

Duta is run by Malaysia's most successful tennis player, V Selvam. He provides different levels of coaching for kids, from intensive coaching for wannabe professionals, to gentle hitting practice for beginners. He also organises some very popular tennis camps and coaching clinics. Prices vary according to whether your child wants to play once, twice or three times a week – check the website for the various packages. Private lessons cost RM60 to RM80 per hour. You can send your child for a free trial lesson before signing up for a package. Take a 15 minute taxi from the station to get there.

Kompleks Sukan
Taman Tasik
Titiwangsa
 Titiwangsa

Titiwangsa Sports Complex

03 4023 9558

Titiwangsa Sports Complex has 10 tennis courts, all hard court and all outdoors, that can be used throughout the day from 08:00 onwards. Booking in advance is required, and the cost varies from RM4 per hour during the day to RM6 per hour during the evening (minimum two hour sessions in the evening). There are a number of freelance coaches who teach regularly at Titiwangsa so if you are looking for lessons, pop down and speak to a few for more information. Lessons are generally about RM60 per hour.

Triathlon

33 Jalan PUJ 7/16
Taman Puncak Jalil
Bandar Putra Permai,
Seri Kembangan
Sungai Besi

Triathlon Malaysia

012 295 9892 | www.triathlonmalaysia.com

Triathlons are popular in Malaysia despite the heat, and there are key events throughout the year, notably in Langkawi, Malacca, Port Dickson and Kenyir Lake, which all invite international triathletes. For most triathlon events, you can register to join the Olympic Distance (swim 1.5km, cycle 40km, and run 10km) or opt for the Sprint Triathlon (usually swim 0.8km, cycle 20km, and run 5km, although this will vary from race to race). Triathlon Malaysia will help put you in touch with fellow triathletes for training at specific venues through the week, and also keep you up to speed with registering for the next event.

Volleyball

95 Jalan
Padang Belia
KL Sentral

YMCA

03 2274 1439 | www.ymcakl.com

Members of the YMCA can use the volleyball court at the YMCA anytime between 07:00 and 19:00. Rates are from RM35 for two hours (during work hours) up to RM55 in the evenings. Daily rental rate is RM210. Membership of the YMCA is open to everyone, at RM80 for the first year. Other sports facilities include basketball courts, tennis courts and an indoor studio for dancing lessons.

Wakeboarding

Wakeboarding and waterskiing are available at the Mines Beach Resort. All levels are welcome and equipment is provided. At weekends, an hour's wakeboarding will cost RM260 per person. Coaching is available for an extra RM60 per hour (03 8944 2866, www.mineswatersports.com).

Watersports

2 Jalan P8 Precinct 8
Putrajaya
Putrajaya

Kelab Tasik Putrajaya (Lake Club Putrajaya)

03 8889 5008 | www.kelabtasikputrajaya.org

Located in an area of the Putrajaya lake where motorised sports are prohibited, the Lake Club has a huge selection of canoes, kayaks, rowing skulls and dinghies for rental. It has a fairly active programme of events including courses, family and corporate events, clinics and competitions. All equipment can be rented out separately, irrespective of whether you are a club member or not. Sail Putrajaya, an associate member of the Malaysian Yachting Association, is also based at the Lake Club.

Mines Beach Resort
Seri Kembangan

Palace Beach & Spa

03 8944 2866 | www.mineswatersports.com

Formerly known as the Mines Beach Resort, this is located on the edge of the salubrious Mines Resort (a 60 hectare site developed from a disused tin mine), the available watersports include wakeboarding, waterskiing (both RM260 per hour at weekends) and banana boat rides (RM65 at weekends for 15 minutes). Coaching is available for wakeboarding and waterskiing at RM60 per hour. By reservation only. Open from 13:00 to 19:00 daily, and from 09:00 to 19:00 at weekends; closed Mondays.

Spectator Sports

No matter how hot it is, you can still stay involved with all your favourite games, largely because of the social nature of the people living here. With many sports, you can simply turn up and watch the game from the sidelines, and then immerse yourself in the apres-sport entertainment if there is any!

Many sports are simply not popular enough among Malaysians yet, so many groups tend to be run by expatriate volunteers. As a result, they are always on the lookout for other people to help them, so if you are knowledgeable about a particular sport and you have some spare time, why not offer to lend a hand?

With the Formula 1 Grand Prix held at Sepang, motorsports is high on the agenda here. On the back of its success, Moto GP and Super GT are also getting a higher profile these days. Like the rest of the world, Malaysians are fairly obsessive about football (or soccer), so the television and newspapers are constantly broadcasting games, keeping residents abreast of player transfers and the European league results. Then there are a large number of sports which are rapidly gaining popularity as access to the man on the street opens up. Sports such as horse riding, tennis and sailing have traditionally been seen as rather elitist here, but no more – with schools and classes readily available they are now becoming more popular and as a result there are an increasing number of international players visiting Malaysia to promote their games.

Royal Selangor Club
Kiara Sports Annexe
Jalan Bukit Kiara
Bukit Damansara
🚇 *Bangsar*

Jonah Jones Rugby 7s Tournament

03 2093 2277 | www.rscrugby.com

The Jonah Jones 7s tournament was initiated before the second world war by a Welshman who simply wanted to play more rugby. It quickly became popular here in KL and before long established itself as an annual event hosted by the Royal Selangor Club. As the sport of rugby became professional, the RSC decided to limit players to only one semi-pro or pro per team, thus keeping the sport competitive among amateurs and retaining the friendly atmosphere off the pitch for spectators too.

FTAAA, 2nd Floor
Wisma OCM
Jalan Hang Jebat

KL International Marathon

03 2715 2843 | www.klmarathon.gov.my

The KL Marathon welcomes a world-class field of runners every year. Runners have an option of a full or half-marathon that is routed through the city centre and around some of the main tourist areas, which makes it very accessible for spectators. The start and finishing point is Dataran Merdeka, in front of the Royal Selangor Club, which makes this area particularly busy. The downside is, of course, the heat and so you need to be prepared with lots of fluids and preferably some shade if you are going to stand out for long. A map of the route is available online at the official website for the event.

14 Jalan 4/76C
Desa Pandan
Selangor
🚇 *Maluri*

Malaysian Golf Association

03 9283 7300 | www.mgaonline.com.my

The MGA's role is to promote golf in Malaysia by making sure the game is played to official R&A rules, and also to encourage more players by bringing international golfers to Malaysia. The Malaysian Open (sponsored by Maybank) is played at different courses around the country, usually around February or March, and attracts top players from Europe and the United States every year. Another high-profile event is the Annual Amateur Championship which similarly draws the crowds out.

National Stadium
Bukit Jalil
Selangor
🚇 *Sri Petaling*

National Sports Complex

03 8994 4660 | www.ksn.com.my

The National Sports Complex was largely purpose-built for the XVI Commonwealth Games held here in KL in 1998, and consists of seven different facilities, each equipped to stage world-class events. The National Stadium hosts athletics events and football matches but, due to its size, also accommodates entertainment events as well. The adjacent indoor Putra Stadium has hosted everything from horse jumping events to table tennis championships and even five-a-side soccer matches. The National Aquatic Centre, the National Hockey Stadium and the National Squash Centre are separate buildings within this complex, all designed to host public events with ease. As with many of these spectacular venues around the world, the National Sports Complex probably doesn't host as many world events as it perhaps could do, but the facilities are open for public use. Enthusiasts can log onto the website and subscribe to a newsletter which provides details on upcoming events.

Jalan Kuda Emas
Selangor
🚇 *Sungai Besi*

Selangor Turf Club
03 9058 3888 | *www.selangorturfclub.com*
The Selangor Turf Club is an institution in Kuala Lumpur with its original race course being established in the late 1800s. The first race meet was held in 1896 and the venue quickly established itself as one of the main places to be seen among the well-to-do in KL society. In 1992, the turf club relocated to Sungei Besi where facilities were purpose built and up to the most modern standards. Racing is held all year round, with around 30 race days scheduled during the year. There are usually around 10 races held on each race day. The most famous of all the races held at the Selangor Turf Club is the Triple Crown Series, which is one of the richest sporting events in Malaysia and consists of a number of high-profile races held during the year. Full listings of all the races can be found on the club's website.

Jalan Pekeliling
Selangor
🚇 *KLIA*

Sepang International Circuit
03 8778 2200 | *www.malaysiangp.com.my*
Sepang was officially opened in 1999 and designed specifically to host the Malaysian F1 Grand Prix each year, typically in March. It can accommodate up to 130,000 spectators at a time, which is just as well because the sport has a huge following here. Hot on the heels of F1 success, the Super GT International series comes to Sepang around June. Making up the trio of motorsports events is the increasingly popular Moto GP which welcomes more colourful characters such as Valentino Rossi to KL for the Malaysian leg of the championship, normally held around October. Tickets for all events are sold via the Sepang website. The website also offers registration to receive free newsletters with updates on upcoming events.

Sepang International Circuit

Selangor Turf Club

263

Sports & Leisure Facilities

KL is fortunate to have so many fantastic facilities. The competition ensures that standards are kept high and it seems that each new development is trying to outdo the last, which is great news for residents. As the city sprawls ever outwards, new luxury suburbs and communities are encouraging more and more country clubs and gyms to be built. When you are looking around, you will notice that the tendency is for places to be either very good or very poor (usually because they are older and haven't been maintained), with little middle ground, so it's easy to decide whether they are going to suit your needs. Clubs and gyms are usually for members only but some welcome walk-in visitors, so ask around. Many of the condominiums around Kuala Lumpur have got their own facilities – usually a swimming pool, a gym and sometimes even squash or tennis courts. It's here that you will usually find groups of residents that have organised their own aqua aerobics classes or swimming lessons. If you would like to start a group, why not put a notice up and find out if anyone else will join you? Some of the outlying, gated residential communities are now planning their houses around such facilities. Valencia at Sungai Buloh and Tropicana in Petaling Jaya are two such places that have built great facilities specifically for their residents.

Sports Clubs

Kuala Lumpur has a multitude of places where you can go and play sports but many are public sports facilities or complexes (and therefore membership is not an option) and others are considered to be country clubs, largely because they have an active social and family-oriented side to their portfolio. What distinguishes a sports club is that they have a number of active amateur sports teams which compete at either a local or national level. In this regard, there really is only one club that can boast this success and that is the renowned Royal Selangor Club which has two premises, one on Dataran Merdeka (Merdeka Square) and the other at Kiara Sports Complex near Bukit Damansara. The Royal Selangor Club requires members to pay a one-off joining fee of RM14,500, and thereafter monthly fees are payable for membership to the sports section that you are particularly interested in.

Kiara Sports Complex ◀
Jalan Bukit Kiara
Off Jalan Damansara
Bukit Damansara
🚇 *Bangsar*

Royal Selangor Club

03 2093 2277 | www.rscweb.org.my

The RSC (or 'The Dog' as it sometimes known) is Kuala Lumpur's most famous sporting club, located in the middle of KL. It was established in the late 1800s by a largely expat contingent that enjoyed sports as well as the social side of colonial life, and quickly established a reputation for polo, cricket, rugby, hashing and, of course, the men-only Long Bar. These days, sports is now played out at the club's Kiara Sports Annexe where you can sit out on the open balcony and watch the RSC play cricket or rugby against visiting teams on a frequent basis. Note that this is a members-only club.

Country Clubs

There are a number of country clubs in and around Kuala Lumpur if you are considering membership. They are all very different, provide some special facilities and are located in different parts of town (worth considering if you don't like sitting in traffic). Importantly, some are more suitable for children and families, but above all, each one has a different aura to it. Membership itself is often costly, but the actual monthly subscription thereafter is very reasonable. Most are accessible to members only, but there are a couple where certain facilities, usually golf, are open to non-members.

Jalan Bukit Kiara
Off Jalan Damansara
Bukit Damansara
🚇 *Bangsar*

Bukit Kiara Equestrian & Country Resort

03 2093 1222 | www.berjayaclubs.com/kiara

One of the Berjaya Club's resorts, Bukit Kiara prides itself as being a 'country club in the city' and this slogan seems fairly accurate. It's located close to Mont Kiara, Bukit Damansara and Bangsar, and it covers a 70 acre site which provides members with a wide choice of sports and recreational activities. It has one of the largest equestrian centres in Malaysia, and a large swimming pool to relax by. Otherwise, the resort can offer over 15 other sports, including archery, badminton, basketball, paintball, squash, table tennis and tennis among others. Aside from sports, members can enjoy a gym and fitness centre, a jogging track, snooker room, a nursery for the young ones and a children's playground. Bukit Kiara has several places to eat, from the casual bite by the pool to Chinese dining in the Oriental Pearl. Bukit Kiara has established itself as a very relaxed and popular country club among families living in KL, largely because there is something for everyone to enjoy.

Taman Tun Abdul
Razak
Jalan Kerja Air
Ampang
🚇 *Putra*

Kelab Darul Ehsan

03 4257 2333 | www.berjayaclubs.com/kde

KDE, another of the Berjaya Club's establishments, is located on the Ampang side of town and its main focus is its nine-hole golf course and 40 bay driving range. However, members can also take advantage of its other sports facilities, including badminton, jogging tracks, squash and tennis courts, table tennis, and three swimming pools. KDE has several places to relax and dine both indoors and alfresco, and even a karaoke lounge to exercise those vocal cords.

3 Jalan Kelab Ukay
Utama
Taman Kelab Uka
Bukit Antarabangsa
Ampang
🚇 *Jelatek*

Kelab Ukay

03 4147 3837

Kelab Ukay is perhaps not the most luxurious country club in KL but it does have a wide variety of facilities and social programmes. Membership is RM1,288 per annum and entitles you to use the swimming pool, gym, squash and tennis courts, jogging track, and participate in the exercise and yoga classes (provided by Candi Soo). It also has a beauty and hair salon to pamper yourself at before eating in the seafood restaurant.

Tasik Perdana
Lake Gardens
🚇 *KL Sentral*

Royal Lake Club

03 2698 7878 | www.royallakeclub.org.my

The Royal Lake Club has a beautiful setting in the middle of the Lake Gardens, and is one of the longest established clubs in KL. With a swimming pool, tennis courts and squash courts, the club has an active calendar of social events, with its own bridge club, hash team, movie nights, children's library, regular live bands, and its own little group of shops for members. This was once a largely expat-dominated club, but these days members are largely permanent residents of KL.

Jalan Kelab Golf
Off Jalan Tun Razak
Ampang
🚇 *Ampang Park*

Royal Selangor Golf Club

03 9206 3333 | www.rsgc.com.my

The Royal Selangor Golf Club is etched in the memories of KL residents from a past era. It was the club to join if you were a golfer, and the club of which to be a member. These days, the club still retains its air of exclusivity and its facilities are constantly modernised to ensure that it remains that way. Aside from its beautifully manicured fairways and greens (there are two 18 hole courses and one nine-hole course), the club has two large swimming pools, tennis courts, squash courts and a billiard room. There are several dining options for families and the Fairway Restaurant overlooking the 18th green has one of the best outlooks. This is a beautiful club for families living on the Ampang side of town.

Saujana Golf & Country Club

Saujana Resort
Section U2
Kelana Jaya
Petaling Jaya
🚇 *Subang Jaya*

03 7846 1466 | www.saujana.com.my
Saujana was established in the 1980s on plantation land, and today the club has a relaxed and country feel to it, despite being only 15 minutes' drive from Bangsar or Damansara. Members are shareholders of the club, but non-members are also permitted to use the facilities here. Aside from two award-winning golf courses (the Palm Course hosted the 2007 Malaysian Open), the club has a large swimming pool, tennis courts, squash courts, a billiards room and several eateries. It's fairly small and quiet, but very friendly, and perfect if you want good facilities away from the hustle and bustle of KL.

Gyms

Celebrity Fitness

4F Bangsar Village II
2 Jalan Telawi 1
Bangsar

03 2092 8000 | www.celebrityfitness.com
Celebrity Fitness has three outlets in KL but its facilities in Bangsar Village II are the most recently opened and it is popular with Bangsar expats. It has a convenient location on the top floor of a popular shopping mall, and it has brand new facilities including over 90 cardio machines (steppers, treadmills and cross-trainers), toning machines and free weights. The gym hosts over 100 classes during the week in their exercise studio. Members can sign up with a personal trainer and schedule one-to-one sessions according to your needs and timeframe. Other branches are in Subang Jaya (03 5163 3000) and Petaling Jaya (03 7718 8000).

Fitness First

Menara Maxis
KLCC
🚇 *KLCC*

03 2026 1828 | www.fitnessfirst.com.my
Fitness First has over 10 branches around KL and they all follow the same successful recipe: access to a great gym (with over 80 cardio machines, a free weights area, stationary weights machines, and a stretching area) with lively music and six Astro channels to watch as you exercise. There are qualified personal trainers who will work with you to achieve your goals, or you can join in one of the Les Mills exercise classes. There is a juice bar if you want to sit and relax, and even a DVD library. This club is for members only, but membership is very reasonable (starting at around RM150 per month). The branch in Menara Manulife is particularly popular among expats.

Gyms		
California Fitness	City Centre	03 2145 1000
	Mid Valley	03 2295 0088
	Petaling Jaya	03 7494 0220
Candi Soo Fitness	Sri Hartamas	03 2300 1253
Celebrity Fitness	Subang	03 5163 3000
	Petaling Jaya	03 7718 8000
	Bangsar	03 2092 8000
Clark Hatch Fitness Centre	Mont Kiara	03 6201 6010
	KL Sentral	03 2260 1688
	Petaling Jaya	03 7957 2939
	Ampang	03 2161 5522
Clark Hatch Fitness Centre Day Thermos	City Centre	03 2141 6800
	City Centre	03 2144 9648
Fitness First	KLCC	03 2026 1828
	Petaling Jaya	03 7728 0077
	Petaling Jaya	03 7956 3320
	City Centre	03 2711 3299
	Damansara Heights	03 2093 8050
	Selangor	03 9133 3311
True Fitness	Petaling Jaya	03 7960 3222
	Selangor	03 8025 0700
	Sri Hartamas	03 6209 3200

When you're lost what will you find in your pocket?

Item 71. The half-eaten chewing gum

When you reach into your pocket make sure you have one of these minature marvels to hand… far more use than a half-eaten stick of chewing gum when you're lost.

Explorer Mini Maps
Putting the city in your pocket

Well-Being

KL hasn't proved immune to the worldwide explosion of interest in health and well-being over the past few years and a host of new spas, Pilates studios and yoga centres have opened around the city. They complement a well-established sector focusing on well-being and holistic therapies that owes its existence to Malaysia's multicultural heritage. So you'll find traditional Chinese medicine and reflexology, ayurvedic therapies and yoga from India, and traditional Malay remedies using massage, plants and herbs. Up until a few years ago, these therapies would have been used primarily by a single nationality group but with the higher profile given to the sector these days it's not uncommon to find people of all nationalities taking a yoga class or sitting having their feet massaged by a Chinese reflexologist.

Modern spas often combine elements from a number of different methodologies offering a wide choice of treatments. You'll find them in five-star hotels, former residential bungalows, shopping streets and malls. Prices, even at the top end, are reasonable compared to many European cities, with a one-hour massage at the Ritz-Carlton's Spa Village costing RM225. There's a trend towards adapting traditional Malay holistic therapies to modern spa treatments, and this is proving very popular.

Beauty Salons

Other options **Health Spas** p.272, **Perfumes & Cosmetics** p.316

You won't have to go far to find a beauty salon in KL – from tiny one-room nail bars to vast temples dedicated to the body beautiful – they're everywhere. Although Malaysians aren't as image obsessed as their neighbours in Singapore, being well groomed is valued and many locals and expats take time to make the best of their appearance. Many spas and hairdressers also offer beauty treatments, so if you're

Beauty Salons

Aveda	2F Bangsar Shopping Centre, 285 Jalan Maarof	Bangsar	03 2284 6423
Beaut'e Fest Salon	2F Bangsar Shopping Centre,285 Jalan Maarof	Bangsar	03 2094 3680
Beauty Affairs	E-01-10 Plaza Mont Kiara	Mont Kiara	03 6201 9196
Hasel's Beauty Care	18 Jalan Setiawangsa 10	Bukit Damansara	03 4252 3522
Jacki's	1F Hock Choon Supermarket, 241-1 Jalan Ampang	Jalan Ampang	03 2142 4954
Jyoti's Beauty Care	86 Jalan Masjid India	Little India	03 2698 1543
Kuku Bar	1st Floor, 20A Jalan Telawi	Bangsar	03 2284 5516
L'Lester Salon	1 floor, Ampwalk 218,	Jalan Ampang	03 2161 2752
Leslie Facial Salon	4B, 2Fl, Lorong Kolam , Ayer Lama 1,	Ampang	03 4251 4437

pushed for time you can get your hair done, eyebrows waxed, your fingers manicured and your toes pedicured all in one appointment! There's a wide range of quality on offer, and beauty salons are not tightly regulated for health and hygiene. This isn't to say a small neighbourhood salon will be a breeding ground for bacteria, but you should satisfy yourself as to the level of hygiene practised by any salon you visit. Neighbourhood salons are often excellent value for money and provide high quality service – manicures start at RM20 and a full leg wax will cost between RM80 and RM120 depending on the salon. Threading is a popular traditional hair removal method and is offered in many salons, and skin whitening or lightening is usually available too. It's a popular myth that Brazilian waxing isn't available in KL. It is, but only a few salons offer this service (see Strip, p.270). Botox is available at some salons but it's not as popular as in Europe and the US.

Well-Being

Level 7 The Pavilion
168 Jalan Bukit
Bintang
Bukit Bintang
🚇 **Bukit Bintang**

128 Faubourg by Sothys
03 2144 1281 | www.sothys.com.my

Offers a full range of highly targeted facial treatments, plus waxing, grooming and makeup services in a female-oriented environment. This group of salons uses Sothys products, a leading professional brand from France, and is positioned at the luxury end of the market. Provides a very reliable service in some key neighbourhood locations including 1Utama (03 7726 1280), Bangsar Village (03 2287 8128), Plaza Mont Kiara (03 6201 2080), as well as the new flagship Pavilion branch (03 2144 1281).

51-G & 51-1
The Boulevard
Mid Valley
🚇 **Mid Valley**

Bella Skin Care
03 2284 8088 | www.bellaskin.com

Bella offers a variety of treatments for women and men, specialising in laser treatment, peels and microdermabrasion, although conventional facials are offered too. They offer a free trial consultation and good packages if you buy a series of treatments. As well as the Mid Valley branch, there are branches at Avenue K on Jalan Ampang (03 2163 8188), Damansara Utama (03 7727 4132) and Subang Jaya (03 8023 3328). Open Monday to Friday from 10:00 to 20:00, and on weekends from 10:00 to 17:00.

**155 Jalan
Aminuddin Baki**
TTDI (Taman Tun Dr
Ismail)
🚇 **Kelana Jaya**

CN Health and Beauty
03 7710 3088 | www.cnbeauty.com.my

This salon has multiple branches covering most areas of KL and Petaling Jaya. It combines advanced cosmetic beauty technology with conventional treatments to provide a complete package for skin care. Facials start at RM80, microdermabrasion is RM340 per session and laser treatments are from RM300 per session. CN uses Dr Murad products and has a good reputation for hygiene and professionalism. Situated 20 minutes by taxi from Kelana Jaya station.

282 Jalan Ampang
Ampang
🚇 **Jelatek**

Gleneagles Intan Medical Centre
03 4257 1300 | www.gimc.com.my

The dermatology department at Gleneagles offers a number of non-surgical treatments to enhance appearance, including Botox injections, laser skin resurfacing to reduce scarring and improve skin texture, collagen injections and other line-filling techniques. It's an expensive option, but you will be treated by a doctor rather than a beautician.

4th Floor, Suria KLCC
KLCC
🚇 **KLCC**

Institut Clarins Paris
03 2382 6800 | http://my.clarins.com

Located in KLCC, this salon is owned and operated by the Clarins brand and uses only its products in treatments. A very luxurious spa with a full range of treatments for all skin types; an Eye Works treatment is RM88. The emphasis is on hands-on therapy, so you won't find lasers and microdermabrasion here. It also offers prenatal and postnatal treatments for women. There is a second branch at 1Utama in Petaling Jaya.

Lot 10
50 Jalan Sultan Ismail
Bukit Bintang
🚇 **Bukit Bintang**

Leonard Drake Skin Care
03 2142 5877 | www.leonarddrake.com.my

An international chain of beauty salons using Dermalogica products in its comprehensive range of treatments for both men and women. You'll find everything from a paraffin hand treatment to advanced pulsed light therapies here, with facials starting at RM48. It's a very professional environment, verging on the clinical rather than pampering, but there are some very effective treatments for problem skin. Other branches are at Suria KLCC (03 2142 5877), Cheras Leisure Mall (03 9132 5322), Taman Maluri Shopping Centre (03 9200 2388), Ampang Point (03 4252 6078), 1 Utama (7726 2433), Jaya Shopping Centre (03 7957 7388) and Plaza Metro Kajang (03 8733 3266).

1st Floor
28 Jalan Telawi 5
Bangsar
 Bangsar

Strip Co-Ed KL
03 2283 6094 | www.strip.com.sg
One of the few salons in KL to offer Brazilian waxing, they'll also wax just about anywhere else too. Catering to both men and women, waxes start at RM38 and go up to RM 88. They say the pain is worth it for that smoothness! IPL permanent hair removal is also on offer, but you won't find any other beauty salon services here. Open Monday to Saturday from 10:00 to 21:30, and Sunday from 10:00 to 19:30.

Hairdressers
Whether you prefer a no-frills trim or a cut and colour session lasting several hours, you'll find a hairdresser to suit you in KL. Many local salons will happily provide a walk-in blow dry service for around RM20, but be aware that 'no appointment necessary' sometimes means 'long wait required'. While many expats visit their local salon for a blow dry or a quick trim, some are a lot more picky about where they go for cutting and chemical processing such as colouring or perms. There's a good reason for this: it can be hard to find a stylist who cuts Caucasian hair well, especially curly or wavy hair. Since many salon products have been especially designed for Asian hair, you'll need someone experienced in colouring or perming Caucasian hair. This is especially true for colour, as most products are designed to lighten black hair, so even brunette tones contain bleach.

Men can get a cut at a local barbers for RM10, rising to RM30 in a smarter salon. Good cuts for women start at around RM50 rising to RM150 for a top stylist at a big salon; with colouring from RM100 and perms at about RM150.

There are a few options for children's cuts. Many regular salons will happily cut children's hair for around RM20. A Cut Above is very popular with younger children who enjoy sitting on the animal-shaped chairs.

Bangsar Village II
Jalan Telawi Satu
Bangsar
Bangsar

A Cut Above
03 2283 2233 | www.acutabove.com.my
Founded by award-winning stylist Winnie Loo, A Cut Above is probably the best known hairdressing chain in Malaysia with branches at several popular malls. The salons are large and clean, and private rooms are available for customers who don't want passers by in the mall seeing them with their hair half cut. It can get very busy at weekends when you will need an appointment, but during the week it's possible to walk in. Several brands of haircare products are available, as well as a wide range of services including cutting (RM40 for a junior stylist to RM200 for Winnie Loo herself), shampoo and blow dry for RM30, perming from RM200, and highlights from RM150. Children's haircuts are around RM25. A Cut Above also offers makeup, manicure and pedicure services. Other branches: Parkson Pavilion (03 2141 3232), Bangsar Shopping Centre (03 2094 9555), Mid Valley Megamall (03 2938 3131), and Sunway Pyramid (03 5635 2222).

Great Eastern Mall
Jalan Ampang
Jelatek

Eco Hair
03 4251 2998
Very popular with expats living in Ampang, Calvin has a loyal following. The salon is a little cramped but this is far outweighed by the excellent cutting and very reasonable

Hairdressers		
A Cut Above	Bukit Bintang	03 2141 3232
	Bangsar	03 2094 9555
	Mid Valley	03 2938 3131
Culture Cut	Bangsar	03 2284 7388
Etec Salon	Bukit Bintang	03 2145 1218
L'Lester Hair and Beauty	Jalan Ampang	03 2161 2752
Lucky Star Barber	Mont Kiara	03 7726 8963
Shunji International	Mid Valley	03 2938 3689
Toni & Guy	Bukit Bintang	03 2145 5569

prices (RM50 for women, RM30 for men). It sells Redken products and is good value for chemical processing too, with relaxing costing RM120 for mid-length hair. Very patient with children, they charge RM25 for a child's cut. They have a loyalty scheme for regular customers who get a discount on cuts and treatments. The salon is open from 11.00 to 19.00, but is closed on Sundays.

Bangsar Shopping Centre
Bangsar
🚊 **Bangsar**

Grace Salon
03 2095 8303 | www.gracesalon.com.my

A flagship salon for L'Oreal, Grace Salon is popular but pricey. The well-equipped salon has private rooms and wireless internet access, plus a small playroom for younger customers. Children's cuts start at RM30 for boys and RM35 for girls, while men's start at RM55 and women's at RM65. Excellent quality colouring services are available from RM200 and relaxing from RM280. For special occasions you can have your makeup done here, or your hair put up. Open weekdays from 10:00 to 20:30, and weekends from 10:00 to 19:00.

46 Jalan Telawi
Bangsar
🚊 **Bangsar**

ISH
03 2287 0920

Michael Marriner runs one of the most popular hair salons in KL for expats, and it's not difficult to understand why. The cutting and colouring advice and results are first class and the salon itself is a friendly and relaxing place to treat oneself. Men, women and children are all welcome. A cut and blow day for ladies is around RM70. L'Oreal products are used. Manicures and pedicures can be arranged if booked ahead.

39-1 Jalan 23/70A
Wisma CKL
Desa Sri Hartamas
Sri Hartamas
🚊 **Bangsar**

Kence Salon
03 6201 0170 | www.kencesalon.com

This very trendy salon is staffed with Korean stylists who trained at Vidal Sassoon, Toni & Guy and Macmillan in London. Kence is well known for its technicians' expertise with the latest digital perming and straightening techniques, which although expensive by KL standards (at RM600 for a digital perm), are excellent quality. Situated about 15 minutes in a taxi from Bangsar LRT.

4th Floor, Suria KLCC
KLCC
🚊 **KLCC**

Saw Hair Salon
03 2171 1881 | www.saw.com.my

After over 20 years working for top London salons, Edwin Saw returned home to Malaysia and opened his own salon. It's very popular with expats and Edwin is highly recommended as a stylist for hard-to-manage curly hair. He charges from RM175 upwards for a cut; junior stylists start from about RM50. Perming, colouring, straightening and conditioning treatments are available, as well as manicures and pedicures, so you can make the most of time spent waiting for your highlights. Perms start at RM150, colour from RM100. Although this salon is on the expensive side it's considered worth the money.

4A Lorong Kolam Air Lama 1
Ampang Jaya
Ampang
🚊 **Ampang**

Winnie Unisex Salon
03 4256 0631

This is a popular family salon in the Ampang area, although strangely, they operate on a 'no appointments' system, which can result in long waits at busy times. The staff are good with children and offer excellent value basic cutting and colouring services, although people tend to go elsewhere for fancy hair-dos or more complicated processing.

Health Spas		
Andana	Ampang	03 2161 3368
Andana (men only)	Selangor	03 7803 2328
Aroma Garden	Mid Valley	03 2287 9809
Be Ratu Spa	Ampang	03 4270 5098
Beaubelle Day Spa	Sri Hartamas	03 6203 2625
Cafe Jamu Spa	Sri Hartamas	03 6203 2990
Cherro Switzerland	Bangsar	03 2287 8480
Oasis Beauty and Spa	Bangsar	03 2093 4200
Sutra's Spa	Ampang	03 4270 3971
Vila Manja	Jalan Ampang	03 2161 5418

Health Spas

Other options **Sports & Leisure Facilities** p.264, **Massage** p.273

The spa industry has taken off in a big way in KL in recent years, with new spas opening up and existing spas upgrading their facilities to compete. You'll find that spas offer mainly body treatments such as scrubs, wraps, massage and hydrotherapy, although some offer facial and beauty treatments too. Larger spas, especially those in hotels, offer spa cuisine to complete your experience. Treatments incorporating elements of traditional Malay remedies are popular, as are those involving aromatherapy, steam and bathing. There isn't a set of safety or hygiene standards for spas to follow, and therapists may not have any formal qualifications. KL spas are generally good value, with a body wrap treatment costing around RM160, body scrub RM180, and massage RM150.

Level 5, Crowne Plaza
Mutiara Hotel, Jalan
Sultan Ismail
City Centre
 Sultan Ismail

Angsana Spa
03 2141 4321 | *www.angsanaspa.com*
Newly reopened, the Angsana now has single and double treatment rooms, two outdoor treatment pavilions with private showers and spa baths, and three rain-mist therapy rooms. Once you've chosen your room, try one of the unique treatments combining the traditions of east and west, such as the body toning Jamu Lore from Indonesia (RM320) or the excellent Fusion massage (from RM210) which blends Thai and Swedish techniques.

6-0-8 Plaza Damas
60 Jalan Sri
Hartamas 1
Sri Hartamas
 Bangsar

Dewi Sri Spa by Martha Tilaar
03 6203 5373 | *www.dewisrispa.com.my*
Owned by a renowned Indonesian company, Dewi Sri Spa brings the Balinese spa tradition to KL. Decorated in natural stone and wood, there are five treatment rooms, each with private bath, shower, steam and Jacuzzi. The signature traditional Golden Lulur treatment, a combination of massage, steam and bathing rituals, is RM240. The spa is open on weekdays from 11:00 to 20:00, and on weekends from 10:00 to 19:00. Take a taxi from Bangsar station (which should take about 15 minutes).

Level 1 Damai Sari
Mont Kiara Damai
Jalan Kiara 2
Mont Kiara
 Bangsar

Energy Day Spa
03 6201 7833 | *www.energymindbodyspirit.com*
A popular spa with expats, the philosophy here is to balance mind, body and spirit to achieve beauty through holistic wellness. The Mont Kiara branch has five treatment rooms, a rooftop rest and relaxation area and a steam room in a light and airy setting. Try the organic brown sugar scrub at RM110 or retexturing skin treatment at RM150. Treatments are available for both men and women. There's a wide range of different massage styles including shiatsu and reflexology. There's another branch at the Great Eastern Mall on Jalan Ampang (03 4256 8833), also very popular with expats. Open from 11:00 to 20:00. Take a 15 minute taxi from Bangsar station to reach it.

Bangsar Village II
Bangsar
Bangsar

Hammam
03 2282 2180 | *www.hammambaths.com*
This Turkish bath is new to the KL spa scene but has already attracted a loyal following. Decorated in traditional style with tiled walls and floors, it's a refreshing change from the standard Balinese-inspired spa look. As well as the straightforward bathing (Hammam, RM100) there are a variety of add on treatments including massage (RM100 to RM145) and

body polish (RM120). A number of packages are available, including two for couples.

Healing Hands At Home

Evelyn is an excellent massage therapist who makes home visits. She brings along her massage table and uses aromatherapy oils to soothe away stress, and the best part is that you don't even have to fight your way through the traffic afterwards. Call 012 614 7508.

Mandarin Oriental
KLCC
🚇 *KLCC*

Mandarin Oriental Spa

03 2380 8888 | www.mandarinoriental.com

The centrepiece of this luxurious spa is the Heat and Water Oasis, a series of steam rooms, dry saunas and hot and cold Jacuzzi. Drawing on natural extracts from around Asia, the therapies soothe and revitalise. The Path to Tranquility treatment (RM430) uses sweet basil and kaffir lime, while the Sikhao treatment (RM160) uses Andaman sea salts. After enjoying the treatments, you're free to make use of the hotel's Vitality Club, and spa cuisine is available to complete your experience. Open daily from 08:00 to 22:00, except for Sundays when it opens at 10:00.

1st Floor, 14 – 16
Jalan Telawi
Bangsar
🚇 *Bangsar*

Ozmosis Health & Day Spa

03 2287 0380 | www.ozmosis.com.my

Ozmosis aims to pamper all five senses to restore your sense of inner health, and fans of this urban spa would say it succeeds. Treatments are a combination of western and south-east Asian traditions, using essential oils blended in Malaysia. A detoxifying body wrap is RM160 and warm stone therapy massage is RM250. Ozmosis also offers a variety of beauty treatments, including waxing and CACI non-surgical face lifts.

168 Jalan Imbi
Bukit Bintang
🚇 *Imbi*

Spa Village at the Ritz-Carlton

03 2782 9090 | www.spavillage.com/kualalumpur

You'll find everything from traditional regional treatments to the latest in multisensory experiences at this top-notch spa. The sensory room is a unique experience where all five senses are engaged to heighten awareness of your inner self. The Spa Village has an excellent range of treatment packages for couples; the Traditional Royal Malay treatment includes scented body steaming that's reputed to delay the signs of ageing.

Massage

Other options **Sports & Leisure Facilities** p.264, **Health Spas** p.272

Spa Village

Even if you've never tried massage before, the wide variety of styles available in KL may tempt you to give it a try. Massage therapy can be helpful in managing stress, easing tired and sore muscles, and to relieve tension in the mind and body. Massage therapists will almost certainly not have any medical training, so if you have any injuries you should consult a doctor first before starting any massage treatments. This is particularly important if you have any back or neck problems. Take your pick from Swedish, Thai, Hawaiian, Japanese Shiatsu, aromatherapy, hot stone massage and a host of others. One very popular treatment is reflexology. At its simplest, this traditional Chinese treatment is presented as a foot massage. However, an experienced practitioner, while massaging your feet, will find out all sorts of other things about your body and lifestyle – whether you drink enough water, eat too much sugar, suffer from headaches or have kidney problems. By applying pressure to particular areas of the sole of the foot, some symptoms can be eased. If you don't like the idea of going to a spa, some therapists make home visits. Many of the spas listed in the Health Spas section offer massage, as well as those listed here.

Pamper Floor
Starhill Gallery
Jalan Bukit Bintang
Bukit Bintang
 Bukit Bintang

Asianel Reflexology Spa
03 2142 1397 | www.asianel.com
Following the belief that regular foot reflexology can help the body to regenerate, Asianel combines traditional reflexology techniques with spa-style pampering. Specific reflexology packages aim to relieve symptoms in certain areas of the body through stimulation of the pressure points in the feet. Popular choices are Headache, Neck and Shoulder Pain (RM85), and Backache, Lower Back and Spine (RM85). Reflexology can be painful as practitioners believe that only by working just above an individual's pain level can real benefits be achieved. With this in mind, Asianel's lavender footbaths and essential oils bring a very welcome soothing touch to the treatments. Open from 10:00 to 21:00, with the last appointment taken at 19:45.

Great Eastern Mall
303 Jalan Ampang
Ampang
Jelatek

Energy Day Spa
03 4256 8833 | www.energymindbodyspirit.com
This spa has well-trained, experienced therapists who offer a number of different massage therapies. Shiatsu (from RM138) is an acupressure technique which uses pressure from the therapist's fingers to relieve energy blockages and restore the optimal flow of qi in the body. It lowers blood pressure and improves circulation. Energy also offers relaxation massage and scalp massage to relieve tension and headaches (RM38). Massage services are available to both men and women.

The Plaza, Northpoint
Mid Valley City
Mid Valley
Mid Valley

Siam Bodyworks
03 2282 0233 | www.siambodyworks.com
Traditional Thai massage doesn't use oils or lotions. You wear pyjama-type garments while the therapist pulls and pushes your limbs in ways you didn't think they could go. Pressure is applied using the hands, fingers, limbs, and at times the therapist's whole body weight. It can be a little painful, but you can always ask the therapist to be more gentle. It's worth the pain as afterwards you'll feel refreshed and rejuvenated. Medical benefits include improved blood and lymph circulation and relief of muscle tension. Siam Bodyworks employs certified and experienced Thai therapists who offer reflexology and aromatherapy too. An hour of Thai massage costs RM65, 45 minutes' reflexology is RM50 and an hour's aromatherapy massage is RM85.

Massages

Blind Massage	No 53M Jalan Thambipillai, Brickfields	KL Sentral	03 2274 0813
Bodhi Sense	E-0-11, Plaza Damas	Sri Hartamas	03 6203 3203
Cah'Ya Aromatherapy	B-03-02 Plaza Mont Kiara	Mont Kiara	03 6203 4500
Samkyya	1 Jalan Abdullah, off Jalan Bangsar	Bangsar	03 2287 2111

Meditation
Meditation as part of yoga has long been practised by Malaysia's Hindu community and is now becoming popular with Malaysians of other races, as well as with expats. Buddhist meditation is part of the Chinese community's tradition and is also practised

by some expats. Regular meditation can help lower blood pressure and reduce the concentration of stress hormones in the blood. From a spiritual perspective meditation can enhance the individual's inner peace by helping to overcome critical mindsets and self-centred behaviour.

Manjushri Kadampa Centre

3-2 Jalan Ara
SD7/3B
Bandar Sri Damansara
Petaling Jaya
🚇 *Taman Jaya*

03 6272 1098 | www.meditateinkl.org

This centre holds weekly meditation classes in English to give an insight into Buddhist thought and practices and to help people find peace and happiness in their lives. Introductory courses are held on Sunday mornings on a drop-in basis: there's no need to register in advance and no charge. For more advanced courses you will need to enrol, but you are allowed to attend trial sessions first. Classes are run on Sundays from 10:00 to 11:30, and from 13:00 to 17:00.

Yogashakti

1 Lorong Damai
13 Kiri
Jalan Ampang
🚇 *Ampang Park*

03 4252 4714 | www.yogashakti.com

A quiet location just outside the city centre provides a peaceful environment in which to meditate. Regular courses are held to introduce beginners to meditation techniques and meditation sessions are held on Sunday evenings. Contact Yogashakti for more details and for course costs.

Pilates

Other options **Yoga** p.277

Pilates is a system of exercises that teaches body awareness, improves posture and helps you increase your control of body movement. Pilates can be performed using special equipment or on the floor using mats. It focuses on strengthening the core abdominal muscles, teaching correct breathing, and moving gracefully. If you commit to a series of classes, your reward will be a more toned, supple body with stronger tummy and back muscles. Pilates can be a useful part of a rehabilitation programme after injury, as many exercises are performed seated and are only partially weight bearing. But you should check with your doctor before taking up any new form of exercise after an injury. You'll find Pilates courses offered at many gyms – these are not usually conducted to a high standard as the class size is generally too large for the instructor to properly observe the participants individually. Look for small classes and an instructor who has undertaken specific Pilates training if you want to see good results.

Nubody

73-1 Jalan Setia Bakti
Damansara Heights
🚇 *Bangsar*

03 2095 8072 | www.nubody.com.my

Instructor Melissa Zecha is certified in the USA and offers group mat classes. The classes are limited to 10 participants and include work with fitballs, therabands, foam rollers and magic circles. Each class costs RM30. Group reformer classes, with a maximum of six participants, are RM60 per person. Nubody can also do private sessions on request.

Pilatique

8-2A Jalan Batai
Damansara Heights
🚇 *Bangsar*

03 2092 5655 | www.pilatique.com

Pilatique offers both equipment and mat classes using instructors certified by Stott Pilates. Private equipment sessions are RM150, and group sessions are RM60 per person. You can form your own group with friends, or Pilatique can help you form a group with other clients of similar ability. Mat classes are RM30 per person. This is a well-run Pilates studio in a good location; before you start Pilates with them they do a postural analysis to identify any problems and discuss your medical history.

Reiki

Reiki is a Japanese hands-on or hands-above healing technique using universal life force energy. Generally, it induces a deep state of relaxation, relieves tension and anxiety, boosts the immune system, increases mental clarity and awakens intuition and consciousness. Reiki is not a traditional practice in Malaysia, but it has many similarities to traditional healing therapies and its popularity is growing. Some spas offer reiki, and it is also available from a number of independent practitioners. A one-hour session will cost around RM120. Courses are available if you're interested in becoming a reiki practitioner. To find an independent practitioner near you, try the website www.reiki.com.my or www.internationalholistictherapiesdirectories.com/malaysia2reiki.htm.

Reiki			
Energy Day Spa	Great Eastern Mall, 303 Jalan Ampang Level 1 Damai Sari, Mont Kiara Damai, Jalan Kiara 2	Ampang Mont Kiara	03 4256 8833 03 6201 7833
Yogashakti	1 Lorong Damai 13 Kiri	Jalan Ampang	03 4252 4714

Lightworks

9 Jalan Mesui
Off Jalan Nagasari
City Centre
Sultan Ismail

03 2143 2766 | www.lightworks.com.my
Lightworks is an inclusive venue offering a variety of new age healing techniques as well as yoga, a new age store, and a cafe. Reiki treatments are offered here, as well as courses for people who are interested in learning more about reiki or becoming practitioners.

Stress Management

Other options **Support Groups** p.135

Stress, or rather your response to stress, can lead to a dizzying array of health problems from high blood pressure to insomnia and appetite loss. Many expats can find that their usual methods for managing stress aren't practical in Malaysia – it's hard to go out for a brisk walk round the block in the heat and humidity, and informal counselling services aren't common. Managing and controlling responses to stress has become an important part of our health and well-being and you may need to find some new techniques. Stress management involves a holistic approach to the problem and what works depends very much on the individual. If you find exercise helps you could join a gym (see p.266). Many people find that learning how to meditate (see p.274) is a good stress buster. Looking after yourself can be a good move; go for a massage (see p.273) a facial (see beauty salons, p.268) or even indulge in a bit of retail therapy (see shopping, p.279). If you like to talk out a stressful situation with friends and family, investing in a cheap international calling card (see p.117) would be a good move.

If your stress has reached the point where it is compromising your ability to live a normal daily life (for example, if it is having an effect on your job or your family), it may be time to see a mental health professional. See p.135 for a listing of counsellors and psychologists who can help.

Tai Chi

Tai Chi is a popular form of exercise among Malaysia's Chinese community. It's actually a martial art, but the emphasis of most Tai Chi practitioners is on the non-combative elements. Tai Chi consists of a series of postures that you move between without pausing, creating a single graceful, fluid movement. Since it's very low impact, Tai Chi is an ideal form of exercise if you have joint problems such as arthritis. Over time it can help to improve balance, increase flexibility and muscle strength and improve agility. Although you can learn Tai Chi on your own, it's better to learn with an instructor who will show you the postures and help with breathing techniques.

Well-Being

Various Locations ## Malaysia Shenlong Tai Chi Chuan Association
03 7983 9868 | www.taichi.org.my

The Malaysia Shenlong Tai Chi Chuan Association runs Tai Chi courses at various venues in KL including schools and community centres. Teaching of Tai Chi is distilled into six key areas; theory, chi, form, Tai Chi Chuan, Tai Chi Sword and internal exercises following the teachings of Grandmaster Cheng Man Ching. See the website for details of current courses and locations.

Yoga
Other options **Pilates** p.275

Many different forms of yoga are practised in KL with the most popular being hatha and astanga. Some yoga practitioners in KL emphasise the spiritual aspects of yoga more than others, but if you're looking for a straight exercise class you'll still have plenty of choice. Yoga practice can be a very personal thing, so it's often a matter of trying out a few classes before you find one that suits you. As well as improving strength, flexibility and muscle tone, yoga can have positive health benefits in reducing stress and lowering blood pressure.

Before starting a course of yoga classes, your studio should give you some guidelines on the correct yoga etiquette. Each studio will have its own set of rules, although there are some that are universal. One of the most important rules of yoga etiquette is to stick to the times of the class. Rushing in five minutes after the class has started is not only disrespectful to the instructor, it won't win you any points with your classmates who are trying hard to concentrate. Similarly, leaving before the end of the class is also frowned upon, not just because of the disruption, but because you will miss out on your savasana – an essential part of the class.

Yoga

Lightworks	City Centre	03 2143 2966
Yoga2Health	Bangsar	03 2282 3866

Plaza Damas
Jalan Sri Hartamas 1
Sri Hartamas
🚇 *Bangsar*

Jiva Yoga
03 6201 1822 | www.jivayogastudio.com

Offering classes in vinyasa yoga, astanga and Pilates, Jiva also conducts regular retreats and workshops to offer students the chance to take the practice to a deeper level. Vinyasa is a flowing class that integrates fluidity and strength and is accompanied by music. The drop-in rate is RM35 for a single class or RM320 for a 12 class package. Six-week special courses designed to give the beginner a solid foundation in yoga are RM180. It's about 15 minutes in a taxi from Bangsar station.

1 Lorong Damai
13 Kiri
Jalan Ampang
🚇 *Ampang Park*

Yogashakti
03 4252 4714 | www.yogashakti.com

Shilpa is particularly popular with expats at this peaceful and centrally located yoga centre. There's a strong focus on the spiritual aspects of yoga. Classes in hatha and astanga yoga are offered, as well as antenatal yoga. A one-time registration fee of RM40 must be paid by all class participants; after that a package of 10 classes is RM350 and a single class is RM45. Private sessions are available at RM250.

The Weld
76 Jalan Raja Chulan
City Centre
🚇 *Sultan Ismail*

Yogazone
03 2161 2222 | www.yogazone.com.my

Yogazone is a chain of yoga clubs – another popular branch with expats is at Plaza Damas in Sri Hartamas (03 6203 2468). Yogazone offers a wide range of yoga classes, including yoga for kids, hatha, astanga and hot yoga. There are also Pilates and fitball classes. Classes are open to members only, but short-term deals are usually available. Contact Yogazone directly for the latest membership rates and promotional offers.

Shopping

Shopping

Shopping

Most expatriates can live like kings in Kuala Lumpur, and this is no exaggeration. It doesn't take a visitor too long after stepping off the aeroplane to realise that living costs here are incredibly affordable. Compared to most western countries, and some Asian nations like Singapore, Korea, Japan and Hong Kong, the costs of housing, communications, transport, local food, holiday accommodation, airfares, clothing, medical expenses, entertainment and recreation are among the lowest in the world. Local food, for starters, is incredibly cheap. A supper of Roti Canai, a griddled bread snack, and milk tea at a local coffee shop barely exceeds RM2.00 (that's less than a dollar). Yes, your dollar, euro or pound sterling can stretch incredibly far in this country. Is it any wonder that more and more expatriates and tourists have decided to make Malaysia their second home?

Capitalising on this burgeoning spending power, shopping malls are mushrooming at a phenomenal rate. With a total retail space of around three million square metres, KL can justifiably be called 'Mall City'. You can shop till you drop, or until you max out your credit card, whichever comes first. Even the Ministry of Tourism gets into the act by organising the Mega Sale Carnival three times a year. During these three sales Seasons (March, August and December), traffic practically grinds to a halt, but the construction of transportation infrastructure like the LRT and monorail links to major retail spaces like the Golden Triangle, KLCC, and Mid Valley Megamall, has provided major relief to traffic woes. If you're a shopaholic who needs a regular fix of retail therapy, you don't need to wait for these three carnivals; there are periodic weekend and seasonal sales throughout the year.

From the antique and the exotic to modern electronic and audio-visual equipment, whether it is within the comfort of a one-stop multi-storey building or browsing through an alfresco pedestrian mall, you can get your hands on just about anything. Goods are available in every price bracket. Imported books, cosmetics and perfumes, watches, computers, leather goods and boats are sold duty free. Even electronics items, traditionally the strong suit of Hong Kong and Singapore, are steadily dropping in price. If for some reason you can't get what you want at any of the myriad shopping malls, there's always online shopping – a burgeoning trend in the local retail industry.

Despite the onslaught of malls, nothing can quite compare to the authentic Asian shopping experience, offered through the shopping streets and markets. Especially popular are the night markets, or *pasar malam*. By evening, dozens of stall holders pile their tables with a dizzying array of fresh produce, flowers, knick knacks and everything you can think of. The city's most famous street market is Petaling Street in Chinatown, where it is joked that everything except the food is fake.

Another growing fad is the flea market, in all probability inspired by their counterparts overseas. Both held indoors and alfresco, these flea markets are operated by both locals as well as expatriates, and are mushrooming all over Klang Valley, especially in the more affluent areas like Sri Hartamas, Bangsar and Mutiara Damansara. The open-air bazaars at Sri Hartamas, Bangsar and The Curve draw huge crowds every weekend who flock here for the lively atmosphere as well as the multifarious offerings of high-street fashion, eclectic jewellery, and home-made pastries laid out in colourful and attractive displays. Apart from the usual kitsch offerings, the indoor flea market Amcorp Mall is a big draw for a different reason; it is a hunting ground for antique collectors scavenging for potentially valuable old records, books and rare toys. A little-known secret that only locals would know is that many intrepid eBay auctioneers actually source their products from here.

Night Owl?

Most shopping malls will close off certain sections of the mall when it is 22:00. So if you are planning to stay on in the mall beyond 22:00, usually to watch a movie or to have drinks in the pub, ensure you park as close as possible to the place you want to go to. Otherwise you may have to walk a long and lonely stretch in the carpark to find your car.

Clothing Sizes

Figuring out your size isn't rocket science, just a bit of a pain. Firstly, check the label – international sizes are often printed on them. Secondly, check the store – they will often have a helpful conversion chart on display. Otherwise, a UK size is always two higher than a US size (so a UK 10 is actually a US 6. To convert European sizes into US sizes, just subtract 32 (so a European 38 is actually a US 6). To convert European sizes into UK sizes, a 38 is roughly a 10, but some countries size smaller so you'll have to try clothes on to be sure. Italian sizing is different again.

With a smorgasbord of shopping alternatives to fit every budget and taste, is it any wonder that Kuala Lumpur is dubbed a shopping paradise? Just a word of advice before you hit the malls: strap on a pair of comfy shoes, and make sure you have plenty of credit limit to spare!

Online Shopping

It was not too long ago that Malaysians were uncomfortable with the concept of online purchasing. With the runaway success of Air Asia, the country's homegrown budget airline, the trend has steadily gained popularity. While the online retail scene is still dominated by companies selling intangible items like theatre and transportation tickets, this niche is increasingly being filled by both major chains and independent shops. Online book businesses are one of the first to embrace the internet revolution, with local book giant MPH (p.290) leading the way. The Malaysia and Singapore-based online shopping mall www.acmamall.com also began by selling English books but has since diversified into a host of other products like Belgian chocolates, DVDs, health and beauty products and flowers. Other notable sites that have steadily built a solid reputation for being reliable and selling quality products are www.lelong.com.my (a local auction site), www.blooming.com.my (the country's pioneer online florist), and www.shashinki.com (camera equipment with international warranty). Most online sites require payment by Visa or MasterCard. At the moment, Paypal facilities are not available here yet but most local online stores offer the option of locally endorsed payment gateways like Maybank2U. Like any country in the world, incoming shipments are subject to search and confiscation by discretion. With conservative Muslim laws in place, it goes without saying that you shouldn't risk shipping your *Playboy* copies here!

Online Shopping	
www.acmamall.com	Books, healthcare products, chocolates
www.airasia.com	Budget flight tickets
www.arthursbooks.com	Books
www.axcess.com.my	Tickets for events and shows
www.blooming.com.my	Flowers and gifts
www.firefly.com	Budget flight tickets
www.lelong.com.my	Local auction website
www.myBBstore.com	Local and imported baby items
www.plal.com	Imported shoes, boots, pipes, men's clothing and winter wear
www.shashinki.com	Cameras and camera equipment
www.ticketcharge.com.my	Tickets for events

Refunds & Exchanges

Refunds and exchanges really depend on the merchant. Generally, international stores tend to be more flexible. Borders (p.344), for example, allows refunds for a period of 14 days on selected merchandise, while hypermarkets like Tesco (p.332), Carrefour (p.331), and Giant (p.331) give a grace period of seven days from the date of purchase. Clothing retailers also tend to be more lenient, as long as you can produce the receipt and product is in a saleable condition. Esprit (p.296) and British India (Lot 10, 03 2142 2127) allow you to return within seven

Refunds

The refund and exchange policies vary from shop to shop. Usually big shops or international brands will have a consumer-friendly policy, but returns have to be done within three to seven days with the receipt and product tag. It is always wise to inspect the product carefully before purchasing it as some shops may not accept the return of faulty goods, especially during the sales period. Some shops do not refund but allow for a product exchange.

days. Shops that do offer these concessions usually display the terms and conditions prominently on the cashier's counter. Most locals merchants will not offer you refunds, but some do make exception for exchanges, as long as the item you wish to exchange it for is of a similar or higher value. Refunds and exchanges are usually not applicable to 'best buy' or 'on sale' items. This is clearly indicated on placards that are displayed in bargain bins.

Consumer Rights

Consumer rights are a sore point here in KL. They are woefully inadequate and the best way to ensure you don't end up regretting your purchase is to buy with caution. If you do have a dispute with a shop, you are unlikely to get any help from the company management or even the police. While existing paper-thin laws overwhelmingly favour traders, you can always fall back on the Consumers' Association of Penang (04 229 3511), a non-governmental body based in Penang that actively champions consumers' rights. To load up on your knowledge of local laws and consumer updates, get a copy of *Utusan Konsumer*, a monthly newsletter that exposes transgressions and highlights general welfare issues. There is also an active one-stop free public service website (www.consumer.com.my) for you to air your woes and share a store's bad service or shoddy products with other shoppers.

Shipping

With a reliable national postal service and a plethora of local and international courier services, you can ship anything from a book to a sofa set anywhere. Both air freight and sea freight are available. You can easily monitor your shipments with the Air Waybill using the online tracking facilities provided. For deliveries to a local destination, Poslaju, the local courier service available at all post offices, provides very reasonable rates. Lightweight packages start at RM4.50. Popular international courier services like DHL, FedEx, and UPS are also widely available. In a latest development that will bring cheer to the customer, TNT has gone one step further and collaborated with local 7-Eleven, KIOSK. Instead of driving to some remote courier agency, you can simply drop off your package at any KIOSK outlet. This service is available for packages up to 25kg.

Credit Where It's Due

MasterCard, Visa, Diners and American Express cards are widely accepted in Malaysia but some small shops, usually eateries and independent boutiques, may only accept credit card payment for purchases above a certain value, usually RM30 to RM50. So it is wise to keep sufficient Ringgit on hand. Many eateries work with credit card companies to offer discounts of up to 30% or give complimentary dishes and drinks, so do ask what offers your credit card has.

Courier Agencies

City-Link Global Network	03 5033 3800	www.citylinkexpress.com
DHL Worldwide Express Malaysia	1800 888 388	www.dhl.com.my
FedEx Express Malaysia	1800 886 363	www.fedex.com/my
Nationwide Express	03 5512 7000	www.nationwide2u.com
Pos Malaysia	1300 300 300	www.pos.com.my
Sure-Reach Worldwide Express	03 7781 8188	www.sure-reach.com
TNT Malaysia	1300 882 882	www.tnt.com
UPS Malaysia	03 7784 1233	www.ups.com

How To Pay

The popularity of credit card purchases is soaring (and so are bankruptcy rates). You won't be able to get through a shopping mall without encountering at least one bankcard sales executive eagerly waving the offer of a 'free lifetime credit card' at you. Nevertheless, cash is still the preferred mode of payment at most outlets. It is advisable to carry some form of cash as many eateries and independent shops don't have credit card machines. If you're paranoid about pickpockets, at least carry your ATM card. ATMs are located in most shopping complexes and increasingly, petrol stations (especially popular banking networks like MEPS, Maybank and Cirrus). Most ATMs operate 24

Useful Numbers

American Express	03 2050 0000
Visa	1800 802 997
Diners Club	03 2730 3388
MasterCard	1800 804 594

hour machines and you can use your credit card to withdraw from these machines. Visa or MasterCard are widely accepted at major shopping malls, hotels, petrol stations and restaurants. Some retailers add on a surcharge of 3% so ask first before you pay. American Express and Diners Club are also accepted, though are not so common. Major travellers' cheques and currencies like dollars and euros may be accepted in hotels, but in most places only the local currency (the ringgit) is accepted. And forget about bringing out your debit cards; the practice has not caught on here yet.

Early Birds &
Late Deals
The best time to
bargain is when
stalls are closing at
the end of the day.
Proprietors tend to
give in especially if
business has been slow.
Alternatively, shop
early. Locals believe
that the first customer
should be given a good
deal as it sets a lucky
precedent for the rest
of the day.

Bargaining

Other options **Markets** p.332

Bargaining is accepted not only in the usual places like street stalls, but many independent shops and speciality stores in shopping malls can be persuaded to give between 5% and 10% discounts off the display (with some cajoling). Though many foreigners may be uncomfortable with the idea of haggling, and may even fear it is rude, in Malaysia the customer is expected to bargain.

Before you embark on any bargaining exercise, do your research. Walk around and check out stores selling similar items, so that you have a benchmark of sorts. In a haggling session, always let the merchant quote the price first. Sure, he will keep badgering for your strike price, but don't fall for this trick. Stand your ground until he caves in and volunteers a price. A poker face always helps; displaying any enthusiasm for the item you desire is strictly a no-no. A trick that always works is to walk away. Very often, vendors give away discounts when a customer is leaving to avoid losing a potential sale. Listen in disbelief as the proprietor reels off a string of prices in descending order, the further you move away.

Places that should carry a 'buyers beware' label are tourist haunts like Petaling Street (p.327). While it is a great place to familiarise yourself with the unique local shopping milieu, it is also a notorious tourist trap, and anybody with blond hair or who speaks with a different accent is regarded as fair game. Mercenary proprietors will not hesitate to rip off any tourist who is too shy to ask for 'cheaper'. The rule of thumb is be thick skinned. If you don't ask, you'll never know!

Tourist Discounts

Visitors' incentive – some retail outlets like Metrojaya (p.330) offer 5% discounts to tourists upon presentation of passports and boarding passes at point of purchase. Pavilion (p.340) and Metrojaya offer tourists flying in on Qatar Airways exclusive privileges. Foreign-issued MasterCard holders may also be entitled to exclusive privileges at participating outlets.

What & Where To Buy – Quick Reference

The Wine Club
(www.wineclub.
my) is a great way to get
a selection of fine wines
delivered to you each
month, free of charge.
After paying the RM75
membership fee you'll
get low prices on wines
from around the world,
invitations to wine
tasting evenings, and
a party service where
you can buy wines on a
'drink or return' basis.

Alcohol

Other options **On the Town**
p.398, **Drinks** p.398

Most hard liquor is imported
from overseas but you can
enjoy locally brewed beer
licensed under famous
brands such as Carlsberg,
Tiger, Heineken and Anchor.
In Malaysia, a shop needs
to apply for a liquor licence
before it can sell alcohol.
The exception is beer,

Alcohol		
Barrique Fine Wines	Bangsar	03 2283 3390
Casa Vino	The Curve, Petaling Jaya	03 7724 2007
Denise	Bangsar	03 2287 8368
Muihua	Bandar Sri Damansara	03 6277 2228
Single & Available	Sri Hartamas	03 6203 2151
Sterling Vines	Sri Hartamas	03 2300 8850
Sur-A	Plaza Mont Kiara	03 6201 0607
Taste Vin	Jalan Berangan	03 2148 8978
The Cellarium	Bangsar	03 2284 4312
Vintry Cellars	Damansara Heights	03 2094 8262
Well Mercury	Bukit Bintang	03 2141 6120
Wine Cellar	Bangsar	03 2093 1919

which comes under the food and beverage licence, and is easily available at most
restaurants (especially Chinese coffee shops and eateries). The government is serious
about battling alcoholism and imposes a hefty tax on alcoholic products. Beer can
cost up to RM7.50. A six-pack of beer is usually around RM25, white wine starts from
RM30, while Smirnoff vodka is upwards of RM55. Selection and prices will depend
on the supermarket or store. Duty-free shops at the airport (KLIA) give you a better
deal than shopping outlets in the city, but you're less likely to drink yourself out of a
fortune if you buy at airport shops in other south-east Asian countries. Fine dining
restaurants that double as liquor stores are a growing trend, especially in the more
affluent suburbs like Bangsar and Taman Tun Dr Ismail. Divino The Wine Bistro (03 2287
9968, One Bangsar) has a well-stocked Denise (p.284). Another hot favourite in Bangsar
is Opus Bistro (p.375) where you get to tuck into authentic traditional Italian fare while
the dishy French sommelier makes recommendations from an extensive wine list,
courtesy of Wine Cellar (p.284).

Art

Other options **Art Galleries** p.183, **Art Classes** p.216, **Art & Craft Supplies** p.286

Art at the Craft Complex

Good news for the art connoisseur: there
is a thriving arts scene in Malaysia. From
Islamic calligraphy and Chinese scroll
paintings to internationally acclaimed
visual art, new and emerging artists
arrive constantly and display every art
concept imaginable. Popular styles of
art are more decorative: the Nanyang
style, with themes like landscapes, fishing
villages and kampung scenes is still a
bestseller. However, interest in abstract
art is burgeoning. Malaysia has a vibrant
contemporary arts market, with works
ranging from lush landscapes in oil and
watercolours to video installations and
performance art. You'll find galleries
throughout the city both in big complexes
and independent galleries. A good place to
get an overview of the Malaysian art scene
is the massive National Art Gallery (p.183)

off Jalan Tun Razak, a stunning building that combines traditional Malay elements with contemporary lines. It holds an open air art market on the first Saturday of every month, where many talented local artists create traditional crafts and there is contemporary art for sale. Galeri Petronas (p.183) at KLCC is renowned for both its traditional and modern multimedia expressions. Visitors also sing the praises of the Islamic Art Museum (p.185), which houses fine collections from Muslim communities from the Middle East, Asia, and Eastern Europe. Commercial and national galleries aside, there are plenty of independent galleries scattered all over the city. Valentine Willie Fine Art (p.183) is renowned for its extensive range of south-east Asian paintings, sculptures and drawings. It also runs the Loft Gallery, which is an entire floor at Starhill (p.341) dedicated to art galleries. If you gravitate towards experimental and expressionist art, NN Gallery has a great collection of works in different media by daring artists. The Gallery at Starhill has an entire upper floor dedicated to art, aptly named 'Muse', with rows of small galleries and art exhibitions showcasing original paintings and sculptures by both established Malaysian artists like Eng Tay, Khalil Ibrahim, Ismail Latiff and Chong Hon Fatt, and upcoming artists like Jack Ting, Kam Woei Yann & Yap Chin Hoe. If you're an art lover, seek out ARTrageously Ramsay Ong The Art Gallery to view Sarawak artworks and handicraft. If Ramsay is around, he'll be happy to chat with you and you'll have a free lesson on Sarawak culture, traditions and art. You can buy straight from art galleries or directly from the artists. Check newspapers and lifestyle publications for listings and articles on selected artists. Prices may range from a few hundred ringgit for small pieces up to RM80,000 or more. Pucuk Rebung Museum Gallery (03 2382 0769, Ampang Mall) is part antique shop, part museum and sells fine quality art pieces. If you're interested in commissioning a painting or family portrait, your best bet is to approach the art galleries individually for recommendations. Otherwise, dozens of street artists are ready to immortalise your image in ink or pencil portraits for RM50 or so at Central Market (p.333).

As for other genres of visual arts, Central Market and Kuala Lumpur Craft Complex (p.188) are treasure troves of traditional crafts like songket (gold thread brocade) weaving, ceramics, silver and brass work, wood carving, and batik painting.

Designer shopping

Suria KLCC

ARTrageously Ramsay Ong has a dazzling range of handicrafts including traditional sleeping mats, wood carvings, and designer textiles.
For the seriously arty, log on to www.kakiseni.com, a community portal organised by passionate artisans which provides both event updates and authoritative write-ups on the local art industry.

Art

Artcase Galleries	Great Eastern Mall, Ampang	03 4257 4007	www.artcase.com.my
ARTrageously Ramsay Ong Galleries	94 Main Bazaar, Kuching Sarawak	03 0824 24346	www.artrageouslyasia.com
Clay Expression	Jalan Subang 3, Petaling Jaya	03 5628 1613	www.clayexpression.com
Galeri Petronas	Suria KLCC	03 2051 7770	www.galeripetronas.com.my
National Art Gallery	2 Jalan Temerloh, City Centre	03 4025 4990	www.artgallery.gov.my
NN Gallery	Jalan Sulaiman 1, Ampang	03 4270 6588	www.nngallery.com.my
Reka Art Space	Kelana Square, Petaling Jaya	03 7880 5982	www.reka-art.com
The Gallery @ Starhill	Starhill Gallery, Bukit Bintang	03 2143 3323	na
The Photographers' Gallery	Starhill Gallery, Bukit Bintang	03 2274 003 0	www.thephotographersgallery.com.m
Valentine Willie Fine Art	17 Jalan Telawi 3, Bangsar Baru	03 2284 2348	www.vwfa.net
Wei-Ling Gallery	8 Jalan Scott, Brickfields	03 2260 1106	www.weiling-gallery.com

Art & Craft Supplies

Other options **Art Classes** p.216, **Art Galleries** p.183, **Art** p.284

Professional artists, you don't have to haul a boatload of supplies to Malaysia to indulge your hobby. Artist Seamus Berkeley declares that Kuala Lumpur is the best place for art supplies. All major stationery chains have some section to offer the city's community of budding and professional artists, though Kinokuniya is better known for its range of eclectic and specialised art supplies. Some of the best gems are the dedicated local stores like Nanyang Art Supplies at Petaling Street or Art Friends at The Gardens.

Starhill Gallery

Art Friends, located at the UE3 complex along Jalan Loke Yew, towards Cheras side, is a popular haunt with budding Michelangelos because of its reasonably priced items. Despite the rise in other prices, this shop has decided to keep prices low for artists. It has earned a good reputation for its impressive array of watercolour choices, from pan colours to tubes, including Daler-Rowney. Prices are pretty competitive at below RM7 for the student colours.
Art Friends also has other items like special water buckets (from RM5 to RM15), box-easels from RM60 above, papers of various poundage and prices, and other watercolour implements. There are other art-related materials sold here, from wall stencils to fashion beads.
Another well-known art shop is Multifilla. Though a little out of the way in Balakong, it has earned a deserving reputation for stocking a wide range of art supplies from basic paint brushes to supplies for glass painting and an extensive array of clay. Presently, most of these shops specialise in retail but they are willing to share advice on which brand is better and why.

Art & Craft Supplies

Art Friends	Gardens, Mid Valley	03 2284 7777
Batik Bintang	Berjaya Times Square	03 2144 8368
Da Vinci	Ikano Power Centre	03 7725 4668
Furcasa Souvenirs & Antiques	Malaysian Tourist Centre	03 2166 3558
House of Silver	Central Market	03 2274 4457
Jadi Batek Centre	30 Jalan Inai, Bukit Bintang	03 2145 1133
Karyaneka Kraf Boutique	Bukit Bintang Plaza	03 2144 1519
Kinokuniya Book Stores	Suria KLCC	03 2164 8133
Lyanne Batik	Malaysian Tourist Centre	03 8061 6084
Mariwasa Pewter	Maju Junction, Jalan Sultan Ismail	03 2698 0418
Multifilla (M) Sdn Bhd	Taman Industri Selesa Jaya	03 8961 3686
Nanyang Art Supplies Sdn Bhd	Petaling St, Chinatown	03 2078 7066
Pink Gui	Plaza Damas, Sri Hartamas	03 6203 3100
Pucuk Rebung	Suria KLCC	03 2282 0769
Ridz Collection & Interior	Malaysian Tourist Centre	03 2166 5057
Royal Selangor Visitor Centre	Jalan Usahawan 6, Off Jalan Pahang	03 4145 6122
Sarakraf	Central Market	03 2273 8868
Songket Sutera Asli	Central Market	03 2273 2728
Talens Fine Art & Frames	Taman Tun Dr Ismail	03 7727 9820
Tom Abang Saufi Boutique	Malaysian Tourist Centre	03 2164 7381
Tuah KTC	Central Market	03 2272 2757
Tumasek Pewter	Jelan Kuang Bulan	03 6274 1225
Venus Art Shop	Petaling St, Chinatown	03 2078 1077
Wau Tradisi	Central Market	03 2274 1906

Baby Items

Congratulations! If you are about to be a parent or are celebrating the new existence of someone else's bundle of joy, you have some great choices in a city brimming with kids.

With dedicated stores and supermarket departments specialising in feeding, nursing, bathing, health and safety you'll find everything you could possibly need here. Sales associates are helpful and registry is available. Diapers, formulas, and trusted baby products by Johnson & Johnson can be picked up at supermarkets and most pharmacies for daily maintenance.

Baby items are available in most department stores, hypermarkets, as well as specialists. You would have more luck at hypermarkets like Carrefour (p.331), Giant (p.331) and Tesco (p.332) for clothes, bottles, toys, cots, rocking chairs and prams. You can get everything remotely related to babies at one go, and at reasonable prices (though not always the best of quality). The spacious Anakku Boutique at The Curve has a whole host of products catering to your baby's needs.

All major shopping malls have lots of baby stores, all clustered together. Baby specialist Chicco has outlets in Mid Valley (p.339), KLCC (p.341) and 1 Utama (p.335). Safe 'n Sound at 1 Utama stocks most well-known European and American brands, like Avent bottles and breastfeeding equipment, and Maclaren and Graco strollers and car seats. It also has its own products for beddings and mattresses.

For a complete range of middle to high-end leading world brands of quality nursery equipment, Planete Enfants megastore is the place to go. Go gaga over literally hundreds of models of strollers, car sets, high chairs and every other necessity you need for bringing up children. Some of the most prominent world brands are found here like Peg-Perego, Maxi Cosi, Maclaren, Playmobil, Philips Baby Care, Bebe Sounds

Retail Therapy

KL has some fab places to shop till you drop, but there are several other cities within easy reach where you can burn a hole in your pocket. Places like Singapore, Dubai and Hong Kong are all shopping hotspots that are not far away. Be sure to take along the relevant Mini Visitors' Guide – it packs in a surprising amount of info, yet it's small enough to fit in any designer handbag.

Baby Items

Anakku	Various Locations	See p.344	www.anakku.com
The Baby Loft	Desa Parkcity	03 6280 7633	www.thebabyloft.com
Baby Sasha & Mom	Online only	na	www.babysashanmom.com
Beverly Kids	Sunway Pyramid	03 7494 0525	na
Chicco	Various Locations	See p.345	www.chicco.com
Ladybird	Sunway Pyramid	03 5622 1823	na
Little Whiz	Online only	na	www.littlewhiz.com
Mia Bambina	Online only	na	http://miabambina.com
Modernmum	Various Locations	See p.348	www.modernmum.com.my
OshKosh B'Gosh	Suria KLCC	03 382 0810	www.oshkoshbgosh.com
Planete Enfants Malaysia	The Atria	03 7724 2424	www.planeteenfants.com.my
Safe 'n Sound	1 Utama	03 7726 8149	www.safensound.com.my
Wonder Tots	Sunway Pyramid	03 7492 0692	na
World of Cartoons & World of Babies	Various Locations	See p.351	na

and much more. Best of all, you can rest assured with their lifetime after-sales service. If you're too lazy to go mall crawling, you can always order with a mouse and click. There is a wealth of online baby stores for the mother who is too harried from chasing her bundle of joy round the house to trek around the shops. Little Whiz, a Malaysia-based online baby and children speciality store, offers a wide range of international brands like Avent, Maclaren, Peg Perego, Fisher-Price, Tommee Tippee, Chicco, Quinny, Evenflo, Safety 1st, Cosco, Leap Frog and many more.

At The Baby Loft, you can get your hands on Carter's and Got Milk brands, which can be a bit difficult to find in department stores. Keep a look out for great bargains at the Loft Exclusives, where you can get a GAP reversible blanket for only RM45.90 or a two-piece Got Milk Blue Onesies Set for only RM29.90. It also has a gift registry service. MiaBambina.com, which carries modern cloth diapers, nursing lingerie, and a range of baby clothing offers flat shipping rate to all over Malaysia at RM10.

Baby showers are popular but they may not be the kind you are accustomed at home. In Malaysia, the 'full moon celebration', which is organised one month after the baby's birth, is very popular especially among Chinese communities. Many bakeries can make full moon hampers which comprise cakes, local sweetmeats called ang koo, saffron glutinous rice and curry chicken.

Surf's up

Beachwear

Other options **Clothes** p.294, **Sports Goods** p.322

With miles of powder-white coastline, thousands of pretty tropical islands and year-round sunny blue skies, it's little wonder that beachwear is sold all year round.

There's swimwear for all shapes, budgets and tastes. Mainstream anchor tenant stores like Metrojaya (p.330), Jusco (p.329) and Parkson (p.330) stock a good range of popular international brands like Arena, Ogival, and Triumph. Specialist beachwear brands like Roxy, Quiksilver and

Beachwear

Arena	1Utama	03 7722 2737
Beach	1Utama	03 7710 8949
Billabong	Sunway Pyramid	03 7491 0597
Island Shop	1Utama	03 7727 8528
Modernmum	Various Locations	See p.348
Quiksilver	Various Locations	See p.349
Reef	KLCC	03 2166 8860
Roxy	Various Locations	See p.349
Sun Paradise	Sunway Pyramid	03 5636 6737
Women'secret	Various Locations	See p.351

Billabong have their own outlets at major malls. You can buy maternity swimwear at Modernmum. Prices and sales at these and other stores vary depending on the season.

If you're not particularly brand conscious, you can get some pretty trendy budget buys at The Street pedestrian mall at the weekend, where a popular beachwear stall retails bikinis for as little as RM39 a pair and recently even introduced made-to-order services.

True fashion-conscious sun worshippers like Beach for their stylish batik pareos that can double up as evening wear. *Cleo*, Malaysia's leading magazine for young women, has rated Women's Secret the best swimsuit boutique for its extensive selection of maillots, tankinis and bikinis. Prices for a bikini top start from RM129, and bikini bottoms upwards of RM69.

Bicycles

You can tell who the crazy people are in KL – they're the ones riding bicycles through the traffic. Kidding aside, you would have to have nerves of steel to take on KL's busy streets on a bike, what with trying to dodge the cars, buses and motorcycles, not to mention the fact that there are no bike lanes. However, in the more suburban areas and in certain recreational areas, bike riding is an enjoyable activity and it's always good to know where you can buy yourself a shiny new bike. If you like the idea of a bum-rattling ride over rocky, muddy terrain, see Cycling (Activities, p.226).

Bicycles

Kim Mun Bicycle	Taman Sri Sinar	03 6272 5530
Advance Bicycle Centre	Taman Sri Damansara	03 6272 4691
Bike-Pro Centre	Petaling Jaya	03 7805 1989
Choon Chen Fook	Jinjang Selatan Tambahan	03 6251 5989
Joo Ngan Bicycle Centre	Jalan Ampang	03 4257 5249
KSH Bicycle	Taman Tun Dr Ismail	03 7727 5173
Liew Yim Lan	Taman Desa Bakti	03 6137 8672
Liew Yoon Ngat	Salak Selatan	03 7982 7615
Syarikat Tak Seng	Taman Muda	03 4291 0464
Syarikat Weng Hong	Taman Kok Lian	03 6258 6252

Books

Other options **Libraries** p.245, **Second-Hand Items** p.318

Books in Malaysia are hardly the cheapest compared to other developing countries like India. No thanks to a weaker currency, English best-selling paperbacks typically go for a steep RM35 at least, and imported magazines cost upwards of RM20, the same price as a good meal in a nice restaurant.

That has not dampened the thriving literary spirit in Kuala Lumpur, nor has it stopped local authors from making it big overseas. Malaysians are very proud of Tash Aw, who was shortlisted for the Booker Prize for his book *The Harmony Silk Factory*.

If you want to get a foot into the community, join any of the active reading groups in Kuala Lumpur who regularly organise meetings, often graced by local and visiting foreign authors. Some of them are spearheaded by expatriates who have made Malaysia their home, most notably Sharon Bakar. For breaking news on the latest book readings, book recommendations, or just to find out who's who in the Malaysian literati, visit her blog at www.thebookaholic.blogspot.com.

Book retailers in Malaysia comprise both mega chainstores like MPH, Borders, Times and Popular, as well as independent shops like Silverfish and Skoob. With ample retail space and financial backing at their disposal, the book chains offer a holistic reading experience by outfitting their stores with cafes (Starbucks at Borders), comfortable sofas and benches for browsers, and increasingly, a CD section with listening posts. They also do pre-ordering. Most book stores offer extensive English and Malay titles, since these are Malaysia's second and first languages respectively. If you are into Chinese, revision books and cookbooks, Malaysian-Singapore chain Popular Book Store is your best bet. For Japanese anime and art books, Kinokuniya at KLCC, the local branch of Japan's largest bookstore chain, is the undisputed leader.

For a more intimate atmosphere and the occasional conversation with like-minded individuals, independent shops like Silverfish are your best bet. It is a gold mine of cultural theory, and periodicals that would satisfy the most erudite Dostoyevsky-quoting literati.

With increased governmental focus, more and more options are available to the reading public. Kinokuniya and Arthur's Books have offered value-added services like online book ordering. The rest of the country envies Kuala Lumpur for the presence of Pay Less Books, which sells a host of books from mainstream best-sellers to hard-to-get niche books, at prices that will send the bibliophile into an ecstatic tailspin. Don't forget to visit The Specialist Bookshop, which has a good range of theological texts.

Various Locations ◀ ## MPH Bookstores

See p.348 | *www.mph.com.my*

Founded by Captain W. G. Shellabear in 1890, Malaya Publishing House (MPH) is Malaysia's leading bookshop chain with about 19 stores in the Klang Valley alone. It stocks a vast variety of books ranging from topics as diverse as horticulture, psychology and life science through to literary criticism. The main stores like the one in Mid Valley Megamall are very reader friendly, with designated special areas like a professional enclave with chairs, 'courtyards' that are like indoor gardens, and a Kidzone that often doubles as a venue for shows, performances and workshops – all in the name of inculcating the reading habit. Its flagship store in Mid Valley Megamall spans a sprawling 36,000 feet and is equipped with PCs so you can search by title, author or ISBN. MPH also offers a host of special services like gift wrapping, doorstep delivery and pre-orders. Becoming a member entitles you to additional savings and promotions. Check the website regularly for the store's event schedule as current and well-known authors frequently give readings.

Various Locations ◀ ## Pay Less Books

See p.349 | *www.paylessbooks.com.my*

Pay Less Books' Warehouse Sales are the most eagerly-anticipated event for all budget-conscious bibliophiles. First set up in The Summit Subang USJ in 2001, before it expanded to five book stores, it has grown into Malaysia's largest used book retailer and was even endorsed by the *Guinness Book of Records*. It sells a phenomenal range of used English books at cheap prices – from antique books like *Frankenstein* or the *Modern Prometheus*, to rare treasures like one of 1,500 numbered copies signed by Everett Henry. Pay Less Books at Ampang Point is particularly noted for children's used books. Online purchase is also available now to fans. And if you self-collect, shipping charges are waived.

Bangsar ◀

Silverfish Books

03 2284 4837 | *www.silverfishbooks.com*

Silverfish Books is both a book boutique and Malaysia's leading publisher of postcolonial and world literature. Every book is produced to the highest standards (albeit in paperback form, due to cost) using wood-free paper. Established in 1999 it emphasises more 'esoteric' subjects like literature, philosophy and Malaysiana. Bona fide book lovers gravitate to Silverfish Books for its eclectic titles as well as to consult its charismatic founder on recommendations and writing advice. To quote Raman, 'We avoid 'management' and 'self-help' books (unless they are exceptionally well written) because we think they are the 'Coca-Cola' of the book world – useless but addictive'. It stocks many titles that cannot be found in any of the mega stores – in fact, not even on Amazon.com. So passionate are its owners about propagating reading that they will deliver online orders free to Malaysian addresses and charge a nominal $4 (by registered airmail) to international destinations.

6-2 Second Floor ◀
Jalan 31/70A
Desa Sri Hartamas
🚇 *Bangsar*

Trisha & Sasha Children Bookstore

03 2300 4399 | *www.trishansasha.com.my*

Trisha & Sasha Children Bookstore opened its door to the community of Klang Valley in July 2000. It is possibly the first and only specialised children's bookstore in Malaysia. Trisha & Sasha was set up to address the problem of getting a range of good quality children's books. It's based on the belief that thousands of good children's books have been mistakenly parked as adult classics, and with this in mind there are plenty of well-selected quality books for babies and toddlers, picture books for pre-school children, stories for early readers, and chapter and series books for teenagers. Reading programmes are also available, and free storytelling sessions and parenting talks are also on offer.

Books		
Arthur's Books	www.arthursbooks.com	na
Borders	Various Locations	See p.344
Kinokuniya	KLCC	03 2164 8133
MPH	Various Locations	See p.348
Pay Less Books	Various Locations	See p.349
Popular Book Store	Various Locations	See p.349
Silverfish Books	Bangsar	03 2284 4837
Skoob Books	Jalan Othman, Petaling Jaya	03 7770 2500
The Specialist Bookshop	Suria KLCC	03 2166 3433
Times Bookshop	Various Locations	See p.350
Trisha & Sasha Children Bookstore	Jalan 31/70A, Desa Sri Hartamas	03 2300 4399

Camera Equipment

Other options **Electronics & Home Appliances** p.298

Camera shops are widely found in malls and tourist areas. Even remote residential areas big or small will have at least one film-processing shop which sells entry-level models. All major brands like Nikon, Canon, Ricoh, Fuji and Sony are well represented in Malaysia. Most shops offer digital photo transfers onto CD (RM10) and print services (29 sen upwards depending on promotional period).

User-friendly point-and-shoot digital models dominate 'mass consumer' areas in hypermarkets and electronics shops. Prices here are lower than their counterparts in Europe and the US. In the past, Singapore was said to offer attractive prices and a wider range, but with market globalisation today the prices are fairly equal.

Notable video camera equipment chains and shops include Foto Shangri-La and Fotokem. Engtong sells Cokin filters and tripods. Digicolor is a good source of third party camera accessories. Applied Imaging sells a good selection of Pro Lab products . Those in the inner circle know that the best hunting ground for camera bargains is in Pudu. If you're willing to brave its relative seediness, you can get great new and second-hand cameras at Keat Camera (on the side of Pudu Jail) and YL Camera at Pudu Plaza. Online shopping is also available. One intrepid Malaysian set up www.shashinki.com. Highly recommended, it ships anywhere in the world and best of all, its products come with an international warranty as standard. Do note that most local stores offer local warranty only, or that they have to send the defective product back to the original manufacturer for servicing, so you may have to wait quite a bit.

www.photomalaysia.com is a good site for shutterbugs, offering you plenty of insider tips on photography, and it regularly organises outings. Although there are no written laws on what you can or cannot photograph or video, use your discretion in religious places. When in doubt ask for permission.

Camera Equipment

Applied Imaging	Taman Tun Dr Ismail	03 7727 5511
Bintang Maju	Maju Junction	03 2692 9166
Digicolor House of Photographic Equipment	Complex Mutiara, Jalan Ipoh	03 6250 7782
Engtong Systems	Jalan SS2/30	03 7875 5211
Foto Shangri La	Various Locations	See p.346
Fotokem	Various Locations	See p.346
Keat Camera Service	Jalan Pudu	03 2148 0447
Key Color	Mid Valley Megamall	03 2282 8960
Selangor Photographers	Pertama Complex	03 2691 7745
ShaShinki	www.shashinki.com	na
YL camera Service	Plaza Pudu	03 2148 7810

Car Parts & Accessories

Where there are cars, there is always a need for car accessories and parts. Eneos (a Japanese chain) in 1 Utama is popular for car accessories. The prices are decent but the range and quality may not be the best. It's the only one worth mentioning in a large mall. For cheap car accessories, you can visit any one of many Brothers outlets spread throughout the Klang Valley, though quality is questionable.

The best place to look for car accessories is Jalan PJS 11/7 in Bandar Sunway (next to the college). This one stretch of road boasts more car shops than anywhere else in Kuala Lumpur or Selangor, and you can find anything you will ever need, from tyres to sound systems to accessories. Due the competition there prices are also usually quite good.

KK Lau in Jalan SS3/59E is well known for stereos. He's won quite a few car stereo competitions and does good work but isn't the cheapest around. Sports rims enthusiasts go to Hupshun Tyres in Jalan PJS 11/7 (Sunway), for its wide range of tyres and wheels at decent prices, too. For tinted windows, everyone gives at least a five-year warranty. True-blue car lovers rave about the quality of workmanship at Sound

Car Parts & Accessories

Brothers	Ampang Plaza	03 4251 1536
Eneos Car Centre	1Utama	03 7726 2777
Giant Ace	Various Locations	See p.346
Hupshun Tyres	11, Jalan PJS 11/7, Bandar Sunway	03 5632 9926
Kakimotor	Mid Valley	03 2282 2118
KK Lau Car Audio Specialist	20 & 22, Lorong SS 3/59E	03 7877 2293
Sound View Auto Accessories	86, Jalan SS 24/2, Taman Megah	03 7805 2889

View Auto Accessories in Jalan SS24/2. When you have car trouble, fear not as there is a very strong AAM presence in Malaysia. They are linked to AAA and other overseas Automobile Associations. The coverage is cheap and most locals renew their member ship without fail every year.

Carpets

Other options **Bargaining** p.283, **Souvenirs** p.320

Carpets are to Middle Easterners what the Rolex represents to Malaysians – enduring value that increases over time. The mushrooming of carpet stores around Kuala Lumpur is a testament to this growing awareness. Although the majority of luxury carpets (read hand-knotted Middle Eastern types) are exported from overseas, their prices are one of the region's cheapest. The answer: local rentals are low, a quarter of what a similar space would fetch in say, Singapore, or Australia. Labour is competitive, and carpets are duty free items. Almost every carpet shop owner will brag that theirs is 'the biggest and offers the widest range', so it makes sense for you to check them out. Most of them are located in prime shopping belts anyway.

Nasim Carpets, which opens up to Jalan Maarof in Bangsar, is like a veritable Aladdin's Cave, featuring a dazzling array of carpets handpicked by the owner, who personally goes from village to village in Iran to select them. He makes it even easier for customers now by offer to deliver samples directly to your residence, look at decor and give his recommendations on how best to flatter your living space.

If the customer is too busy to go to the store, Flying Carpets will bring them to the customer's home. Even a traditional industry moves with the times. Browse through the collection at your own leisure, and with help from specialists you can customise carpets based on your room dimensions, desired

Carpets		
Abbas Nishaburi	The Ampwalk, Jalan Ampang	03 2166 3775
Carpet-Inn	Plaza Ampang	03 2770 0788
Flying Carpets	City Square	03 2166 5510
Kohimaran	Mid Valley	03 4256 9060
Malik's	Jalan 17/13A, Petaling Jaya	03 7956 5403
Nasim Carpets	Jalan Maarof, Bangsar	03 2093 8786
Persian Collections	Desa Sri Hartamas	03 2300 6966
Persian Design	Dataran Palma, Jalan Damai	03 4270 1332
Shalini Carpets	Jalan TAR, Little India	03 2692 7008
Udani Carpets	Jalan TAR, Little India	03 2698 1962
Ziba Carpets	Taman Kosas, Ampang	019 225 3969

size (just make sure you factor in obstacles in the room such as columns and floor air vents). Then voila, the appropriate item will be emailed to you directly, with optional higher resolution and close-up photos for you to peruse before you make your purchasing decision.

Other noteworthy options are Kohimaran at Mid Valley, which has diversified as a lifestyle store and sells clothes and other decorative items. Carpet-Inn, and Persian Collections are noted for their expert washing and repairing services. Udani Carpets and Shalini Carpets, both on Jalan Tuanku Abdul Rahman, also have a pretty extensive range.

Cars

Other options **Buying a Vehicle** p.148

Cars are taxed up to 300% in Malaysia, so expect a vehicle to cost as much as four times the price as in most western countries. That said, fuel is much cheaper – especially compared with Europe – as is insurance, parking and labour rates for repair work, meaning that, overall, it can actually work out cheaper to buy and operate a car here than in your home country. Petrol starts at about RM2 per litre.

Although most major brands are available, the range of models is reduced to reflect the relatively small market. The biggest-selling models are those produced by two Malaysian companies, Proton and Perodua, which enjoy some tax breaks that enable them to price their vehicles lower than most foreign cars. If you are looking for a premium European locally assembled car you will have to choose a model by Mercedes, BMW, Volvo or Audi. BMW and Mercedes are the most popular European brands, while the Japanese companies Toyota and Honda are also favourites.

The risk of buying a fully imported model is in finding places to service it and getting spare parts. Some companies which import cars have a reasonably good servicing network while other sellers (particularly those selling imported second-hand cars) expect you to find your own place to service the car.

In terms of resale value, Japanese cars will always hold their price better than European cars, with Toyota topping the charts. Similarly, you can expect Toyotas to cost the most (relative to new price) to purchase second hand. It's worth remembering that Malaysian car import duties are among the highest in the world. Most cars come with up to three years' warranty, covering parts and labour. This is what is known in the US as a 'bumper-to-bumper' warranty, meaning it covers everything between the front and rear bumper. Extended warranty packages are not available, unlike in most western countries. Whether or not you can ship a Malaysian-registered car overseas would depend on the import regulations of the destination country.

Due to the high price of new cars and poor selection of models actually brought in by local distributors, there is a large grey import market (imports sold at a lower than standard price), especially for high-end luxury and performance cars. Most second-hand car dealers are also grey importers, offering two to three-year-old used cars from Japan and the UK at attractive prices. Locals always recommend buying from private owners as they are the most reliable and you get the best value for money from them.

Clothes

Other options **Beachwear** p.288, **Lingerie** p.310, **Tailoring** p.323, **Sports Goods** p.322, **Shoes** p.319,

From delicate silk cheongsams to rugged jeans and stylish ball gowns, Kuala Lumpur has something for every taste, occasion and budget. It has everything you could possibly need in its independent retail outlets, shopping malls and department stores. Parkson (p.330) and Jaya Jusco (p.347) carry their own in-house fashion brands as well as popular local and international labels. But if you're keen on something more exclusive, it's worth checking out the huge number of independent boutiques scattered around Klang Valley.

Petite & Plus Sizes

The petite needn't worry about ransacking the children's department to fulfil their fashion needs. In fact, many standalone boutiques that carry the latest fashions from Hong Kong, Korea and Taiwan are dominated by XS to M sizes. Conversely, the well-endowed may have some trouble finding clothes that fit here. . Fret not; Kuala Lumpur has a growing number of fashion retailers that cater to the fuller figured. You won't have trouble finding international labels like Marks & Spencer and Liz Claiborne at major shopping malls. Also very popular with the well-endowed is Ms. Read. This homegrown retail chain, which also operates a chain of cafes under the names Dlish and Delicious (p.366), offers

Rent Some Posh Threads
If you're more of a shorts and T-shirt person, and your idea of getting dressed up is pulling on a pair of jeans, you probably don't have a fancy suit or tux stored in the back of your wardrobe for special occasions. You can hire one from the Dynasty Formalwear Centre in the Campbell Complex on Jalan Dang Wangi – call 03 2698 3195.

well-cut clothes that flatter figures ranging from size 12 to 24. For a nominal fee, you can also request alterations.

Designer Labels

The hardcore designer fiend will find Kuala Lumpur's swanky shopping malls a godsend. Most major brands and fashion labels are represented here. Capitalising on an increasingly affluent middle class, all major malls have at least a few designer boutiques in their premises, though Suria KLCC (p.341), Starhill (p.341), Gardens (p.337) and Pavilion (p.340) have arguably more per inch of floor space than others. Starhill, with opulent surroundings that might intimidate the less well-heeled, is the least crowded and offers a more private shopping experience. Fashion devotees can't get enough of the posh Bangsar Village II, which offers shoppers previously unavailable luxury labels like Ted Baker, Warehouse, French Connection and Raoul.

Exclusive brands

Everyday Clothes

T-shirts that equal a month's salary may not be everybody's cup of tarik, but budget-friendly doesn't mean compromising on looking good either. There are plenty of trendy and affordable fashion retailers that flatter your looks without breaking your bank. From anchor tenants that carry in-house brands, to fashion retailers that have an outlet in every shopping mall, you have plenty to choose from: Giordano, Seed, Voir, Colours, P & Co, MNG, Zara, Esprit, British India, Somerset Bay, East India Company … the list is never-ending. Trendy people go gaga over one-stop fashion megastore Nichi Fashion City; chic print dresses start from as low as RM50, while body-hugging knits retail from RM20. Bargain hunters will also love Factory Outlet Store in KL Plaza; get designer jeans in near-flawless condition at a steal, and collar T-shirts and working shirts for between RM29 and RM39. Yuppies love the Padini Concept Store for its sensible workwear; a smart grey linen skirt goes for RM70 and lined jacket for RM129 upwards. If you're willing to fork out a 50% to 100% more, an investment in Edmundser is worth considering for its impeccable tailoring.

Boutique Shopping

Is your biggest nightmare bumping into somebody wearing an identical little black dress? Then how about foraging the many hip boutiques that offer one-off, eclectic pieces at wallet-friendly prices? Shop till you drop in the Jalan Telawi area, the same road that houses Bangsar Village. The area has taken shopaholics by storm with the mushrooming of narrow, quaint boutiques bearing kitschy names like Cats Whiskers and Blook, and carry largely knockoffs but also original designs sourced from Asian fashion hotspots Hong Kong, Korea and Taiwan. Stepping into one of these is like entering a different universe. Cluttered with pastel floral-inspired wallpaper, dramatic candelabras, whimsical lace-trimmed lamps and luxurious velvet armchairs, you'll be forgiven for thinking you've just stepped into an English 18th century ladies' drawing room or a gothic setting in the *Phantom*

Clothes		
Armani	Various Locations	See p.344
Blook	Various Locations	See p.344
British India	Various Locations	See p.344
Calvin Klein	1Utama	03 7726 4292
Carrefour	Various Locations	See p.345
Christian Dior	Various Locations	See p.345
Coast	Bangsar Village II	03 2287 5578
Colours	Various Locations	See p.345
DKNY	Various Locations	See p.345
Dorothy Perkins	Various Locations	See p.345
East India Company	1 Utama	03 7726 2072
Edmundser	Mid Valley	03 2938 3238
Elle	Various Locations	See p.346
Esprit	Various Locations	See p.346
F.O.S.	1Utama	03 7722 5382
Forever 21	Various Locations	See p.346
French Connection	1 Utama	03 7725 0699
Furry Tailes	Dataran Sunway	03 6141 7068
G2000	1Utama	03 7726 4892
GAP	1Utama	03 7726 1255
GAP Kids/Baby Gap	Mid Valley	03 2287 0382
Giordano	Various Locations	See p.346
Guess	Various Locations	See p.346
Isetan	Lot 10	03 2141 7777
Jaya Jusco	Various Locations	See p.347
Levi's	Various Locations	See p.347
Liz Claiborne	1Utama	03 7726 2313
Marks & Spencer	Various Locations	See p.348
Miss Selfridge	Various Locations	See p.348
MNG	Various Locations	See p.348
MS. READ	Various Locations	See p.348
Naf Naf	Mid Valley Mega Mall	03 2282 1318
Nichi Fashion City	178-3, Jalan Sungei Besi	03 9221 6052
P & Co	Mid Valley Megamall	03 2938 3098
Padini	Various Locations	See p.348
Parkson	Various Locations	See p.348
Raoul	Mid Valley Megamall	03 2287 4942
Salabianca	Various Locations	See p.349
Seed	Various Locations	See p.350
Somerset Bay	1Utama	03 7726 2119
Ted Baker	Bangsar Village II	03 2287 1806
Timberland	Mid Valley Megamall	03 2283 1180
Top Shop	Various Locations	See p.350
Travel All	Various Locations	See p.350
Universal Traveller	Various Locations	See p.351
Voir	Mid Valley Megamall	03 2284 8344
Warehouse	1Utama	03 7725 7929
Zara	Mid Valley	03 2287 1517

of the Opera. The enterprising proprietors even provide sofas and lifestyle magazines to entertain the long-suffering boyfriends and husbands. While Jalan Telawi still holds court as indie boutique capital of KL, Damansara Uptown and Dataran Sunway, five minutes away from Mutiara Damansara, are beginning to offer serious competition.

High Street Shopping

Malaysians have embraced high street labels like Topshop and Miss Selfridge, judging from the fact outlets are being opened in virtually every mall. Think twice before splurging on that sequined Topshop tunic though – you can probably get it cheaper back home. Why not indulge your inner adventurer and head out to Sungei Wang Plaza, a treasure trove of cutting edge and funky fashions? If the humungous crowd deters you, still under-the-radar Cineleisure in Mutiara Damansara offers a quieter shopping experience without compromising on range and variety. For the ultimate fashion-cum-social statement, treat yourself to any of Graffi Tee's wide range of Japanese shirts emblazoned with graphics, feel-good slogans and provocative messages. A T-shirt with silver stencils goes for RM70.

Men's Fashion

Not to be outdone, men's fashion is equally well covered in Kuala Lumpur. For off-the-peg well-cut men's shirts, sharp jackets and tailored trousers, you can't go wrong with G2000, while U2 has a great selection of casual wear in linen and cotton. Levi's Dockers are a popular choice with men who want to exude understated elegance. For that all-important Christmas vacation trip back home, get your winter essentials like boots, cardigans, scarves and thermal undergarments at P. Lal Store (p.296), the city's oldest department store. Alternatively, try Travel All (1 Utama), and Universal Traveller for its budget-friendly sweaters, mufflers and parkas.

62 Jalan 8/91
Taman Shamelin Perkasa

Melium Outlet

03 9207 3288

Where can you enjoy posh surroundings, flawless service and most importantly, designer goods for a song? Melium Outlet is a happy bargaining ground for all designer divas who don't mind end-of-season stocks (still in pristine condition). Located about 10 minutes' drive from KLCC, this discount warehouse is a pleasure to browse through, its garments neatly displayed on racks and shelves. Furla handbags from RM700, Stuart Weitzman shoes at RM250, Ermenegildo Zegna suits at RM2,000 and shirts from RM400? Whip out that credit card!

Computers

Other options **Electronics & Home Appliances** p.298

In Kuala Lumpur, you don't have to pay RM10 for designer coffee to surf the net; you can hotfoot over to 24 hour mamak coffee shops and get online for one-tenth of the price. The country's fascination with information technology certainly has grown, with Dell, HP, IBM and Lenovo setting up call centres and manufacturing hubs in Malaysia. Even Apple is rapidly increasing its network of authorised resellers like Machines and EpiCentre. Apple fans will love EpiCentre, the biggest consumer retail centre for Apple products, which offers things such as data backup and software updates.

There are a number of shopping malls completely dedicated to everything that beeps, clicks or has a microprocessor, but the big daddy of them all is definitely Low Yat Plaza at Bukit Bintang. This IT retail hub boasts seven labyrinthine floors of shops selling a staggering array of competitively priced gadgetry. Bargaining is rife and frantic (and expected). Many stores also offer their services to assemble the parts a customer

Computers

Digital Mall	Section 14, PJ	03 7958 2636	www.digitalmall.net.my
EpiCentre	Pavillion Shopping Centre	03 2141 6378	na
House of Notebooks	Various Locations	See p.347	www.houseofnotebooks.com.my
IT World	Mid Valley	03 2938 8000	www.it-world.com.my
Low Yat Plaza	Jalan Alor	03 2148 5141	www.lowyat.net
Machines	Mid Valley Megamall	03 2282 3996	www.machines.com.my

purchases. Having said that, a lot of the products are dubious grey imports. Also, remember that it is better to pay in cash unless you do not mind being charged an extra 3% on top of the price of the product when using a credit card. Digital Mall is another place with numerous IT outlets – you'll often find the store that is right for you through word of mouth or just by luck.

Intensive Care For Your PC
Everyone has experienced that horrible sinking feeling when your computer crashes and you remember you've never got around to backing everything up. Call 'Surgeon Fuad' and he will bring his PC Surgeon 'Mobile Operating Theatre' to your house to fix your poorly PC. Like any good surgeon, he's on call 24 hours a day, seven days a week. Call 016 357 4622.

IT World and Digital Mall are comparatively more streamlined and less chaotic. Multiple access routes via the Federal Highway, as well as the city's Inner and Middle Ring Roads and dedicated LRT service, make them fairly popular among Petaling Jaya residents. There are also specialist shops. House of Notebooks stocks laptops and laptop accessories exclusively. Coverage for computer products generally follows the manufacturer's warranty. PIKOM's PC Fair (03 7955 2922, www.pikom. org.my) which takes place three times a year, is a great place for bargain hunting, especially on the last day.

Electronics & Home Appliances
Other options **Camera Equipment** p.291, **Computers** p.297

From the humble electric shaver to 52 inch LCD TVs, electronics are a staple of the KL retail sector. You won't find western household names like GE, RCA or Maytag as the local market is dominated by Japanese, Korean and Chinese brand names like Sony, Samsung, Toshiba, Hitachi, LG and Sharp. Electronic goods prices used to be a little higher in Singapore and Hong Kong, but with the advent of globalisation, the difference is marginal, although Malaysia still loses out in terms of the latest models, which tend to arrive only three or four months after they debut elsewhere. While there is no shortage of international electronics megastores like Harvey Norman and Courts Mammoth, you might want to check out local chain

Electronics & Home Appliances

Best Denki	Various Locations	See p.344	na
CMY Sound & Vision	Sunway Pyramid	03 7492 8551	www.cmy.com.my
Courts Mammoth	Various Locations	See p.345	www.courts.com.my
Harvey Norman	Ikano Power Centre	03 7718 5200	www.harveynorman.com.au
Hock Sin Leong	Various Locations	See p.347	www.hslg.com.my
Senheng Electric	Various Locations	na	www.senheng.com.my

stores. They stock the latest Hi-Fi equipment, flat screen LCD television sets, gas and electric ovens, washing machines and even computers. Prices are lower by as much as 15%, attractive payment schemes are available, and they're as common as coffee shops – the area SS2 alone has more than a dozen electronics and electrical shops. It is easy to detect them – they often engage in fierce price wars and almost unfailingly bear Chinese-sounding names like Senheng or Hock Sin Leong (HSL). HSL has a huge outlet in Subang Parade as well. Warranty is very much dependent on the manufacturer rather than the retailer, although sometimes stores may offer extended warranty from between five and 10 years on parts, or service warranty, or both. Just make sure you check the terms and conditions on your warranty card at the point of purchase. You can take electronics items overseas depending on voltage. Electrical outlets are rated at 220v, 50 cycles and serve three-pin, flat-pronged plugs. American products do not work here but most supermarkets stock adaptors for about RM50. Unlike the west, second-hand goods aren't popular in Malaysia. Most locals would rather purchase brand new goods unless they inherit them from the previous owner. But you can get second-hand items from people who are moving, who advertise on supermarket noticeboards and in community convenience stores like 7-Eleven, as well as newspapers like *The Star*.

Eyewear

There are plenty of independent stores that stock a good range of eyewear, as well as eyewear chains. The government requires every optical store to have at least one qualified optometrist in the premises, so rest assured, your eyes are in good hands. Because of the huge number of shops, it is quite common to come across store banners or newspaper ads declaring whopping discounts of 90%, or offers of 'free lenses' with every purchase of frames. Even if there isn't any formal sale, try your luck and ask for a 'best price'. Most proprietors are amenable to an additional 5% to 10% off the display price. Focus Point, England and Optical 88 have branches in shopping malls as well as residential areas. England has the biggest number of outlets in the country but prices at Focus Point are known to be lower. A pair of no-frills frames plus prescription lenses can start from as cheap as RM100.

Price increases depend on the cost of the frame and add-ons like UV protection and tinting. Optical stores stock most leading brands of contact lens like Bausch & Lomb, Johnson & Johnson, Acuvue and Boston, with prices beginning from RM45 for

See clearly...

a three-month supply of SofLens 38. It's worth checking out a few shops before making your purchase, especially if you are buying for more than one month's supply. Again, most shops can be cajoled into giving some discount if you buy in bulk, which means anything from three months' supply upwards. Most opticians will do an eye test for free. Should you run out of contact lens solution and no eyewear shop is in sight, fear not. They can be easily obtained at personal care stores like Watson's and most pharmacies. In Malaysia's sunny weather, you'll need a good pair of sunglasses to protect yourself against ultraviolet

Eyewear

Cool Shades	Various Locations	See p.345
D'Image	Mid Valley Megamall	03 2284 3266
EGO	LL2-K-7, Lower Level, Sunway Pyramid	03 5638 0205
England Optical Group	Various Locations	See p.346
Focus Point	Various Locations	See p.346
La Trend Optical	Various Locations	See p.347
Optical 88	Various Locations	See p.348
Pro Vision Express Optical	Sunway Pyramid	03 7492 5336

rays. While you can get a pair of trendy shades for as little as RM10 at street bazaars such as Petaling Street and flea markets, more discerning consumers gravitate towards legitimate optical shops, which stock mostly international brands like Rayban, Oakley, DKNY, Armani and Versace. Cool Shades and D'Image are two sunglass specialists reputed to have a bigger collection than most.

Flowers
Other options **Gardens** p.302

Stuck for gift ideas? There's always the trusty bouquet to fall back on. In Kuala Lumpur, there are plenty of florists with a flurry of imaginative arrangements. Every special occasion you can think of is catered for, from weddings and funerals to Teachers' Day, but beware – prices tend to soar during peak seasons like Valentine's Day. Competition is so stiff – a good thing for customers – that many florists have diversified by bundling their packages with gifts that range from soft toys, to Asian health products. Sunflower, for example, has 'health baskets' or metal baskets filled with Asian health products like snow jelly with ginseng. While some prefer to drop

Flowers

AiFLORiST.com	Petaling Jaya	03 7987 9028	www.aiflorist.com
All Ninety Nine Flowers	Bandar Sunway	03 5631 5877	www.malaysiaflower.com
Bloom	Ikano Power Centre	03 7722 4429	na
Blooming.com	Kelana Business Centre	03 7803 3333	www.blooming.com.my
Eric Choong Flowers	Jalan Telawi 3	03 2283 2113	www.ericchoong.com
Fiori	Bandar Park	03 7987 8888	www.fiori.com.my
Love.com.my	Persiaran Syed Putra 3	03 2272 2222	www.love.com.my
one red lily	Jalan Telawi 6	1800 885 459	www.oneredlily.com
Pure Seed Florist & Gift	Jalan Sultan Ismail	03 2026 2328	www.pureseed.com.my
Sunflower Gifts Boutique	Merdeka Square	03 7954 6686	www.sunflowergifts.com.my
Touch of Eden Florist	Wisma Central	03 2161 6270	www.touchofeden.com

by the physical shop and custom-order a more personalised arrangement, many homegrown florists have taken their business online, and you can order by phone or through the website, and pay with your credit card. International deliveries are also becoming made possible both through global networks like Interflora, and homegrown enterprises like www.blooming.com.my. Pure Seed is a hot favourite for its creative twists on the traditional arrangement. Speedy service is also increasingly becoming a norm in the race to lure customers. If you're in a hurry to spring a last-minute surprise on your sweetheart, www.love.com accepts orders right up until 15:00 for same-day delivery.

Babywear p.98
Bank Loans p.22

Written by residents, these unique guidebooks are packed with insider info, from arriving in a new destination to making it your home and everything in between.

Explorer Residents' Guides
We Know Where You Live

Gardens

Other options **Flowers** p.300, **Hardware & DIY** p.304

With at least six hours of sunshine a day, and an average annual rainfall of 80 inches, it is relatively easy to turn a bare patch into your private eden in the blink of an eye. The best hunting grounds are located out of the city centre, especially in Sungai Buloh, that long belt of road a couple of miles north of shopping hub Mutiara Damansara. There are more saplings per metre here than in any other part of Kuala Lumpur. Other than actual plants, you can obtain a whole gamut of gardening essentials like flower pots, nursery soil, gravels, and so on. Beginners should hotfoot here before descending on hardware hypermarts such as Ace Hardware, which tend to stock more 'professional' materials. The nurseries are run by experienced gardeners who are more than happy to share handy tips, from the right soil for your sunflower plant, to advising you which insecticide to use.

Gardens		
Beleaf Natural	Mid Valley Megamall	03 9368 3023
Chia Nursery	Taman Bukit Maluri	03 6276 4106
Courtyard	Jalan Ampang	03 2163 2868
Damansara Nursery	Jalan Damansara	03 7728 4030
Evergreen Trading & Nursery	Jalan Bukit Lagong	03 6156 2766
Fui Sun Garden	Petaling Jaya	03 7782 6930
Giant Ace	Various Locations	See p.346
Hua May Nursery	Wilayah Persekutuan	03 7981 2278
Ideal Nurseries & Landscaping Designers Sdn Bhd	Puchong	03 8061 1407
Lee Nursery & Bonsai Centre	Jalan Puchong Mukim Petaling	012 378 8761
Nature Décor	Shah Alam	03 7845 0368
RCP Technologies	Kajang	03 8736 9254
Rim Nursery	Sungai Buloh	03 6157 2406
Sungai Buloh Settlement Council	Sungai Buloh	03 6156 1321
Syarikat Kebun Bunga Ah Loke	Sungai Buloh	03 6156 1562
Wellgrow Horticultural Centre	Sungai Buloh	03 6156 2453

There are several gardening hardware superstores that cater to the needs of the professional. Ace Hardware stocks clever tools that you are unlikely to find in nurseries, alongside more conventional articles like flower seedlings (such as the persian carpet dwarf variety) and coconut husk hanging pots. Fix-It is a smaller outfit here but gives Ace a run for its money with its more diversified selection of professional and niche garden tools.

You can get basic stone garden furniture from nurseries but for more aesthetic choices, there are quite a few landscaping stores that can provide you with plenty of ideas for your patch of pride and joy. Courtyard sources stunning designer garden furniture from exotic Vietnam and Thailand, and offers a comprehensive tailor-made design service as well. Nature Décor covers the whole nine yards from initial concept to final completion and can help you with design concept, budget estimation, and site evaluation so that your landscape design realises its fullest potential.

Gifts

With KL's many festivals, you don't need to wait for Christmas to play Santa Claus. From major festive seasons like Chinese New Year and Hari Raya, to more intimate occasions like Valentine's Day and baby showers, there's always an excuse to make someone smile with a thoughtful gift. Don't be caught out turning up at a party with

Gifts

Adam Shahir	www.adamshahir.com	03 4253 2946
Arch	Various Locations	See p.344
Aseana	Suria KLCC	03 2382 9988
Chocolate Mousse	www.mychocolatemousse.com	03 6201 3969
Crystal Corner	Suria KLCC	03 2164 8868
D'Nata	Suria KLCC	03 2382 0271
Davidoff	Suria KLCC	03 2162 2787
Fennel	Mid Valley	03 9368 3383
Gaby Gift Shop	www.gabygiftshop.com	03 7491 8050
Gift Land	Sunway Pyramid	03 7492 6553
Hinode Shop	Various Locations	See p.347
Is Souvenirs	Suria KLCC	03 2382 0757
Legacy	Suria KLCC	03 2171 1851
Living Cabin	Various Locations	See p.348
Lovely Lace	Various Locations	See p.348
Lysha Flora	Suria KLCC	03 2382 0599
Memory Lane	Various Locations	See p.348
Mont Blanc	Suria KLCC	03 2166 2886
Precious Thots	Various Locations	See p.349
Risis Gift Gallery	Suria KLCC	03 2164 2820
Royal Selangor	Various Locations	See p.349
S & J Gift & Collection	Sunway Pyramid	03 7491 0855
Sunflower Gifts Boutique	Merdeka Square	03 7954 6686
Teddy Tales	Suria KLCC	03 2382 0349

just a 'bunch of bananas' (a local colloquial term meaning 'empty handed'). There are many places in KL selling wonderful gifts such as pens, desk accessories and decorative items for the home. Bringing a food gift is acceptable, although if you want to take alcohol, such as a bottle of wine, it is always best to check with the host whether there are any Muslims there who may be offended by such a gift. Walk into any big department store for a huge range of ideas, or if you're looking for something more specialised there are plenty of niche gift shops in the city. The exquisite (though not cheap) knick-knacks at Risis and Royal Selangor Pewter are lovely, while specialist shops like S & J, Living Cabin, Lovely Lace and Teddy Tales do brisk business all year round among children and teenagers for their affordable range of imaginative stationery, mugs, decorative items, and soft toys.

The concept of gift registry has not quite caught on in the local shopping malls, but a number of enterprising Malaysians have brought the idea to KL. Chocolate Mousse (www.mychocolatemousse.com) and Sunflower Gifts (www.sunflowergifts.com.my) are two popular gift registry websites that double up as online florists. For last minute shopping, try online store Gaby Gift Shop that offers free delivery.

Then of course there's always that old safe bet – the gift voucher. Major department stores such as Parkson and Jusco, food chains and bookshops offer gift vouchers in a range of denominations for the thrifty to the extravagant.

Klick A Gift

Klick A Gift is an online shopping site specialising in gifts – they focus heavily on baby gifts, kids' items, jewellery and home decor, although other gifts are available as well. They have regular special offers and if you need gift delivered in a hurry, it's worth browsing the site. www.klickagift.com.

Handbags

A girl can't have enough shoes… or handbags. If that is your mantra, then you've come to the right city. From beaded Chinoiserie purses to elegant Kelly bags, there is an incredible array of stores dedicated to selling gorgeous handbags. Fashion specialists like Bonita, Diva and Vincci carry a good range of evening bags for clubbing and weekend outings; a sequinned bag at Bonita goes for RM169 without discount. If you aren't particularly

Handbags		
Bonita	Various Locations	See p.344
Carrefour	Various Locations	See p.345
Coach	Various Locations	See p.345
Diva	Various Locations	See p.345
Giant	Various Locations	See p.346
Loewe	Starhill Shopping Centre	03 2142 3523
Louis Vuitton	Starhill Shopping Centre	03 2141 8790
Vincci	Various Locations	See p.351
Vincci+	Various Locations	See p.351

brand conscious, check out the weekend flea market at The Curve (p.337). There are a few stalls that display quaint ethnic pieces from Vietnam, Cambodia, Myanmar and India, as well as the designer knockoffs that are practically staples at every open-air bazaar these days. For that all-important business meeting or gala dinner, you might want to get yourself something more exclusive from Starhill (p.341), Pavilion (p.340) and KLCC (p.341), a haven for designer boutiques like Prada, Chanel, and increasingly, Coach.

Hardware & DIY
Other options **Outdoor Goods** p.314

DIY is a relatively new concept in Malaysia. Malaysians still prefer to hire professional contractors to do house painting, carpentry and a host of other residential renovation work, because the cost of labour is very low compared to the west. For example, unplugging a sink may cost you less than RM30. Handyman services are flagrantly advertised just about everywhere – on flyers that jam your mail box, in the local daily newspapers, and even just names and numbers scrawled on walls and telephone poles. You really just need to keep your eyes peeled and ask for word-of-mouth recommendations.

Nevertheless, with the emergence of hardware megastores, more and more DIY wannabes are crawling out of the woodwork. You will have no problem running into hardware shops in any residential neighbourhood. Don't underestimate these – they sell just about everything, often including the kitchen sink.

That said, it is more advisable for the amateur DIY enthusiast to visit specialists, which tend to have better product display, friendly, hands-on, knowledgeable staff and product demonstrations. In Malaysia, it is common to find shops dedicated entirely to customised paint solutions, or power tools, for example. Traditional hardware stores will generally carry more building materials than the DIY chain stores located in malls. For carpentry and design services, go to interior design shops. There are dozens of such shops in Damansara Uptown and Perdana Damansara.

Hardware & DIY		
Giant Ace	Various Locations	See p.346
Hardware House (M)	43, Jalan Perepat 27/95, Section 27	03 5192 7757
Home-Fix The DIY Store	Various Locations	See p.347

At the moment, there aren't many choices when it comes to hardware megastores. Ace Hardware dominates this niche, with outlets in major complexes such as the Ikano Power Centre and Mid Valley. Other outfits like Fix-It and Hardware House cannot rival Ace in terms of size, but sometimes they can surprise with a rare offering in niche areas. Fix-It, for example, carries the hard-to-find starhead screwdriver.

There are plenty of independent wholesalers like wood merchants – a whole cluster of these can be found along the Old Klang Road 'furniture belt'. You can also pay a visit to Jalan Samping, near Pudu Market, which has a few reputable wood merchant wholesalers.

Health Food
Malaysians firmly belief that popping vitamin pills and food supplements can do wonders to boost their immunity and improve well-being. Little wonder then that health products like Kordel's and Blackmores are ubiquitous brand names lining the

shelves of pharmacies and personal care stores. Whether you want increased vitality for your busy life, enhancing your general well being, or burning off flab and replacing it with lean muscles, your pharmacist can prescribe from an assortment of choices like vitamins, speciality supplements, herbal preparations, and special dietary needs such as vegetarian-friendly capsules.

Malaysia, being a vibrant and diverse melting pot of cultures, has more to offer to the adventurous in terms of alternative health foods and treatments compared with western-centric products. Traditional holistic approaches like herbal remedies, unguents, aromatherapy and physical rub-downs are highly popular even among non-Malays. Malaysia has an indigenous answer to Viagra, the aptly named tongkat ali (literally Ali's walking stick), and no, the ladies need not feel left out because they have their own kacip fatimah concoction. These herbal aphrodisiacs are easily available in ready-to-drink preparations and come in the form of sachets, soluble powders and cans.

The culturally steeped traditional Chinese medical cornucopia of herbs, roots, minerals, and organic constituents, including the dried sea horse or 'golden bee', are easily attainable in most Chinese medical halls. Newbies are better off visiting more established set ups like Eu Yan Sang, a veritable supermarket of Chinese medical and health supplies, which has numerous outlets in supermarkets as well as drug stores. Experiment with bottled bird's nest (for promoting general good health), lingzhi cracked spores capsules (to enhance and strengthen the immune system), and hou ning powder (for the relief of coughs). Be forewarned: to unaccustomed palates, they often smell pungent and the aftertaste will usually linger.

Health Food

Country Farm Organics	Various Locations	See p.345
Eu Yan Sang	Shaw Parade	03 2116 8200
Juiceworks	Various Locations	See p.347
Justlife	Various Locations	See p.347

Phang-tastic Service
If the thought of dragging round the supermarket fills you with dread, call Phang Trading, who run a 'mobile supermarket'. Just give them a list of items you want, and they will deliver it all to your home. Call 03 4257 3468 or 03 4257 3467.

Healthy and nutritious food need not be nasty or indifferent to your taste buds. Your french-fry loving tykes will overdose on their daily quota of greens and fruits at Juiceworks and want more; others will surely fall in love with the yummy smoothies and creamy blends of tropical fruits cupped in cheery glasses amid gaily decorated stalls.

Any discussion of health food would be incomplete without mentioning organic food. If in the past, organic food may have been associated with new age hippies, yuppies and spaced-out yoga practitioners, but today more and more people are converting to organic food as their main form of sustenance. In Kuala Lumpur, Country Farm Organics and Justlife dominate the market.

At Country Farm Organics, organic fruits, vegetables, meats, soy products and breads are available, as well as surprisingly delicious soy icecream and smoothies that will leaving you wondering how they could make it without dairy products. Every retail outlet doubles as a cafe serving yummy, healthy food; there's even a nutritionist on hand to offer advice.

The folks at Justlife are just as dedicated to the organic food cause. They sell a complete selection of lifestyle products ranging from parabens-free household cleaners, organic tea from Chile and even France's Babynat label organic infant formula. Organic products are usually higher priced than regular commercially produced items so if you're just dipping your toe into the organic fad, a delicious way to try is with the black soya bean drink which may be found in the refrigerated food section of most supermarkets. Limited varieties of fresh organic produce like vegetables may also be sourced from local wet markets but you will need to ask since most of these premium items are carefully stored away in cooler boxes to retain their natural goodness.

Home furnishings

Home Furnishings & Accessories

Other options **Hardware & DIY** p.304

With a lush tropical rainforest that supplies plenty of raw material, the furniture industry here is thriving. Unsurprisingly, prices are also very affordable. So much so, residents would rather spend a little more on brand new furniture than settle for second-hand stuff, or take the trouble to upholster giveaways. You might spot the occasional ad placed by outgoing tenants in the local classifieds or neighbourhood shop, but they are few and far between. The reason is partly cultural. Locals believe it is auspicious to start off any new endeavour, like moving into a new house, with new possessions, so they would rather buy new furniture than reuse somebody else's, even if it is still in good condition.

From internationally renowned all-rounders to local furniture specialists, there is no shortage of choices for the house-proud. Mutiara Damansara seems to have developed into some sort of a furniture hub for the well-heeled: by some twist of fate or design, the big international names of Harvey Norman, Macy, Courts Mammoth, and IKEA are all clustered at Mutiara Damansara. Conveniently, just five minutes' drive away, are two clusters of interior design and home furnishings stores at Dataran Sunway and Damansara Uptown. They are too numerous to name here, but if they're listed on www.ipdm.org.my, the Malaysian Institute of Interior Designers' website, they should be reliable.

For big ticket items like sofas and bedroom and kitchen furniture, the local stores will give you more choice and better value for your money. Malaysia is a major furniture manufacturer. The large furniture warehouses that line suburban housing estates

especially Old Klang Road and Sungai Buloh, are stacked to the ceiling with everything from office chairs to bedroom sets and dining furniture. Lorenzo, Getha and Fella, which make both locally sold and export-bound furniture, are some of the most trusted local names for their extensive range of designs and quality control. Scour the newspapers, especially the Metro section of *The Star*, for the blizzard of furniture promotions that appear on an almost daily basis.

Chinoiserie antique furniture is another popular local trend. Though not exactly for the budget buyer – a two-seater settee can easily set you back RM2,000 – rosewood furniture inlaid with mother of pearl is in demand because of its exquisite wood finish and is rumoured to retain its coolness cool no matter how hot the day is. Scout around Peter Hoe's at Central Market and Barang Barang at Ikano for eclectic ethnic pieces, while Italian furniture aficionados would do well to look up Benze , which carries a good selection of contemporary brands like Il Loft, Poltromec and Fiam Italia.

Since 2003, HOMEDEC (www.homedec.com.my), the annual home exhibition, has attracted more than 500,000 visitors and continues to be of interest to both the curious and serious bargain hunters.

Ikano Power Centre
Mutiara Damansara
🚇 **Kelana Jaya**

Barang Barang

03 4252 9198 | *www.barang.com.sg*

Outside, the blurb boasts 'World sourced living', but the dim lighting and quiet ambience speaks volumes for its classiness. Don't be intimidated by the fact it seems more art gallery than furniture outlet. The pricier pieces co-exist harmoniously alongside RM32 throw rugs, quirky fluorescent furry lamps, and other affordable but tasteful paraphernalia. The helpful but unobtrusive staff don't hound you, but materialise like magic when you linger over a particular item and look like you need some help in decision making. There is To get here, take the shuttle bus from Kelana Jaya. There is another branch at Great Eastern Mall (03 4292 9198).

Sell Your Store

Have we left out your favourite handbag hangout, or dissed your local shoe shop? Tell us! Make sure the shops you love are in the next edition – visit www.explorerpublishing.com and fill in the Reader Response Form.

Jalan Ampang
City Centre
🚇 **Ampang Park**

Fella Design

03 7726 0041 | *www.fella.com.my*

Synonymous with high-end furniture, this specialist made its name in country and floral themed items. Knock yourself out at the spanking new four-storey concept furniture gallery in Petaling Jaya, a sprawling 40,000 square feet of retail space filled with decor solutions. Fans will go gaga over the elegant French country chic that evokes memories of a bygone era, while Zen lovers are sure to adore their avant garde Morph selection.

Ikano Power Centre
Petaling Jaya
🚇 **Kepong Sentral**

Macy Home Furnishings – Macy The Curtain Shop

03 8947 6060 | *www.macyhomefurnishings.com*

If you have vertigo or are just too lazy to haul yourself up on a chair, the good people at Macy will come and do your window measurement for you, at no obligation. Browse through more than 250,000 metres of fabric at its biggest store in the Ikano Power Centre. Macy offers five years' warranty on sofa frames, foam and springs. If you're really particular about your back, get a top of the range Simmons mattress. There are other branches – check the website for details.

Home Furnishings & Accessories

Asia Moon	Suria KLCC	03 2382 0396
Cavenzi Furniture Outlet	Various Locations	See p.345
Courts Mammoth	Various Locations	See p.345
The Curiousity Shop	11 Jalan Berangan	03 2142 6660
Dynasty Antique Gallery	Suria KLCC	03 2382 0318
Euro Asia Furniture & Lighting	Petaling Jaya	03 7956 2076
Ferro Inspiration	15 Jalan BJ/6, Taman Bukit Jaya	03 4106 5339
IKEA	No. 2 Jalan PJU 7/2, Mutiara Damansara, 47800	03 7726 7777
Jusco Home Centre	1Utama	03 7726 8000
Khazanah	Suria KLCC	03 2382 1055
LDP Furniture Mall	9, Jalan SS8/1	03 7875 2744
Lotus Arte	Suria KLCC	03 2382 9723
Malacca Woodwork	312 C, Klebang Besar 75200	06 315 4468
Nasim Carpets	Suria KLCC	03 2164 2400
Ombak Asia (KL) Sdn Bhd	Suria KLCC	03 2161 9600
Pucuk Rebung Museum Gallery	Suria KLCC	03 2382 1109
Room	Suria KLCC	03 2382 0809

Jalan Hang Lekir
Chinatown
Masjid Jamek

Peter Hoe Evolution
03 2026 0711

Formerly the headquarters for the Japanese secret police during the second world war, Peter Hoe's has received rave reviews for its eclectic home furnishings that marry traditional inspiration with modern sensibilities. From luxurious silk pillows to colourful lanterns and quirky gecko door stoppers that go for only RM29, few can resist its charming combination of unusual designs laced with traditional influences.

Peter Hoe Evolution

Jewellery & Watches
Other options **Markets** p.332

Fashion accessories such as hairpins, scarves, bracelets, jewellery, bags, shoes, purses and ribbons made both locally and overseas are available in many shops located in the city, and in malls. Some famous brands include Tiffany, Bvlgari, Sa Sa, Pearl and Perlini. Kuala Lumpur has plenty of jewellery options for the fashion conscious.

For the budget conscious, make a beeline for shopping malls that abound with affordable yet chic costume jewellery. Bonita and Sinma stock trendy earrings from RM19.90, while AXXEZZ carries interesting ethnic-inspired accessories. If you covet high street looks that grace magazine pages, try international franchises. The Australia-based Diva, UK-originated Topshop, and Miss Selfridge are now practically staples at all major shopping malls. For the diehard bargain hunter, check out the standalone stalls that line the boulevard of all major shopping malls and flea markets at The Curve, Amcorp Mall and Sri Hartamas. Stylish metal and wood earrings typically go for only RM10 for three pairs, and neon-coloured plastic necklaces RM10 apiece.

If you're looking for something that not only looks good but has investment value, how about gold jewellery? Jalan Masjid India is full of jewellery shops. Indian goldsmiths like Little India Jewellers and Madras Jewellers offer competitive prices.

For something less flashy, Diamond & Platinum will win you over with their classic yet elegant designs that come with lifetime cleaning and washing warranty. The first year includes plating, soldering and polishing. If you need a quick fix, just bring your purchase to any of its many outlets. Each one can do repairs and polishing within the hour. Other reputable jewellery specialists are Poh Kong, which also does precious stones, and Goldheart, a favourite with newlyweds-to-be for its platinum wedding bands.

For fine jewellery, locals still tend to favour simple, classic designs, but the landscape is fast changing with the advent of daring new designers. Couture jeweller Cherie Thum (www.cheriethum.com), available at Lotus Arte, has carved a niche in big, bold pieces that incorporates colourful precious stones and diamonds.

For something more individualised, get your trinkets custom made at Love Diamond, which has stores in Suria KLCC and Mid Valley. While many places can allow you to engrave your details (from pen-makers Mont Blanc to jewellery specialists Tomei and Poh Kong), Love Diamond comes up as first choice because custom-making is its fundamental concept.

There is no shortage of watch shops in Kuala Lumpur. Even locals prefer to go for leading international brands of timepieces. Designer brands Tag Heuer, Omega and Longines are widely available in both standalone boutiques and franchises like Watatime, Watchshoppe and City Chain.

But if you're a serious watch collector and nothing less than a Vertu or Cortina will do, there are plenty of options to satisfy your lust for the deluxe. Starhill (p.341) offers more than 100 brands of fine luxury watches. And now the Swiss Watch Gallery has opened the largest standalone Rolex boutique in Pavilion (p.340). Measuring a massive 1,754 square feet, owners and collectors can browse through a comprehensive collection of Rolex and Tudor timepieces in total comfort.

Jewellery & Watches

AXXEZZ	Various Locations	See p.344
Bonita	Various Locations	See p.344
Boutique	Petaling Jaya	03 7710 6087
Bvlgari	Suria KLCC	03 2382 0450
Cartier	Suria KLCC	03 2166 8331
Charriol	Suria KLCC	03 2382 0403
Chopard	Suria KLCC	03 2166 3193
City Chain	Various Locations	See p.345
Diamond & Platinum	Various Locations	See p.345
Diva	Various Locations	See p.345
Emotus	Suria KLCC	03 2163 3841
Franck Muller	Suria KLCC	03 2166 4195
Goldheart	Various Locations	See p.346
Habib Jewels	Various Locations	See p.347
The Hour Glass	Suria KLCC	03 2164 6388
Little India Jewellers	Jalan Masjid India	03 2693 3443
Lotus Arte	Suria KLCC	03 2382 9723
Love Diamond	Suria KLCC	03 2382 2618
Madras Jeweller	Jalan Masjid India	03 2692 6650
Mauboussin	Suria KLCC	03 2163 0113
Mikimoto	Suria KLCC	03 2166 3588
Miss Selfridge	Various Locations	See p.348
Mont Blanc	Suria KLCC	03 2166 2886
Piaget	Suria KLCC	03 2078 7078
Poh Kong	Various Locations	See p.349
PYT Jeweller	Various Locations	See p.349
Rolex	Suria KLCC	03 2382 0431
Selberan	Suria KLCC	03 2382 0305
Sincere Fine Watches	Suria KLCC	03 2166 2181
Sinma	Various Locations	See p.350
Swatch	Suria KLCC	03 2161 2380
Swiss Watch Gallery	Pavilion	na
Tiffany & Co.	Suria KLCC	03 2382 2233
Tomei	Suria KLCC	03 2382 6188
Topshop	Suria KLCC	03 2382 4056
Vincci	Various Locations	See p.351
Watatime	Suria KLCC	03 2166 1268
Watatime (M)	Various Locations	See p.351
Watchshoppe	Various Locations	See p.351
Zurich Timepieces	Various Locations	See p.351

Kids' Items

Kids' items are available at all major shopping malls. For strollers, car seats, potties and carriers, Safe 'n Sound, Mothercare and Chicco at 1 Utama are very popular with mothers. You can easily find children's clothes boutiques like Hallmark, PONEY, OshKosh, GAP and GUESS as well. For all your kids' items under one roof, make a beeline for Wonder Tots. You'll get everything from educational toys and books to clothes that's suitable for both casual and party wear at one venue. Beverly Kids, a specialist in high-quality togs for kids from 3 to 12 years old, offers precious tetron hand-smocked dresses that your little girl would go gaga over. For the boys, there are smart long and short-sleeved cotton (or silk) shirts and linen pants. Both parents and kids will go crazy over the stylish apparel at LIFEbaby. While a tad pricey, you'll be hard-pressed to find similar designs anywhere else. Dress your children up as karate kids in its martial arts-inspired suits, or in designer beachwear. Merry Go Round at Bangsar Village 1 boasts an extensive collection of stylish apparel, leather sandals, scarves and bags. Kids and mothers alike love their Asian-inspired PinkTamarind collection, which boasts fashions made from all-natural fabrics. Expat mothers might want to hook up with ibu (www.ibufamily.org), a family resource site that provides support and information for pregnant women and parents living in Malaysia. Ibu, which means 'mother' in Malay, was initiated by a group of enterprising British expat women and has become

Kids

Anakku	Various Locations	See p.344
Art Attack	1 Utama	03 7729 7155
Bebehaus	1 Utama	03 7729 5008
Beverly Kids	Sunway Pyramid	03 7494 0525
Bubblegummers	1 Utama	03 7724 1296
Carrefour	Various Locations	See p.345
Chicco	Various Locations	See p.345
GAP Kids/Baby Gap	1 Utama	03 7725 5185
GAP kids/Baby Gap	Mid Valley	03 2287 0382
Giant	Various Locations	See p.346
Guess Kids	1 Utama	03 7727 8640
Hallmark	Various Locations	See p.347
Ladybird	Sunway Pyramid	03 5622 1823
LIFEbaby	1 Utama	03 7727 2655
Mom's Care	Mid Valley Megamall	03 2287 1088
Okaidi Obaibi	Sunway Pyramid	03 5635 5886
Osh Kosh B'Gosh	1 Utama	03 7727 2831
Poney Garments	Various Locations	See p.349
Pumpkin Patch	1 Utama	03 7725 4501
Safe 'n Sound	1 Utama	03 7726 8149
Tree House	1 Utama	03 7726 9736
Tumble Tots	1 Utama	03 7710 9188
Wonder Tots	Sunway Pyramid	03 7492 0692
World of Cartoons & World of Babies	Various Locations	See p.351

a very popular site with both locals and foreign residents. It has great resources like playgroups for various age groups, pregnancy support groups, coffee mornings, and a baby equipment loan service, together with maternity wear and a winter wardrobe

Junior fashion

of children's clothes. If you need an outfit for a special occasion, want more variety in casual clothes, or wish to donate an item, visit the Maternity Clothes Loan Service at the ibu drop-in centre during office hours. Ibu also posts ads for members selling things like baby gear, which are always worth checking out because it's much cheaper than buying brand new.

Lingerie
Other options **Clothes** p.294

Kuala Lumpur has a huge range of lingerie outlets. From supermarkets to dodgy corner units at Kota Raya, where you can get a steamy blood-red lacy bikini top for RM20, to hypermarkets like Tesco, you can find lingerie, though it may be the sort that even grandma would be embarrassed to be seen in. Supermarkets stock popular brands such as Triumph, Wacoal and Audrey. Since these are manufactured in the region for the petite Asian woman, the more voluptuous may have difficulty finding fitting sizes. Fear not, there's always Marks & Spencer at Suria KLCC, Berjaya Times Square and 1 Utama. In the last

Lingerie

Lingerie			
Aubade	Lot 10	03 2142 8682	www.aubade.com
Blush	Various Locations	See p.344	www.blush.com.my
La Senza	Various Locations	See p.347	www.lasenza.com
Marks & Spencer	Various Locations	See p.348	www.marksandspencer.com
The Under Shop	Various Locations	See p.350	www.theundershop.com
Women's Secret	Various Locations	See p.351	www.womensecret.com
Xixili	Various Locations	See p.351	www.xixili.com.my

few years, speciality lingerie stores have become very popular with the fashionable, though their shop window displays may be far more modest than their western counterparts. Serious sirens with a mission gravitate towards the eye-popping steamy bodysuits and erotic two-pieces at Blush and Xixili. For a comprehensive range of lingerie that caters for females of all ages, sizes and tastes, La Senza is the overwhelming favourite. You can get anything from functional cotton pyjamas to temperature-raising lacy teddies. Prices are reasonable too. Seamless luxury bras go for RM129. During promotions, you can get five pairs of pants for RM70. Since this brand hails from Canada, its stocks vary according to the Canadian seasons, so you'll find furry boots which may not be suitable for the KL tropical weather. You can be professionally measured at all lingerie stores in KL.

Luggage & Leather

Shopping malls are chock-a-block with luggage and leather shops. You can buy cheap luggage from as little as RM90 from convenience store Watson's, and it isn't difficult to find moderately priced brands like Camel Active and Elle. Premium brand Samsonite is also very popular, and has opened dedicated stores in Mid Valley and Gardens. Some of these luggage specialists, such as Universal Traveller, also stock winter wear. While the crammed layout and display of bags haphazardly arranged across the floor may be no match for the high-end speciality shops, do not underestimate the local independent stores. Standalones like Travel Style at Mid Valley stock luxury brands including DELSEY and Victorinox as well as an impressive range of travelling bags, suitcases, leather bags and briefcases. They usually provide between two and three years' warranty, inclusive of manufacturing defects, as well as a free repair service after point of sales. Another popular luggage store is House of Leather, which sells an impressive range of suitcases, wallets, briefcases and purses both in leather and other materials. Its in-house brands Kaufman and Country & Hide are particularly popular, and items come standard with a one-year product warranty. You will come across plenty of leather knockoffs flooding flea markets and night markets at unbelievably low prices, but these are made of vinyl or PVC and fray easily.

Luggage & Leather		
Black Label	1 Utama	03 7710 7100
Bonia Natural	Suria KLCC	03 2161 0119
Braun Buffel	Various Locations	See p.344
Camel Active	Various Locations	See p.344
Crumpler	Suria KLCC	03 2161 2160
Cuir Boutique	Various Locations	See p.345
Etaly Leather	Sunway Pyramid	03 5634 2539
Furla	Suria KLCC	03 2382 1800
House of Leather	Various Locations	See p.347
Loewe	Suria KLCC	03 2164 8498
Porosus Products	Suria KLCC	03 2162 8890
Samsonite	Various Locations	See p.349
Tearproof	Suria KLCC	03 2166 1893
Travel All	Various Locations	See p.350
Travel Style	Various Locations	See p.350
Universal Traveller	Various Locations	See p.351
Vollez	Sunway Pyramid	03 7492 8896

Maternity Items

Who says pregnancy and looking good are mutually exclusive? Celebrate your motherhood by visiting the staggering array of maternity shops in KL. These combine functionality and fashion to offer a broad range of clothing that encompasses casual and evening wear, swimwear, as well as smart

Maternity Items

The Baby Loft	Desa Park City	03 6280 7633
Belle Belly	Bangsar Village	03 2284 2618
Fabulous Mom	Taman Kinrara	012 295 0396
Funky Mama	Hartamas Shopping Centre	03 6201 2242
Funky Mama Maternity	Gardens	03 2287 5068
Mamalink	Lucky Garden	03 2095 1206
Modernmum	Various Locations	See p.348
Motherclub	Various Locations	See p.348
Runway Maternity	Damansara Intan	03 7727 6873

attire for the working mum-to-be. You won't need to look like a beached whale anymore with the gorgeous collection of swing tops, bootleg pants and bias-cut skirts at Motherclub. Expectant mothers will love local favourite Modernmum for its extensive maternity collection, as well as its lingerie made from silky anti-allergic rubber and cotton that is soft, absorbent and allows skin to breathe easily. Giving these big chain stores a run for their money are several independent shops opened by mothers who couldn't find anything suitable while they were pregnant. The edgy retro stretchable dresses in Funky Mama Maternity at Gardens will definitely inspire you to strut instead of waddle. Try the daring creations of Runway Maternity, which will bring out the Catherine Zeta-Jones in you. To complement your chic maternity outfits, why not take advantage of the many accessories available? Belle Belly at Bangsar is also great for its huge range of stylish yet comfortable options. Mothers-to-be will love their Bella Band, a maternity accessory that conceals unsightly elastic waistbands and expandable panels on maternity outfits. There are also plenty of options for the nursing mum who wants to look effortlessly chic. Fabulous Mom stocks padded and seamless nursing bras that can be worn under halterneck or racer-back tops, while DIVAmom from online retailer The Baby Loft offers a revolutionary nursing tank that provides complete underbust support.

Medicine

Other options **General Medical Care** p.121

At the moment, Kuala Lumpur does not have any 24 hour pharmacies but for that midnight emergency you can easily get over-the-counter medications such as antacids and paracetamol at convenience stores like 7-Eleven. It is no exaggeration to say that pharmacies are found everywhere. You can bet on running into at least one Guardian, Apex or Watson's at major shopping malls and in most neighbourhoods. Guardian offers the broadest range of products. Its prices are usually a little higher than other pharmacy chains, although its sales are worth waiting for. The bigger chains also have the facilities to conduct health services like the blood glucose test, cholesterol checkups, and they can also organise talks and counselling sessions. Independents may not beat the big boys in terms of

Medicine

Apex Pharmacy	Various Locations	See p.344
Caring Pharmacy	Various Locations	See p.345
Guardian Pharmacy	Various Locations	See p.346
Himalaya	Various Locations	See p.347
Primahealth Pharmacy	Various Locations	See p.349
Vitacare	Various Locations	See p.351
Watsons	Various Locations	See p.351

range, but they sell certain niche items at lower prices and are often amenable to further discounts. For example, some medications may vary from as much as RM34 to RM43 in two different pharmacies. It's a legal requirement to have one qualified pharmacist in every outlet, and they are usually on duty from 10:00 to 17:00 on weekdays. A doctor's prescription is usually required for controlled drugs, but some pharmacies are more flexible and merely ask you to register your name and contact details in a logbook for formality. Don't forget to check for expiry dates before you pay up.

Mobile Phones
Other options **Telephone** p.115

While Malaysian phones are competitive in pricing, overseas deals are slightly better because they offer contracts with mobile service providers. This option is available here (Digi pairs up with Samsung, for example) but the selection of phones is limited compared with other countries. Malaysian mobile phones use the GSM network. Where there are computers for sale there are usually mobile phone retailers. Low Yat Plaza,

Mobile nation

BB Plaza, Digital Mall and Sungei Wang Plaza are favourite bargaining grounds. Phone proprietors may operate out of shops or standalone stalls, but for brands like Nokia you're better off buying from authorised resellers. The local market is flooded with grey imports that are frequently found in independent stores. Their prices are usually more tempting and the honey-tongued proprietors will assure you that you can always go back to them if you have any problems with your purchase. But like their products, the stalls are mobile and if they disappear you'll have nobody to turn to when you do encounter a problem. You can get hold of prepaid cards that are very affordable, starting at RM5 for a basic package. These cards allow you to call and text overseas, and can be conveniently topped up at petrol stations, phone shops, convenience stores like 7-Eleven, and newsagents.

Mobile Phones			
Bukit Bintang Plaza (BB Plaza)	Bukit Bintang	03 2148 7411	na
Digital Mall	Petaling Jaya	03 7958 2636	www.digitalmall.net.my
IT World	Mid Valley	03 2938 8000	www.it-world.com.my
Low Yat Plaza	Jalan Alor	03 2148 5141	www.lowyat.net
Sungei Wang Plaza	Bukit Bintang	03 2148 6109	www.sungeiwang.com

Music, DVDs & Videos
Like any other wired nation, Malaysia has been hit by the scourge of illegal downloading. Unfortunately, Malaysia also has the ignominy of being one of the largest producers of bootlegged CDs and DVDs. Petaling Street, for example, is flooded by stalls that openly peddle copies of the latest hit movies, sometimes before they even hit the silver screen. Having said that, original recordings of esoteric music, such as jazz and classical, are still favoured by genuine aficionados due to superior sound and images.

Tower Records, the country's biggest music chain store, caters to both populist tastes and more specialist preferences. Tower is particularly renowned for its back catalogue titles

Music, DVDs & Videos		
Borders	Various Locations	See p.344
Bukit Bintang Plaza (BB Plaza)	111 Jalan Bukit Bintang	03 2148 7411
MPH	Various Locations	See p.348
Popular Book Store	Various Locations	See p.349
Rock Corner	Various Locations	See p.349
Speedy Video	Various Locations	See p.350
Tower Records	Various Locations	See p.350
Video Ezy	Various Locations	See p.351

and range of niche music. Occasionally, Tower Records arrange for artists to appear in store. Recently, Linkin Park delighted KLCC shoppers with a brief appearance. CDs start from RM40 upwards (a little more for those that are imported), but from time to time there are 'best buy' items where three CDs go for the price of two. And if you're intrigued by a snazzy cover but are not sure if it's up your street, make use of the listening posts. For New Age music, try book stores MPH or Borders. If movies are your thing visit Speedy Video and Video Ezy for an up-to-date selection of the latest blockbusters. If you have more discerning indie tastes, BB Plaza with its slew of stores might have something for you.

Musical Instruments

Other options **Music, DVDs & Videos** p.313, **Music Lessons** p.248

There are quite a few music stores that cater to both amateurs and professional musicians. Many music shops double up as schools as well.
Yamaha Music School has a modest collection of beginners' instruments to complement its courses, but for scale and range, you can't beat Bentley. It is the biggest music store not only in the Klang Valley but in Malaysia, and carries everything from Gibson guitars to clarinets.

For professional guitarists and drummers, The Guitar Store wins hands down. It's easy to find – just look for the orange-coloured corner office next to Cheras Leisure Mall. The Guitar Store caters to people who are passionate about their music; the shop itself was opened by avid musicians. The impressive range of guitars and drums are a real draw for strummers and drummers in the area lovingly arranged next to the glass windows can be seen from a distance. It also has an outlet at Jalan Bukit Bintang near The Regent hotel, where you can strum guitars and play on assorted keyboards. Second-hand instruments are not really popular in Malaysia, but you can make enquiries at the music schools. Music Walk is the sole distributor of Viking guitars.

Musical Instruments		
Bentley Music	Bukit Bintang	03 2144 3333
Guitar Collection	Sunway Pyramid	03 7492 6057
The Guitar Store	Taman Segar Cheras	03 9133 2822
Mahogany	Petaling Jaya	03 7873 6388
Mighty Music Store	Petaling Jaya	03 7877 7366
Music Walk	Taipan Crest	03 5633 2822
Rhapsody Valley	Mid Valley Megamall	03 2938 3323
Twinkle Piano	Petaling Jaya	03 7876 3244
Yamaha Music	Petaling Jaya	03 7803 0900

Outdoor Goods

Other options **Sports Goods** p.322, **Hardware & DIY** p.304, **Camping** p.222

With lush tropical forests, seas and mountains galore on KL's doorstep, there are plenty of outdoor goods shops around. Most of the stores carry imported brands, though there are homegrown lovables like Evergreen Adventure that manufacture and export their own products. For the weekend camper, Ace Hardware stocks an adequate range of basic camping and climbing gear. Coleman sleeping bags are available in multiple sizes and Swiss Gear mats go for RM215. You can also get your hands on desert canteens from Academy Broadway, and bungee cords, thermal jugs and other basic equipment for outdoor pursuits.

The rugged camper will prefer specialist outdoor superstores like UFL Adventure, which caters for a wide range of outdoor

Outdoor Goods		
Corezone	42 Jalan SS2/24	03 7873 5560
Dive Station Aquaventure	Mid Valley Megamall	03 2282 1948
Evergreen Adventure	Taman Kepong	03 6277 7778
Giant Ace	Various Locations	See p.346
Outdoor Gear Centre	242-C Jalan Ampang, Federal Territory	03 4251 2423
TCE Tackles	Bandar Baru Seri Petaling	03 9057 7826
UFL Adventure	Bangsar Village	03 2283 3319

needs. You'll can find renowned climbing and backpacking brands like Buck Knives, CAMP mountain gear, backpacks from Eastpak and Deuter, as well as The North Face high-performance equipment and Leatherman multipurpose tools. It also stocks an impressive range of Coleman products including electric lighting, soft and hard coolers, as well as sleeping bags.

Local specialist Evergreen Adventure manufactures and sells products like sleeping bags, tents, bags, protective clothing and reflective gear, and there are several branches around the country.

For dive equipment, you can't go wrong with experts Dive Station Aquaventure. Fishing enthusiasts should head to TCE Tackles for equipment, which carries its own as well as international brands.

Party Accessories

Who doesn't love a good party? The organisers, that's who! And with boisterous, hyperactive bundles to watch over, arranging parties can be a nightmare even for the most devoted parent. If you want to celebrate your child's birthday, but dread the hassle, Kuala Lumpur has plenty of shortcuts. You can always have it at a play centre, or you can outsource the legwork to event organisers who will be more than happy to take care of the dirty work while you sit back and relax.

Supermarkets, stationery shops and even convenience stores like 7-Eleven stock basic party items including balloons and simple decorations, but if you really want to throw a party to remember, get the professionals to handle it. For a reasonable fee, Party Friends can stage a grand *Star Wars* party at the National Planetarium, or you could take the kids to Planet Hollywood where they can behave like rock stars. Another alternative

Party Accessories		
Balloon Buzz	Great Eastern Mall	03 4251 3007
Borneo Rainforest Cafe	Bandar Sunway	016 245 0569
Costume World	Pelangi Damansara	03 7729 7332
Costumes 'N' Parties	City Square	03 2164 8184
Just Heavenly	Bangsar Baru	03 2287 9867
Kizsports	1 Utama	03 7726 6313
LB (Lian Bee) Confectionery	Jalan Sungai Beting	03 3290 2233
Mama Min	Ulu Klang	012 202 5550
MegaKidz	Mid Valley Megamall	03 2282 9300
Mikaliya's Costumes	Jalan, 21/11B Sea Park	03 7877 6401
One-Stop Party Shop	Desa Sri Hartamas	03 2300 2553
Party Friends	Ikano Power Centre	03 2092 2177
Party Princess	Mid Valley Megamall	03 2282 3622
Secret Recipe	Various Locations	See p.350
Zanne Gifts, Hampers & Events	Roving	017 382 6289

is to go tribal at the Borneo Rainforest Cafe in Sunway. If the birthday girl or boy isn't afraid of the limelight, dinner at TGI Friday is always fun. The entire crew gets into the spirit and bursts into birthday song, and you get a cake on the house as well.

Don't be fooled by the modest shoplot size of Party World at The Curve. Its aisles are chock-a-block with pinatas, party bags, streamers, banners, and decorative items for more than 40 party themes. Even the shyest wallflower would love its pink feather boas. Balloon Buzz carries a wide range of party items as well, but its forte is balloons: foil balloons for any occasion, printed balloons, plain ones from as tiny as five inches to three feet, and all sorts of shapes – there are even balloons shaped like champagne glasses and SpongeBob SquarePants. Popular helium balloons go for between RM2.50 to RM95 per piece. To help you get into the party spirit, get the face painters at Zanne Gifts, Hampers & Events to transform your precious tots into Spiderman or Catwoman, while adult guests can opt for the more subdued henna tattoos or funky tribal designs.

For that all-important birthday cake, most bakeries will provide the staple varieties like Black Forest, chocolate fudge, chocolate banana and cheesecake. Secret Recipe is always popular for its range of yummy cheesecakes that go for a very affordable RM60 and upwards. Just Heavenly in Bangsar is a little pricier but it's garnered a legion of fans with its fantastic repertoire of novel designs and yummy flavours. If you're looking for a real conversation piece, give a call to Mama Min. Flavours are limited to butter, chocolate and occasionally strawberry butter, and they may cost a tad more (a two-kilogram cake might cost more than RM150) but her zany creations will have your friends and kids' friends talking for months. She has come up with some truly jaw-dropping designs inspired by Disney cartoons, Barbie, Thomas the Tank Engine and even the Batmobile.

Party Friends is very popular with parents who want to leave their kids in safe hands while they go shopping. With two play areas there's plenty for your kids to keep busy with – they might even protest when you come to pick them up! Prices start at RM15 per hour per child, including a snack, for a maximum of two hours. For playgroup bookings, check out Kizsportz & Gym at 1 Utama with party packages starting at RM36.90 for a minimum of 15 kids.

Perfumes & Cosmetics

Other options **Markets** p.332

If you're the sort who can't bear to leave the house without at least a dab of lipstick and enveloped in a cloud of perfume, you will love Kuala Lumpur malls for their diverse range of cosmetics and fragrances. You can't walk through one without sales promoters waving a free perfume sample at you.

Cosmetics specialists like Sa Sa and Elianto are popular hunting grounds for the younger set with their array of fashionable yet budget-sensitive brands like red earth, Revlon and Maybelline. Popular high-street American brands MAC and Bobbi Brown have taken Malaysia by storm and set up standalone boutiques, but you can easily find other leading international brands like Estee Lauder, Chanel and Christian Dior at just about any shopping mall. Big department stores such as Parkson, Isetan and Jaya Jusco dedicate entire floors to perfumes and cosmetics. The cosmetics consultants will usually be glad to do your makeup at their counter, with no obligation to buy. While mainstream brands have always been popular, environmentally friendly cosmetics have also caught the imagination of trend-spotters here. The Body Shop, Skin Food and H20+ outlets can be found at major shopping malls.

Perfumes & Cosmetics		
The Body Shop	Sunway Pyramid	03 5622 1148
Forest'Secret	The Curve	03 7725 7527
H20+	Sunway Pyramid	03 5622 1139
Isetan	Various Locations	See p.347
Jaya Jusco	Various Locations	See p.347
Just Parfum	Sunway Pyramid	03 7492 2868
L'Occitane	Various Locations	See p.347
MAC	Mid Valley Megamall	03 2284 6490
Metrojaya	Various Locations	See p.348
The Perfume Shop	Sunway Pyramid	03 7492 2868
Sa Sa	Sunway Pyramid	03 7494 0456
Shins	Sunway Pyramid	03 5637 2780
Shu Uemera	Mid Valley Megamall	03 2287 1764
Skin Food	Sunway Pyramid	03 5634 9288

It's not just women who want to smell and look good. With the rise of the 'metrosexual' male, men are no longer content with the traditional pomade or aftershave, and unisex brands like Biotherm are doing a roaring trade with their range of men's toiletries, no doubt inspired by Asian movie idol Takeshi Kaneshiro, whose sultry blemish-free mug graces a giant billboard on the side of 1 Utama.

Cosmetics prices are controlled by distributors and tend to be rather standard in supermarkets and malls. If you can wait a while, it pays to stock up on your supplies at airport shops, as the products fall under the duty-free category and thus offer substantial price savings.

Pets

Other options **Pets (Residents)** p.111

There are many places one can buy cats and dogs, the most common being commercial pet stores, which can be found in major shopping malls and housing estates. Probably the largest and most comprehensive pet shop is the huge Pet Safari at Ikano Power Centre. If you're after a pooch or a kitty, there's lots of cute little furry friends here, and once you've picked out your new best friend the store also offers a range of other services like grooming, boarding and veterinary care (they won't come round to help you clear up house-training booboos, unfortunately). Pet Safari also sells over 10,000 pet products, from food to beds and from medicines to toys. And if you're going for a holiday, you can even send Rover to its De'Ritz Hotel, it is the first of its kind in Malaysia and provides five-star amenities – by animal standards, that is – such as a cool, clean environment with a multitude of kennels and catteries.

These days, you can even buy pets online. Pets More has an innovative concept shop that allows you to suss out the credentials of your potential home buddies by browsing through the repertoire of detailed descriptions and pictures of potential pets in the comfort of your home. Alternatively, you can indulge your animal instinct and play good samaritan by adopting a stray dog or cat from the SPCA (Society for the Prevention of Cruelty to Animals). Another less common way is buying from the breeder directly, but unless you are in the circle, you're better off sticking to a mainstream pet shop. There are some dedicated small-scale breeders who have specialised breeds, but the prices can be expensive. If your taste runs to the exotic, you'll love Pets Wonderland at 1 Utama. From chinchillas to bengal cats, they have a staggering collection of small animals. After your purchase, remember to get a dog licence from the post office and to have your canine companion vaccinated.

Pets

The Pet Family	Ikano Power Centre	03 7727 8771	www.thepetfamily.com
Pet Safari	Ikano Power Centre	03 7724 1578	www.thepetsafari.com.my
Pet World	Sea Park	03 7804 0322	na
Pets More	10 Jalan Sultan	03 2078 6449	www.petsmore.com.my
Pets People	Plaza Damas 60	03 6201 1708	na
Pets Wonderland	Mid Valley	03 2284 3388	www.petswonderland.com.my
Pets' Place	Pandan Indah	03 4297 7577	www.petsplace.com.my
SPCA Selangor	Ampang	03 4256 5312	www.spca.org.my

Portrait Photographers & Artists

Whether it's to commemorate your graduation day or anniversary, or you simply want to indulge in a bit of narcissism, you can easily get a portrait taken at most photography studios in Kuala Lumpur. If you want something that is less cliched and more cutting edge, how about getting an independent photographer to capture you for posterity? Kid Chan (www.kidchan.com) has carved out a reputation with his experimental yet tasteful portraits. Another craze that has dwindled somewhat in popularity but is still worth a gander, is the 'glamorous portrait'. Available at cosmetic counters in shopping malls, this service includes a free makeover by the cosmetics consultant, after which you get to pick from a rack of 'glamorous' outfits that range from a pink feather boa to a Dalmatian-spotted overcoat, and voila, you strike a pose while the resident photographer clicks away. For a cool RM100 or so, you get to take home several photos

Portrait Photographers & Artists

| Abdul Rahim | 012 202 2952 | www.arphotography.com.my |
| Louis Pang | 012 818 1080 | www.louispang.com |

317

as well as discount vouchers on selected products. For a lark, how about a caricature by the artists that roam shopping malls and tourist hubs like Central Market? An A4 sized ink drawing might cost you about RM50, and they can either draw you on the spot or work from a photo.

Second-Hand Items

In Malaysian culture, using other people's cast-offs carries an unspoken stigma, so you won't have much luck finding good or voluminous second-hand stores. Apart from the dusty, dog-eared second-hand books that can be found at the cluster of Indian-Muslim shops around PJ State, there really aren't that many shops dedicated entirely to hand-me-downs. However, it is possible to unearth some rare finds at flea markets. The eclectic weekend bazaar at Amcorp Mall is hugely popular with antique collectors, who faithfully drop by every weekend in the hope of unearthing a rare postage stamp, vintage coin or kitschy Japanese toy. You'll be surprised how many of the items auctioned off for small fortunes on eBay actually originate from here. Factory overruns are another kettle of fish altogether. Malaysia is the manufacturer for many international brands and, from time to time, companies organise big warehouse sales to clear factory overruns. Brands like Fila have been known to give 90% discounts on waist pouches, satchels and golf T-shirts in perfectly decent condition. These warehouses are usually held in industrial areas in Shah Alam, Kepong and Puchong, so finding your way there is half the fun. There is no designated timeframe for these events, so your best bet is to scan newspapers and look out for pennant and banner advertisements on street lamps. *Star Metro* and *Malay Mail* classifieds sections are particularly popular with advertisers.

If you're looking at getting rid of old stuff, there are plenty of stations in housing areas where you can dump unwanted but usable items such as toys, clothes and even recyclable goods like aluminium cans.

Spot the fakes

Petaling Street

What & Where To Buy

Shoes

Adidas	Suria KLCC	03 2162 3475
Adidas Original	Various Locations	See p.344
Aldo	1 Utama	03 7726 5110
Bally	Suria KLCC	03 2382 0306
Bata	1 Utama	03 7727 7698
Birkenstock Boutique	Lot 10	03 2141 3178
Blay	1 Utama	03 7729 1103
Bratpack	Suria KLCC	03 2161 8485
Clarks	1 Utama	03 7726 0180
Cole Haan	Suria KLCC	03 2382 0783
Converse	Suria KLCC	03 2163 0991
Foot Solutions	Subang Parade	03 5621 6831
Hush Puppies	Various Locations	See p.347
Jimmy Choo	Suria KLCC	03 2300 7788
Kickers	Suria KLCC	03 2382 0499
Lewre	1 Utama	03 7726 0298
Moreschi	Suria KLCC	03 2382 0278
Nine West	1 Utama	03 7722 5589
Nose	Various Locations	See p.348
Pedder Red	Suria KLCC	03 2164 4215
Prettyfit	Mid Valley Megamall	03 2284 2090
Primavera	Mid Valley	03 2282 2805
Professional Shoe Repair Shop	Ikano Power Centre	03 7729 4198
Rockin' Reptile	Mid Valley	03 2284 9099
Scholl	Hicom Glenmarie Ind Park	03 5569 2458
Shuz	Suria KLCC	03 2164 4569
Stuart Weitzman	Suria KLCC	03 2164 4569
Vincci	Suria KLCC	03 2166 1985
Vincci+	Various	See p.351

Shoes

Other options **Beachwear** p.288, **Clothes** p.294, **Sports Goods** p.322

Malaysians are mad about shoes, if the plethora of footwear stores that dot the Klang Valley is any indicator. The range of shoes here is simply astounding, from RM5 flip-flops that are sold at any convenience store, through to the sturdy sports shoes from Nike and Adidas and red-carpet stilettos by international couturiers. The market is flooded with a diverse mix of international and local brands and any fashionista will have no trouble finding their favourite names.

The biggest thing here for shoe lovers is definitely Vincci, which recently expanded into its deluxe line Vincci+. It is not much of an exaggeration to say that most girls in KL have about 10 pairs of Vincci shoes. From work pumps to peep-toe patent heels and knee-high boots, girls love the dizzying range of designs as well as the pocket-friendly prices. A decent pair of work pumps starts at RM60 and strappies may go for as little as RM20. Lewre's slip-on leather sandals may not come cheap at RM179, but your feet will thank you for the comfort after hours of mall crawling. For beautifully made and durable workshoes, go for Feliz Primavera, while Hush Puppies are best for comfortable weekend or walking shoes. Crocs are the latest phase – by now you will have seen these on the feet of hundreds of kids and quite a few mums and dads too – they may look a bit funny but they are so comfortable that you won't care.

Apart from local boy made good shoemaker extraordinaire Jimmy Choo, Malaysia's thriving fashion scene has seen the emergence of shoe couturiers who hold their own with red carpet designs at non-designer prices. Rockin' Reptile at Mid Valley, founded by former model and style icon Ming-Shan Tan, is hugely popular for its statement-making conversational pieces, fashioned from exotic materials like snakeskin, lizard, pony hair, carp, and embellished with crystals from the Czech Republic and Australia, Chinese silk and satin and metal mesh. Olde worlde buffs will love poking around in Sole Lovely at Bangsar Village II, where the intimate boutique resembles a lady's drawing room straight out of a Jane Austen novel.

For comfortable walking shoes and specialist supports and powders, you can't go wrong with Clarks, Hush Puppies, Scholl and Birkenstock. Other than in dedicated outlets, these product lines are also available at major anchor tenants like Isetan and Parkson. For something to tide you through all those hours of mall crawling, try Foot Solutions – each store has trained specialists that can insert custom insoles to help foot ailments from arthritis to hammertoes. On-the-spot fixes can be deftly carried out by any of the streetside cobblers at Kota Raya, but if you want something more streamlined try the Professional Shoe Repair Shop at Ikano, which can do just about everything, including rebuilding and polishing old shoes.

Souvenirs
Other options **Gifts** p.302

With the sheer number of souvenir and gift options available, visitors or departing residents have no excuse to go home empty handed. Souvenirs can be obtained just about anywhere – shopping malls, the side of the street, markets, the airport, heritage sites and hotels. You can always do last-minute shopping at souvenir boutiques in the airport and hotels, but you can probably get the same article at souvenir shops at a fraction of the price.

Souvenirs

Arch	Various Locations	See p.344	www.archcollection.com
Aseana	Suria KLCC	03 2382 9988	www.aseanamalaysia.com
Central Market (Pasar Seni)	Jalan Hang Kasturi	03 2031 0339	www.centralmarket-kl.com.my
House of Suzie Wong	Starhill Gallery	03 2143 3220	www.ouseofsuziewong.com
Peter Hoe Evolution	Jalan Hang Lekir	03 2026 0711	peterhoekl@yahoo.com
Pucuk Rebung Museum Gallery	Suria KLCC	03 2382 0769	na
Royal Selangor	Various Locations	See p.349	www.royalselangor.com

Housed in a spacious, air-conditioned art deco building, Central Market was formerly a wet market but is now the best place to look for authentic souvenirs and local handicrafts. Visitors can also watch the local artists and craftsmen at work, and have their profile drawn and portrait painted by the artists, or have intricate glass souvenirs specially made for them by the glass blowers.

Collectables Centre, in the market, is cluttered with every imaginable collectible from old Craven cigarette tin boxes, charcoal irons and oil lamps, to century-old Nyonya tea sets and hairpins. You might stumble upon original prints of Sun Yatsen and old family portraits in this treasure trove.

You can also get your hands on local arts and crafts from all over Malaysia without travelling to their states of origin. Songket & Sutera Asli has beautiful songket, a richly woven brocade textile of silk with gold and silver threads made on the east coast. Be awed by the array of resplendent keris (Malay traditional daggers with ornate carved blades) and Kelantanese tea sets at the House of Silver. Stop by Wau Tradisi for kites of every shape and size, the most popular being wau bulan. Prices here range from RM198 to RM500. Before you head off, refresh yourself with an ice-blended milk tea at the Old Town White Café or have your portrait painted by any of the roving street artists.

Just a stone's throw away is the newly-renovated Petaling Street. Not for the faint-hearted, this open-air bazaar has waned in popularity thanks to the pickpocket scourge, but for lively atmosphere and fabulous street food it's worth the experience. Petaling Street is a vibrant labyrinth of Chinese, Nepalese and Burmese traders touting everything from precious gems and clothes to bootlegged CDs and perfumes. While its merchandise is mainly knockoffs and fakes, you can get kitschy conversation pieces like Malaysian T-shirts with funny captions, locally-made lighters crafted with all sorts of designs, miniature replicas of Kuala Lumpur's buildings such as the Petronas Twin Towers (p.188) and stuffed toys that mimic Malaysia's local wildlife, as well as carpets. Remember to load up on your bargaining tips (p.283) before squaring off with the honey-tongued traders who can do sales pitches in a variety of languages.

If you yearn for something truly classy to impress your arty friends, head out to Pucuk Rebung Museum Gallery (p.320) at Suria KLCC (p.341). It has genuine antiques and artifacts, some dating back over a thousand years. For tasteful, timeless mementos, you can't go wrong with Royal Selangor Pewter (p.303). While they have branches in most major shopping malls, you should check out its sprawling main showroom in Setapak Jaya, where you'll definitely have a hard time choosing from the staggering display of handsome tankards, ornate Chinese astrological figurines and elegant trinket boxes bearing carved Malay motifs. And if you have time, its interesting and free factory tour is always fun. For something unusual, how about exclusively designed miniature replicas of Malaysian icons at ARCH World Miniature?

The upscale Aseana is another treasure trove of handmade clothing from all around the region. Cart home shawls and sarongs by designers Marilyn Tan and Bobby Ch'ng, more silk, teapots and sculptures. You'll also love the pan-cultural eclectic mix of jewellery and gifts at Peter Hoe. If you have a yearning for the exotic, the Tibetan figurines, brush pots, tea sets and incense burners at the House of Suzie Wong in Starhill Gallery (p.341) are worth a look.

Hindu souvenirs

Grass baskets at the Craft Complex

Incense sticks

Sports Goods

Other options **Outdoor Goods** p.314

Malaysia has plenty for the sports buff. Fitness and lifestyle centres dangling enticing free trial memberships are sprouting up every other day, and swimming pools, small-scale gyms and tennis courts are practically a standard fixture in suburban condominiums. Traditionally, residents obtain their shoes, racquets and leg warmers from the sports department in supermarkets, but as living standards increase, they are gravitating to specialist stores that sell a medley of imported athletic clothing and equipment.

Sports equipment is well covered in most shopping malls. All-rounder megastores like Royal Sporting House and Studio R carry clothing and equipment for popular sports like badminton, tennis, football, running, squash and swimming, while international brands such as Nike, Reebok and Adidas have dedicated stores in most major malls. Worth mentioning is local independent store G.S. Gill, which is known for its racquets, soccer balls and McGill golf equipment.

Sports Goods		
Adidas	Suria KLCC	03 2162 3475
Al-Ikhsan	Various Locations	See p.344
Cue Station	Berjaya Times Square	03 2144 3128
Everlast	Suria KLCC	03 2381 0902
Fitness Concept	Various Locations	See p.346
G. S. Gill Sdn. Bhd.	Jalan TAR	03 2698 3477
Golf House	Mid Valley	03 2284 2192
My Dance Shop	Mid Valley	03 2284 4417
Osim Global Healthcare	Suria KLCC	03 2162 3475
Planet Reebok	Mid Valley	03 2284 2576
Pro Billiard Supplies	Sungei Besi	03 9221 8848
Royal Sporting House	Various Locations	See p.349
Studio R	Various Locations	See p.350
Surf Dive 'N' Swim	Mid Valley	03 2284 0431
Why Pay More	Mid Valley	03 2284 2241

For the ambitious fitness fan who wants to set up a home gym, there's always Fitness Concept, a one-stop fitness solution centre with several outlets. Its stock-in trade is the treadmill but it also sells jumping rope, Pilates rings, boxing gloves and weights. The shop assistants are buff beefcakes with impressive pedigrees, including former gold medallists in competitive sports; even a past Mr Malaysia works at one of the branches. With Pro Billiard Supplies, you don't even have to brave the traffic jams to get your shooting fix at the local pub – you can buy your own table and accessories. It has an enormous range of imported billiard and snooker tables. Pool tables start off at around RM3,800, foosball tables are available from RM1,000, while pool cues vary widely from RM40 to RM10,000, depending on make. You can get acclaimed brands like Olhausen, McDermott, Predator and Viking under one roof. My Dance Shop offers trendy apparel for aerobics, yoga, and at the gym, which can also be worn with casual or working attire. For comprehensive archery, gymnastics and watersports equipment, you should to check out Universal Fitness and Leisure.

Stationery

From pencil cases to sketch pads, you won't have trouble spotting stationery shops. All major bookshops stock stationery but students and working adults flock to Popular Book Store, the country's dominant retailer of stationery for school, office and personal use. If you're a stickler for avant-garde design and don't mind shelling out a couple of extra ringgit for a folder, then you should get your supplies at the more arty

Stationery			
Borders	Various Locations	See p.344	www.bordersstores.com
Czip Lee	Bangsar	03 2287 7699	www.cziplee.com
Kinokuniya Book Stores	Suria KLCC	03 2164 8133	www.kinokuniya.com
MPH	Various Locations	See p.348	www.mphonline.com.my
Popular Book Store	Various Locations	See p.349	www.popular.com.my

Kinokuniya. If the humble ballpoint pen doesn't cut it, you can always hotfoot it to KLCC for a dash of Mont Blanc and Tiffany classiness.

Stationery fans love Czip Lee, which began as a humble family enterprise in Kajang before expanding to a sprawling two-storey corner unit in Bangsar Baru. Though it also sells academic books, this multi-purpose store is renowned for its dizzying array of common stationery to more eclectic stuff like electric pencil sharpeners. At any one time, you can find school children browsing its aisles of board games and brightly coloured papers.

Tailoring

Other options **Clothes** p.294, **Textiles** p.323, **Souvenirs** p.320, **Tailors** p.106

Kuala Lumpur has a formidable inventory of professional tailors who are as adept at handling western garb as they are at intricate ethnic costumes like cheongsam, baju kurung and saree. You can easily find a reliable independent tailoring service in any residential area through word of mouth. Any decent tailor will be able to make a garment from scratch, either from a photo or by copying an existing item. You can bring your own fabric, though most reputable tailors will provide sample swatches for you to pick from.

If you don't know anybody in your neighbourhood, make your way to the textile hubs of Jalan

Tailoring		
Alan Michael Fashion Tailor	Jalan Klang Lama	03 7783 0395
Binwani's	Various Locations	See p.344
De Al Fashion	Cineleisure Damansara	012 660 1520
Kaj Chotirmall & Co	Jalan TAR	03 2692 8228
Robert Custom Tailor	Jalan 14/20	03 7957 1732
Spark Manshop	Various Locations	See p.350
Summermen's	City Square Centre	03 2166 2202
Tux & Blazer	Sunway Pyramid	03 7492 2137
Za Altera	Various Locations	See p.351

Masjid India and Jalan Tuanku Abdul Rahman in the city. Many of the textile shops offer professional tailoring services as well, and you can also bring your own materials.

For three-piece suits, try Spark Manshop, practically an institution. They are known for their attention to detail, and all their garments are fitted with the little touches like perspiration shields and lapel buttonholes. They also create men's smart clothing accessories including tie pins and cuff links. Summermen's is also known for its bespoke men's tailoring. Kaj Chotirmall & Co, one of the oldest Indian regional trading firms, specialises in tailoring, menswear, lawyer's gowns and winter clothing. The average price of tailoring a man's suit is RM1,000, while you'll pay RM150 for a shirt and RM80 for a dress.

For garments that are too loose, too long or even too frumpy, look up Za Altera. This alteration specialist goes beyond changing zippers or patching up torn garments. It also makes 'custom-made restyling' such as adding sleeves to tops or jazzing up drab clothes with accessories such as special zippers and buttons. For additional charges of between RM2 and RM5, Za Altera's nifty tailors can shorten your trousers within one or two hours.

Textiles

Other options **Souvenirs** p.320, **Tailoring** p.323

Since pre-Independence days, Jalan Tuanku Abdul Rahman has reigned supreme as the mecca for textiles, from the humble cottons to luxurious silks for special occasions. Dozens of speciality fabric stores flank both sides of the road, mostly run by third-generation Indian and Indian-Muslim families. The office-hour traffic snarl can be daunting but the sheer range and volume is so astounding that rumour has

Textiles

Binwani's	Various Locations	See p.344	www.binwani.com
Euro Moda	Jalan TAR	03 2694 0805	na
Fabritex	Gardens	03 4251 1582	www.fabritex.com.my
IKEA	Mutiara Damansara	03 7726 7777	www.ikea.com.my
Kamdar	Petaling Jaya	03 7877 2870	www.kamdar.com.my
Sakun Silver & Silk	Lot 10	03 2141 8855	www.sakunsilk.com
Summermen's	City Square Centre	03 2166 2202	www.summermens.com

it even Singaporean shop proprietors flock here to purchase their goods in bulk. With four shops at Jalan TAR alone, local institution Kamdar is immensely popular for dress textiles and furnishing fabrics that are affordable without compromising on quality. Also at Jalan Tuanku Abdul Rahman is high-fashion fabric specialist Binwani's, which is noted for its luxurious shantung silk, chiffon and French laces. Equipped with a water

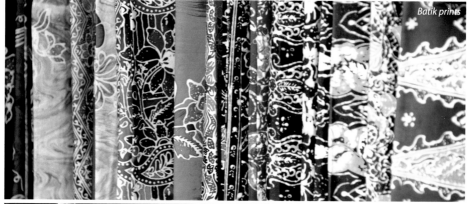

Batik prints

Silk Street

Buying fabrics

fountain, street lamps, park benches, and fauna, its latest concept store Silk Street is a sprawling oasis designed to make your window-shopping experience as decadently pleasurable as possible.

Euro Moda deserves special mention for its exquisite Italian, French, and Indian designer textiles. Easily the poshest textile house in town, prices can rise to an astronomical RM10,000 per metre, but socialites, starlets and politicians' wives flock here for the personalised and attentive service. For the finicky metrosexual who wants the most luxurious fabrics and exclusive tailoring, you can't go wrong with Ermanegildo Zegna, Cerruti and Dormeuil at Summermen's.

For home-furnishings fabric, the ever-dependable IKEA stocks a good range of vibrant fabrics for curtains, bedding and cushions, while Macy is always a great bet for tasteful curtain fabrics. If you feel like pulling out all the stops for your personal palace, you'll want to avail yourself of higher-end brands like Sahco Hesslein and Muirhead at Fabritex, Gardens.

Toys & Games

Keeping little ones amused can be a challenge, especially if you're trying to limit TV time. The secret is a well-stocked toy box – with its wide range of toys and huge stores available at major shopping malls like 1 Utama and Mid Valley Megamall, Toys R Us is always a popular choice. However, if you are more adventurous, you might want to give the niche specialists a go. Early Learning Centre at Gardens and 1 Utama is a UK-origin chain which caters primarily for kids from ages 3 to 8, and which thoughtfully incorporates educational elements into its products. ELC's colourful baby scribblers encourage writing, while the motorcyclettes – that's a mini motorcycle if you haven't guessed already – would definitely make your toddler happy.

For Playstation and video games, Low Yat Plaza and Sungei Wang Plaza have a dizzying range that will leave your tot foaming at the mouth. The bad news is the majority of these shops carry bootlegged copies, but on the plus side, you won't end up burning a hole in your pocket.

Toys & Games		
Early Learning Centre	Various Locations	See p.345
Jigsaw Puzzle World	Mid Valley	03 2938 9199
Low Yat Plaza	Jalan Alor	03 2148 5141
Star Game Station	Mid Valley Megamall	03 2284 3569
Sungei Wang Plaza	Jalan Bukit Bintang	03 2148 6109
Toys R Us	Various Locations	See p.350

Wedding Items

Weddings are big business in Malaysia and there is no shortage of bridal studios to help you capture this once-in-a-lifetime moment for posterity. For tips and recommendations on wedding trousseau, etiquette and general advice for the big day, browse through *Female Brides*, which is available at any major bookshop. Bridal forum www.malaysianbrides.com is another great resource for the cyber-savvy bride. While most reputable hotels offer wedding packages, Concorde and Sunway Hotel are names that come up frequently. Petaling Jaya and Bangsar are replete with bridal houses converted from colonial bungalows which offer everything from bridal gown rental to wedding planning and photography.

You'll also want to capture your once-in-a-lifetime moment for posterity, and a host of bridal studios offer a wedding photography package that can range from a thousand ringgit to tens of thousands, depending on the complexity of the shoot and the number of costumes you want to parade in. In recent years, however, more discerning consumers have begun gravitating to offbeat shots that capture spontaneous moments as well as garden-variety staged studio shots, and Kid Chan (www.kidchan.com) is the last word in occasion photography. With a decade of industry experience, his impressive client list includes members of the Malaysian royal family, government ministers, as well as international corporate figures and celebrities (www.kidchan.com).

Bridal attire can be expensive, running into several thousand ringgits, so thrifty locals prefer to rent their trousseau from bridal shops. Most shops will let you try on as many gowns as you like till you find the perfect white strapless dress. Yuppies like Pretty in White for its elegant yet affordable gowns. That Special Occasion is also a hot favourite for its exclusive, made-to-measure choices for wedding and evening dresses. Mie Couture is fast without compromising on quality – the chief fashion designer can whip up your dream dress in two weeks upon special request.

If you want to pull out all the stops, why not seek the services of Orson Liyu or Eric Choong, Malaysia's answers to Vera Wang? Fashion magazines like Female Brides love their edgy yet sophisticated gowns. If you want something off the traditional white wedding track, you might want to follow the footsteps of Malaysia's number one songstress Siti Nurhaliza, and seek the expertise of Rizalman, who makes the most exquisite baju kebaya, a two-piece richly embroidered body-hugging long blouse and skirt. Turn up the heat and drool over sequins and ruffles conjured up by top local designers, Rizalman Ibrahim and Bernard Chandran. If you are prepared to fork out a pretty penny you'll make heads turn for sure.

Guests and newlyweds alike will love online wedding planner My Chocolate Mousse. From gift registry, drawing up a meticulous directory of wedding venues, photographers, florists, dressmakers, invitation card-makers and an online manager to organise your guest seating – it's all covered for you. For that all-important wedding cake, Just Heavenly is a popular choice for their unusual flavours like butterscotch almandie. You will be hard-pressed to select from over a thousand designs at Choffles Wedding Cake Studio. It also produces bomboniere gifts, given as a token of appreciation for your guests. For exquisite personalised wedding cards, Art is Art has a marvellous selection of classic designs, perfumed cards and even 3D versions.

With so many resources at your disposal, you can concentrate on looking radiant on your big day, while other people do the legwork.

Know It All

At the back of this chapter you'll find a detailed shopping directory. It tells you where to find all the branches of your favourite stores – handy for when you're out of your usual neighbourhood.

Wedding Items

Armadale Weddings	03 2095 5300	www.armadale.com.my
Art is Art	03 3167 8929	www.artisart.com.my
Bernard Chandran	03 2145 0534	na
Carven Ong	03 2142 6232	www.carvenong.com.my
Chocolate Mousse	03 6201 3969	www.mychocolatemousse.com
Choffles Wedding Cake Studio	03 7726 6362	www.choffles.com
Covershots – The Wedding Shop	03 4252 5688	www.covershots.com.my
Eric Choong	03 2283 2113	www.ericchoong.com
Flower Girls	03 7710 5813	na
The Hip List	03 2300 1608	www.the-hiplist.com
Just Heavenly	03 2287 9867	www.justheavenly.biz
Just Married Bridal	03 2032 2663	na
Kidchanstudio	03 2282 0339	www.kidchanstudio.com
Malaysian Brides Forum	na	www.malaysianbrides.com
Mie Couture	03 2282 1618	www.miecouture.com
Orson Liyu	03 2148 2296	na
Picaso Bridal Gallery	03 7492 1989	na
Pretty in White	03 2300 2236	www.prettyinwhite.com.my
Rizalman Ibrahim Couture	03 2141 6149	www.rizalmanibrahim.com.my
That Special Occasion	03 2300 0613	www.thatspecialoccasion.net

Areas To Shop

KL is a major shopping destination and you can find just about anything you will ever need, from cheap tat right up to luxurious international designer brands. The city is a true melting pot, and KLites readily absorb trends from around the world, so the range of goods on offer is quite staggering.

Shopping is part of the culture here, and more and more high-end stores and international brands are setting up in KL all the time. Expats tend to shop in their own neighbourhoods, but many people are also prepared to travel short distances to secure a great bargain or enjoy more variety. Bintang Walk, Suria KLCC and The Gardens are good for luxury brand shopping and for fashionistas. For more choices at affordable prices, Mid Valley Megamall, Sunway Pyramid and 1 Utama are local favourites. Central Market and Petaling Street (Chinatown) are touristy, but still worth a visit, and Little India is interesting for the occasional trip too. Tourist shopping havens are located in the city centre, while major malls are located in the city centre as well as the suburbs of Petaling Jaya. Hypermarkets are usually found in the suburban areas. The mega sales take place before and during festive seasons, and in the middle and end of the year. With mark downs as low as 70%, this is the best time to grab bargains. Most shopping places are built in a way that is friendly for people with disabilities. You will not fail to find an ATM in any shopping area.

Bangsar

Jalan Telawi
Bangsar
🚇 *Bangsar*

Bangsar is a favourite hangout area for expats and tends to cater for higher income groups. Household shopping is made convenient with the Bangsar Shopping Centre, and Bangsar Village I and II, as well as shopping for the latest fashion at independent boutiques that open till 22:00. The atmosphere is casual during the day and glam during the evening, with a host of restaurants and bars. Popular hangout places that have stood the test of time are La Bodega and The Social (both bars) and Devi's Corner mamak stall. Bangsar is also an area in which to see and be seen on Saturday nights, and to hang out on Sunday for the night market. Parking is at the shopping malls, the residential area within walking distance, or along the street. At night, there are unofficial parking attendants who ask for a fee when you park your car along Jalan Telawi 2 and 3, and most people oblige to avoid 'problems'.

Bintang Walk

Jalan Bukit Bintang
Bukit Bintang
🚇 *Bukit Bintang*

Bintang Walk is located along Jalan Bukit Bintang and the area is home to several main shopping malls that cater for every fashion need and budget – Pavilion, Lot 10, Starhill Gallery, KL Plaza, and Sungai Wang Plaza. Apart from non-stop shopping, you will also find alfresco eating, fine dining restaurants, exclusive boutique spas, reflexology centres (to massage those tired feet from walking), and clubs along Bintang Walk. Some of the finest hotels in Malaysia are located here too – The Westin, JW Marriott, and Ritz Carlton, among others. Bintang Walk is definitely one of the happening places for shopping, dining, and clubbing, and is popular with locals, expats and tourists alike. Parking is available at the shopping malls (try Pavilion, since it is newer) or hotels.

Chinatown (Petaling Street)

Jalan Petaling
& Jalan Tun
H.S. Lee
Chinatown
🚇 *Pasar Seni*

This is one of the oldest shopping areas in KL. You'll often hear local Chinese residents affectionately calling Petaling Street 'Chi Cheong Kai' (starch flour street), since the original inhabitants ran tapioca mills here. he bustling market is open throughout the year, day and night, and covers Jalan Petaling through to Jalan Tun HS Lee. It's the place to go if imitation bags are your bag – shop around and you can find pretty good fake handbags, watches, sunglasses and T-shirts, as well as pirated CDs and DVDs under a covered walkway. Bargaining is expected and prices can go

Chinatown

◀ **Jalan Masjid India**
Little India
🚇 **Masjid Jamek**

down to 40% or even more. But you should only make the effort to bargain if you are serious about purchasing, or the vendor may be offended and will scold you. You will also find stalls selling Chinese street delicacies. Perpendicular to Hong Leong Bank, there is a stall selling very smooth tau-fu-fa (bean curd), a must-try. It is reputed to be a favourite of a former prime minister. Surrounding Petaling Street are coffee shops and apparel, shoe and toy shops, and budget hotels (rental by night or by the hour), housed in pre-independence Chinese shophouses. Nearby is the excellent, covered Central Market (see p.333). The area gets particularly crowded during the weekends. You can park at the covered multi-storey carpark in Klang Bus Station (Jalan Sultan) but be advised, the interior of the carpark is dingy. Alternatively, park at Plaza First Nationwide (Jalan Tun HS Lee). It is advisable to take the Putra LRT connection to Pasar Seni, which is a few minutes walk away to the area. Be mindful of personal belongings.

Little India

Little India is located on Jalan Masjid India, the area of shops and stalls that lies around the corner from Masjid Jamek LRT station and Menara OCBC and goes right up to Semua House. In this area, you can find shops selling Muslim clothing such as headscarves and baju kurung, and Indian clothing such as sequined sarees. Prices are informal and by all means you should bargain to get the best deals – it's part of the fun. You can also buy condiments, spices and personal care products imported from India at New Maliga. When it comes to food, the deep fried keropok ikan (fish crackers) and pisang goreng (banana fritters) are must for any visitor. These delicacies can be found among the first few stalls as you walk into Little India. The atmosphere of this bustling area is vibrant and heady, and it is popular with local Malays and Indians, Indian and western expats, and tourists. The best time to go is during the daytime. As with any area of any city in the world, be careful of your belongings, look out for pickpockets, especially when it's busy, and avoid the quiet back lanes. It's not a particularly easy area to get to by car, with not much parking and heavy traffic. It's advisable to take the Putra LRT or Star LRT train to Masjid Jamek.

Department Stores

Department stores are usually located within shopping malls and are often the anchor tenants that pull in the crowds. Most department stores, except for Robinsons and Parkson premium stores in Pavilion and Suria KLCC, cater for the wider market. All department stores sell popular international brands of cosmetics, skincare and fragrances (with some variation among the stores) such as La Mer, Estee Lauder and Lancome, and offer gift wrapping, hamper services and clothes alteration. Some even come equipped with a nursing room. All major credit cards are accepted with no minimum spend required. Personal shopping, or rather personal stylist services, is still a relatively new concept and has traditionally been confined to members of the royal family and VIPs. It is only available to the public at large in Robinsons and selected stores of Parkson and Isetan (arranging an appointment is encouraged). Department stores are usually open from 10:00 to 22:00 every day including major public holidays. During the eve of a major festive day, large department stores may open till 23:00 for last-minute shoppers.

Various Locations ◄

Isetan
See p.347 | *www.isetankl.com.my*

Isetan has been operating in Malaysia since 1990 and remains one of the most popular department stores for its mix of fashionable and conservative work outfits and accessories, and hip casual and party wear, bags and shoes. It also offers beautiful household decorative items for the living room, kitchen and bathroom as well as fittings at mid-range prices onwards. With its strong brand name, any item that comes from Isetan often makes a good gift to a friendly local host. Isetan carries its own line of mid-priced fashion, including Cultivation and Crescendo, which flatters most body shapes, as well as designs for larger women (prices are RM60 and above on average). It houses a mix of foreign brands such as MNG (Mango), Guess, Polo Ralph Lauren, DKNY and BCBG, as well as some local premium brands such as Eclipse for its casual elegant wear. For men there is, among others, Raoul, CK and Oakley for clothes and sunglasses. Spending members of the Isetan Member Club card can get shopping vouchers, two hours of free parking, invitation to sales previews, and weekday discounts at the supermarket. Other branches: Lot 10, 03 2141 7777 and The Gardens 03 2283 1777.

Various Locations ◄

Jusco Department Store
See p.347 | *www.jusco.com.my*

One of the biggest stores in Malaysia, Jusco caters for the needs of the entire family at highly affordable prices. If you are looking for something with no frills and no scary price tags, Jusco is the store to visit. It offers a wide selection of items with basic designs for the home such as curtains, cushions, kitchen utensils and bathroom fittings. Consumer electrical goods can be purchased with a 12 month installment plan using selected credit cards. Its Home Centre in 1 Utama sells lights, paints, and items needed for DIY. It has a children's section for clothes, toys and games, and a section for travel bags and winter wear, sports equipment and apparel. There is a large floor section of comfortable and practical street and work clothes for men and women at decent prices (on average above RM40). Jusco also carries a wide selection of larger sizes. J-card holders enjoy shopping privileges such as 10% to 20% discounts on a regular basis.

Various Locations ◄

Marks & Spencer
See p.348 | *www.marksandspencer.com*

This perennial local favourite is especially popular for its food items such as biscuits, chocolates other non-perishable goods (alas, no full food markets here). It also has a decent selection of reasonably priced wines. And of course, it's the first choice for thousands of women when shopping for lingerie – for something a little saucy or just for daily whites, you can't beat the quality here. It's also a good stop for shoes, handbags and personal care products. And clothes, of course – M&S sells lots of good basic items, so if you're after a pair of black trousers, or a good white blouse, you'll probably hit the jackpot. What you might not find is anything that has featured recently on catwalks or outlandish designs – M&S is the place to go for classic, conservative items. Sizes are usually larger, so for women size 12 and above it's a godsend. Various clothing lines like Per Una and Autograph add a bit of variety. If you give your details to any one of the staff in store, they will add you to the mailing list to be kept informed of impending sales.

Various Locations

Metrojaya

See p.348 | *www.metrojaya.com*

Metrojaya has evolved over the years to stay relevant to the tastes of upmarket residents. It has a wide selection of items for the home which are nicely designed or packaged, and often good value for the quality. It carries a wide range of mid-priced fashion labels for working clothes, sportswear and smart casual wear for women and men (prices on average RM60 and above). Its first fashion concept store, MJ by Metrojaya at The Curve, is meant to appeal to the young adult crowd with funky dresses and office wear at prices starting from RM80. Metrojaya has unique in-house labels, East India Company and Somerset Bay, which feature nice soft prints and feminine dresses. For men, there are brands like Dockers and John Langford. MJ Card members enjoy discounts, sales previews, and free gifts.

Various Locations

Parkson

See p.348 | *www.parkson.com.my*

Parkson was established in the 1980s and has come a long way, evolving from a neighbourhood department store serving the man-in-the-street to creating impressive store concepts. While it has retained its chain of small neighbourhood shops, it has introduced premium stores in Suria KLCC and Pavilion (the newest and most upmarket of the chain), to form one of the largest department store chains in the country. The premium stores have a more contemporary retail feel and wider walkways, offering a comfortable shopping experience. They carry a mix of international designers such as Anya Hindmarch for handbags, and Liz Claiborne, Principles and Warehouse for smart casual wear. In Pavilion, they house a fairly large collection of local high-end independent labels, some with prices starting from RM1,000 for casual elegant wear. The lingerie section is discreetly located away from the public eye so that women can shop in privacy. For men, there are T-shirts by Nautica, and suits from The Saville Row Company and Guy Laroche. Be prepared to spend more than RM200 per item in Parkson. Personal shopping services are available in Pavilion and Suria KLCC. Parkson Elite Cardholders enjoy instant rebates, sales previews, free parking for a limited time, and invitations to exclusive events in Pavilion and KLCC. Its other store, U Parkson at 1 Utama, caters to upper middle class shoppers with its selection of women's and mens' work and casual elegant clothes at premium prices (on average above RM80). Parkson also has a chic selection of bedsheets, curtains and rugs, which are good for those who like to use colours to enhance their homes.

The Gardens
*The Boulevard, Mid
Valley City Lingkaran
Syed Putra*
🚇 *Mid Valley*

Robinsons

03 2089 1111 | *www.robinsons.com.my*

Taking up three floors in The Gardens, Robinsons offers a range of gorgeous household items such as bed linens, kitchen utensils and bathroom fittings, sophisticated casual and glam outfits with fabulous embellishments from labels such as Coast and Trucco, and handbag labels such as Lulu Guinness. Minimum average prices for clothes start from RM300. For an average person living on a regular paycheck in Malaysia, the prices here may seem a little mind-boggling, although those on decent expat packages may enjoy flashing their cash here. Either way, this is a good place to shop for one-off gifts for formal occasions, or for a person that you want to impress, or simply to buy beautiful things for your home. Robinsons ties up with a platinum credit card to offer shopping privileges such as discounts, low interest and the services of a personal stylist.

Hypermarkets

KL is home to some fairly enormous hypermarkets that usually offer better value than smaller supermarkets. They are real 'one-stop shops' where you can wheel your trolley up and down wide aisles full of virtually anything you might need for day-to-day living: fresh produce, frozen foods, cold meats, cakes, beverages, household items, electrical goods, personal care products, plastic shelves, toys, and affordable apparel, sweaters, undergarments, shoes and bags.

Most hypermarkets publish weekly or monthly specials so keep your eyes on the local press for details. It may be worth driving out of your way to stock up on a particularly cheap non-perishable item offered in a hypermarket, although most people tend to shop in their nearest one. Every now and then competitor hypermarkets engage in price wars, which is always good news for consumers.

No hypermarket can be said to have the lowest prices consistently, so the best way to spot lower prices is through the newspapers or in pamphlets which are either handed out in store or distributed in nearby neighbourhoods. The best time to shop in hypermarkets is early mornings or late evenings – otherwise you could find yourself one in a vast crowd of trolley shoppers.

Supermarkets are usually much smaller and often found in shopping malls. They typically only sell foodstuffs, alcohol, personal hygiene items and homecare products. While they may not always offer a lower price, they provide convenience and often stock a wider range of speciality foods such as Japanese, Korean or European items, making them popular with expats.

Various Locations

Carrefour
See p.345 | www.carrefour.com.my

Just like any large hypermarket, French-owned Carrefour sells everything you could possibly need for a family household on a daily basis, from clothing to basic furniture and from electronics to pastries and frozen foods. Carrefour regularly advertises shopping deals in local daily newspapers and its promotional catalogue is also available on its website. Carrefour offers delivery services (charges apply) and ties up with a local credit card company to offer shopping privileges.

Bangsar Shopping Centre
Bangsar
Map 6 E1

Cold Storage Supermarket
03 2094 2900

Cold Storage started out by selling imported fresh meat to expats living in Malaysia, and plenty of foreign residents still shop here for their household needs. The location of most of its branches in expat enclaves, like Bangsar, could partly explain its appeal, but it could also be down to a good selection of breakfast cereals, salads, cheese, yoghurts and wine. You can buy pre-packed salads, sushi and a range of other ready-to-eat foods, so it's a popular haunt for office workers grabbing lunch on the run. Copies of foreign newspapers such as *The Times*, *The Australian* and *Le Monde* are also available here. If you are planning on doing a large shop, you can use the store's delivery service; this comes in particularly handy if you are using public transport.

Various Locations

Giant
See p.346 | www.giant.com.my

Giant is instantly recognisable by its distinctive green and yellow signage and its riot of colourful decorations. It provides an interesting shopping experience for those who do not want to shop in boring, sterile environments. With great monthly deals on household items like electronics, kitchen utensils and affordable clothing, it's a popular destination for those on a budget. These deals are advertised in local newspapers and in pamphlets which are available at in-store information counters, and they are also sent via email newsletter, for which you can sign up on their website. Branches of Giant are usually found in shopping malls or in standalone buildings with plenty of parking. For a list of other branches, see the directory on p.344.

Various Locations ◄

Isetan

See p.347 | www.isetankl.com.my

Isetan supermarkets are popular with Japanese residents as it is one of the best places to get imported Japanese frozen, canned and pre-packed food and liquor. You can buy pre-packed sushi for lunch or dinner. Apart from Japanese items, it also sells mainstream brands for household and personal care products but do not be surprised if some products are more expensive than in the hypermarkets. Cooler bags are also for sale. It is generally pleasant to shop in this supermarket but the walkways may be a bit narrow. .

Various Locations ◄

Jusco

See p.347 | www.jusco.com.my

Apart from the mainstream homecare and personal care items, Jusco also offers a counter that sells organic fresh fruits and vegetables, as well as a selection of Japanese and Korean frozen food, pre-packed food and condiments. J-Card members can get points when they shop at here, and the queues tend to be shorter compared to hypermarkets. Jusco supermarkets are located in shopping malls where the Jusco department stores are found (see p.347).

Various Locations ◄

Tesco

See p.350 | www.tesco.com.my

Many new residents love the idea that they can still pop down to their local Tesco even though they're living miles from home. Apart from mainstream household brands, Tesco also sells products under its own label at a lower price – many of these, except for perishable items, are sold in large quantities. The layout of the stores is generally spacious and shelves are well-stocked, providing a comfortable shopping experience. Special offers are usually promoted with flyers distributed in nearby neighbourhoods. Tesco offers a loyalty card where you can rack up points for each purchase, and redeem them for vouchers. Some Tesco stores are open right up until 23:00.

Markets

Markets add flavour to the shopping scene in Malaysia, particularly the popular all-night markets. You can find trinkets, casual clothes, pashmina scarves, and imitation brands of wallets, handbags and T-shirts, and much more. In spite of local clampdowns by the authorities, you will still be able to find street vendors peddling top-grade Dior, Louis Vuitton and Guess fake handbags, or sometimes imitations with modifications to the logo. Night markets are a haven for local street food at cheap prices. Vendors are compelled by law to show prices, so do not pay more than what is displayed.

Amcorp Mall
Petaling Jaya
🚇 *Taman Jaya*

Amcorp Mall Flea Market

This is the only authentic flea market in the Klang Valley. It is most well known for its local Baba Nyonya antiques, vinyl music records, vintage wine bottles, books and British and American magazine and comic titles that are already out of print, as well as collectibles from Malaysia's pre-independence days. Antique experts caution that it is best to bargain as the prices are likely to be inflated. It is nevertheless a place that still appeals to antique lovers on the prowl for the rare and unusual. Some stalls also sell home-made cakes and cookies, and household Malay decorative items.

Located on the lower ground floor of Amcorp Mall, the flea market has about around 50 stalls, and is open from 10:00 to 18:00 on the weekends. You can park at Amcorp Mall, or take the Putra LRT to the Taman Jaya station. The mall is located across from the station.

Bangsar Night Market

Btn Jalan Maarof & Jalan Telawi 2
Bangsar

Locals call this the Bangsar Pasar Malam (night market). Taking place on Sundays, the casual open-air wet market attracts both locals and expats, the young and old, who predominantly live in the upscale areas such as Bangsar, Damansara Heights, Kenny Hills, Hartamas and Mont' Kiara. Here you can find vegetables, fruits, and flowers that are slightly more expensive than in hypermarkets, but possibly fresher. Prices for foodstuffs are fixed and bargaining is not entertained. Many shoppers here are regulars and they come armed with a basket or trolley to support their favourite vendors. For street food, recommendations are the Chinese sweet snacks such as the peanut pancake (ah pong), and tasty Indian and Malay food such as the murtabak and tandoori chicken. The ancillary stalls sell pashmina scarves, fake wallets, handbags, and watches, and for these goods it is often possible to haggle a discount of up to 30%. The walking area between each row of stalls is narrow and crowded, and vendors continually shout out special offers which adds to the liveliness of the place. Many stalls are set up as early as 15:30 to make up for possible rainy nights. It gets busy from 17:00 to 22:00 (closing time). A note of caution is not to park on this street on Sunday afternoons as the vendors will be setting up their stalls, and it might be difficult for you to move your car.

Central Market (Pasar Seni)

Jalan Hang Kasturi
Chinatown
🚇 *Pasar Seni*
Map 12 C1

03 2031 0339 | *www.centralmarket-kl.com.my*
Central Market, the granddaddy of all markets, was established way back in 1888. It was originally an open wet market but has evolved to become a tourist centre for Malaysian arts, handicrafts, souvenirs and traditional clothing, with a permanent structure having been built to house the vendors. It is such a popular attraction that it has been classified as a heritage site by the Malaysian Heritage Society. It's a one-stop shop for many wonderful items, from sarong and batik cloth to the wau or traditional

Central Market

kite – but there are so many items for sale here that you should set aside some time for a good browse. Occasionally the Central Market is a venue for cultural events such as film screenings, art exhibitions and underground music performances. It is just a few minutes' walk from Petaling Street, and is easy to get to with public transport, being right near the Klang bus stand, the Pudu bus station and the Pasar Seni stop on the Putra LRT line. There is ample parking in front of the market.

The Curve
Petaling Jaya
🚇 *Kepong*

The Curve Street Market

www.thecurve.com.my

Held on Saturdays and Sundays, this large street market offers a range of casual accessories, dresses, T-shirts, handbags, shoes and household decorative items imported from China and Hong Kong. Some amount of bargaining is usually possible when you buy multiple items, but do not expect to pay the lower prices you would pay in China. The market appears quite crowded, but this is mainly down to the limited walking space in between vendors. However, it is very popular with couples and families and there are lots of interesting things to see. The crowd peaks from midday onwards as families come out to do their shopping in nearby Tesco, although the market is open from 10:30 to 22:00 so you should be able to find a time when it is less busy.

Forget Me Not

Some shopping malls are huge and so it is wise to remember where you park your car. Look out for the number on the nearest pillar in the car park, or take note of the name of the shop which is closest to the entrance you came out. If you are lost, do seek help from the security guards. There are patrol officers who can go around the parking area to help you locate your car.

Fountain Courtyard
Plaza Mont'Kiara
Mont Kiara

Mont' Kiara Fiesta Nite

This night market is held every Thursday in the fountain courtyard of Plaza Mont'Kiara, and offers an array of local Malaysian food like fried rice, chicken rice, street delicacies, cakes and fruits, as well as fresh flowers and plants. Prices are similar to those at hawker centres in KL. The environment is clean, the atmosphere is carnival-like, and there is ample walking space, so no need to jostle with the crowd to get from one stall to the next. The market is open from 18:00 to 22:00, but it gets harder to drive to after about 19:00 when traffic picks up. Parking along Jalan Mont'Kiara is free but hard to find. The best option is to park inside the Plaza.

Fountain Courtyard
Plaza Mont'Kiara
Mont Kiara

Mont' Kiara Sunday ABC Market

www.plazamontkiara.com.my

ABC stands for arts, bric-a-brac and crafts, and this open-air market is held every Sunday in the upmarket suburb of Mont'Kiara. The stalls sell a lot of mass-market, imported, casual womenswear from the far east, as well as accessories and shoes. It's a good place to shop for branded handbags at knockdown prices, as well as hand-painted decorative items for the home. Vendors are usually friendly and you'll see many expats with their own stalls here. The atmosphere is casual, and there is a definite 'cosy neighbourhood' feel to the place. Bargaining is acceptable at some stalls or if you buy several items, although vendors don't usually go lower than the first discounted price they offer, which is usually just 10% (or sometimes 20%) off the original price. After browsing the stalls you can grab a cold beer at the Deutsches Bierhaus, and relax while you watch the world go by. The market is open from 10:00 to 18:00, but it is best to go before 11:00 or from 16:00 to 18:00 because it is cooler and there are less people. Parking along Jalan Mont'Kiara is free, and you might find a lucky parking spot during quieter hours. At peak times you can forget it though; it's best to park inside Plaza Mont'Kiara.

Shopping Malls

Shopping malls are the place to be if you've got money to burn. On the ground floor, you will find the premium tenants such as the higher end brands and designer labels. Anchor tenants usually take up a portion at both ends of each mall and occupy at least two or three floors. Suria KLCC and Bukit Bintang (Starhill Gallery and Pavilion) are high-end, while Mid Valley Megamall caters for the mass market and families. Malls are usually open from 10:00 to 22:00 every day, including public holidays. Most malls are friendly for people with disabilities unless mentioned otherwise in the following sections.

Lebuh Bandar Utama
Bandar Utama
Petaling Jaya
🚇 *Kelana Jaya*
Map 4 A4

1 Utama

03 7710 8118 | *www.1utama.com.my*

This suburban mall caters to families living in the neighbourhoods of Bandar Utama, Tropicana, Kota Damansara, Mutiara Damansara and Bandar Sri Damansara, and gets extremely crowded at weekends. The old wing caters more for teenagers and kids, while the new wing features international brands and swanky restaurants. In the old wing you'll also find Jusco department store, Marks & Spencer, Edmunser and Tanjung Golden Village (TGB) Cineplex. In the new wing, you will find Parkson, Giant, GSC Cineplex, MPH Bookstore (two floors) and some international designer brands such as BCBG Maxazria, CK, DKNY, Dockers, Zara, as well as Ms Read for larger sizes, and British India (its store in 1 Utama is the largest). You will find high quality funky street wear and smart casual outfits. Khazanah offers a beautiful selection of colourful organza table runners, curtains and cushion covers in a fusion of Indian and Middle Eastern styles. You can find organic foods and toiletries at Country Farm Organics, or work out in Celebrity Fitness, a popular gym with a hip environment and evening yoga and dance classes. Dragon I in the new wing, Oriental Cravings and Peranakan Place are all excellent restaurants if you're stopping for dinner. At peak times, the easiest place to find parking will be the lot outside the new wing (Giant) where there is a flat rate (hourly rate applies for indoor parking). There is a taxi stand outside. The mall adjoins One World Hotel. The Aeroline coach to Singapore leaves from 1 Utama, and there is also a bus service to Genting Highlands.

1 Utama

Maju Junction

Amcorp Mall

Bangsar Shopping Centre (BSC)

285 Jalan Maarof
Bangsar
🚇 *Bangsar*
Map 6 E1

03 2094 7700

Despite being one of the smallest malls Bangsar Shopping Centre (BSC) serves the expats and the locals who live in this area well. It has had somewhat of a makeover in recent years, with new front retail outlets such as La Bodega, the popular open format Spanish pub and cafe, and Dome, a place loved for its pies and desserts. Other eateries include the posh-looking Alexis bistro and wine bar, a popular hangout for young urban professionals. There is Cold Storage as well as Mr Ho's Fine Meats, which offers a great selection of meats and condiments (bookings are accepted). Cigars can be bought from Wain & Cerut. There is a shoemaker where you can get shoes custom-made (Thomas Chan), as well as a shoe and bag repair shop in the basement that offers independent advice and services at reasonable prices. Tasteful fine furniture is available in Janine, which can also custom make furniture using imported fabrics from the UK and India. The Actors Studio here is for theatre lovers. BSC offers valet services, basement parking, and has a taxi stand located outside the main entrance.

Bangsar Village I (BVI)

Jalan Telawi 1
Bangsar
🚇 *Bangsar*
Map 6 E2

03 2282 1808

BVI is a relatively small but popular neighbourhood mall that serves the local and expat communities living in the affluent neighbourhoods of Bangsar, Bukit Tunku (Kenny Hills), Damansara Heights, Hartamas and Mont'Kiara. Interesting eateries are the Hong Kong-style Chatterbox, DLish for its sandwiches, quiches and fresh juices, and Bakerzin for its heavenly cakes in tiny portions (so that you can sample more varieties). BVI houses a supermarket called the Village Grocer, which sells the basic day-to-day essentials for the household as well as copies of foreign newspapers such as *Daily Mail*, *The Independent* and *The Times*. There are shops that sell clothes, toys and learning aids for kids. Other notable shops are the Farm Organics shop and a whiskey specialist. Parking is available in the basement or for free in the residential area nearby.

Bangsar Village II (BVII)

2 Jalan Telawi 1
Bangsar
🚇 *Bangsar*
Map 6 E2

03 2288 1200 | www.bangsarvillage.com

The first thing you'll notice about Bangsar Village (BVII) is its fabulous indoor perfumed scent. BVII is connected by a bridge to Bangsar Village I. While BVI is for the family, BVII is entirely devoted to fashion and a leisurely lifestyle. It houses an eclectic mix of chic local boutiques and international labels, namely Mumbai Se, Trucco, Ted Baker, Massimo Dutti, and Guess, as well as the favourite Spanish brand, Zara. Here, you will find a range of casual, elegant and formal wear. You can also get quirky and retro T-shirts, dresses, shoes and purses at Khai and Marmalade Boutique at premium prices. Indulge yourself at the Hammam, the Turkish-inspired baths, or at Lancome Beauty Institute for a relaxing facial. Or for something at home, Harnn Natural Home Spa offers a wide selection of relaxing aromatherapy oils. There are also some nice restaurants here, notably Delicious, which is hugely popular among professionals and expats, and Suchan, which is famous for its banoffie pie. For more casual dining, drop by at Marmalade for its gorgeous salads in generous portions. The MPH bookstore occupies two floors. The most famous upmarket local hair salon, A Cut Above, is also here. Parking is in the basement or for free at the nearby houses.

Berjaya Times Square

1 Jalan Imbi
Bukit Bintang
🚇 *Imbi*
Map 13 B2

03 2144 9821 | www.timessquarekl.com

Berjaya Times Square is the largest shopping mall in Malaysia, covering an area of 3.45 million sq ft, with 10 floors. It houses the biggest Borders bookshop, Metrojaya, Cold Storage Supermarket, Ampang Superbowl, the largest IMAX Theatre (3D viewing) in south east Asia, and Cosmo's World Theme Park, the largest indoor theme park in the country. At Cosmo's, there are many fun rides available including rollercoasters. As well as being a popular hangout for teenagers and families with young children, it boasts an impressive number of independent stores, mainly selling affordable street wear, and in some shops like Wearhaus, you can buy Abercombie & Fitch and Dolce & Gabana items at factory prices. Interesting shops are Cue Station, which sells snooker equipment, while the High Tech game area has gaming slots. For something grungy or non-mainstream, I-Socks Boutique sells alternative fashion items like netted and lacy leggings. Parking is in the basement or alternatively, you can take a taxi – there is usually a long queue of taxis waiting outside. The Imbi monorail station is also connected to the mall. Security is hardly a concern, with a police hut located outside. Next to the mall is the Berjaya Times Square Hotel & Convention Centre and, across the road is the Melia Hotel.

111 Jalan Bukit Bintang
Bukit Bintang
🚇 **Bukit Bintang**
Map 13 B1

Bukit Bintang Plaza (BB Plaza)
03 2148 7411
Bukit Bintang (BB) Plaza plays second fiddle to the adjoining shopping centre, Sungei Wang Plaza (p.341). Here, you will find an assortment of stores and standalone stalls, some selling phones, street wear and trinkets. There are speciality shops like Basheer Graphics Books, which stocks coffee table books, and T-Shirt Republic, which sells T-shirts with quirky wordings. Just outside the entrance is Al-Turka Ice-Cream, where the vendor will entertain you each time he scoops home-made Turkish ice-cream. Parking is available in the plaza and there is a taxi stand outside. There are lifts in the plaza but the entrance into the plaza is not friendly for people with disabilities.

No.6 Jalan PJU 7/3
Mutiara Damansara
Petaling Jaya
🚇 **Kepong**

The Curve
03 7710 6868 | www.thecurve.com.my
The Curve started on a rather low note when it first opened but traffic has picked up significantly thanks to residents living in Mutiara Damansara and Kota Damansara. The place is busy on weekends and during the run-up to public holidays. This is a foodie place: slightly more than 50% of its space is filled with independent eateries serving local, Japanese and western food. Laundry, an open-air pub and restaurant which is packed at nights, is worth a special mention. It closes at 01:00 at weekends, and at midnight on other days. The IT area is a place where you can find PCs and peripherals but the prices are fixed and usually higher than Low Yat Plaza (p.339). The Curve connects to Ikano Power Centre, Tesco and IKEA.

Mid Valley City
Lingkaran Syed Putra
Mid Valley
🚇 **Mid Valley**

The Gardens
03 2297 0288 | www.midvalleygardens.com.my
The Gardens, located across from Mid Valley Megamall, is dedicated to the sophisticated, discerning and to those who seek a luxurious lifestyle. It was opened at the same time as Pavilion in 2007. The receptionists in their smart uniforms welcome you with big smiles, and are extremely friendly and helpful. Anchor tenants are Isetan and Robinsons. Some big international brands are here – Coach, Karen Miller and DKNY. Interesting stores are Wedgwood, Left (custom-made shoes for men), Yogitree (healthy food cafe and sells yoga apparel), Justlife (organic food), The Address (find unusual decorative items hand picked by a chic French designer), LifeBaby (quirky kids' wear), and 2201 Fashion Avenue, which showcases the fashion works of talented local designers. For the foodies, there is Delights of Gurney Drive where you can supposedly get the best of Penang food, and Din Tai Fung for its wonderful dumplings, albeit in small portions for the price. For a luxurious movie experience, you can check out GSC Signature where you can wine and dine before watching a

movie in a posh setting. For relaxation, members of the top floor yoga centre, spa and hair salon can use the guest lounge to rest and read in privacy. The VIP lounge is by invitation only. Valet services are provided and there is also premium taxi service just outside The Gardens. Mid Valley is on the KTM Komuter line, so it's easy to get to even without a car.

Ikano Power Centre

2 Jalan PJU7/2
Petaling Jaya
Kepong Sentral

03 7720 7333

Ikano receives a spillover of the visitors that throng IKEA, Tesco and The Curve, and is lively during the weekends. Its concept is family oriented with shops such as Cold Storage, Guardian pharmacy, Popular bookstore (good if you are looking for books in Mandarin), and various types of eateries ranging from Italian, Japanese, local Kopitiam, and fast food (A&W). Popular outlets are Manhattan Fish Market, a homegrown fish & chips restaurant, and Kluang Station, which offers a mix of local and western options. Kluang Station's signature dish is its chicken chop. For furnishings, there is an eclectic mix of Balinese-type decorative fixtures and fittings available at Barang Barang. The Pet Safari, the largest pet store in Malaysia, has a huge selection of petfood and fish, an in-house veterinarian, and a grooming and training salon. Other places of interest are the shoe repair shop on the ground floor, but its services are pricey. Several independent stores, located in the area that connects Ikano to IKEA, sell clothes and handbags at low prices for young adults. The Brands Outlet also sells a range of casual clothes, shoes and bags at low prices. A free shuttle bus links Ikano to the Kelana Jaya LRT station, or you can take a 15 minute cab drive from Kepong Sentral.

Kuala Lumpur Plaza (KL Plaza)

179 Jalan Bukit
Bintang
Bukit Bintang
Bukit Bintang
Map 13 C1

03 2141 7288

KL Plaza is relatively quiet these days and mainly houses independent boutiques selling casual elegant outfits. Worth a notable mention is the boutique owned by Bernard Chandran, Malaysia's top couturier. The shoe boutique on the ground floor, Pedal Works, has shoes as small as size three. The Coffee Bean outlet next to the entrance is also a popular hangout. KL Plaza is worth a visit if you are in the area and on the lookout for casual or elegant wear, or when you are on your way to Starhill Gallery and Pavilion. Above the shopping area are office suites and condominiums.

Lot 10

50 Jalan Sultan Ismail
Bukit Bintang
Bukit Bintang
Map 13 C1

This is a landmark shopping area synonymous with fashionable stores, as the first Isetan in Malaysia was established here. This is a must-visit place for fashionistas. You won't miss the building with its striking green colour facade. Its main attraction is Isetan, the anchor tenant, which continues to carry various lines of fashionable clothing, and remains the busiest part of Lot 10, especially during the sales. Lot 10 also houses premium local brands such as Eclipse and Tangoo, and you will also find Andy Ho Haute Coiffure (Andy Ho is one of the leading hairstylist in Malaysia). There is a taxi stand outside the mall.

Low Yat Plaza

7 Jalan Bukit Bintang
Bukit Bintang
Imbi
Map 13 B2

03 2148 3651 | *www.plazalowyat.com*

Low Yat Plaza is probably the closest thing to heaven for tech geeks. With its brightly-lit six floors, you will find whatever you need from any brand of personal computers, including generic brands (Dell is also here), handphones, DVDs, games and peripherals. People come here for the selection of products, low prices and to seek advice. Bargaining is encouraged – you may be able to get discounts of up to 40% in the stalls or smaller stores. There is bound to be variation in some prices for certain items and shops located in higher floors may be cheaper at times because they do not throw in goodies or they stock a cheaper line of product. Hence, it is recommended that you diligently compare prices in several stores to see what they have, and that you ask for a discount and freebies before deciding on where to buy. Low Yat provides valet services, although it is easy to get to using public transport. Do not be intimidated by the bouncer-looking chaps who managed the valet counter – they're quite harmless really.

Mid Valley City
Lingkara Syed Putra
Mid Valley
🚇 *Mid Valley*
Map 6 F3

Mid Valley Megamall
03 2289 8688 | *www.midvalley.com.my*

Mid Valley Megamall is one of the largest shopping malls in South East Asia, possibly one of the busiest too, and is reputed to be located in one of the best feng shui spots in the Klang Valley. Whether you're looking for food, entertainment, beauty services, clothes or speciality items, you'll find it here, along with great service and a huge variety. The anchor tenants are Jusco, Metrojaya and Carrefour, and the mall also has discount stores like the Factory Outlet Store and Why Pay More. You can find affordable fashion accessories at shops like Sinma and Bonita. The World of Feng Shui shop on the top floor stocks all kinds of paraphernalia, including trinkets, charms and books. Leisure options within the mall include bowling alley Cosmic Bowl, with 38 lanes, the GSC Cineplex showing the widest selection of foreign films in Malaysia, and California Fitness gym, with a 25m swimming pool. Pets Wonderland stocks interesting reptiles like iguanas and snakes, as well as a huge range of pet products and pet food. Megakidz is a fun centre where you can drop the kids off while you go shopping. Dining options are many: notable mentions are Annalakshmi, where you decide how much to pay for your vegetarian meal, Finnegan's Irish Pub for a bit o' craic, Kim Gary Restaurant for a great Chinese meal, and Spring Valley Chinese Restaurant for more formal occasions. The mall's two money changers here are reputed to have the best rates in town. There are taxi and bus stands outside the mall, and it is on the KTM Komuter line. The mall is attached to Cititel, a popular business hotel for its decent rates, and the newer hotel, the

Lot 10

Mid Valley Megamall

Boulevard Hotel. It also adjoins Menara IGB and is across from Boulevard offices and The Gardens. Valet services are available at both hotels.

Pavilion

Jalan Bukit Bintang
Bukit Bintang
🚇 *Bukit Bintang*
Map 13 C1

03 2716 1088 | *www.pavilion-kl.com*

This fairly new mall features bright, bold and swanky stores selling an exciting range of international brands such as Hermes, Gucci, Jean-Paul Gaultier, Juicy Couture, Versace, and Liuligongfang. There is Tangs, with a wonderful collection of chic and glam dresses, but you can expect to pay at least RM300 for an item. High street shops like Topshop are here also, and carry the full range. Although everything here looks upmarket (due to the classy interior), it is possible to find some good bargains, especially during the sales, and that's why Pavilion attracts a steady flow of discerning shoppers. In terms of dining, there is a small selection of restaurants on the top floor, and on the lower ground floor you will find the popular Food Republic which consists of small independent food stalls selling Japanese, western and local food at decent prices. Just next to the entrance is The Loaf, a bakery co-owned by one of Malaysia's former prime ministers, bakes heavenly breads and pastries using Japanese techniques. Another interesting store is The C.Club, where you can preview diamond jewellery while having champagne and caviar. Other stores of interest are Harvey Norman for consumer electronics, Epi Centre (Malaysia's largest Apple reseller), and Furniture Section for its retro and contemporary art and decorative pieces. The mall's stunning courtyard was especially designed to collect chi, and it is characterised by beautiful visuals. Parking is free for the first two hours if you spend above a certain amount in a single receipt.

Starhill Gallery

Jalan Bukit Bintang
Bukit Bintang
🚇 *Bukit Bintang*
Map 13 C1

03 2782 3855 | *www.starhillgallery.com*

Definitely one of the most elegant shopping centres in Malaysia, this is the place where the rich and famous shop at designer stores. Here you will find Dior, Louis Vuitton (usually the busiest), Van Cleef & Arpels, Asprey, Porsche Design, and many more luxurious boutiques. It's also a haven for horologists, with beautiful time pieces available from Audemars Piguet, Corum, Chopard, Patek Philippe and Jaeger le Coultre. The pamper section houses various wonderful spas, while the top floor is devoted to small independent art galleries where you can check out the works of

Pavilion

emerging artists. Shook! and MyThai are just two of the lovely eateries within the centre – head down to the 'Feast' floor to find more. Starhill adjoins JW Marriott Hotel, where you can catch a taxi. Parking is available, or the nearest monorail station is Bukit Bintang.

Jalan Bukit Bintang
Bukit Bintang
🚇 *Bukit Bintang*
Map 13 B2

Sungei Wang Plaza

03 2148 6109 | www.sungeiwang.com

Built in 1977, Sungei Wang Plaza is a household name, popular for its affordable, trendy, and bohemian street wear. Perpetually busy, it is a regular hangout for local teenagers and young adults looking for imitation shoes (Gucci under a different label name is popular) and handbags or something tacky and grungy to add to their wardrobe. Some refreshing local designers such as Khoon Hooi, Jonathan Cheng and Michael Ong have set up stores here too. G2, on the lower ground level, is stacked with clothes, and has a regular following for its marked-down dresses and tops. With its narrow and confusing walkways, and faux-decadent-looking cosy stores, being in Sungei Wang Plaza is an experience not to be missed when you are in the Bukit Bintang area. There are lifts in the plaza but the entrance into the plaza itself is not friendly for people with disabilities.

No 3 Jalan PJS 11/15
Bandar Sunway
Petaling Jaya
🚇 *Setia Jaya*

Sunway Pyramid

03 7492 9998 | www.sunwaypyramid.com

Sunway Pyramid mainly serves the burgeoning neighbourhoods of Sunway and Subang. Popular among private college students with generous allowances, you can find trendy clothes for young adults at mid-prices (average RM60 and above), all-day entertainment and an array of fast food joints. Anchor tenants are Giant, Jusco and Parkson. Its unique feature is the ice-skating rink. Other interesting shops are Bread Papa (great cream puffs), J.Co Donuts & Coffee (long queue), Marks & Spencer, Sun Paradise (large collection of bikinis), Rest & Relax (for its signature spaghetti stretchable dresses), panne3.com (Buddhism books), and Kohimaran (Middle Eastern rugs and decorative items). The standalone stalls located in pockets of the mall lend character to the place. Here you can find earrings priced as low as RM2 and handbags as low as RM15. There are four entrances into the Pyramid, and valet services are available. Taxi stands are located outside at the main entrance, and indoor parking is available. Nearby is the Sunway Theme Park and Sunway Hotel Resort & Spa. Sunway is a 10 minute cab drive from Setia Jaya station.

Jalan Ampang
Nxt to Petronas Twin Towers
🚇 *KLCC*
Map 11 C2

Suria KLCC

03 2382 2828 | www.suriaklcc.com.my

Suria KLCC is Malaysia's premier shopping destination, flanked by the Petronas Twin Towers and located on the most expensive real estate in Malaysia. This must-visit shopping centre offers six levels of retail outlets and houses major international designer brands such as Burberry, Chanel, Hermes and Salvatore Ferragamo, as well as anchor tenants Isetan and Parkson. Kinokuniya bookstore, which occupies two floors in KLCC, sells a wide range of books and CDs, and there is also a cafe inside. At Aseana, a section within KLCC, you can find sophisticated traditional and ultra glam outfits. A well-kept secret is the cafe in Aseana – a quiet oasis away from the centre's constant hustle and bustle. Ombak and Malaysian Heritage & Style are recommended places to buy interesting Asian decorative and Malaysian antique collectibles. The Royal Selangor Pewter store also offers a definitive range of pewter items, always popular as gifts for formal occasions. Electronic consumer goods can be found in Sony Style and Best Denki. There are international luggage brands such as Braun Buffel and Loewe, and visitors will be spoilt for choices in terms of jewellers with Bvlgari, the Love Diamond, Mikimoto and Tiffany & Co. For timepieces, there are Franck Muller and Piaget among others. There is an amazing array of gourmet choices, including local, western, Italian, Japanese, Vietnamese and Thai food, as well as a selection of cafes and bakeries. A definite must-try is the Rotiboy bun from Rotiboy Bakeshoppe on the concourse level. Entertainment includes the largest TGV Cineplex (12 screens), and for kids, the Petrosains centre, an interactive science discovery centre that showcases the science and technology behind the petroleum industry. Other services available are alteration services, an internet cafe, shoe repair, a duplicate key maker, a travel agency and numerous money changers. KLCC is well-served by taxis and buses, and its Putra LRT stop is KLCC. If you are planning to be in KLCC for a while, it is worthwhile getting there on the LRT as hourly parking rates apply.

Suria KLCC

Starhill Gallery

Malay Tea

Small but indispensable…

Perfectly proportioned to fit in your pocket, these marvellous mini guidebooks make sure you don't just get the holiday you paid for, but rather the one that you dreamed of.

Explorer Mini Visitors' Guides
Maximising your holiday, minimising your hand luggage

Ace Hardware ◄ See Giant Ace

Adidas ◄ Suria KLCC (03 2162 3475)

Adidas Original ◄ KLCC (03 2163 2041), KLCC (03 2171 2928)

Al-Ikhsan ◄ Sunway Pyramid (03 7492 0599), The Curve (03 7727 5258)

Aldo ◄ Bangsar Village II (03 2283 2210), 1 Utama (03 7726 5110)

Anakku ◄ Amcorp Mall (03 7492 2638), The Curve (03 16226 0372), Mines Shopping Fair (016 226 0197), Jalan Nenas (03 5161 8822), Taman Pandan Indah (03 4295 2863)

Apex Pharmacy ◄ Ampang Point (03 4257 4691), Little India (03 2693 7164), Metrojaya (03 2072 7735), Sunway Pyramid (03 5636 2929)

Arch ◄ Taman Industri Bukit Permai (03 4296 9970), 1 Utama (03 7725 0512), KLCC (03 2382 0489)

Armani ◄ Pavilion (03 2148 3448), Suria KLCC (03 2163 2692), Lot 10 (03 2143 2205), The Gardens (03 2287 6171), 1 Utama (03 7726 8620)

AXXEZZ ◄ Mid Valley Megamall (03 2287 4779), The Curve (03 7728 9755), Suria KLCC (03 2383 0245), 1 Utama (03 7726 6300)

Barang Barang ◄ Ikano Power Centre (03 7726 4198), Great Eastern Mall (03 4252 9198)

Bata ◄ Mid Valley Megamall (03 2284 5773), Suria KLCC (03 2382 0306), 1 Utama (03 7727 7698)

Best Denki ◄ Little India (03 2698 4188), Mines Shopping Fair (03 8948 5325), Mid Valley Megamall (03 9368 3288), 1 Utama (03 7722 1933), Berjaya Times Square (03 2144 1878), Lot 10 (03 2144 1833), Suria KLCC (03 2382 1233), The Summit (03 8023 6593)

Binwani's ◄ Jaya Shopping Centre (03 7958 6128), The Curve (03 www.binwani.com), Ampang Park (03 2161 2887), Little India (03 2694 0402)

Blook ◄ Jalan Telawi (03 2287 7128), 1 Utama (03 7725 5178), Subang Parade (03 5636 1138)

Blush ◄ Berjaya Times Square (03 2141 6416), The Curve (03 6436 2202), Great Eastern Mall (03 4253 3778), Bangsar Shopping Centre (03 2092 5375), Sunway Pyramid (03 7492 2265)

Bonita ◄ Sunway Pyramid (03 5635 4328), Mid Valley Megamall (03 2283 1500), 1 Utama (03 7728 0318)

Borders ◄ The Curve (03 7725 9303), Berajaya Times Square (03 2141 0288)

Braun Buffel ◄ 1 Utama (03 7727 0172), Suria KLCC (03 2382 0172)

British India ◄ 1 Utama (03 7724 1822), Lot 10 (03 2142 2127), Mid Valley Megamall (03 2938 3826), Great Eastern Mall (03 4253 5266)

Calvin Klein ◄ Pavilion (03 2142 0019), Gardens (03 2287 6272), KLCC (03 2171 2115), Lot 10 (03 2143 1785), 1 Utama (03 7726 4292)

Camel Active ◄ Sunway Pyramid (03 7492 1315), Taman Bukit Malurin (03 6277 8833)

Caring Pharmacy — Sunway Pyramid (03 5632 7928), Subang Parade (03 5632 9928), Petaling Jaya (03 7957 7928), Pavilion (03 2142 2928), Hartamas Shopping Centre (03 6201 0879), Bangsar Village (03 2287 8928), 1 Utama (03 7728 1928), TTDI (03 7710 4928)

Carrefour — Mid Valley Megamall (03 2282 6899), Kepong (03 6254 6600), Sungai Pinang (03 3361 8000), Putrajaya (03 8889 3318), Jalan Peel (03 9282 9200), Bandar Baru (03 9543 0188), Section 5 (03 4149 4200)

Cavenzi Furniture Outlet — Carrefour Mid Valley (03 9074 4792), Taman Desa (03 9058 1871), Megamas Business Centre (03 6140 7807), Damansara (03 7722 5653), Jalan Memanda (03 4252 2300)

Chicco — 1 Utama (03 7728 6113), Pavilion (03 2143 2278), Suria KLCC, (03 2161 8919), Metrojaya (03 2283 3002), Mid Valley Gardens (03 2089 1111), Spring Kuching (03 7982 8355)

City Chain — Berjaya Times Square (03 2143 1794), Bandar Puchong Jaya (03 5882 1869), Maju Junction (03 2694 8327), Mid Valley (03 2284 1894), Suria KLCC (03 2382 1603), The Curve (03 7728 9687)

Coach — KLCC (03 2300 1122), Pavilion (www.coach.com)

Cold Storage — Berjaya Times Square (03 2142 6875), Great Eastern Mall (03 4252 9620), Ikano (03 7722 5614), Jaya (03 7957 0964), Subang Parade (03 5632 5202), Suria KLCC (03 2166 2439), The Gardens (03 2287 4420), The Mall (03 4043 5815), The Summit (03 8023 2295), Bangsar Shopping Centre (03 2094 2900)

Colours — Utama (03 7724 2282), Sunway Pyramid (03 7492 2682), Mid Valley (03 2284 0429), Sungei Wang Plaza (03 2142 5736)

Cool Shades — Suria KLCC (03 7880 3181), Mid Valley Megamall (03 2287 5105)

Country Farm Organics — 1 Utama (03 7724 2166), Bangsar Village I (03 2284 2094), Hartamas Shopping Centre (03 6201 2993)

Courts Mammoth — Persiaran Subang Permai (03 5631 0053), Jalan Barat (03 7958 4166), Jalan Sultan Abdul Samad (03 3187 3210), Ampang Point (03 4260 4751), Giant Hypermarket (03 5510 9073), Mutiara Damansara (03 7726 9251)

Cuir Boutique — Berjaya Times Square (03 2148 1118), Mid Valley Megamall (03 2938 8118), Sunway Pyramid (03 7492 8118)

Diamond & Platinum — 1 Utama (03 7725 3478), Mid Valley Megamall (03 2938 3478), Sungei Wang (03 2148 3478), Sunway Pyramid (03 7492 2478), The Curve (03 7728 2478)

Dior — Surya KLCC (03 2070 0294), Starhill Gallery (03 2143 1886)

Diva — Sunway Pyramid (03 5632 6054), 1 Utama (03 7728 9386), Mid Valley (03 2282 0735)

DKNY — Starhill Gallery (03 2144 0042), 1 Utama (03 7722 5660), Pavilion (03 2141 9770)

Dorothy Perkins — 1 Utama (03 7726 6645), Mid Valley Megamall (03 2287 9308), Sunway Pyramid (03 5632 5946)

Early Learning Centre — Gardens (03 2282 1805), The Curve (03 7725 5958)

Edmundser — Mid Valley (03 2938 3238), 1 Utama (03 7726 3720)

Elle	1 Utama (03 7727 7594), Mid Valley (03 2284 3290)
England Optical Group	Sunway Pyramid (03 7492 1066), Jalan Klang Lama (03 7785 6666), Suria KLCC (03 2166 6166)
Esprit	1 Utama (03 7724 1887), Berjaya Times Square (03 2142 9460), KL Plaza (03 2148 6295), KLCC (03 2382 5702), Lot 10 (03 2142 7519), Mid Valley Megamall (03 2938 3839), Pavilion (03 2141 4768), The Gardens (03 2287 4427)
Fitness Concept	KLCC (03 2382 1218), Mid Valley (03 2282 3200), Taman Perindustrian UEP (03 8026 2271)
Focus Point	Dataran Prima (03 7880 5520), Sunway Pyramid (03 7492 5155), Pandan Indah (03 4296 0053), Taman Putra (03 4295 2310), Tesco Ampang (03 9285 7767), Ampang Point (03 4252 0758)
Foot Solutions	Great Eastern Mall (03 4251 6831), The Curve (03 7727 6831), Subang Parade (03 5621 6831)
Forever 21	1 Utama (03 7728 7550), Sunway Pyramid (03 7494 3000)
Foto Shangri La	Mid Valley Megamall (03 2283 3133), Bangsar Village (03 2287 7306)
Fotokem	Sunway Pyramid (03 7492 1061), Mines Shopping Fair (03 8942 3201), Sungei Wang Plaza (03 2145 5011), Plaza Metro Kajang (03 8734 4688), Klang Parade (03 3343 7833), IOI Mall (03 5891 9104), 1 Utama (03 7722 1011)
Giant	Sunway Pyramid (03 5632 6903), Metro Plaza Complex (03 8733 1712), Puchong (03 8068 2952), Pandamaran (03 3323 5518), Jalan Mega (03 7980 0637), Batu Caves (03 6137 1420), Balakong (03 8962 6398), Maju Junction (03 2694 7622), Mines Shopping Fair (03 8942 2523), Petaling Jaya (03 7956 9053), Petaling Jaya (03 7803 2345), Prima Saujana (03 8374 5179), Taman Serdang Perdana (03 8945 8944), Taman Connaught (03 9101 1227), Taman Permata (03 4016 5673), Pusat Bandar Rawang (03 6092 9152), Shah Alam Mall 2 (03 5512 7831), Klang Parade (03 3344 1800), 1 Utama (03 7725 4923), Paramount (03 7874 3263), Subang Jaya (03 5631 0633), Amcorp Mall (03 7955 0575), Damansara Jaya (03 7725 5079), Ampang Point (03 4256 8853), Damansara (03 2095 5094), Jalan Setiawangsa (03 4252 7394), Cheras Leisure Mall (03 9130 7506), Jalan Kepong (03 6277 0585), Kelana Jaya (03 7880 2523), Sungei Wang Plaza (03 2143 4045), Kawasan Perniagaan (03 5541 0112), Gombak (03 6187 5785), Jalan Dagang (03 4270 6653), Jalan Wangsa Ukay (03 4106 1623)
Giant Ace	Persiaran Kewajipan USJ 1 (03 41057 2231), Mid Valley Megamall (03 41057 2231), Lucky Plaza (03 41057 2231), Taman Melawati (03 41057 2231), Ikano Power Centre (03 41057 2231)
Giordano	Mid Valley (03 2284 9391), Sungei Wang Plaza (03 2145 0393)
Goldheart	Mid Valley Megamall (03 2282 8198), KLCC (03 2161 1198)
Guardian Pharmacy	1 Utama (03 7726 1916), Bangsar Baru (03 2284 5463), Bangsar Shopping Centre (03 2094 0309), Ikano (03 7722 4301), Jalan Bukit Bintang (03 2145 7553), KLCC (03 2382 0208), KL Sentral (03 2279 8778), Lot 10 (03 2142 4770), Mid Valley Megamall (03 2284 3844), Sunway Pyramid (03 7492 8115)
Guess	1 Utama (03 7725 2453), Mid Valley Megamall (03 2284 2739)

Shopping Directory

The Guitar Store
Desa Sri Hartamas (03 2300 2822), Taman Segar Cheras (03 9133 2822), Bandar Damansara Perdana (03 7710 5822)

Habib Jewels
Ampang Point (03 4252 7777), Bangsar Village II (03 2282 8188), Central Market (03 2274 7242), Suria KLCC (03 2166 7677), The Curve (03 7710 2888)

Hallmark
1 Utama (03 7726 0161), Mid Valley Megamall (03 2282 8161), Sunway Pyramid (03 5636 3161)

Himalaya
KLCC (03 2164 1296), Sunway Pyramid (03 7491 0915)

Hinode Shop
Mid Valley (03 2284 0885), Sunway Pyramid (03 7492 2408)

Hock Sin Leong
Wilayah Persekutuan (03 7980 8133), Subang Parade (03 5633 9623), Mid Valley Megamall (03 2282 6848), Cheras Leisure Mall (03 9132 2433), Bukit Bintang Plaza (03 2142 5630), The Curve (03 7722 2852)

Home-fix The DIY Store
1 Utama (03 7729 1829) , Bangsar Village (03 2283 1628), Great Eastern Mall (03 4242 1828)

House of Leather
KL Plaza (03 2142 1045), Sungei Wang Plaza (03 2148 3718), The Curve (03 7722 5621), Suria KLCC (03 2166 6721), Sunway Pyramid (03 4041 5261), The Mall (03 4944 6796), Subang Parade (03 5635 2930), Low Yat Plaza (03 2145 3294), Berjaya Times Square (03 2143 1898), 1 Utama (03 7726 8336), Mid Valley Megamall (03 2284 1899)

House of Notebooks
Low Yat Plaza (03 2145 0833), Mid Valley Megamall (03 2938 3110)

Hush Puppies
Mid Valley Megamall (03 2938 3319), Sunway Pyramid (03 7492 0157), Subang Parade (03 5636 0981), Ampang Mall (03 2163 0991), Maju Junction (03 2694 8063), Sungei Wang Plaza (03 2141 6319), Bandar Utama Damasara (03 7726 1845)

Isetan
Suria KLCC (03 2282 7777), The Gardens (03 2283 1777), Lot 10 (03 2141 7777)

Jaya Jusco
1 Utama (03 7726 6033), Mid Valley Megamall (03 2284 4800)

Juiceworks
Suria KLCC (03 2161 3157), The Curve (03 7722 2066), Mid Valley Megamall (03 2287 7066), 1 Utama (03 7710 5654), The Gardens (03 2287 4492)

Jusco
Bukit Tinggi Shopping Centre (03 3326 2370), Cheras Selatan Shopping Centre (03 9080 3498), Taman Equine Shopping Centre (03 8945 2700), Alpha Angle Shopping Centre (03 4149 5288), Bukit Raja Shopping Centre (03 3343 2166), Kepong (03 6259 1122), Taman Maluri (03 9200 1004)

Justlife
Subang Jaya (03 5632 0868), Ikano Power Centre (03 7728 5503), Queen's Park Retail Centre (03 9205 5209)

aryaneka Kraf Boutique
KL Craft Complex (03 2164 2987), Bukit Bintang Plaza (03 2144 1519)

L'Occitane
Sunway Pyramid (03 5631 9881), Bangsar Village II (03 2283 3828)

La Senza
Avenue K (03 2161 6288), Pavilion (03 2143 2278), Suria KLCC (03 2164 0291), Mid Valley Megamall (03 2284 9890), The Gardens (03 2141 6508)

La Trend Optical
1 Utama (03 7726 4686), Wilayah Persekutuan (03 6275 8833), Mid Valley (03 2284 6210)

Levi's
Mid Valley Mega Mall (03 2282 2501), 1 Utama (03 7725 8381)

Lewre Mid Valley Megamall (03 2283 2773), The Gardens (03 2283 1373), 1 Utama (03 7726 0298)

Living Cabin Jalan Sultan (03 2026 5069), Jalan Cheng Lock (03 2078 8867), Ampang Point (03 4257 3761), Berjaya Times Square (03 2142 8507), Mid Valley City (03 2282 6408), Mines Shopping Fair (03 8945 0841), Sunway Pyramid (03 7492 9689), Tesco Mutiara Damansara (03 7726 7742)

Lovely Lace Mid Valley Megamall (03 2283 1363), Suria KLCC (03 2161 0375)

Marks & Spencer The Gardens (03 2287 4252), 1 Utama (03 7762 0177), Sunway Pyramid (03 5637 3292), Suria KLCC (03 2162 0177)

Memory Lane Mid Valley Megamall (03 2288 1300), Sunway Pyramid (03 7492 5895), Suria KLCC (03 2166 5677)

Metrojaya Avenue K (03 2161 6288), Berjaya Times Square (03 2148 5599), Bukit Bintang Plaza (03 2144 1751), Mid Valley Megamall (03 2283 3002), The Curve (03 7728 2230)

Miss Selfridge 1 Utama (03 7728 6084), Mid Valley Megamall (03 2287 9319), Sunway Pyramid (03 7492 0701)

MNG MidValley Megamall (03 2938 3901), Sunway Pyramid (03 7492 2057)

Modernmum 1 Utama (03 7726 2339), Ampang Point (03 4251 3766), IOI Mall (03 8075 3912), Metro Prima Shopping Centre(03 6252 2655), Mid Valley Megamall (03 2283 2317), Sunway Pyramid (03 7494 0388), Suria KLCC (03 2382 0288), TTDI (03 7728 8911)

Motherclub 1 Utama (03 7728 6833), KLCC (03 2162 0833), Mid Valley Megamall (03 2287 0833)

MPH Mid Valley Megamall (03 2938 3800), Bangsar Village I (03 2283 1098), Alpha Angle (03 4142 1246), Bangsar Village II (03 2287 3600), Bukit Bintang Plaza (03 2142 8231)

Ms. Read 1 Utama Shopping Centre (03 7712 1990), Midvalley Megamall (03 2295 3593)

Nichi Fashion City Jalan Sungei Besi (03 9221 6052), The Curve (03 7710 8331), Maju Junction (03 2698 0718), IOI Mall (03 8075 3363)

Nichii Maju Junction (03 2698 0718), The Curve (03 7710 8331), Berjaya Times Square, (03 2148 6330)

Nine West Avenue K (03 2163 5899), 1 Utama (03 7722 5589)

Nose KLCC (03 2164 9445), Mid Valley Megamall (03 2284 9778), 1 Utama (03 7724 2636)

Optical 88 The Curve (03 7726 9916), Sunway Pyramid (03 5638 8903), Mid Valley City (03 2283 4749), Berjaya Times Square (03 2148 7586), Cheras Leisure Mall(03 9132 2080)

P & Co Sungei Wang Plaza (03 2145 6017), Mid Valley Megamall (03 2938 3098)

Padini 1 Utama (03 7727 5535), Mid Valley Megamall (03 2938 3884), Sungei Wang Plaza (03 2145 8640)

Parkson 1 Utama (03 7728 1369), The Mall (03 4042 1188), Suria KLCC (03 2161 8919), Subang Parade (03 5633 9390), Sunway Pyramid (03 5636 9198), Sungei Wang Plaza

	(03 2142 4622), OUG Plaza (03 7982 2488), Kajang (03 8734 4225), Klang (03 3343 6599), Selayang Mall (03 6138 2889)
Pay Less Books	Subang (03 5632 9882), Summit USJ (03 8023 5259), Ampang Point (03 4257 5214), Amcorp Mall (03 7957 9729), 1 Utama (03 7724 2402)
Poh Kong	The Mall (03 4041 0542), Mid Valley Megamall (03 2284 9636), Tesco Mutiara Damansara (03 7710 5528), Sunway Pyramid (03 7492 0972), Summit City (03 8024 7350), Subang Parade (03 5635 1087), Sogo Pernas Complex (03 2698 5275), Mines Shopping Fair (03 8943 7835), 1 Utama (03 7726 3868), Cheras Leisure Mall (03 9132 2417), Bangsar Shopping Centre (03 2093 3161), Ampang Point (03 4252 7375), Amcorp Mall (03 7958 6391), Alpha Angle (03 4142 1688), Jaya Shopping Centre (03 7957 4271)
Poney Garments	1 Utama (03 6332 0578), The Mall (03 016332 0571), Suria KLCC (03 0163320 569), Mines Shopping Fair (03 6332 0572), Alpha Angle (03 016332 0575)
Popular Book Store	Jalan Hang Lekir (03 2070 0687), Jaya Shopping Centre (03 7958 1694), The Summit (03 8024 3588), Amcorp Mall (03 7958 5101), Sungei Wang Plaza (03 2145 8848), Ikano (03 7725 9188)
Precious Thots	1 Utama (03 7710 0198), Bangsar Village (03 2287 7160), Sunway Pyramid (03 7492 1311)
Primahealth Pharmacy	Mines Shopping Fair (03 8024 2116), Summit (03 8024 2116), Mid Valley (03 2283 6362), Sunway Pyramid (03 7492 8119)
Primavera	KLCC (03 2166 3309), Mid Valley (03 2282 2805)
PYT Jeweller	Subang Jaya (03 5633 6922), Jalan SS2/55 (03 7876 7922)
Quiksilver	Pavilion (03 2141 8043), Mid Valley (03 2284 0431), KLCC (03 2166 2984)
Raoul	1 Utama (03 7728 0849), Sunway Pyramid (03 5622 1936), Mid Valley Megamall (03 2287 4942)
Rock Corner	Gardens (03 2283 4893), Mid Valley (03 2284 7423)
Roxy	1 Utama (03 7722 1568), Pavilion (03 2141 8184), Bukit Bintang Plaza (03 2144 4393), Mid Valley (03 2287 1876)
Royal Selangor	Pavilion (03 2141 8150), The Gardens (03 2287 4642), Suria KLCC (03 2382 0240), Sunway Pyramid (03 582 7668), Setapak Jaya (03 4145 6000), Subang Parade (03 5636 2763), Mines Shopping Fair (03 8945 8168), Mid Valley (03 2282 0039), KLIA (03 8787 3094), Petaling Jaya (03 7874 7290), 1 Utama (03 7727 0476), Bangsar Shopping Centre (03 2287 3290)
Royal Sporting House	Starhill Gallery (03 2144 9476), Bangsar Shopping Centre (03 2094 2717), Mid Valley Megamall (03 2284 2098)
Salabianca	1 Utama Shopping Centre (03 7725 3560), Mid Valley (03 2287 7694)
Samsonite	Mid Valley Megamall (03 2284 2900), The Gardens (03 2283 3820)

Secret Recipe	IOI Mall (03 8075 6946), KL Sentral (03 2274 7557), The Mall (03 4044 5011), The Curve (03 7710 3159), Tesco Mutiara Damansara (03 7725 7540), Suria KLCC (03 2171 2686), Sunway Pyramid (03 7492 1900), Subang Parade (03 5632 0117), Sogo Pernas Complex (03 2698 1691), Plaza Mont' Kiara (03 6201 9178), Mid Valley Megamall (03 2284 0877), Lot 10 (03 2143 9304), Berjaya Times Square (03 2145 4406), Avenue K (03 2161 8736), Alpha Angle Shopping Centre (03 4143 7166), Jalan Burhanuddin Helmi (03 7726 6944), Jalan Setiabakti (03 2095 8678), Jalan Tun Mohd Fuad 1 (03 7725 3918), 1 Utama (03 7726 7499), Jalan Bukit Bintang (03 2148 8108), Menara The Weld, (03 2163 3418)
Seed	Mid Valley (03 2938 3028), Sungei Wang Plaza (03 2145 0516)
Sinma	IOI Mall (03 5882 0238), Maju Junction (03 2694 7951), Mid Valley (03 2284 9587), Sungei Wang Plaza (03 2142 3096), Sunway Pyramid (03 7492 6318), Tesco Mutiara Damansara (03 7727 3601), The Mall (03 4042 2268), Alpha Angle (03 4142 1342)
Spark Manshop	Suria KLCC (03 2166 2185), The Gardens (03 2287 4860), Mid Valley Megamall (03 2284 5476), Jaya Supermarket (03 7956 9700), Bangsar (03 2282 9369), Taman Shamelin Perkasa (03 9283 2255), 1 Utama (03 7726 5866), Lot 10 (03 2141 4324)
Speedy Video	1 Utama (03 7726 2453), Ampang Point (03 4256 0618), Bangsar Village (03 2284 1012), Great Eastern Mall (03 4257 9681), Ikano Power Centre (03 7722 5491), Mid Valley Megamall (03 2287 6501), Mines Shopping Fair (03 8942 6353), Pavilion (03 2141 6567)
Studio R	1 Utama (03 7728 0978), Sunway Pyramid (03 7492 2088), Mid Valley (03 2284 6392), KLCC (03 2161 7193)
Ted Baker	Bangsar Village II (03 2287 1806), The Pavillion (03 2141 5517)
Tesco	Bandar Bukit Tinggi (03 3323 1100), Dataran Pandan Prima (03 9281 1266), Mutiara Damansara (03 7726 1600), Cheras (03 9132 6688), Seksyen 13 (03 5512 0698), Seksyen 13 (03 5512 2600), Mukim Kajang Saujana Impian (03 8734 1369), AIM Point Plaza (03 3187 2909), Puchong (03 8076 2166), Selayang (03 6259 1279)
Times Bookshop	Hartamas Shopping Centre (03 6201 6871), 1 Utama (03 7727 4368), KLCC (03 2382 3359), Bangsar Shopping Centre (03 2095 3509), Pavilion (03 2148 8813)
Top Shop	Mid Valley Megamall (03 2287 9308), Pavilion (03 2141 4293), 1 Utama (03 7727 5691)
Tower Records	Mid Valley Megamall (03 2282 8081), 1 Utama Shopping Centre (03 7722 1416), KL Plaza (03 2141 8881), Suria KLCC (03 2382 1009)
Toys R Us	Subang Parade (03 5634 1550), City Square (03 2161 3822), 1 Utama (03 7726 2766), The Mall (03 4041 8388), Mid Valley Megamall (03 2284 3770), Bangsar Village (03 2287 9880), Avenue K (03 2162 0188), Pavilion (03 2141 4782)
Travel All	Bangsar Village II (03 2283 6322), Ikano (03 7727 2744), Lot 10 (03 2143 0430), Subang Parade (03 5631 3529), 1 Utama (03 7722 3766)
Travel Style	1 Utama (03 7725 1288), Mid Valley (03 2282 8388)
The Under Shop	Berjaya Times Square (03 9288 1888), Sunway Pyramid (03 7492 1168), Bukit Bintang Plaza (03 9288 1888), Mines Shopping Fair (03 9288 1888)

Universal Traveller Berjaya Times Square (03 2145 0900), Bukit Bintang Plaza (03 2143 3900), Mid Valley Megamall (03 2283 6900), Sunway Pyramid (03 5637 6900), Suria KLCC (03 2163 3900), The Mall (03 4044 0900)

Video Ezy TTDI (03 7728 0617), Sungei Wang Plaza (03 2144 8758), Suria KLCC (03 2161 4830), Plaza Mont Kiara (03 6201 9327)

Vincci Ikano Power Centre (03 7710 1711), Sungei Wang Plaza (03 2148 4978), Mid Valley Megamall (03 2938 3108), Pavilion (03 2141 4330), Sunway Pyramid (2 outlets) (03 5622 1629), Suria KLCC (03 2166 1985), Alpha Angle (03 4143 0240), Concourse Level, Suria KLCC (03 2166 1985)

Vincci+ Mid Valley Megamall (03 2282 5931), Pavilion (03 2141 4330), Bangsar Village II (03 2287 2668), Sunway Pyramid (03 5622 1629)

Vitacare Amcorp Mall (03 7958 7731), Subang Jaya (03 5632 5506), KLCC (03 2166 2469), Mid Valley (03 2284 2010), The Gardens (03 2282 4641)

Voir 1 Utama (03 7725 6450), Pavilion (03 2141 6609), Mid Valley Megamall (03 2284 8344)

Watatime (M) Sdn Bhd Sungei Wang Plaza (03 2148 1818), Subang Parade (03 5633 9263), Sunway Pyramid (03 7492 2368), Mid Valley Megamall (03 2938 3000), 1 Utama (03 7726 3318)

Watchshoppe 1 Utama (03 7729 1172), Mid Valley (03 2938 3266), Sunway Pyramid (03 7492 8665)

Watson's Sunway Pyramid (03 7492 9003), KL Plaza (03 2148 5467), Pusat Bandar Damansara (03 2095 7098), Mid Valley (03 2282 4632), Mines Shopping Fair (03 8943 9461), Pavilion (03 2141 4923), Subang Parade (03 5635 0723), Sungei Wang Plaza (03 2141 1096), Jaya Shopping Centre (03 7960 1763), The Curve (03 7724 1685), The Mall (03 4044 5510), The Weld, Jalan Raja Chulan (03 2161 4341), Summit (03 8024 7261), Amcorp Mall (03 7958 2754), Section 14 (03 7968 3324), KLCC (03 2161 7533), Alpha Angle (03 4143 8320), Hartamas Shopping Centre (03 6201 4301), Ampang Park (03 2164 4864), Ampang Point (03 4251 2825), Avenue K (03 2162 5211), Berjaya Times Square (03 2145 5211), Central Market (03 2031 7186), Cineleisure Damansara (03 7727 4130), Jalan Maarof (03 2094 3614), Great Eastern Mall (03 4251 3825), 1 Utama (03 7726 2646)

Women'secret Mid Valley (03 2284 1566), 1 Utama (03 7727 8587), Sunway Pyramid (03 7492 0645)

World of Cartoons & World of Babies Mid Valley Megamall (03 2282 2673), Sunway Pyramid (03 7492 6102)

Xixili 1 Utama (03 7729 1669), Sunway Pyramid (03 5622 1181)

Za Altera Sunway Pyramid (03 5637 2927), Ikano (03 7720 7333)

Zara 1 Utama (03 7724 1028), Bangsar Village II (03 2287 1480), Mid Valley (03 2287 1517)

Zurich Timepieces Bangsar Shopping Centre (03 2092 4389), The Gardens (03 2282 5572)

Our mission is to help you succeed overseas by providing you with a first-stop website to share stories, network globally, develop personally and find the best resources!

Visit Now: www.ExpatWomen.com

Going Out

Going Out

Malaysians love to go out – they call it 'jalan, jalan'. Home entertaining isn't as common as in some countries, so families and groups of friends or colleagues will usually go out to socialise either to a restaurant or pub or both. Eating out is not expensive and it's easy to see why many choose to dine out rather than at home. Some will also eat near work and then drive home later in the evening to avoid the traffic jam.

Larger Malaysian cities like Penang, Johor Bahru, Ipoh, Kota Kinabalu, Kuching and Miri also have places to dine, drink and dance (karaoke is another popular pastime). Restaurants in the capital range from fine dining, atmospheric restaurants to the simplest of hawker stalls down some alleyway. Not so long ago, fine dining was restricted to the international hotels, but an increasing number of free-standing restaurants now offer excellent food in atmospheric surroundings.

Many Malaysians are quite liberal in their views on alcohol. While it is freely available in most parts of Kuala Lumpur and Malaysia, expats need to be sensitive to those who don't drink. A truly halal restaurant will not serve alcohol and there are many Muslim or mamak (Indian Muslim) restaurants and coffee shops in the city where alcohol is neither served nor welcome in the restaurant.

Other outlets are best considered pork free in that they serve alcohol but not pork. Most hotels are at least pork free so that they can cater to all sections of the Malaysian public. You can find Malaysians in restaurants and coffee shops during the daylight hours and into the late evening. Some places operate around the clock and in the centre of KL there are food streets and outlets that open into the wee hours. Most large restaurants open for dinner by 18:00 but the kitchens of many of those will take their last orders by 22:30. After that, hungry diners will have to seek out snacks in those restaurants that carry on as bars later in the evening or in a coffee shop or hawker stall.

Discount Delights

Generally food in Kuala Lumpur is cheap if you stick to hawker stalls and avoid alcohol. Even more refined restaurants offer value for money on a global scale. Dining is made easier by promotional incentives and some of the best are offered by credit card companies, with discounts ranging from 10% to 30% being common. The large hotels may also have a hotel discount card where guests get a range of discounts on accommodation and meals in return for an annual fee which tends to be around RM600. This may include a free night's stay, discounts on subsequent stays, gym discounts and discounts of up to 50% on restaurant dining as long as at least two people eat at the same time. These cards offer good value if they are from an international chain involving more than one restaurant and hotel and if you frequent upmarket hotels on a regular basis.

Cuisine List – Quick Reference

African	359	Indian	370	Pizzerias	383
American	359	International	372	Seafood	383
British	360	Italian	374	South East Asian	384
Brunch	360	Japanese	376	Spanish	385
Chinese	361	Korean	378	Steakhouses	386
Contemporary Asian	364	Latin American	378	Thai	387
European	365	Malay	379	Vegetarian	389
French	367	Mediterranean	380		
German	369	Middle Eastern	382		

Eating Out

Visitors and recently arrived expats to Malaysia will learn two words of the local lingo very early in their stay – 'sudah makan' or 'have you eaten?'. These are two of the most widely used words in a country where eating is almost the national sport. Malaysians constantly discuss food rather than the weather, which rarely changes anyway. For example, taxi drivers will ask whether you have eaten. If you have, the topic will centre on what you ate. However, if you haven't eaten, the conversation will revolve around what you could eat next.

Malaysians just love to eat, and while servings are not always large they are plentiful, with most people eating breakfast, morning tea, lunch, afternoon tea and dinner. A snack before dinner and a late night supper of a snack and drink are not uncommon for those who go out late.

Being the national capital, Kuala Lumpur has the nation's most diverse dining options with an extensive array of local dishes as well as an increasing number of regional and international cuisines. Malay, Chinese and Indian foods combine to make up what could be called Malaysian food, but there are many variations on the theme with different interpretations of well-known Malay dishes being found in various states. There's also a myriad of regional Chinese cuisines and many different styles of Indian food.

Malaysians are very patriotic about their various local dishes and visitors and expat residents will love the variety and the value for money this offers. Some very creditable international fare such as Japanese, Korean, Italian, Spanish, French, German, Thai, Vietnamese and fusion restaurants have recently become popular. Many of these will offer halal food in order to cater to all Malaysians, but there are some that stick to original recipes, so pork is offered.

Local delicacies are available throughout the city and all suburbs have a range of restaurants and coffee shops. Cheap prices mean that many dine out rather than at home. Most outlets in both KL and the country generally are also family friendly, and eating out as a family is very popular at weekends. There are several famous locations, food streets and areas in KL where food is abundant. These include Jalan Bukit Bintang, Petaling Street, Jalan Alor, Changkat Bukit Bintang, Tengkat Tong Shin, Brickfields and Bangsar (but most only come to life in the early evening).

Food courts are also located within shopping malls, where a satisfying lunch can be had for less than a cup of coffee in the west.

Some atmospheric dining places achieve greatness not necessarily for their food but more for their ambience. The Coliseum Cafe (p.360) is one of these. It's located in an old and somewhat dilapidated building, but has a long history of catering to colonial planters and nowadays to travellers from all over the world. The food is traditionally British, with a team of no-nonsense staff who add to the overall ambience. Start the evening with a drink in the adjoining bar and then order a sizzling meat dish and watch the theatre unfold.

Another experience from the colonial past is Sunday tiffin curry at Gulai House (Carcosa Seri Negara, p.23). Buffet lunch, taken on the veranda of this superb boutique hotel, is a journey back to a bygone era. Afterwards, take a turn around the expansive gardens while contemplating afternoon tea. The Dining Room (p.368) in another part of the Carcosa is an excellent French-inspired restaurant with the degustation menu recommended, along with a bottle of fine vintage wine from an extensive list.

Old China Café (p.363), tucked away in Chinatown, is another fantastic culinary journey. While the Nyonya cuisine is good, it is the photos of the clothes washing association adorning the walls and the antiques that will distract diners for hours.

Restaurant Or Bar?

Several restaurants in KL transform into bars as the evening progresses, and the character of most changes accordingly. Food is served in most city restaurants until about 22:30, but they then close or continue to serve drinks (and possibly snacks) up until closing time. In some the drinks are more important than the food – often having a great night out in a restaurant does not always mean the food has to be sensational. Frequently it is a combination of various factors including the company, the ambience, entertainment, price and restaurant location.

Arguably the city's finest restaurant, Cilantro, recently closed for at least 12 months while it is being renovated. The team has moved to Sage located in The Gardens Hotel and Residences in Mid Valley where they now craft their magic to produce excellent Italian-Japanese fusion cuisine.

Delivery & Takeaways

With food being so popular in the city it's not surprising that it's available in many different forms including home or office catering. Outside catering is big business for almost every city hotel and for many restaurants. Hotel catering is well organised and the hotel food and beverage section should be contacted for more details. Check out the hotel list on p.22 for more details. Normally they will offer a one-stop service that takes care of the food, cutlery, tables and chairs, marquee and staff. As a general rule, the more exclusive the hotel, the higher the charge.

While not all restaurants offer home catering, most will consider any offer so don't be afraid to ask at your favourite restaurant. They may not be able to offer as comprehensive a range of services as the hotels, and may just provide the food. It isn't unusual for Malaysians to entertain at home for weddings and to celebrate festivals – this is called a 'kenduri'. Streets may be partially closed while temporary marquees are erected.

Room Service Deliveries (03 6201 2400, www.roomservicedeliveries.com) offers a delivery service from a number of restaurants in the city and suburbs. It operates seven days a week, from 11:00 to 22:00, and charges RM10 to RM15 (depending upon distance from the city) in addition to the cost of the meal.

Most of the international fastfood operators in Kuala Lumpur operate a free meal delivery service, with some operating 24 hours a day. McDonald's (1300 12 1300) offers a home delivery service but KFC does not (it has many stores in Kuala Lumpur that are open 24 hours a day).

Hygiene

Many Malaysians and expats enjoy eating in cheap hawker stalls, and outlets selling bad or adulterated food do not stay in business for very long. The health authorities check regularly and some even issue cleanliness ratings to outlets. However, makeshift stalls on the side of the road do not receive the same scrutiny but as they usually rely upon a regular clientele, it's in their interest to see all patrons remain healthy.

Tax & Service Charges

Meals in large establishments normally have a 10% service charge and 5% government tax added to the bill. By law, this should be written on the menu and receipt (normally in fine print at the bottom) or listed as '+ +'. Smaller establishments such as coffee shops will not add this. Some outlets may not add the government tax. The government tax should not be imposed in duty-free destinations such as the islands of Langkawi and Labuan.

Tipping

Most large establishments add a 10% service charge to the final bill so customers are 'forced' to some extent to pay for service – either good or bad. This money is divided up among the staff based upon service in the establishment, so not only will a restaurant waiter benefit, but so will the most lowly kitchen staff. Additional tipping is not expected, nor is tipping in hawker stalls, but most patrons will leave loose change behind. Exceptional service could be rewarded with a few extra ringgit, as wages for many restaurant staff are quite low.

Dine With The Wind In Your Hair

Enjoy the sunshine by eating in an alfresco restaurant. Top ones to try include Bijan (p.379), Chinoz on the Park (p.365), La Terrasse (p.368), Sao Nam (p.384), 7atenine (p.373) and Telawi Street Bistro (p.367).

Independent Reviews

All of the outlets in this book have been independently reviewed by a team of food and nightlife experts who are based in Kuala Lumpur. Their aim is to give clear, realistic and, as far as possible, unbiased views of each venue, without back-handers, hand-me-downs or underhandedness on the part of any restaurant owner, nightclub promoter, crafty PR guru or persuasive barista.

The Yellow Star

This pretty yellow star seen highlights places that merit extra praise. It might be the atmosphere, the food, the cocktails, the music or the crowd, but any review that you see with the star attached marks somewhere that's a bit special.

Restaurant Listing Structure

There are so many places offering varied cuisine in Kuala Lumpur that choosing the perfect place to eat out can be an arduous task. Reviewing every single restaurant, bar, nightclub and coffee shop would fill an entire book in itself, so this section of the Kuala Lumpur Explorer features around 200 outlets that have been carefully selected by a team of food and nightlife experts who live and breathe the social scene.

Each review attempts to give an idea of the food, service, decor and ambience, while those venues that are particularly brilliant earn the coveted 'Explorer Recommended' big yellow star.

Primarily the restaurants have been categorised according to cuisine (in alphabetical order), but if you want to go out for a special occasion, such as to watch the game, each outdoors, impress a date, get sozzled on cocktails or eat on a budget, see Dine With The Wind In Your Hair (p.356), Make It A Manhattan (p.400), Drinking For Sport (p.406), and Sweethearts Of KL Unite (p.373).

Vegetarian Food

With vegetarian-friendly religions like Hinduism being so prevalent in Malaysia, there are a lot of vegetarians; and a lot of vegetarian restaurants. Many Indian and some Chinese restaurants cater well to vegetarians, and hotel restaurants always have some vegetarian options on their menus. Just a word of warning: many outlets apply a rather loose definition of vegetarian preparation, so you may find yourself choking down a spoonful of chicken broth or swallowing a rogue shrimp. If you are at all in doubt about whether or not a restaurant uses non-vegetarian products in its vegetarian dishes, speak to the manager about the exact ingredients. A popular southern Indian meal is banana leaf curry, which consists of at least three vegetable dishes. The happy cow website (www.happycow.net) has a comprehensive listing of vegetarian restaurants and health food stores located in KL.

Street Food

Malaysia is a gourmet paradise, where affordable food is available around the clock at reasonable prices. Hawker stalls offer the best value, with many operating with minimal overheads – a wok and a few plastic chairs, tables, plates and cutlery. They have taken specialisation to an art form and many concentrate on just one dish. They often congregate in foodcourts and coffee shops so diners can go to specific stalls to choose from the variety on offer. Many have become famous and patrons will travel long distances to eat at specific stalls.

Popular local specialities include satay made from marinated and barbecued chicken or beef served with a peanut sauce; rendang (chicken or beef cooked in spicy coconut milk), nasi lemak (rice cooked in coconut milk and served with anchovies, egg and cucumber) and a wide range of noodle and rice dishes. Some other popular dishes to try include dim sum, roti canai (Indian bread), nasi kandar (a smorgasbord of various meats and vegetables served with rice) and teh tarik (literally, 'stretched tea' or tea with condensed milk that has been passed from cup to cup to create a frothy head).

There are various famous food and restaurant streets in Kuala Lumpur, but few are as famous or as atmospheric as Jalan Alor in the Golden Triangle, running parallel to Jalan Bukit Bintang. While some of the stalls or street-side restaurants operate around the clock, the street really only hits top gear when the sun sets. All afternoon, vendors start wheeling their various cooking stations into place and setting up plastic chairs and tables along a street that has seen similar action for decades.

Most of the food served here is Chinese although there are a few Malay stalls. The stalls stretch from the top of the street (Jalan Sultan Ismail end) down to the Nova Hotel (towards Chinatown). A Baptist Church located next to the Imperial Hotel and a Sport Toto (lucky numbers outlet) looks out of place in the crowded and busy street.

Restoran Dragon View (03 2142 4111) is located immediately opposite the church. This is one of the largest and most popular restaurants along the street probably because it operates around the clock. It serves non-halal dishes with roasted duck, chicken and pork being the most popular but there other options such as bak kuh teh (herbal pork ribs), frogs, fish, porridge and some vegetarian dishes. The open-sided restaurant gets crowded as patrons spill out onto the street beneath a protective awning.

Immediately in front of the restaurant is a hawker stall selling fresh durian and mangosteen. Continue down Jalan Alor to a shop called Long Kee that serves chicken and pork floss. Staff barbecue the thinly compacted meat at the front of the shop.

Restoran Ch Cha is open for lunch and dinner, with Hainanese chicken rice being the speciality dish of one of the hawker carts there. Other restaurants on the Bukit Bintang side of the street include Restoran Sai Woo, which offers popular dishes like Penang lobak, bak kuh teh, Penang fried kueh teow and Restoran Sun Chui Yueh, which serves barbecued fish and eel in the evening.

Cross the street where there is a stall in front of Budget Inn serving deliciously sweet sugar cane juice. Next door, Warung Tom Yam Melayu Kita serves another popular Malay dish called roti bakar, or toasted bread. Alor Food Court has an extensive selection of local drinks including Malaysia's famous teh tarik (tea with condensed milk) and some unusual juices such as banana or carrot.

Street food vendor

Streetside juice bar

Restaurants

African

Kelab Syabas
1 Lorong Sultan
Petaling Jaya
🚇 *Asia Jaya*
Map 6 C4

Out Of Africa

03 7955 3432 | *www.outofafrica.com.my*

You saw the movie, now it's time to experience the hearty food of South Africa. After a good feed you'll soon appreciate why the Springboks are so formidable on the rugby field. This place has been feeding large portions to hungry sportsmen and their families for over a decade so they must be doing something right. Try any braai dish (African BBQ) to discover the big attraction and there's an interesting selection of South African wines to wash it down. The adjoining Kudu Bar is guaranteed to show any live sporting event, especially those featuring South Africans. Located within a private sporting club called Kelab Syabas in suburban Petaling Jaya, the restaurant can be hard to find so check the map on its website. The outdoor play equipment makes it a good spot for children.

Hot peanuts

American

Suria KLCC
City Centre
🚇 *KLCC*
Map 11 C2

Chili's

03 2164 1400 | *www.chilis.com*

If you don't like dining surprises head to Chili's for consistently good comfort food. This Tex-Mex joint is a crowd pleaser and Chili's is popular with families, especially those on shopping forays into Suria KLCC (p.341). Booths are available and window tables overlook the KLCC parklands or you can opt for the island bar for drinks. The decor is American 50s drugstore with its associated paraphernalia to get you in the mood for Big Mouth Burgers. You'll also find nachos, fajitas, flame-grilled steaks, ribs and salads on the menu, but save room for the molten chocolate cake. Margaritas in various forms and international beers are available along with draught beer.
There are other branches at Mid Valley Megamall (03 2287 6788), Bangsar (03 2092 2023) and Petaling Jaya (03 7725 7277).

KL Plaza
179, Jalan Bukit Bintang
Bukit Bintang
🚇 *Bukit Bintang*
Map 13 C1

Planet Hollywood

03 2144 6562 | *www.planethollywood.com*

Dining in Planet Hollywood satisfies those looking for a lively atmosphere, hearty and tasty comfort food, entertainment, branded merchandise and an excellent selection of drinks. It takes on different forms during the day, from a place to snack at lunchtime to a restaurant in the evening, and then a bar and party place until early morning. Its central location and line of special, limited-edition merchandise makes it popular with tourists.
Expect burgers, pasta and steaks with various promotions such as evening BBQ buffets from 19:00 to 23:00 and, 'kids eat for free on Sunday' when a main course is ordered by an accompanying adult. Guests can dine on two levels and the outdoor area is a great spot for happy hour drinks and people watching. A band swings into action at 22:30 from Monday to Saturday. Ladies' Nights are every Monday and Wednesday (from 21:00 onwards) for women over 21, who receive complimentary drinks inclusive of champagne, wine, sangria and strawberry margaritas.

TGI Friday's

The Curve
TTDI (Taman Tun Dr Ismail)
🚇 *Kepong*

03 7726 6899 | *www.fridays.com.my*

Shoppers at The Curve (p.337) can take time out from the retail action and slip into a welcoming environment where guests are greeted by staff wearing colourful uniforms covered in badges of unknown significance. The retro American decor, with musical memorabilia like old record covers on the wall, reminds kids that music existed before iPods. Children will love the atmosphere and the special menu while adults will find comfort in dishes like buffalo wings, cajun chicken pasta and Jack Daniel's grilled salmon. Three-course meals from RM39.90 offer great value. A limited selection of wine is available as are beers, juices and margaritas. The Curve is a 15 minute cab ride from Kepong station. Friday's has other KL outlets at the Pavilion (03 7957 3245), Subang Parade (03 734 2956), 1 Utama (03 7729 4822) and the Life Centre (03 2163 7761).

British

Coliseum Cafe

98-100 Jalan
Tuanku Abdul
Rahman
Little India
🚇 *Bandaraya*
Map 10 D3

03 2692 6270

In a previous era, the Coliseum (pronounced col-ee-zee-um by most Malaysians), was the place to dine in KL. Present day diners can just imagine Somerset Maugham or Joseph Conrad sitting in a corner penning a tome. The cafe and bar and upstairs hotel opened in 1921 and, while all have seen better days, they don't come much more atmospheric than this. Some of the staff look like they've been waiting tables here forever and very little seems to have changed. Start the evening with a drink in the bar and soak up the ambience. The old cafe is famous for its sizzling steaks which arrive at the table on hot plates onto which a dollop of butter and gravy are placed. The ensuing cloud of steam and splattering fat fills the air; luckily patrons are supplied with a bib to protect their clothing. There's an extensive menu of local and western dishes, with the baked crabmeat in its shell, creme caramel and fried icecream all highly recommended. The Coliseum may not be a gourmet haven but go for the atmosphere if nothing else.

Tanner's

H2 Taman Tunku
Off Langgak Tunku
Bukit Tunku
🚇 *KL Sentral*
Map 4 E3

03 6201 2333

Tanner's offers traditional international cuisine with a British bias cooked by a UK-trained chef. Finding Tanner's in a row of shops in Taman Tunku is a navigational challenge for many, but it's worth finding for the excellent caesar salad, moussaka and cheesecake. Try the three-course Sunday lunch for a very reasonable RM45. A compact but good wine and beverage list provides another great reason for visiting, but another plus is the abundant and free off-street parking in front of the restaurant.

Brunch

Weekends are popular times for friends and families to get together over a meal. Most Malaysians will do this at least once over the weekend and most expats will follow suit. Large Chinese restaurants are well-equipped for family gatherings with tables capable of serving eight diners or so available in most restaurants.

Many hotels have capitalised on diners who like to relax over Sunday brunch, and offer various buffets with or without alcohol included. In most cases, if a free flow of either champagne or table wines is offered, diners can opt to eat just the food or pay a premium for the alcohol. Most brunches in hotels last from 11:00 to 15:00.

Brunch

Iketeru	Hilton Kuala Lumpur	03 2264 2264	www1.hilton.com
Kampachi	Hotel Equatorial Kuala Lumpur	03 2161 7777	www.equatorial.com
La Terrasse	33 Jalan Berangan	03 2145 4964	www.laterrassekl.com
Latest Recipe	Level 5, Le Meridien Kuala Lumpur, 2 Jalan Sentral	03 2263 7888	www.lemeridien.com
Pacifica Grill	Mandarin Oriental Kuala Lumpur	03 2179 8882	www.mandarinoriental.com
Prego	The Westin Kuala Lumpur, 199 Jalan Bukit Bintang	03 2731 8333	www.starwoodhotels.com
Tanner's	H2 Taman Tunku off Langgak Tunku	03 6201 2333	na
Uncle Chillis	Hilton Petaling Jaya	03 7955 9122	www.hilton.com
Zipangu	Shangri-La Hotel Kuala Lumpur, 11 Jalan Sultan Ismail	03 2074 3900	www.shangri-la.com

Chinese

Hilton Hotel
3 Jalan Stesen Sentral
KL Sentral
🚇 *KL Sentral*
Map 7 A2

Chynna

03 2264 2264 | www.kl-studio.com

The Hilton really is a place to see and be seen. Not surprisingly, Chynna serves up Chinese food in an opulent setting of Shanghai splendour circa 1920, with staff dressed accordingly. The dishes are suited to celebratory nights with high-priced Chinese specialities and sadly only a few moderately priced dishes. Peking duck is served with all the ceremony it deserves and a selection of dim sum dishes is also available. Choosing Chinese tea (with all the theatrics of a long-spout pourer) to accompany your meal is a good option as the wine list features excellent wines with equally impressive prices.

Renaissance KL
Cnr Jalan Sultan Ismail
& Jalan Ampang
City Centre
🚇 *Bukit Nanas*
Map 10 F2

Dynasty

03 2771 6728 | www.marriott.com

This smart Chinese spot is a great choice for a big night out. Dynasty offers authentic Cantonese and non-halal food including the signature dish of barbecued suckling pig. Celebratory Chinese dinners usually involve premium quality dishes and the Dynasty doesn't disappoint with a selection of lobster, abalone, foie gras, shark's fin and bird's nest options. Desserts like durian fritters, Chinese pancakes and Chinese herbal jelly shouldn't be missed. While there's an extensive wine list, promotional wine offers or Chinese tea appear quicker than wines from the full wine list which are retrieved from distant cellars.

The Emperor

Sheraton Subang
Jalan SS12/1
Subang Jaya
Subang
🚇 *Subang Jaya*
Map 1 B3

The Emperor

03 5031 6060 | www.sheraton.com

The Emperor is an upmarket Chinese restaurant located in suburban Subang Jaya. Being in one of the few five-star hotels in the area, The Emperor is popular for big night out celebrations, with private dining rooms available. While many dishes are big ticket items there's a healthy balance with many more accessible and cheaper items listed. Most dishes are cooked Cantonese style, but there are several spicier Szechuan dishes. Some dishes include meats such as ostrich and venison which are not commonly seen in other restaurants,

while tanks containing live fish are an indication of just how fresh some of the seafood items can be. Various Chinese teas, juices, beers and a small selection of wines are on offer.

Gu Yue Tien

Lot B5-A, Chulan Sq
92 Jalan Raja Chulan
Bukit Bintang
🚇 *Bukit Bintang*
Map 13 D1

03 2148 0808

Award-winning chef and owner Frankie Woo fuses Chinese and western flavours in a creative style. Discover this with dishes such as scallop served on yam cake or foie gras with soft-boiled egg. Being non-halal, there are several tasty pork dishes including pork fillet and daikon accompanied by a buttery wasabi sauce. One of the more traditional dishes is local chicken lightly flavoured with ginseng. Dessert of chilled avocado cream, sago and ginseng is as creative as many of the mains and many agree that Gu Yue Tien is probably the most innovative of all the Chinese restaurants in KL.

Hakka Restaurant

6 Jalan Kia Peng
City Centre
🚇 *Raja Chulan*
Map 11 C4

03 2143 1907

This well-established Chinese restaurant is popular with tour groups and the business community due to its downtown location. The best place to dine is in the semi-outdoors (a moveable canopy encloses the restaurant when it rains) with glimpses of the Petronas Twin Towers (p.288). Avoid the harshly-lit interior which is a little sterile. For a restaurant that's been open for almost half a century, it's obviously doing something right. Hakka food originates from Guangdong and Fujian Provinces and is typically simple with home-cooked presentation. Dishes mostly come in three sizes and staff will advise on how much to order, with some steering towards the more expensive items. The extensive menu covers most bases with some outstanding dishes being country chicken and yong tau foo, claypot drunken tiger prawns, and roasted pig's trotters. There's a sizeable car park with valet parking.

Ka-Soh

136 Jalan Kasah
Medan Damansara
Bukit Damansara
🚇 *KL Sentral*
Map 6 D1

03 2093 7388

Ka-Soh is a little known Chinese restaurant that gets a little noisy when well-heeled Damansara families dine at the weekends. It is a no-frills spot, with a bright orange interior and crowded seating, but diners come to eat and not to soak up the ambience. The large menu features more than 100 items, some of which are non-halal. There are several dishes with pig innards but more conventional dishes like butter prawns and honey pork are popular. One of the more unusual, but very tasty dishes, is deep-fried frog legs with ginger. Beer is served but patrons can bring their own wine and corkage is not charged. An excellent selection of wine is obtainable from Vintry (03 2094 8262) next door. There are two other outlets in Kuala Lumpur at Jalan Bukit Bintang (03 2148 2207) and Jalan Delima (03 2207 2723).

Mandarin Palace

Federal Hotel
Bukit Bintang
🚇 *Bukit Bintang*
Map 13 B2

03 2148 9166 | *www.fhihotels.com*

Walking into the Mandarin Palace is like entering a museum, with walls and ceilings lined with intricately-carved wooden panels that have remained unchanged since the restaurant opened in 1957. It is on the second floor of the Federal Hotel which was, in its day, the city's only hotel of international standard. Things have since changed, but, for those who like tradition and heritage, this is the place to dine. Cinema buffs will revel in the knowledge that the restaurant featured in the 1964 movie Seventh Dawn starring William Holden and Susannah York. No doubt they enjoyed the classic Hong Kong dim sum, which is still one of the big attractions, especially at lunch. This is a non-halal restaurant serving Cantonese and Szechuan favourites, with outstanding dishes such as siew mai, har gau and steamed barbecue pork buns.

Old China Cafe

11 Jalan Balai Polis
Chinatown
🚇 **Masjid Jamek**
Map 12 D3

03 2072 5915 | www.oldchina.com.my

Another of the city's most atmospheric dining outlets is the Old China Cafe, tucked away in a backstreet away from the Petaling Street action. The building was once the trade guild headquarters for the Selangor & Federal Territory Laundry Association and the walls are lined with old photos and paraphernalia. The antique furniture creates a great atmosphere, ideal when guests come to town and you want to impress them with something really Asian. The menu mostly features the unique Nyonya cuisine style, the food of the Peranakan or Straits Chinese. Try dishes such as a Portuguese beef semur (spiced with cinnamon and pepper originating from Malacca which is still home to a Portuguese community), ginseng soup and assam prawns. There are various tofu and vegetable dishes for those who don't eat meat.

Qing Zhen Chinese Muslim Restaurant

Novotel Hydro Majestic
Bukit Bintang
🚇 **Raja Chulan**
Map 11 C4

03 2147 0888 | www.novotel.com

Qing Zhen conjures up images of some remote outpost along the Silk Road, with decor reminiscent of far western China where the influence is more Islamic than Chinese. The restaurant interior is lined with decorated arches and columns and intricately-carved wooden partitions. The food is typical of that found in western China and the style is best known as Muslim Chinese. However, with the chef originating from Yunnan, there are some spicy overtones and Szechuan flavours in several dishes. Some of the dishes from the far west of China are inspired by the Middle East, so guests can also choose kebabs and various naan breads. The fusion of several styles and the ornate decor creates an exciting venue. Halal dim sum is served at lunch.

Si Chuan Dou Hua

Parkroyal KL
52 Jalan Sultan Ismail
Bukit Bintang
🚇 **Bukit Bintang**
Map 13 C2

03 2147 2303 | www.kualalumpur.parkroyalhotels.com

If nothing else, go to watch the tea-pouring theatrics of the restaurant's own tea master. Using a metal tea pot with a metre-long, narrow pouring spout he delivers piping hot tea with pinpoint accuracy into cups on your dining room table. Tea is essential as the wines are expensive and the food is extra spicy. Szechuan food dominates and, as the hottest of all the Chinese styles, it's quite popular with Malaysian diners. Two signature dishes in this style are the stir-fried beef and braised fish. Cantonese cuisine provides support to the more piquant dishes. Vegetarians will enjoy several dishes made from beancurd. The setting is upmarket and contemporary yet not obviously Chinese, with minimal gold and red to be seen. Four private rooms for up to 15 people are also available.

Woo Lan

19 Jalan Scott
KL Sentral
🚇 **KL Sentral**
Map 7 A2

03 2274 8368

This inconspicuous establishment is a real find, with some delicious food and great prices. There's no menu and, while not all the staff speak English, it's possible to be understood. It's worth the effort with the various seafood, pork, chicken, tofu and vegetable dishes available. Try deep-fried tofu, deep-fried belly pork, Guinness pork ribs, steamed fish and curried prawns to discover the taste of authentic home-cooked food. The setting is nothing spectacular with harsh lighting, plastic tables and chairs and paintings of horses galloping through the surf, and it can get noisy with kids running around, but nobody seems to mind. Finding the place is a little difficult, but the Hindu temple opposite is a useful landmark. Beer, soft drinks and tea are served and corkage isn't charged for those who bring their own wine. If in doubt about food prices ask when ordering but don't expect to pay more than RM25 per head.

Contemporary Asian

The Westin KL
199 Jalan Bukit Bintang
Bukit Bintang
🚇 **Bukit Bintang**
Map 13 C1

EEST
03 2731 8333 | www.starwoodhotels.com

The Westin has pulled out all stops to impress KL diners. If you can't decide between culinary styles, then the extensive pan-Asian selections at EEST (pronounced 'east'), makes for a happy compromise. Diners can choose Chinese, Japanese, Thai, Vietnamese and Malay dishes, with an emphasis on seafood. The selection of Cantonese dim sum is very good and great value for money. There's a Zen-like interior and several private dining rooms for meetings or family gatherings. The various open kitchens ensure a lively setting that enables guests and staff to interact, especially on Saturdays when cooking classes are held in the restaurant. EEST made it onto Condé Nast World Hot Table List for 2006.

Hilton KL
3 Jalan Stesen Sentral
KL Sentral
🚇 **KL Sentral**
Map 7 A2

Senses
03 2264 2264 | www.kl-studio.com

This is the signature restaurant of local-chef-done-well Cheong Liew. Cheong calls his cooking style 'global food' as it is a synthesis of Australian, international and Asian styles. There is an a la carte menu or the chefs can specially prepare a degustation menu of up to eight courses. Try the signature dish 'sea dance plate' which represents milestones in Chef Cheong's culinary journey. Expect premium items such as oysters, crabs, scallops, lobster, crayfish and wagyu beef. In line with its name, a sensory approach is taken with the restaurant's ambience; aromatic candles burn and soft music is played. While the wine list is superb, there are few bargains to be had and each dish on the menu is matched with a wine sold by the glass. This is one for serious diners who enjoy creative food that crosses several cooking styles.

Starhill Gallery
181 Jalan Bukit Bintang
🚇 **Bukit Bintang**
Map 13 C1

Shook!
03 2782 3875 | www.ytlcommunity.com/shook

While it's been around for some time, Shook! still manages to attract a sophisticated clientele of locals, celebrities and international travellers. Despite being in a shopping

Shook!

centre, it is the high-end Starhill Gallery (p.341), and attracts shoppers who can afford to eat in the restaurants on its Feast Level in the basement. Prime people-watching territory, Shook! is considered one of the city's most prestigious restaurants. However, there are two private dining spaces for those who don't want to be seen. The menu takes in many of the great global cuisines, with dishes from Japan, China and Italy as well as western grills. There is an inspiring walk-in wine cellar with some incredible vintages at equally impressive prices, including bottles Château Mouton Rothschild from every vintage between 1945 and 2003.

Top Hat

7 Jalan Kia Peng
City Centre
🚇 **Raja Chulan**
Map 11 C4

03 2142 8611 | *www.top-hat-restaurants.com*

The 1930s downtown bungalow where you'll find Top Hat was once home to the original Bon Ton (p.414). It's a great location with abundant parking in spacious gardens and spectacular, floodlit evening views of the Petronas Twin Towers (p.188). The menu features a la carte international and Asian dishes and set meals of Nonya, Malay, Thai and western cuisines, and there's also a healthy selection of vegetarian dishes. The wine list is very good and the desserts are worth saving space for. Jazz fans can hear live music in The Top Room above the restaurant every Friday to Sunday (22:30 to 02:00 and 18:00 to 02:00 on Sundays).

European

Other options **Spanish** p.385, **German** p.369, **Italian** p.374, **Mediterranean** p.380, **Pizzerias** p.383, **French** p.367

Chalet

Hotel Equatorial KL
Jalan Sultan Ismail
City Centre
🚇 **Raja Chulan**
Map 11 B3

03 2161 7777 | *www.equatorial.com*

This place is caught in a time warp, appealing to those who like traditional, international and classic cuisine. The Chalet does what it does well and customers keep coming back. The lighting is subtle with sofa seating providing secluded, romantic spaces around the European-styled restaurant. Expect classic Swiss-Continental dishes like beef fondue, lobster bisque, sliced veal, raclette cheese and baby lamb served with flair. It has an enticing dessert trolley, and those made at the table with lots of theatrics are a speciality. Some of the staff have been here almost as long as the hotel (more than 35 years) but that's a bonus – they know the menu backwards and how to impress with little touches. The comprehensive wine list is one of Malaysia's best. The restaurant is open for lunch and dinner from Monday to Friday, and for dinner only at weekends.

Chinoz on the Park

Suria KLCC
KLCC
🚇 **KLCC**
Map 11 C2

03 2166 8277

Chinoz is a landmark within a landmark. Once in the epicentre of Bangsar's cafe society it now commands a premier location overlooking the parklands that surround the two peaks of the Petronas Towers (p.188). It's a stylish yet relaxed bistro with leanings to sophisticated dining inside, but casual dining outside. There are plans to raise the standards inside so watch out for some more upmarket dining there. Chinoz kicks off with breakfast and serves international dishes and a comprehensive selection of mezze starters throughout the rest of the day. It offers wood-fired pizzas, pastas, salads, sashimi, sushi and seafood. To complement the food, a serious range of wines, including some grand crus from Burgundy, is available at reasonable prices from an octagonal wine cellar. Chinoz is open daily from 08:00 to 23:30 and has another outlet in the Gardens, Mid Valley (03 2287 8277).

Bangsar Village II
2 Jalan Telawi 1
Bangsar
🚇 *Bangsar*
Map 6 E2

Delicious

03 2287 1554 | www.delicious.com.my

Queues formed when this restaurant opened in Bangsar Village II and it didn't take diners long to realise that this Malaysian-owned concept was worth it. The white and sky blue interior looks like an IKEA showroom, punctuated by oak furniture to achieve a sense of space. The freshness flows through to the menu items, which include both Asian and western favourites with a tendency towards the latter. Diners can choose from pies, quiches, sandwiches, burgers, pastas as well as a tantalising selection of desserts (kids will love the cup cakes). Vegetarians are not neglected with some very nutritious salads. There's a good drinks list and a selection of wines by the glass and bottle. Try the traditional English afternoon tea for two from 15:00 to 18:00. Delicious and its offshoot DLish have an outlet in Marc Residences (03 2166 9099) and the soon-to-open Dua Residences on Jalan Tun Razak.

Bangsar Puteri
Condominium
Jalan Medang Serai
Bukit Bandaraya
Bangsar
🚇 *Bangsar*
Map 6 E1

Karl's Beisl

03 2094 0628 | unitedlinks2003@yahoo.com

This casual restaurant is named after the chef/owner and offers authentic, home-style, non-halal, Austrian fare. The cosy setting is made more homely by the owner's collection of antiques and artefacts gathered from his travels. The menu includes a selection of soups, mains and desserts with the house specialities including hand-crafted bratwurst sausages, roasted pork knuckle, whole roasted suckling pig, Hungarian beef goulash with spätzle, Weiner schnitzel and lamb shanks. It's near impossible to eat Austrian food without apple strudel and Karl's interpretation of this national dish is excellent. Austrian and German wines as well as a selection of international and German beers provide further authenticity.

6-5 Jalan Batai
Damansara Heights
Bukit Damansara
🚇 *KL Sentral*
Map 4 D4

Klimt's

03 2092 1978

Klimt's is a small, owner-chef operated Austrian restaurant in suburban Damansara. The service is hands-on and the home-cooked, hearty food is popular with expats. It's also a family-friendly restaurant with a kids' menu and relaxed atmosphere. The restaurant walls are decorated with prints from Austria's most celebrated artist, Gustav Klimt. The cuisine has changed over the years from being almost exclusively Austrian to continental, but has retained several famous Austrian dishes like schnitzel, strudel and spätzle (noodles). The Hungarian goulash is very popular, as is 'znaimer rinds rouladen' or rolled beef with dumplings and red cabbage. The restaurant is pork free and there are a few dishes for vegetarians. There's a small selection of wines (mostly Chilean and Australian) by the glass and bottle as well as various schnapps and German wheat beers.

One Bangsar
63C Jalan Ara
Bangsar
🚇 *Bangsar*
Map 6 E2

Rick's Cafe Casablanca

03 2287 1618 | www.rickscafe.com.my

One Bangsar is a collection of upmarket restaurants in trendy Bangsar. Away from the main restaurant and bar strip, there's abundant parking with access to the 10 dining concepts. If you can't decide upon a food style, drop by One Bangsar and have a dish in several restaurants. Rick's is one of the newest and the sophisticated ambience is enhanced with posters from the famous movie the restaurant is named after. Try dishes like kemia (Moroccan tapas), pertuna ocean trout, Japanese butterfish, steak tartare and lamb with creamy mash. There are several creative dishes catering to vegetarians like twice-baked mushroom souffle. Desserts such as tiramisu and creme brulee are almost staples in restaurants of this calibre but both are executed extremely well at Rick's. Wines are taken seriously but priced reasonably. There's a Moroccan-inspired lounge upstairs where a live jazz band performs every Thursday.

Telawi Street Bistro

03 2284 3168 | *www.telawi.com.my*

Despite the constantly changing Bangsar restaurant landscape, 'TSB' is a popular venue for young, trendy urbanites who dine in the downstairs restaurant and later hit the lively bar upstairs. It's associated with the group of La Bodega restaurants and bars so everything is done to exacting standards. Contemporary cuisine is on offer with greek salad, mediterranean-style seafood soup, chicken tikka masala and rack of lamb on the menu. There's an adjoining informal cafe and a trendy upstairs bar that swings into top gear as the evening progresses.

Third Floor

03 2141 3363 | *www.thirdfloor.com.my*

Chef Ken Hon is a legend in KL after putting Cilantro Restaurant (temporarily closed for renovations) into restaurant guides some years ago. Start your dining experience with an aperitif at the stone bar or in a comfortable lounge. The dining space is minimalist, as is the plate presentation. Diners can expect an explosion of taste sensations with every bite. This is a restaurant all devotees of fine dining should try at least once while in KL. The seasonal menu changes regularly but expect dishes such as Jerusalem artichoke soup scented with truffle, wagyu beef, and baked banana and cheese in filo pastry. The dining pinnacle is a six-course degustation menu. The wine list is suitably impressive with a reserve selection of French grand crus from Bordeaux and Burgundy. As you would expect, the service is faultless and discreet.

Twentyone Kitchen + Bar

03 2142 0021 | *www.twentyone.com.my*

During the day and in the early evening, Twenty One serves interesting dishes from a list called 'the passion' instead of the menu. Later in the evening it becomes an upmarket cocktail lounge that grooves to house music or a DJ on Wednesday, Friday and Saturday nights. The menu has been carefully designed to offer trendy, inner-city fare. Start the day with an all-day 'brekkie baby yeah!' and progress to dishes like blue cheese risotto, lamb shank and pan-fried sea bass. Expect desserts like espresso creme brulee and apple crumble and there is a serious cheese platter at a serious price. Sharing platters and tapas are also available and popular. The power tables are at the front overlooking the busy strip of Changkat Bukit Bintang. This is one of the most recent additions to the urban landscape and is a cut above some of the other outlets nearby.

French

Tropicana Golf &
Country Club Resort
Jalan Kelab Tropicana
Petaling Jaya
Kelana Jaya
Map 1 B2

Cuisine Studio

03 7805 3088 | *www.cuisine-studio.net*

Cuisine Studio combines a restaurant, gourmet shop and show kitchen to offer a unique environment where you can dine, shop and learn. It was established by a group of professional French chefs who offer modern French dishes based upon traditional recipes. Look for seasonal specials on the menu, all made from premium and organically-sourced ingredients. A range of healthy breads, rich pastries and unique jams are made on the premises. The restaurant walls are lined with cooking utensils and ingredients which are all for sale. A well-considered wine list complements the food. The show kitchen and surrounding seating make this a great venue for foodies to learn new cooking skills while dining on the fruits of their labour. It also operates Urban Picnic (03 2026 5040) in Menara IMC. To gain access to this private, gated estate just inform security that you are dining in Cuisine Studio.

Carcosa Seri Negara
Lake Gardens
KL Sentral
🚇 **KL Sentral**
Map 6 F1

The Dining Room
03 2295 0888 | www.carcosa.com.my

This is the dining domain of corporate captains, socialites and people celebrating. You can expect refined dining in KL's most exclusive and lavish restaurant. There are two degustation menus as well as international a la carte with the five-course or seven-course menus particularly recommended. The menus are in French and English, and diners can choose dishes such as grilled wagyu beef tenderloin and crispy mashed potato mille feuilles. A chariot-sized trolley has a sumptuous selection of mostly Alsatian cheeses. There are some very impressive wines from both the Old and New World with leanings to the former, including five reds, five whites and a few sparklers by the glass. English afternoon teas are popular with KL's socialites and expats impressing visitors with their grand lifestyle in the tropics.

33 Jalan Berangan
Bukit Bintang
🚇 **Raja Chulan**
Map 13 A1

La Terrasse
03 2145 4964 | www.laterrassekl.com

There's no place for nouvelle cuisine at La Terrasse; it offers everyday French cuisine at reasonable prices in comfortable surroundings. The somewhat spartan exterior is for drinkers and devotees of French television, which is projected onto a large screen. The air-conditioned interior, decorated with historic travel posters, seats 30. For those who like their pork (and an extensive selection of other dishes) cooked in a French home-style way, this is the place to dine. The atmosphere is relaxed although the tables are formally set with an array of wine glasses. Upstairs, Tastevin Cellars (www.mytastevinkl.com) has a superb and reasonable wine selection with bottles costing from just RM48 up to the stratosphere with Chateau Petrus. This is the place for Sunday champagne brunch with room for the kids to play on the outside terrace.

Shangri-La KL
11 Jalan Sultan Ismail
City Centre
🚇 **Bukit Nanas**
Map 11 A3

Lafite
03 2074 3900 | www.shangri-la.com

Adam Tihany, one of the world's leading hospitality designers, was responsible for the innovative design of Lafite. His interior makeover a few years ago repositioned the restaurant towards contemporary dining rather than traditional French. Lafite

Lafite

Dine with a beautiful view

was once KL's big night out restaurant and, while the competition has caught up, the wine list and impeccable service still make it stand out. The extensive list of premium and reserve wines is the envy of many connoisseurs but mere mortals can still find an affordable drop. The current chef likes to dabble in molecular gastronomy so expect the unexpected like prawn laksa bubble. It offers degustation menus of six and 12 dishes, with or without wine or champagne pairings. While dinner isn't cheap, if you stay away from the 12 course menu and Romanèe Conti wines, there will be change for the taxi home.

14-16 Changkat
Bukit Bintang
Bukit Bintang
🚇 *Raja Chulan*
Map 13 A1

Le Bouchon

03 2142 7633 | *www.lebouchonrestaurant.com*

This is La Terrasses's big brother so you know it's good. The main differences are that it is pork free with a smarter ambience and menu offering premium ingredients. An elegant and cosy spot for a rendezvous, this fine French restaurant is reminiscent of an old country home, with traditional cuisine. Wines are taken seriously and it's possible to enjoy a premium selection ranging from Petrus to Petaluma at reasonable prices.

One Bangsar
63-F Jalan Ara
Bangsar
🚇 *Bangsar*
Map 6 E2

Le Francais

03 2282 2510 | *www.lefrancaisfrenchdining.com*

This smartly decorated restaurant only seats about 50 and uses splashes of curtains to provide a little privacy for those who need it. The tables are covered in deep burgundy cloths and a selection of fine glassware. The cooking style is traditional but the French chef changes the menu regularly to keep the taste buds of his regulars continually tantalised. However, diners can expect the usual line up of traditional French fare like escargot, scallops, foie gras, duck, cheese, souffles and creme brulee. While it is not necessarily cheap, many of the items are imported which makes them expensive. It also has a cigar divan and a good selection of wines.

German

46 Changkat
Bukit Bintang
City Centre
🚇 *Bukit Bintang*
Map 13 A1

Deutsches Haus

03 2143 2268 | *www.deutscheshaus.com.my*

Lots of German kitsch gives this place a cosy feel and, with a good stretch of the imagination, you could be in a German beer hall. Sipping the beers will definitely help. Alcohol is certainly the biggest draw to this busy street but the non-halal food in Deutsches Haus provides excellent support. Patrons can sit at tables along an open veranda or inside at tables and booths surrounding the bar. The dishes on offer include a plate for two of honey-glazed pork knuckle with smoked bacon, sausage and Bavarian meatloaf. Soups, schnitzels and strudel complete a menu that is reasonably faithful to German cuisine. Paulaner and Hoegaarden beers are especially popular during happy hour from 18:00 to 20:00. Parking in this part of the city is a challenge but the restaurant has a subsidised arrangement with the hotel immediately opposite.

12 Jalan Telawi 5
Bangsar
🚇 *Bukit Bintang*
Map 6 E2

Frankfurt House

03 2284 1624

Frankfurt House has stood the test of time in Bangsar, where restaurants and bars come and go as frequently as monsoonal storms. The entrance is open to the street and many diners choose to sit there to watch the busy street life. The restaurant changes to a popular bar later in the evening and is well supported by its regulars who come to watch sporting fixtures on the large screen. The menu is fairly authentic with dishes including goulash, pork or chicken schnitzel, bratwurst, grilled pork knuckle and smoked pork. Sadly, vegetarians will have to make do with a plate of mixed vegetables but there is a kids' menu for young diners. Various German beers are available as are a few wines including a small selection of German vintages.

Indian

215 Jalan Tun Razak
KLCC
🚇 *Ampang Park*

Bombay Palace
03 2145 4241

While it may not be Bollywood, you can imagine Indian lovers serenading each other at this popular former bungalow on Jalan Tun Razak. Bombay Palace can seat a large number of patrons over its two storeys and is considered to be the best Indian restaurant in KL for a big night out. The award-winning cuisine comes from northern India and includes an extensive selection of tandoori meats. Regulars rave about the handi biriyani, butter chicken, kashmiri naan (crammed with dried fruits) and, the garlic kulcha. While Indian icecream is very sweet, and has an acquired taste, it is lapped up here. The large, free on-site carpark is a bonus.

21G Jalan Telwai 2
Bangsar
🚇 *Bangsar*

Chutney Mary
03 2282 9923 | *nickey_harry@yahoo.com*

This little Indian restaurant may appear unassuming from the outside, but inside it has beautiful decor and an impressive range of Indian cuisine. The smallish dining area is made to look bigger with a fascinating blend of decorative features, such as the ceiling detail or the white wall with tiny little mirrors embedded into it. It also features an open kitchen, where you can see the roti breads being spun in the air and giant skewers of marinated meat waiting to be cooked in the tandoor oven. The menu is diverse and caters for those who love all the spices the cuisine has to offer, as well as those with milder tastes. The range of starters is large enough that you can select a few and enjoy a 'tapas-style' Indian meal. Chutney Mary has a decent wine list and the Tiger beer flows on tap – the perfect accompaniment to those dishes with a bit of a kick. If you're in the area at lunchtime, try the set menu, ranging in price from RM6.90 to RM12.90.

138 Jalan Kasah
Medan Damansara
Bukit Damansara
🚇 *KL Sentral*
Map 6 D1

Gills
03 2092 5403

Gills is one of the most popular suburban Indian restaurants, located in a semi-secluded part of Medan Damansara just off busy Jalan Damansara. It can't be seen from the main road but is situated behind the popular Victoria Station Restaurant. Diners can sit in the somewhat clinical but comfortable interior, or in the open air along a covered veranda. The north Indian food keeps the loyal customers coming back. Lamb rogan josh is one of the most popular dishes but others include chicken tikka, tandoori prawns and a rather hot lamb vindaloo. There are several rice dishes, lots of vegetables and Indian breads like chapati and naan. The staff are happy to adjust the spice levels or assist those who have ventured into unknown territory. Kids are both welcome and offered a special menu. While wines are available, the list is limited but there are juices and an excellent selection of coffees and teas.

**51 11/4 Jalan Dato
Mahmud**
Petaling Jaya
🚇 *Universiti*
Map 6 D3

Grand City
03 7958 4223

There are many southern Indian restaurants in KL offering meals served on a banana leaf. Grand City in suburban Petaling Jaya near University Hospital is well established and once had a monopoly, but similar outlets have opened in the area. There is a menu, but regulars rarely make reference to it so staff will assume you want a banana leaf curry and will place foliage on the table to act as a plate. White rice and three scoops of vegetables form the basis, with curry sauce, chutney, pappadams and yoghurt completing the basic meal. Carnivores can add curried meats of chicken, seafood and mutton from one of several platters lining the kitchen bench. They serve tea, coffee, juices and a tasty mango lassi but no alcohol. There's nothing lavish about the surroundings but this is reflected in the modest prices.

Plaza Mont'Kiara ◄
2 Jalan Kiara
Mont Kiara
🚇 **KL Sentral**
Map 4 D3

Khaana Peena
03 6201 3355 | *www.khaanapeena.net*
Don't be put off by its secluded location in a corner of busy Plaza Mont' Kiara; seek this place out for its excellent north Indian cuisine and uncluttered interior. As with other restaurants surrounding the plaza, diners can eat inside with air conditioning or in the open air. Try dishes like kebabs, chicken dilruba, tandoori specialities and varieties of naan and chapati breads. Dishes with generic ayurvedic qualities are marked on the menu and vegetarians will find several dishes to their liking. Therapeutic teas, coffees and power drinks are available, as is Kingfisher beer for just RM8. Diners are welcome to bring their own wines but RM25 is charged for corkage. One of KL's best value breakfasts is available for just RM8 (weekdays from 08:00 to 10:00). Go if only to use the 'ordering buzzer' where diners can page the waiters via the on-table buzzer.

13-15 Jalan Gasing ◄
Petaling Jaya
🚇 **Universiti**
Map 6 D4

Lotus
03 7782 8795 | *www.lotusgroup.com.my*
This is one of KL's best Indian outlets and it now has 15 branches throughout the city. The interior is a rabbit warren of low-ceiling rooms that seem to have been added as business rapidly expanded. Menus seem unnecessary with prices this cheap but they are available if you prefer. The south Indian food is very popular; the banana leaf curry is the house speciality and many claim the food tastes better on a leaf than a plate. Various vegetables form the basis of the curry to which various meats can be added. Vegetarians will enjoy the basic curry which is accompanied by white rice or biryani. While the decor is nothing special, the regulars come for the food and not the ambience.

Chutney Mary

Khaana Peena

C14 Plaza Damas
Hartamas Shopping
Centre
Jalan Sri Hartamas
Mont Kiara
KL Sentral
Map 4 D3

Nasi Kandar Bestari

Mamak stalls or Indian Muslim restaurants are known for their interpretation of popular dishes, and nasi candar or mixed rice is a good example of one of these. Meals start with breakfast and finish late in the evening with supper. When important football matches are played, the big screen TV comes out and the crowd may stay until early morning. There's nothing subtle about the strong lights and plastic furniture but diners can eat in or outside under umbrellas. Select various types of tandoori, prata, thosai and chapati from the wall-mounted menu with fresh juices, coffees and teas also on offer. The food is affordable, so many Malaysians choose to dine at Nasi Kandar Bestari for all three meals of the day.

Crown Princess KL
KLCC
Ampang Park
Map 9 E4

The Taj

03 2162 5522 | *www.crownprincess.com.my*

While there are many north Indian restaurants in the city, few offer the refinement and comfort of The Taj on the 11th floor of the Crown Princess Hotel. The restaurant and long-serving chefs have won many awards since it opened some years ago. Panoramic windows offer an elevated view of the city and it's worth asking for a window seat when making a reservation. The restaurant serves many popular dishes with some fine tandoori and naan offerings. Vegetarians can also dine well. Beer, a good selection of wines and various yoghurt-based lassi drinks are available. A small group of musicians performing traditional Indian tunes complete the authentic experience.

International

Le Meridien KL
2 Jalan Sentral
KL Sentral
KL Sentral
Map 12 A4

Latest Recipe

03 2263 7888 | *www.lemeridien.com*

Latest Recipe in Le Meridien is a new addition to the city's popular buffet dining scene. The setting is rather grand with two large private dining areas and window tables overlooking extensive parklands, offering a refreshing view of the city. Portions are small and chefs in the open kitchen frequently replenish dishes for freshness. The Indian selection is comprehensive and supported by Chinese, Malay, Western, Japanese and Thai favourites including a spicy green papaya salad. There's an excellent cheese selection and desserts are enticing, with an innovative icecream teppanyaki counter where chef makes icecream desserts on a cold plate. Considering the premium ingredients and variety offered, Latest Recipe provides one of the best lunch buffet selections in the city, with prices starting from RM68 for adults and RM38 for kids.

Latest Recipe

Pavilion KL
168 Jalan Bukit Bintang
Bukit Bintang
Bukit Bintang
Map 13 C1

The Loaf

03 2145 3036 | *www.theloaf.net*

The Loaf has a split personality; a Japanese bakery and patisserie at street level and a French-Japanese fine dining restaurant upstairs in the evening. The tempting range of breads, cookies and pastries in the bakery are creative and can be enjoyed in the open air at the restaurant's entrance. In the evening diners can indulge in fusion dishes like beef tenderloin with sauteed portabella mushrooms and wasabi herb butter. Both up and downstairs are on the pricey side but the restaurant is very particular about using only the finest imported ingredients. Rumour has it that this is former Malaysian Prime Minister Tun Mahathir's favourite KL restaurant. It also has some excellent packaging for offering pastries and cakes to friends as gifts.

7atenine

The Ascott KL
9 Jalan Pinang
KLCC
🚇 *KLCC*
Map 11 B3

7atenine
03 2161 7789 | www.sevenatenine.com

This elegant outlet is a restaurant by day, and a bar then a chill-out lounge by night. The stunning white decor attracts KL's beautiful people, who dine and party with cool drinks and funky music. While a few local dishes are listed on the menu, the food is mostly contemporary European with dishes such as three pepper squid, pizza, fresh oysters and venison giving some indication of the chef's cooking direction. Save room for desserts which are listed here as 'sins', with the fried icecream guaranteed to be wickedly good. There is also a serious cheese platter. Wines, cocktails (with lots of showmanship), detox mocktails and great champagne deals are equally impressive. Reservations are essential and you should stick around for the late night partying.

20 Jalan 30/70A
Desa Sri Hartamas
Sri Hartamas
🚇 *KL Sentral*
Map 4 D3

SOULed OUT
03 2300 1955 | www.souledout.com.my

SOULed OUT is an expat institution but is also well loved by locals who like to eat well and party hard. It has one of the city's best restaurant/bar combinations and has been around for over a decade. SOULed OUT offers great comfort food, a fantastic atmosphere, snappy and happy service, and drinks of every conceivable concoction. A wide variety of food is served, from western to north Indian cuisine but there is also a choice of thin-crust pizzas cooked in a wood-fired oven. The restaurant spreads over a large area with two floors of dining, and the best tables are under an expansive glass sunlight. There's a giant TV screen for sports events which adds to SOULed OUT's mass appeal. The management is not one to rest on

Sweethearts Of KL Unite

For a romantic dinner that will impress your beloved, try Al Nafourah (p.382), La Bodega (p.385), Lafite (p.368), Nerovivo (p.374), The Dining Room (p.368), Soi 23 (p.388), Le Bouchon (p.369), Sky Bar (p.404), Villa Danieli (p.376), CoChine (p.409) or Chalet (p.365).

its laurels and constantly initiates new promotions to keep the punters returning. The restaurant has abundant parking and even a booze cruiser for those who need assistance home.

Italian

Other options **Mediterranean** p.380, **Pizzerias** p.383

Sunway Resort
Bandar Sunway
Petaling Jaya
🚇 **Setia Jaya**
Map 1 B3

Avanti

03 7492 8000 | www.sunwayhotels.com

Sunway Lagoon (p.192) is a popular 'resort within the city' in the KL suburbs and the water park, shops and restaurants make it a one-stop entertainment hub. Avanti is one of its dining outlets with a lively atmosphere and Italian-inspired dishes. The dual-level outlet has pressed-metal ceilings and stained-glass windows, and diners can eat in booths or at tables. The food includes popular Italian favourites such as pizza, pasta and mains such as beef tenderloin and sea bass. The Sunday smorgasbord brunches are well worth the drive into the suburbs. Diners are entertained by a resident pianist, while guest artists perform on special occasions. This is a popular spot for groups and families, and you can hire the upstairs space for private functions.

3 Jalan 26A/70A
Plaza Prisma Ville
Desa Sri Hartamas
Mont Kiara
🚇 **KL Sentral**
Map 4 C4

Il Divo

03 6201 4445 | www.ildivokl.com

Il Divo is located in suburban Desa Sri Hartamas, close to Mont' Kiara and is the Italian of choice for many. The inviting exterior has a glassed entrance, mood lighting and planter boxes to soften the harshness of this commercial precinct. An all-white interior gives the impression of space and is creatively broken up with several colourful paintings. While no pizza is served, most other standard Italian dishes are on the compact menu which is more fine dining than casual trattoria. Select from dishes like beef carpaccio, seafood risotto, homemade pastas, angus tenderloin and several salads. Desserts like homemade gelati, panna cotta and tiramisu are supported by a high-quality cheese platter. There's a respectable all-Italian wine list with reasonable prices. A good map is on the website and may be required for first-time diners.

Somerset
8 Lorong Ceylon
City Centre
🚇 **Raja Chulan**
Map 13 A1

Neroteca

03 2070 8530 | www.neroteca.com

This vibrant restaurant has a unique concept and diners could be mistaken for thinking they were in an Italian trattoria or corner store. Every inch of wall space is taken up with shelves of Italian produce like olive oils, pastas, herbs and an enticing selection of Italian wines. At the far end display fridges are full of pastries, cheeses, sausages and hams. The restaurant is non-halal and a speciality item is whole roasted suckling pig, although this must be ordered two days in advance. The sit-up bar is popular for those seeking coffee, grappa or some reading space. While the mood is relaxed, there's nothing casual about the food preparation and diners can order sandwiches, cold plates, pastas and mains such as grilled Italian sausages and mash, and fried spare ribs in mushroom sauce. Wines are available at realistic prices and are even cheaper for takeaway. Neroteca's trendy feel attracts young urbanites but it's the food that keeps them coming back.

3A Jalan Ceylon
City Centre
🚇 **Raja Chulan**
Map 13 A1

Nerovivo

03 2070 3120 | www.nerovivo.com

This trendy, inner-city bungalow boasts authentic Italian dishes, many of which are prepared in an open-air pizza oven. Guests can dine inside with air conditioning, alfresco with views of Menara KL or enjoy an aperitif at the bar. The owner and host orchestrates the evening with great gusto to ensure everyone is content upon leaving. The menu features creative cuisine and regional specialities, various pastas with traditional sauces, and meat and fish mains. Meat dishes are based upon northern Italian recipes, while the seafood leans to Sicilian cooking styles. Try dishes like bistecca florentia and chocolate flan to appreciate the skill of the kitchen staff. There's a superb selection of well-priced wines with an inevitable Italian bias. Nerovivo offers one of the city's best set lunches at just RM20 for antipasto or RM48 for antipasto, main, dessert and tea or coffee.

67 Jalan Bangkung
Bukit Bandaraya
Bangsar
🚇 **Bangsar**
Map 6 E1

Opus Bistro
03 2092 4288 | www.opusbistro.com

Opus is in a quiet neighbourhood near Bangsar with ample and free parking. The menu features a wide range of authentic Italian appetisers, salads, soups, pastas, mains and desserts. Enjoy dishes like seafood antipasti, bruschetta, soups, clams in white wine, seafood risotto and lobster thermidor. A signature dish is roasted cod with lemon caper sauce. Desserts include tiramisu and honey affogato (espresso, icecream and violet crumble). Cocktails and a wide selection of wines are available, with Wine Cellars (03 2093 1919) next door ensuring a good flow of booze. While the restaurant is situated in the area of Bangsar, the map on its website is useful. The ambience is as relaxed as the location, with seating for just 50 patrons. Guests can dine inside or alfresco on the sidewalk veranda.

The Westin KL
199 Jalan Bukit Bintang
Bukit Bintang
🚇 **Bukit Bintang**
Map 13 C1

Prego
03 2731 8333 | www.starwoodhotels.com

Prego is a contemporary Italian restaurant in an upmarket and design-oriented downtown hotel. The open kitchen and wood-fired pizza oven are the heart and hearth of the action. While the staff don't take themselves too seriously, they are one of the city's more professional outfits lead by a manager who knows his stuff. Guests can dine in a covered area that flows onto the busy Bukit Bintang pavement or inside on one of two levels. The cooking leans to northern Italian cuisine and don't be surprised if staff appear with slices of complimentary pizza between courses. A few lesser known dishes like braised oxtail add variety to the menu, while king prawns served with arugula, olive oil and a dash of chilli add some spice. There's a well considered wine list by the glass or bottle and this is supported by several types of grappa. Kids are also well looked after with their own menu. The Sunday, free-flow champagne brunch at just RM168 per person is always busy and great value, with a clown providing distraction for the kids.

Neroteca

Prego

Hotel Imperial KL
Jalan Sultan Ismail
City Centre
🚇 **Medan Tuanku**
Map 10 E1

Villa Danieli

03 2717 9900 | *www.starwood.com*

True to its five-star hotel location, Villa Danieli is beautifully decorated with hand-blown light fittings and commissioned artwork from California. While many dishes follow traditional Italian recipes, others have been given a modern Californian twist. The cooking revolves around an open kitchen and a wood-fired pizza oven where various dishes are prepared. Pre-dinner drinks are available in the stylish bar or alfresco near the hotel's swimming pool. The menu changes every few months but diners can expect some excellent dishes of beef, seafood, lamb, pasta, pizza and poultry. The seafood platter is recommended, as is a dessert sampler for two and the complimentary chocolates at the end are worth waiting for. Wines are an important part of the Villa Danieli dining experience and one table is even inside the open wine vault.

Japanese

Hotel Nikko KL
165 Jalan Ampang
KLCC
🚇 **Ampang Park**
Map 11 D1

Benkay

03 2782 6118 | *www.hotelnikko.com.my*

This Japanese restaurant in Nikko Hotel (p.24) has garnered strong support in the city, especially for its range of seafood dishes. Like most Japanese restaurants in KL there's a tranquil, minimalist approach to the decor, providing a soothing dining experience. The restaurant is deceptively large, seating 140 patrons with many tucked away in one of five private rooms. The sashimi and sushi are guaranteed fresh with many seasonal items flown in from Japan. Set menus range in price from RM40 to RM150 with an all-you-can-eat option of sushi, teppanyaki, sukiyaki and shabu shabu on Friday evening and the weekend for RM88.

Eastin Hotel
Jalan 16/11
Pusat Dagang
Petaling Jaya
🚇 **KL Sentral**
Map 6 C2

Eyuzu

03 7665 1111 | *www.eastin.com*

Eyuzu offers a good selection of a la carte and set meals in a cosy but functional space on the second floor of the Eastin Hotel. Despite its suburban location it has won several national awards and is popular with those who work or live in the area. Diners can choose to dine in the main part of the restaurant, in two private dining rooms,

Benkay

Zipangu

or two tatami rooms. The sushi counter offers fresh imported and local sashimi and sushi selections. There is also a teppanyaki counter for those who like to be part of the cooking action. The soft-shelled Californian rolls, tempura and noodle dishes also make for a memorable meal.

Genji

Hilton Petaling Jaya
2 Jalan Barat
Petaling Jaya
🚇 Asia Jaya
Map 6 C4

03 7955 9122 | *www.hilton.com*
Genji, located in the five-star Hilton (p.22) in suburban Petaling Jaya, serves excellent Japanese cuisine to predominantly the Japanese business community. The seating is comfortable and there is a teppan suite and tatami rooms for those seeking a little privacy. The sushi bar is a popular place for those dining alone or those requiring a quick snack. The restaurant's emphasis is on fresh seafood and it doesn't get any fresher than the sushi and sashimi on offer. Those dining on an expense account may want to savour the fresh lobster hauled live from in-restaurant tanks minutes before being delivered to your table. Despite being expensive, the kobe beef is another house speciality. There is a comprehensive variety of sake, beers and wines, but with the usual Hilton mark-up.

Kampachi

Hotel Equatorial KL
City Centre
🚇 Raja Chulan
Map 11 B3

03 2161 7777 | *www.equatorial.com*
Kampachi has been around for over 30 years and has a well-deserved reputation particularly among Japanese businessmen. The semi-darkened interior and several private tatami rooms make this a great venue for deals. The superb wine list is shared with the adjoining Chalet Restaurant (p.365) and there is a lounge area between the two for pre-dinner drinks. The Japanese menu is one of the city's most comprehensive with sashimi, sushi, teppanyaki, tempura and hot pot selections. The sashimi is air-flown fresh from Tokyo's famous Tsukiji Market. Set menus offer good value for money and monthly promotions keep regular diners satisfied. Sunday's buffet lunch is one of KL's most popular and reservations are essential. Kampachi is also located on level six of the Pavilion Kuala Lumpur (03 2148 9608).

Still Waters

Hotel Maya KL
KLCC
🚇 KLCC
Map 11 A1

03 2711 8866 | *www.hotelmaya.com.my*
While the waters in the feng shui pool at the entrance may be calm, the chefs whip up some tsunami-force dishes in the open kitchen. Their cooking roots are traditional Japanese but the interpretation is contemporary and fused with other Asian and some western styles. The Japanese call the cooking style sosaku and some examples include foie gras served with daikon, and grilled lamb chops with truffle miso. These are accompanied by a selection of international wines at reasonable prices. This smart downtown restaurant deserves to see more customers; don't be surprised if you dine here with just a handful of other people. However, this does mean you can be assured of attentive service.

Zipangu

Shangri-La KL
11 Jalan Sultan Ismail
City Centre
🚇 Bukit Nanas
Map 11-A3

03 2074 3900 | *www.shangri-la.com*
One of the world's leading interior design teams, Super Potato from Japan, was responsible for Zipangu's dining space. It also did the fit out for Shook! (p.364) in the Starhill Gallery. A bar at the front door awaits diners and an extensive wine wall is off to one side. Natural stone and wood provide a warm ambience and partially open kitchens keep the place lively. Two large private dining rooms are available but there is a charge. Eight semi-private rooms are available at no charge and booked on a first come, first served basis. The menu includes a la carte items and

various set dinners including sushi, sashimi and teppanyaki. The chefs don't mind fusing traditional Japanese ingredients with western items such as foie gras. While the wine list is decent it's not as good as the selection at Lafite (p.368), also in the Shangri-La, but a comprehensive array of sake and cigars make this is a good place to celebrate.

Korean

Starhill Gallery
181 Jalan Bukit Bintang
Bukit Bintang
🚇 *Bukit Bintang*
Map 13 C1

KoRyo Won
03 2143 2189

Despite its indoor location, Korean barbecue is the house speciality at KoRyo Won. Packed each evening, the interactive dining around barbecue plates set into tables is very popular. A unique exhaust system above each table extracts most of the fumes. A large, central, glassed-in barbecue pit is where dishes for those who don't want to do their own cooking are prepared by chefs. Korean food uses spices such as chilli, garlic, ginger and sesame oil but the staff are helpful, guiding diners towards soups, hot pots and noodles. Korean beer and wines are available so try soju (fermented sweet potato wine similar to sake) or plum wine with real gold flecks in it. They have other outlets in KL including Wisma Antarabangsar (03 2142 7655).

Plaza Mont' Kiara
2 Jalan Kiara
Mont Kiara
🚇 *KL Sentral*
Map 4 D3

Maehwa Maul
03 6203 2345

It's fair to say the food at Maehwa Maul is better than the ambience, with its tiled floor and no-nonsense benches. The food is non-halal and centred on various interpretations of pork, chicken, seafood and beef. The barbecue is popular, as is the steamboat which involves diners cooking various meats and vegetables in a broth at the table. It's a fun way for groups to eat cheaply and it's hard to blame the chef if the food isn't cooked to your liking. Various set meals are available including a fusion set of pork cutlet, fruit sauce and rice. The restaurant is associated with another Korean restaurant called Shin in downtown KL's Sungei Wang Plaza (03 2145 6717).

Latin American

35 Changkat
Bukit Bintang
City Centre
🚇 *Bukit Bintang*
Map 13 A1

Bom Brazil Churrascaria
03 2144 8763 | www.bombrazil.com

The bright green and yellow flags give the location of Bom Brazil away. While it may not be a good place for a romantic dinner when Brazil is playing football, the food is good. Meat lovers will enjoy the Brazilian churrascaria style, with cooked meats sliced from long skewers by the chefs at the table. The barbecue buffet is the best value at RM65 and includes soup, unlimited helpings from a salad bar and all-you-can-eat meat including beef, lamb and chicken. You can select New Zealand shoulder lamb, charbroiled steaks, pan-fried dory and tiramisu from the a la carte menu. However, there's a Brazilian creme caramel for those looking for some authentic cuisine. Brazilian cocktails of caipiroska are available and a few wines from around the world are also served. Diners can eat inside or under an open-sided canopy facing the lively street.

Lot 85, Chulan Sq
92 Jalan Raja
Bukit Bintang
🚇 *Bukit Bintang*
Map 13 D1

Gaucho Grill
03 2145 4268 | gauchogrill@savagerestaurants.com

Supposedly, the pampas grasslands of Argentina are the best grazing pastures for beef cattle and the steaks produced by such beasts are leaner, healthier and more flavoursome than the fed-lot animals from other nations. The cowboys who tend to these cattle are called gauchos and this restaurant aims to be the kind of place they hang out in, including brick walls lined with images of smiling amigos, misplaced cart wheels and old saddles. It's a pleasant place to eat and the steaks are all chargrilled to perfection. Try the rib eye steak to appreciate just how tasty the meat is. Other dishes include seafood, pasta, lamb and chicken and there is a help-yourself salad bar. Look for the life-sized red and black cow at the front entrance.

1 Jalan Telawi 5
Bangsar
Bangsar
Map 6 E2

Maredo's Steakhouse
03 2282 0314

Maredo's has a prime corner in busy Bangsar and the best tables are on the outside veranda, cooled by ceiling fans. The decor is stylish with the interior favoured by courting couples or business diners. The concept is Argentinian, from the steaks and chini-churri sauce to the large gaucho images on the wall. The house speciality is the mixed parilla for two, which includes various meats and plump lobster grilled on skewers. There is a variety of steaks (try the El Feugo with black pepper sauce) and burgers, plus a walk-in wine cellar with a reasonable selection of Argentinian, Chilean and Australian wines. There is also a branch in the city in the Crown Regency Apartments on Jalan P Ramlee (03 2162 8268).

Malay
Other options **Chinese** p.361, **Thai** p.387

3 Jalan Ceylon
City Centre
Bukit Bintang
Map 13 A1

Bijan
03 2031 3575 | *www.bijanrestaurant.com*

While most Malay food is consumed in value-for-money hawker stalls, Bijan offers an oasis for those seeking relaxed dining in smart surroundings. The converted inner-city bungalow has been brightly decorated in orange and burgundy with large orange dragonfly murals, and a bamboo-lined bar awaits spicy food fans. It is surrounded by tropical plants with open sides and ceiling fans keeping temperatures comfortable. Bijan has nurtured a popular menu with a healthy selection of traditional Malay dishes that are complemented by a few contemporary twists. A cautionary word; most dishes are large so some waiter guidance is recommended for the uninitiated and it's advisable to order several dishes for sharing. The chefs have introduced some local ingredients to the great selection of icecreams with flavours such as durian, coconut, bandung and teh tarik. The must-order dessert is the chocolate cake with durian. Service is friendly, smart and efficient and the wine selection is good but a tad expensive. While the food prices are reasonable it's no surprise that they come with a heftier price tag than those found in hawker stalls.

Bijan

Enak KL

Starhill Gallery
181 Jalan Bukit Bintang
Bukit Bintang
Bukit Bintang
Map 13 C1

03 2141 8973 | www.enakkl.com

Enak KL is a quiet space for those who want to sample some tasty, home-cooked Malay food presented in a modern style. The spacious restaurant is decorated with bright red batik wall hangings and intricately-designed mirrors. A few private couples' nooks and a pillowed section on the floor make for a relaxing evening. Enak KL offers a small selection of wines, beers and cocktails but several refreshing, 100% fruit juice drinks and Malaysia's famous teh tarik tea are also available. Many of the halal recipes are from Johor on Malaysia's southern

Enak KL

peninsula and have been sourced from old recipes of the owner's family. This is a great place to learn more about the intricacies of Malay cuisine for those who are new to town, and staff are on hand to guide. While tradition reigns supreme for the appetisers and mains, the chefs have a little fun with the desserts; try the blended avocado and chocolate whip.

Seri Angkasa

Menara KL
Jalan Punchak
Off Jalan P. Ramlee
City Centre
Bukit Nanas
Map 10 F3

03 2020 5055 | www.serimelayu.com

For those who like the earth to move, Seri Angkasa is one of two revolving restaurants in KL. Most KL residents and visitors should go at least once to appreciate the city's skyline at night. From its lofty perch of 282 metres above the ground, it's a formidable sight. Because of its tourist appeal diners will be joined by lots of hungry tour groups who make the most of the extensive buffet offerings. The restaurant also offers set menus and a la carte with both local and international selections. It is advisable to make early reservations as the restaurant is popular and gets booked out early.

Mediterranean

Other options **Spanish** p.389, **Italian** p.374

Basque Lane

Plaza Mont' Kiara
2 Jalan Kiara
Mont Kiara
KL Sentral
Map 4 D3

03 6201 6028 | www.basquelane.com.my

This place is often neglected by diners who are attracted to the newer restaurants in this busy commercial and social hub. The food in this Mediterranean-inspired spot is pretty good, with an eclectic menu and some dishes from Switzerland, Hawaii and even Japan. The bulk of the dishes come from Spain and Italy. Expect tapas, paella, pasta and meats, and seafood for mains. How fondue crept onto the menu remains a mystery but you can choose from Swiss cheese and chocolate. The sangria is worth sampling and there are happy hour jugs of beer at just RM28. There is a small and safe wine list with well-known labels and a few quirky choices like 'Goats do Roam' from South Africa.

MED.@Marché

Renaissance KL
Cnr Jalan Sultan Ismail
& Jalan Ampang
City Centre
Bukit Nanas
Map 10 F2

03 2162 2233 | www.marriott.com

While the name suggests Mediterranean, contemporary European may be a better description of the food. The setting in this leading hotel is excellent with a trendy bar, very attentive, professional service, pleasant background music and some excellent dishes. Try creative dishes like fillet of beef, pineapple compote and vanilla bean sauce or poached black cod with grilled baby leek. Desserts of chocolate tortino are worth waiting for. There's a walk-in wine cellar offering a good selection of international wines.

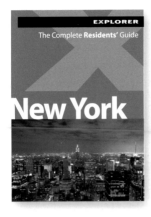

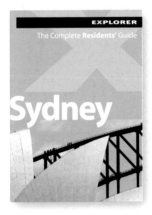

Tired of writing your insider tips…

…in a blog that nobody reads?

The Explorer Complete Residents' Guide series is growing rapidly, and we're always looking for literate, resident writers to help pen our new guides. So whether you live in Tuscany or Timbuktu, if writing's your thing, and you know your city inside out, we'd like to talk to you.

Apply online at www.explorerpublishing.com

Middle Eastern

Le Meridien KL
2 Jalan Stesen Sentral
KL Sentral
🚇 KL Sentral
Map 12 A4

Al Nafourah
03 2263 7888 | www.lemeridien.com/kualalumpur
Fancy dining in an Arabian tent? This unique Middle Eastern-themed restaurant serves delicious food in luxurious and exotic surroundings reminiscent of the Arabian Nights. The atmospheric ambience includes the privacy of dining like a Bedouin in various candle-lit tents or the exclusive Blue Salon dining room for 10. Diners enter the restaurant by passing through into a contemporary Arabian oasis. Choose dishes that showcase the delicious cuisines of Lebanon, Turkey, Tunisia and Morocco including lamb, chicken and fish, with set meals also available. A belly dancer performs every evening apart from Sunday and shisha smoking completes a memorable evening.

138 Jalan Bukit
Bintang
Bukit Bintang
🚇 Bukit Bintang
Map 13 B1

Tarbush
03 2142 8558 | www.tarbush.com.my
This restaurant in central KL is home to some good Lebanese food. Located on busy Jalan Bukit Bintang, Tarbush is one of several Middle Eastern restaurants that have opened recently to serve the growing numbers of holidaymakers from the Arab world. The restaurant opens onto a busy street and diners can expect a lively atmosphere rather than intimate dining. The fans and air conditioning work overtime to cool the place as the front entrance is open to the outside. Lebanese music, tiled walls, artwork and shisha pipes complete the surroundings. Traditional Lebanese dishes such as hummus, tabouleh, kebabs and falafel are served, but salads and french fries are available as well. While no alcohol is served, there's a good selection of juices, ice-blended coffees, teas and lassi drinks. Tarbush has a more stylish outlet on the Feast Level of the Starhill Gallery (03 2144 6393).

Al Nafourah

Tarbush

Pizzerias

Other options **Italian** p.374

Never underestimate the value of a good takeaway pizza – when you're sat in for a cosy night in front of the telly and you get that pizza craving, you've got to know who to call.

Pizzerias	
Canadian 2 for 1	1300 880 241
Dominos	1300 888 333
Pizza Hut	1300 882 525
Shakey's	1300 881 818

Seafood

Starhill Gallery
181 Jalan Bukit Bintang
Bukit Bintang
Bukit Bintang
Map 13 C1

Fisherman's Cove

03 2782 3848 | *www.ytlcommunity.com/fishermanscove*

Take a seat inside this replica fisherman's houseboat and choose from virtually every type of seafood. The two-storey structure has comfortable wooden chairs and is completed by an active open kitchen with the rear of the kitchen lined with glass fish tanks. While rustic in appearance, the food presentation is stylish and clean. The chefs believe in letting the flavours of the seafood do the talking, so the preparation is orchestrated to complement and not dominate. Spices and sauces are still used in dishes like spicy steamed barramundi with eggplant and pumpkin jus. Adventurous diners can expect dishes containing items such as sea urchin and ocean trout caviar. Those with an aversion to seafood can select meat and pasta dishes from the menu or order from any of the other restaurants in Feast Village and have it delivered to the table. The creative desserts include home-made icecream flavoured with rice, olive oil and beetroot.

51-53 Jalan SS2/30
Petaling Jaya
Taman Bahagia
Map 6 A3

The Lobsterman

03 7877 6772 | *www.lobsterman.com.my*

For those who love crustaceans, this is the place to sink your claws into the finest available. Not surprisingly, live lobster in all its culinary glory is the hero at this speciality restaurant in suburban SS2, Petaling Jaya. There is a myriad of cooking styles offered including staples like Thermidor and some unusual offerings such as porridge, curry and tom yam soup. Servings come in various sizes from quarter to whole and the prices are reasonable, despite the fact much of the seafood is flown in live from overseas. While it's hard to imagine that someone would not order lobster, there are other dishes such as pasta, rice, beef, lamb and chicken. The Lobsterman is tucked away in a row of suburban shops but there's an excellent website with a detailed map that should be consulted by first-timers.

28 Changkat
Bukit Bintang
City Centre
Bukit Bintang
Map 13 A1

The Magnificent Fish and Chips Bar

03 2142 7021

A lot of people rave about the seafood served in this small outlet along busy Changkat Bukit Bintang. It operates as both a restaurant and a bar with the crowd changing as the evening progresses. Unlike some other places along the strip, it has a very lively setting and the decor makes it a magnet for diners. There is an open-fronted pavement and casual seating upstairs best suited for drinking and a game of pool. Diners choose from the blackboard menu with its extensive selection including traditional battered fish, oysters, prawns and salmon. Fish such as dory, barramundi and coral trout are served in a variety of ways, but curries and vegetarian pies are also available. Alcohol is an important component, with margarita offers on Friday night for ladies and men in skirts and cheap bloody mary pitchers on Sundays. This is a great place to chill out, read a book, shoot some pool and dine on delicious seafood.

51 Jalan Barat
Off Jalan Imbi
KLCC
🚇 **Bukit Bintang**
Map 13 D2

Yu Jia Village Seafood

03 2143 9966 | *www.orientalrestaurants.com.my*

This restaurant is located in an inner city area dominated by several large Chinese restaurants. Rarely can Chinese dining in KL be called intimate and Yu Jia Village is typically set up for large groups. It is advisable to find out whether the restaurant is booked out for a function before visiting, as the occasional karaoke session can be distracting. The range of high-quality seafood is the main attraction; if it swims or lurks anywhere near salt or freshwater, Yu Jia Village is sure to serve it. The chef's special is giant garoupa fish head soup with noodles, or you could try braised sea cucumber with abalone sauce for something more unusual. However, it's not all seafood, and barbecued duck is a popular signature dish. Suitable wines to accompany the food are available from a compact wine list. The restaurant is owned by the Oriental Group which operates another six restaurants in KL, including the well-respected Noble House (19 Jalan Delima, 03 21 45 88 22).

South East Asian

Asian Heritage Row
64 Jalan Doraisamy
City Centre
🚇 **Medan Tuanku**
Map 10 E1

CoChine

03 2697 1180 | *www.indochine.com.sg*

The lush ambience makes Cochine and Bar SaVanh (downstairs) a popular venue for KL's beautiful people. The decor comprises carved stone Buddhas, colourful textiles and unusual artefacts sourced from neighbouring Indochina.. Cochine offers some very creditable Vietnamese, Lao and Khmer dishes. Pre and post-dinner drinks can be enjoyed in the smart Bar SaVanh where the music moves up a few decibels later in the evening. A good introductory choice for those unfamiliar with the subtleties of Indochinese cuisine is the Cochine platter which features spring rolls and rice paper duck rolls. Vegetarians will enjoy the extensive salad selection. The owning group has a great website with details on Cochine and all its other outlets. It has recently opened a larger but similar concept in Plaza Mont' Kiara.

63 D-G, One Bangsar
Jalan Ara
Bangsar
🚇 **Bangsar**
Map 6 E2

Cungdinh

03 2283 5088 | *www.cungdinh.com*

Cungdinh is the Vietnamese contribution to the One Bangsar international dining scene. The restaurant is Vietnamese owned and the chefs all come from Malaysia's northern neighbour to ensure authenticity. While the name means 'royal place', commoners will feel at home in the comfortable surrounds of the restaurant, that spreads over two storeys. You can choose the upstairs, open-sided balcony on a balmy evening or the air-conditioned space downstairs. Seafood is the speciality, with barbecued king prawns, lobster with a crunchy lotus salad, steamed crab and deep-fried fish all available. The dishes come from various parts of Vietnam, with some emphasis on the cuisine of central Vietnam centred on Hué. Try the spicy rice noodle soup. Beers and wines are available, as is traditional Vietnamese coffee served from an aluminium immerser. Open Monday to Thursday, 11:00 to 15:00 and 18:00 to 23:00; Friday to Sunday, 11:00 to 15:00 and 18:00 to 00:00.

25 Tingkat Tong Shin
City Centre
🚇 **Bukit Bintang**
Map 13 A1

Sao Nam, Kuala Lumpur

03 2144 1225

This smart Vietnamese restaurant is so hot diners are advised to make both reservations for tables and specific signature dishes. The mangosteen and prawn salad is so popular it's usually sold out early in the evening, so place an order when booking. For those unfamiliar with mangosteen, it is considered the queen of tropical fruits, while durian is the king. Its fruitiness combined with fresh prawns and a topping of dried, salted squid is adored by many. This dish is the creation of the young award-winning chef who has maintained a solid team in the kitchen for a few years now. A well-considered wine list with some vintages from Austria and Germany is the perfect accompaniment to the subtly spiced Vietnamese food. The designer chic of the restaurant, with yellow ochre walls lined with revolutionary Vietnamese posters, also makes it popular with KL's trendy young urbanites. Sao Nam is located along one of KL's new food streets and has ventured to suburban Plaza Damas (03 62 01 02 25).

Jalan 1, Taman TAR
Ampang
⚇ *Ampang*
Map 1 A2

Tamarind Springs

03 4256 9300 | www.tamarindrestaurants.com

Diners arrive in a secluded and forested part of suburban Ampang to be greeted by an avenue of flickering candles lining the path to this enchanting venue. The lighting is subtle and the chic regional furnishing complements the Khmer, Lao and Vietnamese cuisine served. Relax in the bar lounge and contemplate the menu while cooling off with a cocktail. A Tamarind Springs platter for entrees makes for a good introduction to the various cuisines. Other specialities include chicken and fresh coconut sour soup, watermelon salad, snakehead fish steamed in spicy green chilli and lime sauce, and amok fish curry. Diners will need good directions to find Tamarind Springs but there's an excellent map on its website and it has a transfer service from downtown hotels.

Spanish

Other options **Mediterranean** p.380

14-16 Jalan Telawi 2
Bangsar
⚇ *Bangsar*
Map 6 E2

La Bodega

03 2287 8318 | www.gastrodome.com.my

Bullfighting posters, siestas, sangria and paella – it's all on display in this tapas and wine bar in trendy Bangsar. Cliched or not, its interpretations of many popular Spanish dishes are as good as they get in KL. There are several options in one complex – a full restaurant, tapas bar and adjoining deli. In the bar, start with an extensive selection of tapas and choose a glass or bottle of Spanish wine. Move onto paella or order from the decadent menu offered in the dining room. There are various La Bodegas located throughout Bangsar and Kuala Lumpur and the standards are both high and consistent.

Starhill Gallery
181 Jalan Bukit Bintang
Bukit Bintang
⚇ *Bukit Bintang*
Map 13 C1

Sentidos Tapas

03 2145 3385 | www.ytlcommunity.com/tapas

The restaurant is stylish, sensuous and Spanish with the inclusion of some other Mediterranean cuisine. Sentidos is more a bar that offers tapas, but you can eat here and be fully satisfied by sampling the snack-sized portions and refreshing drinks. Try the signature tapas such as homemade pate, oxtail and scallops with caviar. More filling mains of pasta and paella are available and there are tables for those who want a full dining experience. Exposed rustic wooden beams provide a welcoming ambience, and with an open bar it's a great venue for single females to enjoy a drink and a meal. A TV showing sports provides a distraction for drinkers who visit for the generous and tasty servings of sangria. House-pouring, happy hour drinks are served on a buy-one, get-one-free basis from 17:00 to 21:00. The same people own Flamenco (03 2093 0032) in suburban Damansara Heights, which is similar but offers more formal dining.

Steakhouses

Other options **American** p.359

21 Jalan Setiapuspa
Medan Damansara
Bukit Damansara
🚇 *KL Sentral*
Map 6 D1

Jake's

03 2094 5677 | *www.jakes.com.my*

Jake's is a themed restaurant with staff dressed as cowboys and Indians. It has been in suburban Medan Damansara for over 25 years, attracting three generations of KL families with its relaxed atmosphere. Jake's has now opened another outlet on the Feast Floor of the Starhill Gallery (03 2148 1398). Charbroiled steaks are the house speciality, with other staples like smoked salmon, prawn cocktail, lobster thermidor and beef on offer. Some Mexican offerings, which appeal to vegetarians, are also available. Seafood, burgers, and lamb and chicken dishes complete the menu. There are few surprises in the desserts, with apple pie, pecan pie, cheesecake and a fruit plate available, but save room for the buttery cashew nut brittle.

Bangsar Village
1 Jalan Telawi 1
Bangsar
🚇 *Bangsar*
Map 6 E2

Outback Steakhouse

03 2287 7850 | *www.outback-sea.com*

This Australian concept restaurant may have dishes with cliched names, but the food is mostly standard international fare that offers comfort to many. Take away the boomerangs and photos of the Australian outback, and you could be in any number of similar restaurants. Booth seating is popular but there is also seating outside under a protective awning. While each dish appears to have an Australian prefix, diners can expect salads, soups, steaks, burgers, pasta, chicken, ribs and sandwiches. There's a special kids' menu and the place is great for families. The drinks list is extensive but the wine component is small and, surprisingly, contains wines from almost everywhere but Australia. There is another outlet in BB Park (03 2144 9919).

Le Meridien KL
2 Jalan Stesen Sentral
KL Sentral
🚇 *KL Sentral*
Map 12 A4

Prime

03 2263 7888 | *www.lemeridien.com*

Some steak restaurants can be a little stiff and formal but Prime in Le Meridien offers a contemporary atmosphere where guests can comfortably dine with a degree of privacy. Imported grain-fed steaks are the main attraction but the wine list is equally impressive with 12 wines offered for the starters, which include several seafood offerings such as oysters, caviar (at RM648) and prawns. Steak dishes are listed by age (from 80 days to 200 days), country of origin, weight and cut. Wagyu prime rib from Australia is about as good as it gets and various sauces are available, with the truffle or porcini mushroom sauce recommended. Vegetarians will feel like a fish out of water and probably shouldn't give this place a second look. For many, this will be a big night out as five-star grazing on imported beef does not come cheaply.

Prime

Prime Grill Room

03 2775 1022 | www.crownprincess.com.my

If you want a juicy steak or other popular international fare, Prime Grill Room in the Crown Princess Hotel is a good place to dine. The recently refurbished outlet provides an upmarket but understated retro look. The menu features classic favourites like steaks, oysters and seasonal delicacies prepared from a show kitchen. Select dishes include grilled medallion of beef, roast loin of lamb cooked in port jus, and gratinated scallops and mussels. The wine list features Australian vintages from some interesting boutique vineyards at reasonable prices. Enjoy these with dinner or in the cosy bar and lounge at the entrance.

San Francisco SteakHouse

03 7118 2988 | www.ttrb.com.my

Damansara Intan is home to the original San Francisco Steakhouse which has now spread to three other KL locations: Mid Valley Megamall (03 2938 2882), The Summit USJ (03 8023 5518) and Suria KLCC (03 2382 0329). The setting, menu and concept are basically the same with the emphasis naturally being on meat, especially prime steaks. The menu offers a comprehensive selection of steaks as well as some international favourites such as seafood, pasta, salads, soups and desserts. While premium steaks are expensive, there are other options and the set three-course dinner plus coffee for under RM40 is excellent value. Damansara Intan is easily accessed via several freeways and there's a good map on its website.

Victoria Station

03 2094 9406 | www.victoriastation.com.my

Victoria Station has earned a good reputation for its charbroil steaks and other well-known international dishes. It covers two floors and there's a private dining room for 10 people. The restaurant has resisted the temptation to contemporise its menu, and if dishes such as caesar salad, lobster thermidor, mulligatawny soup, bombe alaska and crepe suzette get your gastronomic juices fired up, then this is the place to dine. The interior has lots of paraphernalia associated with trains and you can even dine inside a mock train carriage. The staff are also dressed like station personnel to add to the experience. The menu covers traditional international dishes and diners can also select satay, lobster bisque, carpetbag steak, cheesecake, Weiner schnitzel and T-bone steak. While it may appear to be in a culinary time warp, the regulars would have it no other way. In line with the food, the wine list is also safe and a little predictable. There are other KL outlets in Ampang (03 4257 3388), USJ Taipan (03 5637 3388) and Petaling Jaya (03 7955 8988).

Thai

mythai

03 2148 6151 | www.jimthompson.com

Jim Thompson was the one who kickstarted the Thai silk industry and now the group has moved into a collection of restaurants called mythai, not to be confused with the drink. Jim Thompson disappeared over 30 years ago in the jungles of the Cameron Highlands, some two hours north of KL. One side of this very trendy restaurant is lined with silk items from the Jim Thompson boutique located in another part of the Starhill Gallery (p.341). The food in mythai is as impressive as the merchandise and remains traditional central Thai cuisine without the essential tastes being modified to satisfy Malaysian palates. Try a sampler appetiser dish to appreciate several taste sensations, and move on to mains such as noodles, vegetables, seafood (lots of sea bass done in various styles), soups (15 kinds), chicken, beef and rice. There are many vegetarian dishes and a mouthwatering selection of desserts. The designer interior offers several seating options including some curtained pavilions beneath large rattan lights. There is a comprehensive selection of beers, wines and juices.

6-8 Jalan Telawi 2
Bangsar
🚇 *Bangsar*
Map 6 E2

Planter Jim's

03 2282 4084

Like many of the Bangsar restaurants, Planter Jim's sprawls across the pavement underneath a canvas awning that provides protection from the elements. Planter Jim's is in a quieter stretch of the normally busy Bangsar. It specialises in both Thai and Malaysian cuisine and has been keeping hungry Malaysians fed for over a decade. While the open-fronted interior is dimly lit, it's a pleasant place to relax, and the colourful Vietnamese lights provide localised light. Signature dishes include crispy duck, chargrilled tenderloin, pineapple rice and the ever-popular Thai dishes of tom yam soup and Thai fried noodles (or pad thai). A tasting platter of several small appetiser portions is offered and there is a decent selection of vegetarian dishes. Mango, sweet rice and coconut milk is the most popular dessert. The kitchen staff can also moderate the level of spices, especially chilli, for those who don't like too much spice in their life. Drinks are reasonably priced and happy hours last from 12:00 to 20:00.

Pavilion KL
Jalan Raja Chulan
Bukit Bintang
🚇 *Bukit Bintang*
Map 13 C1

Rain Nudle House

03 2141 8708 | www.seacuisine.com.my

Malaysians love to dine in shopping malls and it's not surprising that food courts in malls are popular places to eat out. The recently opened Pavilion offers great retail action and restaurants like Rain Nudle House provide a serene setting to rest between it all. The casual, cafe ambience is a contemporary space full of bright colours. The concept was tried and tested for several years in Suria KLCC and now refined in its new Pavilion home. While the major focus is on noodles, there are many supporting acts including Thai fish cakes, salads, tom yam soups, and rice dishes such as pineapple-fried rice with chicken or prawns. On the menu, signature dishes are marked with a heart and spicy dishes with a chilli. Juices, soft drinks, smoothies, Lavazza coffee, teas and beer (including Singha from Thailand) round out a quick but wholesome meal. It's possible to snack here for just RM15 or have a more substantive meal for RM45.

Pacific Regency
Menara Pan Global
Jalan Punchak off
Jalan P Ramlee
City Centre
🚇 *Raja Chulan*
Map 11 A3

Soi 23

03 2332 7777 | www.pacific-regency.com

Soi 23 is located on the 23rd floor of the Pacific Regency Hotel Suites, opposite the entrance to the Kuala Lumpur Tower. This is the same venue as the mega trendy, partially open-air Luna Bar (p.403). Those in the know dine here and adjourn for some after-dinner chilling out at Luna Bar. The restaurant is semi-darkened to enable diners to peer through the windows to see some of the city's sights, but sadly not the Petronas Twin Towers. The menu offers all one expects from a Thai restaurant. Start with spicy and creamy prawn soup with lemongrass and mushroom. There are various other starters such as fried air-dried beef with kaffir leaves and the old standby, chicken cooked in pandan leaves. The signature dish is steamed seabass with lemon and chilli. Desserts include the ever-popular chilled water chestnut in coconut milk, as well as mango and sticky rice. Mains range from RM25 to RM55. Singha beer is the perfect accompaniment to the food's chillis and spices. There's also an excellent wine list but a few cheaper offerings would be welcomed by most diners.

3 Jalan Setiapuspa
Medan Damansara
Bukit Damansara
KL Sentral
Map 6 D1

Sri Ayutthaya
03 2094 2333

Sri Ayutthaya is located in suburban Medan Damansara in an epicentre of restaurants beside busy Jalan Damansara. The staff are all decked out in Thai costumes and the decor varies on each floor, but is mostly Thai in design. An indoor waterfall and koi pond are guaranteed to distract the kids for hours. The restaurant has an expensive look and the menu does not disappoint with its somewhat high pricing. There is a broad interpretation of Thai cuisine, with fried New Zealand oysters and sizzling New Zealand steak creeping in among more traditional dishes such as tom yam soup, fish cakes and various curries. There's an abundance of seafood dishes but most are priced according to market rates, which may put some diners off. The staff will bring a display of desserts that are on offer for that evening. A very small selection of wines and beers is available including Thailand's national beer, Singha. There are also branches in USJ (5631 0928) and Putrajaya (8888 9128).

Vegetarian

Plaza Mont'Kiara
2 Jalan Kiara
Mont Kiara
KL Sentral
Map 4 D3

Marmalade
03 6201 1743

While not strictly vegetarian, Marmalade is very popular with fans of refreshing and healthy salads, invigorating juices and rejuvenating teas. The fresh interior of white and orange is clean and minimalist, and an obvious attraction is the kids' play area at the rear. Diners can eat casual meals inside or out. The salads are excellent and come in two sizes. Homemade soups, sandwiches, burgers, stews, pizza, pasta and vegetable lasagne are also offered. Delicious cakes are served from the cake fridge, with cupcakes for the kids, and there's also a dedicated kids' menu.

24 Jalan Telawi 3
Bangsar
Bangsar
Map 6 E2

Nature's Vegetarian
03 2283 5523

Some Chinese vegetarian restaurants in Malaysia simulate various meats and seafood from tofu, which might seem a little odd at first. However, many of the creations bear a close resemblance to the real thing. In fact, many meat-eaters could eat in places like Nature's Vegetarian in Bangsar and not notice that they weren't eating the real deal. The restaurant's interior is rather sterile, with an abundance of rosewood and a tiled floor. Regulars swear by the place and vegetarians pining for Chinese food should drop by. It serves dishes like shark's fin soup, fried chicken with black pepper sauce, and deep-fried goose and butter prawns – but remember, it's all make believe. The various set menus make it popular with large groups. Dim sum is also served all day on Saturday. Various teas and juices are available, but no alcohol.

Fresh coconut juice

Street food

Cafes & Coffee Shops
Other options **Afternoon Tea** p.397

With cafes and coffee shops that serve good, hearty and extremely affordable food at all times of the day, it is no wonder that some streets in Kuala Lumpur are like 24 hour buffets. The cafe culture is more varied than some may be used to – not all establishments peddle premium coffee beans or designer blends.

Local coffee shops are usually budget Chinese eateries that offer affordable fare. There's no air conditioning – ceiling fans are the only method of cooling. There is no fancy silverware and they have mostly budget furniture made mainly of plastic. Recently, the coffee shop has experienced a revival in the guise of the kopitiam, basically a swankier version of the traditional Chinese coffee shops of old. They serve the same things, while preserving the traditional charm of marble-top tables and porcelain cutlery.

Giving the kopitiams and coffee shops a run for their money is the mamak stall. This quintessential part of Malaysian cafe culture is where nocturnal locals congregate in the early hours of the morning, savouring roti canai (flat bread) with curry and teh tarik (pulled tea) after a late night at the office or at one of Kuala Lumpur's swinging nightspots. Most are open around the clock and offer a huge range of local snacks and non-alcoholic beverages.

While it is difficult to imagine the colourful mamak culture ever dying out, the younger set has acquired a taste for more cosmopolitan digs like Starbucks or Coffee Bean and in recent years the designer cafe scene has boomed. Kuala Lumpur has a dizzying range of bistro and gourmet outlets that rival any western country. They're a godsend to the first-time visitor hankering for the look, feel and taste of home.

It is impossible to understand the bewildering subtleties of the Malaysian cafe culture, especially if you are here for the first time. But you can get a glimpse of the wide spectrum of tastes and flavours by just walking into any coffee shop in Kuala Lumpur.

Bangsar Village
Bangsar
🚇 *Bangsar*

Bakerzin
03 2284 7514 | *www.bakerzin.com*

Bakerzin is a brazen attack on the five senses – just like its desserts. The furniture is funky, the menus are like recipe books with loving, detailed descriptions that will make you even hungrier, and even the crockery is asymmetrical and quirky. Styled after French teahouses, Bakerzin originated in Singapore and serves popular French bistro food, from cakes, pastries, breads, soups and salads to sandwiches. Its menu has been tweaked to cater for local tastebuds, so don't be surprised to see rendang lamb shank (this tender lamb in a thick curry stew is a hot favourite) on the menu alongside fish and chips or spaghetti carbonara. Still, its desserts are the real crowd-pleaser. Walk into any outlet and you'll first be greeted by the colourful display of freshly baked cakes and pastries. If you can't make up your mind whether to have the warm chocolate cake (its top seller), banana pizza, creme brulee or panna cotta (so many desserts, so little time), fret not, the inventive owners serve you a solution on a tapas platter. You can have all your cakes and eat them too if you order the dessert tapas, where you can enjoy three desserts in miniature sizes for a cool RM22. There is another branch in 1 Utama in Petaling Jaya (03 7729 4493).

1 Jalan Kamunting,
Off Jalan Dang Wangi
City Centre
🚇 *Dang Wangi*

The Bodhi Tree Cafe & Restaurant
03 2692 2011

Near the Dang Wangi LRT station and past the Klang River canal lies this culinary gem that serves top-notch food at down-to-earth prices. Above square wooden tables, antique fans with ornate wooden and bronze blades whir softly. The muted decor is set off by chipper canary yellow walls. The set lunch of duck confit, vegetable cream soup and coffee costs a mere RM25. Chef usually recommends Bodhi Tree neophytes to begin, with creamy wild mushroom soup, chilli cheese baked mussels, and baked teriyaki mushroom salad. For mains, try the Moroccan chicken which has been marinated in yoghurt, cumin, fennel, coriander and chilli powder overnight. Meat lovers might take a fancy to the pan-seared lamb burger pate on a bed of

D'lish

tempura-style pumpkin and broccoli, and topped with mint cucumber yoghurt (RM20). Finish off with the signature apple tart, and go home happy.

KL Plaza
Bukit Bintang
🚇 **Bukit Bintang**

Coffee Bean & Tea Leaf

03 2142 9488 | www.coffeebean.com.my

Although this giant coffee chain was the first to arrive, its business has been somewhat affected by Starbucks' almost viral presence. It also doesn't help that Wi-Fi isn't provided as standard for all outlets. Nevertheless, Coffee Bean is still rated as one of the best coffee-makers in town. Its cappuccino and cafe latte are reputed to be creamier than its competitors. In addition to a respectable coffee menu, it also serves delicious sandwiches using breads like stone-ground pita, panini, foccacia or ciabatta. And come Christmas, everybody looks forward to its delectable Yule log creations. Other branches can be found in KLCC (03 2161 2507), Sungei Wang Plaza (03 2144 5587), Mont Kiara (03 2093 3635), Mid Valley (03 2284 2932), Sunway Pyramid II (03 7491 0721), The Curve (03 7728 7598), 1 Utama (03 7726 7833), Gardens (03 2287 8977) and Pavilion (03 2144 3788).

Bangsar Village
Bangsar
🚇 **Bangsar**

D'lish

03 2288 1770 | www.dlish.com.my

Will it be the caramel fudge slice with the chunky nut base, or the raspberry brownie cheese cupcake with the gigantic chocolate curls? Like the donut craze, cupcake fever is raging through the valley like wildfire and you will be hard pressed to find any bakery that matches the shameless decadence offered here. Bigger, creamier and available in more flavours than anywhere else, they are great value for RM6.50 (and if you can hold your horses, come back after 21:00, when all leftovers go for half price). If you can't decide, order a steaming flat white, plonk yourself at one of the long tables and watch some football on the TV. You may, however, find yourself sneaking a peek at the menu scrawled on the wall and drooling further. Who would have thought you could incorporate Japanese wagyu beef into puff pastry pie? You'd never expect Japanese fine food to be manipulated quite like this, but it works. There's another outlet at Mid Valley Megamall (03 2287 5770).

Dome Cafe

03 2141 5971 | *www.domecafe.com.my*

While many lifestyle cafes have opened and then fizzled out, Dome consistently retains a loyal following by consistently reinventing itself with delightful new creations. A chic hangout with wood tables and comfortable sofas, this Australian-bred cafe is a great place to enjoy a brew while browsing through its many magazines. For the ultimate indulgence, order the shamelessly decadent and aptly named Death by Chocolate, washed down with a flat white. Dome is deservedly known as the best fine coffee place in town. If you're hankering for some hearty grub, try the flaky fish and thick cut chips, or bulging sandwiches that come with a healthy side of salad. Its gourmet pies are popular, with a choice of seafood, beef, or chicken stew served in a deep bowl of thick gravy and topped with lightweight puff pastry. For an essentially western-centric joint, its take on local fare is surprisingly authentic: the nasi lemak, fragrant rice cooked with coconut milk and pandan leaves served with flavourful sambal and chicken or beef rendang, is sublime. Other outlets can be found in KLCC (03 2166 1948) and Mid Valley (03 2938 3081).

Étoile Bistro

Hotel Equatorial KL
Jalan Sultan Ismail
City Centre
 Sultan Ismail

03 2161 7777 | *www.equatorial.com*

Long before the Starbucks and Coffee Bean craze hit Malaysia, this cosy bistro inside Hotel Equatorial was serving up lifestyle-based coffees. Coffee lovers will be spoilt for choice by the menu: it offers a dizzying 50 blends, including dark roasts, flavoured varieties, decaf and espresso (they have whimsical names like Monkeys in the Mist, Spice Song and Banana Mania). Regulars recommend Cafe Caramel Mocha, a heady blend of Java Coast brew supplemented by caramel and chocolate, and topped with steamed milk. Latte Tarik, designer coffee with a Malaysian twist, is also worth a try. Apart from coffee, Etoile serves a great range of freshly baked breads, cakes, sandwiches, pastas, crepes and other confectioneries. For the geeks who can't step into a cafe without scanning for a Wi-Fi sign, there are two wireless Apple iBooks available for diners to surf the net with, at no cost for the first half hour.

Food Foundry

Happy Mansion
Jalan 17/13
Petaling Jaya
 Taman Jaya

03 7955 3885 | *www.foodfoundry.us*

From pastas in a range of unique sauces, freshly-made sandwiches and tasty soups, to light salads, fluffy pancakes and decadent cream cakes, Food Foundry offers something for all tastes and fancies. But what truly is special is something that you'll probably not find anywhere else in Kuala Lumpur (unless they are shameless copycats): its signature Mille Crepe Cake. Literally meaning a thousand layers crepe, this now-infamous dessert is a delectable confection comprising 15 to 20 light layers of crepe sandwiched together with fresh custard cream. It tastes as good as it sounds. Food Foundry also offers standard bistro fare like tapas, sandwiches and pasta. Shaded by leafy old trees, it's snug enough to have a quiet cuppa with friends or simply to enjoy a comfortable meal with the family.

J. CO Donuts & Coffee

Pavilion
Bukit Bintang
 Bukit Bintang

03 2141 7761 | *www.jcodonuts.com*

Donut culture is catching on nationwide, with donut shops popping up in shopping malls a dime a dozen. Nevertheless, true donut connoisseurs will tell you the best ones are found at J. CO Donuts & Coffee, where there is always an absurdly long queue, no doubt inspired by the sight of them being freshly made. The vast array of flavours and colours is staggering. Shall it be the award-winning alcapone, a basic donut with white chocolate topping, dipped in almond shavings? Or will you sink your teeth into heaven berry, a mouthwatering concoction that oozes a succulent lava of strawberry filling? Why not all, since buying half a dozen entitles you to a bulk discount? To make things even more irresistible, at J.CO any drink that you order will come with a free serving of a glazzy donut. If you're willing to queue at least 25 minutes, donut heaven awaits you at the end of the snaking line. There's another outlet at Sunway Pyramid (03 5634 0377).

Kluang Station

1Utama
Petaling Jaya
Kepong Sentral

03 7710 1039

Since 1938, the Kluang Station coffee shop in Johor has been offering traditional homemade favourites such as toasted buns, half-boiled eggs and its famous coffee, which has gained a strong following. The first branch of this family-run establishment was opened at the 1 Utama shopping centre at Kluang Station. The decor is reminiscent of the original shop at the railway station and the casual, open layout and kopitiam-style wooden furniture simply beckons you in.

A variety of tasty family recipes are also available alongside the signature kopitiam fare. The Hainanese chicken chop, with its crispy, deep-fried battered chicken and brown sauce is a recognised crowd-pleaser. Other favourites are the Kluang laksa, a bowl of rice noodles in spicy gravy, and the Assam fish curry featuring a deep-fried dory fillet with a crispy crust, served in a tantalising sauce. Lighter appetites will find succour with dishes like the Kluang mee siam, curry puffs and nasi lemak, the breakfast staple of many. Coffees are priced at RM2.60 while toast starts at RM1.80 for a slice. The main courses are priced between RM7.90 and RM9.90.

Marmalade

Bangsar Village II
Bangsar
Bangsar

03 2282 8301

Lip-smacking food needn't be sweet, loaded with fat or decadently unhealthy, and Marmalade proves this point in a bevy of mouthwatering ways through its impressive array of healthy but tasty smoothies and detox drinks concocted from fresh juices. It also offers wholemeal sandwiches using healthy but flavoursome ingredients like pine nuts and alfalfa sprouts, and pasta that makes the best of light dressings and olive oil. In keeping with the trippy new age vibe, this place gives off a cheeriness that's palpable even before you set eyes on the giant Beatles-inspired kaleidoscopic mural that leaps out from the white wall. The location is great, particularly if you manage to grab a table by the window sill. The side of the cafe is panelled from floor to ceiling, with glass windows bathing the interior in balmy sunlight and providing a bird's eye view into Bangsar's most happening street. Service is superlative; Jason, the restaurant manager, knows his customers by name and schools his solicitous waiters on the 10 commandments of table waiting. Prices are as friendly as the waiters; coffees hover around the RM6 to RM10 range and mains rarely exceed RM30. Even the spicy Moroccan lamb shank, a gigantic portion big enough for two, only costs RM22.

OLDTOWN White Coffee

23 Jalan Hang Lekir
Chinatown
Masjid Jamek

03 2031 4321 | www.oldtownwhitecafe.com

A runaway hit since its inception barely three years ago, this food chain that hails from Ipoh, a sleepy hollow up north, is practically as ubiquitous as 7-Eleven. Locals and visitors alike love its hearty comfort food, marble top tables and dainty porcelain tableware that recreates the old world charm of traditional eateries.

Open for breakfast until dinner, its bestseller hands down is the set all-day breakfast. Its healthy omega soft boiled eggs, paired with charcoal-toasted bread sandwiched with thick slices of butter and kaya (a creamy coconut jam) is appealing for lunch or dinner. For a more substantial meal, try the curry noodles, kway teow (flat rice noodles with chicken shreds and bean sprouts served in a clear soup) or nasi lemak (fragrant coconut rice served with spicy chicken and other condiments). Craving something sweet? Go nuts over the sinfully good French toast – thick bread spread with peanut butter, dipped in egg batter and then deep fried, topped with a knob of butter, a layer of honey and condensed milk – your waistline will pay. The enterprising owners now stock three-in-one drink sachets for those who can't get enough of their coffee.

2A-1 & 2-1 (GF)
Jalan PJU 5/7 PJU 5
Dataran Sunway
Kota Damansara
Petaling Jaya
🚇 *Kelana Jaya*

Restaurant Sun Yin Loong
013 398 8310

For some time, Klang Valley folks had to make do with watered down, if not rather insipid imitations of Ipoh white coffee sold at fancy kopitiams. With the latest addition to Dataran Sunway, however, they don't have to make the two-hour trip to Ipoh anymore. The runaway success of the SYL franchise prompted the owners to open an outlet here. SYL coffee is smoother and creamier because of its copious amounts of condensed and evaporated milk, and the coffee is sharper and more fragrant because the beans are deep-fried with butter and margarine. The high concentration of caffeine will give even a double shot of espresso a run for its money, and if you're unaccustomed to it, anything more than two cups is pushing your luck. Kick-ass coffee aside, there's hearty hawker fare you won't find at other coffee shops in Kuala Lumpur: chee cheong fun (flat white rice noodles in mushroom sauce) and tan chi, or poached egg on buttered toast, dribbled with soy sauce. You can even find spaghetti with an Asian twist.

Various Locations

Secret Recipe
www.secretrecipe.com.my

Secret Recipe is a homegrown lifestyle cafe chain that is so wildly successful that it has spread its wings to Singapore, Indonesia, Thailand, China and the Philippines since its 1997 debut. Its bulging menu boasts an impressive array of local, western and fusion food, cake creations and pastries, icecream and beverages. Its award-winning lamb shank is hugely popular for its fall-off-the-bone consistency, while the tom yam spaghetti is always a crowd pleaser. The set lunches are good value for money; you can choose fish and chips, tom yam spaghetti, or roast duck to go with a brownie and an iced lemon tea. Its most deadly weapon is its cakes which keep the crowds (and new outlets mushrooming). Ask where you can find a good birthday cake and more often than not, the answer will be Secret Recipe. There is such a huge variety you'll need many visits to try them all. Those with a sweet tooth will love the perennial bestsellers: chocolate banana cake, moist chocolate cake and Oreo cheesecake. Cakes start from RM5.50 per slice while a whole cake typically goes for RM65. Other outlets can be found in KLCC (03 2171 2686), Lot 10 (03 2143 9304), TTDI (03 7725 3918), Berjaya Times Square (03 2145 4406), 1 Utama (03 7746 4950), Sunway Pyramid (03 7492 1908), Tesco (03 5632 3431), Section 14 PJ (03 7957 3431) and The Curve (03 7710 3159).

Singled Out
If you're out to meet people, you've got to know where to mingle. You'll find all the other beautiful people at places like Chinoz on the Park (p.365), D'lish (p.391), La Bodega (p.402), Marmalade (p.389), Neroteca (p.374), Out of Africa (p.359), Planet Hollywood (p.359), 7atenine (p.373), SOULed OUT (p.373), Telawi Street Bistro (p.411), twentyone (p.411) or Velvet Underground (p.411).

Cafes & Coffee Shops

43 Jalan Telawi 3 ◀
Bangsar
🚇 *Bangsar*

Sri Nirwana Maju

03 2287 8445

Tucked away in upscale Bangsar is a little jewel that seems like a non sequitur among its posher neighbours, but you'll never know from the masses of locals and expats who spill from its crammed shop lot into the corridor. Word has it that the owner used to work with an automobile company and one fine day he gave that up to open a restaurant in Rawang. Armed with recipes and the cooking skills of his wife and mother-in-law, he expanded to Bangsar in 2001 and has been drawing fans from all corners of the Klang Valley. While you can get equally good curry gravies, meat and fish dishes at other similar outfits, regulars come here for his legendary deep-fried bitter gourd. Other than lunch and dinner, Sri Nirwana also whips up a splendid array of traditional breads like roti canai, thosai and appam for the breakfast crowd. Try the highly rated rawa thosai (griddled bread with chilli and onion flakes) dipped in dhal sauce. Washed down with a steaming cup of the tarik (pulled tea), you'll agree that this is one of the most soul-satisfying breakfasts you can ever have.

Various Locations ◀

Starbucks

03 2145 9593 | *www.starbucks.com.my*

Malaysians and their love for all things American extend well beyond Hollywood blockbusters and Guess apparel. Starbucks is the new McDonald's, with an outlet in just about every trendy mall; Berjaya Times Mall and 1Utama have at least two each. Though initially shunned by old-school folks, Starbucks are no longer just the domain of college sophomores who yearn for some hip quotient, but are increasingly popular among corporate shills who take advantage of the free internet connection and accessible locations to organise business meetings. The menu isn't very different from its American counterpart – staples like cafe Americano, espresso and cafe latte are all there – but some new items have been added in to titillate the Asian palate, like green tea frappuccino. The outlet at Berjaya Times Square is the biggest in the country. Find other outlets at KL Plaza (03 2148 6842), Bangsar Baru (03 2287 6842), Mid Valley (03 2283 6842), Damansara Uptown (03 2092 5842), Mont Kiara (03 6201 8842), The Weld (03 2032 3351), KL Sentral (03 2274 6842), Bangsar Village (03 2287 1849) and KLCC (03 2383 6346).

Jalan Hujan
Rahmat Dua ◀
OUG, Jalan Kelang
Lama

Steven's Corner

03 7781 9762 | *www.stevenscorner.com.my*

Named after its founder, this mamak stall is practically a Klang Valley institution. Rising from its humble beginnings as a roadside stall, today it is the mecca for hungry, night-owlish residents in the neighbourhood looking for a good, affordable meal with a congenial atmosphere. During the English football season, televised matches are played on a widescreen TV. Standard fare like roti canai, thosai and naan are available, but what really sets Steven's Corner apart from your average mamak shop is its incomparable roti john – halved sausage roll which is soaked in beaten egg before being toasted over a griddle and smothered with a range of condiments and more fillings than a Subway sandwich. Another famous offering is deep-fried quail, a delicacy that even draws visitors from overseas to this unfashionable part of KL. Then there's the golden brown, deep-fried fish roe, iffy to the unadventurous, but heavenly with generous lashings of chilli sauce. A tandoori oven standing proudly near the front door offers the promise of hearty hunks of perfectly baked marinated chicken. You can also find Steven's Corner at 31 – 39, Jalan Pandan Indah 1/22, Pandan Indah (03 9274 9018) and Lot 9136, Jalan 2/23D, Prima Setapak, Batu 4, Jalan Genting Klang.

Teh Tarik

016 213 8854

A shopping mall is the last place Malaysians would find a mamak shop but, Teh Tarik, located in The Curve, Mutiara Damansara, defies such expectations. Named after the nation's favourite beverage, menus here have been dispensed with – ask for one and the uniformed waiters will nod eloquently towards items and their prices scrawled onto wall-mounted chalkboard. Service is brisk and prices are a bit higher than Pelita or Khalifa (hot drinks start at RM1.60). Its repertoire of mamak-style staples is limited to sardine and planta-flavoured variations of roti canai, although it offers a good spread of hot dishes and the fried catfish is delectable with a side of sambal. Opening hours are from 08:00 to 12:30, as opposed to the more egalitarian 24 hour mamak stalls, so the party animals pouring out of The Curve's numerous nightclubs may have to go elsewhere for their hangover cures. For exhausted shopaholics, however, there couldn't be a more ideal pit stop for reasonably priced fare after a shopping marathon.

Vishal Food & Catering

03 2274 0502

Brickfields, the curry mecca of Kuala Lumpur, can be confusing for a newcomer – you can't walk 10 paces without bumping into an 'authentic South Indian cuisine' sign. Real hardcore fans, however, weave through dodgy roads and pull up at a squat building facing a cul-de-sac. In this spartan establishment, tables are laid out 'soldiers' mess' style, bare except for the banana leaves placed before expectant customers. Onto these plate replacements a waiter ladles fluffy steamed basmati rice from giant metal vats. The mutton masala is so spicy that one spoonful might send you lunging for the hot, thick, bru coffee made with creamy fresh cow's milk. You're likely to emerge from the shop with hair smelling of vindaloo spices, and sweating so much you'll look like you just bathed in the Ganges River. Certainly not a place for the delicate and swoonsome, Vishal is nevertheless the last word for hardcore Indian curry fans.

Yut Kee

03 2698 8108

No mention of coffee shops would be complete without a nod to Yut Kee, practically an institution for its longstanding tradition of hearty, honest Hainanese fare. Colonial families during pre-independence Malaya hired Hainanese chefs for their homes, where they were exposed to western cuisine and added a bit of Malaysian flair to it. Yut Kee is like a blast from the past: think round marble tables with rickety chairs, old-fashioned wooden shutter windows, winding wooden staircases and simple hand-written menus that comprise of unfussy, down-to-earth grub. There is standing room only during lunch and scores of articles and blogs have paid homage to its roti babi, bread pocket fried in egg batter and stuffed with minced pork, onions, carrots, crab meat and spices. Equally addictive is its pungent kopi kau (extra strong coffee), marble cake and Hainanese chicken chop. Also excellent is the stewed beef with rice or noodles (RM5.50), which comes with soft tender radish pieces to soak up the beef broth. Yut Kee also sells takeaway butter cake, swiss rolls, coffee powder, kaya (coconut jam) and belacan (fermented shrimp paste that tastes a lot better than it sounds) Service may be mechanical, but with the never-ending flow of customers streaming in and out of the shop, the harried waiters can't really afford to engage in any extended tableside pedantry. For a walk down memory lane, it's hard to beat Yut Kee.

Shisha Cafes

The influx of Middle Eastern tourists in recent years spurred the introduction of elements of Middle Eastern culture into the country, which includes the cuisine, fashion and the shisha. The government has curbed the proliferation of establishments offering the water-cooled, flavoured tobacco after it found school-going teenagers were among the clientele. Some restrictions have also been placed on the sale of shisha equipment and tobacco. Nevertheless, shisha can still be found at Middle Eastern-themed restaurants, and is a great way to start or end a sumptuous meal from the exotic, faraway lands of dunes and damask. One such place is Sahara Tent (03 2144 8310, http://saharatent.com), where the giant mezze platter will leave two feeling stuffed. It's located in Ain Arabia (KL's Little Arabia), a small enclave in the heart of KL. Al Nafourah on the eighth floor of KL Sentral's Le Meridien Hotel serves authentic Lebanese cuisine and offers a semi-buffet that includes Arabic coffee and shisha. The restaurant decor here is as Middle Eastern as it gets, with large brass ornaments adorning the entrance and walls, colourful floor tiles, and Moorish architecture. Serving authentic Lebanese cuisine, dinner is made even more exotic with a Middle Eastern belly dancer moving to sultry music.

Afternoon Tea

Other options **Cafes & Coffee Shops** p.390

Carcosa Seri Negara
Lake Gardens
KL Sentral
KL Sentral
Map 6 F1

The Drawing Room

03 2295 0888 | *www.carcosa.com.my*

If something quieter and more dainty is up your street, KL has no shortage of places that serve the traditional English high tea, where you have finger sandwiches, pastries and petits fours with a fancy pot of tea. And for the ultimate indulgence, you can't possibly surpass an afternoon tea treat in The Drawing Room at Carcosa Seri Negara. An iconic mansion atop a hill overlooking Kuala Lumpur's Lake Gardens, its history dates back to 1904, when it was built as the official residence of Sir Frank Swettenham, then the senior British representative to the Malay states. You'll be bowled over by its luxurious Victorian-styled suites and sprawling landscape. Sit on rattan chairs on the al fresco terrace facing manicured lawns and enjoy the selection of fine teas, savouries, pastries and scones (which are to die for). Enjoy it just like its original resident, Sir Frank Swettenham, did once. Oh, and in a nod to modernisation, the building now has Wi-Fi.

169 Jalan SS2/24
Petaling Jaya

The Teapot Cafe

03 7875 3024 | *www.teapotcafe.com*

If you want a taste of English gentility without breaking the bank, why don't you head out to The Teapot Cafe? It has a warm, cosy atmosphere evoked by quaint-looking teapots, lace-inspired wallpaper, and precious decorative plates. The Devonshire Tea set (RM20.50) is hugely popular; it consists of two scones served with strawberry jam and real clotted cream, a dainty tuna sandwich, a slice of cake, and a pot of tea which can be shared by two people. The Teapot Cafe is also one of the few places in town that serves authentic Victorian jam cake. If you're keen to indulge your inner Anglophile, come here for lunch or tea (as by dinnertime, most of the popular items will have been sold out). While the menu is primarily western, there are local options as well, like the popular roti jala (lattice-like pancake accompanied by curried chicken).

Internet Cafes

Kuala Lumpur is wired – no doubt about it. If you have your laptop handy, you can use the Wi-Fi in many establishments around the city. Most branches of Starbucks, Délifrance and Coffee Bean & Tea Leaf have Wi-Fi, and in some cases you don't even have to pay for it. Alternatively, you can use one of the many internet cafes in KL. You'll find one in most shopping malls, and there are plenty of stand-alone internet cafes as well. Rates vary greatly: the internet cafe in Suria KLCC charges RM8 per hour, for example, whereas internet cafes in slightly less glossy locations charge as little as RM4 per hour.

**It's Stupid &
You Know It Is**

*It's an offence to drive a
vehicle while exceeding
the proscribed amount
of blood alcohol
content (0.08%). Fines
range from RM1,000
to RM6,000 or jail
of up to 12 months.
Police roadblocks are
set up but aren't that
common – mostly at
weekends and after
23:00. But rather
than play a game
of avoiding these
roadblocks, it's a far
better idea to drive
responsibly and not
to drink excessively
– if you aren't worried
about your life, think
of other road users.
There's an abundance
of taxis to ferry home
those who have
consumed too much.
Outlets like Souled Out
in Desa Sri Hartamas
have a 'booze cruiser'
to ensure patrons get
home safely.*

On The Town

While Malaysia is a country that prides itself on its Islamic principles, you will never have to worry about going thirsty in Kuala Lumpur. You could visit a different pub, bar, nightclub, hawker, or live music venue for a beverage every night for months. Most pubs will deliver the standards you would expect: efficient menu, cold draft, storable bottles of spirits, and ongoing football coverage. Nightclubs are for the young, pretty, decibel tolerant and 'loose-walleted'. Many bars will have happy hours that generally run between 16:00 and 20:00, and offer reasonable drink deals. Most bars still welcome smokers for those that indulge, and for those that don't, you will have difficulty in finding escape from the smoke. Kuala Lumpur's nightlife varies as much as its clientele, as some bars look as though they haven't seen a paintbrush for decades and others are obvious in their dedication to their appearance. Bangsar and Desa Sri Hartamas are areas known for their expat patronage, but the diversity of Malaysia ensures that the bars are kept busy by locals and foreigners alike. For those who enjoy an 'alternative' lifestyle, there are gay-friendly places for you to wet your whistle such as Relish Bar and Frangipani on Changkat Bukit Bintang, and Liquid Bar in Central Market. Whatever your tastes, Kuala Lumpur has something that will suit your nightlife expectations.

Dress Code

It is the tropics and dress codes are reasonably casual and liberal, but then again it's also a Muslim country so some places may require modest dress. Being the cosmopolitan capital that it is, dress codes in KL are the most liberal in the country, but in smaller villages around the countryside women especially should take into consideration the possible sensitivities of the local community. Some restaurants in KL may insist that patrons don't wear shorts or flip-flops. While not always stated, hotel restaurants and leading independent restaurants expect that their guests are smartly attired, but for men this rarely means a tie or jacket. Formal functions will state the dress, which is usually national dress (for men, a batik shirt) or lounge suit. Others may state either office attire (which would equate to a suit, collar and tie) or smart casual.

Drinks

Other options **Alcohol** p.284

Alcohol is readily available in downtown Kuala Lumpur, but as you head further out of the city, be prepared to search for your favourite alcoholic beverage as alcohol becomes increasingly difficult to find. The legal drinking age is 18, but with alcohol available rather inexpensively at many convenience stores and grocery stores in KL, it is seldom enforced among expats.

On nights out, prices for drinks vary depending on the establishment. Beer prices can fluctuate between RM8 to RM50, with the local favourites of Carlsberg and Tiger being readily available. Beer imports can be found at many bars but premium prices are to be expected. Bottles of wine from many of the popular regions (Australia, France, South Africa) start at around RM80 and can go as high as your imagination. Bottles of standard spirits (vodka, gin and whisky) can be found for between RM250 and RM600. Visit one of the many Denise Wine (p.401) retail locations scattered throughout KL for an excellent selection of imported wines and reasonable deals. Many bars, lounges and nightclubs offer an impressive list of cocktails and wines to suit every taste.

Go Big Or Go Home

There ain't no party like a KL party 'cos a KL party don't stop – if you're up for a big night out, be sure to head for Zouk (p.411), Velvet Underground (p.411), Ruums (p.410), Bar Club (p.408), Aloha Club (p.408), Ibiza (p.410) or Rum Jungle (p.410).

Work Visas p.54
Weekend Breaks p.155

Written by residents, these unique guidebooks are packed with insider info, from arriving in a new destination to making it your home and everything in between.

Explorer Residents' Guides
We Know Where You Live

Bars

Absolute Chemistry

3 & 5, Jln Telawi 2
Bangsar
 Bangsar
Map 6 E2

03 2282 7242

The interior of this spacious spot wraps around a circular bar that serves up a mix of Guinness, house wines, and the standard spirits. Wednesday night is Bollywood night and if you can't get your fix of traditional Indian audio delights, come back on Sunday for some Bhangra. Ladies enjoy the free wine and champagne on Fridays and Saturdays until 22:00, while men can watch football. The music is loud and boasts a playlist of top tunes from the past 40 years, so guessing which song is next can be fun. To escape the noise, head to the outdoor patio and enjoy some of the cheapest happy hour beers on the Bangsar strip.

Alexis

303 Jalan Ampang
Great Eastern Mall
Ampang
Jelatek
Map 5 D4

03 4260 2288 | *www.alexis.com.my*

Part fine dining restaurant and part jazz club, Alexis manages both very well, offering contemporary dining and a sophisticated night out. The decor is very modern with standard table seating, bar seating, and booths for a more relaxed evening. Live jazz performances from both local and international artists grace the stage on Friday and Saturday nights. The performances are charmingly intimate, and this is one of the best places for live jazz. Cover charges vary so check the website for artists and costs. It is advisable to arrive early or call to reserve seating for live shows. The wine list is extensive and the delicious menu also makes it a handy choice for a pre-show dinner.

Bangkok Jazz

Chulan Square
Jalan Raja Chulan
City Centre
Raja Chulan
Map 13 D1

03 2145 8708

Those looking for a laid back, trendy venue for great live jazz should visit Bangkok Jazz. It is an ideal date spot to rekindle a dimming romance. The seats are comfy, the music is groovy and no one seems in a hurry. There is no house band; instead Bangkok Jazz opts to import Malaysia and Asia's top talent to entertain the masses. For major events there is an entrance fee that includes a soft drink, and you should call ahead to reserve a table. You can even start your night of tunes with a feat of delicious Thai food at the restaurant upstairs. For non-jazz fans, there are flatscreen TVs showing football to entertain as you feign interest in the music.

Blackhole Bistro

22 Jln 25/70A
Sri Hartamas
Bangsar
Map 4 D3

03 2300 1180

Located in the heart of Desa Sri Hartamas' entertainment region, the Blackhole Bistro is an outdoor drinking spot, great for starting the evening's activities. The decor is solid, there is ample indoor and outdoor seating, and the patrons make for attractive people watching. At times, the lack of effort by the staff can be disappointing but it shouldn't ruin your night. The crowd is a thirsty one and make up for the lack of a dancefloor by boogying where they choose. Be warned; if you are heading to Blackhole then go to the bathroom first, and if you are leaving it's advisable to wait until your next watering hole before you take a break.

Make It A Manhattan

The cocktail scene continues to flourish, as Kuala Lumpur prides itself on its cosmopolitan offerings and continually evolving nightlife scene. If you can drink it, you can find it in Kuala Lumpur. The popular rooftop, cocktail scene offers attractive options in Kuala Lumpur where discerning drinkers can enjoy a colourful beverage, attractive people watching and views of Kuala Lumpur's impressive skyline. Check out Luna Bar (p.403) on the 35th floor of the Pan Pacific Hotel and the new SkyBar (p.404) atop the Trader's Hotel.

Jalan Selaman
1/1 Dataran Palma
Ampang
🚇 **Ampang**
Map 5 F4

Chestnuts Bar & Bistro

03 4270 2159

Nestled among a row of shophouses in the expat neighbourhood of Ampang is Portuguese-influenced bistro, Chestnuts. The service is delightfully friendly and extremely efficient. Daily happy hours attract a local and expat after-work crowd who relax with live music or a game of pool. Standard drinks are available, with Tiger draught served cold. A menu offers a diverse range of local and western dishes. There is a limited selection of drinking establishments in the Ampang area, so Chestnuts happily fills the thirsty void.

11 & 15 Jalan Telawi 2
Bangsar
🚇 **Bangsar**
Map 6 E2

Club 11:15

03 2284 1310

Club 11:15's confusing interior, seemingly inspired by a schoolhouse, sports bar and India might be what provides its unique flair. There are two pool tables for the conversationally challenge and seating for over 200 in indoors and fan-cooled outdoor areas. Cheap alcohol is the main selling point with jugs of Tiger going for RM21 during the daily happy hour (16:00 to 19:00). There is a small dancefloor if you are moved by the house DJ's peculiar selection of R&B tunes and ladies can enjoy free wine and champagne on Thursdays until 22:00.

Desa Sri Hartamas
Sri Hartamas
🚇 **Bangsar**
Map 4 D3

Denise Wine Bar

03 2300 1648 | www.denisewine.com

This is a wonderfully unique addition to the wine bar concept. Denise is a wine retail shop, stocked with a healthy selection focusing mainly on Australia and France. The prices are reasonable and range from approximately RM40 a bottle to curious vintages that retail for RM7,000. Once you've made your selection, enjoy it on site with generous crystal glasses in the members' lounge area at the back. The rustic tasting area can accommodate up to 25 people. The idea that you must be a member to use the member's tasting area is enforced, but membership is free with one RM500 purchase. You can store your wine there or take it home. Your membership card also entitles you to discounts on wine at one of the 14 Denise Wine outlets in Kuala Lumpur (p.401).

37 & 39, Changkat
Bukit Bintang
Bukit Bintang
🚇 **Bukit Bintang**
Map 13 A1

Flam's Restaurant & Wine Bar

03 2145 8222 | www.flams.com

Luxurious ambience and an exhaustive wine list make Flam's an exquisite choice to taste a few vintages. With marble counters and dimmed lighting, this place caters to an affluent, well-informed crowd that enjoys what they drink. The main focus is on French and Australian wines but there is a greater selection available. There are two function rooms that can accommodate 30 and 15 wine lovers respectively. The service is incredibly friendly and while the music isn't very inspiring, it is easy to ignore. Flam's is open daily for lunch from 12:00 to 14:30 and in the evenings for tastings and dinner at 18:30.

25 Changkat Bukit
Bintang
Bukit Bintang
🚇 **Bukit Bintang**
Map 13 A1

Frangipani

03 2144 3001 | www.frangipani.com.my

Frangipani is the most upscale option on the popular Changkat Bukit Bintang circuit. With a fine-dining restaurant below and posh nightclub upstairs, it is a good destination to both begin and end your evening. It boasts an impressive cocktail list satisfying even the most discriminating of drinkers. It is easy to try a different drink with every visit and walk away with a new favourite. Take a tip from the bartender and try one of its house specialities. Frangipani offers an inviting dancefloor with a DJ spinning house and retro music, cosy lounge seating for intimate conversations, and basic bar stool seating for those interested in a more casual evening. The crowd is diverse and often mature. Friday nights cater to the alternative crowd but everyone is always welcome.

1-1, Jalan 22A/70A
Desa Sri Hartamas
Sri Hartamas
🚇 *Bangsar*
Map 4 D3

Groove Junction

03 6201 8990 | www.groove-junctionkl.com

Located in the trendy Sri Hartamas area, Groove Junction is an excellent venue to experience local and international musical acts in a cosy setting with great sound. Although there is a house focus on jazz, the venue does have a variety of acts on its stage. Live acts tend to start nightly around 22:00. There isn't a bad seat in the house as the stage flanks one end of the bar and the seats are spread throughout two levels. The staff are excellent and there is a great selection of cocktails and beers available. There is also a diverse menu to satisfy your late night cravings, or for a pre-party feast. The line up of artists is continually changing so be sure to check the website for updates.

56 Jalan Doraisamy
City Centre
🚇 *Dang Wangi*
Map 13 E1

Kristao Restaurant & Bar

03 2691 8768

Kristao is definitely one of the more laid back options on the radically trendy Asian Heritage Row strip. Reservations aren't needed but are encouraged. The atmosphere is geared more towards chatting rather than dancing. Kristao's dark ambience and delicious wild sangrias lubricate the conversational topics as you sample the menu or move on to dance somewhere along the strip. Kristao hosts a mixed crowd of 20 to 30 year-old professionals, and while the dress code isn't extremely strict, it is worth noting that patrons dress to impress.

14-16 Jalan Telawi 2
Bangsar Baru
Bangsar
🚇 *Bangsar*
Map 6 E2

La Bodega

03 2287 8318 | www.gastrodome.com.my

Those craving a little Spanish flair to should stop at La Bodega. Great service, a soothing vibe and the refreshing white sangria are the main selling points of this lounge. Two floors of seating usually ensure access to a table at one of its indoor or outdoor seating areas. There is a massive Spanish-inspired drinks list to cater to the diverse, fun-seeking clientele of young and old that journey to La Bodega every night. There is also a 50 foot bar where you can complement your conversation and sangria with a dish of tasty authentic paella.

Italiannies
The Curve
Petaling Jaya
🚇 *Kepong Sentral*
Map 4 D4

Laundry

03 7728 1715 | www.laundrybar.net

Music fans head to Laundry Bar for the latest and best on the KL independent scene. Whether it is rock, hip-hop or an acoustic groove you want, this venue has something to offer. In addition to the great local acts that grace the stage, the bar also showcases international talent. The dancefloor is large enough to accommodate many music fans and there are plenty of places to just chill out with friends and enjoy a drink. The crowd is mainly young and local but music is the common passion. Open nightly from 17:00 until 01:00; check the website for listings of who is playing and when.

2 & 4 Lorong Sahabat
Bukit Bintang
🚇 *Bukit Bintang*
Map 13 A1

Little Havana

03 2144 7170 | www.mylittlehavanakl.com

Anchoring the popular Changkat Bukit Bintang strip, Little Havana has a little something for everyone. The main floor has a great outdoor patio with a bar, big screen TV, outdoor pool table and ambience perfect for conversation. Inside, you can choose from a small selection of cigars and sample from a menu of local and western dishes. The food is satisfactory but if you are looking for something special then eat at one of the many restaurants on CBB and go to Little Havana afterwards. There are special nights that include salsa dancing and live music by local acts.

Luna Bar

Pacific Regency
Menara Pan Global
Jalan Punchak
City Centre
🚇 *KLCC*
Map 11 A3

03 2026 2211 | *www.pacific-regency.com*
Kuala Lumpur's first rooftop nightclub is still considered by many to be its best. Luna Bar gives off both that necessary exclusive vibe yet attracts a wide range of local and foreign visitors. The mood inside is nothing short of tranquil as the dim lights, comfortable booths and inviting pool create a great atmosphere. There is an outdoor bar upstairs that offers a cool breeze while you absorb the panoramic views of the downtown skyline. You won't be the only one taking pictures and, although it is allowed, you should be discreet. The staff are helpful and pleasant by KL service standards. Although there isn't an actual dress code, wear something smart to accommodate the crowd and the evening KL air. Luna Bar is closed on Sundays.

Mojo Bar

42 Jalan Doraisamy
City Centre
🚇 *Dang Wangi*
Map 13 E2

03 2697 7999
Mojo Bar is a cool, relaxed bar situated in the middle of Asian Heritage Row. It provides a nice transition bar between nightclubs on the strip or a great place to hang out, have a drink and do some people watching. Once the dinner crowd rolls out, a dancefloor opens up to allow for the DJ's mix of hip and R&B music. Fortunately, with two floors and an outside seating area, there are numerous places to go for good conversation. The decor is 70s chic with hanging beads and appropriate mood lighting. The staff are friendly and efficient. There is never a cover charge, which makes it a low risk venture.

No Black Tie

17 Jalan Mesui
Bukit Bintang
🚇 *Bukit Bintang*
Map 13 A1

03 2142 3737
Located just off the Changkat Bukit Bintang path, No Black Tie is definitely worth finding. Built specifically for live music, it is hard to beat the sound that emanates nightly. Whether it is classical, jazz or local independent rock, it all sounds incredible. The owner Evelyn, a classical piano player, wanted to create a space where musicians love to play and music lovers want to come to listen. There is an upstairs balcony that offers a great perspective on the artist performing below and, while there is no dancefloor, if the music calls for it people will dance wherever they can find room. Expect to pay a cover to see the performances that showcase Malaysian and international talent, but music lovers will get their money's worth.

Planet Hollywood

KL Plaza
179 Jalan Bukit Bintang
Bukit Bintang
🚇 *Bukit Bintang*
Map 13 C1

03 2144 6562 | *www.planethollywood.com*
If you have ever been to a Planet Hollwood anywhere else on the planet then you are certain to know what to expect at KL's branch. Movie posters and memorabilia grace the walls while the drinks and menu charge western prices for huge portions. The saving grace of Planet Hollywood is the cold beer and incredible live music set up in the nightclub downstairs. Many great local and international rock acts have graced the stage and the large dancefloor makes it a great place to catch a show.

6-8 Jalan Telawi 2
Bangsar
🚇 **Bangsar**
Map 5 E2

Planter Jim's

03 2282 4084

Located in the trendy Bangsar area, expats and locals alike visit Planter Jim's for the extensive wine list and fully stocked cigar bar. Tastefully decorated, the interior has a range of comfortable seating options, including booths and bar stools where you can watch premiership football matches. There is a wide variety of cocktails with mai tais and margaritas considered to be the tastiest specialities. Attractive happy hour prices and additional menu of Thai and local fare make it a good place to stop after work.

64 Jalan Tun HS Lee
Chinatown
🚇 **Pasar Seni**
Map 12 D2

Reggae Bar

03 2070 5333

Catering mostly to the backpacking crowd, Reggae Bar is a chill-out pub located in the heart of Chinatown. The food is surprising good but pricey by local standards, and the same goes for the beer. As expected, the music is of the island-vibe variety, with Bob Marley and Jack Johnson getting daily spins in the DJ's rotation. It claims every night is ladies' night. Arrive early to escape the hustle and bustle of the market shopping, or stay late to dance with touring strangers.

22 Changkat
Bukit Bintang
Bukit Bintang
🚇 **Bukit Bintang**
Map 13 A1

Relish Bar

03 2145 3321 | *www.relishworld.com*

Relish is continuing its quest to change how the public feels about hamburgers. The atmosphere is crisp, the seats are comfortable, and the service is always incredible. There is bar seating available or you can choose from plenty of tables indoors or out. Fridays make for a popular night for drinks with the alternative crowd before many head over to Frangipani's (p.401) for some music and mingling. There is an adequate wine and cocktail selection and many talk highly of the dessert menu. And of course, if the mood hits, try one of Relish's amazing burgers from the late-night kitchen. There is another branch in Bangsar (03 2283 3321).

Traders Hotel KL
City Centre
🚇 **KLCC**
Map 11 C3

SkyBar

03 2332 9888 | *www.shangri-la.com*

On the 33rd floor of the elegant Traders Hotel (p.25) is KL's newest addition to the rooftop club scene. SkyBar's extensive cocktail menu and cosmopolitan vibe caters to the young, hip and trendy in addition to those who wish they were. Large viewing windows surround the club allowing guests stunning views of downtown. Seats are comfortably scattered throughout, leaving a dancefloor wherever you can find it, and there is a large pool in the centre. Remember to dress to impress and be prepared to pay upscale prices for your upscale evening.

SkyBar

18 Jalan Telawi 3
Bangsar
🚇 *Bangsar*
Map 6 E2

T Club Bar & Bistro
03 2284 0403

As the unusual name suggests, it is difficult to determine what kind of watering hole this small, dark, yet comfortable, venue is. The service is friendly and quick, catering mainly to the thirsty crowd of regulars. The drinks are reasonably priced for the area but the cocktail menu is not great. Fortunately, the music is not as loud as other bars on the Bangsar strip making it a good place to have a drink with friends before any evening action begins. As with most pubs and bars in the area, there is a big screen TV perpetually tuned into sports.

22 Jalan Telawi 3
Bangsar
🚇 *Bangsar*
Map 6 E2

The Talk
03 2284 3242

Trendy, talkative locals and expats enjoy this bohemian, multi-concept escape. Cigars and an extensive Eurasian wine list are available, with a sushi bar providing the light meal to complement the evening's conversation. The prices are reasonable, so you can put your money towards a piece of art (the walls are dotted with paintings from local artists). There is seating both indoors and outdoors, making it an excellent place to people watch.

Pubs
Other options **Bars** p.400

No. 28 Jalan Sri
Hartamas 8
Sri Hartamas
Map 4 D4

Backyard Pub & Grill
03 6201 0318 | *www.backyardpub.com*

Locals and expats alike gather at the Backyard for cold beer, live music and Jerry, the pub's friendly owner. With big screen TVs mainly showing sport, two pool tables, and ample seating both indoors and outside, the Backyard is a favourite for both after-work drinks and a full-on Friday night out. Prices are reasonable, and the food is satisfactory. There is live music every night of the week showcasing local talent, which keeps the dancefloor busy and the regulars coming back for more.

31 & 31-1 Jalan
Sri Hartamas 7
Sri Hartamas
Map 4 D4

Bulldog Restaurant & Pub
03 6201 4484

Modelled on the traditional British pub, Bulldog caters to an older, professional expat crowd, the sort that enjoys Guinness and fine English fare. Low-key music that complements the tabled conversations is the order of the day, except for Friday and Saturday nights when a covers band cranks up the volume (the upstairs section offers a comfortable retreat for those looking for a quieter experience). The owner insists that premium spirit brands only are used, assuring the regulars of quality refreshment. When the beer starts tickling the appetite, indulge in some of Britain's finest, such as the popular toad in the hole. Come early on Sundays for a traditional full-English breakfast, served from 10:00.

6 Jalan Telawi Lima
Bangsar
🚇 *Bangsar*
Map 6 E2

Finnegan's
03 2284 0476 | *www.finneganspubs.com*

When you're homesick in KL, head for an Irish pub. You don't even have to be Irish – there's just something comforting about being in a pub where the folk are friendly, the walls are covered in nostalgic paraphernalia, and, most importantly, the Guinness flows on tap. Finnegan's is a real 'home from home' venue, where you'll find solace in getting exactly what you're expecting, every single time. Wooden stools, numerous TVs showing football matches, dartboards and a sturdy pub-grub menu complete the comfort. The weekly quiz night on Wednesdays is a crowd-puller. On the downside, prices can be steep and the service is a bit hit and miss, but when you've got a hankering for distant shores, this is the place to be. Other branches can be found in Desi Sri Hartamas (03 2300 0538), Bukit Bintang (03 2145 1930) and Mid Valley (03 2284 8157).

The Green Man

40 Changkat
Bukit Bintang
Bukit Bintang
🚇 *Bukit Bintang*
Map 13 A1

03 2141 9924 | *www.greenman.com.my*

The Green Man is a popular, British-style pub catering to locals and expats who appreciate great beer, delicious, well-prepared food and televised sports in a relaxed environment. As well-known as the Green Man is on the Changkat Bukit Bintang strip, it's not exactly spacious, but there always appears to be enough seating both indoors and out. As with all pubs in KL, there is a nightly happy hour, but most patrons let the beer tell them when they are happy. Pub games are aplenty, and the free Green Man lighters are a nice touch. For those into old motors, a group of classic car enthusiasts hold monthly meetings here.

Home & Away

37 Jalan 23/70A
Sri Hartamas
Map 4 D3

03 6203 5262

If you're in the mood to watch the big game in the company of others rather than on your couch, Home & Away in Desa Sri Hartamas is the place to head. The pub is small, and the numerous TVs scattered throughout make every seat a good one. Beamish and Tetley's are on tap, a welcome break from the standard local offerings. There are a few pool tables, in case your team is losing, and the management will periodically stage billiard tournaments for the competitive-minded. Home & Away has all the elements you'd expect from a traditional pub: aromas of day-old beer, a sticky floor, and, most importantly, someone close by to strike up a conversation with.

Karma

1 Jalan 22A/70A
Desa Sri Hartamas
Sri Hartamas
Map 10 E2

03 6203 2111

Karma is the type of venue best suited to starting a night in, not for ending one. Very simple in design and concept, it caters to the local and expat community with the standard selection of beers, spirits and wines. Happy hour jugs of beer for RM 37 delight customers, and there's a selection of tapas and Mediterranean specialities to satisfy your nibbling appetite. Small acoustic bands have been known to play in the evenings, unfortunately drowning out any opportunity to hold a conversation, and a DJ also mixes retro and contemporary music.

Ol Skool Bistro

No. 125 & 125A
Jalan Gasing
Petaling Jaya
Map 6 D4

03 7960 5855 | *www.olskool-bistro.com*

From the outside, Ol Skool is the venue you were scared of as a kid: black, ominous doors, no windows, seemingly no one ever going in or coming out. Inside, however, it's a different world. Varying live bands and an extremely friendly, predominantly local clientele inject wonderful colour to this long-serving pub. There isn't much else out at this end of town, so coming to Ol Skool means staying at Ol Skool. The owner divides his time between spinning great records (retro and rock) and chatting to customers. The menu isn't fantastic, so a good option is to try some great Indian food at one of the nearby hawker stalls before making your way here to play pool, darts or dance until closing time.

> ### Drinking For Sport
>
> There are numerous sports bars scattered around Kuala Lumpur but almost every pub, bar and even local hawker stall will have numerous TVs where you can enjoy watching international sports, specifically football, at all hours of the evening. Popular sporting hangouts include Home & Away (p.406) in Desa Sri Hartamas and The Green Man (p.406) on the popular Changkat Bukit Bintang strip.

Ronnie Q's
03 2689 4807

Expats and locals may come into legendary Ronnie Q's for a refreshing Kilkenny or to catch the latest premiership match, but they often stay for Frank's (manager, social director, master of brews) unique presence. Ronnie Q's is a classic British pub. Everyone is welcome at this charming place but it is advised that you come thirsty and with an opinion. It might be one of the rare places in Malaysia where conversations about politics and religion are actually encouraged. Wednesday is quiz night and all-day happy hours on Sunday ensure that you always have a reason for visiting.

Gay & Lesbian
Other options **Gay & Lesbian** p.18

Malaysia isn't the top destination of choice for gay and lesbian visitors looking for the freedom they may have in western countries. It's a Muslim nation, homosexuality is illegal, and hanging out a rainbow flag is not exactly a good idea.
Nevertheless, Kuala Lumpur is decidedly more cosmopolitan then the rest of the country, with a wider acceptance of the gay community that is more akin to attitudes in Thailand and Singapore. The community is becoming more open and nightlife choices for the gay community are burgeoning, without blatantly advertising this.
The city is peppered with gay-friendly eateries, spas, saunas, bars and clubs, and even 'straight clubs' organise gay and lesbian nights.
As a former British colony, Malaysia has similar anti-gay laws to Singapore and India. The penal code prohibits sex between men of any age, whether in public or in private. Religious and secular laws frown on public displays of affection from same-sex couples (or couples of the opposite sex, for that matter). Shariah law (which applies only to Muslims) forbids sodomy and cross-dressing.
If all you have in mind is a night of dancing and drinking, then head on to any of the clubs. For pure cruising, your best bets are Liquid and La Queen, where the rule is 'anything goes' – and that may refer literally to the shirt on your back. Just go easy on the public displays of affection.
While remembering that homosexuality is outlawed in KL, there are certain bars and nightclubs that are gay friendly or that hold popular 'alternative' nights that draw the crowds. Shook! (p.364) and Frangipani (p.401) are both established restaurants and bars that are popular with the gay crowd on certain nights. Rahsia (03 2142 5555, www.rahsia-kl.com) feels surprisingly secluded considering its city centre location, and the free cocktails and half-price drinks every day from 16:00 to 20:00 keep its patrons smiling. Other venues to try are Nuovo on Jalan P Ramlee (017 325 9985), La Queen Club (012 658 6831), which is a fantastic dance venue, and Blue Boy (03 2142 1067, 50 Jalan Sultan Ismail), which has been around for years, but is still very popular.

Zouk (p.411)

Nightclubs

Other options **Belly Dancing** p.219

Nightclubbers will be spoilt for choice with a variety of nightlife options in KL, as new clubs open and old ones evolve to meet the ever-changing needs of Kuala Lumpur's dance set. There are popular areas in town where you can find a variety of hot spots that will suit the laid-back loungers and the hard-core clubbers. Check out Asian Heritage Row, Bangsar and the Zouk Complex (p.411) for Kuala Lumpur's most popular clubbing options. Most KL nightclubs insist that you dress to impress, and the prices for entrance and drinks are much higher than you would expect to pay at pubs or restaurants. Be prepared to dish out between RM10 and RM100 depending on the night, venue or visiting DJ. Often this cover expense includes a drink upon entry. Expats rarely have difficulty gaining entry to nightclubs, but it is recommended that you bring identification with you regardless. Most clubs are diverse in clientele, and locals and expats share the dancefloor and conversation. While the atmosphere and vibe at most is welcoming, there are instances of violence and theft, so take precautions as necessary. It is advisable to tour KL's nightclub circuit with a buddy.

Jalan P Ramlee
City Centre
Map 11 B2

Aloha Club

03 2711 7266 | www.alohakl.com

The Aloha Club on Ramlee is a large club based on three levels, each catering to a specific need or fantasy. This appears to be the flagship location of several Aloha clubs around Kuala Lumpur and Malaysia. The main floor sports an imported cover band playing top 40 covers to the packed dancefloor. The second floor offers the VIP experience, where for the low price of RM10,000 (not a typo) you can purchase a lifetime VIP membership. This VIP status will grant you the right to make a reservation, bypass any nightly lines and to start consuming your RM10,000 automatic bar credit. The basement nightclub requires a bit of tolerance for darkness and loud house music. Ladies can expect special treatment on Wednesdays, and Aloha's is open until 03:00 in the morning. There is even an outdoor seafood bar to satisfy the hunger developed throughout the evening.

21 Jalan Doraisamy
City Centre
🚇 *Medan Tuanku*
Map 13 E2

Atrium

03 2694 1318 | www.atrium.com.my

Atrium is one of the main dance clubs on Asian Heritage Row in terms of size and consistency. The service is surprisingly friendly and with an extensive beverage list, the clientele tends to be quite friendly too. The attractive, mostly local crowd has two music options to choose from while in this tastefully decorated, upscale club. Enjoy house music upstairs or stay on the main level for some danceable R&B. Atrium is open from Wednesdays to Saturdays and you should expect to pay the standard nightclub cover charge except on Wednesdays, when women enjoy the standard perks of ladies' night. Atrium's dress code requests that you look good in your smart casual attire. There is seating outside the club, which allows you to get some air before continuing with your dancing.

No. 44, 46 & 48
Jalan Doraisamy
City Centre
🚇 *Medan Tuanku*
Map 13 E2

Bar Club

03 2693 2270

One of the larger dance clubs on Asian Heritage Row, Bar Club's nightly mix of R&B tunes keeps the dancefloor moving. Tastefully decorated in warm reds and hideaway blacks, the ambience suits the champagne-sipping set. There are two floors that offer a wide range of lounging options, dance spaces and a pool table.

Wednesday is ladies' night and as such the drinks and cover are free from 22:00 to 01:00 for women. Otherwise, expect to pay standard club entrance cover charges between RM25 and RM35, which will include one alcoholic beverage. The crowd is a mix of locals and foreigners in their 20s and 30s. There is a dress code, so throw on your Saturday night bests.

97 Jalan P Ramlee
City Centre
KLCC
Map 11 A2

Beach Club
03 2170 9919

The Beach Club is one of those glorious institutions that you have to experience once, and for many that is enough. Sometimes a walk in front is even enough for those that aren't feeling brave enough to face the masses of thirsty expat and local men looking for more than beer to satisfy their cravings. A cover charge is required if you arrive later and the place is always packed from the bar to the dancefloor. An energetic band that performs nightly will sing the songs you never want to admit you know the words to. Located at the end of Jalan Ramlee, you can always go to one of the many nearby bars or nightclubs to continue your evening if need be.

18 Jalan Liku
Bangsar
Bangsar
Map 6 E2

Club 18
03 2283 1091 | *www.club18bangsar.com*

Club 18 is another example of the large KL nightclub that has many faces. As you enter, floor-to-ceiling mirrors welcome you to the massive dancefloor. Bars and drink stations with courteous and swift staff are spread conveniently throughout the club. Anchored at the rear is a massive stage where you'll find live music and special events. There is a plush VIP area upstairs with friendly service and talkative people. The DJ and clientele enjoy hits from the 80s and 90s as crowds stay past 03:00 dancing the night away. The kitchen offers delicious choices and stays open until 02:00 for your convenience.

Asian Heritage Row
64 Jalan Doraisamy
City Centre
Medan Tuanku
Map 13 E2

CoChine
03 2697 1180 | *www.indochine.com.sg*

Decorated in traditional Buddhist style, CoChine (also known as Bar Savanh) is a popular choice among KL's ever-changing nightclub scene. Each room is designed perfectly to fit the intended mood, with soothing fountains, pillow-filled opium beds and the many watchful eyes of Buddha. Relax in the front bar or upstairs over a well-made martini; hit the dancefloor to some contemporary house music, or just hang back and wait to get noticed by another of the attractive clientele. Stay at CoChine late to take advantage of its well-thought-out club culture, but feel free to come early for a tempting menu of Vietnamese, Laotian and Cambodian cuisine. The food is light, spicy and relatively guilt free, perfect before a solid night of clubbing on the Heritage Row trail. The crowd is quite mixed, with both locals and a sprinkling of foreigners enjoying the great vibe. There don't seem to be any boundaries when it comes to the dress code, but save the flip-flops and the hat for the beach.

18-1 Jalan P Ramlee
City Centre
KLCC
Map 11 B2

Havanita
03 2141 8888

Located in a bar adjacent to Poppy, Havanita seems like a good idea turned bad. Originally created seemingly as an escape for Poppy dancers and partygoers, it feels a bit unfinished. It is pleasant enough, but the darkness and low ceilings don't quite achieve the intended effect. There's a small area with a cover band. It isn't that the cover band is bad, it's just that there is no room for sound to move and the result is tragic. It's ok just to come to for a drink with your friends at the start of your evening.

Ibiza

Jalan P Ramlee
City Centre
KLCC
Map 11 B2

03 2713 2333

Based below the trendy Modesto's restaurant on the Ramlee strip, Ibiza caters mostly to local Malaysian trendsetters and clubbers. The dancefloor is massive and the service staff helpful. beers and spirits are reasonably priced and the music is standard R&B and house. Although it is open from Wednesday to Sunday, Saturdays are the big nights to be seen here. Worth checking out if you are interested in immersing yourself in a different scene.

The Loft

113 Jln Ampang
City Centre
KLCC
Map 11 A2

03 2171 1997 | www.zoukclub.com.my

The Loft plays the music that other clubs don't: rock, punk, indie and house. The crowd is younger and the interior is loft-like. It is often crowded which makes movement difficult, and the dancefloor is centre stage. The drinks are priced according to KL nightclub rates, which means you could get a beer cheaper somewhere else. People don't come to The Loft for the bargains, but rather to see, be seen and get sweaty. Open Wednesdays to Saturdays.

Poppy

18-1 Jln P Ramlee
City Centre
KLCC
Map 11 B2

03 2141 8888

Poppy is the kind of place that Vanity Fair would rent out to hold its monthly 'party-so-we-can-take-your-picture' event. It is tastefully decorated in white, and there is a sunken dance floor that is often filled with gyrating, sweaty revelers dancing to the latest in house, R&B and top 40 dance music. The second floor allows for an uninterrupted view of the party and the bars are ideally scattered throughout the bar making it rather easy to grab a drink. There is an outdoor area which makes for a nice view on a clear night.

Qba

The Westin KL
199 Jalan Bukit Bintang
Bukit Bintang
Bukit Bintang
Map 13 E1

03 2731 8333 | www.starwoodhotels.com

Qba is a prime venue for salsa music. It has a well-stocked cigar lounge, diverse and delicious wine menu, international live acts and a dancefloor which is always packed. Party on two floors of Cuban opulence with crystal chandeliers, decorative ceilings and efficient service staff. The crowds is mixed; all come to dance. The vibe is friendly: just be sure to respect others on the dancefloor. Perhaps you may just meet someone you can share one of the dark romantic hideaways in the corner with. Be sure to dress appropriately for a night of dancing in an upmarket hotel. If you have no intention of dancing, don't bother coming, as there's nowhere really just to be an observer.

Rum Jungle

Jalan P Ramlee
City Centre
KLCC
Map 11 B2

03 2148 0282

Rum Jungle picks up where the Beach Club ends. It is almost identical: it's crowded, there's a live band, and a fish tank (with the obligatory shark) above the bar. There's a drink-included cover charge of RM20 to RM30. Happy hours boast an adequate deal of beers for RM8. If you get sick of the crowds and noise, you can always chill outside on the patio for some entertaining people-watching. Rum Jungle is surrounded by numerous bars on the Ramlee Strip that contribute to a night of bar hopping.

Ruums

Bangunan Life Centre
Jalan Sultan Ismail
City Centre
KLCC
Map 11 A3

03 2162 8163 | www.ruumsclub.com

Ruums has everything you like in your massive dance halls: a huge dancefloor, numerous satellite bars to quench your thirst, ample spacious areas to satisfy your craving for personal space, an upstairs lounge area, and a beautiful, albeit young, crowd. Ruums is also famous for bringing in top international live music acts including

Napalm Death, NOFX and Pop Shuvit. It is located conveniently near many nightclubs and bars, in case you wish to take your night elsewhere.

Telawi Street Bistro

1-3 Jalan Telawi 3
Bangsar
🚇 *Bangsar*
Map 6 E2

03 2284 3168 | *www.telawi.com.my*

Start or end your night at this popular Bangsar hangout. After dinner on the main level, head upstairs where the house DJ offers great dance and house music to an appreciative crowd. Enjoy the cocktail of the month on the spacious outdoor balcony overlooking the Bangsar strip. Catering largely to an expat crowd, there is never a cover charge, which helps offset the drink prices. However, at TSB you tend to get what you pay for: friendly service, attractive energetic crowds, and a fun night.

Twentyone Kitchen + Bar

20-1 Changkat
Bukit Bintang
City Centre
🚇 *Bukit Bintang*
Map13 A1

03 2142 0021 | *www.twentyone.com.my*

This bar's stylish, sleek and sexy interior brings in the lookers, the dancers and the partygoers. Above the main floor's elegant restaurant is a bar where you can dance to excellent house music, enjoy well-mixed cocktails, and chat to strangers on the comfortable, breezy balcony overlooking the street below. The drink prices are welcomingly inexpensive and there's no cover charge. Dress to impress, not because it's a house rule, but because the other clientele expect it.

Velvet Underground

113 Jalan Ampang
City Centre
🚇 *KLCC*
Map 11 A2

03 2171 1997 | *www.zoukclub.com.my*

Velvet Underground is Zouk's classy, older sister. It is a darker, slightly more stylish nightclub catering to an older clubbing crowd that still loves the music but also the conversation. The only place you can actually move in Velvet Underground is the dancefloor, as there seem to be tables and chairs everywhere you try to go. Mambo Jambo nights on Wednesdays are extremely popular, as people flock to dance to the best in retro music. There is always a cover charge for entry, but the drink that is included in the deal offsets the hit your wallet takes. There are dark areas in the bar, which can foster an uncomfortable feeling, and there have been too many stories of violence to ignore. Dancers beware. Open Wednesdays to Saturdays.

Zeta Bar

Hilton KL
3 Jalan Stesen Sentral
KL Sentral
🚇 *KL Sentral*
Map 7 A2

03 2264 2264 | *www.kl-studio.com*

Located in the upmarket Hilton Hotel, Zeta Bar caters to the wealthy, uber-trendy, 30 plus night owls that don't mind paying shocking prices for their drinks. The international live bands are always spot on and guarantee an entertaining show until the wee hours of the morning. It's one of KL's friendliest dancefloors. Call to reserve a table to make sure you aren't using your elbows all night. Ordering a bottle of spirits is the best way to stay refreshed. The staff will ensure that your glasses are always refreshed (after all, you paid a hefty price for it). Open Monday to Saturday.

Zouk

113 Jalan Ampang
City Centre
🚇 *KLCC*
Map 11 A2

03 2171 1997 | *www.zoukclub.com.my*

Zouk is the originator of Kuala Lumpur's dance club scene. Known for bringing in world class DJs, it's packed with Kuala Lumpur's trendy clubbers looking to get their weekly dance fix. The sound system is world class and there is ample space to dance, sweat and be seen. The crowd is a mix of young and old, energetic locals and expats. The wrong words or attitudes may bring unwanted and often undeserved attention. Drinks are predictably pricey and always expect a cover charge for entry that will vary depending on the talent entertaining the masses. Open Thursdays to Saturdays.

Casinos

Depending upon your definition of gambling, the only legalised casino in the country is located in the Genting Highlands, 2,000 metres up in the clouds, and an hour's drive from KL. Horse racing and 'four-digit' systems (which work like a lottery where four numbers are randomly selected and payouts made based upon the number of holders of the lucky numbers) operate freely throughout the country, but if punters want to chance their hand on the tables they have to make the journey up to the Genting Highlands. An alternative is to sail into international waters on a cruise ship and enjoy gambling freely in the on-board casinos. There are people who also play mahjong, especially around Chinese New Year, and there is a good chance that a few dollars change hands on some games (but the authorities turn a blind eye).

To use an old cliche, the Genting Highlands Resort (www.genting.com.my) or 'City of Entertainment' has something for everyone. When it was established over 40 years ago the intention was to provide a place in the cool mountain air where Malaysians could relax and enjoy themselves and where non-Muslims could gamble. While the gambling still exists around the clock, the resort has expanded to become a complete entertainment city with theme parks (indoor and outdoor), live shows, shopping, restaurants, numerous hotels (over 6,000 rooms), convention facilities and a championship golf course at neighbouring Awana Genting Highlands Golf & Country Club (03 6436 9000). It gets crowded especially during holidays and it is a bit over the top so it may not appeal to everyone. Visitors can drive to the summit or ride an 11 minute cable car from Goh Tong Jaya halfway up the mountain. Entry to the gaming rooms is restricted to non-Muslims over 21 years of age, who are reasonably attired (shoes not sandals).

Cinemas

Malaysia is one of the cheapest places to watch movies. In the past, you could watch them for a couple of ringgit at independent theatre halls like the Odeon and the Rex – quaint cinema halls with narrow musty seats – but today, they have been taken over by conglomerates like Golden Screen Cinemas and Cathay.
Cinema watching is a popular activity, so queues can be intimidatingly long, especially during the weekends. Most people beat the long queues by booking online through www.cinemaonline.com.my or using the telephone, for which you

Cinemas			
Cineleisure Damansara	Mutiara Damansara	03 7727 8051	www.cathaycineplexes.com.
Golden Screen Cinema	1 Utama Shopping Centre	03 8312 3456	www.gsc.com.my
	Berjaya TImes Square		
	Cheras Leisure Mall		
	IOI Mall		
	Mid Valley Mega Mall		
	Selayang Capitol		
	Summit USJ		
IMAX – Times Square	Berjaya Times Square, 1 Jalan Imbi	03 2117 3046	www.timessquarekl.com
MBO Cinemas	Galaxy Ampang	03 4270 1938	www.mbocinemas.com
Smile Theaters	Amcorp Mall	03 7958 8119	na
Tanjong Golden Village	1 Utama Shopping Centre	03 7492 2929	www.tgv.com.my
	Bukit Raja Shopping Centre		
	Mines Shopping Fair		
	Sunway Pyramid Shopping Centre		
	Suria KLCC		

pay a nominal RM1 service charge. Tickets go for RM10 to RM12 at the weekends (depending on the popularity of the movie), but some cinemas offer discounts on weekdays when it is also less crowded. Lovebirds can upgrade to RM15 for a couple-seat at selected cinemas (do call up to check for availability), while RM20 buys you your own table. Berjaya Times Square (p.336) offers a 3D alternative through its IMAX Theatre (p.182). Movie listings are available in all major newspapers and websites (listed in the accompanying table).

The most popular offerings are Hollywood blockbusters as well as Hong Kong and Korean hits, though you can get art house films. Expatriate organisations like Alliance Française periodically stage collaborations with cinema operators to run foreign movie festivals which show award-winning titles like *Children of Heaven*. Generally, non-Malay language movies carry subtitles in Chinese and Malay. Sometimes, blockbusters are released even earlier than their counterparts in the US, UK and Hong Kong, to curb video piracy.

Censorship can be quite strict. Scenes with excessive violence, sexual overtones and religious connotations are snipped out due to cultural sensitivities, though the government is keen to educate the public by allowing in acclaimed movies that carry R-rated classifications like *Brokeback Mountain* and *Lust, Caution*.

Entrapment

The film *Entrapment*, starring Catherine Zeta Jones and Sean Connery, famously included footage of the Petronas Twin Towers shortly after they were constructed. There was some outrage, however, at the way the towers were depicted as being surrounded by river-side slums that were superimposed into the shots at the editing stage. Then again, there's no such thing as bad publicity...

Comedy

There really aren't any comedy clubs here in the strictest sense of the word, at least not in the way comedy is perceived overseas.

The closest thing Kuala Lumpur has to a comedy club of sorts is the Instant Café Theatre Company (www.instantcafetheatre.com, 03 7960 2214). Staffed by a band of passionate local artists whose day jobs comprise everything from writing children's books to penning satirical columns in mainstream papers, its hugely popular productions poke fun at political and social establishments and have sometimes resulted in it getting into trouble with the powers that be. The controversial nature of the plays makes it well worth the effort to drop by whenever there is a show, if only to get an insight into the current political and social issues that resonate with the locals. The plays are mostly staged in English of a pretty high standard. Despite the controversy, information on upcoming shows is publicised in the mainstream media. Other avenues of information include its website, as well as blogs. Some of the scriptwriters and actors for the theatre use blogs to advertise and engage their audiences.

Petronas by night

Arts portal Kakiseni (www.kakiseni.com) provides comprehensive information on the local arts scene as well as insightful reviews, while alternative lifestyle magazine Off The Edge gives a provocative and incisive commentary on the arts and lifestyle scene in Malaysia.

Concerts & Live Music

Everyone's A Critic

If you like eating out or frequenting bars, and then you like to critique them for all your friends, why not join the KL community on www. explorerpublishing. com? It's the ultimate meeting point for the latest updates, sharing information, and recommending your favourite restaurants and nightlife venues.

There is never a shortage of live music options in Kuala Lumpur. Many pubs and bars offer music at the weekends and there are special venues that provide live music seven days a week. Be prepared to experience a range of original and cover music artists (hard rock, acoustic, classical, rap, salsa) as the local music scene continues to grow. Depending on the artist and the venue, admission prices will vary as pubs will rarely charge a cover to see the live bands, but international acts can charge upwards of RM500.

The annual Rainforest Music Festival (p.39) in Sarawak in July is a must-see and Kuala Lumpur continues to attempt to attract international artists. However, at times it can be difficult to witness international acts as Malaysian performance restrictions often deter popular musicians from entertaining in Malaysia.

Local bars and clubs that continue to supply great live music are Laundry Bar (p.402), Little Havana (p.402), Backyard Pub (p.405), Qba (p.410), Zouk (p.411) and Ruums (p.410).

The local independent music scene in Kuala Lumpur is experiencing an incredible revival. Acoustic singer-songwriters, metal bands, punks, hip hop heads, and even perfect-pitch chanteuses grace Kuala Lumpur with their presence. Local acts to watch out for include the rock and rap hybrid of Pop Shuvit (www.myspace.com/popshuvit), the local rocking expats, Benchmarx (www.myspace.com/thebenchmarx), peace-of-mind musicians Estrella (www.myspace.com/estrellaband), the percussive acoustic stylings of Reza Salleh (www.myspace.com/rezasalleh) and the sonically fuelled They Will Kill Us All (www.myspace.com/twkua).

Theatre

Other options **Drama Groups** p.229

Kuala Lumpur is the epicentre of the contemporary drama scene in Malaysia. There is no shortage of fodder for the culture vulture, from avant garde plays to West End

Benchmarx in action

National Theatre

comedies and satirical parodies. In recent years, interest in theatre has revived thanks chiefly to the small coterie of local performing arts enthusiasts who have fervently championed the nurturing of the performing arts. Recent years have seen the staging of internationally acclaimed productions like Cats, Saturday Night Fever and Fame, as well as local dramas. Arts portal Kakiseni (www.kakiseni.com) provides comprehensive information on the local arts scene as well as insightful reviews, while alternative lifestyle magazine Off The Edge provides provocative and incisive commentary on the arts and lifestyle scene of Malaysia. You can now indulge your theatre appetite from the comfort of your home by booking tickets online.

Sentul Park
Jalan Strachan
Ampang
🚉 *Sentul*

The Actors Studio
03 4047 9060 | www.theactorsstudio.com.my
A small contemporary performing arts space run by the country's top theatre company and featuring mainly local productions, it was set up by a husband-and-wife thespian team Joe Hasham and Faridah Merican. It also has a training academy responsible for churning out many of today's leading theatre practitioners. There are three venues: The Actors Studio Theatre, a 153 seat proscenium space at Plaza Putra, The Actors Studio Box, a 100 seat experimental space catering for the younger performing arts groups (this is a very popular venue for music, dance, drama and comedy), and The Actors Studio at Bangsar Shopping Complex, a 260 seat venue which is often credited as being responsible for bringing 'real' theatre to the mainstream public.

Jalan Tun Razak
City Centre
🚉 *Titiwangsa*

Istana Budaya (National Theatre)
03 4026 5558 | www.istanabudaya.gov.my
Breathtaking architecture aside, the country's largest theatre, modelled after the Kelantan kite, is the platform for big-ticket local and international acts. In recent years, Broadway musicals and West End plays have been shown here regularly, and there have also been performances by symphonic orchestras. Interest in local musicals has been revived by the recent success of Puteri Gunung Ledang, a legend about a princess.

Sentul Park
Jalan Strachan
Ampang
🚉 *Sentul*

Kuala Lumpur Performing Arts Centre
03 4047 9000 | www.klpac.com
Though a little out of the way, this award-winning space is a gem of an arts centre, which uses part of an abandoned 1930s railway godown as its architectural backbone. Set within the grounds of a landscaped area, it boasts a 500 seat main auditorium and a slew of auxiliary performing spaces. Managed by the Actors Studio, it stages a good mix of local and international performances. You can also have a picnic in the grounds or catch a light bite at the adjoining Japanese garden restaurant.

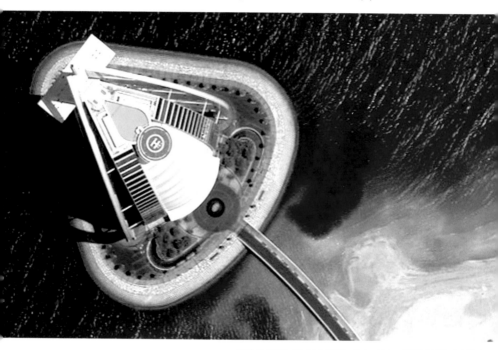

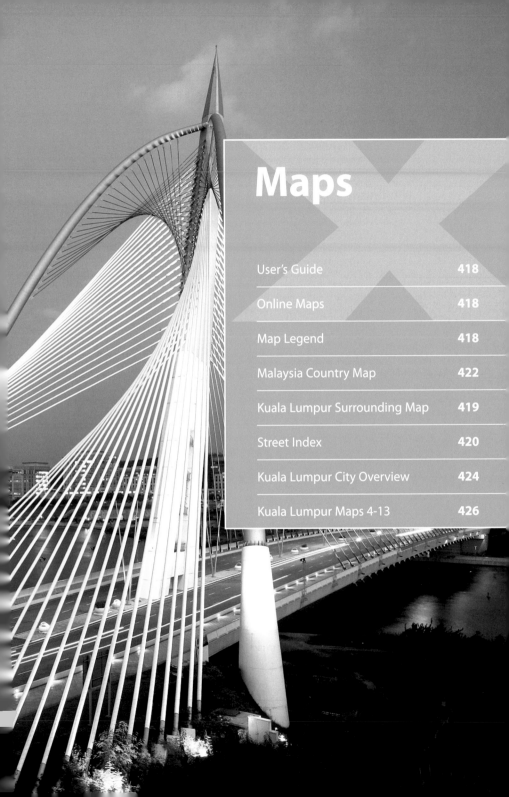

Maps

User's Guide

This section has detailed maps of Kuala Lumpur. They are intended to help you get your bearings when you first arrive, and give you an idea of where we're talking about in the main chapters of the book. The Kuala Lumpur City Overview on Map 3 shows the areas of the city covered. The maps are blown up nice and big, with the central areas (Map 8 to Map 13) on a 1cm=80m scale. The rest of the city (Map 4 to Map 7) has a scale of 1cm=300m. We've included the main hotels from the General Information chapter (see p.22) along with schools, hospitals, shopping malls, heritage sites and parks. See the legend below for an idea of which is which. We've also put on the Monorail and LRT stations.

The Area & Street Index (see p.420) should provide a quick way to find KL's best known places, and for the bigger picture there's even a map of the whole of Malaysia (1cm=90km) sitting on Map 2. The inside of the back cover has an easily accessible map of the city's Monorail and LRT stations.

More Maps

Beyond these maps and our own very nifty Kuala Lumpur Mini Map there are a number of street directories to be found in KL's bookshops and newsagents. 5 Simple Steps Using Kuala Lumpur Transit System, published by Far East Trading & Supplies, is a really handy guide to getting around the city, with a user-friendly layout.

Word On The Street

Citymap Publishing's Road Maps of Kuala Lumpur & Its Surroundings provides an authoritative geographical guide to the city.

Need More?

We understand that this residents' guide is a pretty big book: it needs to be, to carry all the info we have about living in KL. But, unless you've got the pockets of a clown, it's unlikely to be carried around with you on day trips. With this in mind, we've created the *Kuala Lumpur Mini Map* as a more manageable alternative - it packs the whole city into your pocket. It's part of a series of Mini Maps that includes cities as diverse as London, Dubai, New York and Barcelona. Wherever your travels take you, you'll never have to ask for directions again. Visit our website, www.explorerpublishing.com for details of how to pick up these little gems, or nip into any good bookshop.

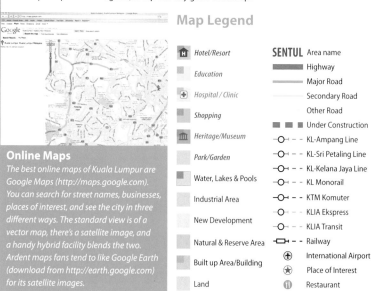

Map Legend

🏨	Hotel/Resort	**SENTUL**	Area name
▪	Education	▬▬▬	Highway
✚	Hospital / Clinic	▬▬	Major Road
▪	Shopping	▬	Secondary Road
🏛	Heritage/Museum		Other Road
	Park/Garden	■ ■ ■	Under Construction
	Water, Lakes & Pools	–O⊣ – –	KL-Ampang Line
	Industrial Area	–O⊣ – –	KL-Sri Petaling Line
	New Development	–O⊣ – –	KL-Kelana Jaya Line
	Natural & Reserve Area	–O⊣ – –	KL Monorail
	Built up Area/Building	–O⊣ – –	KTM Komuter
	Land	–O⊣ – –	KLIA Ekspress
		–O⊣ – –	KLIA Transit
		–▢⊣ – –	Railway
		⊕	International Airport
		⊛	Place of Interest
		ⓘ	Restaurant

Online Maps

The best online maps of Kuala Lumpur are Google Maps (http://maps.google.com). You can search for street names, businesses, places of interest, and see the city in three different ways. The standard view is of a vector map, there's a satellite image, and a handy hybrid facility blends the two. Ardent maps fans tend to like Google Earth (download from http://earth.google.com) for its satellite images.

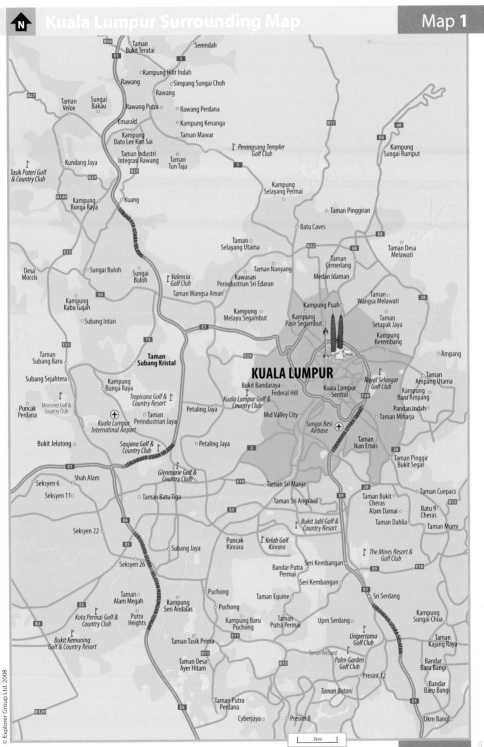

KUALA LUMPUR

Street Name	Map Ref
Federal Highway	6-D3 To 6-E3
Jalan 1 Au 3/1	5-F2
Jalan 1/48a	5-A2
Jalan 1/56	5-F1
Jalan 10/91	7-E2
Jalan 14/48	6-B4
Jalan 14/49 Jalan 51a/227	6-B4
Jalan 14/53 Jalan 22/32	6-A4
Jalan 16/6	6-C2
Jalan 17/1	6-C2
Jalan 17/21	6-B2
Jalan 17/22	6-B2
Jalan 19/70a	4-C3
Jalan 19/8	6-B3
Jalan 2/62	4-A1
Jalan 21/1 Jalan 19/1b	6-B3
Jalan 3/56	5-F1
Jalan 3/62 B	4-C1
Jalan 34/26	5-D1
Jalan 4/91	7-D2
Jalan 5/91	7-E2
Jalan 51a223	6-B4
Jalan 8/27a	5-E1
Jalan 9/48a	5-A1
Jalan Abang Haji Openg	6-B1
Jalan Ampang	5-D4
Jalan Ampang Hilir	5-E4
Jalan Ara	6-E2
Jalan Baidur	6-A4
Jalan Barat	6-C4
Jalan Beringin	4-D4
Jalan Besar	7-B4
Jalan Bukit 11/2	6-C3
Jalan Bukit Bintang	7-C1
Jalan Bukit Keramat	5-D3
Jalan Bukit Kiara 1/70 C	4-D3
Jalan Bukit Pandai	6-E2
Jalan Bunga Mawar	7-F3
Jalan Bunga Mewar 3	7-F3
Jalan Bunga Raya	7-F3
Jalan Burhanuddin Helmi	4-A4
Jalan Burung Hantu	4-B1
Jalan Cangkat Thambi Dollah	7-C1
Jalan Cempaka	7-F1
Jalan Cenderai	6-E2
Jalan Changgai 6/22	6-D4

Street Name	Map Ref
Jalan Chaya 1	7-F1
Jalan Cheras	7-C2
Jalan Cochrane	7-D2
Jalan Conlay	5-C4
Jalan Damansara	7-A1
Jalan Dato Abdul Aziz 14/29	6-B4
Jalan Dato Abu Bakar	6-C3
Jalan Datojamilrais15	6-B4
Jalan Datuk Sulaiman 2	4-B4
Jalan Davis	7-C1
Jalan Desa	6-F4
Jalan Desa Utama	6-F4
Jalan Duta	4-E3
Jalan Enggang	5-E3
Jalan Gombak	5-B1
Jalan Gurney	5-D3
Jalan Hangjebat	7-B1
Jalan I Poh	4-F1
Jalan Imbi	7-C1
Jalan Indah	7-E2
Jalan Istana	7-A2
Jalan Jejaka	7-D2
Jalan Jelawat	7-C3
Jalan Kampung Pandan	7-D1
Jalan Kelang Lama	6-F4
Jalan Kemajuan	6-C3
Jalan Keramat	5-E3
Jalan Kerinchi	6-E3
Jalan Kia Peng	5-C3
Jalan Kinabalu	7-A1
Jalan Kovil Hillir	5-A2
Jalan Kuantan	5-B2
Jalan Kuari	7-D4
Jalan Kuching	8-B3
Jalan Kuri	7-F3
Jalan L Yew	7-C2
Jalan Lang Emas	4-C1
Jalan Lang Perut Putih 8	4-C1
Jalan Latif (Jalan Tenteram)	7-D4
Jalan Leong Yew Koh	6-B1
Jalan Lingkaran Tengah 2	7-E1
Jalan Loke Yew	7-B2
Jalan Maarof	6-E1
Jalan Mahkota	7-D2
Jalan Majlis	6-A4
Jalan Makmur	6-A4

Street Name	Map Ref	Street Name	Map Ref
Jalan Pahang	5-B3	Jalan Taman Setiawangsa 37/56	5-E2
Jalan Pahang	5-C1	Jalan Titiwangsa	5-B2
Jalan Pahang Berat	5-A2	Jalan Tun Ismail	5-A3
Jalan Panadan Indah	7-F1	Jalan Tun Razak	8-C1
Jalan Pandan 1	5-E1	Jalan Tunku	4-F4
Jalan Pandan Aman	7-F2	Jalan Universiti	6-C3
Jalan Pandan Indah	7-F2	Jalan Universiti Jalan Gasing	6-D3
Jalan Pandan Kemajuan	7-F1	Jalan Utara	6-C4
Jalan Pandan Utama	7-F2	Jalan Wira	7-D1
Jalan Pantai Permai	6-E4	Jalan Yap Kwan Seng	5-C3
Jalan Parlimen	5-A4	Jalanchan Sow Lin	7-C3
Jalan Peel	7-C2	Jalanpa Ntai 9/7	6-D4
Jalan Penage	6-E1	Jalan Semantan	4-E4
Jalan Perkasa	7-E2	Jalan Tempinis	6-E2
Jalan Perkasa 1	7-D2	Jaya(22/43)	6-A2
Jalan Pertiwi	7-D1	Lebuh Raya Utara Selatan	4-B2
Jalan Pinang	5-C3	Lebuhraya Bertingkat Ampang	9-B4
Jalan Pju 7/9	4-A3	Lebuhraya Damansara - Punchong	6-A1
Jalan Pria	7-D1	Lebuhraya Hubungan Timuraa-Barat	7-A4
Jalan Pudu	7-B1	Lebuhraya Kuala Lumpur Seremban	7-B4
Jalan Raja Abdullah	5-B3	Lebuhraya Persekutuan Hwy	6-D3
Jalan Raja Laut	5-A4	Lebuhraya Sprint	4-D3
Jalan Raja Muda Abdul Aziz	5-B3	Lebuhraya Sungai Besi Hwy	7-B4
Jalan San Peng	7-B2	Persiaran Ampang Hilir	5-D4
Jalan Segambut	4-D2	Persiaran Ara	4-A1
Jalan Sekilau	7-C3	Persiaran Kenanga	4-A1
Jalan Semangat	6-B3	Pesiaran Dato Shamsuddin Naim	4-A1
Jalan Semarak	5-C3	Ss 22/ 11	6-A2
Jalan Sentul	5-A2		
Jalan Setia Bakti	4-D4		
Jalan Sri Hartamas 1	4-D4		
Jalan Sri Permaisuri	7-C4		
Jalan Sri Permaisuri 6	7-B4		
Jalan Ss 2/ 24	6-A3		
Jalan Ss 2/55	6-A3		
Jalan Ss 2/75	6-A3		
Jalan Ss 21/23	6-A1		
Jalan Ss 21/64	6-A2		
Jalan Ss 22/41	6-A2		
Jalan Ss 24/13	6-A3		
Jalan Ss 3/39	6-A4		
Jalan Sultan	6-C4		
Jalan Sultan Ismail	10-D1		
Jalan Sultanabdulsamad	7-A2		
Jalan Syed Putra	6-F3		
Jalan Taman Bukit Maluri Jalan Lang Emas	4-B1		

Map **2**   Malaysia Country Map

Map **2**

PHILIPPINES

Sulu Sea

Pulau Balambangan   *Pulau Banggi*

Kudat○

Pulau Jambongan
Beluran

○ Kota Marudu

○ Kota Belud

Kota Kinabalu

Kota Kinabalu   ○ Ranau   ⊕ Sandakan
Penampang

Kuala Penyu

Tambunan   Beluran

Labuan   ○ Beaufort   ○ Keningau   Tongod   A5

○ Tenom   ⊕   ○ Lahad Datu
Bunut
Telisai○ ○Bangar   ○Labu   Kunak○
Kuala Belait○ ○Bukok   ○ Sipitang   Nabawan   Tawau○   *Pulau Timbun Mata*
Limbang   ○   Tawau   ○Sempoma
○Pulau Sebatik
BRUNEI   *Tarakan*
DARUSSALAM
○Miri

○ Marudi   Celebes Sea

Bintulu○ ○ Bintulu

○Daro   ○Mukah   Tatau○   **MALAYSIA**
Dalat○   Sibu○
Meradong○   ○Sibu   ○ Belaga
Sarikei○
○Kanowit
Saratok○   ○Julau
Kuching○   ○Asajaya   ○Betong   ○ Kapit
Bau○   ○Simunjan
Sri Aman○   ○Lubok Antu
Ledo○   ○Serian   ○Donao Luar
Benkayang○   Donao Genali○
Sidas○   Ngabang○
○Sosok
Sanggau○   ○Sintang   Mahakam○   Muarabadak
Meliau○   ○Sekadau   Tenggarong○   ○Samarinda
○Nangah Pinoh   Loakulu○
INDONESIA   Lohjanan○

○Nanga Tayap   Balikpapan○

○Ketapang   Barito○   Makassar Strait

Tanahgrogot○
○Kendawangan   ○Tanjung
Amuntai○   ○Tabudarat
Kandangan○
○Rantau
Bandjermasin○
Java Sea   ○Martapura   ○Pagatan

100km

Map **2**

Map **3** Kuala Lumpur City Overview

N

4

BANDAR SRI DAMANSARA

BANDAR MANJALARA

TAMAN SRI MANJALARA

TAMAN NOVA 2

TAMAN SRI KEPONG BARU

TAMAN SRI SEGAMBURT

TAMAN KOK DOH

TAMAN RAINBOW

KG PASIR SEGAMBUT

TAMAN BAMBOO

SEGAMBUT LUAR

Menaru Multiara

KG SEGAMBUT BAHAGIA

SEGAMBUT MILLION

TAMAN MILLION

TAMAN SEGAMBUT

NORTH SOUTH EXPRESSWAY

JALAN KUCHING

BUKIT SEGAMBUT

KG SEGAMBUT TENGAH

KG KASIPILLAY

KG SEGAMBUT

HARTAMAS HEIGHTS

JALAN DUTA JALAN DUTA

KG PALIMBAYAN

MONT KIARA

DUTA NUSANTARA

BUKIT LANJAN

SRI HARTAMAS

BUKIT TUNKU

KG SUNGAI PENCALA

Plaza Damas

TAMAN DESA SRI HARTAMAS

SPRINT HIGHWAY

TAMAN SRI HARTAMAS

JALAN DUTA

TAMAN DUTA

The Curve The Royale Bintang

Tesco

IKEA

TAMAN TUN DR ISMAIL

DAMANSARA HEIGHTS

JALAN SEMANTAN

BANDAR UTAMA

I Utama

Lembah Kiara Park

Plaza Damansara

Duta Vista

6

One World

DAMANSARA HEIGHTS

Giant MENOM MILLERURM

JELUTUNG VILLAS

TAMAN SA

Carcosa Sri Negara

PETALING JAYA

TAMANTUN DR ISMAIL

Kiara Forest Park

Bangsor Shopping Centre

Centre Point

DAMANSARA UTAMA

Plaza Ibm

Kuala Lumpur Golf & Country Club KLGCC

SPRINT HIGHWAY

MEDAN DAMANSARA

BANGSAR HILL

TAMAN BANDARAYA

FEDERAL HILL

JALAN DAMANSARA

Dansara Specialist Hospital

JALAN SS 21/64

Kelab Golf Perkhidmatan Awam Malatsia

BANGSAR

Hilton

Atria

E11

TAMAN SENTOSA

E23

Eastin

JALAN DAMANSARA

BANGSAR BARU

Bangsar Village

Bangsar

TAMAN BAN LEE

UNIVERSITI MALAYA

SPRINT HIGHWAY

BUKIT PANTAI

JALAN SYED PUTRA

TAMAN SEA

LEBUHRAYA DAMANSARA PUNCHING

HAPPY GARDEN

Lisa De Inn

Abdullah Hukum

Boulevard Cititel Mid Valley

Ritz Garden

TAMAN PESIARAN DESA

Kerinchi

Taman Bahagia

Jaya Shopping Centre

Crystal Crown

LEBUH RAYA PERSEKUTUAN (FEDERAL HIGHWAY)

Universiti

KG KERINCHI

2

SEPUTEH

TAMAN PARAMOUNT

Asia Jaya

Armada

Taman Jaya

TAMAN BUKIT ANGKASA

NEW PANTAI EXPRESSWAY

TAMAN SRI LEMBAH

Taman Paramount

Crystal Plaza

PJ Hilton

Shah Village

PANTAI HILL PARK

SERI PANTAI

JALAN KELANG LAMA

KG TUNKU

TAMAN LEAN SEAN

Giant Colirts Mamnath

DESA AMAN 2

TAMAN SHANGHAI

TAMAN UNIVERSITY

KG PANTAI

Taman Desa Medical Centre

© Explorer Group Ltd. 2009

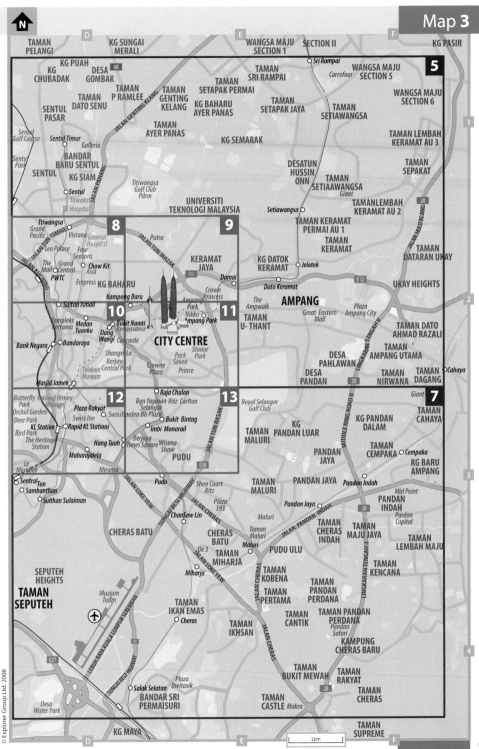

Map **3**

N

TAMAN
PELANGI

KG SUNGAI
MERALI

WANGSA MAJU
SECTION 1

SECTION II

KG PASIR

5

KG PUAH

KG
CHUBADAK

DESA
GOMBAK

68

TAMAN
SRI RAMPAI

Sri Rampai

Carrefour

WANGSA MAJU
SECTION 5

TAMAN
P RAMLEE

TAMAN
GENTING
KELANG

TAMAN
SETAPAK PERMAI

WANGSA MAJU
SECTION 6

TAMAN
DATO SENU

KG BAHARU
AYER PANAS

TAMAN
SETAPAK JAYA

TAMAN
SETIAWANGSA

SENTUL
PASAR

TAMAN
AYER PANAS

KG SEMARAK

TAMAN LEMBAH
KERAMAT AU 3

Sentul
Golf Course

Sentul Timur

Galleria

DESATUN
HUSSIN
ONN

TAMAN
SEPAKAT

Sentul
Park

BANDAR
BARU SENTUL

Titiwangsa
Golf Club
Pdrm

TAMAN
SETIAAWANGSA
Giant

SENTUL

KG SIAM

Sentul
Tawakal
TB Hospital

UNIVERSITI
TEKNOLOGI MALAYSIA

Setiawangsa

TAMANLEMBAH
KERAMAT AU 2

28

TAMAN
DATARAN UKAY

Ttiwangsa
Grand
Pacific

8

Putra

TAMAN KERAMAT
PERMAI AU 1

9

Vistana

General
Hospital

KERAMAT
JAYA

TAMAN
KERAMAT

Leo Palace

Four
Seasons

E12

The
Mall

Grand
Central

Chow Kit

Damai

KG DATOK
KERAMAT

Jelatek

UKAY HEIGHTS

PWTC

Empress

KG BAHARU

Crown
Princess

Dato Keramat

E12

AMPANG

Sultan Ismail

Kampong Baru

Ampang
Park

The
Ampwalk

Great Eastern
Mall

Plaza
Ampang City

TAMAN DATO
AHMAD RAZALI

Kompleks
Pertama

10

Medan
Tuanku

Bukit Nanas

Nikko

Park

TAMAN
U- THANT

TAMAN
AMPANG UTAMA

Bank Negara

Bandaraya

Dang
Wangi

Renaissance

Concorde

Ampang Park

11

CITY CENTRE

Shangri La

Berjaya
Central Park

Park
Seven

Stonor
Park

DESA
PAHLAWAN

TAMAN
NIRWANA

TAMAN
DAGANG

Cahaya

Masjid Jamek

Telekom
Museum

Crowne
Plaza

Prince

DESA
PANDAN

28

Butterfly
Park

National History
Museum

12

Raja Chulan

Bgn Yayasan Ritz Carlton
Selangor

13

Royal Selangor
Golf Club

Giant

7

Orchid Garden
Deer Park

Plaza Rakyat

Swiss Inn

SwissGarden Bb Plaza

Bukit Bintag

TAMAN
MALURI

KG
PANDAN LUAR

KG PANDAN
DALAM

TAMAN
CAHAYA

Bird Park

The Heritage
Station

KL Station

Rapid KL Stationi

Imbi Monorail

Berjaya
Times Square Wisena
Shaw

PANDAN
JAYA

TAMAN
CEMPAKA

Cempaka

KG BARU
AMPANG

Hang Tuah

PUDU

Maharajalela

Mirama

E38

TAMAN
MALURI

PANDAN JAYA

Pandan Indah

PANDAN
INDAH

Le
Merkdek

Pudu

ChanSow Lin

Shen Court
Ritz

Plaza
393

Maluri

Pandan Jaya

JALAN PANDAN INDAH

Mid Point

28

Pardon
Capital

Sentral
Sambanthan

Tun

CHERAS BATU

JALAN CHERAS

TAMAN
CHERAS
INDAH

TAMAN
MAJU JAYA

Sulthan Sulaiman

CHERAS
BATU

Taman
Maluri

Maluri

PUDU ULU

TAMAN
LEMBAH MAJU

SEPUTEH
HEIGHTS

Muzium
Tudm

Ije 3

TAMAN
MIHARJA

TAMAN
KOBENA

TAMAN
PANDAN
PERDANA

TAMAN
KENCANA

TAMAN
SEPUTEH

Miharja

TAMAN
IKAN EMAS

Cheras

TAMAN
PERTAMA

TAMAN
CANTIK

TAMAN PANDAN
PERDANA
Pandan
Safari

TAMAN
IKHSAN

KAMPUNG
CHERAS BARU

E27

Plaza
Dwitasik

TAMAN
BUKIT MEWAH

TAMAN
RAKYAT

Desa
Water Park

Salak Selatan

BANDAR SRI
PERMAISURI

TAMAN
CASTLE

Makra

TAMAN
CHERAS

KG MAYA

TAMAN
SUPREME

1km

© Explorer Group Ltd. 2008

Map **4**

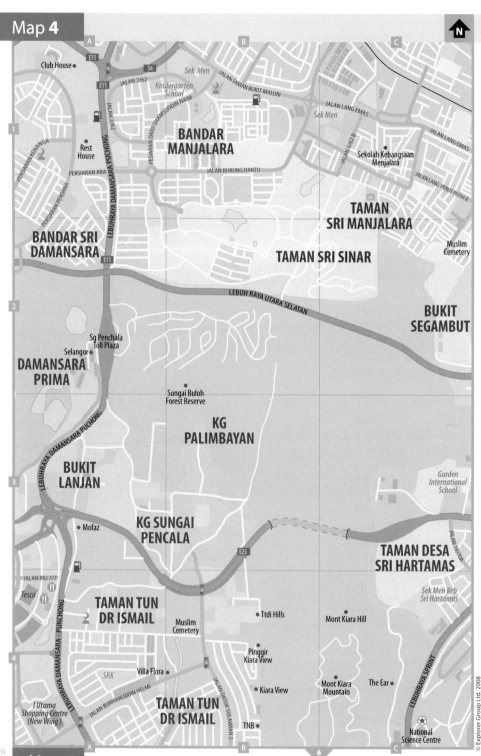

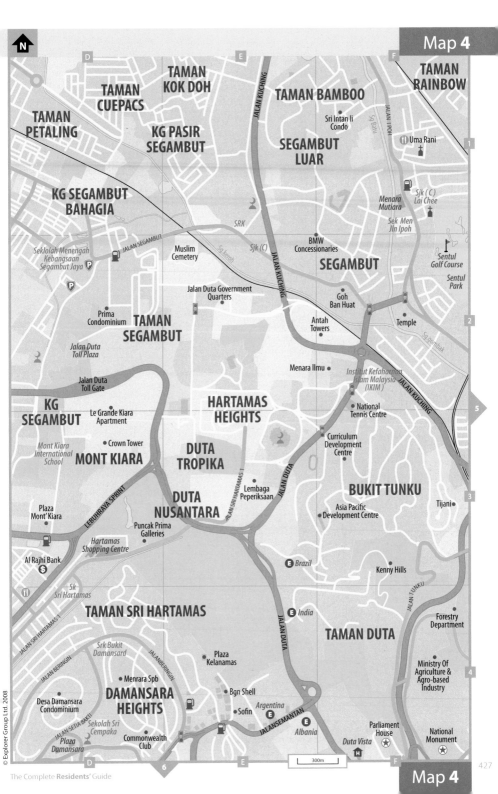

Map **4**

N

TAMAN
RAINBOW

TAMAN
KOK DOH

TAMAN
CUEPACS

TAMAN BAMBOO

Sri Intan Ii
Condo

Uma Rani

TAMAN
PETALING

KG PASIR
SEGAMBUT

SEGAMBUT
LUAR

KG SEGAMBUT
BAHAGIA

Menara
Mutiara

Sjk (C)
Lai Chee

Sek Men
Jln Ipoh

SRK

Sjk (C)

BMW
Concessionaries

SEGAMBUT

Sentul
Golf Course

Sekolah Menengah
Kebangsaan
Segambut Jaya

JALAN SEGAMBUT

Muslim
Cemetery

Sentul
Park

Jalan Duta Government
Quarters

Goh
Ban Huat

Temple

Prima
Condominium

TAMAN
SEGAMBUT

Antah
Towers

Jalan Duta
Toll Plaza

Menara Ilmu

Institut Kefahaman
Islam Malaysia
(IKIM)

Jalan Duta
Toll Gate

HARTAMAS
HEIGHTS

National
Tennis Centre

KG
SEGAMBUT

Le Grande Kiara
Apartment

Curriculum
Development
Centre

Crown Tower

Mont Kiara
International
School

DUTA
TROPIKA

BUKIT TUNKU

MONT KIARA

Tijani

Plaza
Mont'Kiara

DUTA
NUSANTARA

Lembaga
Peperiksaan

Asia Pacific
Development Centre

Puncak Prima
Galleries

Hartamas
Shopping Centre

Al Rajhi Bank

Brazil

Kenny Hills

5k
Sri Hartamas

India

TAMAN SRI HARTAMAS

Forestry
Department

TAMAN DUTA

Srk Bukit
Damansard

Plaza
Kelanamas

Ministry Of
Agriculture &
Agro-based
Industry

Menrara Spb

DAMANSARA
HEIGHTS

Bgn Shell

Desa Damansara
Condominium

Sofin

Argentina

Sekolah Sri
Cempaka

Albania

Parliament
House

National
Monument

Plaza
Damansara

Commonwealth
Club

Duta Vista

300m

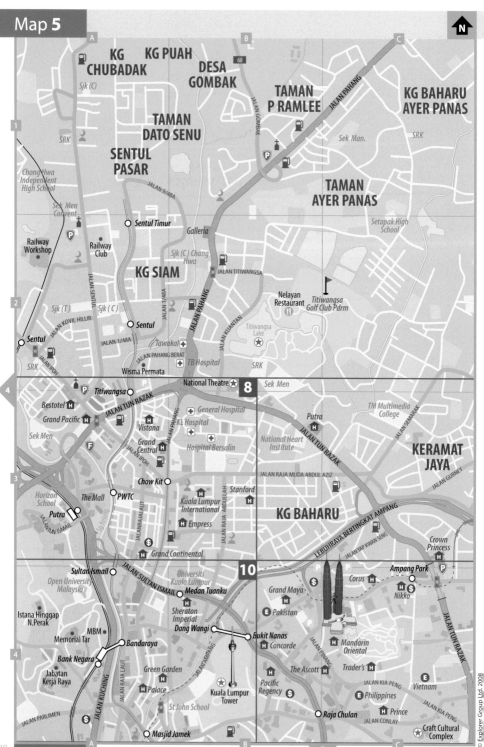

Map **5**

Map **5**

Kuala Lumpur Explorer 1st Edition

© Explorer Group Ltd. 2008

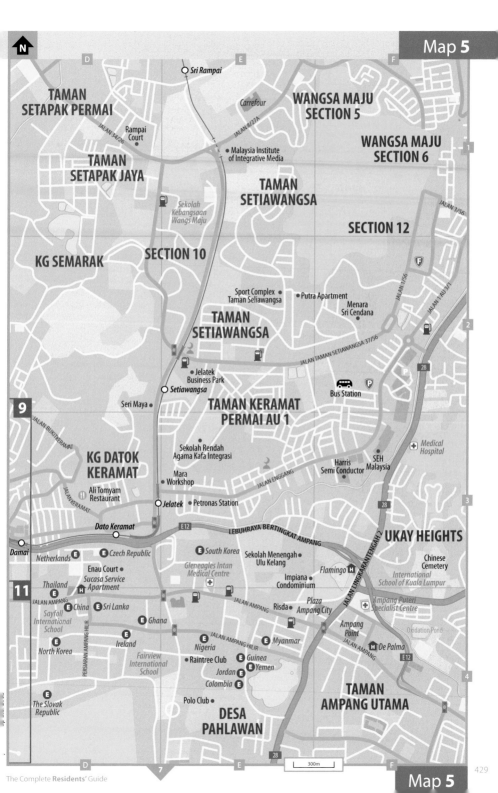

Map 6

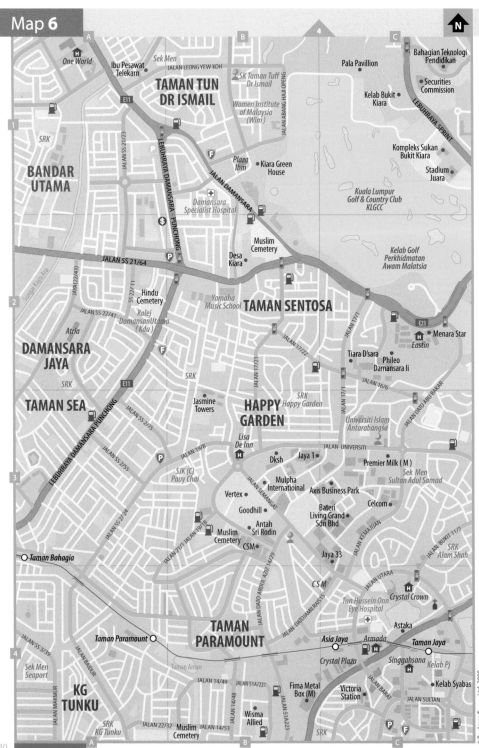

DAMANSARA
TOWN CENTRE

✝ Calvary Church

TAMAN SA

Kelab Perdana

Carcosa
Seri Negara

DAMANSARA
HEIGHTS

Desa Bistari

Famnah View

Bangsar
Shopping Centre

Galeri
Sri Perdana

Sek Men

Lake Gardens

Istana
Tetamu

Institut Tadbiran Awam
Negara Malaysia
(Intan)

BANGSAR
HILL

JALAN MAAROF

Bangsar Indah

FEDERAL HILL

MEDAN
DAMANSARA

TAMAN
BANDARAYA

Istana Hinggap
N Kedah

Sri Bayu

JALAN DAMANSARA

JALAN PINGGE

BANGSAR
BARU

JALAN MAAROF

Sek Men

Nusa
Rhu

Institute of Public
Health

Akademi
Pengajian Islam

The
Tuscany

JALAN ARA

Maktab
Kesihatan Umun
Dental Clinic

Kolej Kediaman
Ke 10

Kompleks
Squash

JALAN CENDERAI

Bangsar
Village

Universiti Malaya
Sports Club

SRK

Bangsar

DbkI Sports
Club

SRK
SJK (C)

Kolej Kelapan

SPRINT HIGHWAY

TAMAN BUKIT
PANTAI

JALAN TEMPONG

UNIVERSITI
MALAYA

Kotej
Kelino

JALAN BUKIT PANDAI

Bangsar
Heights

Police
Quarters

Robson
Court

Kolej Ketujuh

Jabatan
Fizik

Institute Pengojian
Tinggi Soins

JALAN SYED PUTRA

Ritz
Garden

Rumah Naib
Canselor

Jabatan
Botani

Makma
Sains

Pantai Tower

TNB

Casa Elilta

Kesatuan Mahasitwa

Institute Bahasa
Malaysia

Pantai Hospital

Abdullah Hukum
Boulevard

Mid Valley

The Japan
Club of KL

Sri Seputih

Fakulti
Undang - Undang

Padang Hockey &
Cricket

Mid Valley

Asrama
Penuntut Penuntut

Menara
Atlas

Kerinchi

LEBUHRAYA PERSEKUTUAN HWY

Seputeh

Kota
Darul Ehsan

Universiti

KG KERINCHI

Angkasapuri

SEPUTEH

JALAN UNIVERSITI

University
Tower

LEBUHRAYA PERSEKUTUAN HWY

Trinity
Methodist Church

Pusat Siaran
Antarabangsa

Madrasah
Al-insaniyah

PETALING
LAMA

JALAN KERINCHI

Faber Ria

JALAN GASING

Gemilong Indah

JALAN DESA UTAMA

Assembly
Of God

JALAN PANTAI PERMAI

Faber
Heights

Dera
Plaza

DESA
AMAN 1

Muslim
Cemetery

JALAN KELANG LAMA

Sek Men
Assunta

Sek Men
La Salle

Selangor

Indah Water
Konsortrum

TAMAN
SHANGHAI

Danau
Idaman

JALAN CHANGGAI 6/22

KG PANTAI

OXIDATION
POND

Desa Business
Park

300m

© e.xplorer Group Ltd. 2008

Map **7**

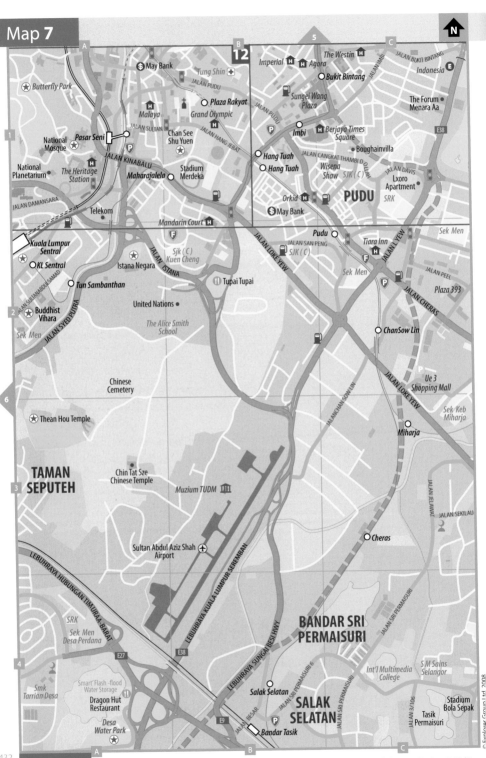

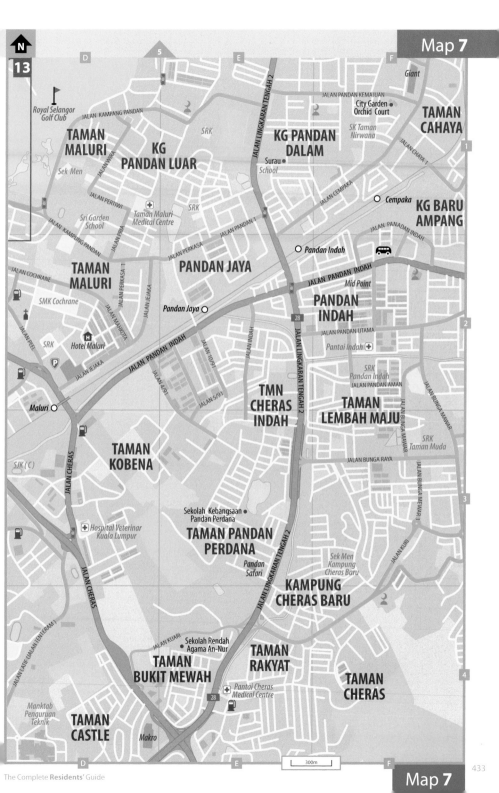

Map 7

N

13

Royal Selangor
Golf Club

TAMAN
MALURI

Sek Men

JALAN WIRA

JALAN KAMPANG PANDAN

KG
PANDAN LUAR

JALAN PERTIWI

Sri Garden
School

JALAN PRIA

JALAN KAMPUNG PANDAN

SRK

Taman Maluri
Medical Centre

SRK

Giant

JALAN PANDAN KEMAJUAN

City Garden
Orchid Court

TAMAN
CAHAYA

SK Taman
Nirwana

KG PANDAN
DALAM

Surau
School

JALAN LINGKARAN TENGAH 2

JALAN CEMPAKA

JALAN CHAYA 1

Cempaka

KG BARU
AMPANG

JALAN PANADAN INDAH

1

JALAN COCHRANE

TAMAN
MALURI

SMK Cochrane

JALAN PERKASA 1

JALAN MAHKOTA

JALAN JEJAKA

JALAN PERKASA

PANDAN JAYA

Pandan Jaya

Pandan Indah

JALAN PANDAN INDAH

JALAN PANDAN 1

Mid Point

PANDAN
INDAH

JALAN PANDAN UTAMA

Pantai Indah

2

JALAN PEEL

SRK

Hotel Maluri

JALAN JEJAKA

P

JALAN PANDAN INDAH

JALAN 10/91

JALAN 4/91

JALAN 5/91

JALAN PANDAN INDAH

28

JALAN LINGKARAN TENGAH 2

TMN
CHERAS
INDAH

SRK
Pandan Indah

JALAN PANDAN AMAN

TAMAN
LEMBAH MAJU

JALAN BUNGA MAWAR

JALAN BUNGA MAWAR

SRK
Taman Muda

Maluri

JALAN CHERAS

SJK (C)

TAMAN
KOBENA

JALAN BUNGA RAYA

JALAN BUNGA MEWAR 3

JALAN KURI

3

Hospital Veterinar
Kuala Lumpur

Sekolah Kebangsaan
Pandan Perdana

TAMAN PANDAN
PERDANA

Pandan
Safari

JALAN LINGKARAN TENGAH 2

Sek Men
Kampung
Cheras Baru

JALAN CHERAS

KAMPUNG
CHERAS BARU

JALAN LATIF (JALAN TENTERAM)

JALAN KUARI

Sekolah Rendah
Agama An-Nur

TAMAN
BUKIT MEWAH

TAMAN
RAKYAT

Pantai Cheras
Medical Centre

TAMAN
CHERAS

4

Manktab
Penguruan
Teknik

TAMAN
CASTLE

Makro

28

300m

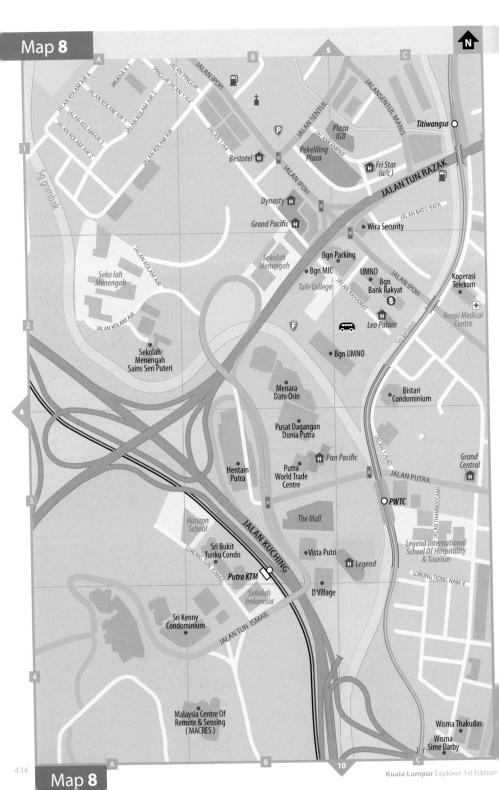

Map 8

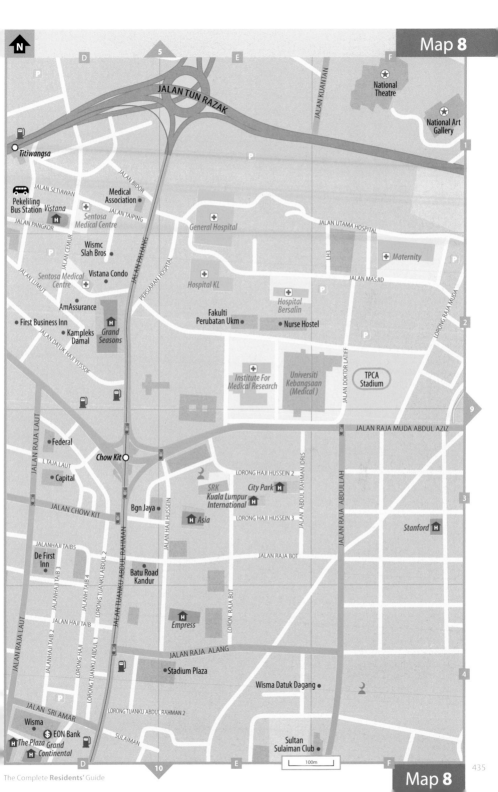

Map **8**

N

JALAN TUN RAZAK

D

E

F

National
Theatre

National Art
Gallery

JALAN KUANTAN

1

Titiwangsa

JALAN SETIAWAN

Pekeliling
Bus Station Vistana

JALAN PANGKOR

Medical
Association ●

JALAN TAIPING

Sentosa
Medical Centre

JALAN BIDOR

General Hospital

JALAN UTAMA HOSPITAL

Maternity

JALAN CEMUR

Wismc
Slah Bros ●

JALAN LUMUT

Sentosa Medical
Centre

Vistana Condo

Hospital KL

JALAN MASJID

Hospital
Bersalin

LORONG RAJA MUDA

P

AmAssurance

● First Business Inn

JALAN DATUK HAJI YUSSOF

● Kampleks
Damal

Grand
Seasons

Fakulti
Perubatan Ukm ●

● Nurse Hostel

2

JALAN PAHANG

PERSIARAN HOSPITAL

Institute For
Medical Research

Universiti
Kebangsaan
(Medical)

JALAN DOKTOR LATIEF

TPCA
Stadium

9

JALAN RAJA MUDA ABDUL AZIZ

JALAN RAJA LAUT

● Federal

L TAJA LAUT

● Capital

Chow Kit ○

JALAN CHOW KIT

Bgn Jaya ●

JALAN HAJI HUSSEIN

LORONG HAJI HUSSEIN 2

SRK
Kuala Lumpur
International

City Park

Asia

LORONG HAJI HUSSEIN 3

JALAN ABDUL RAHMAN IDRIS

JALAN ABDUL RAHMAN

JALAN RAJA ABDULLAH

Stanford

3

JALANHAJI TAIBS

De First
Inn

JALANHAJI TAIB 3

JALAN H TAIB 4

JALAN HAJI TAIB

JALANHAJI TAIB 2

LORONG TUANKU ABDUL 1

LORONG TUANKU ABDUL 2

JALAN TUANKU ABDUL RAHMAN

Batu Road
Kandur

JALAN RAJA BOT

LORON RAJA BOT

Empress

JALAN RAJA ALANG

JALAN RAJA LAUT

LORONG HAJI

JALAN SRI AMAR

Wisma

The Plaza

EON Bank

Grand
Continental

LORONG TUANKU ABDUL RAHMAN 2

SULAIMAN

● Stadium Plaza

Wisma Datuk Dagang ●

Sultan
Sulaiman Club ●

4

D

E

F

100m

Map **8**

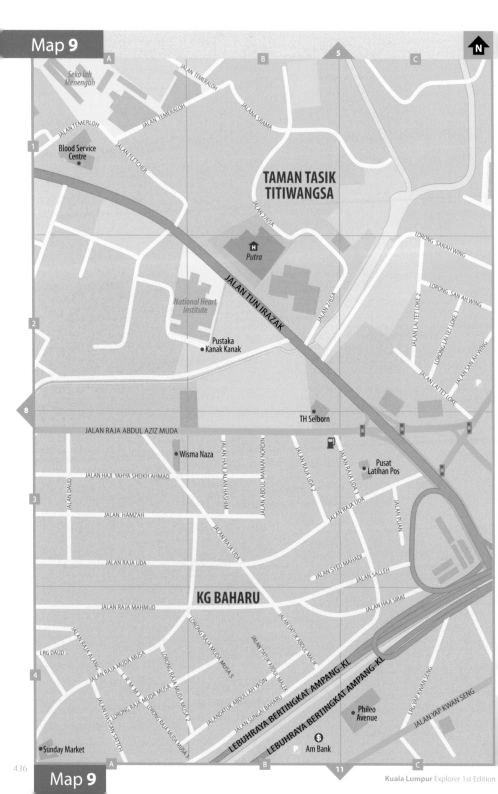

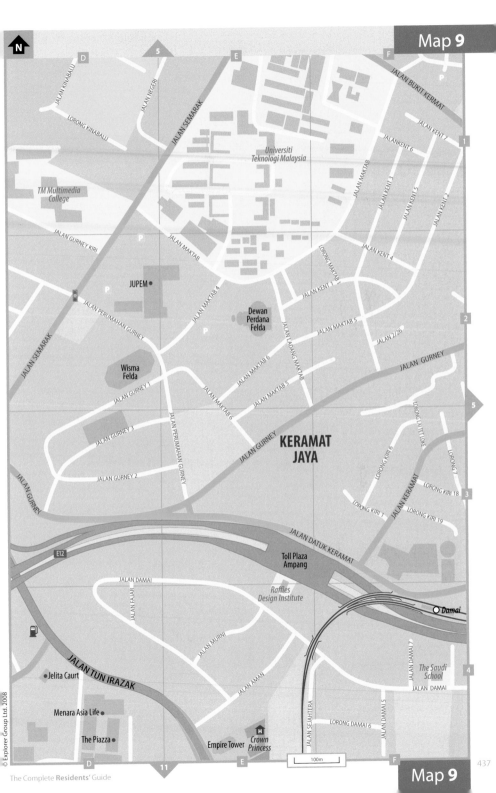

Map **9**

© Explorer Group Ltd. 2008

Universiti Teknologi Malaysia

TM Multimedia College

JUPEM ●

Dewan Perdana Felda

Wisma Felda

KERAMAT JAYA

Toll Plaza Ampang

Raffles Design Institute

○ Damai

The Saudi School

Jelita Caurt ●

Menara Asia Life ●

The Piazza ●

Empire Tower

Crown Princess

JALAN TUN IRAZAK

JALAN KINABALU
LORONG KINABALU
JALAN NEGERI
JALAN SEMARAK
JALAN BUKIT KERMAT
JALAN KENT 7
JALANKENT 6
JALAN MAKTAB
JALAN KENT 3
JALAN KENT 5
JALAN KENT 2
JALAN KENT 4
JALAN KENT 1
LORONG MAKTAB 1
JALAN GURNEY KIRI
JALAN MAKTAB
JALAN MAKTAB 4
JALAN PERUMAHAN GURNEY
JALAN MAKTAB 5
JALAN 2/26
JALAN SEMARAK
JALAN MAKTAB 6
JALAN LADANG MAKTAB
JALAN MAKTAB 5
JALAN GURNEY
JALAN GURNEY 1
JALAN MAKTAB 6
JALAN PERUMAHAN GURNEY
JALAN GURNEY
LORONG C KIRI 6
LORONG LAUTET LOKE
LORONG 7
JALAN GURNEY 3
LORONG KIRI 18
LORONG 7
JALAN GURNEY 2
LORONG KIRI 1
JALAN KERAMAT
LORONG KIRI 19
JALAN GURNEY
JALAN DATUK KERAMAT
E12
JALAN DAMAI
JALAN FAJAR
JALAN DAMAI 7
JALAN MURNI
JALAN DAMAI
JALAN AMAN
JALAN DAMAI 5
JALAN SELAHTERA
LORONG DAMAI 6

100m

N

Map **10**

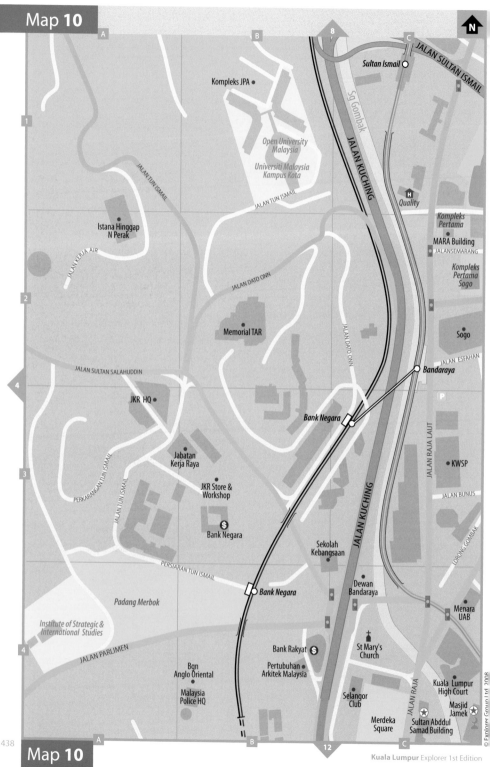

© Explorer Group Ltd. 2008

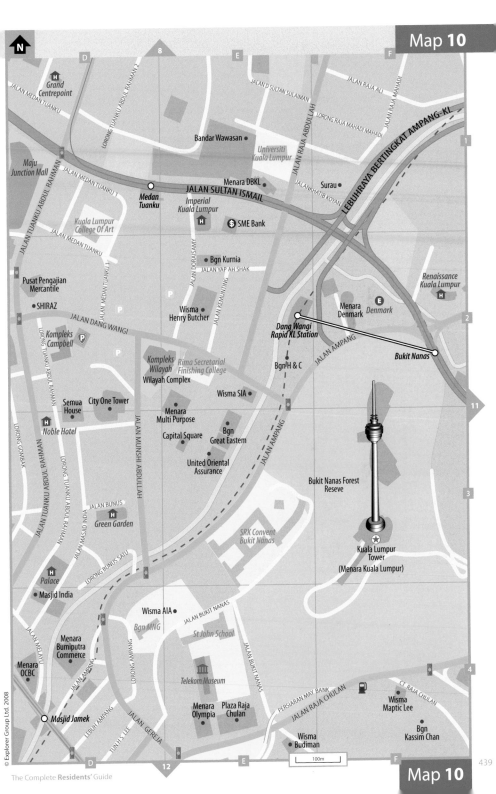

Map **10**

Map **11**

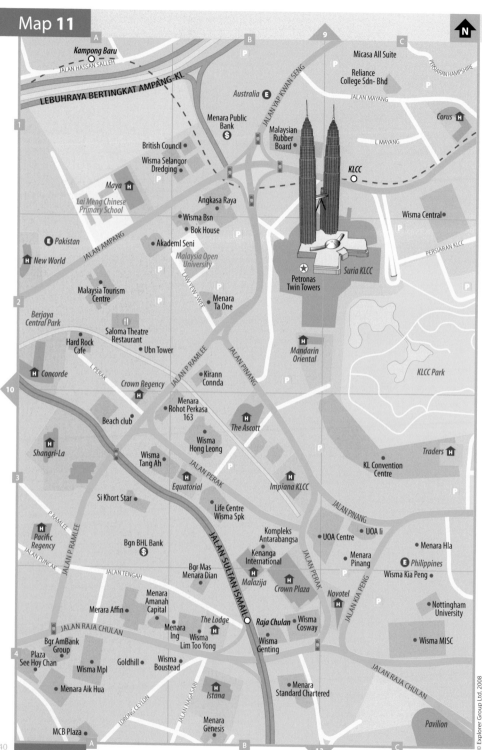

Kampong Baru

JALAN HASSAN SALLEH

LEBUHRAYA BERTINGKAT AMPANG-KL

Australia

Micasa All Suite

Reliance
College Sdn- Bhd

Menara Public
Bank

JALAN MAYANG

Corus

Malaysian
Rubber Board

L MAYANG

British Council

Wisma Selangor
Dredging

KLCC

Wisma Central

Maya

Lai Meng Chinese
Primary School

Angkasa Raya

Wisma Bsn

Bok House

Pakistan

Akademl Seni

New World

JALAN AMPANG

Malaysia Open
University

PERSIARAN KLCC

JALAN YEW SWEE

Menara
Ta One

Petronas
Twin Towers

Suria KLCC

Berjaya
Central Park

Saloma Theatre
Restaurant

KLCC Park

Hard Rock
Cafe

Ubn Tower

JALAN P. RAMLEE

JALAN PINANG

Mandarin
Oriental

Concorde

L PERAK

Crown Regency

Kirann
Connda

Traders

Beach club

Menara
Rohot Perkasa
163

The Ascott

Shangri-La

Wisma
Tang Ah

Wisma
Hong Leong

KL Convention
Centre

JALAN PERAK

Equatorial

Impiana KLCC

Si Khort Star

Life Centre
Wisma Spk

JALAN PINANG

P RAMLEE

Kompleks
Antarabangsa

UOA li

Pacific
Regency

JALAN P RAMLEE

Bgn BHL Bank

UOA Centre

Menara Hla

JALAN PUNCAK

JALAN TENGAH

Kenanga
International

Menara
Pinang

Philippines

Wisma Kia Peng

Bgr Mas
Menara Dian

JALAN SULTAN ISMAIL

Malazija

Crown Plaza

JALAN PERAK

Novotel

JALAN KIA PENG

Nottingham
University

Menara
Amanah
Capital

Merara Affin

Raja Chulan

Wisma
Cosway

Wisma MISC

JALAN RAJA CHULAN

Bgr AmBank
Group

Menara
Ing

The Lodge

Wisma
Genting

Plaza
See Hoy Chan

Wisma
Lim Too Yong

JALAN RAJA CHULAN

Wisma Mpl

Goldhill

Wisma
Boustead

Menara Aik Hua

JALAN NAGASARI

Istana

Menara
Standard Chartered

LORONG CEYLON

Pavilion

MCB Plaza

Menara
Genesis

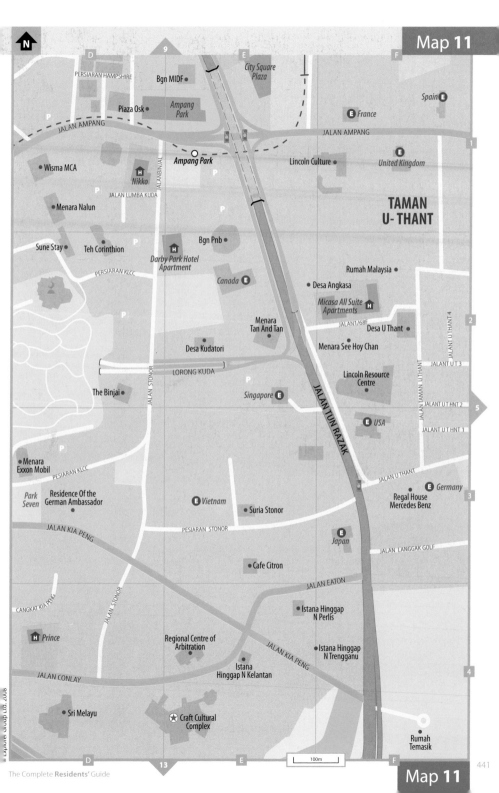

Map **11**

N

PERSIARAN HAMPSHIRE

Bgn MIDF ●

City Square Plaza

Spain **E**

Piaza Osk ●

Ampang Park

E France

JALAN AMPANG

JALAN AMPANG

● Wisma MCA

H Nikko

○ Ampang Park

Lincoln Culture ●

E United Kingdom

JALAN LUMBA KUDA

● Menara Nalun

TAMAN U-THANT

Sune Stay ●

● Teh Corinthion

Bgn Pnb ●

H Darby Park Hotel Apartment

PERSIARAN KLCC

Rumah Malaysia ●

Canada **E**

● Desa Angkasa

Micasa All Suite Apartments **H**

Menara Tan And Tan

JALAN1/68F

Desa U Thant ●

JALANT U THANT 4

Desa Kudatori ●

Menara See Hoy Chan

LORONG KUDA

Lincoln Resource Centre

JALANT U T 3

JALAN TAMAN U THANT

The Binjai ●

Singapore **E**

JALANT U T HNT 2

E USA

JALANT U T HNT 1

● Menara Exxon Mobil

PESIARAN KLCC

JALAN U THANT

E Germany

Park Seven

Residence Of the German Ambassador

Regal House Mercedes Benz

E Vietnam

● Suria Stonor

PESIARAN STONOR

JALAN KIA PENG

JALAN LANGGAK GOLF

E Japan

● Cafe Citron

JALAN EATON

● Istana Hinggap N Perlis

CANGKAT KIA PENG

● Istana Hinggap N Trengganu

H Prince

Regional Centre of Arbitration

JALAN KIA PENG

JALAN STONOR

Istana Hinggap N Kelantan

JALAN CONLAY

● Sri Melayu

★ Craft Cultural Complex

Rumah Temasik

100m

Map **12**

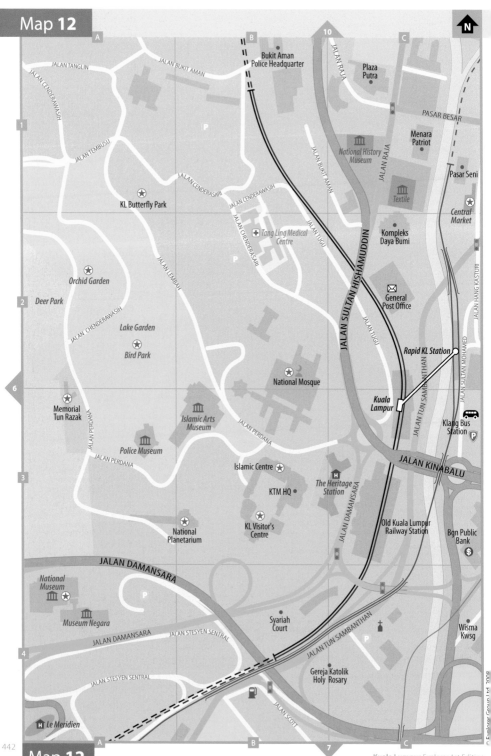

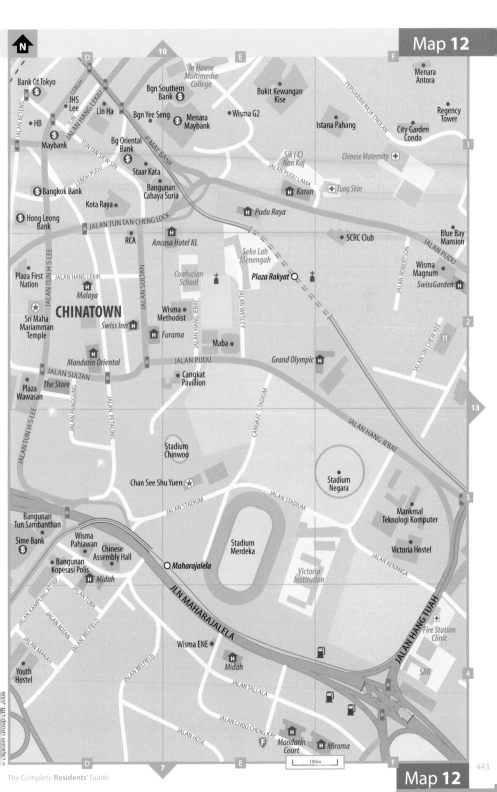

Map **12**

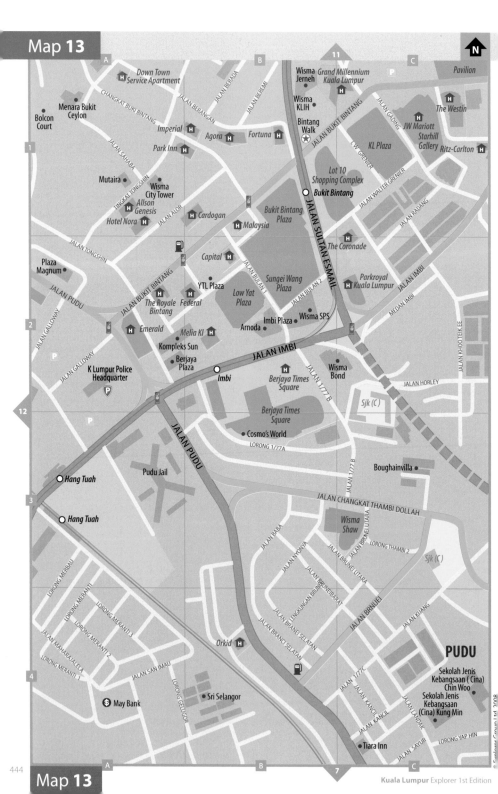

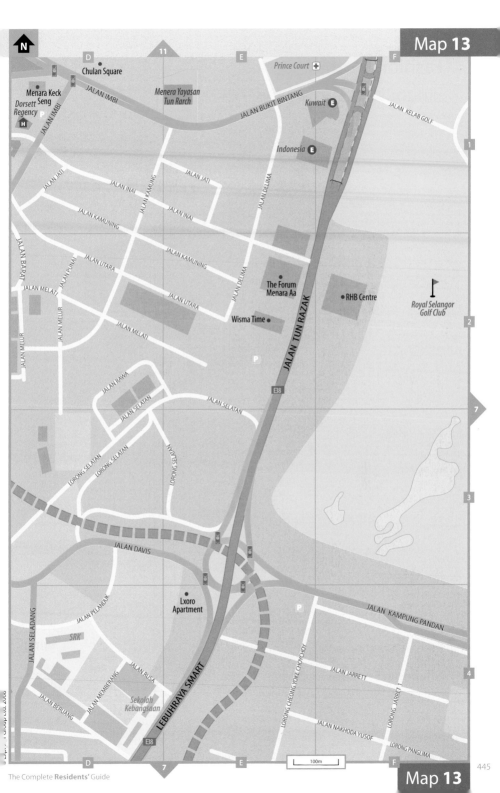

Map **13**

Fashion Boutiques p.123
Financial Advisors p.95

Written by residents, the Shanghai Explorer is packed with insider info, from arriving in the city to making it your home and everything in between.

Shanghai Explorer Residents' Guide
We Know Where You Live

Index

Index

Index

Index

Index

W

X

Y

Z

Residents' Guides

All you need to know about living, working and enjoying life in these exciting destinations

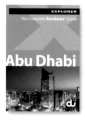
Abu Dhabi

Amsterdam

Bahrain

Barcelona

Beijing

Berlin

Dubai

Dublin

Geneva

Hong Kong

Kuala Lumpur

Kuwait

London

Los Angeles

New York

New Zealand

Oman

Paris

Qatar

Shanghai

Singapore

Sydney

Tokyo

Vancouver

Coming in 2008/9: Bangkok, Brussels, Mexico City, Moscow, San Francisco, Saudi Arabia and Taipei

Mini Guides

The perfect pocket-sized
Visitors' Guides

Coming in 2008/9: Bangkok, Brussels, Mexico City, Moscow, San Francisco and Taipei

Mini Maps

Wherever you are,
never get lost again

Check out www.explorerpublishing.com/products

Photography Books
Beautiful cities caught through the lens

Calendars
The time, the place, and the date

Maps
Wherever you are, never get lost again

Activity and Lifestyle Guides
Drive, trek, dive and swim... life will never be boring again

Retail sales

Our books are available in most good bookshops around the world, and are also available online at Amazon.co.uk and Amazon.com. If you would like to enquire about any of our international distributors, please contact retail@explorerpublishing.com

Bulk sales and customisation

All our products are available for bulk sales with customisation options. For discount rates and further information, please contact corporatesales@explorerpublishing.com

Licensing and digital sales

All our content, maps and photography are available for print or digital use. For licensing enquiries please contact licensing@explorerpublishing.com

Check out www.explorerpublishing.com/products

Ahmed Mainodin
AKA: Mystery Man
We can never recognise Ahmed because of his constantly changing facial hair. He waltzes in with big lambchop sideburns one day, a handlebar moustache the next, and a neatly trimmed goatee after that. So far we've had no objections to his hirsute chameleonisms, but we'll definitely draw the line at a monobrow.

Andrea Fust
AKA: Mother Superior
By day Andrea is the most efficient manager in the world and by night she replaces the boardroom for her board and wows the pants off the dudes in Ski Dubai. Literally. Back in the office she definitely wears the trousers!

Ajay Krishnan R
AKA: Web Wonder
Ajay's mum and dad knew he was going to be an IT genius when they found him reconfiguring his Commodore 64 at the tender age of 2. He went on to become the technology consultant on all three Matrix films, and counts Keanu as a close personal friend.

Bahrudeen Abdul
AKA: The Stallion
Having tired of creating abstract sculptures out of papier maché and candy canes, Bahrudeen turned to the art of computer programming. After honing his skills in the southern Andes for three years he grew bored of Patagonian winters, and landed a job here, 'The Home of 01010101 Creative Freedom'.

Alex Jeffries
AKA: Easy Rider
Alex is happiest when dressed in leather from head to toe with a humming machine between his thighs – just like any other motorbike enthusiast. Whenever he's not speeding along the Hatta Road at full throttle, he can be found at his beloved Mac, still dressed in leather.

Ben Merrett
AKA: Big Ben
After a short (or tall as the case may have been) career as a human statue, Ben tired of the pigeons choosing him, rather than his namesake, as a public convenience and decided to fly the nest to seek his fortune in foreign lands. Not only is he big on personality but he brings in the big bucks with his bulk!

Alistair MacKenzie
AKA: Media Mogul
If only Alistair could take the paperless office one step further and achieve the officeless office he would be the happiest publisher alive. Wireless access from a remote spot somewhere in the Hajar Mountains would suit this intrepid explorer – less traffic, lots of fresh air, and wearing sandals all day – the perfect work environment!

Cherry Enriquez
AKA: Bean Counter
With the team's penchant for sweets and pastries, it's good to know we have Cherry on top of our accounting cake. The local confectioner is always paid on time, so we're guaranteed great gateaux for every special occasion.

Annabel Clough
AKA: Bollywood Babe
Taking a short break from her successful career in Bollywood, Annabel livens up the Explorer office with her spontaneous dance routines and random passionate outpouring of song. If there is a whiff of drama or a hint of romance, Annabel's famed vocal chords and nifty footwork will bring a touch of glamour to Al Quoz.

Claire England
AKA: Whip Cracker
No longer able to freeload off the fact that she once appeared in a Robbie Williams video, Claire now puts her creative skills to better use – looking up rude words in the dictionary! A child of English nobility, Claire is quite the lady – unless she's down at Rock Bottom.

Darwin Lovitos

AKA: The Philosopher
We are firm believers in our own Darwinism theory at Explorer – enthusiasm, organisation and a great sense of humour can evolve into a wonderful thing. He may not have the big beard (except on weekends) , but Darwin is just as wise as his namesake.

Hashim MM

AKA: Speedy Gonzales
They don't come much faster than Hashim – he's so speedy with his mouse that scientists are struggling to create a computer that can keep up with him. His nimble fingers leave his keyboard smouldering (he gets through three a week), and his go-faster stripes make him almost invisible to the naked eye when he moves.

David Quinn

AKA: Sharp Shooter
After a short stint as a children's TV presenter was robbed from David because he developed an allergy to sticky back plastic, he made his way to sandier pastures. Now that he's thinking outside the box, nothing gets past the man with the sharpest pencil in town.

Helen Spearman

AKA: Little Miss Sunshine
With her bubbly laugh and permanent smile, Helen is a much-needed ray of sunshine in the office when we're all grumpy and facing harrowing deadlines. It's almost impossible to think that she ever loses her temper or shows a dark side... although put her behind the wheel of a car, and you've got instant road rage.

Derrick Pereira

AKA: The Returnimator
After leaving Explorer in 2003, Derrick's life took a dramatic downturn – his dog ran away, his prized bonsai tree died and he got kicked out of his thrash metal band. Since rejoining us, things are looking up and he just found out he's won $10 million in a Nigerian sweepstakes competition. And he's got the desk by the window!

Henry Hilos

AKA: The Quiet Man
Henry can rarely be seen from behind his large obstructive screen but when you do catch a glimpse you'll be sure to get a smile. Lighthearted Henry keeps all those glossy pages filled with pretty pictures for something to look at when you can't be bothered to read.

Enrico Maullon

AKA: The Crooner
Frequently mistaken for his near-namesake Enrique Iglesias, Enrico decided to capitalise and is now a regular stand-in for the Latin heartthrob. If he's ever missing from the office, it usually means he's off performing for millions of adoring fans on another stadium tour of America.

Iain Young
AKA: 'The Cat'
Iain follows in the fine tradition of Scots with safe hands – Alan Rough, Andy Goram, Jim Leighton on a good day – but breaking into the Explorer XI has proved frustrating. There's no match on a Mac, but that Al Huzaifa ringer doesn't half make himself big.

Firos Khan

AKA: Big Smiler
Previously a body double in kung fu movies, including several appearances in close up scenes for Steven Seagal's moustache. He also once tore down a restaurant with his bare hands after they served him a mild curry by mistake.

Ieyad Charaf

AKA: Fashion Designer
When we hired Ieyad as a top designer, we didn't realise we'd be getting his designer tops too! By far the snappiest dresser in the office, you'd be hard-pressed to beat his impeccably ironed shirts.

Grace Carnay

AKA: Manila Ice
It's just as well the office is so close to a movie theatre, because Grace is always keen to catch the latest Hollywood offering from Brad Pitt, who she admires purely for his acting ability, of course. Her ice cool exterior conceals a tempestuous passion for jazz, which fuels her frenzied typing speed.

Ingrid Cupido
AKA: The Karaoke Queen
Ingrid has a voice to match her starlet name. She'll put any Pop Idols to shame once behind the mike, and she's pretty nifty on a keyboard too. She certainly gets our vote if she decides to go pro; just remember you saw her here first.

Johny Mathew
AKA: The Hawker
Caring Johny used to nurse wounded eagles back to health and teach them how to fly again before trying his luck in merchandising. Fortunately his skills in the field have come in handy at Explorer, where his efforts to improve our book sales have been a soaring success.

Ivan Rodrigues
AKA: The Aviator
After making a mint in the airline market, Ivan came to Explorer where he works for pleasure, not money. That's his story, anyway. We know that he is actually a corporate spy from a rival company and that his multi-level spreadsheets are really elaborate codes designed to confuse us.

Joy Tubog
AKA: Joyburgh
Don't let her saintly office behaviour deceive you. Joy has the habit of jumping up and down while screaming 'Jumanji' the instant anyone mentions Robin Williams and his hair sweater. Thankfully, her volleyball team has learned to utilize her 'uniqueness' when it's her turn to spike the ball.

Jake Marsico
AKA: Don Calzone
Jake spent the last 10 years on the tiny triangular Mediterranean island of Samoza, honing his traditional cooking techniques and perfecting his Italian. Now, whenever he returns to his native America, he impresses his buddies by effortlessly zapping a hot dog to perfection in any microwave, anywhere, anytime.

Juby Jose
AKA: The Nutcracker
After years as a ballet teacher, Juby decided on mapping out a completely different career path, charting the UAE's ever-changing road network. Plotting products to illuminate the whole of the Middle East, she now works alongside the all-singing, all-dancing Madathil brothers, and cracks any nut that steps out of line.

Kate Fox
AKA: Contacts Collector
Kate swooped into the office like the UK equivalent of Wonderwoman, minus the tights of course (it's much too hot for that), but armed with a superhuman marketing brain. Even though she's just arrived, she is already a regular on the Dubai social scene – she is helping to blast Explorer into the stratosphere, one champagne-soaked networking party at a time.

Jane Roberts
AKA: The Oracle
After working in an undisclosed role in the government, Jane brought her super sleuth skills to Explorer. Whatever the question, she knows what, where, who, how and when, but her encyclopaedic knowledge is only impressive until you realise she just makes things up randomly.

Kathryn Calderon
AKA: Miss Moneypenny
With her high-flying banking background, Kathryn is an invaluable member of the team. During her lunchtimes she conducts 'get rich quick' seminars that, she says, will make us so much money that we'll be able to retire early and spend our days reading books instead of making them. We're still waiting...

Jayde Fernandes
AKA: Pop Idol
Jayde's idol is Britney Spears, and he recently shaved his head to show solidarity with the troubled star. When he's not checking his dome for stubble, or practising the dance moves to 'Baby One More Time' in front of the bathroom mirror, he actually manages to get some designing done.

Katie Drynan
AKA: The Irish Deputy
This Irish lass is full of sass, fresh from her previous role as the four leaf clover mascot for the Irish ladies' rugby team. Katie provides the Explorer office with lots of Celtic banter and unlimited Irish charm.

Kelly Tesoro
AKA: Leading Lady
Kelly's former career as a Korean soapstar babe set her in good stead for the daily dramas at the bold and beautiful Explorer office. As our lovely receptionist she's on stage all day and her winning smile never slips.

Kiran Melwani
AKA: Bow Selector
Like a modern-day Robin Hood (right down to the green tights and band of merry men), Kiran's mission in life is to distribute Explorer's wealth of knowledge to the fact-hungry readers of the world. Just make sure you never do anything to upset her – rumour has it she's a pretty mean shot with that bow and arrow.

Laura Zuffa
AKA: Travelling Salesgirl
Laura's passport is covered in more stamps than Kofi Annan's, and there isn't a city, country or continent that she won't travel to. With a smile that makes grown men weep, our girl on the frontlines always brings home the beef bacon.

Lennie Mangalino
AKA: Shaker Maker
With a giant spring in her step and music in her heart it's hard to not to swing to the beat when Lennie passes by in the office. She loves her Lambada… and Samba… and Salsa and anything else she can get the sales team shaking their hips to.

Mannie Lugtu
AKA: Distribution Demon
When the travelling circus rode into town, their master juggler Mannie decided to leave the Big Top and explore Dubai instead. He may have swapped his balls for our books but his juggling skills still come in handy.

Maricar Ong
AKA: Pocket Docket
A pint-sized dynamo of ruthless efficiency, Maricar gets the job done before anyone else notices it needed doing. If this most able assistant is absent for a moment, it sends a surge of blind panic through the Explorer ranks.

Matt Farquharson
AKA: Hack Hunter
A career of tuppence-a-word hackery ended when Matt arrived in Dubai to cover a maggot wranglers' convention. He misguidedly thinks he's clever because he once wrote for some grown-up English papers.

Mathew Samuel
AKA: Mr Modest
Matt's penchant for the entrepreneurial life began with a pair of red braces and a filofax when still a child. That yearning for the cut and thrust of commerce has brought him to Dubai, where he made a fortune in the sand-selling business before semi-retiring at Explorer.

Michael Samuel
AKA: Gordon Gekko
We have a feeling this mild mannered master of mathematics has a wild side. He hasn't witnessed an Explorer party yet but the office agrees that once the karaoke machine is out, Michael will be the maestro. Watch out Dubai!

Mimi Stankova
AKA: Mind Controller
A master of mind control, Mimi's siren-like voice lulls people into doing whatever she asks. Her steely reserve and endless patience mean recalcitrant reporters and persistent PR people are putty in her hands, delivering whatever she wants, whenever she wants it.

Mohammed Sameer
AKA: Man in the Van
Known as MS, short for Microsoft, Sameer can pick apart a PC like a thief with a lock, which is why we keep him out of finance and pounding Dubai's roads in the unmissable Explorer van – so we can always spot him coming.

Najumudeen Kuttathundil
AKA: The Groove
If it weren't for Najumudeen, our stock of books would be lying in a massive pile of rubble in our warehouse. Thankfully, through hours of crunk dancing and forklift racing with Mohammed T, Najumudeen has perfected the art of organisation and currently holds the title for fastest forklift slalom in the UAE.

Rafi Jamal
AKA: Soap Star
After a walk on part in The Bold and the Beautiful, Rafi swapped the Hollywood Hills for the Hajar Mountains. Although he left the glitz behind, he still mingles with high society, moonlighting as a male gigolo and impressing Dubai's ladies with his fancy footwork.

Noushad Madathil
AKA: Map Daddy
Where would Explorer be without the mercurial Madathil brothers? Lost in the Empty Quarter, that's where. Quieter than a mute dormouse, Noushad prefers to let his Photoshop layers, and brother Zain, do all the talking. A true Map Daddy.

Rafi VP
AKA: Party Trickster
After developing a rare allergy to sunlight in his teens, Rafi started to lose a few centimeters of height every year. He now stands just 30cm tall, and does his best work in our dingy basement wearing a pair of infrared goggles. His favourite party trick is to fold himself into a briefcase.

Richard Greig
AKA: Sir Lancelot
Chivalrous to the last, Richard's dream of being a medieval knight suffered a setback after being born several centuries too late. His stellar parliamentary career remains intact, and he is in the process of creating a new party with the aim of abolishing all onions and onion-related produce.

Pamela Afram
AKA: Lady of Arabia
After an ill-fated accident playing Lawrence of Arabia's love interest in a play in Jumeira, Pamela found solace in the Explorer office. Her first paycheque went on a set of shiny new gleamers and she is now back to her bright and smiley self and is solely responsible for lighting up one half of the office!

Roshni Ahuja
AKA: Bright Spark
Never failing to brighten up the office with her colourful get-up, Roshni definitely puts the 'it' in the IT department. She's a perennially pleasant, profound programmer with peerless panache, and she does her job with plenty of pep and piles of pizzazz.

Pamela Grist
AKA: Happy Snapper
If a picture can speak a thousand words then Pam's photos say a lot about her - through her lens she manages to find the beauty in everything – even this motley crew. And when the camera never lies, thankfully Photoshop can.

Sean Kearns
AKA: The Tall Guy
Big Sean, as he's affectionately known, is so laid back he actually spends most of his time lying down (unless he's on a camping trip, when his ridiculously small tent forces him to sleep on his hands and knees). Despite the rest of us constantly tripping over his lanky frame, when the job requires someone who will work flat out, he always rises to the editorial occasion.

Pete Maloney
AKA: Graphic Guru
Image conscious he may be, but when Pete has his designs on something you can bet he's gonna get it! He's the king of chat up lines, ladies – if he ever opens a conversation with 'D'you come here often?' then brace yourself for the Maloney magic.

Shabsir M
AKA: Sticky Wicket
Shabsir is a valuable player on the Indian national cricket team, so instead of working you'll usually find him autographing cricket balls for crazed fans around the world. We don't mind though – if ever a retailer is stumped because they run out of stock, he knocks them for six with his speedy delivery.

Shan Kumar
AKA: Caped Crusader
Not dissimilar to the Batman's beacon, Explorer shines a giant X into the skies over Al Quoz in times of need. Luckily for us, Shan battled for days through the sand and warehouse units to save the day at our shiny new office. What a hero!

Steve Jones
AKA: Golden Boy
Our resident Kiwi lives in a nine-bedroom mansion and is already planning an extension. His winning smile has caused many a knee to weaken in Bur Dubai but sadly for the ladies, he's hopelessly devoted to his clients.

Shawn Jackson Zuzarte
AKA: Paper Plumber
If you thought rocket science was hard, try rearranging the chaotic babble that flows from the editorial team! If it weren't for Shawn, most of our books would require a kaleidoscope to read correctly so we're keeping him and his jazz hands under wraps.

Tim Binks
AKA: Class Clown
El Binksmeisterooney is such a sharp wit, he often has fellow Explorers gushing tea from their noses in convulsions of mirth. Years spent hiking across the Middle East have given him an encyclopaedic knowledge of rock formations and elaborate hair.

Shyrell Tamayo
AKA: Fashion Princess
We've never seen Shyrell wearing the same thing twice – her clothes collection is so large that her husband has to keep all his things in a shoebox. She runs Designlab like clockwork, because being late for deadlines is SO last season.

Tom Jordan
AKA: The True Professional
Explorer's resident thesp, Tom delivers lines almost as well as he cuts them. His early promise on the pantomime circuit was rewarded with an all-action role in hit UK drama Heartbeat. He's still living off the royalties – and the fact he shared a sandwich with Kenneth Branagh.

Sobia Gulzad
AKA: High Flyer
If Sobia's exam results in economics and management are anything to go by, she's destined to become a member of the global jet set. Her pursuit of glamour is almost more relentless than her pursuit of success, and in her time away from reading The Wealth of Nations she shops for designer handbags and that elusive perfect shade of lipgloss.

Tracy Fitzgerald
AKA: 'La Dona'
Tracy is a queenpin Catalan mafiosa and ringleader for the 'pescadora' clan, a nefarious group that runs a sushi smuggling operation between the Costa Brava and Ras Al Khaimah. She is not to be crossed. Rival clans will find themselves fed fish, and then fed to the fishes.

Sunita Lakhiani
AKA: Designlass
Initially suspicious of having a female in their midst, the boys in Designlab now treat Sunita like one of their own. A big shame for her, because they treat each other pretty damn bad!

Zainudheen Madathil
AKA: Map Master
Often confused with retired footballer Zinedine Zidane because of his dexterous displays and a bad head-butting habit, Zain tackles design with the mouse skills of a star striker. Maps are his goal and despite getting red-penned a few times, when he shoots, he scores.

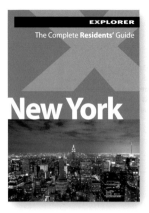

Flick back a few pages and ask yourself.

...would you like to see your face

Explorer has grown from a one-man operation a decade ago to a 60+ team today and our expansion isn't slowing down. We are always looking for creative bods, from PR pros and mas marketers to daring designers and excellent editors, as well as super sales and support staff.

So what are you waiting for? Apply online at www.explorerpublishing.com

The *Kuala Lumpur Explorer* Team
Lead Editor Jane Roberts
Deputy Editor Richard Greig
Editorial Assistant Mimi Stankova
Designer Rafi VP
Cartographers Sree Kala Ravindran, Raghunath Melethil, Noushad Madathil, Juby Jose
Photographers Victor Romero, Jane Roberts

Publishing
Publisher Alistair MacKenzie
Associate Publisher Claire England
Assistant to Associate Publisher Kathryn Calderon

Editorial
Group Editor Jane Roberts
Lead Editors David Quinn, Matt Farquharson, Sean Kearns, Tim Binks, Tom Jordan
Deputy Editors Helen Spearman, Jake Marsico, Katie Drynan, Pamela Afram, Richard Greig, Tracy Fitzgerald
Senior Editorial Assistant Mimi Stankova
Editorial Assistants Grace Carnay, Ingrid Cupido

Design
Creative Director Pete Maloney
Art Director Ieyad Charaf
Design Manager Alex Jeffries
Senior Designer Iain Young
Junior Designer Jessy Perera
Layout Manager Jayde Fernandes
Designers Hashim Moideen, Rafi VP, Shawn Jackson Zuzarte
Cartography Manager Zainudheen Madathil
Cartographers Juby Jose, Noushad Madathil, Sunita Lakhiani
Traffic Manager Maricar Ong
Production Coordinator Joy Tubog

Photography
Photography Manager Pamela Grist
Photographer Victor Romero
Image Editor Henry Hilos

Sales & Marketing
Media Sales Area Managers Laura Zuffa, Stephen Jones
Corporate Sales Executive Ben Merrett
Marketing Manager Kate Fox
Marketing Executive Annabel Clough
Marketing Assistant Shedan Ebona
Digital Content Manager Derrick Pereira
International Retail Sales Manager Ivan Rodrigues
Retail Sales Coordinators Kiran Melwani, Sobia Gulzad
Retail Sales Supervisor Mathew Samuel
Retail Sales Merchandisers Johny Mathew, Shan Kumar
Sales & Marketing Coordinator Lennie Mangalino
Senior Distribution Executives Ahmed Mainodin, Firos Khan
Warehouse Assistant Najumudeen K.I.
Drivers Mohammed Sameer, Shabsir Madathil

Finance & Administration
Finance Manager Michael Samuel
HR & Administration Manager Andrea Fust
Admin Manager Shyrell Tamayo
Junior Accountant Cherry Enriquez
Accountants Assistant Darwin Lovitas
Administrators Enrico Maullon, Kelly Tesoro
Drivers Rafi Jamal, Mannie Lugtu

IT
IT Administrator Ajay Krishnan
Senior Software Engineer Bahrudeen Abdul
Software Engineer Roshni Ahuja

Contact Us
Reader Response
If you have any comments and suggestions, fill out our online reader response form and you could win prizes. Log on to **www.explorerpublishing.com**

General Enquiries
We'd love to hear your thoughts and answer any questions you have about this book or any other Explorer product. Contact us at **info@explorerpublishing.com**

Careers
If you fancy yourself as an Explorer, send your CV (stating the position you're interested in) to **jobs@explorerpublishing.com**

Designlab & Contract Publishing
For enquiries about Explorer's Contract Publishing arm and design services contact **designlab@explorerpublishing.com**

PR & Marketing
For PR and marketing enquries contact **marketing@explorerpublishing.com**
pr@explorerpublishing.com

Corporate Sales
For bulk sales and customisation options, for this book or any Explorer product, contact **sales@explorerpublishing.com**

Advertising & Sponsorship
For advertising and sponsorship, contact **media@explorerpublishing.com**

Explorer Publishing & Distribution
PO Box 34275, Dubai, United Arab Emirates
www.explorerpublishing.com

Phone: +971 (0)4 340 8805
Fax: +971 (0)4 340 8806

Emergency Numbers

Ambulance	999
Fire & Rescue	994
Civil Defense	991
Civil Defense from mobile phone	112
National Poison Centre	1800 888 099
Police	999
Breakdown	15454
American Express	03 2050 0000
Diners Club	03 2161 1055
HSBC	03 2072 8608
MasterCard	1800 804 594
Maybank	03 2070 3333
Visa	1800 802 997

Landmark Hotels

Carcosa Seri Negara	03 2295 0888
Crowne Plaza Hotel	03 2148 2322
Federal Hotel	03 2148 9166
Hotel Istana	03 2141 9988
Hotel Maya Kuala Lumpur	03 2711 8866
Hotel Nikko	03 2161 1111
Impiana KLCC Hotel & Spa	03 2147 1111
Mandarin Oriental	03 2715 8818
Novotel Hydro Majestic	03 2147 0888
Parkroyal Hotel Kuala Lumpur	03 2147 0088
Putrajaya Shangi-La	03 8887 8888
Renaissance Hotel KL	03 2163 6888
Shangri-La	03 2032 2388
Sunway Resort Hotel & Spa	03 7492 8000
Traders Hotel	03 2332 9888

Embassies & Consulates

Australia	03 2146 5555
Belgium	03 2162 0025
Canada	03 2718 3333
China	03 2142 8585
Denmark	03 2032 2001
France	03 2053 5500
Germany	03 2142 9666
India	03 2093 3507
Indonesia	03 2142 1151
Ireland	03 2161 2963
Italy	03 4256 5122
Japan	03 2142 7044
Korea (South)	03 4251 2336
New Zealand	03 2078 2533
Philippines	03 2148 4233
Russia	03 4256 0009
Singapore	03 2161 6277
South Africa	03 2168 8663
Spain	03 2142 8776
Sweden	03 2052 2550
Thailand	03 2148 8222
The Netherlands	03 2168 6200
United Kingdom	03 2148 2122
United States	03 2168 5000

Airport Information

Airport / Flight Infoline	03 8777 8888
MAS Reservation	03 7846 3000
Limousine Service	03 8787 4490
Bus Service Enquiries	03 7982 7060
Customs KLIA	03 8787 2312

Public Holidays

Awal Muharram (Maal Hijrah)	20 Jan
Birthday of SPB Yang di-Pertuan Agong	02 Jun
Chinese New Year	18 & 19 Feb
Christmas Day	25 Dec
Deepavali	08 Nov
Hari Raya Aidiladha	01 Jan
Hari Raya Aidiladha	20 Dec
Hari Raya Puasa	13 & 14 Oct
Labour Day	01 May
National Day	31 Aug
Prophet Mohamed's Birthday	31 Mar
Wesak Day	02 Jun

Medical Services

Ampang Puteri Hospital	03 4270 2500
General (Besar) Hospital	03 2692 1044
National Poison Centre	1800 888 099
Pantai Medical Centre	03 2296 0888
Selangor Medical Centre	03 5543 1111
St. John Ambulance of Malaysia	03 6928 5157

City Information

www.bernama.com	News & Media
www.dinemalaysia.com	Nightlife
www.gov.my	Directories
www.imi.gov.my	Living & Working
www.kualalumpur.gov.my	City Information
www.mm2h.com	Living & Working
www.thestar.com.my	News & Media
www.miti.gov.my	Business & Industry
www.kualalumpur-city.com	City Information

Airlines

Air Asia	1300 889 933
British Airways	03 21676188
Cathay Pacific	03 20783377
China Airlines	03 21427344
Emirates Airlines	03 20585888
Japan Air	03 21611722
Korean Airlines	03 21428460
Lufthansa	03 21614666
Malaysian Airlines	03 78433300
Qantas Airways	03 21676000
Royal Brunei Airlines	03 20707166
Singapore Airlines	03 87766425
Swiss International Airlines	03 21635885
Thai Airways	03 20311913
United Airlines	03 21611433